MUSHROOMS
of WESTERN CANADA

DEC 2 0 1994

MUSHROOMS
of WESTERN CANADA

Helene M.E. Schalkwijk-Barendsen

LONE
PINE

First printed in 1991   5 4 3 2

Printed in Singapore

The Publisher: Lone Pine Publishing

#206, 10426–81 Avenue   202A–1110 Seymour Street
Edmonton, Alberta   Vancouver, British Columbia
Canada T6E 1X5   Canada V6B 3N3

16149 Redmond Way, #180
Redmond, Washington 98052
USA

Canadian Cataloguing in Publication Data
Schalkwyk, Helene M. E., 1921–
Mushrooms of Western Canada
Published also as: Mushrooms of Northwest North America
Includes bibliographical references and index.
ISBN 0–919433–47–2

1. Mushrooms—Canada, Western—Identification. 2. Mushrooms—Northwest, Pacific—Identification.3. Mushrooms—Alaska—Identification. I. Title. II. Title: Mushrooms of Northwest North America
QK617.S33 1991   589.2'22'09712   C91–091189–4

Editorial: Elaine Butler, Glenn Rollans
Design: Yuet Chan
Production: Yuet Chan, Elaine Butler, Brian Stephens, Bruce Timothy Keith
Printing: Kyodo Printing Co. (S'pore) Pte. Ltd.

The publisher gratefully acknowledges the assistance of Alberta Community Development and the Department of Canadian Heritage, and the financial support provided by the Alberta Foundation for the Arts.

WARNING: The author and publisher have made every effort to provide accurate information in this volume, but **we warn readers that eating any wild fleshy fungi with which you are unfamiliar carries some risk of poisoning, and that some mushrooms are acutely toxic and can cause death.** The author and publisher cannot accept any responsibility for the correct identification by readers or the edibility of any mushroom, or for any harm resulting from eating any fungi. If you have any doubt about the safety of mushrooms you have collected, we advise that you and others refrain from eating them until you have confirmed their safety with an experienced collector.

This book is dedicated to my husband,
Johan August Schalkwijk.
Not only have we always gone on walks together at home
and wherever we travelled, but with drying paintings and drying,
often smelly mushrooms in cabin, car, tent, house,
truck and trailer, not to mention four children, he has shown
much restraint. What is more, when Lone Pine Publishing
asked me to "do" this book, he offered to teach
himself to use a computer to put the text on discs.
I am very grateful for the wonderful willing help of
my husband, my best friend.

Contents

Acknowledgements

I am thankful to the many mycologists I have had contact with, either in person or through correspondence, over the past twenty years.

My first contact was with D. W. Malloch (University of Toronto). He wrote to me in 1973 when he was a mycologist at the Biosystematics Research Centre (BRC), Ottawa, in answer to my letter, in which I offered him my data. "What we really need at BRC are actual specimens, along with full records and descriptions. The fungus flora of Alberta is very poorly known. Almost anything you can collect will be a new Alberta record. I usually hesitate to put somebody to work on these things, but if you are in the habit of making notes on your mushrooms, it would be extremely valuable to have specimens sent along with your data."

I took up the challenge, and as a result, I can proudly say that almost all specimens in the illustrations are documented in the National Mycological Herbarium, of which J.H. Ginns is the curator. From him and especially from S.A. Redhead (BRC), I have learned a lot. I received reprints of their publications, in addition to identification of specimens.

Other Canadian mycologists who were very supportive are: E. Silver Keeping (died in 1991), the first mycologist in Alberta; H.J. Brodie, who specialized in bird's nest fungi (died in 1989); and R.S. Currah who has taught courses in mycology at the University of Alberta since 1989. I deeply appreciate the support of K.N. Egger (Memorial University, St. John's, Newfoundland). I owe a special debt to him for reading the manuscript (which he did during his holiday) as well as for writing a foreword.

From 1976 to 1981, I corresponded with A.H. Smith (Ann Arbour, Michigan). I sent him species of *Lactarius*, *Cortinarius* and *Leccinum* at his request. I was an honour to have contact with the great American mycologist, who died in 1986.

In 1974 I joined the Netherlands Mycological Society to have more mycological contacts, and through this organization started a long, happy correspondence with A.J.P. Oort (Wageningen University, where I studied long ago). He died in 1987. He had been a member of the Dutch mycological society for 64 years. Through him, I came in contact with other Dutch mycologists: E.J.M. Arnolds, Biological Research Station, Wijster, connected with Wageningen; C. Bas, Rijksherbarium, Leiden University; and Else C. Vellinga, a mycologist at the Rijksherbarium. She quickly found information for me in the "best mycological library in the world" when I needed it.

Helene M.E. Schalkwijk-Barendsen

Foreword

What is the appeal of mushrooms? Is it their surprising overnight appearance in unexpected places, their provocative shapes and exotic colours, or is it the rich folklore associated with them? Throughout history, mushrooms have tantalized us. They beckon some as culinary delicacies, others as avenues into psychic wonderlands, despite their deadly potential. Even those of us who study mushrooms and other fungi professionally usually admit to a sense of wonder at their fundamental beauty and inexplicable mystery as the source of our attraction to mycology.

Mushrooms seem to invite us to discover more about them. The sheer delight of discovering a new species or finding an "old friend" during a walk in the woods often inspires people to learn more about their diversity and complex life-history. However, in some cases, as with Leni Schalkwijk, such encounters cement a lifelong relationship.

I became acquainted with Leni while working at the Biosystematics Research Centre in Ottawa, where I had the enjoyable task of identifying some of the specimens of mushrooms she sent in for identification. I remember that each specimen was accompanied by careful notes and often a small, detailed colour sketch. In discussions with my colleagues, I came to realize the value of her mushroom specimens as a contribution to our scientific knowledge of mushroom ecology and distribution. However, it wasn't until I moved to Edmonton and met Leni personally that I discovered that she had been carefully collecting and documenting mushrooms and submitting them to Ottawa since the early 1970s. This book represents the cumulative observations of twenty years!

Building upon her scientific training in horticulture, Leni has combined the discipline of a scientist with the creative hand of an artist. Her plates are drawn with meticulous care so that characteristics necessary for identification are accurately represented. She has also painstakingly researched the scientific names of each mushroom, taking full advantage of her training in Latin and Greek. In addition to the colour illustrations, Leni has provided identification keys, a glossary, a reading list and notes on edibility and ecology, making this book a valuable resource for mycologists and field naturalists alike.

Even if your interest does not lie in scientific study, you can enjoy the vivid beauty of the artwork. The colour illustrations present the full range of exotic shapes and hues found in mushrooms, seen through the eyes of an artist and dedicated mushroom enthusiast. Feast upon the wealth of detailed information or on the rich artistry and allow yourself to become infected by the enigmatic appeal of mushrooms!

Keith N. Egger, Professor of Mycology
St. John's, Newfoundland

Introduction

On my eleventh birthday, one of my aunts sent me a postcard picturing hundreds of fly amanitas in a forest. That was my best gift! I still have the card. Walking in the woods near our cabin in 1969 with my paints and canvas, I suddenly found myself in my childhood postcard and was absolutely delighted. For two days I painted fly amanitas as they emerged from their "egg", then as they developed, lost their colour and fell over. I have never stopped.

This book is the result of that work. It contains the descriptions and my illustrations of 550 species. The Kingdom of Fungi is so large that the macrofungi, species with a fruiting body large enough to see with the naked eye and which run into the thousands, only represent a small percentage of that kingdom. Thus any mushroom guide can only contain a limited number of species.

Most specimens for my illustrations were found by my husband and myself, and some by friends or people attending my field identification sessions at the Edmonton Nature Centre.

In the literature list, in addition to a selection of field guides, I included checklists, which make it possible to get an idea of the distribution of species. A checklist to accompany this book can be ordered from the author. It gives additional locations of the illustrated species plus their location in herbaria. Also included are books which only treat certain groups, e.g., *Fungi On Wood* by Hermann Jahn, *Bird's Nest Fungi* by Harold Brodie and *Ascomycotina* (*Fungi of Switzerland*, Vol. 1)

I like to collect publications on fungi. My hobby is collecting local books from all over the world to learn about exotic native mushrooms. The scientific names are always present, and even if I cannot read the text, the book is still of great value. One of my favourite books is *Fungi, Delight of Curiosity*, written by Harold J. Brodie. The book describes in a wonderful way how a lot of us are attracted to Fungi.

What is a Mushroom?

A mushroom is the fruiting body of a fungus. Unlike a green plant, a fungus cannot produce its own food and must obtain its nutrition from other living things. Fungi are essential in nature's housekeeping; not only for the role they play in the recycling of dead organic material, but also for their role as symbiotic partners to all trees, shrubs and most herbs. In this latter role, the fungi's below-ground system of fine threads, called mycelium, envelopes, or grows into, the roots of the green plants and supplies them with needed minerals, trace elements and water from the soil. The green plant, in turn, supplies the fungus with food from its own supply, which it produced through photosynthesis. This makes it possible for forests to survive on poor soils. A third lifestyle is parasitism. Certain fungi attack living or damaged plants and exist at the expense of the victim. The relevant roles are mentioned in the description for each species.

Taxonomy

Taxon: dividing in orderly groups (Greek)

Taxonomy, the scientific classification of organisms, is built upon the binomial nomenclature system, in which each creature has two names: a genus name and a species name which is descriptive. Carolus Linnaeus (1707-1778) worked very hard all his life to develop the binomial system, but he did not include the Fungi in it. Not until almost a century later, was the modern study of mycology founded, by Christiaan Hendrik Persoon (1755-1837) and Elias Magnus Fries (1794-1878). In Fries' final system there were five series of gilled mushrooms: groups with white, pink, purple, brown or black spore prints. This is an artificial division, but it is time honoured and is very handy in giving directions to certain specific groups of fungi. In my lifetime many changes have been made in the taxonomic systems of Botany and Mycology.

The taxonomic system is hierarchical with Kingdom as the highest rank and species (which includes subspecies, variations and forms) as the lowest.

> Kingdom
> > Division
> > > Subdivision
> > > > Class
> > > > > Order
> > > > > > Family
> > > > > > > Genus
> > > > > > > > Species

The Kingdom of Fungi has two Divisions: the Eumycota, or true fungi, and the Myxomycota, which contains no fleshy fungi. The Eumycota is composed of five Subdivisions, two of which contain fleshy mushrooms and which will be addressed in this book: the Basidiomycotina and the Ascomycotina.

The Basidiomycotina produce spores or basidiospores, usually four, on a club-shaped cell called a basidium, and this group includes the boletes, gilled mushrooms, and puffballs.

Ascomycotina produce their spores, usually eight, in asci or miniature sacs. The morels, false morels, cup mushrooms and truffles are found in this group.

There are three Classes in Basidiomycotina: Teliomycetes, Gasteromycetes and Hymenomycetes. Teliomycetes contains the fungi responsible for the important plant diseases (e.g., rusts and smuts), which are not part of this guide. The Gasteromycetes contains the puffballs and their allies, and the Hymenomycetes includes the boletes, gilled and non-gilled mushrooms.

In the Ascomycotina there are six Classes, but most of the thousands of species of these Classes are not of interest to the mushroom hunter because they are microscopic. The two Classes which do contain species of interest are the Discomycetes, in which the morels and truffles belong, and Pyrenomycetes, which include the lobster mushrooms.

Each class is divided into orders; each order contains one or more families and each family contains at least one genus, often many genera and each genus in turn contains species. Species is the lowest rank in the system, but the most important for the mushroom hunter! To make things somewhat clearer, I will give an example. Imagine that you find a gilled mushroom growing on a log. It has a pink spore print. It is a "deer mushroom" or *Pluteus cervinus*. The second word is the species name, which is descriptive (*cervinus*, meaning of the deer) and is not written with a capital first letter. *Pluteus* is the name of the genus. This name and the name of all the higher ranking groups are started with capital letters. *Pluteus* belongs to the family of Pluteaceae together with another genus, that of *Volvariella*. The family Pluteaceae belongs to the order Agaricales or gilled mushrooms.

Note that order names all end in -ales and the family names in -aceae.

Common or ethnic names exist for certain well-known, edible or poisonous species, but they are only valid locally, whereas scientific names, usually in Latin or Latinized Greek, are valid world wide. I derived great pleasure from translating and from finding out the reasons for the scientific names, making use of my classical education in Holland. These translations may help people remember the names or help them form their own names for favorite species.

Only well-known common names are listed in the index. Indexes for genera and species are separated because name changes for the genera and species may take place in the future as the taxonomy of mycology continues to evolve.

Changes in scientific names have to be approved by an international commission on nomenclature which regularly holds conferences. Strict rules have been established for the naming of species. When a change is being proposed, mycologists search for the earliest legitimate name. In the past certain mushrooms had different names in different countries. The conferences are held to resolve the resulting confusion and also to solve taxonomic changes.

Field Identification

When you find a mushroom, note down the locality, substrate (on the ground, wood, etc.), habitat and date. Remove it from its substrate with care, so that the base is intact. Collect a young and a mature specimen. Describe it, following the example of species described in the text. See page 14 for a diagram of the parts of a mushroom and examples of longitudinal sections. To prepare a mature specimen for spore printing, put the cap of a gilled mushroom on a piece of white paper with a bowl over top to protect it from drafts. Obtaining a spore print takes several hours or overnight, but it is essential in identifying mushrooms; looking at gill colour is not enough.

If you have identified the species, or think you have (or when you do not know what it is), you can dry the specimens over a 20 watt lightbulb. Ask for information from a mycologist if you need help. When you think it is important, put the specimens with spore print (folded) and relevant information in a small paper bag and label it. Keep a list and number each species collected. Your records and specimens can be used to help establish distribution information for fungi species. In Europe many volunteers from mycological clubs do this.

Many forests in European countries are dying from pollution. With this volunteer help, scientists are finding that mushroom populations have changed completely because of this. Mycorrhizal species disappear, while species growing on dying and dead wood increase in number. The disappearance of certain species may be a warning signal in polluted areas.

A good number of species can be identified with the help of a field guide, but for many species a microscope is needed. I have mentioned in the text when that is the case. As far as edibility is concerned, you have to be very careful. No guessing is permitted. **All characteristics have to fit.**

Climate, Fruiting Bodies & Distribution

Some fungi fruit yearly, others rarely. In dryer climates, that can be a matter of available moisture at the right time. In climates with a true winter, like the prairies and the arctic, everything becomes dormant for six months or longer. In the arctic, because of the short growing season, it is possible to find many species fruiting at the same time, which at lower latitudes would fruit during different seasons. Mushrooms fruit when humidity and temperature conditions are just right. The mycelium survives well under snow cover.

In milder climates along the Pacific coast, for instance in Victoria, B.C., fungi may have their rest period in a hot dry summer, and fruiting bodies may be found throughout a mild winter, in addition to the spring and fall.

Each species has a favorite fruiting time. You just have to find out how circumstances influence things in your area. Fruiting time is mentioned in the text, while, in the illustrations, I have noted when and where species were found. There are some exotic places among them, but I used those specimens only if I knew that they occured in northwest North America as well.

Distribution can be Worldwide, Cosmopolitan (widely distributed), North American, Pacific Northwest, or Circumpolar.

Certain species occurring in Arctic bogs of the Northwest Territories, the Yukon and Alaska may also occur in montane regions as far south as California. This happens because of the general direction of our mountain ranges and spores that are carried by the prevailing North-South winds. Dutch professor Dr. L.G.M. Baas Becking, said: "Everything is everywhere, but the environment selects." There are enormous amounts of spores in the stratosphere; even though most spores are not viable. On the other hand, certain mycorrhizal species just grow on, or near, one type of tree, and this is the only place where that mushroom will occur.

Classification

Classification is based on evolution and species may be grouped together which don't always have obvious visual features in common.

In the classification of fungi, the genus is the most important group. Genera are grouped into families and families into larger groups.

In this overview it can be noted that two families of gilled mushrooms are combined with the bolete family into one order. An explanation for this is given in the text.

I have placed the illustrations and detailed descriptions for the class of Gasteromycetes in the middle of the illustrations and detailed descriptions for the class of Hymenomycetes (as is explained in the text). This is not because I meant to split up this class. In the overview the class of Hymenomycetes is left in one continuous group.

The overview can be used to find the various groups when you are comfortable with the book and want to find known specimens. I cannot do without a system like this myself. Do not consider it rigid; scientists work on classification all the time. It is a good filing system, but the files can be put in other drawers.

The Keys to the families of gilled mushrooms have been traditionally based on the colour of the spore print, and this system is still used, but there are exceptions. You will experience this when you follow the keys (see Bolbitiaceae).

A Note to the Reader

A scale bar of 5 cm appears on each colour illustration. Most of the time the size is about half the natural size. There are four exceptions: pages 27 and 28 containing boletes, and page 163 with stalked puffballs are reduced more. Page 161 with the bird's nest fungi shows natural size.

The keys give the page numbers to the colour illustrations and short descriptions. The page numbers for detailed descriptions are given in the short descriptions. The index gives page numbers for the detailed descriptions and colour illustraions. Colour illustrations are listed in bold.

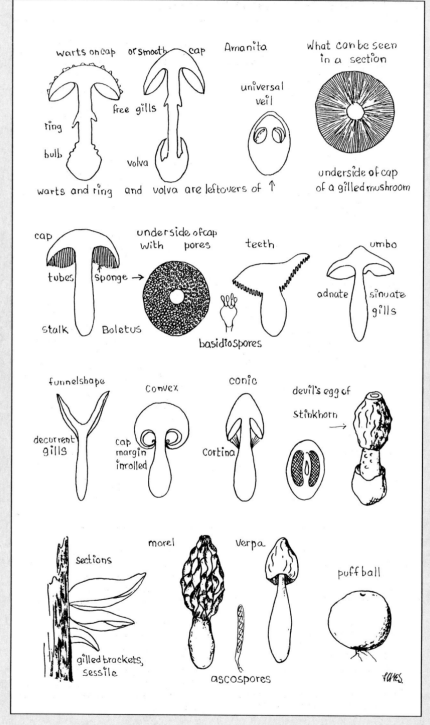

warts on cap or smooth cap Amanita

What can be seen in a section

ring

bulb

free gills

volva

warts and ring and volva are leftovers of ↑

universal veil

underside of cap of a gilled mushroom

cap

tubes sponge →

stalk Boletus

underside of cap with pores

teeth

umbo

adnate sinuate gills

basidiospores

funnel shape

decurrent gills

Convex

cap margin inrolled

conic

Cortina

devil's egg of Stinkhorn →

sections

gilled brackets, sessile

morel Verpa

ascospores

puff ball

Various Shapes of Fruiting Bodies

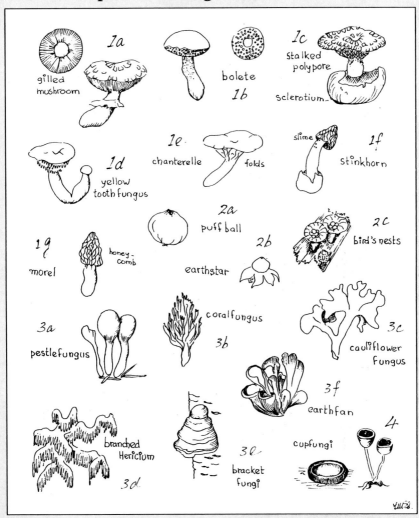

1a gilled mushroom

1b bolete

1c stalked polypore

sclerotium

1d yellow tooth fungus

1e chanterelle — folds

slime *1f* stinkhorn

2a puff ball

1g morel

honey-comb

earthstar

2b

2c bird's nests

3a pestle fungus

coral fungus *3b*

3c cauliflower fungus

3f earthfan

branched Hericium *3d*

3e bracket fungi

cupfungi *4*

1. **Fruiting Bodies: fleshy stalked mushrooms**
   a. with gills under the cap
   b. with pores under the cap: detachable sponge
   c. with pores under the cap: non-detachable sponge
   d. with teeth under the cap
   e. with blunt ridges under the cap
   f. with caplike, smelly, slimy top
   g. with honeycomb or brainlike top

2. **Fruiting bodies: round or pear shaped when immature**
   a. round or pear shaped, spore sac enclosed
   b. opening into a star shape with a thin-skinned spore sac in the centre
   c. spore-filled capsules seen inside a "nest" when top disintegrates

3. **Fruiting bodies in other shape; fleshy, sturdy, tough or woody, but not fragile**
   a. club or pestle shaped
   b. repeatedly branched - upright
   c. repeatedly branched - with lobes
   d. repeatedly branched - with hanging teeth
   e. brackets with pores underneath
   f. small leathery warty shapes

4. **Fruiting bodies fragile: in the shape of a cup, ear, saddle, or spatula; with or without stalk**

Classification Overview

Page numbers in bold refer to colour illustrations;
other numbers refer to listing in text.

Kingdom Fungi
   Division Eumycota
      Subdivision Basidiomycotina
         Class Hymenomycetes
            Order Boletales

Keys to Colour Illustrations

The major group of fungi — stalked, fleshy mushrooms with gills or a sponge — are keyed out first. The families of gilled mushrooms are arranged according to spore print colour, starting with white, then pink; yellow to orange; medium brown; purplish to chocolate brown and ending with greyish black to black. The Russulaceae family precedes the others in this list, even though the spore colour varies from white to almost orange in a few species. It is not practical to do it otherwise. With gilled mushrooms you have to look at a spore print; looking at the gill colour is not enough.

Separate keys for species which form their spores inside a skin are next. These are puffballs, earthstars, bird's nests or stinkhorns. All keys point to plates with closely related species on it.

Non-gilled mushrooms with many different shapes are keyed out in the next section. Here shapes like teeth at the underside of the cap, branched structures, etc., are important, as well as spore colour.

In the last group, morels, false morels and cup fungi are keyed out. For the limited number of species of this group that are treated in this book, directions to the plates of related species is sufficient.

The two families in the Boletales that have gilled fruiting bodies (Gomphidiaceae and Paxillaceae) are keyed out with the Agaricales, according to the spore print colour.

I. Boletes and Stalked Polypores

Fleshy stalked mushrooms with tubes underneath the cap, showing pore openings in the surface of the sponge:

1. sponge or fertile layer not detachable see fleshy stalked ------ POLYPORES -- 175-177
2. fruiting bodies with detachable sponge --------------------------- BOLETACEAE ------ 27-33
   a. muted colours; flesh, when cut, does not change colour -- genus BOLETUS --------- 27
   b. strong colours, including flesh, when cut -------------------- genus BOLETUS --------- 28
   c. sticky caps; smooth stalks with ring --------------------------- genus SUILLUS --------- 29
   d. slimy caps, smooth stalks, no ring ---------------------------- genus SUILLUS --------- 31
   e. dry caps, rough stalks --- genus LECCINUM --------- 32
   f. large angular pores, radially arranged ------------ genus FUSCOBOLETINUS --------- 33

II. Gilled Mushrooms

Fleshy stalked mushrooms with gills underneath the cap; list of families arranged according to spore print colour as follows:

A. white, creamy, buff or yellowish
B. white
C. pink or peach
D. yellow ochre to orange
E. medium brown in many shades but not purple brown
F. purplish brown to chocolate brown
G. greyish to black

A. Spore print white, creamy, buff, yellowish; mushrooms with a brittle consistency, confluent cap and stalk; no ring or volva; with or without latex.
-- RUSSULACEAE -- 38-49

1. no latex -- genus RUSSULA -- 38-43

2. latex -- genus LACTARIUS -- 44-49

B. Spore print white

1. gills free, ring present, no volva, most have scaly caps and stalks
--LEPIOTACEAE -- 51-52

2. gills free; ring present or absent, volva, or remnants of it on a bulbous base; universal veil may be membranous or slimy ------------------------------- AMANITACEAE -- 53-57

3. gills attached, soft, thick gills, feeling waxy when crushed, colourful species, sticky or slimy -- HYGROPHORACEAE -- 58-63

4. gills attached, thick, distant, not waxy; cap and stalk coloured as well as gills.
-- LACCARIACEAE -------- 98

5. gills attached, not thick, many small species included; no ring, no volva; all with rhizomorphs or rhizoid bundles at the stalk base; living on duff and woody substances, e.g., cones, dead moss -- XERULACEAE -- 93-97

6. gills attached, fleshy brackets and stalked mushrooms of various shapes and colours; recyclers of dead wood--- PLEUROTACEAE   99-102

7. gills attached, the rest of white-spored mushroom species with attached gills, most of them with cap and stalks, with or without rings; the largest of white-spored species: an artificial group. For direction to the plates of the genera of Tricholomatacea see page 23.
-- TRICHOLOMATACEAE -- 64-91

C. Spore print pink

1. gills free, becoming pink, with or without volva ---------------- PLUTACEAE   103-105
with volva--- genus VOLVARIELLA ------ 105
no volva --- genus PLUTEUS   103-105

2. gills attached, pink, no rings, no volva -------------------- ENTOLOMATACEAE ------ 107

3. gills attached, spore print buff, pinkish or peach
-- genus LEPISTA, TRICHOLOMATACEAE -------- 81

D. Spore print yellow ochre to orange. All are one of a kind in various families.

1. yellow ochre to orange in *Phaeolepiota aurea*---------- TRICHOLOMATACEAE -------- 91

2. orange in *Lactarius deliciosus* in RUSSULACEAE, all parts inside and out, including latex are orange in this species -- 47

3. the monotype *Rhodotus palmatus*, RHODOTACEAE and *Phyllotopsis nidulans*, PLEUROTACEAE. These two completely orange species can be found on this plate. -------------- 99

E. Spore print medium brown, in many shades, but not purple brown

1. spore print rust brown in -------------------------------------- STROPHARIACEAE   129-136
-- genus PHOLIOTA   130-133
--- and genus KUEHNEROMYCES ------ 136

2. spore print rust to cinnamon brown, dull brown and bright orange brown; the largest brown spored family, most species with cortina and attached gills.For direction to the plates of the genera of Cortinariaceae, see page 23. ------ CORTINARIACEAE   109-123

3. spore print yellow to orange brown, cinnamon brown to dark brown. The three genera have more microscopic than macroscopic .things in common-- BOLBITIACEAE 124-127

   a. rust to reddish brown spore print, adnexed gills, covered in slime
-- genus BOLBITIUS ------ 124

   b. dark brown spore print, resembling Agaricus but with attached gills; with or without ring -- genus AGROCYBE ------ 125

   c. rustbrown spore print, small fragile species, adnexed gills, conic caps, slender stalks
-- genus CONOCYBE ------ 127

4. spore print rust brown (creamy in one species), gills decurrent, forked with connecting veins and often anastomosing. This group is related to the Boletaceae and belongs in the order of Boletales, even though they have gills. ---------------------- PAXILLACEAE -------- 37

F. Spore print purplish brown to chocolate brown

1. free gills, first pale or bright pink, then changing to brown as the spores ripen; dark brown spore print -- AGARICACEAE 137-142

2. attached gills and purplish brown spore print ----------------- STROPHARIACEAE 129-136
-- genus STROPHARIA ------ 129
--- genera HYPHOLOMA & PSILOCYBE 135-136

G. Spore print greyish black to black

1. strongly decurrent gills, slimy cortina; peg shaped mushrooms closely related to Boletaceae. This gilled group belongs to Boletales ------------- GOMPHIDIACEAE -------- 35

2. gills free of adnexed, four genera in ------------------------------- COPRINACEAE 143-151

   a. gills free and usually delinquescing ----------------------------- genus COPRINUS 143-145

   b. gills adnexed in ---------- genera ANELLARIA, PANAEOLINA & PANAEOLUS ------ 147

   c. gills adnexed, with annulus & inclined to deliquesce -------------------------------
-- genera PSATHYRELLA & LACRYMARIA 149-151

III. True and false puffballs, earthstars, bird's nests and stinkhorns

A. True and false puffballs

1. closed fruiting bodies, round or pear shaped; various ways of releasing spores; true puffballs, 4 genera in --- LYCOPERDACEAE 153-157

   a. smooth round balls, loosing outer skin layer, staying closed for a long time, eventually apical pore.

     (1) without sterile base --- genus BOVISTA ------ 155

     (2) with sterile base and division between spore mass and base
-- genus VASCELLUM ------ 155

   b. pear-shaped with shorter or longer sterile base, various surface decorations, apical pore --- genus LYCOPERDON ------ 153

   c. large puffballs with or without base; disintegrating their tops at maturity to relaease spores --- genus CAVALATIA 155-157

2. odd shapes, not unlike a malformed *Coprinus*, often with rudimentary gills and a continuation of the stalk inside the gleba; probably an evolutionary stage between gilled mushroom and puffballs; these are false puffballs in SECOTIACEAE & PODAXACEAE
-- genera ENDOPTYCHUM & PODAXIS ----- 152

B. Earthstars, bird's nests and stinkhorns
When immature, fruiting bodies are puffball shaped, but they open up in various different shapes

IV.Non-gilled mushrooms: coral, clubs, teeth, folds and pores

A. hymenium on gill-like structure

B. hymenium on teeth

C. hymenium on pestle, club or coral-shaped fruiting body

D. hymenium in tubes, not detachable

   1. stalked fleshy fruiting bodies, several or many with fused bases; tough when older; tube layer thin; rhizomorphs ---------------- BONDARZEWIACEAE, POLYPORACEAE ------ 175

   2. stalked, tough or fleshy fruiting bodies, hexagonal or angular pores, growing from wood or sclerotium --- POLYPORACEAE ------ 177

   3. soft or woody brackets with pores on the bottom; a variation of colours, but spore colour white --- POLYPORACEAE ------ 177

   4. brackets with red brown, lacquered crust and a white waxy layer covering brown tubes; brown spores -- GANODERMATACEAE ------ 180

E. hymenium on repeatedly branched structures

   1. hymenium covering "leafy lobes" on flat branches forming a cauliflower-like structure --- SPARASSIDACEAE ------ 165

   2. branched structure has hanging teeth on all branches -------- HERICIACEAE ------ 173

F. warted hymenium on stalked or irregularly shaped structures

   1. warted hymenium on leathery fruiting bodies, which can be stalked, lobed, cup-like or like coral ---------------------------- genus THELEPHORA, THELEPHORACEAE ------ 169

V. Morels, false morels and cup mushrooms

A list of the seven illustrations of sac fungi, rather than keys, seems more practical. The majority of Ascomycotina are micro-fungi, not visible with the naked eye. These are some of the macro-fungi.

page 181   MORCHELLACEAE True morels: fruiting body with distinct stalk and head, which is either honeycombed in *Morchella*, or like a thimble in *Verpa* and *Ptychoverpa*.

page 183   HELVELLACEAE False morels: fruiting body with distinct stalk and convoluted brain-like head. Genus *Gyromitra*.

page 185   HELVELLACEAE: Fruiting body with distinct, often pitted, stalk and a head which may be saddle shaped; irregular and one cup-shaped head. Genus *Helvella*.

page 186   PEZIZACEAE: Fruiting body cup shaped or ear shaped, sessile or with very short stalk, no hairs on rim.

page 187   HUMARIACEAE: Fruiting body cup to saucer shaped, sessile and with hairy underside and margin.

page 189   PEZIZALES & HELOTIALES: Fruiting body a stalked cup or other stalked shapes belonging to various families in the orders of *Pezizales* and *Helotiales*.

page 191   SPHAERIALES: Fruiting bodies of flask fungi often parasitic on fruiting bodies of other fungi in the order of *Sphaeriales*.

Genera of TRICHOLOMATACEAE

page 64-69   TRICHOLOMA: medium to large mushrooms with cap, stalk (some with ring) and sinuate gills, terrestrial.

page 70-75   CLITOCYBE: small to large , funnel shaped mushrooms; stalked, decurrent gills, terrestrial.

page 76   COLLYBIA: small to medium thin-fleshed species with hollow often hairy, cartilaginous stalks, growing in tufts or groups, terrestrial.

Genera of CORTINARIACEAE

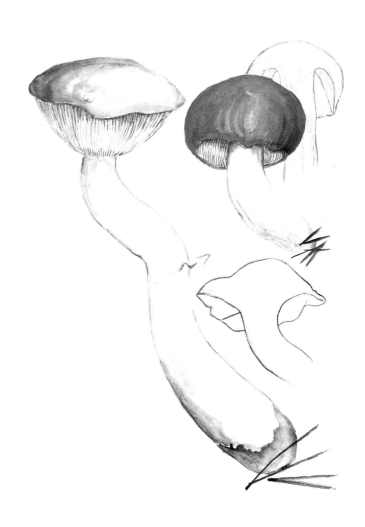

Colour Illustrations

Page 27

BOLETACEAE

Members of this family are solid, fleshy mushrooms with a sponge-like structure on the cap bottom. Three large edible species of the genus *Boletus* are shown on this plate, including the king bolete, enjoyed by Europeans since Roman times and well known on our continent.

1. **yellow cracked bolete** *Boletus subtomentosus* p.195
   Yellow-brown cap, often with cracked cuticle, angular pores; these continue the pattern on the top of the stalk.

2. **Zeller's bolete** *Boletus zelleri* p.195
   Dark brown, almost black cap; large angular pores are yellow; whitish stalk with reddish blush.

3. **king bolete of cep** *Boletus edulis* p.195
   Red-brown cap, massive stalk with raised network particularly at top; the yellowish sponge with small round pores.

Page 28

BOLETACEAE

Three inedible to poisonous species of *Boletus* and *Suillus*; strong colours, especially in the flesh.

1. **Eastwood's bolete or red-pored bolete** *Boletus pulcherrimus* p.196
   This magnificent colourful bolete is an example of a poisonous species. It is especially dangerous when eaten raw. It is easily recognized by its red pores and the fact that its flesh and tubes immediately change from yellow to blue-green when cut. Be careful with any bolete with strong colours like that. It is closely related to the equally poisonous *Boletus satanas*.

2. **peppery bolete** *Boletus piperatus* p.196
   The pepper bolete is a species that is easily recognized with its red pores, sponge, small stature and orange-yellow stalk with red streaks. It has a peppery acrid taste and is unpalatable.

3. **peaked Suillus** *Suillus umbonatus* p.197
   See genus description in the next paragraph. Small and soft species with a domed, slimy cap, sticky ring and large, angular, yellow pores. Easy to recognize; not poisonous but unpalatable.

Page 29

BOLETACEAE

Suillus, a sticky bolete; 6 species with sticky or slimy caps; smooth stalks with ring.

1. **slippery Jill** *Suillus subolivaceous* p.197
   Associated with pine; the stalk shows a flaring ring, is white above, brown below ring; medium-sized olive-yellow cap. Edible but not palatable.

2. **western painted bolete** *Suillus lakei* p.197
   Associated with Douglas fir; colourful hairy cap; broad, wooly, white ring.

3. **heavy bolete** *Suillus ponderosus* p.197
   Associated with Douglas fir and pine; sticky salmon-coloured cap; broad sticky ring.

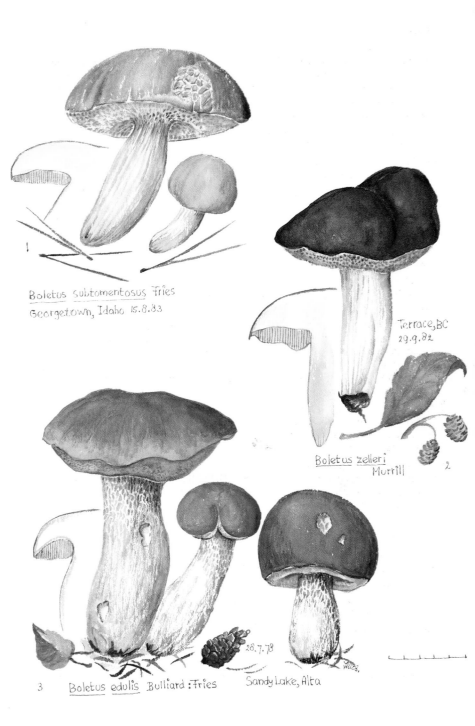

Boletus subtomentosus Fries
Georgetown, Idaho 15.8.83

Terrace, BC
29.9.82

Boletus zelleri
Murrill   2

3   Boletus edulis Bulliard : Fries

28.7.78

Sandy Lake, Alta

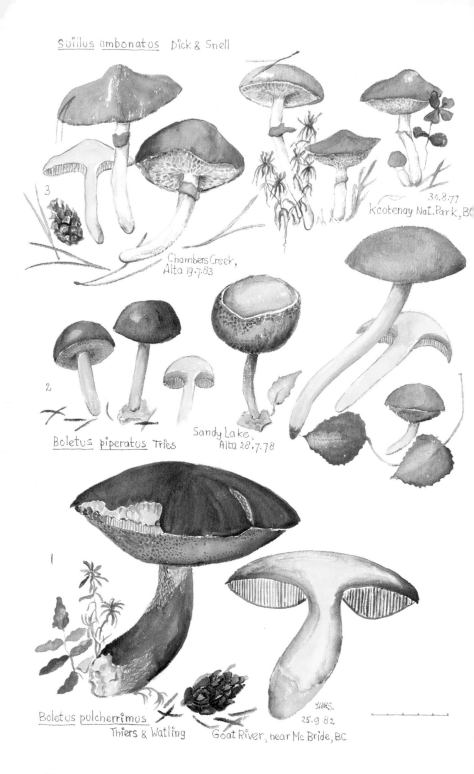

Suillus umbonatus Dick & Snell

3

30.8.77
Kootenay Nat. Park, BC

Chambers Creek,
Alta 19·7·83

2

Boletus piperatus Fries

Sandy Lake,
Alta 28·7·78

1

Boletus pulcherrimus
Thiers & Watling

YWRS.
25·9·82
Goat River, near Mc Bride, BC

Suillus subolivaceus
Smith & Thiers

Glacier National Park, BC
4.8.74

1

Suillus ponderosus
Smith & Thiers

King George
Park, BC

2

6.8.74

3

Suillus Lakei (Murrill)
Smith & Thiers
Shoswap lake, BC. 12.10.82

4

Suillus cavipes
(Opatowski) Smith & Thiers

Sprucegrove, Alta
7.9.82

5

6

Edmonton,
Alta
31.8.78
Suillus grevillei (Klotzch)
Singer

Jasper, Alta   22.8.87
Suillus luteus (Fries) S.F. Gray

• 29 •

4. **hollow-stalked larch bolete** *Suillus cavipes* p.198
Associated with tamarack; dry and hairy cap and a hollow stalk.

5. **tamarack Jack** *Suillus grevillei* p.198
Associated with tamarack; very slimy cap in damp weather, orange to auburn; large flaring ring.

6. **slippery Jack** *Suillus luteus* p.198
Associated with pine; sticky purple-brown cap; ring brown on top and purple below; dots on the stalk.

Page 31

BOLETACEAE
Suillus or sticky bolete; slimy caps; no ring; all but one are edible.

1. **variable Suillus** *Suillus subvariegatus* p.199
Sticky, smooth, orange-brown cap; smooth relatively tall stalk because of high undergrowth in coastal forests; yellow flesh discolouring to blue; grows under hemlock and western red cedar. Edibility unknown.

2. **woolly pine bolete** *Suillus tomentosus* p.199
Sticky, hairy, orange-yellow cap; glandular dots on the stalk; yellow flesh discolouring slightly to blue-green; grows under pine. Edible.

3. **milk bolete** *Suillus granulatus* p.199
Sticky, smooth, streaky yellow-brown cap; glandular dots on stalk; often cloudy droplets on pore surface, hence the common name; grows under pine. Edible.

4. **northern pine bolete** *Suillus albivelatus* p.199
Very sticky, hairy, yellow-brown cap; hairy edge of cap leaves a sticky zone on the stalk which turns reddish, as do the holes left in the flesh by insects; grows under pine. Edible.

5. **short-stemmed bolete** *Suillus brevipes* p.200
Very sticky, smooth reddish-brown cap; white short stalk; grows under pine. Edible.

6. **small short-stemmed bolete** *Suillus brevipes* var. *subgracilis* p.200
A variation of the short-stemmed bolete; sticky, smooth, tan to ochre cap; bright yellow stalk with small white base; grows under pine. Edible.

Page 32

BOLETACEAE
Leccinum or roughstem; easily recognized by the ornamentation on the stalk; dry caps; the sponge shows small round pores. No. 1 and no. 5 are often called orange caps; all are edible.

1. **northern roughstem** *Leccinum boreale* p.200
Big, massive stalk with coarse ornamentation, orange-brown cap with generous skin flap. Earliest fruiting roughstem. Edible.

2. **brown roughstem** *Leccinum snellii* p.201
Often medium size, this species has a dull-brown cap and a relatively slim stalk. Edible.

3. **ochre roughstem** *Leccinum ochraceum* p.201
Medium to large ochre-coloured bolete; the sponge tends to change in colour to orange-ochre. Edible.

Suillus subvariegatus Snell & Dick

Lakelse lake, 28.9.82
near Terrace, BC.

3.8.74
Wabasso,
Jasper N.P
Alta

Saskatchewan crossing, Alta 27.7.82

Suillus tomentosus (Kauffman) Singer, Snell & Dick

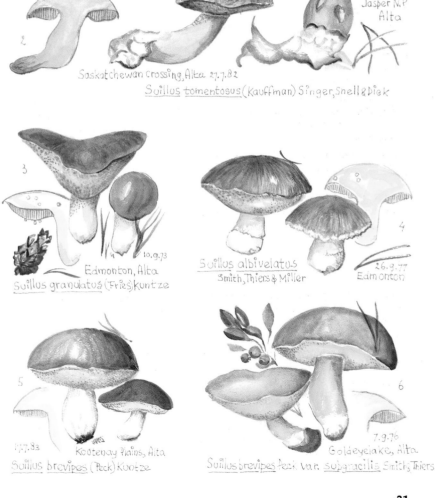

10.9.73

Edmonton, Alta

Suillus granulatus (Fries) Kuntze

Suillus albivelatus
Smith, Thiers & Miller

26.9.77
Edmonton

Kootenay Plains, Alta

Suillus brevipes (Peck) Kuntze

7.9.76
Goldeye lake, Alta

Suillus brevipes Peck var. subgracilis Smith, Thiers

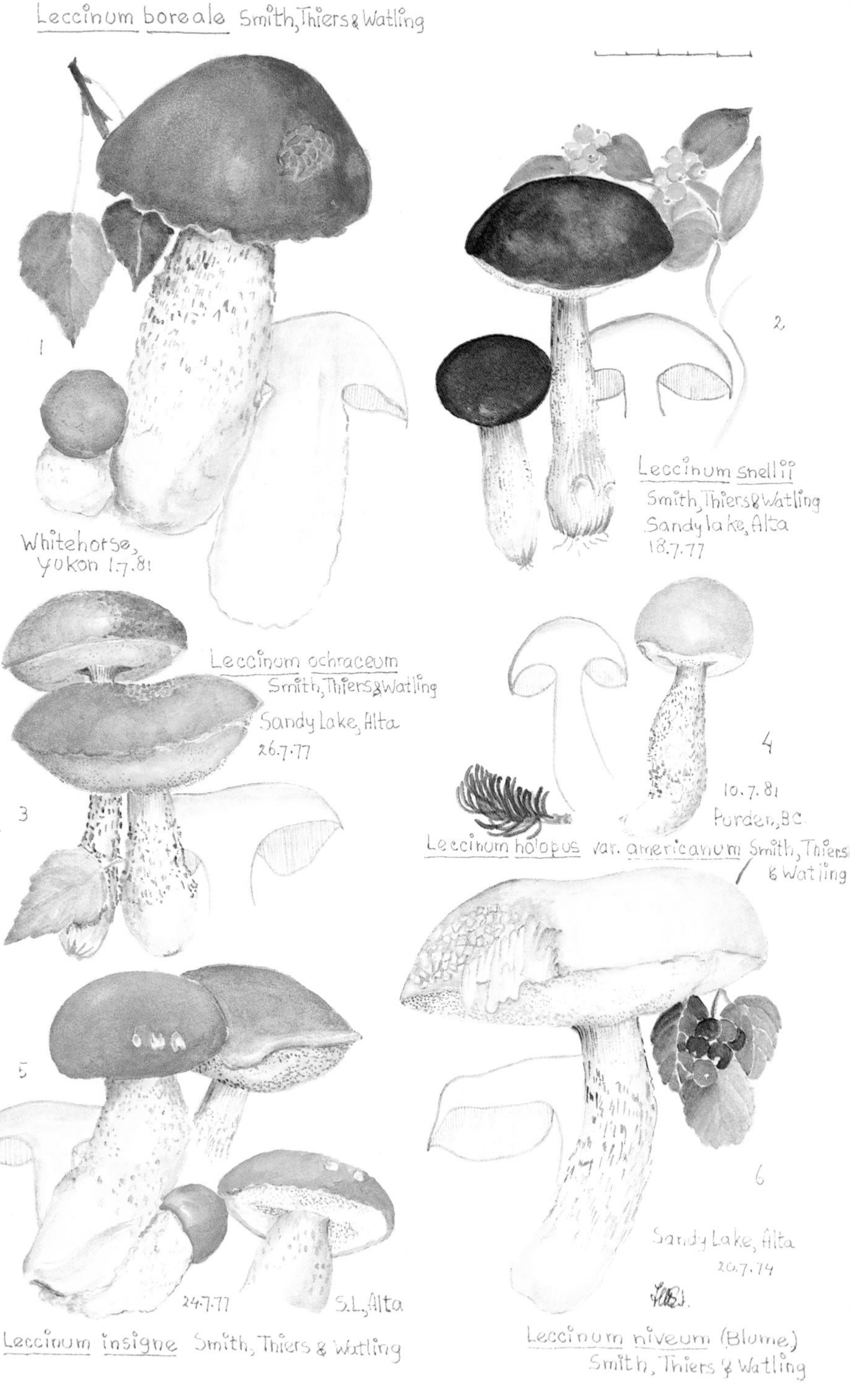

Leccinum boreale Smith, Thiers & Watling

1

Whitehorse,
Yukon 1.7.81

2

Leccinum snellii
Smith, Thiers & Watling
Sandy Lake, Alta
18.7.77

Leccinum ochraceum
Smith, Thiers & Watling
Sandy Lake, Alta
26.7.77

3

4

10.7.81
Purden, BC
Leccinum holopus var. americanum Smith, Thiers
& Watling

5

6

Sandy Lake, Alta
20.7.74

24.7.77   S.L., Alta

Leccinum insigne Smith, Thiers & Watling

Leccinum niveum (Blume)
Smith, Thiers & Watling

Fuscoboletinus spectabilis
(Peck) Pomerleau & A.H. Smith
Dorset, Ont.
22.9.84

Fuscoboletinus
sinuspaulianus
Pomerleau & Smith

E. of Princeton,
BC.
9.6.80

near Princeton, BC   2.9.76

Fuscoboletinus ochraceoroseus (Snell) Pomerleau & Smith

4. **pale roughstem**   *Leccinum holopus*   p.201
Small to medium size, pale-capped bolete; unlike the other five, this one grows
under conifers. Edible.

5. **aspen roughstem**   *Leccinum insigne*   p.202
Medium to very large in size and brightest in colour. Not only is the cap the
brightest orange, but there is often green discolouration on the outside as well as
the inside flesh of the stalk base. Edible.

6. **white roughstem**   *Leccinum niveum*   p.202
Large white roughstem, which turns blushing pink after being nibbled on by
squirrels; coarse dark scabers on the stalk. Edible.

Page 33

BOLETACEAE

Three species of *Fuscoboletinus*. They have fibrillose or hairy caps; have large
radially arranged angular pores and have a ring on the stalk.

1. **admirable bolete**   *Fuscoboletinus spectabilis*   p.202
A very elegant mushroom, recognized by its red double ring, the outside of which
is gelatinous; its grey-red, floccose patches (veil remnants) on the mature cap and
its hollow stalk. Edible but not good.

2. **hairy bolete**   *Fuscoboletinus sinuspaulianus*   p.203
An interesting mushroom recognized by its brown, hairy cap; large size; fibrous
ring which disappears and red net-like pore design at the top of the heavy stalk.
Edible.

3. **rosy larch bolete**   *Fuscoboletinus ochraceoroseus*   p.203
The rosy larch bolete has yellow-ochre and red colours in its cap and stalk. The cap
is hairy and dry; the heavy stalk has a yellow top, a disappearing white ring and
colourful base. Inedible because it is bitter.

Page 35

GOMPHIDIACEAE

Peg-shaped mushrooms with more or less sticky caps and decurrent gills; in the
genus *Gomphidius*, the flesh in the stalk base is yellow.

1. **pegtop**   *Chroogomphus rutilus*   p.204
Cap colour varies, but usually reddish and with small umbo; gills decurrent; the
lengthwise section shows clearly the shape of an old-fashioned nail or peg; flesh
pale-ochre. Edible, not very good.

2. **winepeg**   *Chroogomphus vinicolor*   p.204
Cap colour darker than no. 1, is dark burgundy or chestnut; gills decurrent; the
flesh is also darker than flesh of no. 1; cap shape either rounded or with umbo.
Edible, not very good.

3. **rosy Gomphidius**   *Gomphidius subroseus*   p.205
Striking mushroom, recognized by its rounded, pinkish cap, often with pine needles
stuck to it; its bright yellow stalk base and its black wispy fringe of partial veil
remnants. Edible.

4. **slimy Gomphidius**   *Gomphidius glutinosus*   p.205
Somewhat less obvious than its rosy sister, because of its delicate, fading lilac
colour.This mushroom differs from the above by its thicker glutinous layer, the
annular zone lower on the stalk and its generally darker colours. Edible.

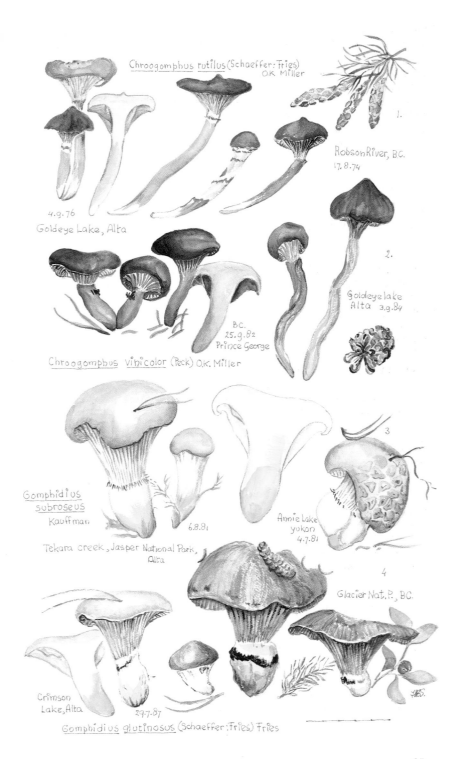

Chroogomphus rutilus (Schaeffer: Fries) O.K. Miller

1.

RobsonRiver, B.C.
17.8.74

4.9.76
Goldeye Lake, Alta

2.

Goldeye lake
Alta 3.9.84

B.C.
25.9.82
Prince George

Chroogomphus vinicolor (Peck) O.K. Miller

Gomphidius
subroseus
Kauffman

6.8.81

3

Annie Lake
yukon
4.7.81

Tekara creek, Jasper National Park,
Alta

4

Glacier Nat.P., B.C.

Crimson
Lake, Alta

29.7.87

Gomphidius glutinosus (Schaeffer: Fries) Fries

Page 37

PAXILLACEAE
Peg mushrooms with dry caps; the decurrent gills show a tendency to form angular pores near the stalk or forked gills as in the false chanterelle. All are inedible.

1. **spring Paxillus**   *Paxillus vernalis*   p.206
A large sandy-coloured mushroom; despite its name, it simply fruits in cool weather — spring and fall. It could be mistaken for a *Lactarius*, but the spore print is cinnamon-brown, not white. Gills and stalk stain reddish-brown when handled; grows under deciduous trees. Inedible.

2. **poison Paxillus**   *Paxillus involutus*   p.206
Usually medium-sized, can occasionally grow quite large; marbled brown; the inrolled margin persists for a long time. Dangerous species to eat (see detailed description). Grows in spruce bogs or mixed woods, very common. **Poisonous.**

3. **blackfoot Paxillus**   *Paxillus atrotomentosus*   p.206
A medium to large mushroom, easily recognized by its thick, dark, velvety stalk and often irregular cap; growing singly or in clumps on wood debris or decaying stumps in coniferous forests in the mountains or along the coast. Inedible.

4. **false chanterelle**   *Hygrophoropsis aurantiaca*   p.207
A small orange mushroom of which the gills especially are different. They are brilliant orange and forked in a very regular pattern. Widely distributed under spruce on squirrel middens or old wood. Not recommended.

Page 38

RUSSULACEAE
Eight *Russula* species with warm-coloured caps; yellowish spore prints ranging from very pale to deep warm yellow; unchanging white flesh; all edible.

1. **rainbow Russula**   *Russula olivacea*   p.208
Can be recognized by its multicoloured cap (including olive green), yellowish gills with red edges, and pink or blushing stalk; mild taste.

2. **leathery Russula**   *Russula alutacea*   p.208
Can be recognized by its vinaceous pink colour and wrinkly, leathery looking, chamois-coloured discolouration. Has yellow gills and white stalk; taste is mild.

3. **Peck's red Russula**   *Russula peckii*   p.208
A blood-red cap; pale gills with red edges; pink stalk; flesh discolouring pink under the cuticle; mild taste.

4. **fishy-smelling Russula**   *Russula xerampelina*   p.209
The fishy odour; dusty, somber, dark brownish-purple cap, yellow-ochre gills; and vinaceous pink stalk make this one easy to recognize; mild taste.

5. **bog Russula**   *Russula paludosa*   p.209
Orange and buff in the illustration, but they can also be red; there are fading spots on the cap; pale buff gills when mature;mild taste; not easily recognizable.

6. **northern Russula**   *Russula borealis*   p.209
Large deep-red *Russula*; white gills changing to bright yellow when spores ripen; gills often have red edges; blushing stalk; mild taste. Not difficult to recognize.

7. **small yellow Russula**   *Russula chameoleontina*   p.210
This butter-yellow *Russula* is very easy to identify, with its unchanging small bright yellow cap, yellow spores and white stalk (see detailed description); taste mild.

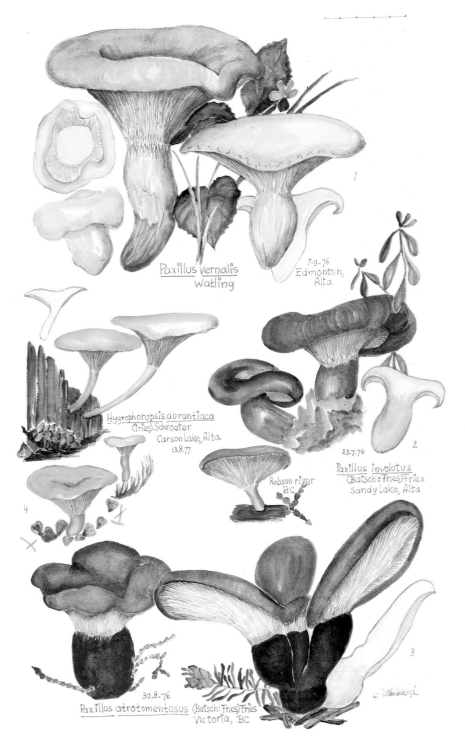

Paxillus vernalis
Watling

7.9.76
Edmonton,
Alta

1

Hygrophoropsis aurantiaca
(Fries) Schroeter
Carson Lake, Alta
13.8.77

Robson river
B.C.

Paxillus involutus
(Batsch: Fries) Fries
Sandy lake, Alta

23.7.76

2

4

Paxillus atrotomentosus (Batsch: Fries) Fries
Victoria, BC

30.8.76

3

Russula olivacea (Secretan) Fries
Victoria, BC
11.8.74

Russula alutacea (Fries) Fries
Sandy Lake
Alta, 26.7.80
2

1

Russula velenovskyi
Melzer & Zvara

Sandy Lake
Alta 26.7.80
8

Russula
peckii
Singer
9.8.82
S. L.
3

S.L.
18.7.77
Russula chamaeleontina (Fries) Fries
7

Russula
xerampelina
(Schaeff.: Secr.)
Fries
26.8.83
S.L.
Alta
4

Russula borealis Kauffman
6

1.8.77
Devon, Alta

S.L.
30.7.72
Russula paludosa Britzelmayr
5

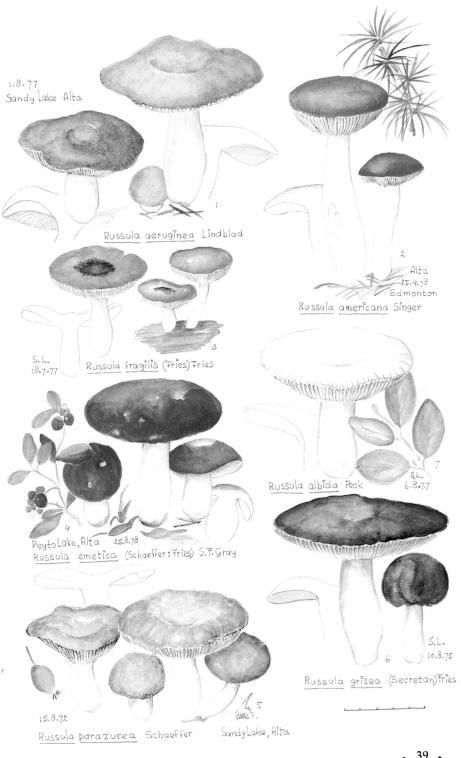

1.8.77
Sandy Lake Alta

Russula aeruginea Lindblad

2
Alta
25.9.78
Edmonton
Russula americana Singer

S.L.
18.7.77
Russula fragilis (Fries) Fries

3

4
Peyto Lake, Alta   25.8.78
Russula emetica (Schaeffer: Fries) S.F. Gray

7
S.L.
6.8.77
Russula albida Peck

6
S.L.
10.8.75
Russula grisea (Secretan) Fries

15.8.72
Russula parazurea Schaeffer

5
Sandy Lake, Alta

• 39 •

8. brown velvet Russula   *Russula velenovskyi*   p.210
A medium-sized *Russula* with a velvety-appearing brown cap and a salmon-pink stalk base; yellowish gills. This is an interesting find; mild taste.

Page 39

RUSSULACEAE

Russula species with cooler colours; the pink and red species with white spore prints are very sharp tasting and inedible; the white, grey and green species taste milder.

1. **green Russula**   *Russula aeruginea*   p.210
Can be recognized by its green cap, which can range from apple green to blue-green, creamy or yellowish gills and white stalk; mild taste, edible.

2. **American Russula**   *Russula americana*   p.210
Red-capped *Russula* with white gills and white spore print; very sharp taste. Can be recognized by its extremely fragile flesh. Inedible.

3. **fragile Russula**   *Russula fragilis*   p.211
Small, vinaceous, pink *Russula*; usually but not always with a dark cap centre; white gills; white spores; white stalk and very sharp taste. Not edible; it is too small to be of interest for eating purposes anyway.

4. **the sickener**   *Russula emetica*   p.211
Medium-sized, red-capped mushroom; fading, older specimens have whitish spots; white stalk, white gills, white sporeprint; taste very bitter and burning; causes vomiting. **Poisonous.**

5. **blue Russula**   *Russula parazurea*   p.211
Slate blue or a bit green blue; dip in the cap centre tan coloured; off-white gills, cream spores; mild taste; edible.

6. **grey Russula**   *Russula grisea*   p.212
Dark, metal or elephant grey with violet tinges; centre of the cap tan coloured; white stalk, sometimes with violet tinges; light tan gills; mild taste, edible.

7. **soft white Russula**   *Russula albida*   p.212
In contrast to the big, coarse, white Russulas of p. 43, this one belongs to a colourful fragile group; all parts are white, except the gills, which turn from white to buff as the spores ripen; mild taste; edible.

Page 41

RUSSULACEAE

Four *Russula* species with some unpleasant characteristics: they are smelly and/or the flesh colours grey on cutting.

1. **greying Russula**   *Russula decolorans*   p.212
The cap is bright orange, fading with age; yellowish gills; flesh turns grey when cut; mild taste, edible.

2. **chrome-yellow Russula**   *Russula claroflava*   p.212
Another greying *Russula*, this one with a chrome yellow cap (greenish where covered by leaves); this specimen had a very tall stalk, because it was growing in very dense undergrowth under conifers. Related to no. 1, the flesh also discolours to grey, when cut; mild taste; edible.

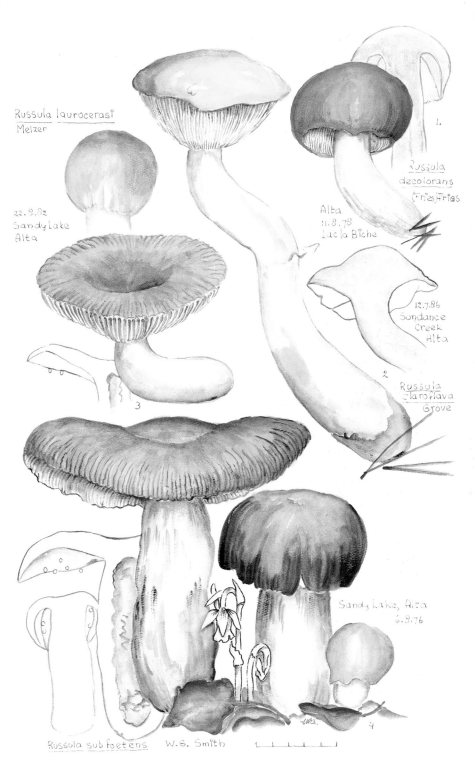

Russula laurocerasi
Melzer

23.9.82
Sandy Lake
Alta

1.

Russula
decolorans
(Fries)Fries

Alta
11.8.78
Lucla Biche

12.7.86
Sundance
Creek
Alta

2

Russula
claroflava
Grove

3

Russula subfoetens   W. S. Smith

Sandy Lake, Alta
6.8.76

4

3. **almond Russula**   *Russula laurocerasi*   p.213
Stands out by its conspicuous striations or ridges on the margin of the cap; the sporeprint is creamy; has an odour of fruit or almonds, but later becomes faintly fetid; not edible.

4. **stinking Russula**   *Russula subfoetens*   p.213
Resembles no. 3 but larger, darker and dirty looking. It grows in damp places and has a nasty chemical odour; not edible.

Page 43

RUSSULACEAE

These three large *Russulas* belong to a coarse-fleshed group that look like *Lactarius* but lack the latex. Inedible to poisonous.

1. **Cascade Russula**   *Russula cascadensis*   p.213
Very large , coarse, white *Russula*, resembling a large *Lactarius*, but it contains no latex; developing underground, it emerges with a lot of duff and earth on the cap; the gills are coarse and distant, discolouring from white to ochre; white spores; thick heavy stalk; acrid taste. Not edible.

2. **short-stalked Russula**   *Russula brevipes*   p.214
Another *Lactarius*-like *Russula*; it has narrower gills; at the base of the gills small drops of water are often found; it has a short stalk as the name indicates; considered to be edible elsewhere, but there is a western variety that is very acrid.

3. **blackening Russula**   *Russula nigricans*   p.214
A very interesting, large, tough *Russula*; it changes from almost white when young, through buff to brown and finally to black and the dried mummy can still be found in spring; when cut, the flesh changes to red, sometimes just partly; after a while it changes to grey and black as well; it has an unpleasant odour, especially when drying.

Page 44

RUSSULACEAE

The *Lactarius* species on this page are inedible to poisonous; they have hairy caps and white, milky latex, and the flesh does not change colour when exposed to air.

1. **woolly milkcap**   *Lactarius torminosus*   p.215
Medium-sized mushroom; can be recognized by its zoned, very woolly cap in shades of creamy orange and red. Milky latex with sharp taste. **Poisonous.**

2. **downy milkcap**   *Lactarius pubescens*   p.215
Medium to small in size, this is a smaller, less hairy version of *L. torminosus*. Milky latex, tastes slowly peppery. Inedible.

3. **poplar milkcap**   *Lactarius controversus*   p.215
Medium to very large mushroom; white, sticky cap, often with leaves sticking to it. Recognized by its pink gills, white latex and very sharp taste. Inedible.

4. **tan wool milkcap**   *Lactarius subtorminosus*   p.216
Small to medium-sized *Lactarius*; lighter in colour than *L. torminosus* but with a mild taste; white latex. Not recommended for eating because it is easily confused with poisonous species.

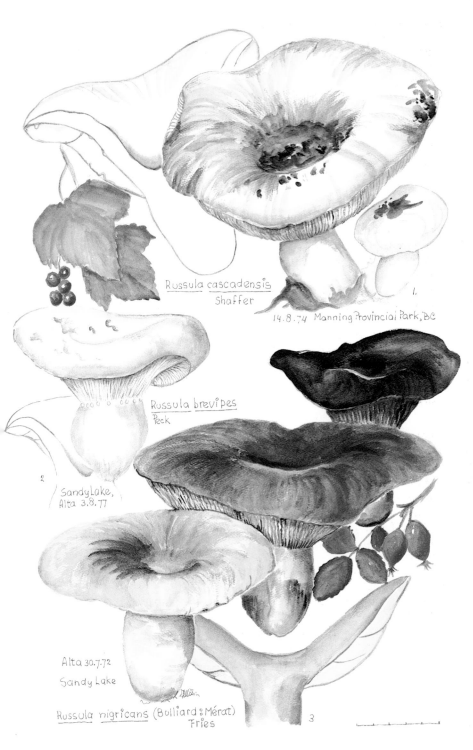

Russula cascadensis
Shaffer

14.8.74 Manning Provincial Park, BC

1.

Russula brevipes
Peck

2

Sandy Lake,
Alta 3.8.77

Alta 30.7.72
Sandy Lake

Russula nigricans (Bulliard : Mérat)
Fries

3

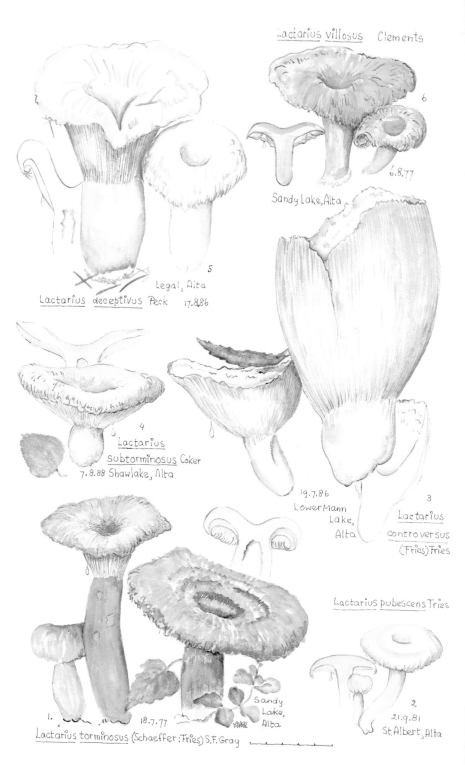

Lactarius villosus Clements

6

6.8.77

Sandy Lake, Alta

5

Legal, Alta

Lactarius deceptivus Peck   17.8.86

4

Lactarius subtorminosus Coker
7.8.88 Shaw Lake, Alta

19.7.86
Lower Mann
Lake,
Alta

3

Lactarius controversus (Fries) Fries

Lactarius pubescens Fries

1.

18.7.77

Sandy Lake, Alta

2

21.9.81
St. Albert, Alta

Lactarius torminosus (Schaeffer : Fries) S.F. Gray

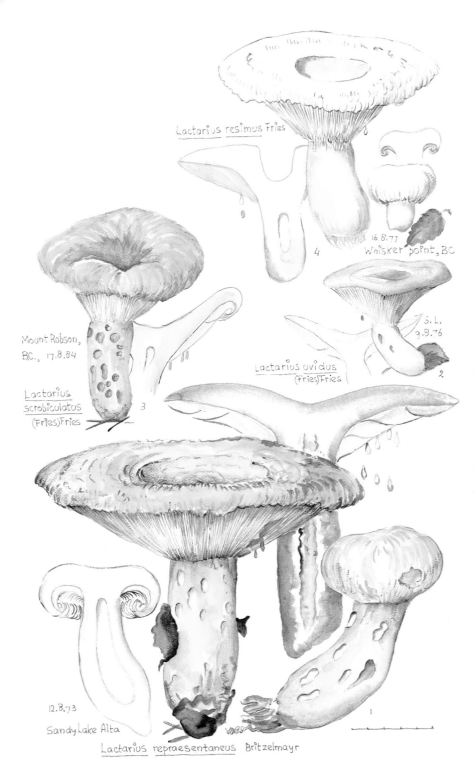

Lactarius resimus Fries

16.8.77
Whisker point, BC

4

Mount Robson,
BC., 17.8.84

Lactarius
scrobiculatus
(Fries) Fries

3

S.L.
9.8.76

2

Lactarius uvidus
(Fries) Fries

12.8.73
Sandy Lake Alta

Lactarius repraesentaneus Britzelmayr

1

• 45 •

5. **deceptive milkcap**   *Lactarius deceptivus*   p.216
   A big coarse *Lactarius*, dirty white in colour; bearded margin; velvety stalk; white latex; slowly acrid taste and coarse flesh. Not recommended.

6. **hairy milkcap**   *Lactarius villosus*   p.216
   Small, very hairy, pale salmon-orange milkcap; unchanging white latex; very sharp taste. Inedible.

Page 45

RUSSULACEAE

Lactarius species with hairy caps; latex and flesh stain yellow or purple; watery depressions present in the stalks of some species. **Poisonous.**

1. **northern milkcap**   *Lactarius repraesentaneus*   p.217
   An impressive, very large mushroom; slimy; hairy and bearded; pale yellow; easy to recognize. Associated with deciduous trees. **Poisonous.**

2. **purple-staining milkcap**   *Lactarius uvidus*   p.217
   Another purple-staining *Lactarius* with milky latex changing to purple when exposed to the air. This one is not woolly but has a sticky purplish cap. Causes gastro-intestinal disturbances. **Poisonous.**

3. **pitted milkcap**   *Lactarius scrobiculatus*   p.217
   Like the northern milkcap, this mushroom is slimy, woolly and yellowish and has a pitted stalk — even more so than no. 1. The flesh and latex stain a sulphur yellow on exposure to air. It is associated with coniferous trees. **Poisonous.**

4. **yellow-staining bearded milkcap**   *Lactarius resimus*   p.218
   A species of the north and the mountains, it resembles *L. repraesentaneus* and *L. scrobiculatus*, but it has a white bearded cap, no erosions in the stalk and has white latex, which stains the gills yellow. It is not recommended to eat any species containing latex that changes colour, since these mushrooms are usually **poisonous.**

Page 47

RUSSULACEAE

Six brightly coloured, smooth-capped *Lactarius* species; they may have zoned caps but are not hairy. The famous, orange delicious milkcap is included, as well as some poisonous species.

1. **delicious milkcap**   *Lactarius deliciosus*   p.218
   This is the most famous *Lactarius*; it is very easy to recognize, although it can be overlooked when it has green discolouration on a faded cap and grows in moss in a coniferous forest. The mushroom is orange all over, including the gills and the latex. Edible.

2. **sweetish milkcap**   *Lactarius subdulcis*   p.218
   Sweetish milkcap is a terrible name. It looks a lot like a smaller version of the red-hot milkcap, but grows in a different habitat: under alder, willow or poplar in damp spots, and is mild tasting. Try a small piece on the tongue and spit it out again. Edible.

3. **gold drop milkcap**   *Lactarius chrysorrheus*   p.219
   This mushroom has a yellowish-pinkish cap with darker spots in concentric zones and does not look special until checked for latex, which, unexpectedly, is a bright sulphur yellow and stains the injured parts yellow. Inedible.

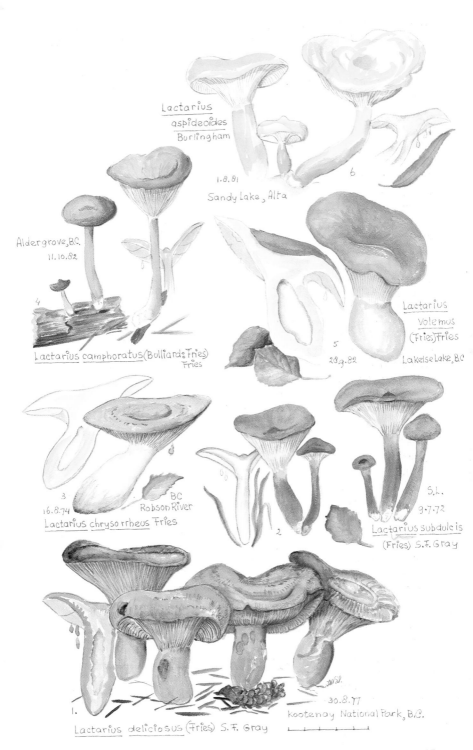

Lactarius
aspideoïdes
Burlingham

1.8.81

Sandy Lake, Alta

6

Aldergrove, B.C.
11.10.82

4

Lactarius camphoratus (Bulliards Fries)
Fries

Lactarius
volemus
(Fries) Fries
Lakelse Lake, BC

5

28.9.82

3

16.8.74

BC
Robson River

Lactarius chrysorrheus Fries

2

S.L.
9.7.72

Lactarius subdulcis
(Fries) S.F. Gray

1.

Lactarius deliciosus (Fries) S.F. Gray

30.8.77
Kootenay National Park, B.C.

4. **spicy milkcap**   *Lactarius camphoratus*   p.219
Can be recognized by its spicy odour, especially when dried. It is a species of
northern coniferous or mixed forests. A slender reddish brown or rufous coloured
mushroom fading to pale salmon; with rufous flesh and white, unchanging latex. It
is said to be edible.

5. **apricot milkcap**   *Lactarius volemus*   p.219
Beautiful apricot-coloured mushroom with copious, white, unchanging latex; mild
taste, but somewhat fishy odour when drying. A good **edible** mushroom when well
cooked.

6. **bright yellow milkcap**   *Lactarius aspideoides*   p.220
This very bright yellow, slimy milkcap with white latex, which stains the injured
parts purple, is easy to recognize. **Poisonous**.

Page 49

RUSSULACEAE
Five smooth-capped, pinkish to brown *Lactarius* species; unchanging latex; inedible
to **poisonous**.

1. **red-hot Lactarius**   *Lactarius rufus*   p.220
Can be recognized by its lovely reddish brown colour, its red-hot taste, white
unchanging latex and spruce habitat. **Poisonous**.

2. **sticky milkcap**   *Lactarius affinis*   p.220
Similar in shape to no. 1; it has a pale pinkish, buff colour all over and is sticky; the
latex is copious, white, unchanging and the taste is mild, very slowly a bit sharp.
Not edible.

3. **smoky milkcap**   *Lactarius fumosus*   p.220
A striking mushroom, not immediately recognized as a Lactarius. It does have
white latex, which colours the flesh light pink. Velvety, smoky brown cap stalk.
Although it has a mild taste, it is not recommended for eating.

4. **pale milkcap**   *Lactarius pallidus*   p.221
The baby-pink *Lactarius* is sticky; has a lot of unchanging milky latex; pale salmon-
coloured gills. Despite its innocent, baby-pink looks it is said to be **poisonous**.

5. **Waterdrop Lactarius**   *Lactarius aquifluus*   p.221
This is a *Lactarius* which can be easily recognized by its clear colourless latex; the
fragrant, sugary odour, especially when it is dried; and its reddish brown cap,
which shows a fine areolate pattern in age. Edibility unknown.

Page 51

LEPIOTACEAE
Parasol mushrooms have a scaly cap, free white gills; a white spore print; a ring on
the stalk, no volva. Watch out for small *Lepiota* species. They can be **deadly
poisonous**.

1. **sharp-scaled Lepiota**   *Lepiota acutesquamosa*   p.223
Easily recognized by its sharp warts on the cap, the large white ring with brown
scales on the margin and its smooth stalk. **Poisonous**.

2. **shaggy-stalked parasol**   *Lepiota clypeolaria*   p.223
There is quite a lot of variation in colour and shagginess. This is a lovely, delicate
mushroom, with small scales on the cap, which is shaped like a Chinese hat. The
stalk has a woolly, shaggy ring and shaggy lower stalk. **Poisonous**.

Lactarius
aquifluus Peck

5

St. Albert, Alta   21.9.81

19.9.76
Sandy
Lake, Alta

Lactarius pallidus
(Persoon: Fries) Fries

4

2

Lactarius
affinis Peck
WolfLake, Alta
28.8.78

Elk
Island
Nat. Park
Alta 15.8.81

Lactarius fumosus Peck
var. fumosoides (Smith & Hesler)
Hesler & Smith

3

30.8.77
Kootenay National
Park, B.C.

1.

Lactarius rufus (Schaeffer: Fries) S.F. Gray

3. **small white Lepiota**   *Lepiota alba*   p.223
Easily recognized as one of the small Lepiotas, this one is pure white . It may have a light brown umbo. Closely related to *L. clypeolaria*, it is almost smooth; may have a few bits on the lower stalk. Not recommended for eating.

4. **very small brown Lepiota**   *Lepiota castanea*   p.223
The small chestnut-coloured *Lepiota* is hard to find in moss under spruce. Darker than the others and smaller, it has a typical *Lepiota* shape. It is **deadly poisonous**; contains *Amanita* toxins.

5. **brown-eyed parasol**   *Lepiota helveola*   p.224
This *Lepiota* does not have as pronounced an umbo as the others. Its crown draws attention like a brown eye, the scales around it are lighter in colour. It has a smooth stalk and a brown ring. **Deadly poisonous.**

6. **shaggy parasol**   *Macrolepiota rhacodes*   p.224
The word *rhacodes* refers to the shagginess of the cap. The cuticle breaks up in large pieces, which hang on by threads or fall off. The large stalk is smooth and reddish brown and the flesh turns, first, saffron-yellow and then changes to a beautiful red. Edible but extreme caution needed because a similar tropical species is very poisonous. Both turn up in atria. See text or long description.

Page 52

LEPIOTACEAE

Five parasol mushrooms, belonging to three genera, which are somewhat different: the flowerpot and yellow parasols are tropical species and grow with houseplants or in atria in temperate climates; one without scales and two with cobwebby veils. None of these are edible. One is deadly.

1. **deadly Lepiota**   *Lepiota josserandii*   p.225
Small but **deadly** Lepiota, recognized by its cinnamon-coloured concentric scales, showing pink in between its cobwebby veil and quite sturdy stalk. Another **deadly**, small Lepiota, *L. helveola* (former name: *L. brunneoincarnata*), looks very much like this one.

2. **cobweb parasol**   *Lepiota cortinarius*   p.225
This is a typical *Lepiota* except for the hairy ring left by the cobwebby veil; both the deadly Lepiota and the cobweb parasol have a cortina. Edibility unknown.

3. **flowerpot parasol**   *Leucocoprinus longistriatus*   p.225
This species has long striations or grooves on the cap and is mostly white and very fragile. A tropical species, sometimes found with houseplants. Edibility unknown.

4. **yellow Lepiota**   *Leucocoprinus luteus*   p.225
Butter to sulphur yellow mushroom with a strongly grooved cap. An exciting find in midwinter in indoor gardens in Canada. **Poisonous.**

5. **smooth Lepiota**   *Leucoagaricus naucinus*   p.226
Leuco means white in Greek and this species looks very much indeed like a white *Agaricus* except that the gills stay white instead of turning pink and then brown. It has white spores, white cap, flaring ring on a sturdy stalk. Edible, but caution is needed because it could be confused with the destroying angel, (p. 53).

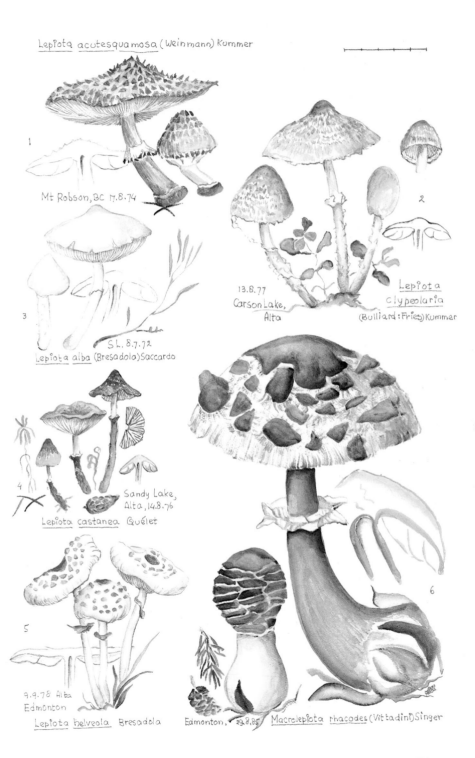

Lepiota acutesquamosa (Weinmann) Kummer

1

Mt Robson, BC 17.8.74

3

S.L. 8.7.72
Lepiota alba (Bresadola) Saccardo

13.8.77
Carson Lake,
Alta

2

Lepiota
clypeolaria
(Bulliard : Fries) Kummer

4

Sandy Lake,
Alta, 14.8.76
Lepiota castanea Quélet

5

9.9.78 Alta
Edmonton
Lepiota helveola Bresadola

6

Edmonton, 29.8.85   Macrolepiota rhacodes (Vittadini) Singer

Sandy Lake, Alta
17·9·79

Lepiota josserandii
Bon & Boilfard

Lepiota cortinarius
3.8.77   J. Lange
Sandy Lake, Alta

2

1.

2.11.86
Edmonton,
Alta
in atrium

Leucocoprinus longistriatus
(Peck) H.V. Smith & Weber

3

Leucocoprinus luteus
(Bolton) Godfrin
West Edmonton Mall
25.3.87

4

Leucoagaricus naucinus (Fries) Singer   15.7.85 Radville, Sask.

5

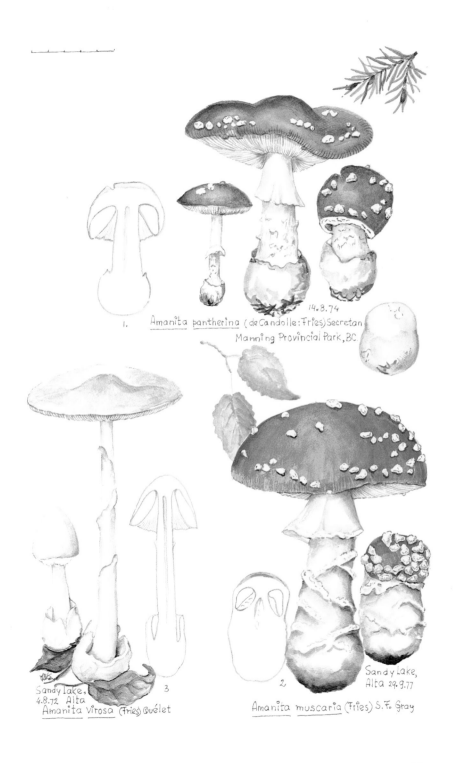

1. Amanita pantherina (de Candolle: Fries) Secretan
Manning Provincial Park, BC
14.8.74

Sandy Lake,
4.8.72 Alta
Amanita virosa (Fries) Quélet
3

Sandy Lake,
Alta 29.9.77
2
Amanita muscaria (Fries) S.F. Gray

Page 53

AMANITACEAE

Three poisonous and deadly *Amanita* species; all have free, white gills; white spore print, a ring and a volva.

1. **the panther** *Amanita pantherina* p.227
Medium to large mushroom; cap in various shades of smoky brown; partial veil leaves a drooping ring; universal veil leaves white spots on cap and a collar around the bulbous base. Very **poisonous** and hallucinogenic.

2. **fly amanita** *Amanita muscaria* p.227
Large mushroom; cap in shades of red, orange and yellow; the colour fades in bright sunshine and is almost white, just before decay. The well-known white spots are loose parts of the volva, which wash off in a rainshower. Large drooping ring and ridges instead of a cup on the swollen stalk base characterize this beautiful species. **Poisonous** and hallucinogenic.

3. **destroying angel** *Amanita virosa* p.228
Tall, stately, slim mushroom; the whole mushroom is white; smooth cap, large basal cup; drooping ring, sometimes shaggy. **Deadly poisonous**.

Page 55

AMANITACEAE

Four species of *Amanita* with free, white gills, a white spore print, a volva but no ring.

1. **grisette** *Amanita vaginata* p.228
Characterized by its dark, shiny, grey-brown or smoky-brown cap and its grey flame-patterned, ringless stalk with its slim, soft cup. Edible but not recommended.

2. **Battarra's Amanita** *Amanita battarrae* p.228
Characterized by its yellowish-brown cap with a large volval patch; its white ringless stalk and its slim, soft cup; a mountain mushroom. Its edibility is not known.

3. **tawny grisette** *Amanita fulva* p.229
Characterized by its fox-coloured cap and stalk, ringless like the others and the large floppy cup. Said to be edible but not recommended. I don't recommend any *Amanita* since it could be deadly to make a mistake.

4. **smelly Amanita** *Amanita roanokensis* p.229
Characterized by its tall, white, flame-patterned, ringless stalk buried deep in the ground; its white domed cap with a bit darker crown and its obnoxious odour. Not edible.

Page 57

AMANITACEAE

The two *Amanita* species shown here have a straight stalk with a suddenly thickening base and the two *Limacella* species have a slimy universal veil (not a fibrous one as the *Amanita*s have).

1. **purplish Amanita or booted Amanita** *Amanita porphyria* p.229
Characterized by its smooth, greyish-brown cap with a purplish tinge, its grey ring and round (abruptibulbous) base of the stalk; collared bulb. **Poisonous**.

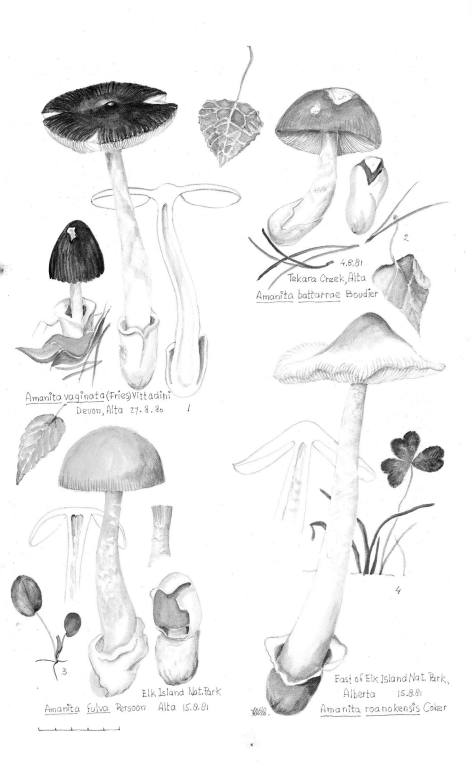

Amanita vaginata (Fries) Vittadini
Devon, Alta 27.8.80   1

4.8.81
Tekara Creek, Alta
Amanita battarrae Boudier

2

Amanita fulva Persoon   Alta 15.8.81
Elk Island Nat. Park

3

East of Elk Island Nat. Park,
Alberta   15.8.81
Amanita roanokensis Coker

4

2. **the blusher**   *Amanita rubescens*   p.230
   Characterized by its smoky red cap with raised white and pink volval patches; its
   sturdy pink stalk; lined droopy ring and abruptibulbous base. It is called the
   blusher because handling deepens the blush, and insect bites cause the flesh to turn
   pink. Said to be edible but not recommended. Deadly species could easily be
   mistaken for this one.

3. **white to yellow, slime-veiled Limacella**   *Limacella illinita*   p.230
   Characterized by its thick, slimy, universal veil covering the white or yellow cap
   and white stalk; the partial veil is slimy as well. The universal veil does not leave a
   cup.

4. **fox-coloured, slime-veiled Limacella**   *Limacella glioderma*   p.230
   Characterized by its slimy universal veil covering a fox-coloured mushroom; the
   slime is not as thick as in species no. 3. The stalk cuticle breaks up in patches
   (originally slimy); superior ragged ring.

Page 58

HYGROPHORACEAE
Hygrophorus species with sticky to slimy caps; thick, soft gills; slimy or fibrous rings
and soft colours.

1. **spruce waxgill**   *Hygrophorus piceae*   p.231
   Snow white mushroom with a sticky cap and dry, silky stalk. Grows exclusively
   under spruce.

2. **sheathed waxgill**   *Hygrophorus olivaceoalbus*   p.232
   Easily recognized by the brown sticky cap with decurrent gills and zigzag pattern
   on the lower stalk.

3. **small grey waxgill**   *Hygrophorus morrisii*   p.232
   Small, grey, elegant mushroom; white gills; small ridge just below the gills; small
   pointed grey scales on the stalk.

4. **veiled waxgill**   *Hygrophorus velatus*   p.232
   When a fresh specimen of this species is found, it will not be easily forgotten by a
   true mycophile. It has a beautiful, shiny, slimy, pink cap; white decurrent gills;
   white scaly stalk and a ridge below the gills.

5. **smoky waxgill**   *Hygrophorus camarophyllus*   p.232
   Smoky, greyish-brown, squat mushroom, with white distant gills; growing under
   spruce.

6. **golden-fringed waxgill**   *Hygrophorus chrysodon*   p.233
   The golden-fringed Hygrophorus is paler than no. 7 and does not have such a
   pronounced sheath.

7. **golden waxgill**   *Hygrophorus aureus*   p.233
   The golden Hygrophorus is more golden and orange than no. 6 and it has a more
   woolly-looking stalk with definite annular ridge.

Page 59

HYGROPHORACEAE
Large *Hygrophorus* species in shades of pink; not slimy; attached, thick, soft gills.

1. **blushing waxgill**   *Hygrophorus pudorinus*   p.233
   There is a lot of variation possible in this medium-sized mushroom, but it can be
   recognized by a flesh-coloured to orange cap, darker in the centre; thick, decurrent,
   intervenose gills; and a white blushing stalk. Inedible.

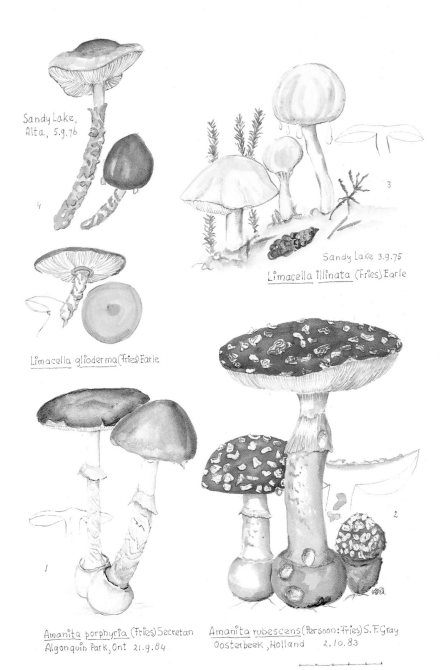

Sandy Lake,
Alta, 5.9.76

4

3

Sandy Lake 3.9.75
Limacella illinata (Fries) Earle

Limacella glioderma (Fries) Earle

1

2

Amanita porphyria (Fries) Secretan
Algonquin Park, Ont 21.9.84

Amanita rubescens (Persoon:Fries) S.F. Gray
Oosterbeek, Holland   2.10.83

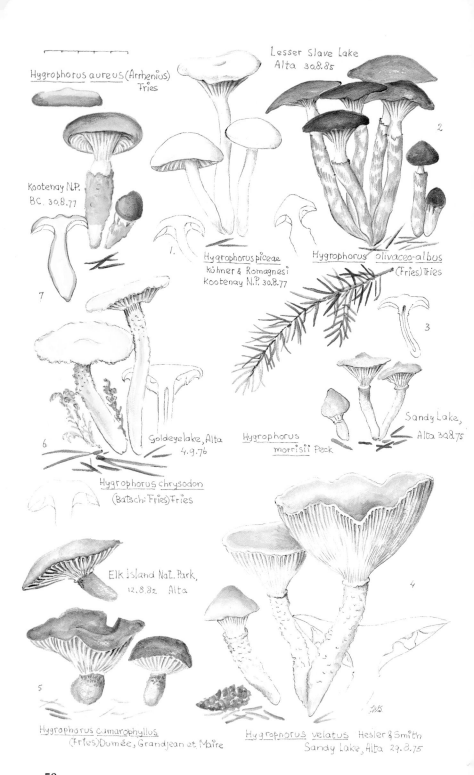

Hygrophorus aureus (Arrhenius) Fries

Kootenay N.P. B.C. 30.8.77

7

Lesser Slave Lake Alta 30.8.85

2

1.

Hygrophorus piceae Kühner & Romagnesi Kootenay N.P. 30.8.77

Hygrophorus olivaceo-albus (Fries) Fries

3

6

Goldeyelake, Alta 4.9.76

Hygrophorus chrysodon (Batsch: Fries) Fries

Hygrophorus morrisii Peck

Sandy Lake, Alta 30.8.75

Elk Island Nat. Park, 12.8.82 Alta

4

5

Hygrophorus cumarophyllus (Fries) Dumée, Grandjean et Maire

Hygrophorus velatus Hesler & Smith Sandy Lake, Alta 27.8.75

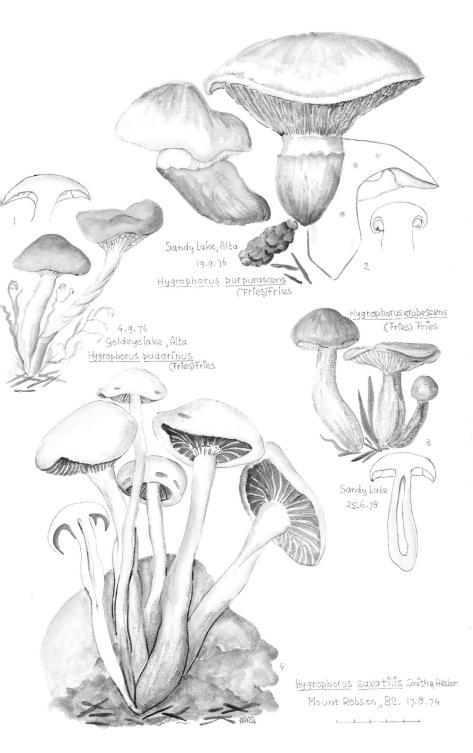

Sandy Lake, Alta
19.9.76
Hygrophorus purpurascens
(Fries)Fries

4.9.76
Goldeyelake, Alta
Hygrophorus pudorinus
(Fries)Fries

Hygrophorus erubescens
(Fries) Fries

Sandy Lake
25.6.78

Hygrophorus saxatilis Smith& Hesler
Mount Robson, BC. 17.8.74

2. **purplish waxgill**   *Hygrophorus purpurascens*   p.234
Large, squat mushrooms with streaky, purplish-pink cap and heavy stalk. In young specimens the presence of a white cortina results in a narrow ring. The sporeprint is white as in all waxgills. Said to be edible.

3. **reddening waxgill**   *Hygrophorus erubescens*   p.234
Medium-sized mushrooms, looking remarkably like no. 2, but smaller in size, with no cortina and the flesh of the stalk stains yellow. While no. 2 is said to be edible, this one is inedible and bitter.

4. **waxgill of the Rockies**   *Hygrophorus saxatilis*   p.234
Growing on rocky mountain slopes on decaying conifer stumps and duff, these mushrooms, with rosy red gills and white spores, are very striking and certain to attract attention.

Page 61

HYGROPHORACEAE
Ten very bright, small *Hygrocybe* species; caps and stalks can be sticky or viscid but not slimy; no veil; gills waxy. Numbers 9 and 10 can be relatively large.

1. **chanterelle waxgill**   *Hygrocybe cantharellus*   p.235
Small mushroom with dry red cap and stalk; thick deep yellow to orange, decurrent gills; reminiscent of a chantarelle but smaller and brighter in colour.

2. **pointed waxgill**   *Hygrocybe cuspidata*   p.235
Small red-capped mushroom; pointed like *H. conica*, but does not blacken when touched and is more sticky; fruits in spring.

3. **orange-brown waxgill**   *Hygrocybe laeta*   p.235
Very slimy, orange-brown mushroom with a fishy odour.

4. **tiny waxgill**   *Hygrocybe minutula*   p.236
Very small waxgill; can be recognized by its viscid orange cap with yellow border.

5. **small waxgill**   *Hygrocybe parvula*   p.236
Small apricot-coloured mushroom; slightly larger generally than no. 4; can be recognized by its orange, decurrent gills and non-viscid surface.

6. **vermilion waxgill**   *Hygrocybe miniata*   p.236
This species can easily be recognized by its overall bright scarlet to vermilion colouring; even the flesh of the cap and stalk is red.

7. **golden yellow waxgill**   *Hygrocybe ceracea*   p.236
Every part of this species is coloured yellow, making it easy to recognize.

8. **parrot waxgill**   *Hygrocybe psittacina*   p.237
The shiny, olive green cap makes this mushroom easily recognizable; it looks like an emerald in the sun. When it dries, there are always green traces left.

9. **sharply conic waxgill**   *Hygrocybe acutoconica*   p.237
Can be recognized by its viscid, golden yellow cap; yellow gills; and twisted stalk; does not stain black, when touched.

10. **blackening waxgill**   *Hygrocybe conica*   p.237
The blackening waxgill comes in a variety of colours and sizes, but every part of it turns black when touched or when aging.

Hygrocybe cantharellus (Schweinitz) Morrill

1

30.6.85
Ann Prior, Ont.

Hygrocybe cuspidata (Peck) Morrill
Sandy Lake, Alta 29.6.71

2

3

S.L. 9.9.73
Hygrocybe laeta (Persoon:Fries) Kummer

Hygrocybe minutula (Peck) Morrill

4

Jasper, Alta 11.6.71

5

Hygrocybe parvula (Peck) Morrill
Sandy Lake, Alta
30.8.80

6

25.9.82

Hygrocybe miniata (Fries) Kummer
Goat River, B.C.

8

7

Hygrocybe ceracea (Fries) Kummer
S.L. 6.9.75

Hygrocybe psittacina
(Schaeffer: Fries) Wünsche

3.7.85
North Hatley,
Québec

10

21.8.76
Sandy Lake, Alta

Hygrocybe conica (Fries) Kummer

Alta,
28.7.78
Sandy Lake

9

Hygrocybe acutoconica
(Clements) Singer

• 61 •

Page 63

HYGROPHORACEAE

The five species of *Camarophyllus* or arch-gilled waxcaps are less sticky than either *Hygrophorus* or *Hygrocybe*; there is no ring; sometimes there are interconnecting veins between the gills.

1. **snow-white waxgill**   *Camarophyllus niveus*   p.238
Small white mushrooms with decurrent, thick gills, which have a lot of interconnecting veins. The waxy feeling of crushed gills and the thickness of the gills show it is a waxgill.

2. **meadow waxgill**   *Camarophyllus pratensis*   p.238
Medium-sized mushrooms; characterized by the apricot colour, fading to buff, and distant interveined, decurrent gills, which stay arched most of the time.

3. **virginal waxgill**   *Camarophyllus virgineus*   p.239
Another medium-sized waxgill; in shape much like no. 2, but completely white; dries up yellowish, unlike no. 1 which is much smaller and dries up snowy white.

4. **violet waxgill**   *Camarophyllus subviolaceus*   p.239
The unusual colour of the gills for a waxgill makes this mushroom stand out; the purple arched, thick gills and white spore print make this one readily recognizable.

5. **northern white waxgill**   *Camarophyllus borealis*   p.239
The smallest of the white species described. Sometimes it is suggested that *C. borealis* and *C. niveus* are so close, that they could be one species; others suggest that *C. niveus* and *C. virgineus* could be one. I leave this up to the experts to decide.

Page 64

TRICHOLOMATACEAE

Two large "booted" or sheathed *Tricholoma* species. The top of the sheath forms the ring. This is unusual in Tricholomas.

1. **Zeller's mushroom**   *Tricholoma zelleri*   p.240
Large fleshy mushroom; cap up to 20 cm across; stalk tapering down; flaring ring; brownish colour with scales on the disc; growing in mixed coniferous forest under Douglas fir and spruce. Taste and odour variable.

2. **pine mushroom**   *Tricholoma magnivelare*   p.241
Equally large mushroom with stalk tapering down, but this one is predominantly white and has a smooth cap and a very large partial veil, as the Latin name indicates. Forms a mycorrhizal relationship with pine (see the common name). Excellent taste and pleasant odour.

Page 65

TRICHOLOMATACEAE

Five medium-sized, mostly yellow species of *Tricholoma*. Some good edible species and some look-a-like **poisonous** ones.

1. **earthy Tricholoma**   *Tricholoma terreum*   p.241
Can be recognized by its grey, felty or fibrous cap and white, easily splitting, stalk. Not recommended for eating because it is difficult to recognize accurately.

2. **western chevalier**   *Tricholoma leucophyllum*   p.241
Can be recognized by its chinese-hat-like cap with a chestnut crown, light margin and white gills; the flesh is white. Tastes good.

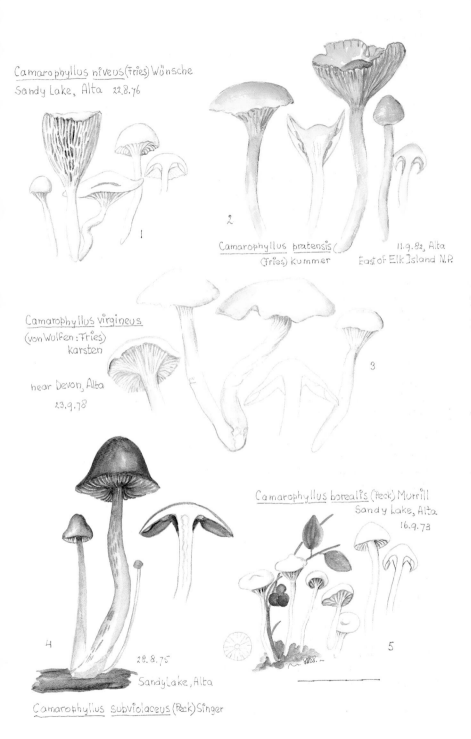

Camarophyllus niveus (Fries) Wünsche
Sandy Lake, Alta   22.8.76

1

2

Camarophyllus pratensis   11.9.82, Alta
(Fries) Kummer   East of Elk Island N.P.

Camarophyllus virgineus
(von Wulfen : Fries)
Karsten

near Devon, Alta
23.9.78

3

Camarophyllus borealis (Peck) Murrill
Sandy Lake, Alta
16.9.73

4

28.8.75

Sandy Lake, Alta

Camarophyllus subviolaceus (Peck) Singer

5

24.8.78   Lac Beauvert, Jasper N.P., Alta

Tricholoma zelleri (Stuntz & Smith) Ovebro & Tylutki

2

Valemount, B.C.

28.8.87

Tricholoma magnivelare (Peck) Redhead

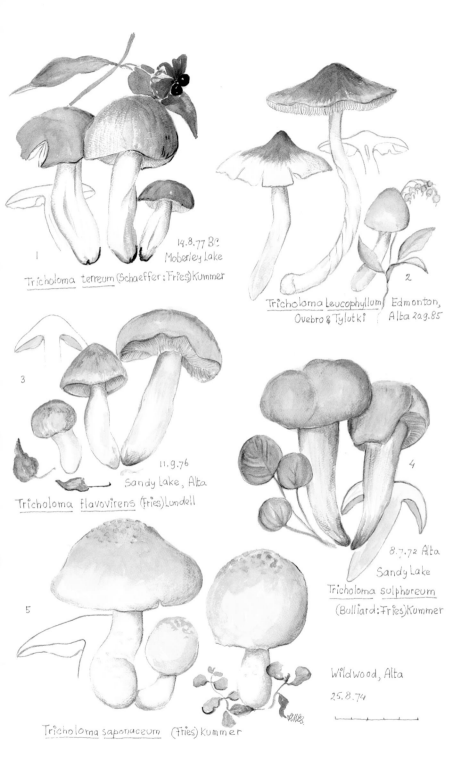

1

14.8.77 BC
Moberley Lake

Tricholoma terreum (Schaeffer: Fries) Kummer

2

Tricholoma Leucophyllum   Edmonton,
Ovebro & Tylutki   Alta 2ag.85

3

11.9.76
Sandy Lake, Alta

Tricholoma flavovirens (Fries) Lundell

4

8.7.72 Alta
Sandy Lake

Tricholoma sulphoreum
(Bulliard: Fries) Kummer

5

Tricholoma saponaceum   (Fries) Kummer

Wildwood, Alta

25.8.74

3. **chevalier or man on horseback**   *Tricholoma flavovirens*   p.242
This is a well-known, excellent-tasting, edible mushroom. The name may have
something to do with "fit for a knight or chevalier". Bright yellow gills are
characteristic; the flesh is white. Excellent taste. Edible.

4. **narcissus Tricholoma**   *Tricholoma sulphureum*   p.242
This mushroom resembles no 3. The difference is the bright yellow colour of the
flesh. It frequently has a nasty coal-tar odour and it is **poisonous.**

5. **soapy Tricholoma**   *Tricholoma saponaceum*   p.242
A very variable species in colour as well as odour. Can be yellowish to grey-brown.
Has been reported as **poisonous.** Too variable in colour and shape to experiment
with.

Page 67

TRICHOLOMATACEAE

These two *Tricholoma* species have many characteristics in common. They grow in
dense masses, developing underground. When they emerge, earth and leaves stick
to their viscid caps. Thick, firm flesh; almost "rooting" stalk; irregular caps from
pushing in the crowd; pink-staining gills; and their very large size (up to 20 cm
across) apply to both species. Among the red- and pink- staining species there are
some which can cause gastro-intestinal disturbances. *T. pessundatum* is one of them
(see p. 69). Caution is advised in this group. Renée Pomerleau describes both
species in *Champignons de Québec*. American authors either describe one or the other
or neither.

1. **"the sandy"**   *Tricholoma populinum*   p.243
The common name refers to the soil and leaves on the caps when they emerge in a
group. **Always** found under poplar; light-coloured caps, dirty reddish brown with
white border; white stalks and white flesh which stays white. A popular edible in
the Pacific Northwest.

2. **burnt Tricholoma**   *Tricholoma ustale*   p.243
The dark brown to maroon caps look burnt and dirty with earth and leaves sticking
to them. They may grow under poplar but not exclusively; they also grow under
various deciduous trees. The massive stalks are ventricose and dirty white, staining
pink or pinkish brown; flesh white, staining pink, particularly around holes made
by insects.

Page 69

TRICHOLOMATACEAE

Four pink-staining and two whitish species of *Tricholoma*, all growing under
coniferous trees; inedible to **poisonous.**

1. **slimy, orange Tricholoma**   *Tricholoma aurantium*   p.243
Recognized by its gelatinous covering on cap and stalk when wet, its foxy colour
and the interesting pattern on the stalk. Unpalatable.

2. **girdled Tricholoma**   *Tricholoma cingulatum*   p.244
Recognized by its blue-grey colour, small size and its small ring on the stalk. Too
small to be considered for eating.

Tricholoma populinum   J. Lange   3.9.78   Sandy Lake, Alta

2   Gibbons, Alta, 12.9.85

Tricholoma ustale (Fries) Kummer

. 67 .

3. **ill-scented Tricholoma**   *Tricholoma inamoenum*   p.244
Almost white *Tricholoma*, characterized by its distant forked, or crossveined, gills and its unpleasant scent. Unpalatable.

4. **scaly Tricholoma**   *Tricholoma vaccinum*   p.244
Recognized by its reddish-brown, scaly cap, same colour stalk and pink-staining gills. Growing in groups under spruce. Inedible.

5. **reddish-brown Tricholoma**   *Tricholoma pessundatum*   p.244
Characterized by its sticky, smooth, dark brown cap, lighter stalk with reddish, woolly fibres on it and pink-staining gills. **Poisonous.**

6. **false Tricholoma**   *Pseudotricholoma umbrosum*   p.245
Characterized by its golden brown cap and short, red-brown, hollowed-out stalk. Inedible. *Pseudotricholoma* is related to *Tricholoma*.

Page 70

TRICHOLOMATACEAE
The genus *Clitocybe* contains funnel-shaped mushrooms with decurrent gills. **Do not** try to eat small, white or grey Clitocybes even if they smell good. See also p. 71 where very **poisonous** species are shown.

1. **mountain avens Clitocybe**   *Clitocybe candicans* var. *dryadicola*   p.245
Small *Clitocybe* which is found only with *Dryas drummondii* or yellow mountain avens and so can be recognized by the company it keeps. Edibility unknown.

2. **slim anise mushroom**   *Clitocybe fragrans*   p.246
Small white mushroom with a strong scent of anise seed; not poisonous but can easily be mixed up with other small poisonous Clitocybes.

3. **sweet-smelling Clitocybe**   *Clitocybe suavolens*   p.246
Small brown mushroom with pale grey gills; growing in grassy areas, often in the ring of *Marasmius oreades*, the fairy ring mushroom (see remarks with no. 2).

4. **slim Clitocybe**   *Clitocybe tenuissima*   p.246
Slim, small, pale grey mushroom with woolly stalk base; grows in moss under pine.

5. **bruised Clitocybe**   *Clitocybe vibecina*   p.246
Medium small mushroom; growing under spruce in mixed woods; brownish fading to white, looking bruised in the process; deep navel.

6. **white anise-scented Clitocybe**   *Clitocybe odora*   p.247
White, medium-size mushroom with decurrent gills and a strong anise scent; growing in deciduous and mixed forest. A very common mushroom in boreal mixed forest and aspen parkland. Edible with caution because of the chance of confusing it with the poisonous *C. cerussata* (see p. 71).

7. **green anise-scented Clitocybe or funnel Clitocybe**   *Clitocybe odora*   p.247
The green-capped form occurs only in coniferous forests on the prairies; the blue-green cap, white gills and white stalk, in addition to the strong anise scent, make it unmistakable. Edible.

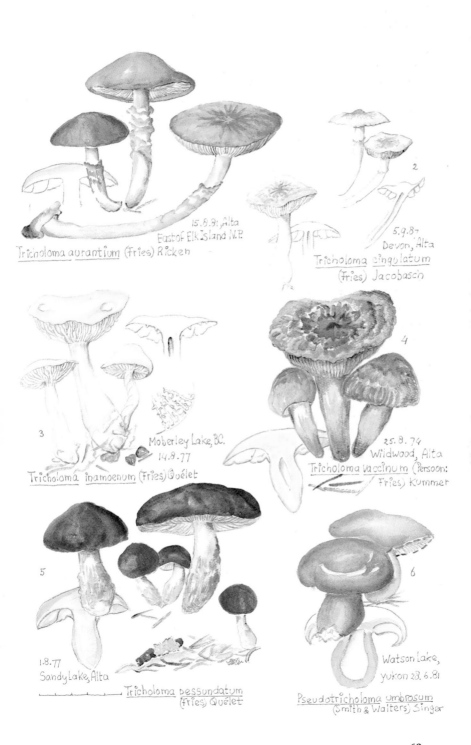

15.8.81, Alta
East of Elk Island N.P.
Tricholoma aurantium (Fries) Ricken

2

5.9.87
Devon, Alta
Tricholoma cingulatum
(Fries) Jacobasch

3

Moberley Lake, BC.
14.8.77
Tricholoma inamoenum (Fries) Quélet

4

25.8.74
Wildwood, Alta
Tricholoma vaccinum (Persoon:
Fries) Kummer

5

1.8.77
Sandy Lake, Alta
Tricholoma pessundatum
(Fries) Quélet

6

Watson Lake,
Yukon 23.6.81
Pseudotricholoma umbrosum
(Smith & Walters) Singer

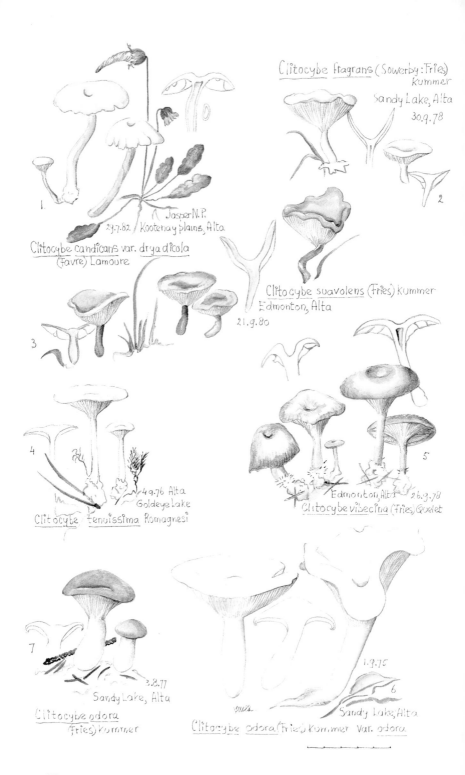

Clitocybe fragrans (Sowerby:Fries) kummer

Sandy Lake, Alta
30.9.78

2

1.

Jasper N.P.
23.7.82 Kootenay plains, Alta

Clitocybe candicans var. dryadicola
(Favre) Lamoure

Clitocybe suavolens (Fries) kummer
Edmonton, Alta
21.9.80

3

4

4.9.76 Alta
Goldeye Lake

Clitocybe tenuissima Romagnesi

5

Edmonton, Alta 26.9.78
Clitocybe vibecina (Fries) Quelet

7

3.8.77
Sandy Lake, Alta

Clitocybe odora
(Fries) kummer

1.9.75

6

Sandy Lake, Alta

Clitocybe odora (Fries) kummer var. odora.

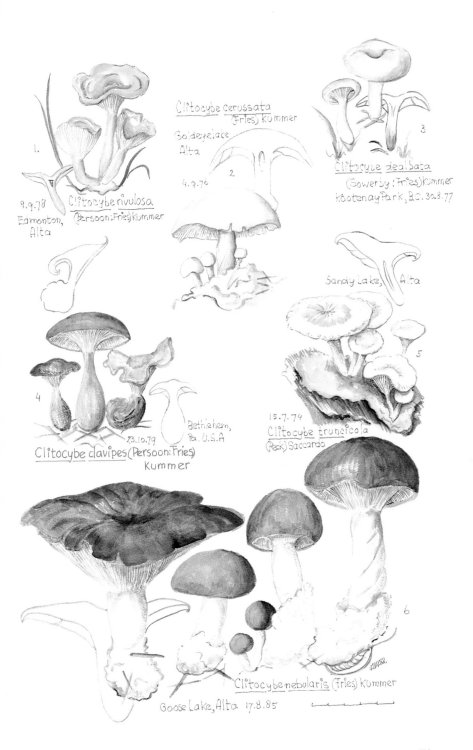

1. 8.9.78 Edmonton, Alta
Clitocybe rivulosa (Persoon: Fries) Kummer

2. *Clitocybe cerussata* (Fries) Kummer
Goldeye lake Alta
4.9.76

3. *Clitocybe dealbata* (Sowerby: Fries) Kummer
Kootenay Park, B.C. 30.8.77

4. *Clitocybe clavipes* (Persoon: Fries) Kummer
23.10.79
Bethlehem, Pa. U.S.A

5. Sandy lake, Alta
15.7.74 *Clitocybe truncicola* (Peck) Saccardo

6. *Clitocybe nebularis* (Fries) Kummer
Goose Lake, Alta 17.8.85

Page 71

TRICHOLOMATACEAE

Six small to large , **poisonous** to **deadly** species of *Clitocybe* growing in the forest or in fairy rings in lawns or parks.

1. **deadly Clitocybe**   *Clitocybe rivulosa*   p.247
Small mushroom with a pattern of pink and white concentric circles on the cap when damp; drying up whitish; growing in grassy areas; **very poisonous.**

2. **lead-white Clitocybe**   *Clitocybe cerussata*   p.247
Recognized by its lead-white cap; medium small; growing in tufts in the forest. **Poisonous.**

3. **sweating mushroom**   *Clitocybe dealbata*   p.248
Small greyish mushroom, bleaching white; may grow with fairy ring mushroom. Contains muscarine and causes sweating and other miseries when eaten. **Poisonous.**

4. **clubfooted Clitocybe**   *Clitocybe clavipes*   p.248
Very neat, brown mushroom with heavy stalk base; occurring in conifer woods. Related to no. 6. Only **poisonous** when used with alcohol. **Caution.**

5. **log Clitocybe**   *Clitocybe truncicola*   p.248
Off-white, small to medium-sized mushrooms growing in groups on mossy old logs which is unusual for a *Clitocybe*; *C. truncicola* has some brownish pink on the cap disc. **Poisonous.**

6. **cloudy Clitocybe**   *Clitocybe nebularis*   p.249
Large strong mushrooms growing in fairy rings under conifers. The name indicates that the smoky, greyish-brown cap looks a little frosty. Can be recognized by this and its pale yellow gills. It is related to the clubfooted Clitocybe. **Poisonous.** See detailed description.

Page 73

TRICHOLOMATACEAE

Five *Clitocybe* species (or funnel mushrooms) with woolly-white mycelium at the stalkbase. Edibility of these is unknown.

1. **small scaly Clitocybe**   *Clitocybe squamulosa*   p.249
Small brown mushroom with an interesting sudden dip in the cap; the scales referred to in the name are not very obvious.

2. **strong or sturdy Clitocybe**   *Clitocybe robusta*   p.249
Medium-sized, sturdy, off-white mushroom resembling the poisonous cloudy Clitocybe in shape (p. 71).

3. **slim funnel mushroom**   *Clitocybe gibba*   p.250
Small to medium-sized, dainty, pale buckskin, funnel mushroom growing in deciduous forest.

4. **brick-red Clitocybe**   *Clitocybe sinopica*   p.250
Small to medium-sized funnel mushroom, darker in colour than no. 3 and somewhat sturdier. Occurs on burnt ground and along roads.

5. **streaked Clitocybe**   *Clitocybe ectypoides*   p.250
Medium to large funnel mushroom; can be recognized by its cap with scaly centre, pinkish decurrent gills and auburn stalk.

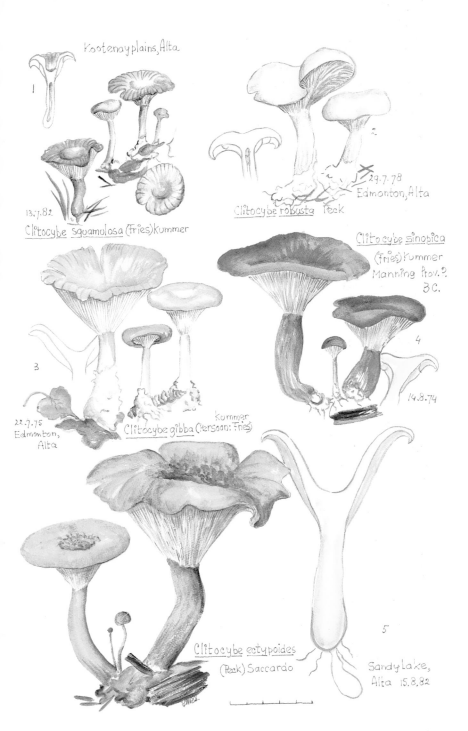

Kootenay plains, Alta

1

13.7.82

Clitocybe squamulosa (Fries) Kummer

2

29.7.78
Edmonton, Alta

Clitocybe robusta Peck

Clitocybe sinopica
(Fries) Kummer
Manning Prov.?
B.C.

3

4

22.7.75
Edmonton,
Alta

14.8.74

Clitocybe gibba (Persoon: Fries) Kummer

5

Clitocybe ectypoides
(Peck) Saccardo

Sandy lake,
Alta 15.8.82

Page 75

TRICHOLOMATACEAE

Two very large *Clitocybe* species, edible when young. I have eaten *Clitocybe maxima* and found the young ones tasty. Young *C. geotropa* are said to be good, too, but I have not eaten them myself. Both are long living and get tough. They grow in enormous fairy rings, rows or part rings. In dry areas they are found when no other mushrooms are around, simply because they survive for a long time.

1. **large white Clitocybe** *Clitocybe maxima* p.250
Can be recognized by its large size; narrow, long-decurrent gills; white colour; stringy stalk; and white mycelium in the duff.

2. **trumpet mushroom** *Clitocybe geotropa* p.251
Can be recognized by its large size; straw and peach colour all over; woolly mycelium halfway up the stalk; and mature cap with splitting cuticle and holes between the gills. Besides that, the mushroom has a proud and erect stance. As the name "geotropa" indicates, it is perfectly perpendicular to the earth.

Page 76

TRICHOLOMATACEAE

Seven small to medium-sized *Collybia* species; thin-fleshed with hollow, cartilaginous stalks. They are tough and inedible, including the spotted one which is bitter. Collybias tend to grow in groups.

1. **insignificant Collybia** *Collybia ingrata* p.251
Can be recognized by its very small size and strong aromatic odour. Grows in groups on leaves.

2. **tufted Collybia** *Collybia confluens* p.252
Another species growing in tufts, but it is somewhat bigger in size than *C. ingrata* when mature. The velvety stalks are first pinkish but fade. Grows on leaves, needles or old wood.

3. **dark Collybia** *Collybia obscura* p.252
The dark Collybia is small too, but everything is brown — gills included; the dark stalk is velvety, like nos. 1 and 2.

4. **clustered Collybia** *Collybia acervata* p.252
Beautiful, very tight, large clusters. Easily recognized when fresh by reddish-brown, smooth stalks and caps. Grows on stumps or buried wood. They fade with age.

5. **forest-loving Collybia or June mushroom** *Collybia dryophila* p.252
Grows only in spring while other Collybias grow in spring or fall. It is a very variable complex group, which grows in small groups on duff. Chestnut to golden yellow colouring; white spores.

6. **hard-to-know Collybia** *Collybia confusa* p.253
Another dark hard-to-identify species as the name indicates. Dark, velvety, twisted stalk; very narrow brown gills, but a white spore print.

7. **spotted Collybia** *Collybia maculata* p.253
The spotted Collybia is the easiest to recognize as a *Collybia* because it is bigger than the others and gets pinkish to rusty spots on cap and gills as it ages. Pinkish-buff spore print.

6.9.75

Sandy Lake, Alta

<u>Clitocybe maxima</u> (Fries) Kummer

Edmonton, Alta
10.8.80, in ravine

<u>Clitocybe geotropa</u> (Bulliard: St Amans) Quélet

• 75 •

Collybia ingrata (Schumacher: Fries) Quélet
Sandy Lake, Alta 2.7.76

1

2

Collybia obscura Favre
Kootenay plains, Alta

4

3

31.7.82

Collybia confluens (Persoon: Fries) Kummer
Sandy Lake, Alta 30.6.74

Sandy Lake, Alta 20.8.73

Collybia acervata (Fries) Kummer

5

Collybia dryophila (Bulliard: Fries) Kummer
Sandy Lake, Alta 15.7.81

6
12.9.82

Collybia confusa Orton
Elk Island National Park, Alta

7

Shaw Lake, Alta
6.8.80

Collybia maculata (Albertini & Schweinitz: Fries) Kummer

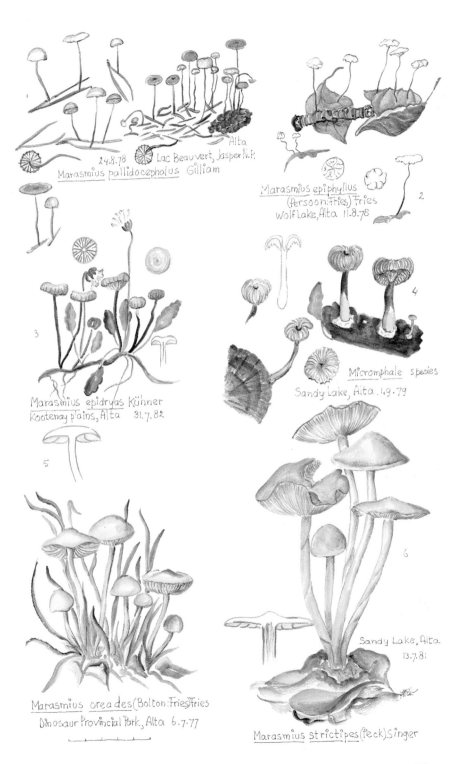

24.8.78 Lac Beauvert, Jasper N.P.
Alta
Marasmius pallidocephalus Gilliam

Marasmius epiphyllus
(Persoon:Fries) Fries
Wolf Lake, Alta 11.8.78

2

3

Marasmius epidryas Kühner
Kootenay plains, Alta   31.7.82

5

4

Micromphale species
Sandy Lake, Alta . 1.9.79

6

Sandy Lake, Alta
13.7.81

Marasmius oreades (Bolton:Fries) Fries
Dinosaur Provincial Park., Alta 6.7.77

Marasmius strictipes (Peck) Singer

Page 77

TRICHOLOMATACEAE

Five *Marasmius* and one closely related *Micromphale* species, which are able to dry up or wither (meaning of the name *Marasmius*) in dry periods and then revive and sporulate again when it rains.

1. **conifers pinwheels** *Marasmius pallidocephalus*   p.253
Small reddish-brown caps soon fading to buff or almost white; thin, dark, tough stalks; growing on conifer needles.

2. **white pinwheel** *Marasmius epiphyllus*   p.254
Even daintier than no. 1, the white pinwheels grow on dead leaves in the forest. Although the fruiting bodies are small, the mycelial network is far-reaching and they are mighty recyclers of leaves and branchlets.

3. **Dryas pinwheel** *Marasmius eprdryas*   p.254
A very specialized species of pinwheel. These little mushrooms grow only on the dead part of the bark of Dryas (or mountain avens).

4. **small mushroom with navel** *Micromphale* sp.   p.254
Growing on old wood and bark, these brown mushrooms have a deep navel in their cap centre. Hygrophanous, their caps looked ribbed soon after they were picked, showing the gills through the thin cap.

5. **fairy ring mushroom** *Marasmius oreades*   p.255
Small buff-coloured mushrooms growing in rings in grassy areas. Edible, but watch for small white poisonous Clitocybe and poison pie (*Hebeloma crustiliniforme*) which also form rings and sometimes join the fairy ring mushroom.

6. **tightly bunched Marasmius** *Marasmius strictipes*   p.255
Very similar to no.5 but grows on dead leaves in the forest. It grows in tight bunches; has a fuzzy stalk; is taller and pinkish-tan in colour.

Page 79

TRICHOLOMATACEAE

honey mushroom *Armillaria mellea*   p.256
woolly stalk mushroom *Floccularia albolanaripes*   p.256

The honey mushroom grows in groups at the base of both deciduous and coniferous trees or on the wood of dead-standing trees or stumps, in which case the mushrooms are larger. Caps are honey-coloured or brown with or without scales; stalks often club shaped, at other times equal; rings present. A lemon yellow colour under the ring is an important characteristic when collecting for the pot. In the illustration are six variations in colour and shape of this complex species, and there is one cluster belonging to the related genus *Floccularia*. The parasitic honey mushrooms are the favorite late-fall edible mushrooms of many people.

1. Honey mushrooms growing from the roots of a living birch in mixed boreal forest. To the right is one specimen (and section) which I found in Holland under fir, very similar but with different gill attachment.

2. Honey mushroom specimens growing on the dead wood of the balsam poplar tree the fungus killed. Fruiting bodies are bigger when growing on dead wood. To the right is a small pale specimen with adnate gills, while the big one has decurrent gills.

3. Specimens portrayed here are overmature. They have turned dark brown, almost black, but the white woolly ring stayed white, and the mushrooms were still sporulating! Found under hazelnut in Edmonton ravine.

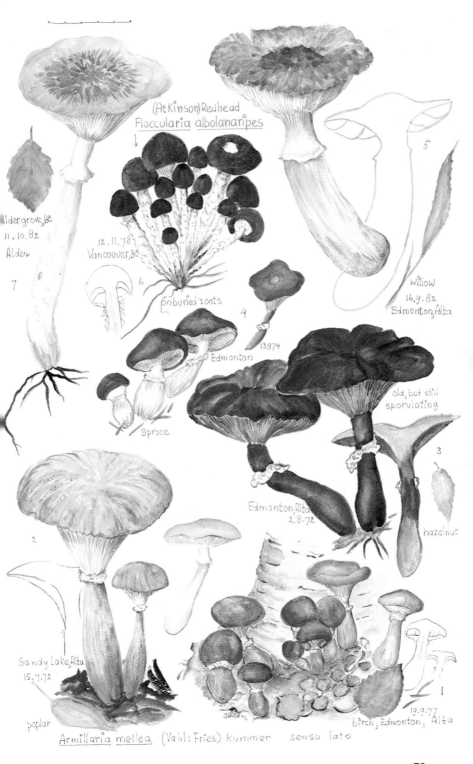

(Atkinson) Redhead
Floccularia albolanaripes

Aldergrove, BC
11.10.82
Alder

7

12.11.78?
Vancouver, BC

6

on buried roots

4

5

Willow
16.9.82
Edmonton, Alta

13.8.74

Edmonton

Spruce

old, but still
sporulating

3

Edmonton, Alta
2.8.72

hazelnut

2

Sandy Lake, Alta
15.7.72

poplar

13.9.77
birch, Edmonton, Alta

1

Armillaria mellea (Vahl: Fries) Kummer   sensu lato

• 79 •

4. Found these under a spruce tree in an Edmonton garden in 1974. They are a beautiful chestnut colour. They have the characteristic woolly ring and lemon yellow under the ring but not the honey colour of nos. 1 and 2. This spruce won; it looks healthy 15 years later.
5. Big specimens found on willow wood near the North Saskatchewan river. Large in size but they still have the basic honey mushroom shape. Instead of a streaked, more-or-less smooth cap, it has a scaly cap with lovely yellow, pink and brown colours; the gills have a bit of a pinkish tinge (like the ones growing under spruce). The ring is woolly and the stalk under the ring is streaky with yellow, pink and brown colours but is not scaly. The gills are adnate.
6. A tight bunch was found in a Vancouver garden in the winter. The caps are a beautiful coffee colour with very small scales. The stalks completely white and woolly all over; growing out of buried wood. This is *Floccularia albolanaripes*, a related species.
7. Tall specimens were found in winter in Aldergrove, B.C., growing under alder. Also with a white, more-or-less woolly stalk and a pale brown squamulose cap. The ring was slightly more fibrous than woolly. Only when you are sure of recognizing the honey mushroom in its various forms, should you collect it for eating. When in doubt, ask an expert. Collect a small amount, including young, mature and old ones, for identification purposes. They always grow in groups.

Page 81

TRICHOLOMATACEAE

Lepista species have a dull cap surface resembling chamois; the spore prints are cream, pink or flesh coloured. The blewit can be cultivated and is a good edible mushroom when young. The edibility of the others is unknown.

1. **orange funnel cap** *Lepista inversa*   p.257
Small to medium; recognized by its colourful cap, which with age becomes a deep, irregular funnel in foxy orange to brick colour; its long decurrent gills and short brown stalk. Grows under spruce.

2. **woolly Lepista** *Lepista irina*   p.257
Medium to large; recognized by its pale cap; pale flesh-coloured gills; whitish stalk with fluffy top and its general resemblance to the well-known blewit but without the blewit's purple colouring; does have pale pink spore print.

3. **blueleg** *Lepista saeva*   p.258
Medium to large; the blueleg really has a wine-coloured, not blue, stalk; pale tan cap and pale buff gills with vinaceous tints in it.

4. **golden Lepista** *Lepista gilva*   p.258
Small to medium; the golden Lepista resembles the orange species but is pale golden all over. Young caps have just a depression in the centre, and the funnel is very shallow.

5. **blewit** *Lepista nuda*   p.258
Recognized by lilaceous or purple colour of cap, stalk, gills and flesh, and by a peach-pink spore print. The intensity of colour varies. In California I have found specimens which were much darker than those in Alberta. The long-living mushrooms fade with age. Can be mixed up with *Cortinarius albo-violaceus*, but that one has a cortina and brown spores. Edible when cooked.

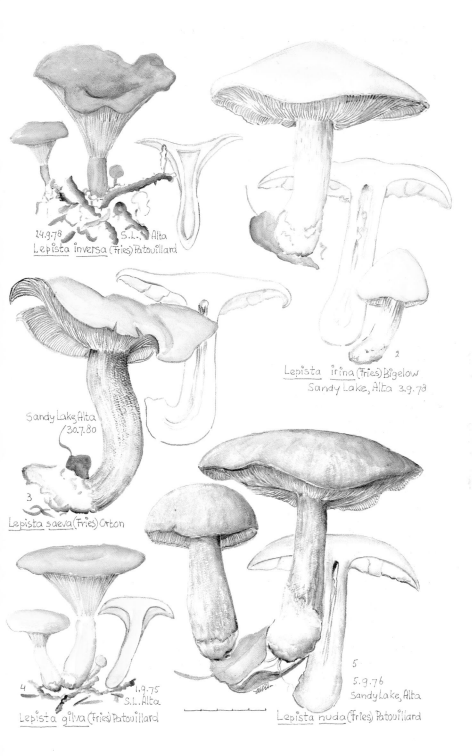

24.9.78   S.L., Alta
Lepista inversa (Fries) Patouillard

Lepista irina (Fries) Bigelow
Sandy Lake, Alta 3.9.78

2

Sandy Lake, Alta
(30.7.80

3
Lepista saeva (Fries) Orton

4   1.9.75
               S.L. Alta
Lepista gilva (Fries) Patouillard

5
5.9.76
Sandy Lake, Alta
Lepista nuda (Fries) Patouillard

• 81 •

Page 83

TRICHOLOMATACEAE

Leucopaxillus species are solid, long-lasting mushrooms with dry caps like soft leather; narrow decurrent gills, often somewhat forked or with cross connections; white cottony mycelium shows in the duff at the stalk base. The long lasting mushrooms often drop a dusting of white spores on the surrounding plants.

1. **spruce leucopax**   *Leucopaxillus piceinus*   p.259
Grows in mixed forest, usually near spruce in fairy rings or part rings; perfectly hemispherical tan caps; seem very short because the bulbous part of the stalk is buried in the duff. There is always a white dusting of spores on neighbouring plants.

2. **northern leucopax**   *Leucopaxillus septentrionalis*   p.259
Grows under spruce or generally conifers. This species has a massive stalk compared to its cap; very narrow anastomosing gills; tan cap; quickly gets dingy from handling.

3. **bitter leucopax**   *Leucopaxillus amarus*   p.259
Grows under conifers. This species has a foxy reddish-brown cap with lighter margin; short, white stalk; and, like the others, copious white mycelium in the duff.

4. **giant leucopax**   *Leucopaxillus giganteus*   p.260
Grows in mixed forest. This species is the biggest of this genus; easily more than 30 cm across. Recognized by its decurrent, narrow gills; caps which are often cracked in a circular pattern; stalk with fine brown hairs in maturity. It grows in fairy rings with a large diameter.

Page 84

TRICHOLOMATACEAE

The six Melanoleucas are characterized by their stiff, straight, slim stalks; no ring or volva; spore print is white, cream or buff depending on the species. Some are said to be edible, but edibility is mostly unknown.

1. **mountain Melanoleuca**   *Melanoleuca evenosa*   p.260
Recognized by its light-coloured overall appearance and its clean smell; occurs in spring in the mountains. May look like *Collybia*, but is sturdier; white spores.

2. **yellowish-white Melanoleuca**   *Melanoleuca alboflavida*   p.261
Recognized by its very tall, streaky stalk; light brown cap and white gills. Occurs in groups in meadows in the fall; creamy spores.

3. **dark Melanoleuca**   *Melanoleuca melaleuca*   p.261
Darkest of this genus, it almost looks black when wet; can also be dark blackish-brown; white gills; creamy spores.

4. **small Melanoleuca**   *Melanoleuca humilis*   p.261
Very small mouse-coloured species; grows in moss in bogs; rarely found because of its protective colouring and habitat; white spores.

5. **striped-stalk Melanoleuca**   *Melanoleuca grammopodia*   p.261
Can be recognized by its lined stalk, brown cap and white gills; spores creamy.

6. **peach-gilled Melanoleuca**   *Melanoleuca cognata*   p.262
Most easily recognized *Melanoleuca*, although there is a lot of variation; can be recognized by its rigid, straight stalk, peach-coloured gills; stringy flesh in stalk and the spore print, which is creamy white to ochrish cream.

Leucopaxillus piceinus (Peck) Pomerleau

18.7.77
Sandy Lake, Alta

Leucopaxillus amarus (Albertini & Schweinitz) Kühner
Lacla Biche,
Alta

3

22.8.86

Cookinglake,
Alta.18.8.78

2

Leucopaxillus sestentrionalis
Singer & A.H.Smith

4   Leucopaxillus giganteus (Fries) Singer   Sandy Lake, Alta

20.7.76

13.7.81
Melanoleuca evenosa
(Saccardo) Konrad
Maligne Lake, Jasper N.P. Alta

Melanoleuca melaleuca
(Fries) Murrill

3

Edmonton
Alta 27.9.79

S.L. 5.9.76
Melanoleuca humilis (Fries)
Patouillard

4

5

6.7.75
Sandy Lake
Melanoleuca grammopodia
(Bulliard) Patouillard

Sandy Lake,
Alta 11.9.76
Melanoleuca alboflavida
(Peck) Murrill

18.6.88
Ministik Lake, Alta

6

6

28.6.81
Watson Lake, Yukon
Melanoleuca cognata (Fries) Konrad & Maublanc

Lesser Slave Lake, Alta 26.8.85

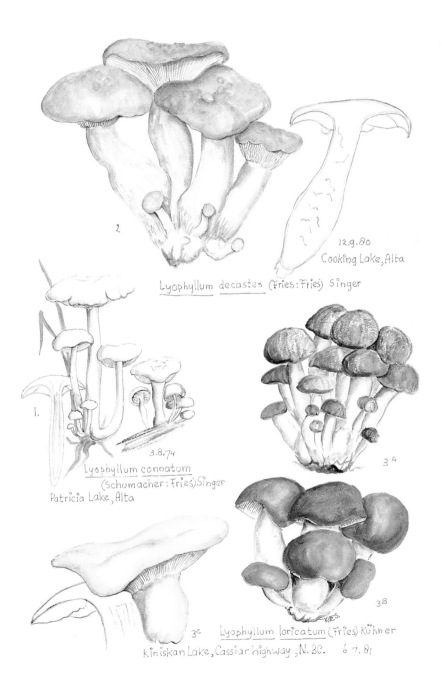

2

12.9.80
Cooking Lake, Alta

<u>Lyophyllum decastes</u> (Fries:Fries) Singer

1.

3.8.74
<u>Lyophyllum connatum</u>
(Schumacher:Fries)Singer
Patricia Lake, Alta

3ᴬ

3ᴮ

3ᶜ   <u>Lyophyllum loricatum</u> (Fries) Kühner
Kiniskan Lake, Cassiar highway, N.BC.   6.7.81

Page 85

TRICHOLOMATACEAE

Lyophyllum species grow in tight tufts, strongly joined at the base of the stalks; white spore prints.

1. **white tuft**   *Lyophyllum connatum*   p.262
   Grows in caespitose groups. These white mushrooms stand out in grassy areas and disturbed places. Not recommended for eating, can be confused with poisonous *Clitocybe*.

2. **fried chicken mushroom**   *Lyophyllum decastes*   p.263
   Grows in very large tufts in disturbed areas, like city parks, and other grassy areas where there usually is buried wood present. Greyish or brownish caps. Edible with caution, because it is not easily recognized.

3. **frosty Lyophyllum**   *Lyophyllum loricatum*   p.263
   Growing in the same kind of habitat as the other two, this species goes through more colour changes in its development than the first two. Grows in large tufts in ditches and disturbed areas. Edible with caution because it is not easily recognized.

Page 87

TRICHOLOMATACEAE

Calocybe means beautiful head. The four species shown have colourful round caps and a white spore print. They often grow in fairy rings. Edibility of the orange, pink and violet Calocybes is unknown.

1. **orange Calocybe**   *Calocybe fallax*   p.264
   Small, bright yellow, ochre and orange mushroom with very interesting irregular gills.

2. **pink Calocybe**   *Calocybe carnea*   p.264
   Small, flesh-coloured mushroom with white gills. I have found it in fairy rings in grass and in moss in conifer woods.

3. **violet Calocybe**   *Calocybe ionides*   p.264
   Medium to small, violet mushroom with bone-coloured gills. Grows in fairy rings in grass.

4. **cream Calocybe**   *Calocybe gambosa*   p.264
   Large cream-coloured mushroom. In England they are called St. George's mushrooms because they fruit around St. George's Day, April 23. In Alberta, they fruit in the fall because spring is usually very short. Edible, but not very good.

Page 89

TRICHOLOMATACEAE

The five species on this plate represent four small genera. They have the following in common: a white spore print; and growing on dead wood. The angelwings or *Pleurocybella* are stalkless.

1. **angel wings**   *Pleurocybella porrigens*   p.265
   Pliable, very thin, white brackets — like butterflies ready to fly away. These are hard to mistake for anything else, especially since they grow mostly west of the Great Divide in old conifer forests. Edible; good.

1

Calocybe fallax (Saccardo)
Singer

8.8.76
Sandy Lake, Alta

2

Calocybe ionides
(Bulliard:Fries)Donk

17.9.77 Edmonton, Alta

3

Sandy Lake, Alta   8.8.76
Calocybe carnea (Bulliard:Fries)
Kühner in Donk

4

Calocybe gambosa (Fries)Donk
Sandy Lake, Alta 9.9.73

2. **king's coat (konings mantel)** *Tricholomopsis rutilans* p.266
Granted, a very small king with a tiny fur coat, it is still a nice Dutch common name for this mushroom. Alizarin crimson hair on a yellow background and yellow gills make this an easy to recognize mushroom.

3. **queen's coat** *Tricholomopsis decora* p.266
Quite similar to the king's coat, but smaller and yellow all over with some dark hair on the cap which is denser in the centre. Both this one and no.2 occur on conifer logs, but this one is rarer.

4. **velvet foot** *Flammulina fennae* p.266
Easily recognized by it velvety, dark brown stalk, its colourful cap with a yellow edge and orange-brown centre. It grows in caespitose clusters. This is one of our two velvet foot species, which closely resemble each other. Edible; good tasting.

5. **western Hypsizygus** *Hysizygus marmoreus* p.267
Can be recognized in clusters on poplar wood (in the west); often has tall stalks; marbled buff caps.

Page 90

TRICHOLOMATACEAE
The ten species belonging to eight genera of Tricholomataceae have in common that they are small funnel-shaped mushrooms and resemble *Omphalina*. All but one have a white spore print, but one has a brown one. Edibility is unknown, but they are too small in any case.

1. **orange pin mushroom** *Rickenella fibula* p.267
Can be recognized by its colour; small cap with navel and fringed edge; thin stalk. Grows in mossy environment.

2. **small, white umbrella mushroom** *Phytoconis ericetorum* p.268
Small white mushroom growing on old wood, rocks or the ground, but always with lichens and mosses. It is a lichenized gilled mushroom.

3. **very dark Omphalina** *Omphalina obscurata* p.268
Can be recognized by its small size; very dark brown, overall colour; small umbrella shape and white spore print; occurs in grassy areas.

4. **brown goblet** *Omphalina epichysium* p.268
This small brown funnel mushroom is not so dark as no. 3 and the rim of the cap is lifted up. Grows on deacying wood in moss and lichens.

5. **burn site mushroom** *Myxomphalia maura* p.268
Can be rocognized by its typical cap shape and its habit of growing on burn sites on old wood.

6. **brown-spored navel mushroom** *Ripartites tricholoma* p.269
Characterized by its pale, pink hairy cap and its similarity to the others but it has a brown spore print, which is unexpected for a member of the Tricholomataceae family. Grows on dead leaves.

7. **Leather-brown Clitocybe** *Clitocybe diatreta* p.269
This little brown mushroom (L.B.M.) looks a lot like an Omphalina with its navel in the centre of the cap. It needs to be studied under a microscope to identify it. Grows on spruce needles.

8. **fork-gilled funnel** *Cantharellopsis prescotii* p.269
A white, small, funnel-shaped mushroom often with forked gills. Grows on leaves and needles on the ground or between spagnum moss.

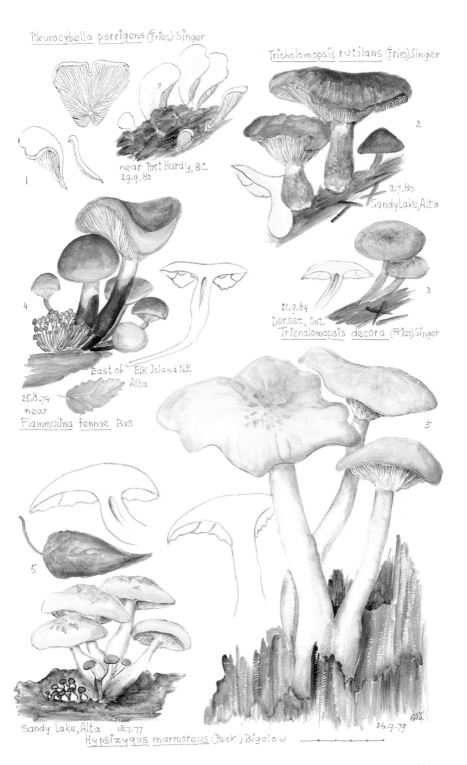

Pleurocybella porrigens (Fries) Singer

Tricholomopsis rutilans (Fries) Singer

2

1

near Port Hardy, B.C.
29.9.82

3.7.80
Sandy Lake, Alta

4

21.9.84
Dorset, Ont.

3

Tricholomopsis decora (Fries) Singer

East of Elk Island N.P.
Alta

25.8.74
near
Flammulina fennae Bas

5

5

Sandy Lake, Alta   18.7.77

24.9.79

Hypsizygus marmoreus (Peck) Bigelow

• 89 •

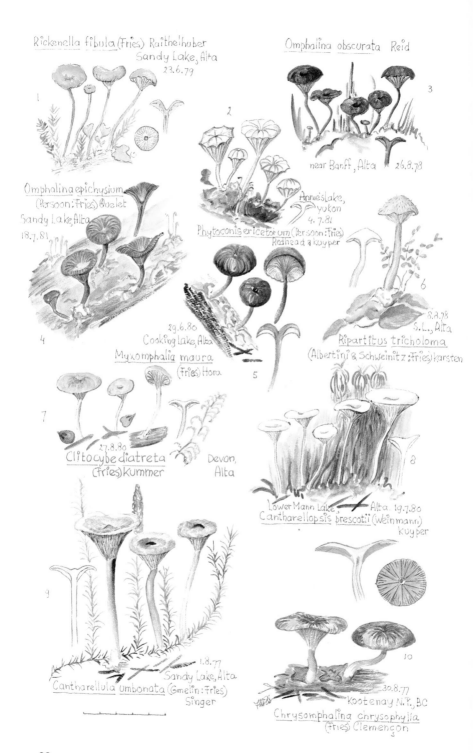

Rickenella fibula (Fries) Raithelhuber
Sandy Lake, Alta
23.6.79

1

Omphalina obscurata Reid

3

near Banff, Alta   26.8.78

Omphalina epichysium
(Persoon: Fries) Quélet
Sandy Lake, Alta
18.7.81

4

2

Annie's Lake,
Yukon
4.7.81

Phytoconis ericetorum (Persoon: Fries)
Redhead & Kuyper

29.6.80
Cooking Lake, Alta

Myxomphalia maura
(Fries) Hora

5

6

8.8.78
S.L., Alta
Ripartitus tricholoma
(Albertini & Schweinitz: Fries) Karsten

7

27.8.80
Clitocybe diatreta
(Fries) Kummer

Devon,
Alta

8

Lower Mann Lake,   Alta. 19.7.80
Cantharellopsis prescotii (Weinmann)
Kuyper

9

10

1.8.77
Sandy Lake, Alta
Cantharellula umbonata (Gmelin: Fries)
Singer

30.8.77
Kootenay N.P., BC
Chrysomphalina chrysophylla
(Fries) Clémençon

Cystoderma amiantinum (Scopoli : Fries)
Fayod fm montanum

5

Sandy lake, Alta 1.8.77

Vancouver
Island, BC

15.11.78

Goldeye lake
Alta

4.9.74

4

Cystoderma amiantinum (Scopoli :
Fries) Fayod

21.8.76

3

Sandy lake, Alta
Cystoderma cinnabarinum (Albertini
& Schweinitz : Secretan)
Fayod

2

Devon, Alta
4.7.87

Cystoderma fallax
A.H. Smith & Singer

1.

2...9.80

Jasper Nat. Park, Alta

Phaeolepiota aurea (Mattirolo : Fries) Maire : Konrad & Maublanc

9. **grayling** *Cantharellula umbonata* p.269
The grayling can be recognized by its overall grey colour, its conspicuously forked gills and its preference for conifer bogs.

10. **golden gilled mushroom** *Chrysomphalina chrysophylla* p.270
Characterized by its apricot-orange, distant gills; orange stalk; rounded cap with navel; and its occurrence on rotting conifer wood.

Page 91

TRICHOLOMATACEAE

The four *Cystoderma* species resemble *Phaeolepiota* very much in shape and skin texture. Both are "booted" or "sheathed". This means that the ring — when still covering the gills — is a part of the skin of the stalk. When it loosens from the cap edge, it stands up like a collar. *Phaeolepiota* is much larger than the others and has a yellow-ochre spore print. Edibility of the four *Cystoderma* species is unknown.

1. **goldcap** *Phaeolepiota aurea* p.270
The large golden mushroom cannot be mistaken for anything else because of its granular or powdery coating, its collar-like ring, sheathed stalk and yellow ochre spore print. Edible for some, but may cause gastric distress in some people.

2. **conifer Cystoderma** *Cystoderma fallax* p.271
Medium-sized chestnut brown mushroom; looks like a smaller, brown version of no. 1, with white spores; grows on conifer debris, needles and bits of wood.

3. **vermilion Cystoderma** *Cystoderma cinnabarinum* p.271
Grows singly, or in small groups, in moss under spruce. This medium-sized mushroom can be recognized by its colourful granular cap, its sheathed, scaly stalk, very small ring and lighter colour at the top of the stalk.

4. **unspotted Cystoderma** *Cystoderma amiantinum* p.271
A smaller paler version of the previous one. There is quite a bit of variation in this species. There is a sheath and a collar-like ring but both can be evanescent (see no. 5 for more variation).

5. **mountain cystoderma** *Cystoderma amiantinum* forma *montanum* p.272
The mountain form is brighter in colour and has a more scaly stalk. It looks most like a mini version of *Cystoderma cinnabarinum*.

Page 93

XERULACEAE

Eight species from six Xerulaceae genera are included. All grow on dry material — leaves, cones, needles, rotten wood or near old stumps, and all have rhizomorphs or rootlike mycelium bundles at their base and white spore prints. The first seven are inedible.

1. **slender white bog mushroom** *Hemimycena gracilis* p.273
Small, completely white mushrooms with striate hemispherical caps and thin, tall stalks.

2. **miniature Mycena** *Mycenella margaritispora* p.273
Very small, dainty mushrooms; grey all over; grow in moss at the base of stumps.

3. **western cone mushroom** *Strobilurus occidentalis* p.273
Very small mushrooms in shades of brown; grow on conifer cones and needles. They fruit in late summer and fall.

Strobilurus occidentalis
Wells & Kempton
26.9.78   Sandy Lake,
           Alta

3

Strobilurus
trullisatus
(Murrill) Lennox

4

Spruce   Robson River,
          BC 16.8.74 Rocky
                       Mtns

Mycenella margaritispora
(Lange) Singer

18.7.81
Sandy Lake,
Alta
2

88.76
S.L.

Hemimycena
gracilis
(Quélet) Singer

Alta,
Lac la Biche
22.8.86   6A

5   Xeromphalina
     campanella
     (Fries) Kühner & Maire
     Carson Lake, Alta

30.8.80

9.8.82
Sandy Lake,
Alta

6D

2.9.77, S.L.   6B

23.9.78, S.L.   6C

Xeromphalina
fraxinophila
A.H.Smith

7

A.H.Smith
Baeospora myriadophylla
Edmonton, Alta 21.7.80

8

North Hatley, Québ.
2.7.85

Mt.Robson,BC
17.8.74

Megacollybia platyphylla (Persoon:Fries) Kotlaba & Pouzar

• 93 •

4. **Douglas fir cone mushroom**   *Strobilurus trullisatus*   p.273
Small mushrooms, but bigger than no.3. Grows on conifer cones, with preference for Douglas fir; profuse orange fluffy mycelium at the stalkbase is a characteristic.

5. **orange fuzzyfoot**   *Xeromphalina campanella*   p.274
Early in spring, late in summer or fall, large numbers of small orange bell-shaped mushrooms can be found on moss-covered, well-decayed spruce stumps; overall orange and ochre colour; distant, interveined gills; caps with a navel; velvety stalk.

6. **rufus fuzzyfoot**   *Xeromphalina fraxinophila*   p.274
Slightly bigger mushrooms with a round cap and a deep navel, like no.5. Cap colour ranges from orange to yellowish-brown and rufous; dark brown stalk; grow on leaf and needle debris of various trees.

7. **lavender Baeospora**   *Baeospora myriadophylla*   p.274
Lavender-coloured mushroom with very crowded gills; grows on wood; with a long pseudorhiza, which may grow into the ground under the wood.

8. **rooting braodgill**   *Megacollybia platyphylla*   p.275
Large sturdy mushroom; grey-brown cap with radial fibres, broad off-white gills; sturdy, off-white stalk that is often twisted and large rhizoids; grows in groups on well-decayed stumps. Not recommended for eating because some people cannot tolerate this mushroom, and it has a poor taste.

Page 95

XERULACEAE
Members of the genus *Mycena* have elegant, colourful caps resembling miniature chinese hats; fragile mushrooms; thin flesh; narrow gills; white spore print. The six species on this plate all live on wood. None are edible.

1. **bleeding Mycena**   *Mycena haematopus*   p.275
Very apt name, because rich blood-red juice drips from the stalk when it is broken; easily recognized as well by its elegant chinese-hat-shaped cap with crimson tinges; grows on decaying stumps.

2. **orange Mycena or Lea's Mycena**   *Mycena leaiana*   p.275
Also easily recognized by its bright orange cap, gills and stalk, although they fade quite easily; found on deciduous logs in caespitose clusters.

3. **toque Mycena**   *Mycena galericulata*   p.276
In England it's called a bonnet Mycena, but I thought that for us, toque is more appropriate! Easily recognized by the gills, which turn pink in maturity and by its habit of growing in caespitose clusters on deciduous wood; relatively big for the genus.

4. **Algerian Mycena**   *Mycena algeriensis*   p.276
A very dark brown or black, small, bell-shaped mushroom which grows on wood debris, sometimes on buried wood. A rhizomorph, as shown in one specimen, frequently occurs in Mycena species growing on buried, decayed wood.

5. **yellow-edged Mycena**   *Mycena citrinomarginata*   p.276
Small pointed-cap mushroom which grows on conifer debris. It has white gills with yellow edges.

6. **parabola Mycena**   *Mycena parabolica*   p.276
Not only is the cap section of a young specimen shaped like a parabola, but the cap is completely grooved (not just the margin), so that the striations are parabolic too! The colour is grey.

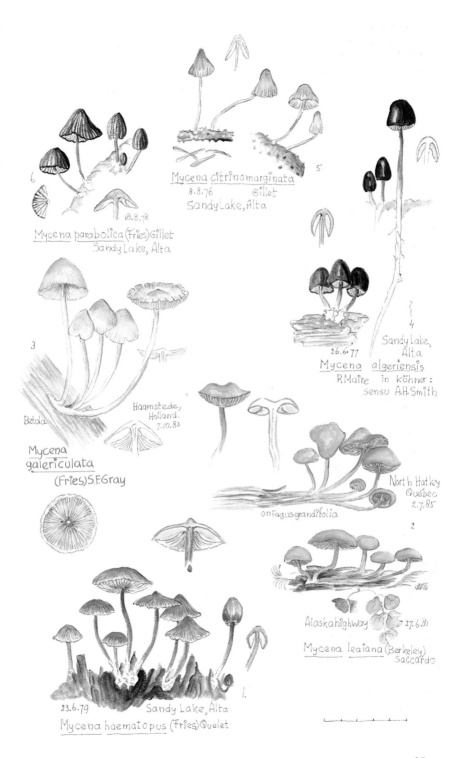

Mycena citrinomarginata
8.8.76   Gillet
Sandy Lake, Alta

5

6

18.8.78

Mycena parabolica (Fries) Gillet
Sandy Lake, Alta

3

Betula

Haamstede,
Holland.
7.10.83

Mycena
galericulata
(Fries) S.F. Gray

Sandy Lake,
Alta
26.6.77

?
4

Mycena algeriensis
R. Maire   in köhner:
sensu A.H. Smith

North Hatley
Québec
2.7.85

on Fagus grandifolia

2

Alaska highway   27.6.81

Mycena leaiana (Berkeley)
Saccardo

23.6.79   Sandy Lake, Alta
Mycena haematopus (Fries) Quelet

1.

Page 97

XERULACEAE

Seven more species of *Mycena* (Greek for mushroom), of which all are decomposers of needles, leaves, old wood, and duff in general. All the Mycenas need to be microscopically examined in order to make sure what they are.

1. **pink or lilac Mycena**   *Mycena pura*   p.277
Both common names are applicable because the colour varies between pink, lilaceous pink and lavender. This species is reported to be **poisonous**.

2. **white-stemmed Mycena**   *Mycena niveipes*   p.277
Grey-capped *Mycena* with a white stalk. Like many Mycenas it has beautifully spaced gills. There are several grey *Mycena* species, but this one has an unpleasant chemical odour.

3. **dark brown Mycena**   *Mycena macrocystidia*   p.277
A rare species, characterized by its dark brown convex cap, lighter stalk, but especially by microscopic features, e.g., the large cystidia as the species name implies. Cystidia are sterile cells, which keep the gills beautifully spaced.

4. **sand Mycena**   *Mycena psammicola*   p.277
Small brownish, bell-shaped mushroom with brown gills; looks like a *Galerina* which is poisonous. The sand Mycena has a white spore print while the *Galerina*'s is brown.

5. **pewter Mycena**   *Mycena stannea*   p.278
A pewter-coloured Mycena; the whole mushroom — cap, stalk and gills — is grey.

6. **conical Mycena**   *Mycena pectinata*   p.278
Narrowly conical, greyish-brown cap and brown stalk; grows under deciduous trees.

7. **common Mycena**   *Mycena vulgaris*   p.278
Not as common as the name implies; this small mushroom is different from the other mushrooms in this group in that it has adnate, arched gills and a reddish-brown centre of the cap.

Page 98

LACCARIACEAE

The four *Laccaria* species on the plate are all brightly coloured and have thick distant gills in the same bright colours, but the spore print is white. Not edible.

1. **auburn Laccaria**   *Laccaria purpureo-badia*   p.279
Recognized by its dark auburn colour tinged with purple; this mushroom resembles no. 3 in shape but not in colour. Powdery-looking, thick, distant gills.

2. **amethyst Laccaria**   *Laccaria amethystea*   p.279
Called red cabbage Laccaria in Holland; very fitting because it is that colour. This mushroom can be confused with the purple Mycena (see p. 97). *Laccaria* has a much tougher stalk and is **poisonous**.

3. **orange Laccaria**   *Laccaria laccata*   p.279
Very common species, but has great variations in colour and size, which makes it difficult to identify; look for colour clash between pink gills and a cap in shades of orange; thick, pink, powdery-looking gills.

4. **two-coloured Laccaria**   *Laccaria bicolor*   p.280
Not as common as nos. 2 and 3. This is a paler *Laccaria* version, with some of the colours of the other species; grows in the same habitat.

5
Alta
Sandy Lake, 3.10.81
Mycena stannea (Fries) Quélet

Mycena vulgaris (Fries) Quélet
Kootenay Nat. P. B.C.
29.8.77   7

6
Morrill
Mycena pectinata
8.8.76
S. L. Alta

Mycena
psammicola
(Berkeley & Broome) Saccardo
8.8.76
S. L.
Alta
4

3
Mycena macrocystidia
26.9.78   Singer
Sandy Lake, Alta

2
Mycena niveipes Morrill
Sandy Lake, Alta
2.9.75

spruce

aspen
5.9.76

birch

8.8.76
Sandy Lake, Alta
1.
Mycena pura (Fries) Gillet

4

Laccaria *bicolor* (Maire) Orton
Devon, Alta 4.7.87

3

Robson
River, BC
17.8.74

30.9.78
Sandy lake Alta
Laccaria *laccata* (Scopoli: Fries) Cooke

Sandy Lake, Alta.

4.8.75

12.9.82
Elk Island N.P. Alta

2

Laccaria *amethystea*
(Bulliard: Mérat) Murrill

Laccaria *purpureo-badia* D. Reid

1

15.8.82
Sandy Lake, Alta

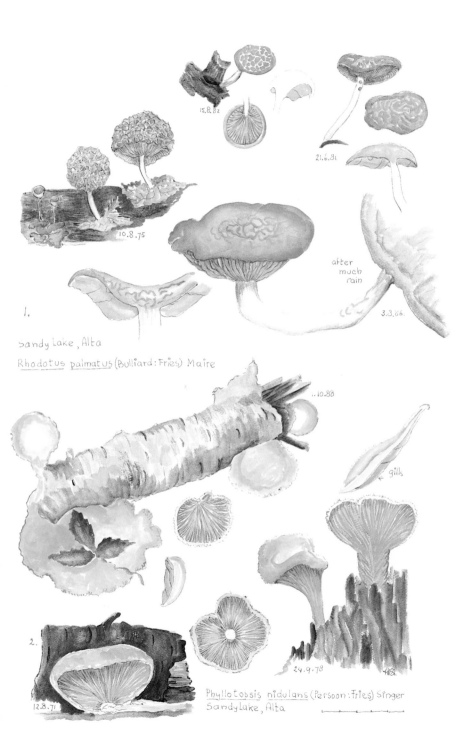

15.8.82

21.6.81

10.8.75

after
much
rain

3.3.86.

1.

Sandy Lake, Alta

Rhodotus palmatus (Bulliard: Fries) Maire

..10.88

gills

2.

24.9.78

12.8.71

Phyllotopsis nidulans (Persoon: Fries) Singer
Sandy Lake, Alta

Page 99

The two species illustrated here have the same colours — even the spores (pink to salmon) — but they do belong to different families.

RHODOTACEAE
1. **netted Rhodotus**   *Rhodotus palmatus*   p.280
Apricot-pink to orange mushroom with a raised network of veins on its cap; a short or long white stalk; salmon-coloured gills and a pinkish sporeprint; grows on decaying deciduous wood. Rare in the west — only three collections are recorded: one from Washington State, one from Manitoba, and mine from Alberta. Tough and inedible.

PLEUROTACEAE
2. **smelly oyster**   *Phyllotopsis nidulans*   p.281
A beautiful, orange, soft-bracket mushroom; felty on top and with saffron-coloured gills, but it has a really dirty odour. I was sitting in the forest, painting, when the smell from this mushroom suddenly hit me. This happened when the sun hit them. The heat brings out the rotting cabbage odour; you can follow your nose to find the culprits. The spore print is salmon-coloured. Grows on old wood. Inedible.

Page 101

PLEUROTACEAE
All Pleurotaceae grow on wood. The oyster mushroom of northwest North America is white, stalkless and grows on dead wood. The veiled oyster has a stalk with a ring and grows on a dead part or wound of a living tree.

1. **oyster mushroom**   *Pleurotus ostreatus*   p.281
Oyster-shaped mushroom, grows in shelving groups on dead wood; all white, somewhat yellowing with age; no stalk; with a strong anise odour, especially when warmed by the sun; good tasting and edible when young.

2. **veiled oyster**   *Pleurotus dryinus*   p.282
The veiled oyster is a sturdy mushroom with a stalk; a partial veil leaving a fringe around the cap edge, but not much of a ring; a scaly cap. It grows in clusters high up in trees, often from a hole in the trunk where a dead branch has fallen off a living tree; also on logs; good tasting and edible when young.

Page 102

PLEUROTACEAE
Six species belonging to six small genera of the family Pleurotaceae. They are all very different in shape and colour, but all have white spore prints, live on wood and are extremely persistent.

1. **black jelly oyster**   *Resupinatus applicatus*   p.282
Rubbery, black, small brackets growing on the underside of old logs; gills and white spore print are proof that this is not a jelly fungus. Not edible.

2. **late fall oyster**   *Panellus serotinus*   p.283
Orange and olive-green colours and its appearance late in the season make this an easily identifiable bracket mushroom; good tasting and edible.

3. **sunray mushroom**   *Heliocybe sulcata*   p.283
A tough, small mushroom growing on dry, barkless logs; can be recognized by its sunray pattern (radially ribbed) on the cap. Inedible and tough.

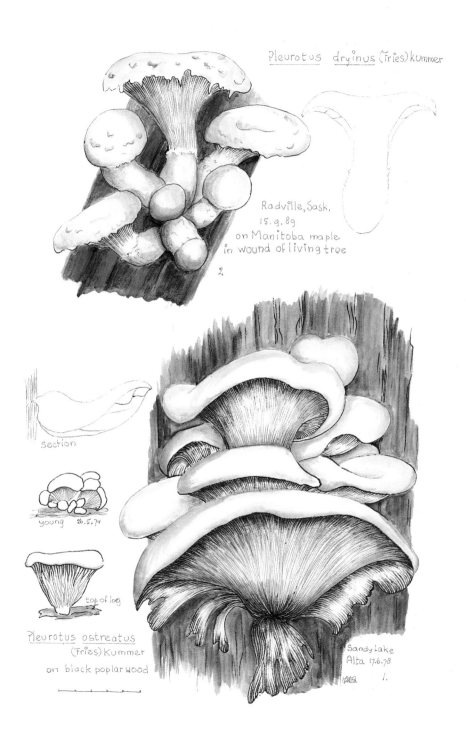

Pleurotus dryinus (Fries) Kummer

Radville, Sask.
15.9.89
on Manitoba maple
in wound of living tree
2

section

young 26.5.74

top of log

Pleurotus ostreatus
(Fries) Kummer
on black poplar wood

Sandy Lake
Alta 17.6.78
1.

3 bottom of log section

top

Sandy Lake, Alta.

under-side of log

1.

24.9.78

Resupinatus applicatus
(Batsch: Fries) S.F. Gray

19.11.78
Vancouver, BC

2.

Panellus serotinus (Persoon: Fries) Kühner

3.

yukon   2.7.81

Heliocybe sulcata
(Berkeley) Redhead & Ginns

4.

1.6.77

Winterburn, Alta
Neolentinus lepideus
(Fries: Fries) Redhead & Ginns

5.

Lentinus strigosus
(Schweinitz) Fries

6.

S.L.
5.8.79

Sandy Lake, Alta 12.7.75

Hohenbuehelia petaloides (Bulliard: Fries)
Schulzer

Edmonton
Alta 21.8.74

Pluteus patricius
(Schulzer) Boudier

1.

10.7.80
Sandy lake, Alta

Pluteus leoninus
(Fries) kummer

Moberley lake P.P.
Bc

2

15.8.77

6

3

Pluteus lutescens (Fries) Bres adola

4.7.87
Devon, Alta

3.7.80
Sandy lake, Alta
Pluteus tomentosulus
Peck

5

Pluteus cervinus
(Fries) kummer

4

Sandy lake
Alta, 6.8.77

Pluteus pellitus (Persoon: Fries) Kummer

11.9.76
Sandy lake, Alta.

4. **train wrecker**   *Neolentinus lepideus*   p.283
Another tough, strong mushroom, which does not decay easily; recycles wood, including railroad ties. It is said to be edible when young (requires long cooking).

5. **shoehorn oyster**   *Hohenbuehelia petaloides*   p.283
Somewhat leaf-shaped fruiting bodies with long decurrent gills in irregular form; edible but poor quality of taste and texture.

6. **hairy oyster**   *Lentinus strigosus*   p.284
Tough, very hairy mushroom with an elegant shape; very narrow gills. Inedible.

Page 103

PLUTEACEAE
Six species of the genus *Pluteus*. Easily recognized as stalked mushrooms that grow on wood; no ring; free gills turning pink and with a pink spore print.

1. **patrician deer mushroom**   *Pluteus patricius*   p.285
Sturdy mushroom with design on its cap of dark fibres on a lighter background. Said to be edible.

2. **golden deer mushroom**   *Pluteus leoninus*   p.285
Small yellow mushroom with hygrophanous cap which changes colour when it dries up. Its edibility is unknown.

3. **small white deer mushroom**   *Pluteus tomentosulus*   p.285
Small to medium mushroom with white, umbonate, floccose cap. Edibility is unknown.

4. **deer mushroom**   *Pluteus cervinus*   p.286
The original name "deer mushroom" was given to this species; pale to dark brown; radially streaked; often with uneven surface. Said to be edible and good.

5. **white deer mushroom**   *Pluteus pellitus*   p.286
Like the deer mushroom; quite tall; silky white cap and eventually salmon-coloured gills. Edibility is unknown.

6. **yellow-stalked deer mushroom**   *Pluteus lutescens*   p.286
Small mushroom with dark olive-brown cap and bright yellow stalk. Edibility is unknown.

Page 105

PLUTEACEAE
Three small *Pluteus* species on this plate as well as two species of *Volvariella*. The latter have a cup or volva at the stalk base which originally envelopes the whole mushroom; no ring; all with free gills and pink spore print.

1. **bulbous-stalked Pluteus**   *Pluteus semibulbosus*   p.286
Small white mushroom with bulbous stalk and floccose cap; grows on wood. Edibility unknown.

2. **pink and grey Pluteus**   *Pluteus atriavellaneus*   p.287
Small pink and grey mushroom with bell-shaped cap; white mycelium around the base; quite rare; grows on wood. Edibility unknown.

3. **small deer mushroom**   *Pluteus exiguus*   p.287
Small, fibrous, grey mushroom; also rare; with twisted stalk; grows on buried wood.

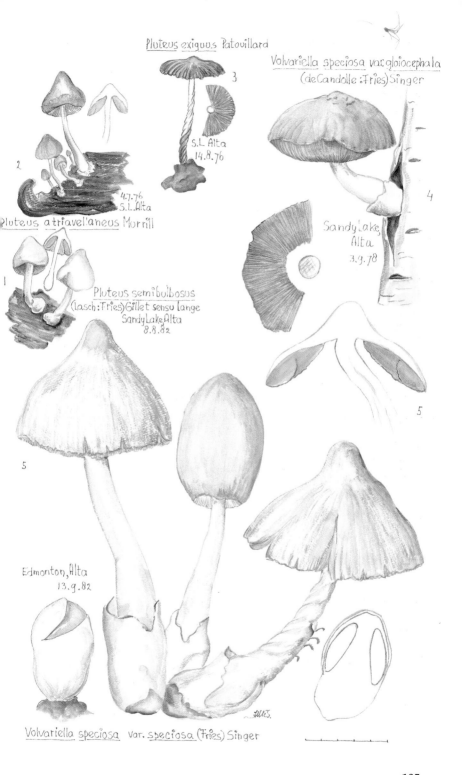

Pluteus exiguus Patouillard

3

S.L. Alta
14.8.76

Volvariella speciosa var. gloiocephala
(deCandolle : Fries) Singer

2

4.7.76
S.L. Alta

4

Pluteus atriavellaneus Morrill

1

Sandy Lake,
Alta
3.9.78

Pluteus semibulbosus
(Lasch : Fries) Gillet sensu Lange
Sandy Lake, Alta
8.8.82

5

5

Edmonton, Alta
13.9.82

Volvariella speciosa var. speciosa (Fries) Singer

4. **grey Volvariella**   *Volvariella speciosa* var. *gloiocephala*   p.287
Medium to large, sticky, grey-capped mushroom; usually grows on decaying wood. The conspicuous volva and remote gills stand out.

5. **beautiful Volvariella**   *Volvariella speciosa* var. *speciosa*   p.288
Usually a large beautiful mushroom; sticky, fibrous, white cap or white with light greyish-brown fibers; remote gills; found in forests on decaying leaves, on rich soils or in cultivated fields. Neither the grey nor the white large Volvariella are recommended for eating; cases of poisoning have occurred.

Page 107

ENTOLOMATACEAE

It is important to know the difference between the two pink-spored families: Pluteaceae which have free gills and are safe to eat, and Entolomataceae which have attached gills and are **dangerous**.

1. **earth Entoloma**   *Entoloma rusticoides*   p.289
Small brown mushrooms, with scaly cap and brown adnate gills; very easy to overlook because of earth colour; its pink spore print and adnate gills should alert you that it is from a group that is not well known and it may be dangerous.

2. **strong-scented Entoloma**   *Entoloma nidorosum*   p.289
Medium-sized pale mushrooms, fading to almost white; pink spore print and adnate gills mark it as an *Entoloma*; **poisonous**.

3. **shield Entoloma**   *Entoloma clypeatum*   p.289
Silky looking with radial fibres on the cap; persistent umbo. This mushroom got its name from its resemblance to a Roman shield; adnate-sinuate gills; pink spores; not recommended for eating.

4. **rosy Entoloma**   *Entoloma rhodopolium*   p.289
This *Entoloma* can be recognized by its very shiny, white, irregular stalk; the cap is quite variable; **poisonous**.

5. **slate-grey Entoloma**   *Entoloma madidum*   p.290
Dark, slate-grey, *Russula*-shaped mushrooms; often found under spruce; pink spores and adnate-sinuate gills help in recognizing this species. Edibility not known; consider it **poisonous**.

6. **redhead**   *Rhodocybe* sp.   p.290
Smoky cap, round first, then flattens and becomes depressed; inrolled edge; gills long, decurrent, narrow, becoming pink; club-shaped stalk; pink spore print.

7. **slim Nolanea**   *Nolanea juncina*   p.290
Dark brown, small neat mushroom; cap with umbo; adnate-sinuate gills and pink spores; grows on spruce needles. Edibility unknown.

8. **silky Nolanea**   *Nolanea sericea*   p.290
Another dark brown *Nolanea*; bell shaped when young, but hemispheric when mature; hygrophanous, fading to buff; grey brown stalk with white base. **Poisonous**.

9. **bell-shaped Entoloma**   *Nolanea mammosa*   p.291
Dark brown and hygrophanous; unlike the two previous species, it is taller and has narrow gills. **Poisonous**.

Edmonton, Alberta
23.7.82

1

Entoloma rusticoides (Gillet)
Noordeloos

Nolanea juncina (Kühner & Romagnesi)
Orton

7

Sandy lake,
Alta 8.8.76

8

Alta,
Edmonton   26.8.87

Nolanea sericea
(Micrat) Orton

Nolanea salmonea
(Peck)   Pomerleau

11

20.9.84
Dorset, Ont.

Nolanea mammosa
(Fries) Quélet
S.L. Alta 1.8.77

9

10

28.8.78
Sandy L, Alta
Nolanea species

2

Entoloma   hidorosum (Fries) Quélet
2.8.86   Sandy Lake, Alta

3

Sandy Lake,
Alta 9.7.72

Entoloma clypeatum
(Fries) kummer

S.L., Alta
5.9.75

4

Alta, 18.6.88
Ministik lake
(Fries) kummer
Entoloma rhodopolium

5

6

Atrium   4.4.86
Rhodocybe species   Edmonton, Alta

Sandy Lake, Alta
2.9.73
Entoloma madidum (Fries) Gillet

• 107 •

10. **yellow Nolanea**   *Nolanea* sp.   p.291
   To show that Nolaneas are not always brown, I include a yellow one, with adnexed pink gills; found in a bog.

11. **salmon-coloured Nolanea or unicorn Nolanea**   *Nolanea salmonea*   p.291
   Lovely bright Nolanea; all parts are the same apricot orange, and it has rosy salmon spores as well. Although it has not been found in the West, it is included to show another bright-coloured *Nolanea*.

Page 109

CORTINARIACEAE

Genus *Cortinarius*, subgenus *Myxacium*; with attached gills, cobwebby veil and medium-brown spore print. In the subgenus *Myxacium* both cap and stalk are slimy. There are more than eight hundred known species in the genus *Cortinarius*, but it is not known of many whether they are edible or not. There are quite a few poisonous species known. It is inadvisable to try to eat *Cortinarius* species. When a species is known to be either edible or poisonous, it will be mentioned. Identification is difficult.

1. **slimy violet Cortinarius**   *Cortinarius iodeoides*   p.293
   Grows under spruce; a slim slimy mushroom with a violet cap and a white stalk.

2. **very slimy Cortinarius**   *Cortinarius subbalteatus*   p.293
   This extremely slimy species with its deep reddish-brown colour, pale gills and interesting shape, can be easily recognized. Rare.

3. **early Cortinarius**   *Cortinarius trivialis*   p.293
   The orange-ochre cap, the pattern on the tall straight stalk and the fact that usually it is the first of *Cortinarius* species to appear, should make it recognizable. Common.

4. **slimy yellow-brown Cortinarius**   *Cortinarius mucosus*   p.294
   Another very slimy species, stalk and cap. Not as easily recognized as no. 3, but this one also occurs frequently in the Pacific Northwest under conifers.

5. **pale Cortinarius**   *Cortinarius pallidifolius*   p.294
   Quite large, very pale *Cortinarius*, occurring in the prairie provinces as well as in the Rocky Mountains. One other species of the subgenus *Myxacium* is presented on p.112.

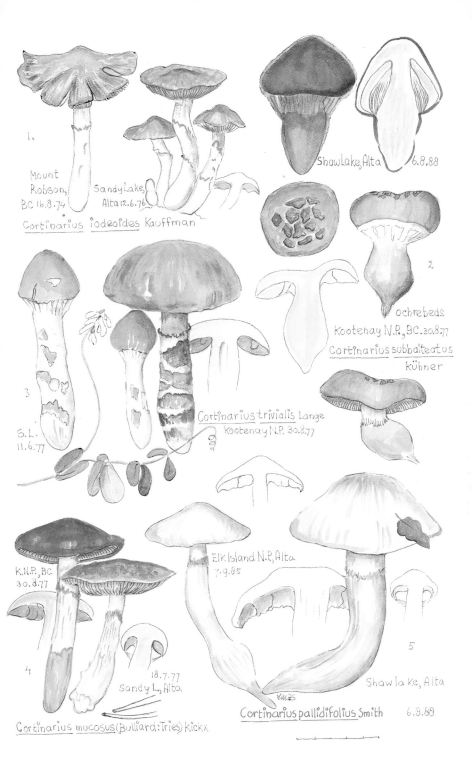

1.

Mount
Robson,
BC 16.8.74

Sandy Lake,
Alta 12.6.76

Cortinarius iodeoides Kauffman

Shaw Lake, Alta

6.8.88

2

ochrebeds
Kootenay N.P., BC. 30.8.77
Cortinarius subbalteatus
Kühner

3

S.L.
11.6.77

Cortinarius trivialis Lange
Kootenay N.P. 30.8.77

K.N.P., BC
30.8.77

Elk Island N.P., Alta
7.9.85

5

4

18.7.77
Sandy L., Alta

Shaw lake, Alta

Cortinarius pallidifolius Smith   6.8.88

Cortinarius mucosus (Bulliard:Tries) Kickx

Page 111

CORTINARIACEAE

Six species of the subgenus *Phlegmacium*, genus *Cortinarius*; they have a slimy cap and dry stalk, when young.

1. **beautiful Cortinarius** *Cortinarius calochrous* p.294
   A colourful species with violet gills, yellow cap and both colours on the bulbous stalk; this is a nice one to find.

2. **mountain Cortinarius** *Cortinarius montanus* p.295
   The shiny, streaked, greenish-brown cap is very striking; stalk is a pale colour and not very bulbous.

3. **variable Cortinarius** *Cortinarius multiformis* p.295
   Pale sandy-coloured species; the shape varies a lot. Often grows in big crowds with both short, bulbous specimens and longer-stemmed specimens with an almost equal stalk; cap is sandy yellow, but very pale at first; basal bulb has no pronounced edge.

4. **yellow spinning-top Cortinarius** *Cortinarius autoturbinatus* p.295
   Much brighter, yellow mushroom than no. 3 but has the same kind of serrate, pale gills; the stalk has a strongly rimmed, large, bulbous base.

5. **purple-staining Cortinarius** *Cortinarius purpurascens* p.296
   This *Cortinarius* also varies considerably in shape, but there is a mixture of brown and purple on cap, stalk and gills, and the flesh is purple. There are quite a few *Cortinarius* species with purple on the outside or inside.

6. **cedar Cortinarius** *Cortinarius cedretorum* p.296
   This *Cortinarius* of the Pacific Northwest is striking. The cap of the immature specimen is slimy yellow, soon changing to deep red; it has lavender flesh and an abruptibulbous stalk. This mushroom is easily recognized.

Page 112

CORTINARIACEAE

The *Cortinarius* with the pointed cap belongs to *Myxacium* (slimy all over when small), but the booted Cortinarius and bracelet Cortinarius have caps which change colour when they dry, and have "belts". They are members of the subgenus *Telemonia*.

1. **pointed Cortinarius** *Cortinarius vanduzerensis* p.296
   This mushroom is not hard to recognize, with its dark, pointed cap and booted stalk, all streaked in deep dark brown, maroon and purplish colours. When young it is covered in slime and the gills are tan coloured — later they turn brown. It grows under conifers and is rare.

2. **booted Cortinarius** *Cortinarius torvus* p.296
   Not common, but easy to recognize with its white boot and purplish-pink top half of the stalk; purple gills at first; a brown cap with light edge (sometimes streaked with purple); and double membranous ring. It grows under deciduous trees.

3. **bracelet Cortinarius** *Cortinarius armillatus* p.297
   This *Cortinarius* can be identified without any trouble. It grows singly or in small groups and shows its red bracelets on the stalk. It is said to be edible.

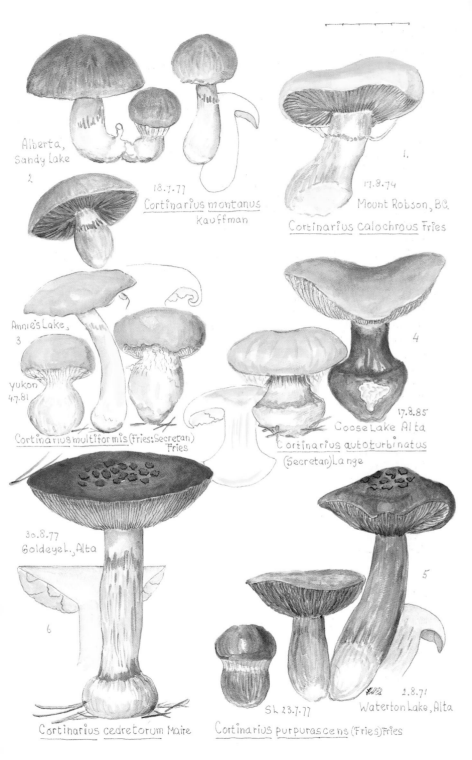

Alberta,
Sandy Lake
2

18.7.77
Cortinarius montanus
Kauffman

1.

17.8.74
Mount Robson, BC.
Cortinarius Calochrous Fries

Annie's Lake,
3

Yukon
47.81

Cortinarius multiformis (Fries:Secretan)
Fries

4

17.8.85
Goose Lake Alta
Cortinarius autoturbinatus
(Secretan)Lange

30.8.77
Goldeye L., Alta

6

Cortinarius cedretorum Maire

5

2.8.71
Waterton Lake, Alta
SL 23.7.77
Cortinarius purpurascens (Fries)Fries

• 111 •

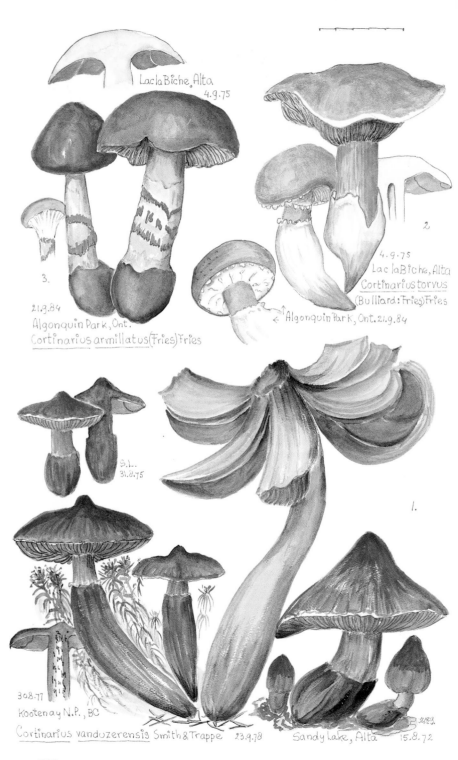

Lac la Biche, Alta
4.9.75

3.
21.9.84
Algonquin Park, Ont.
Cortinarius armillatus (Fries) Fries

2.
4.9.75
Lac la Biche, Alta
Cortinarius torvus
(Bulliard: Fries) Fries
← Algonquin Park, Ont. 21.9.84

S.L.
31.8.75

1.

30.8.77
Kootenay N.P., BC
Cortinarius vanduzerensis Smith & Trappe   23.9.78

Sandy Lake, Alta   15.8.72

4

Cortinarius sanguineus
(von Wolfen : Fries) Fries
Sandy L. Alta 17.8.70

3

Valemount
B.C. 12.7.86

Cortinarius semisanguineus
(Fries) Gillet

5

13.8.72
Sandy L.

Cortinarius uliginosus
Berkeley   4.7.81 Yukon

Cortinarius croceofolius
Peck

2

6

Sandy L.
Alta 9.8.82

Yukon
3.7.81

2.9.72
Sandy L., Alta

Cortinarius cinnamomeobadius
Henry

Cortinarius castaneus
(Bulliard : Fries) Fries
Pyramid Lake,
Alta 20.5.74

1.

7

Dorset
Ont.
20.9.84

Cortinarius violaceus (Fries) Fries

8

13.8.77 Carson Lake, Alta
Cortinarius alboviolaceus (Fries) Kummer

Page 113

The eight *Cortinarius* species on this plate belong to the subgenera *Telamonia*, *Dermocybe*, *Cortinarius* and *Seriocybe*. All are colourful species. The brightest are easiest to recognize.

1. **little brown Cortinarius** (Telamonia)   *Cortinarius castaneus*   p.297
   Small brown mushroom with cortina when young; cinnamon-coloured spores; fruits in spring or fall.

2. **yellow Cortinarius** (Dermocybe)   *Cortinarius croceofolius*   p.297
   Tall slim mushroom growing in coniferous forest; with almost decurrent, yellow to saffron-coloured gills, yellow brown cap and yellow flesh. **Dangerous**.

3. **red-gilled Cortinarius** (Dermocybe)   *Cortinarius semisanguineus*   p.298
   Not at all "half blood-red", nevertheless this ordinary little brown mushroom does not look at all ordinary when you see its bright red gills! Only the gills have this interesting colour; the spore print is rusty brown.

4. **blood-red Cortinarius** (Dermocybe)   *Cortinarius sanguineus*   p.298
   Not common, but this species is not hard to identify with all parts blood-red. Though it resembles a *Hygrocybe*, the rusty spore print points to *Cortinarius* instead. **Poisonous**.

5. **bog Cortinarius** (Dermocybe)   *Cortinarius uliginosus*   p.298
   One of the yellowish-brownish group of *Cortinarius*. This one grows in wet areas under willow and poplar, while the others of the subgenus *Dermocybe* grow under conifers. This one is mostly orange with yellow gills. **Dangerous**.

6. **brown-stalked Cortinarius** (Dermocybe)   *Cortinarius cinnamomeobadius*p.299
   A typical species of the group to which nos. 2 and 5 belong; with brown coloration, yellow gills and yellow flesh; growing under conifers in moss. **Dangerous**.

7. **purple Cortinarius** (Cortinarius)   *Cortinarius violaceus*   p.299
   Strong purple mushrooms, outside and inside, including gills. The only thing not purple is the spore print. Edible but **caution** advised.

8. **silvery violet Cortinarius** (Seriocybe)   *Cortinarius alboviolaceus*   p.299
   Beautiful violet mushroom, with a white universal veil, giving it a silvery appearance; white sheathed base; pale lilaceous flesh; violet gills changing to rusty from spores; no other colour changes. Edible with **caution**.

Page 115

Eight species that are **dangerous** to **deadly**. The cobwebby veil in both *Galerina* and *Hebeloma* is less obvious than in *Cortinarius*, and the spore print in *Galerina* is yellow ochre to rust and in *Hebeloma* dull brown.

1. **bog Galerina**   *Galerina paludosa*   p.300
   Always grows in sphagnum bogs. This mushroom has a small bell-shaped cap with minute umbo and a very tall, slim stalk; fruits from spring to fall. **Dangerous**.

2. **fall Galerina**   *Galerina autumnalis*   p.300
   Grows in coniferous forests on bits of decaying wood; this small brown mushroom with a hairy ring on the stalk is **deadly**.

Galerina autumnalis (Peck) Smith & Singer

Yoho N.P., BC. 4.9.76

2

Galerina paludosa (Fries) Kühner

Sandy Lake, Alta 23.7.77

1.

Sandy L, Alta 11.9.76
Hebeloma sordidulum (Peck) Saccardo

4

Haamstede, Holland
10.10.83

5

Edmonton, Alta   8.9.79
Hebeloma mesophaeum (Persoon: Fries) Quélet

Hebeloma strophosum (Fries) Saccardo
Lytton, BC. 23.5.80   Sand

6

3

Galerina venenata A.H. Smith
Sturgeon Lake, Alta 20.8.85

Elk Island, Alta
21.8.87

7

Sandy Lake, Alta
14.8.76

8

Hebeloma crustuliniforme
(Bulliard: St. Amans) Quélet

Hebeloma sinapizans (Paulet: Fries) Gillet sensu
Am. authors

• 115 •

3. **deadly lawn Galerina** *Galerina venenata* p.300
The cap can be buff to pale bay-brown to reddish cinnamon; hygrophanous and fading when drying; this one is difficult to identify; it has a superior ring. It is found more often because it grows in grass. **Deadly.**

4. **small poison pie mushroom** *Hebeloma sordidulum* p.301
Small reddish-brown *Hebeloma*, looks like "poison pie" (see no. 8). Small **poisonous** mushrooms can be found growing in city lawns, so be careful before picking mushrooms from the lawn and watch small children carefully so they don't eat any.

5. **dark-centred Hebeloma** *Hebeloma mesophaeum* p.301
This is a *Hebeloma* which can easily be identified. The cap has a dark brown center and a buff margin; light yellowish-brown gills, covered by a cortina in young specimens; white stalk; in groups or rings in lawns. **Dangerous.**

6. **veiled Hebeloma** *Hebeloma strophosum* p.301
Small ochrish mushroom with a woolly sheath as partial veil, resulting in a thick cortina-like annular zone, which is exceptional in *Hebeloma*; clay-brown spore print and radish odour. Like all Hebelomas, consider it **dangerous.**

7. **scaly-stalked Hebeloma** *Hebeloma sinapizans* p.302
Large species with pink cap, dark dots on the gills and white, sturdy, woolly stalk with a bulbous base. **Poisonous.**

8. **poison pie** *Hebeloma crustuliniforme* p.302
Small buff mushrooms growing in forests but often in grass in city parks. Always take a spore print and check the odour (radish).It can be mistaken for the fairy ring mushroom *Marasmius oreades*. The name "poison pie" does not lie. **Poisonous.**

Page 117

CORTINARIACEAE
Inocybe, or fibrehead is the largest genus of dangerous and deadly mushrooms in the Kingdom of Fungi. The three species on this plate show an unusual variation in size. They often have pointed, fibrous, radially splitting caps and the spore prints are dull brown.

1. **cornsilk Inocybe** *Inocybe sororia* p.303
The caps are blond and silky; the gills become yellowish to greenish ochre before changing to dull yellowish-brown when spores ripen. When humid enough, it can grow to very large size. Odour of unripe corn. **Poisonous.**

2. **deadly Inocybe** *Inocybe fastigiata* p.303
Somewhat darker than no. 1; the cap is not always as pointed as shown; variation in size occurs with this species also; they are not always easy to identify. The odour is unpleasant, fetid. **Deadly poisonous.**

3. **full-breasted fibrehead** *Inocybe eutheles* p.304
A very light-coloured, almost white Inocybe, with a very pointed cap; it can be dull yellow in colour. The odour is earthy, like radish. **Dangerous.**

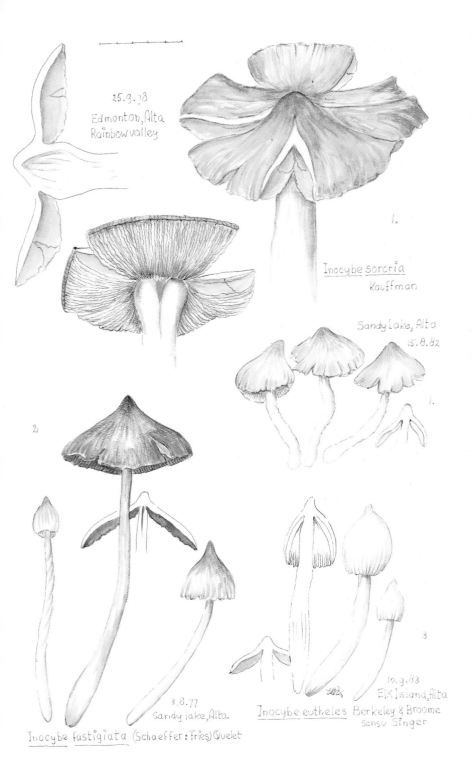

25.9.78
Edmonton, Alta
Rainbow valley

1.

Inocybe soraria Kauffman

Sandy Lake, Alta
15.8.82

1.

2.

Inocybe fastigiata (Schaeffer: Fries) Quelet

3.8.77
Sandy lake, Alta.

3

10.9.83
Elk Island, Alta

Inocybe eutheles Berkeley & Broome
senso Singer

Page 119

CORTINARIACEAE

Ten more small fibreheads; **poisonous and dangerous**. Not all of these have pointed caps, but all have attached gills and dull brown spore prints.

1. **bog Inocybe**   *Inocybe paludinella*   p.304
   Very small yellow-capped *Inocybe*; fine radial striations on slightly umbonate cap; greyish gills, pale yellowish-brown spore print. **Dangerous.**

2. **lilac and grey Inocybe**   *Inocybe griseolilacina*   p.304
   Small amethyst-coloured mushrooms, which fade to grey. Some of the small dried up mushrooms still had the youthful colours of this species. **Poisonous.**

3. **miniature Inocybe**   *Inocybe petiginosa*   p.304
   Another very small *Inocybe*, occurring on and around the fungus *Thelephora terrestris*, (see p. 169). It is not parasitic, however. Dull brown spore print. It is so small, nobody would try to eat it. **Dangerous** like the big ones.

4. **little white Inocybe**   *Inocybe geophylla*   p.305
   Completely white, small mushroom in typical *Inocybe* shape, but when the white gills become mud-coloured, *Inocybe* comes to mind. The gill colour is not enough for identification; it just points in a direction. A spore print needs to be made. **Poisonous.**

5. **little violet Inocybe**   *Inocybe geophylla* var. *violaceus*   p.305
   A violet-coloured duplicate of no. 4; they often occurs in each other's company. The species grows in mixed forests. **Poisonous.**

6. **brown scaly Inocybe**   *Inocybe dulcamara*   p.305
   One of the four hairy brown Inocybes. It could be mistaken for a *Cortinarius* with its convex cap and cortina! It has a mud-brown spore print. **Dangerous.**

7. **blonde, hairy Inocybe**   *Inocybe mixtilis*   p.305
   Somewhat smaller, hairy species; this one has a more felty cap with a scaly crown, an off-white stalk and a somewhat bulbous base. **Dangerous.**

8. **black nipple Inocybe**   *Inocybe fuscodisca*   p.306
   This is one which can be very easily recognized by its startling dark brown umbo and split fibrous cap. **Poisonous.**

9. **small woolly fibrehead**   *Inocybe ovatocystis*   p.306
   Small, woolly, brown *Inocybe*. Like the much larger no. 6, it also has remnants of a cortina. **Dangerous.**

10. **woolly fibrehead**   *Inocybe lanuginosa*   p.306
    This is the fourth woolly fibrehead. The special feature of this one is that it grows on very decayed, mossy logs (also on forest humus or duff).This one has a cortina but it completely disappears. **Poisonous.**

1.
SL 18.7.81
Inocybe paludinella Peck

2
Sandy L. Alta 1.8.81
Inocybe griseolilacina J. Lange

3
Inocybe petiginosa (Fries) Gillet
Sandy Lake, Alta 2.9.81

10
old log
Sandy L. 9.6.82
Inocybe lanuginosa
(Bulliard: Fries) Kummer

9
14.8.76
Sandy L., Alta
Inocybe ovatocystis
Boursier & Kühner

4
Moberley L., BC 14.8.77
Inocybe geophylla
(Sowerby : Fries) Kummer

5
Devon, Alta 4.7.87
Inocybe geophylla
(Sowerby: Fries) Kummer
var. violaceus Patouillard

8
Inocybe fuscodisca
(Peck) Massée
Sandy Lake, Alta 15.7.80

7
Inocybe mixtilis Britzelmayr
sensu Kühner
Siffleur Falls, Alta 18.7.83

6
Inocybe dulcamara (Albertini
& Schweinitz: Persoon) Kummer
Sandy Lake, Alta 25.7.81

Page 121

CORTINARIACEAE

Eight species of four genera of Cortinariaceae are shown here. All are growing on logs, wood debris or buried wood. *Crepidotus* is the only genus in the family with a bracket-shaped fruiting body. *Cerrena*, no. 9, belonging to the Polyporaceae, happened to be growing on the same log.

1. **red Crepidotus** *Crepidotus cinnabarinus* p.307
   Beautiful red, small, gilled, fleshy brackets; grows on deciduous logs or stumps; reddish-brown spore print.

2. **small white Crepidotus** *Crepidotus ellipsoideus* p.307
   Small white brackets; grows on deciduous branchlets and logs; fan-shaped gills, light brown spore print.

3. **flat Crepidotus** *Crepidotus applanatus* p.307
   These brackets are bigger than those of no. 2; only white when young, then turn brown, starting from the edge; grow on decayed wood; medium brown spore print.

4. **soft Crepidotus** *Crepidotus mollis* p.308
   The brackets of this species are bigger than the first three and are yellowish-brown; hairy at first (velevety or in tufts); later lose the hair and fade to dirty white; gills greyish at first, then cinnamon brown from the spores.

5. **American Simocybe** *Simocybe serrulatus* p.308
   Small, yellowish-brown gilled mushroom with curved stalk; grows on decaying deciduous wood; medium brown spore print.

6. **brown alder mushroom** *Alnicola melinoides* p.308
   Small scruffy mushroom; grows in sand near alder — surprisingly late in the fall; brown spore print.

7. **spring Tubaria** *Tubaria conspersa* p.309
   Small, early spring, brown mushroom with white fluffy base of stalk; hygrophanous cap, which is decorated with white patches along the rim. Grows on poplar branchlets, chips and other debris; yellowish-brown spore print.

8. **fringed Tubaria** *Tubaria furfuracea* p.309
   Small to medium-size mushroom; more vinaceous or cinnamon brown than no. 7; with a reddish brown spore print. Fruits late in the fall, sometimes early in spring; also grows on woody debris in forest and field.

9. **grey polypore** *Cerrena unicolor* p.376
   A different fungus all together; this one belongs to the Polyporaceae. It grew along the grooves of the bark of the old poplar log, which housed the red and the white Crepidotus and several lichen species.

Page 123

CORTINARIACEAE

The five *Gymnopilus* species portrayed here have a bright orange-brown spore print and grow on wood; the gypsy (*Rozites*) has a rusty brown spore print, a true membranous ring and lives on the ground on humus.

1. **golden-gilled Gymnopilus** *Gymnopilus luteofolius* p.310
   Can be recognized by golden gills; dark red fibrils on the yellow cap; cortinal zone on stalk and habit of growing on decaying wood.

Shuswap L., BC. 12.10.82

7

Tubaria conspersa
(Persoon:Fries) Fayod

8

24.9.78 S.L.
Tubaria
furfuracea
(Persoon:Fries)
Gillet

Sandy L. 20.5.72

Alnicola melinoides (Fries) Kühner

14.11.78
Victoria, BC

6

Simocybe serrulatus (Murrill) Singer

18.7.77
Sandy Lake, Alta

5

Crepidotus applanatus (Persoon:Persoon)
Kootenay N.P. BC. 29.8.77   Kummer

3

7.9.84
Alta
Shaw Lake,

Crepidotus mollis
(Fries) Staude
Sandy Lake Alta
26.8.73

4

Crepidotus ellipsoideus
Hesler & Smith
Sandy Lake, Alta

2

2.8.87   top
bottom of birch branchlet

Cerrena unicolor (Fries)
S.L. Alta 8.8.76   Murrill
3

2

old poplar log

8 8 76
Sandy Lake, Alta
Crepidotus cinnabarinus Peck

1.

• 121 •

2. **laughing mushroom**   *Gymnopilus spectabilis*   p.310
A well known mushroom; recognized by its habit of growing in bundles at the base
of or near trees; the overall orange and yellow colours; the orange-brown spore
print. Inedible. Sometimes hallucinogenic, but not in western North America. The
name "laughing mushroom" is used in Japan.

3. **small yellow Gymnopilus**   *Gymnopilus penetrans*   p.310
Grows in conifer forests, this mushroom can be recognized by the bright orange-
buff gills, yellowish cap and stalk with reddish brown staining; the disappearing
cortina is not often noticed.

4. **bitter Gymnopilus**   *Gymnopilus liquiritiae*   p.311
A typically lignicolous species, growing on old logs in tight tufts. Can be recognized
by its close buff-orange gills, orange-brown cap and bright rust-brown spore print.

5. **spruce Gymnopilus**   *Gymnopilus sapineus*   p.311
Small brown and orange mushroom, occurring under spruce on lignin-rich duff or
rotten wood; rusty orange spore print.

6. **the gypsy**   *Rozites caperata*   p.311
It has been called the veiled Cortinarius. It definitely belongs to the Cortinariaceae,
but it has a true membranous ring and, even if it is difficult to see, a very thin
universal veil.

Page 124

BOLBITIACEAE
Bolbitius, or dung mushroom, is slimy and soft; the species have rust to reddish-
brown spore prints. Edibility unknown.

1. **grey Bolbitius**   *Bolbitius aleuriatus*   p.312
Small grey-capped mushroom with lilac tinges; white or yellow stalk and rust-
brown spore print; slimy.

2. **white Bolbitius**   *Bolbitius sordidus*   p.312
White mushroom; slimy, with a very pointed cap; medium brown spore print like
the others.

3a. **yellow dung mushroom**   *Bolbitius vitellinus*   p.312
Bright yellow mushroom; slimy with an interesting colour change in the mature
mushroom — the cap margin changes to violet grey; strongly striate surface.

3b. **green dung mushroom**   *Bolbitius vitellinus*
A yellow-green, slimy cap and a yellow stalk make this *Bolbitius* stand out. The only
difference from 3a is the colour; probably a different form of the yellow dung
mushroom.

Page 125

BOLBITIACEAE
Five *Agrocybe* species, generally growing in grassy areas in field or forest, or on an
old stump; the gills are attached to the stalk and the sporeprint is dark brown; often
a ring is present.

1. **plains Agrocybe**   *Agrocybe pediades*   p.313
Smallest *Agrocybe*; buff to orange, hemispherical cap; thin, stiff stalk; no ring; it
fruits in summer after rain; occurs in grassy areas. Inedible.

Gymnopilus luteofolius (Peck) Singer

1. near Elk Island, Alta 12.8.80

Gymnopilus spectabilis (Fries) Smith

2. Sandy Lake, Alta 2.8.87

Gymnopilus penetrans (Fries:Fries) Murrill

3. 17.8.74 Robson falls, Alta

Gymnopilus liguiritiae (Persoon: Fries) Karsten
Sandy Lake, Alta
11.8.73

4.

5. Sandyl.. 8.8.76
Gymnopilus sapineus
(Fries) Maire

6. Rozites caperata (Fries) Micheli   12.9.87   near Elk Island Park, Alberta

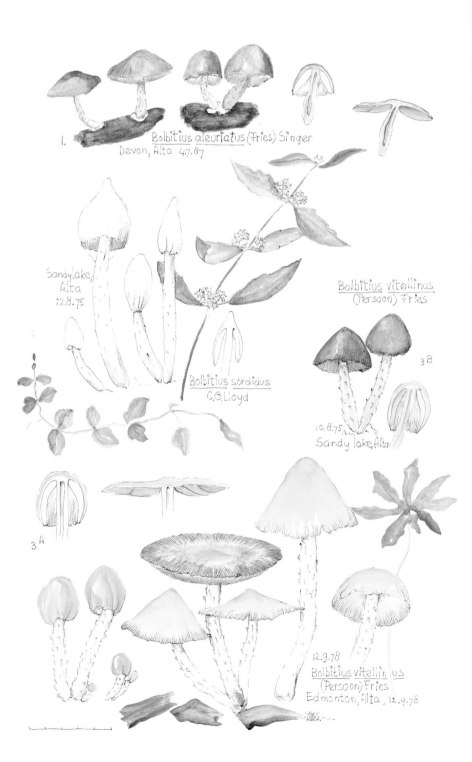

1. *Bolbitius aleuriatus* (Fries) Singer
Devon, Alta 4.7.87

Sandy lake,
Alta
22.8.75

Bolbitius sordidus
C. G. Lloyd

Bolbitius vitellinus
(Persoon) Fries

3B

10.8.75
Sandy lake, Alta

3A

12.9.78
Bolbitius vitellinus
(Persoon) Fries
Edmonton, Alta, 12.9.78

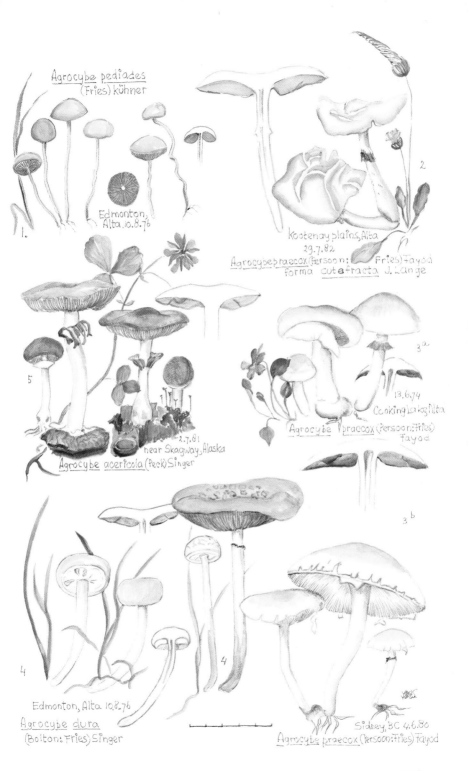

Agrocybe pediades
(Fries) Kühner

Edmonton,
Alta. 10.8.76

1.

Kootenay plains, Alta
29.7.82
Agrocybe praecox (Persoon: Fries) Fayod
forma cutafracta J. Lange

2

13.6.74
Cooking lake, Alta
Agrocybe praecox (Persoon: Fries)
Fayod

3ᵃ

3ᵇ

2.7.81
near Skagway, Alaska
Agrocybe acericola (Peck) Singer

5

4

Edmonton, Alta 10.8.76
Agrocybe dura
(Bolton: Fries) Singer

4

Sidney, BC 4.6.80
Agrocybe praecox (Persoon: Fries) Fayod

• 125 •

2. **mountain Agrocybe**   *Agrocybe praecox* forma *cutefracta*   p.313
Early mushroom; a form of the early *Agrocybe* with a cap that has a broken cuticle as the name says. Fruits in summer in the mountains. Said to be edible and mediocre.

3. **spring Agrocybe**   *Agrocybe praecox*   p.313
One of the earliest gilled mushrooms; a quite common and widespread species. It does look like *Agaricus* but it has attached gills. The partial veil is large; sometimes it becomes an annulus (3a), sometimes scraps of it fringe the cap edge (3b). Edibility (see No. 2).

4. **rough Agrocybe**   *Agrocybe dura*   p.314
The name of the species originates with the rough surface of the mature cap. The cuticle breaks into small patches. The partial veil is very thin and often disappears completely. Occurs in grassy areas; fruits in spring and summer. Not recommended for eating because of possible confusion.

5. **stump Agrocybe**   *Agrocybe acericola*   p.314
Found in areas of North America where maples grow; this mushroom prefers old maple stumps (*Acer*, Latin for maple). In the west it grows on other decaying hardwood species, e.g., poplar. The young specimens have brown caps (pale in the other species), and the partial veil leaves a big flaring ring. Edible with caution.

Page 127

BOLBITIACEAE

The genus *Conocybe* contains small fragile mushroom species with a conical cap and a rust-brown spore print. There exist some dangerous, even deadly species in this genus. *C. lactea* is said to be edible but is too small and fragile to be worth it. Better to leave them in the lawn. They are difficult to identify; a microscope is needed.

1. **white dunce cap**   *Conocybe lactea*   p.314
Easily recognized by its tall, slim conic cap; its pinkish narrow gills; and its extreme fragility; immediately falls apart when it is picked; cap and stalk white.

2. **slim Conocybe**   *Conocybe siliginea*   p.315
The smallness of the cap, reminding one of wheat cornels, separates this *Conocybe* from the brown dunce cap; in this one the small conic cap hardly expands; cap and stalk light brown.

3. **short-stemmed Conocybe**   *Conocybe mesospora*   p.315
Like the others, this very short-stemmed mushroom grows in grassy areas; the cap expands to a broad bell shape; brown cap, white stalk.

4. **brownie cap or brown dunce cap**   *Conocybe tenera*   p.315
Another all-brown *Conocybe*; on average, it is larger than no. 2 and the conic cap is striate; reddish-brown cap fades to buff or yellow-ochre.

5. **Kühner's Conocybe**   *Conocybe kuehneriana*   p.315
A long-legged species with a hemispherical cap, which looks very much like one of the long-legged Psathyrellas; its rusty gills and spore print are some of the characteristics of the *Conocybe* connection, while Psathyrellas have dark purple-brown spore prints; yellow-ochre cap fading to almost white; white stalk.

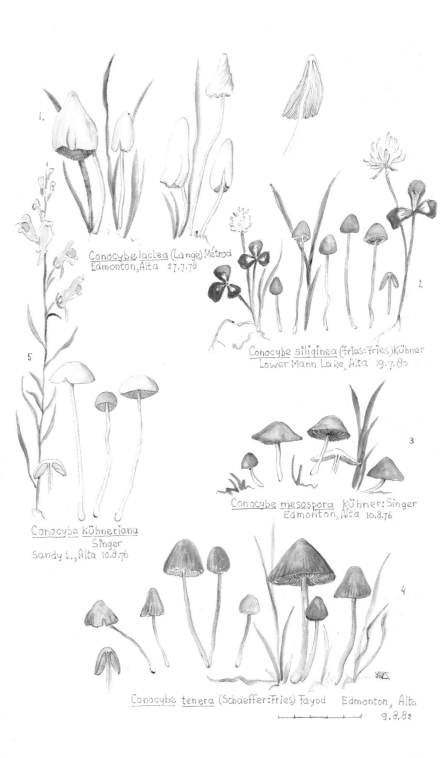

Conocybe lactea (Lange) Métrod
Edmonton, Alta 27.7.78

Conocybe siliqinea (Fries:Fries) Kühner
Lower Mann Lake, Alta 19.7.80

Conocybe mesospora Kühner:Singer
Edmonton, Alta 10.8.76

Conocybe Kühneriana
Singer
Sandy L., Alta 10.8.76

Conocybe tenera (Schaeffer:Fries) Fayod   Edmonton, Alta
9.8.82

Page 129

STROPHARIACEAE

Species of the genus *Stropharia* have a conspicuous ring. They are colourful mushrooms with a deep purplish-brown spore print and attached gills.

1. **dung roundhead**   *Stropharia semiglobata*   p.316
These slender round-capped mushrooms grow on cow, horse or wild animal manure in meadows during rainy periods. Especially when young, they are covered with a bright yellow gel. Inedible.

2. **ochre-yellow Stropharia**   *Stropharia coronilla*   p.317
The cap of this species is a dull yellowish colour; it is not slimy like the dunghead, and it grows on disturbed ground and on road berms; looks somewhat like a small *Agaricus* but the gills are adnate. This one is **poisonous**.

3. **Kauffman's Stropharia**   *Stropharia kauffmanii*   p.317
Can be recognized by its strongly squamulose cap; its adnate grey gills, before they turn purple brown; and its persistent grooved ring. Often a solitary fruiting body grows at the edge of a forest. Edibility unknown.

4. **verdigris Stropharia**   *Stropharia aeruginosa*   p.317
Easily recognized by its glistening blue-green slimy cuticle with rusty or yellow-ochre crown in older specimens. Edibility unknown.

5. **winecap Stropharia**   *Stropharia rugoso-annulata*   p.318
Largest of the Stropharias, the winecap grows in man-made environments: damp cultivated places, on compost, woodchips, gardens and greenhouses. The cap can be wine-red to brown red and, in cultivation experiments, some tan forms have been developed. The grey gills turning purplish-brown; the prominent, grooved double ring; its size and habitat make this an easily recognizable species. This is a choice edible mushroom.

Page 130

STROPHARIACEAE

Pholiota species grow on wood or are connected to buried wood. Generally they have scaly caps and rust-brown spore prints; attached gills; partial veil, leaving either a ring or bits on the cap edge. There are a few edible species of mediocre quality in this very large genus, some poisonous species and a lot of unknown edibility. Best to avoid the thought of eating them.

1. **golden-skinned Pholiota**   *Pholiota aurivella*   p.318
Easily recognized by its warm yellow to orange cap; often growing high up on deciduous trees out of cracks or wounds. Cap, as well as stalk, sticky when wet. Inedible, because of gastric upsets.

2. **pointed Pholiota**   *Pholiota acutoconica*   p.319
Easily recognized by its sharply conic yellow cap with sparse, flat-lying brown hair tufts; grows in clusters on conifer wood. Rare, edibility unknown. Smells like a skunk.

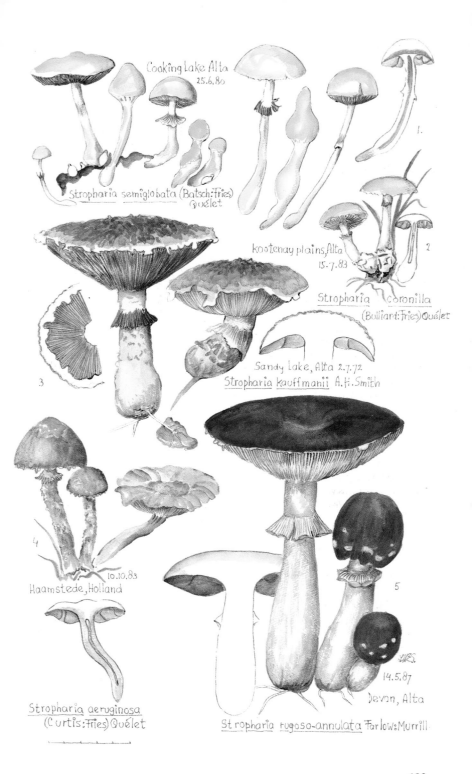

Cooking Lake Alta
25.6.80

Stropharia semiglobata (Batsch:Fries)
Quélet

kootenay plains, Alta
15.7.83

1.

2

Stropharia coronilla
(Bulliard:Fries) Quélet

3

Sandy Lake, Alta 2.7.72
Stropharia kauffmanii A.H.Smith

4

Haamstede, Holland
10.10.83

Stropharia aeruginosa
(Curtis:Fries) Quélet

5

CURS.
14.5.87

Devon, Alta

Stropharia rugoso-annulata Farlow:Murrill

• 129 •

Pholiota aurivella (Fries) Kummer
Sandy Lake, Alta
1.8.88

1.

Pholiota acutoconica
Smith & Hesler
Edmonton, Alta
19.9.60

2

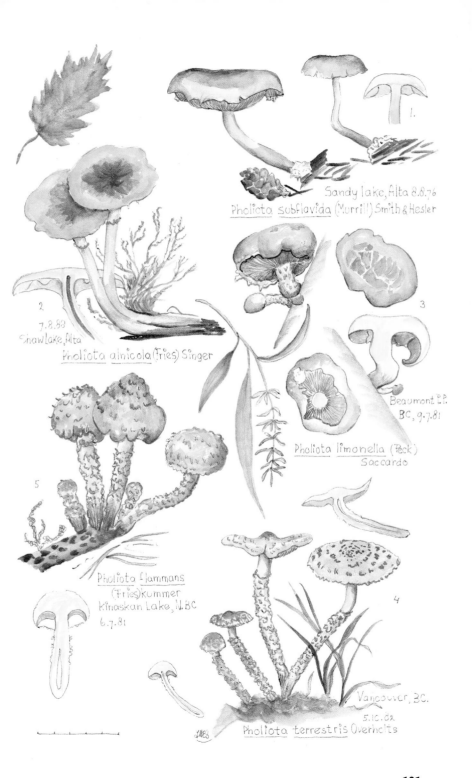

Sandy lake, Alta 8.8.76
Pholiota subflavida (Murrill) Smith & Hesler

2
7.8.80
Shaw Lake, Alta
Pholiota alnicola (Fries) Singer

3

Beaumont P.P.
BC, 9.7.81

Pholiota limonella (Peck)
Saccardo

5

Pholiota flammans
(Fries) Kummer
Kinaskan Lake, N.BC
6.7.81

4

Vancouver, BC.
5.10.82
Pholiota terrestris Overholts

• 131 •

Page 131

STROPHARIACEAE

Five species of *Pholiota*; grow mostly in tufts on wood. The size of the tuft varies as does the scaliness in various species.

1. **slender Pholiota**   *Pholiota subflavida*   p.319
Slender and smooth; this *Pholiota* is without scales and ring (the veil vanishes). Yellow cap; brown crown and stalk base. Grows on conifer debris. Edibility unknown.

2. **alder tuft**   *Pholiota alnicola*   p.319
Resembles *P. subflavida*; the difference is that the gills of *P. alnicola* tend to be greyish at first; the ring is more obvious; and the alder tuft grows on deciduous wood, preferring alder. Edibility unknown.

3. **lemon yellow Pholiota**   *Pholiota limonella*   p.320
The yellow mushroom grows in tufts, as most of the Pholiotas do. It is very slimy when damp. Grows on living or dead wood of deciduous trees. A species of wet climates. Edibility unknown.

4. **ground Pholiota**   *Pholiota terrestris*   p.320
Grows in groups in park lawns and along paths; this *Pholiota* appears to be terrestrial. It grows more along the west coast than inland. Inedible.

5. **flaming Pholiota**   *Pholiota flammans*   p.320
Can be recognized by its bright yellow colour, overall scaliness and habit of growing on coniferous wood. Said to be edible but not choice.

Page 133

STROPHARIACEAE

Two *Pholiota* species which destroy a lot of wood. *Pholiota destruens* can destroy poplar woodpiles. In northern forests this is a very useful species for decomposing dead wood. *Pholiota squarrosa* is a parasite as well as a saprophyte, attacking living trees, which produce leaves for a long time before succumbing.

1. **poplar Pholiota**   *Pholiota destruens*   p.320
Large, pale *Pholiota* with heavy stalk; grows on standing dead trees and logs, but also on worked wood, of which it can make short shrift. That is why it is called destructive! Overall colour is white. Inedible.

2. **scaly Pholiota**   *Pholiota squarrosa*   p.321
Yellow-ochre species occurs in large bunches at the base of both coniferous and deciduous trees, doing them harm. Was considered edible but now known to cause gastric upsets in some people. Not advisible to combine it with alcohol either.

Page 135

STROPHARIACEAE

The three *Hypholoma* species on this plate are decomposers of wood. Colourful species growing in tufts, they have a cobwebby veil like *Cortinarius*, but the spore print is purplish brown. The name *Hypholoma* means fringed margin and refers to the veil remnants on the cap edge.

1. **sulphur tuft**   *Hypholoma fasciculare*   p.321
Easily recognized by the sulphur yellow gills (which darken as the spores ripen), the yellow caps, brown crown and veil remnants on the margin. Grows on stumps of both deciduous and coniferous trees. **Poisonous.**

Pholiota destruens (Brondeau) Gillet
Sandy lake, Alta 23.8.75

1.

19.8.84
Jasper N. P. Alta
Pholiota squarrosa (Fries) Kummer

2

2. **conifer tuft**   *Hypholoma capnoides*   p.322
Not as easily recognized as the sulphur tuft. This species grows **only** under conifers or on decayed conifer wood; it lacks the strong yellow to olive-yellow gill colour of the sulphur tuft. Said to be a good edible mushroom.

3. **bricktop**   *Hypholoma sublateritium*   p.322
Although varying in size, shape and colour, the yellowish-grey gills, the brick colour and its habit of growing on deciduous wood, make identification unmistakable. Said to be a good edible species.

Page 136

STROPHARIACEAE
These six species, from three genera, all belong to the Strophariaceae family. There are one more *Hypholoma* species, smaller than those on p. 135, and a decomposer of moss; three species of *Psilocybe*, growing on dung or rich soil, with a purplish-green or purplish-brown spore print; and two *Kuehneromyces* species, closely related to *Pholiota*, with cinnamon-brown spore print, that grow on wood.

1. **long-legged Hypholoma**   *Hypholoma elongatum*   p.323
Resembles the long-legged Psathyrellas but has a reddish-brown spore print; grows in sphagnum bogs.

2. **round dung mushroom**   *Psilocybe coprophila*   p.323
or **meadow muffin mushroom** (acc. to Arora)
Small mushroom with brown sticky cap; semispherical, short stalk; no annular zone; grows on horse manure. Slightly hallucinogenic.

3. **dung mushroom**   *Psilocybe merdaria*   p.324
This mushroom can be small or medium sized. It is lighter in colour than no. 2 and usually has an annular zone dark from spores; grows on manure (3a) or manure-rich soil (3b).

4. **liberty cap**   *Psilocybe semilanceata*   p.324
Small mushrooms with pointed, narrowly conical brownish cap and thin whitish stalks; grow in grass in coastal areas during late fall. This is the famous or infamous hallucinogenic species hunted worldwide along seacoasts.

5. **changeable tuft mushroom**   *Kuehneromyces mutabilis*   p.324
Can be recognized by its smooth hygrophanous cap, which shows two colour zones very clearly; its stalk with membranous ring; and scaly surface below the ring. Grows in dense tufts on decaying deciduous wood. Good-tasting and edible. Caution, because it can easily be confused with deadly *Galerina* species.

6. **small, changeable tuft**   *Kuehneromyces lignicola*   p.325
This species is similar to no. 5, for instance, the two-toned cap, but *K. lignicola* is smaller, has narrower gills, a very small ring and smoother stalk. Grows on decaying coniferous and deciduous wood. Edibility unknown and too small to consider.

1.

1.10.83
Hypholoma fasciculare
(Hudson:Fries) Kummer
Oosterbeek, Holland

Hypholoma capnoides
(Fries:Fries) Kummer

2

Lake Louise, Alta
28.8.78

3

Hypholoma sublateritium (Fries) Quélet   Hoogsoeren, Holland 9.11.83

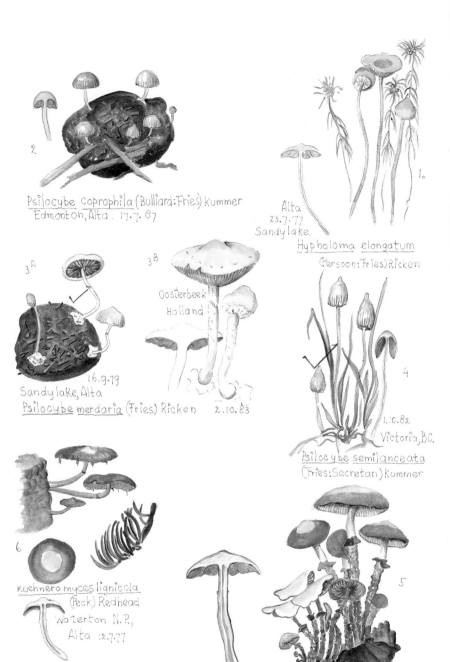

2

Psilocybe coprophila (Bulliard:Fries) kummer
Edmonton, Alta . 17·7· 87

Alta
23.7.77
Sandy lake.

Hypholoma elongatum
(Persoon:Fries) Ricken

3ᴬ

3ᴮ

Oosterbeek
Holland

16.9.79
Sandy lake, Alta
Psilocybe merdaria (Fries) Ricken   2.10.83

4

1.10.82
Victoria, B.C.
Psilocybe semilanceata
(Fries:Secretan) kummer

6
kuehneromyces lignicola
(Peck) Redhead
Waterton N.P.,
Alta 12.7.77

5

Kuehneromyces mutabilis (Fries) Singer & Smith
Kootenay plains , Alta 27.7.82

3

Victoria, B.C. 11.8.74
Agaricus augustus Fries

Agaricus crocodilinus Murrill
Edmonton, Alta 26.7.78

1.

Agaricus perrarus Schulzer

6.7.81

Cassiar highway
Kininaskin Lake, N. BC.

Page 137

AGARICACEAE

Agaricus species, easily recognized by their free gills which change from a shade of pale to deep pink to dark brown as the spores ripen; ring always present. The three species on this plate can be recognized as being edible by the white or white-changing-to-pink flesh.

1. **Sitka spruce Agaricus**   *Agaricus perrarus*   p.325
   Can be recognized by its large size; ochrish-coloured cap; pink gills, turning brown; gills remote from the stalk; and its preference for Sitka spruce habitat. Edible and good tasting.

2. **crocodile Agaricus**   *Agaricus crocodilinus*   p.326
   Very large *Agaricus* with very thick flesh, which is white or turning slightly pink; cap is white at first with very large scales; relatively narrow pink gills turning brown; double ring which is brown underneath; grows in disturbed areas; an urban species. Edible and good.

3. **"the Prince"**   *Agaricus augustus*   p.326
   A large *Agaricus*, up to 30 cm across; can be recognized by its numerous brown scales on the cap; very large droopy ring and woolly fibres below the ring. Very pale pink gills, turning brown. Edible and good.

Page 139

AGARICACEAE

Three large *Agaricus* species, all edible. All have the *Agaricus* characteristics but the differences are quite obvious: surface of the cap smooth, scaly or hairy; flesh slowly turning from white to pale pink in nos. 1 and 2 but turning quickly to red in no. 3.

1. **spring Agaricus**   *Agaricus bitorquis*   p.326
   This city dweller is easily recognized by its wide collar-like ring, with loose top and bottom; very narrow gills; thick hard flesh that turns pink; and overall white appearance. Because of its excellent edibility and resistance to pests, it is used in cultivation experiments.

2. **Patterson's Agaricus or dark scaly Agaricus**   *Agaricus pattersonae*   p.327
   An *Agaricus* with a very dark scaly cap, this is an urban species as well. The mushroom has bunched mycelium at the stalk base encrusted with hard dry soil. It grows in places where other mushrooms would not thrive. Edible but often infested with bugs.

3. **bleeding Agaricus**   *Agaricus haemorrhoidarius*   p.327
   Characterized by its reddish-brown hairy cap, often with a white woolly edge; bright salmon-pink gills before browning; and flesh that turns red very quickly. Grows in woods as well as in grassy areas of city parks. Edible and choice.

Page 141

AGARICACEAE

Five more *Agaricus* species. The first three are edible but nos. 4 and 5 are not recommended, because they are small and harder to recognize.

1. **wild button mushroom**   *Agaricus brunnescens*   p.327
   Unmistakebly an *Agaricus* with its pink free gills, changing to brown, and its ring midway on the stalk. Edible and choice.

1.

Agaricus bitorquis (Quélet) Saccardo
Edmonton, Alta   30.6.72

2.

Edmonton,
Alta, 29.5.75
Agaricus pattersonae Peck

3

Edmonton, Alta 26.9.77

Agaricus haemorrhoidarius Fries

2. **field mushroom**   *Agaricus campestris*   p.328
Characterized by its silky, white cap; fringed cap edge; vividly pink free gills
changing to dark brown; and narrow evanescent ring. Edible and choice.

3. **wine Agaricus**   *Agaricus semotus*   p.328
Small mushroom with the colour of pale red wine; appressed hair on the cap;
narrow ring on the stalk; free and remote pink gills, changing to brown. Edible.

4. **small slender Agaricus**   *Agaricus comptulus*   p.328
Characterized by its small size; slender stalk; silky, creamy cap; pale pink, free gills
changing to brown. Not recommended for eating.

5. **atrium Agaricus**   *Agaricus fusco-fibrillosus*   p.329
Characterized by its very dark, radially fibrillose cap; loose ring; and pink gills
turning brown. In northern climates it turns up in atria. Not recommended for
eating.

Page 142

AGARICACEAE

The last plate of *Agaricus* shows yellow-staining species. If there is only a little
yellow on the outside, as on the horse mushroom (no. 1), it doesn't matter, but if the
flesh shows yellow discolouration, watch out because it could be a poisonous
species.

1. **horse mushroom**   *Agaricus arvensis*   p.329
A very large, coarse mushroom; grows in grassy areas in city parks, along roads
and in fields; often collected. Recognized by its mostly white cap and stalk, double
ring and white hard flesh, which stays white. Edible and good.

2. **yellow-staining Agaricus**   *Agaricus xanthodermus*   p.329
A poisonous *Agaricus*, growing in urban areas and along roads. Can be recognized
by the yellow discolouration of its flesh and its nasty odour. **Poisonous.**

3. **felt-ringed Agaricus**   *Agaricus hondensis*   p.330
A poisonous *Agaricus* growing in the woods. Can be recognized by its silky,
pinkish-grey cap, thick felty ring and flesh with yellow discolouration. **Poisonous.**

4a. **wood Agaricus**   *Agaricus silvicola*   p.330
The wood Agaricus looks a lot like the horse mushroom, but it grows in the forest
under spruce. Bruises yellow on the outside, but the flesh is white and stays white.
Edible with **caution** (watch out for resemblance to very poisonous white Amanitas).
   This is a very variable species and is considered to be a complex of species. It may
be compact and sturdy with convex cap; much slimmer with a domed cap; stalk
equal or abruptibulbous.

4b. **brown form, with brown squamulose cap**   *Agaricus silvicola*   p.330
Not recommended because the species is so variable.

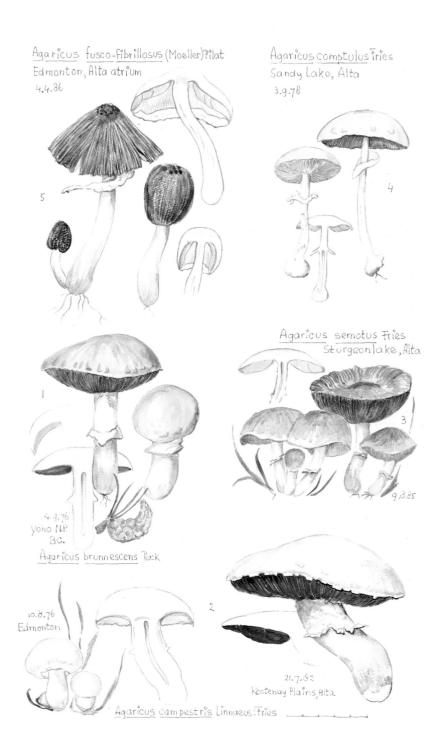

Agaricus fusco-fibrillosus (Moeller) Pilat
Edmonton, Alta atrium
4.4.86

5

Agaricus comptulus Fries
Sandy Lake, Alta
3.9.78

4

Agaricus semotus Fries
Sturgeon Lake, Alta

3

9.8.85

1

4.7.76
Yoho NP
BC.

Agaricus brunnescens Peck

10.8.76
Edmonton

2

21.7.82
Kootenay Plains, Alta

Agaricus campestris Linnaeus : Fries

. 141 .

Agaricus arvensis Schaeffer: Fries
Edmonton, Alta
24.8.76

1.

2

1.7.81
Whitehorse, yukon
Agaricus xanthodermis
Genevier

3

Agaricus shondensis
Murrill

5.9.87
Redwater, Alta

4B

brown form
Sandylake, Alta
Agaricus silvicola
Vittadini (Fries)

19.9.76

4A

1.8.77
Sandylake, Alta

Agaricus silvicola (Vittadini) Fries

25.9.82
Prince George,
B.C.

whiteform

1. Coprinus radiatus
(Fries) S.F. Gray
Ministik Hills,
Alta, 19.9.82

2. Coprinus domesticus
(Fries) S.F. Gray

Edmonton, Alta
23.6.81

3. Coprinus flocculosus
de Candolle: Fries

Sandy lake,
Alta, 25.8.78

4. Coprinus plicatilis
(Curtis: Fries) Fries
S.L. Alta 18.6.72

5. Edmonton, Alta 8.9.78
Coprinus comatus (Müller in Oeder: Fries)
S.F. Gray

6. Coprinus quadrifidus Peck
Dinosaur Prov. Park 7.7.77

Page 143

COPRINACEAE

Inky caps or *Coprinus* species usually have egg-shaped caps when young, with the cap edge touching the stalk; the gills are free, turning black when they mature and the spores ripen; the caps often don't expand but turn into an inky liquid from the edge towards the centre.

1. **miniature woolly inky cap**   *Coprinus radiatus*   p.331
   Grows on manure of herbivores. It can be recognized by its small size, woolly cap and radiating mycelium, visible at the stalk base.

2. **domestic inky cap**   *Coprinus domesticus*   p.331
   Grows on all kinds of things, e.g., hulls of sunflower seeds left under birdfeeders, damp rugs, plaster, furniture, even in mines. It can be recognized by its deeply grooved, conic, yellow-ochre cap and its homely habitat; may be poisonous.

3. **woolly inky cap**   *Coprinus flocculosus*   p.332
   Grows in gardens, dirt, dug up from basements and in flowerpots. It can be recognized by a very flocculose cap and an odd-looking base of the stalk. Edible.

4. **Japanese umbrella**   *Coprinus plicatilis*   p.332
   Grows on old leaves, wood debris and also in flowerpots in houses and greenhouses. It can be recognized by its Japanese-umbrella shape when it is mature; very fragile and short lived.

5. **shaggy mane**   *Coprinus comatus*   p.332
   Grows on heavily manured soil in meadows, parks and along roadways. It can be recognized by its shaggy cylindrical shape, like an unopened standing umbrella. It is grown commercially in a very limited way because it is hard to keep as the enzyme which causes autodigestion keeps working even in cold storage. Edible and good.

6. **scaly inky cap**   *Coprinus quadrifidus*   p.333
   It grows in bundles on old roots or chips and can be recognized by its resemblance to *C. atramentarius*. *C. quadrifidus*, however, has scales on the cap and the base of the stalk. Its gills turn pinkish-violet before turning black and it grows in tight caespitose bundles. Edible but the taste is not very good.

Page 145

COPRINACEAE

Six *Coprinus* species; the tall slim species, like the magpie and the hare's foot, are especially fragile, with very narrow gills and an almost see-through cap; they can be blown over. Mature mushrooms of *C. lagopus* last only one hour or less.

1. **magpie inky cap**   *Coprinus picaceus*   p.333
   It grows on or near rotten wood. It is a rare species; I found it in a hole in the ground made by the hoof of an animal where it was protected. It is recognized by the tall, dark, translucent, fragile cap, which, in the early stages, has large white patches, reminding one of a magpie.

2. **woodchip Coprinus**   *Coprinus ellisii*   p.333
   It grows on wood debris or mossy logs in the forest. It is closely related to *C. domesticus* and *C. micaceus*. It can be recognized by its small, yellow-ochre cap with brown bits on the crown and grooved bottom half.

Coprinus picaceus (Bulliard) Fries
Wainwright, Alta   19.9.87

Coprinus alisii Orton 3.0.-8.5l, Alta

1.

Coprinus lagopus
(Fries) Fries
Vermilion, Alta 2.6.74

27.6.85
near Fort Nelson, BC.
Coprinus micaceus (Bulliard : Fries) Fries

4

Coprinus truncorum (Schaeffer) Fries
Sandy Lake, Alta 3.7.80

Kootenay Plains, Alta
Coprinus atramentarius
(Bulliard : Fries) Fries
19.7.80

5

6

3

2

3. **hare's foot**   *Coprinus lagopus*   p.334
It grows on the ground in the forest, but also on compost heaps and woodchips; can be recognized by its small, hairy, grey young mushrooms that look like hare's feet and the lacy Chinese hats of mature ones.

4. **glistening inky cap**   *Coprinus micaceus*   p.334
It grows on or near rotten wood and can be recognized by the bright orange-brown crowns with glistening granules on it which soon disappear; grows in dense clusters.

5. **tree Coprinus**   *Coprinus truncorum*   p.334
It grows on the ground close to living trees. Closely related to *C. micaceus*, which it resembles, but it is slightly bigger and the lower part of the stalk shows a thin annular zone.

6. **smooth inky cap**   *Coprinus atramentarius*   p.335
It grows on or near rotten stumps. One of the most well-known species. It can be recognized by its smooth cap and stalk; greyish white colour; and its characteristic of growing in groups. It is edible if you do not drink any alcohol for several days before and after eating it.

Page 147

COPRINACEAE

Three closely related genera are combined on this plate: *Anellaria* looks like *Panaeolus*, but has a ring. They have black spore prints. *Panaeolina* grows in lawns and hayfields; it has a purple-brown spore print. All species portrayed contain small amounts of psilocybin; *P. subbalteatus* is the most consistently psychoactive *Panaeolus* of the west.

1. **dung mottle gill**   *Anellaria semiovata*   p.335
Grows on horse or sheep dung; can be recognized by its sticky cap and persistent ring; black spore print.

2. **belted Panaeolus**   *Panaeolus subbalteatus*   p.336
Grows in grass or well-manured gardens; can be recognized by its dark marginal band on the cap and pinkish-brown stalk; spore print is black.

3. **haymaker's mushroom**   *Panaeolina foenisecii*   p.336
Growing on dry grass in lawns or hayfields. This variable small mushroom is not easily distinguished from no. 2; the spore print is dark purplish-brown.

4. **pinched Panaeolus**   *Panaeolus sphinctrinus*   p.336
Grows on dung of domestic and wild animals; recognized by its constricted cap margin; black spore print.

5. **bellcap Panaeolus**   *Panaeolus campanulatus*   p.336
Grows on dung; can be recognized by its fox-red stalk (sometimes the stalk is grey and the flesh fox-red). Another characteristic is the toothlike margin of the young cap. Black spore print. **Poisonous.**

3
Edmonton, Alta
18.7.86
Panaeolina foenisecii (Fries) Maire

2
Edmonton, Alta   16.7.86
Panaeolus subbalteatus Berkeley & Broome

4
Sandy Lake
Alta 21.9.75
Panaeolus sphinctrinus (Fries) Quélet
Carson Lake, Alta
13.8.77

1.
Cooking Lake, Alta
13.6.74
Anellaria semiovata (Sowerby: Fries)
Pearson & Dennis

5
Moberly Lake P.
B.C. 14.8.77
Panaeolus campanulatus
(Linnaeus) Fries

· 147 ·

Page 149

COPRINACEAE

Psyathrella is a very large genus with many fragile small species in it. All eight species shown here are ringless. Six of these have very tall slim stalks. Edibility is unknown. The spore prints are dark-brown to black. A microscope is needed for identification.

1. **bell-shaped** *Psathyrella conopilea*   p.337
   Grey-brown bell-shape to broadly conical cap; fades to pale buff; tall, thin, white stalk; grows in deep duff.

2. **rooted Psathyrella** *Psathyrella microrhiza*   p.337
   Cap like small Chinese hat; deeply "rooted," thin, white stalk; grows in leaves and lignin-rich humus.

3. **big-spored Psathyrella** *Psathyrella megaspora*   p.338
   Small brown, bell-shaped, striate cap, fading to buff; short thin stalk; grows in leaves or on decayed wood.

4. **path Psathyrella** *Psathyrella limicola*   p.338
   Brown convex cap, fading to buff; gills are white before turning dark brown; long, thin white stalk; grows on paths or in duff.

5. **crowned Psathyrella** *Psathyrella pseudocoronata*   p.338
   Brown conical cap, maturing in a somewhat crown shape; sometimes slightly bigger than the others; very early mushroom.

6. **smooth-capped Psathyrella** *Psathyrella subnuda*   p.338
   Smooth brown cap fading to very light buff; the thin white stalks are very crooked.

7. **date-coloured Psathyrella** *Psathyrella spadicea*   p.339
   Chestnut-brown cap fading to tan; gills are reddish-brown at first; grows in tufts on very decayed wood.

8. **bog Psathyrella** *Psathyrella uliginicola*   p.339
   Medium to large mushroom with a beautiful silky grey cap — not hygrophanous; gills pearly-grey at first; stalk heavier than most; almost becoming liquid in the end.

Page 151

COPRINACEAE

The seven *Psathyrella* species shown on this plate all have a partial veil covering their gills in youth, resulting in a ring or remnants of the veil on the cap edge. Many Psathyrellas are hygrophanous (this means "seeming wet"). The colour changes when the caps dry up. The cap colour has to be noted down immediately when found, for identification.

1. **clustered Psathyrella** *Psathyrella hydrophila*   p.339
   Grows in large clusters on or around decaying stumps; dark brown at first, hygrophanous; partial veil leaving fringe on cap edge, sometimes an annulus.

2. **dubious Psathyrella** *Psathyrella incerta*   p.340
   Grows in small groups on or near hardwood debris; dainty, almost-white mushroom; fringe on cap edge, sometimes an annulus.

3. **moist disc Psathyrella** *Psathyrella madeodisca*   p.340
   Grows in large groups on decaying wood; young specimens have a conspicuous partial veil; hygrophanous.

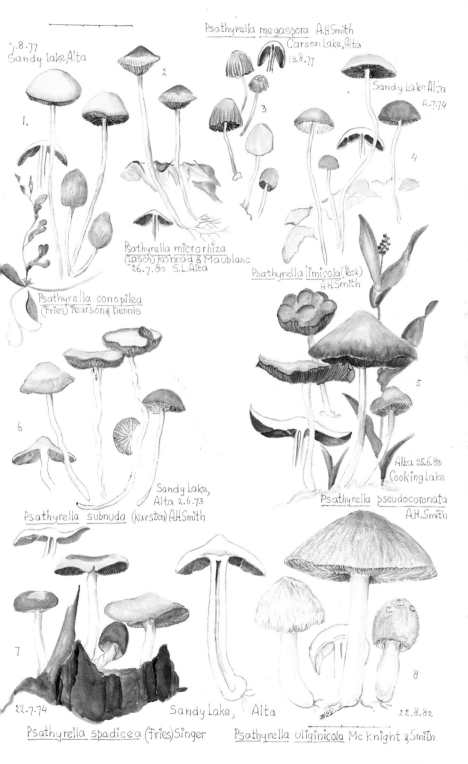

7.8.77
Sandy Lake, Alta

1.

2

Psathyrella megaspora A.H.Smith
Carson Lake, Alta
13.8.77

3

Sandy Lake, Alta
12.7.74

4

Psathyrella microrhiza
(Lasch) Konrad & Maublanc
26.7.80 S.L.Alta

Psathyrella conopilea
(Fries) Pearson & Dennis

Psathyrella limicola (Peck)
A.H.Smith

5

Alta 25.6.80
Cooking Lake

Psathyrella pseudocoronata
A.H.Smith

6

Sandy Lake,
Alta 2.6.73

Psathyrella subnuda (Karsten) A.H.Smith

7

22.7.74

Psathyrella spadicea (Fries) Singer

Sandy Lake, Alta

8

22.8.82

Psathyrella uliginicola Mc Knight & Smith

4. **stiff-leg Psathyrella**   *Psathyrella rigidipes*   p.340
Grows on dead grass in lawns, along roads, etc.; light yellowish-brown hairy cap; smooth stalk.

5. **weeping widow**   *Lacrymaria velutina*   p.340
Grows in groups on dead grass in lawns or on leaves in the forest; young specimens are quite hairy and orange-brown; cortina-like remains of partial veil on stalk which is often black from the spores.

6. **parasitic Psathyrella**   *Psathyrella epimyces*   p.341
Grows in clusters exclusively on shaggy manes and causes deformation of these mushrooms.

7. **suburban Psathryella**   *Psathyrella candolleana*   p.341
Grows in groups on dead grass in lawns; pale hygrophanous mushroom with a striate cap.

Page 152

GASTEROMYCETES
Although both species on this plate are related to gilled mushrooms, in particular to *Coprinus*, they are put in the class Gasteromycetes or stomach fungi, because the gills are either not developed, or they are rudimentary. The spores stay inside the skin and are not forcefully discharged. The part of the stalk which extends into the "puffball", has a different name: columella.

SECOTIACEAE
1. **false puffball**   *Endoptychum agaricoides*   p.342.
Looking like a shaggy, pointed puffball when no stalk is showing, or a small, somewhat leaning shaggy mane, these mushrooms grow in arid regions after rain, up to 3000 m elevation in the Rocky Mountains as well as in cultivated areas. The fruiting body does not open up; the spores are dispersed when the mushroom is eaten by an animal or when it disintegrates.

PODAXACEAE
2. **false shaggy mane**   *Podaxis pistillaris*   p.343
Looking like a tall, tough shaggy mane, this mushroom has a very tough stalk and usually a closed cap, which does not liquify like true shaggy manes. I found the one in the illustration in Africa on a termite hill. It puffed out some black spores at the time.

Page 153

LYCOPERDACEAE
Seven species of small puffballs are shown. They have a short sterile base, and when they are mature, the spores escape through a hole in the top. True puffballs have a two-layered skin. They grow in open forests. Edible when young and the flesh is white.

1. **snow-white puffball**   *Lycoperdon candidum*   p.344
Outer skin consists of long white spines dropping off in patches showing the dark spore sac when maturing. Grows in mixed forest on very decayed wood or on the ground.

2. **soft puffball**   *Lycoperdon molle*   p.345
Outer skin has a beautiful regular pattern of short gray-brown spines on a lighter background; note the elegant stalk-like extension in the spore sac. Grows on the ground in mixed forest.

1.

Psathyrella hydrophila (Fries) A.H.Smith
Sandy Lake, Alta 12.5.78

Falconlake, Man. 23.6.85

2

Psathyrella incerta (Peck) A.H.Smith

3

Psathyrella madeodisca (Peck) A.H.Smith
Kledo Creek, B.C.
27.6.81

4

13.8.81
Sandylake, Alta
Psathyrella rigidipes (Peck)
A. H. Smith

5

16.7.81
Sherwood P., Alta
Lacrymaria velutina (Persoon: Fries) Konrad & Maublanc

7

Edmonton, Alta
18.8.84

Psathyrella candolleana (Fries) Maire

Psathyrella epimyces
(Peck) A.H.Smith
Edmonton,
Alta 24.9.77

6

on Coprinus comatus

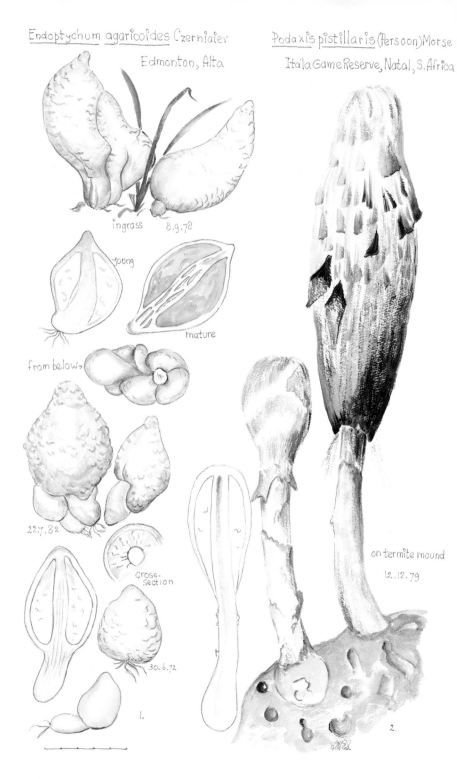

Endoptychum agaricoides Czerniaiev
Edmonton, Alta

Podaxis pistillaris (Persoon) Morse
Itala Game Reserve, Natal, S. Africa

in grass   8.9.78

young

mature

from below →

22.7.82

Cross-section

30.6.72

1.

on termite mound
12..12.79

2.

152

Lycoperdon candidum Persoon
Sandy Lake, Alta
6.8.77

1.

Lycoperdon moile Persoon: Persoon
Chambers Creek, Alta
19.7.83

2

Morganella   subincarnata
(Peck) Kreisel & Dring
Sandy Lake, Alta
28.9.78

3

29.8.78, Alta
Sandy Lake
Lycoperdon echinatum
Persoon: Persoon

4

Lycoperdon perlatum
Persoon

3.9.70
Sandy Lake, Alta

6

5

Sandy Lake, Alta 23.7.78
Lycoperdon umbrinum Persoon

7

on Fomes fomentarius
Lycoperdon pyriforme Persoon

on wood
1.9.79
Sandy Lake, Alta

7

3. **flesh-coloured puffball**   *Morganella subincarnata*   p.345
Outer skin is brown with longer spines than no. 2, grouped in pyramidal bunches;
when they fall off, a lovely netlike pattern is left; short or nearly absent sterile base.
Grows on the ground or sometimes on decayed wood.

4. **spiny puffball**   *Lycoperdon echinatum*   p.345
Outer skin consists of long dense spines, light to dark brown, quite persistent,
looking like a mini porcupine. Grows on the ground in moss or humus in mixed-
wood forests.

5. **umber puffball**   *Lycoperdon umbrinum*   p.345
Outer skin is brown with medium-long spines in pyramidal groupings like no. 3 but
interspersed with granular warts. When the spines fall off, the inner skin, or spore
sac, is smooth, yellow to brown, with a sturdy base. Grows on the ground in open
spots in mixed forest.

6. **warted or gem-studded puffball**   *Lycoperdon perlatum*   p.346
Outer skin is white with conical spines and different sized warts in between; large
conical sterile base and round head. Often found in large groups in open woods, on
the ground.

7. **pear-shaped puffball**   *Lycoperdon pyriforme*   p.346
Outer skin is light brown to bronze with granular warts; the pear-shaped fruiting
bodies are often found in large groups on old decaying stumps. The white mycelial
cords are easily visible.

Page 155

LYCOPERDACEAE

Five puffballs of the genera *Bovista*, *Vascellum* and *Calvatia*. All of them occur in
grassy areas. Edible when young and the flesh is completely white.

1. **lead-coloured puffball**   *Bovista plumbea*   p.346
Easily recognized by its white, round shape (which later turns grey) after the white
outer skin has peeled away like an eggshell; found loose in meadows in the fall
where it is blown around by the wind; no sterile base.

2. **small tumbling puffball**   *Bovista pusilla*   p.347
Recognized by its small size; dotted pattern where it has lost its outer skin; quite
similar to no. 1 but smaller; no sterile base.

3. **Curtis' puffball**   *Vascellum curtisii*   p.347
Another small puffball which is not smooth but covered with numerous fine spines;
pear-shaped with a rudimentary base.

4. **golden puffball**   *Bovista colorata*   p.347
Very easily recognized by its bright yellow colour. It is bigger than the first two and
has yellow rhizoids.

5. **western lawn puffball**   *Vascellum pratense*   p.347
White, tall, medium-sized puffball; its sporemass turns yellow before it changes to
olive brown. Persistent, can be found in spring (left over from the previous fall),
looking like a small garbage can with its deflated head and still-intact sterile base.

6. **box puffball**   *Calvatia excipuliforme*   p.348
Another species with a tall sterile base. It is not easy to decide exactly what species
this is, but the beautiful round head, the yellowish brown colour and its tall shape
make it stand out. The persistent base, left over after most spores have been
dispersed, looks like an old-fashioned birdbath.

Bovista pusilla (Batsch) Persoon
Roger's pass, BC.
4.8.74

1
Cooking Lake, Alta 28.9.78
Bovista plumbea (Persoon) Persoon

2

3
Alta
Waterton Nat Park
Vascellum curtisii
(Berkeley) kreisel
10.8.83

Bovista colorata (Peck) kreisel
Sandy Lake; Wolflake; Carson Lake; Sturgeon lake,
Alberta, August '75-'85

4

Calvatia excipuliformis
(Persoon) Perdeck
Haamstede Holland
7.10.83

5
Sandy Lake,
17.9.79, Alta
Vascellum pratense
(Persoon em. Quélet) Kreisel

6

• 155 •

Page 157

LYCOPERDACEAE

Three large puffballs belonging to the genus *Calvatia*. When the spores of these three species are ripe, the top disintegrates, leaving a bowl-shaped remnant. Species of dry climates, e.g., the giant western puffball, stay closed longer. (See p. 155 for one more *Calvatia*.)

1. **checkered puffball**   *Calvatia utriformis*   p.348
   The common name indicates the pattern the disappearing outerskin leaves on the long-lasting, bowl-shaped remnant of the fruiting body.

2. **tall puffball**   *Calvatia elata*   p.348
   This one looks like *C. excipuliformis* but is whitish and granular while *C. excipuliformis* is covered with fine spines, is coloured ochrish to brown and the top comes off more easily.

3. **giant western puffball**   *Calvatia booniana*   p.349
   Easily recognized by its large scales and curry smell when it matures.

Page 158

GEASTRACEAE

Earthstars are puffballs with a multilayered skin. The outer layers open up into pointed rays and a thin-skinned puffball in the centre holds the spores.

1. **four-pointed earthstar**   *Geastrum quadrifidum*   p.349
   Stands tiptoe on four tall rays (sometimes five) and has its "nest" attached to the tips; has a halo (see detailed description).

2. **sitting earthstar**   *Geastrum sessile*   p.350
   Sits in the duff on 6 - 11 bent rays; long fringe around mouth; no halo.

3. **flower-shaped earthstar**   *Geastrum floriforme*   p.350
   Hygroscopic species (stays closed in dry weather, opens up when it rains); small round mouth; no halo; has 5 - 10 rays.

4. **rounded earthstar**   *Geastrum saccatum*   p.350
   Sits in the ground like nos. 2 and 3; sessile spore sac as well (no neck); halo; 5 - 8 rays.

5. **beret earthstar**   *Geastrum pectinatum*   p.350
   This earthstar has a spore sac which looks like a plumed beret; grooved base; 6 - 8 rays, stands on tiptoes.

6. **collared earthstar**   *Geastrum triplex*   p.351
   This earthstar has a fleshy collar under the spore sac; 5 - 8 rays; halo; eventually it becomes loose from the ground and is not attached to its mycelial nest.

Calvatia utriformis (Bulliard:Persoon) Jaap

Calvatia elata (Massée) Morgan

1.

2.

16.9.73 Sandy Lake, Alta

5.5.73 Sandy Lake, Alta

Edmonton ravine Alta 21.8.79

3

Calvatia booniana A.H.Smith

• 157 •

1.

Sandy Lake, Alta
3.9.79

Geastrum quadrifidum Persoon:
Persoon

2

3

Alta
20.6.87
Kananaskis

Geastrum sessile
(Sowerby) Pouzar

Arizona
19.2.78

Geastrum floriforme (Vittadini) Cunningham

4

Wabamun
Lake, Alta
28.9.77

Geastrum saccatum Fries

Alta 13.8.77
Moonshine Lake

5

Geastrum
pectinatum
Persoon

opened up

6

young: underground.

mature,
collar
left

Collar forming

St Albert,
Alta
26.9.81

Geastrum triplex Junghuhn

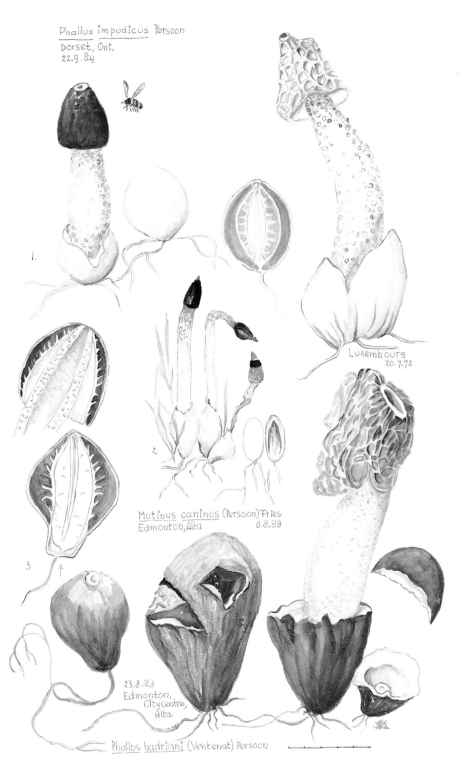

Phallus impudicus Persoon
Dorset, Ont.
22.9.84

1.

Luxembourg
20.7.73

Mutinus caninus (Persoon) Fries
Edmonton, Alta   8.8.88

2.

3

23.8.83
Edmonton,
City centre,
Alta

Phallus hadriani (Ventenat) Persoon

Page 159

PHALLACEAE

Stinkhorns are very interesting fungi: the spores sit on top of the stalk in a smelly gel which attracts flies who eat the gel and disperse the spores. All have rootlike structures underground (rhizoids). The youthful form is in the shape of an egg.

1. **stinkhorn**   *Phallus impudicus*   p.351
White egg, commonly referred to as devil's egg; olive-green gel on honeycombed, caplike top; white porous stalk.

2. **dog's stinkhorn**   *Mutinus caninus*   p.352
Soft small oblong egg; white chambered stalk with bright orange-red top and almost black gel. No reticulum (caplike top).

3. **Hadrian's stinkhorn**   *Phallus hadriani*   p.352
Purple devil's egg; brown gel on honeycombed reticulum; white, porous or chambered stalk.

Page 161

NIDULARIACEAE

Bird's nest fungi are very small. On the plate they are shown life size. The little "eggs", filled with spores, are attached to the "nest" by a miniature cord in nos. 1, 2 and 3 and imbedded in gel in nos. 4 and 5.

1. **deep splash cup**   *Cyathus olla*   p.353
Flaring cup with smooth outer surface and relatively large white eggs. Immature fruiting bodies are brown, hairy little barrels.

2. **ribbed splash cup**   *Cyathus striatus*   p.353
Flaring cup with ribbed inner surface and hairy outside. Relatively large white eggs. The immature fruiting body is a brown, woolly little barrel, smaller than no. 1.

3. **yellow bird's nest fungus**   *Crucibulum laeve*   p.354
Yellow conical cup with numerous white eggs in it. The immature fruiting body is round, velvety, yellow.

4. **white barrel bird's nest**   *Nidula niveo-tomentosa*   p.354
Very small, white, hairy, cylindrical cups with mahogany-coloured "eggs," attached by sticky secretions to inner wall of the cup (or nest). Immature fruiting body is a very small white barrel.

5. **jellied bird's nest fungus**   *Nidula candida*   p.354
Brown, shaggy, flaring cup with light brown "eggs", attached by a sticky secretion to the inner wall of the cup. Much larger than no. 4 and despite the name (candida) it is only white inside.

Cyathus striatus Hudson: Persoon

8.10.80
Edmonton, Alta   2

1. Cyathus olla Batsch: Persoon
    Edmonton, Alta
    18.9.78

Lake Louise
Alta
26.8.78

3

Crucibulum laeve (Bulliard: de Candolle) Kambly

4   14.8.76   Brentwood Bay, BC

Nidula nivea-tomentosa (Hennings) Lloyd

5

30.8.84
Cowichan Lake, B.C.
Nidula candida (Peck) White

5 cm

Page 163

The stalked puffball, the tough-skinned puffball and dyemaker's puffball are all very interesting creatures, built for survival in dry climates. This includes underground development, tough thick skin and the staggered ripening of spores, not all at once! (Look at the marbled spore mass.) None of the tough-skinned and dyemaker's puffballs are edible, and the pigskin puffball is **poisonous.**

TULOSTOMATACEAE

1. **stalked puffball**   *Tulostoma simulans*   p.355
Grows in sandy areas; they look like rabbit droppings because only the spore sac is visible. Once it is found, it cannot be mistaken—the wiry rufus stalk underground, the small round puffball with the raised ostiole (or opening through which spores are released). *Simulans* refers to imitating a true puffball, which has no stalk.

2. **desert drumstick**   *Battarraea stevenii*   p.355
Occurs in arid and semi-arid areas. Can be recognized by its tough, often twisted, ragged stalk topped by the remains of a sporecase which looks like a hat; sticky brown spores on top. Inedible.

SCLERODERMATACEAE

3. **small potato**   *Scleroderma areolatum*   p.356
Occurs on poor soil in gardens and woods. Looks like a small potato; has a short, lined stalk, very thick skin. Inedible.

4. **pigskin poison puffball**   *Scleroderma citrinum*   p.356
Occurs on sandy soil in dry areas. another potato-like tough-skinned puffball; widespread. The tough skin turns pinkish when cut. The gleba is soon marbled purplish. The scales are bigger than those of no. 3. The peridium is a deeper yellow; there is no stalk; but there is a strong "rooting" mycelium clump. **Poisonous.**

5. **rooting toughskin**   *Scleroderma verrucosum*   p.357
Occurs in sandy soil in dry areas. Again a potato-like tough skin, that is characterized by it extremely large "rooting" structure. Inedible.

PISOLITHACEAE

6. **dyemaker's puffball**   *Pisolithus tinctorius*   p.357
Occurs in forests in dry climates. It is perfectly camouflaged by its brownish colour. It develops underground and emerges partially at maturity. Once it is spotted, it is unmistakable because of its pear shape, heaviness and interesting yellow-orange colours in the base. Inedible.

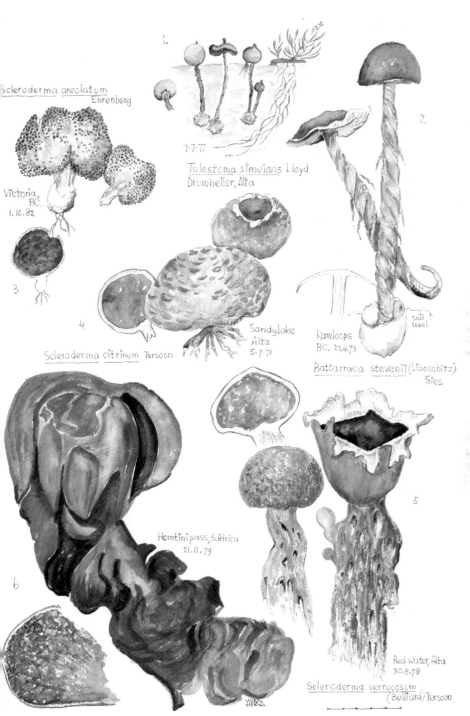

Scleroderma areolatum
Ehrenberg

Victoria,
BC.
1.10.82

3

1.

7.7.77

Tolostoma simulans Lloyd
Drumheller, Alta

2

4

Sandy lake
Alta
5.7.77

Scleroderma citrinum Persoon

soil
level

Kamloops
BC. 23.4.73

Battarraea stevenii (Liboschitz)
Fries

Homtinipass, S.Africa
21.11.79

5

Red water, Alta
30.8.78

Scleroderma verrucosum
(Bolliard) Persoon

6

Pisolithus tinctorius (Micheli: Persoon) Coker & Couch

Page 165

Representatives of the two families on this page belong to the non-gilled mushrooms. Superficially, the chanterelle looks like a gilled mushroom but on closer inspection (by cutting across the top) folds can be seen rather than gills. Absence of gills in the others is obvious.

CANTHARELLACEAE

1. **golden chanterelle**   *Cantharellus cibarius*   p.358
Fleshy orange and yellow mushrooms with cap, stalk and gill-like ridges, rather than gills, which carry the hymenium where ochre-coloured spores are formed. Edible and excellent-tasting.

2. **trumpet chanterelle**   *Cantharellus tubaeformis*   p.359
Thin-fleshed, hollow-stalked chanterelle; grows in bogs. This mushroom of cool northern woods can be recognized by its perforated cap; cut the fruiting body lengthwise to see this well. Edible but does not agree with everybody; caution is advised.

3. **horn of plenty**   *Craterellus cornucopioides*   p.359
   deceptive horn   *Craterellus fallax*
These two species of *Craterellus* look alike. Both are dark smoky brown on top and inside the horn-shaped fruiting body. On the outside they are purplish brown. The horn of plenty has whitish spores; *Craterellus fallax* has salmon or yellowish spores. Good-tasting, edible species although thin-fleshed.

SPARASSIDACEAE

4. **sponge fungus or cauliflower fungus**   *Sparassis crispa*   p.360
Various names are used for this species: cauliflower mushroom, brain fungus or sponge. This mushroom cannot be mistaken for anything else. It grows at the foot of coniferous trees in cauliflower shapes with a heavy rooting base; flat, lobed, whitish to yellowish, curly branches and a fragrant odour. Edible and excellent.

Page 166

CLAVARIACEAE

Simple pestle-shaped fruiting bodies which are easy to recognize. The spores form on the surface of the clubs or pestles. A puffball may look like it, but its spores are inside. Another mushroom with a similar form is *Podostroma* (p. 191) but it forms ascospores on its surface (all these produce basidiospores).

1. **pestle fungus**   *Clavariadelphus pistillaris*   p.360
Generally a large simple pestle-shaped mushroom; when encountered for the first time, a *Lycoperdon* may come to mind, but the spores of the pestle are formed on the outside and the flesh stays white, while in the puffball the spores are formed inside and are coloured. Edible but not good.

2. **strap-shaped pestle**   *Clavariadelphus sachalinensis*   p.361
Small to medium-sized, worm to pestle-shaped fruiting bodies. *Calocera cornea,* a jelly fungus, looks somewhat like this one, but it grows on wood and its consistency is gelatinous. Reported as being edible.

3. **northern pestle**   *Clavariadelphus borealis*   p.361
Not as big as the pestle fungus. The northern pestle looks like *C. pistillaris,* but has a flatter, very wrinkled top. The specimens I found had an excellent taste.

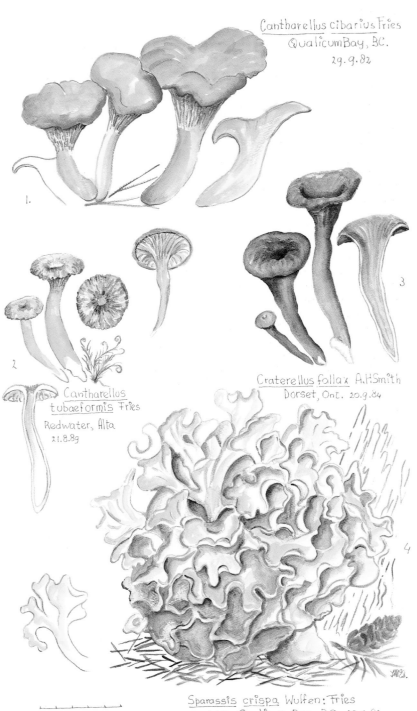

Cantharellus cibarius Fries
QualicumBay, BC.
29.9.82

1.

2

Cantharellus
tubaeformis Fries
Redwater, Alta
21.8.89

3

Craterellus fallax A.H.Smith
Dorset, Ont. 20.9.84

4

Sparassis crispa Wulfen:Fries
near Qualicum Bay, BC. 29.9.82

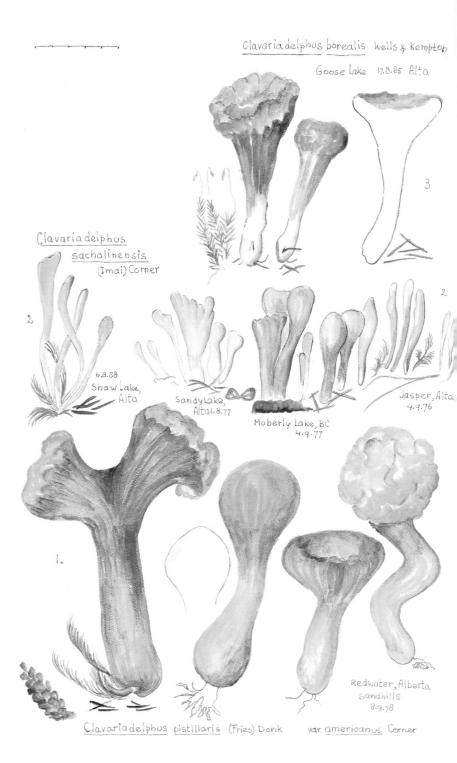

Clavariadelphus borealis Wells & Kempton

Goose Lake 17.8.85 Alta

3

Clavariadelphus
sachalinensis
(Imai) Corner

2

6.8.88
Shaw Lake,
Alta

Sandy Lake,
Alta. 1.8.77

Moberly Lake, BC
4.9.77

Jasper, Alta
4.9.76

2

1.

Clavariadelphus pistillaris (Fries) Donk   var. americanus Corner

Redwater, Alberta
sandhills
8.9.78

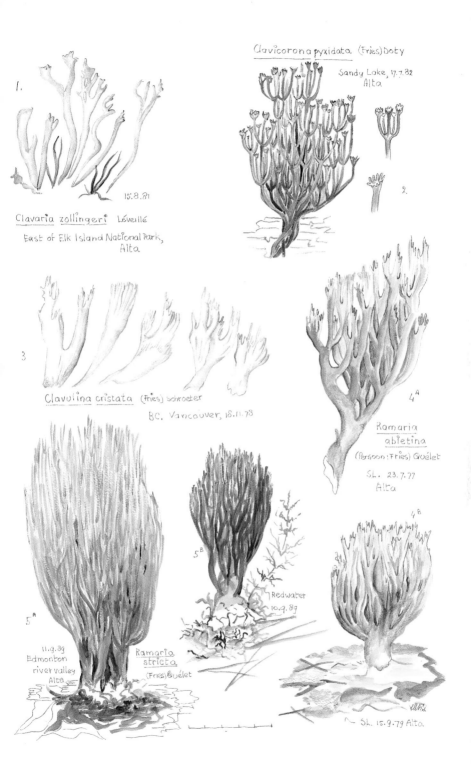

1.

Clavaria zollingeri Léveillé

East of Elk Island National Park,
Alta

15.8.81

Clavicorona pyxidata (Fries) Doty

Sandy Lake, 17.7.82
Alta

2.

3

Clavulina cristata (Fries) Schroeter

BC. Vancouver, 18.11.78

4^A

Ramaria abietina
(Persoon : Fries) Quélet

SL. 23.7.77
Alta

5^A

11.9.89
Edmonton
river valley
Alta

Ramaria stricta
(Fries) Quélet

5^B

Redwater
10.9.89

4^B

SL. 15.9.79 Alta.

· **167** ·

Page 167

CLAVARIA AND SPECIES OF RELATED FAMILIES

Club and coral-shaped fungi belonging to various related families are shown on this plate; they grow on the ground, old wood, leaves or needles. These are all decomposers of organic matter.

1. **purplish Clavaria**   *Clavaria zollingeri*   p.361
There is more than one purplish coral mushroom, but this one is not as dense or regular as many of the others; white spore print.

2. **crowned coral**   *Clavicorona pyxidata*   p.362
Can be recognized by its pyxidate branching (see detailed description); white spore print; tender flesh; edible.

3. **white-crested coral fungus**   *Clavulina cristata*   p.362
The white-crested coral fungus has less branches than nos. 2, 4 or 5, but more teeth on its flattened branch tips; often infected by parasitic fungi, therefore not recommended for consumption. White spore print.

4. **green-staining coral**   *Ramaria abietina*   p.363
Yellowish coral fungus, stains green when handled and with age, which makes it easy to recognize; grows in coniferous forests; bitter tasting; inedible. Yellow spore print.

5. **straight coral**   *Ramaria stricta*   p.363
Greyish orange and yellow; stains wine red when handled and with age; this coral mushroom is recognized by its very tight, erect, parallel branches ending in 4 - 5 thin points; edible but not palatable. Yellow spore print.

Page 169

Both families represented here get more interesting the closer you look at them. The tough, small fruiting bodies are long lasting and have very interesting features, but they are not easy to spot.

SCHIZOPHYLLACEAE

1. **splitgill**   *Schizophyllum commune*   p.364
Hairy, grey-white, tough brackets which are more interesting below than on top; can be recognized by the "split" gills; cannot be confused with anything else. Inedible.

THELEPHORACEAE

2. **zoned Phellodon**   *Phellodon tomentosus*   p.364
The velvety-zoned caps, joined together when growing in groups; separate stalks; spined fertile surface; white spore print and fragrant odour make this fungus easy to recognize. Inedible.

3. **fetid false coral**   *Thelephora palmata*   p.365
Can be recognized by its purplish-brown, upright tufts with pale tips, growing from a solid base and by its dirty odour. The odour disappears when it dries. Inedible.

4. **funnel-shaped Thelephora**   *Thelephora caryophylla*   p.365
Small brown rosettes with light edges; growing on leaf or needle debris; very nice shapes but hard to spot. Inedible.

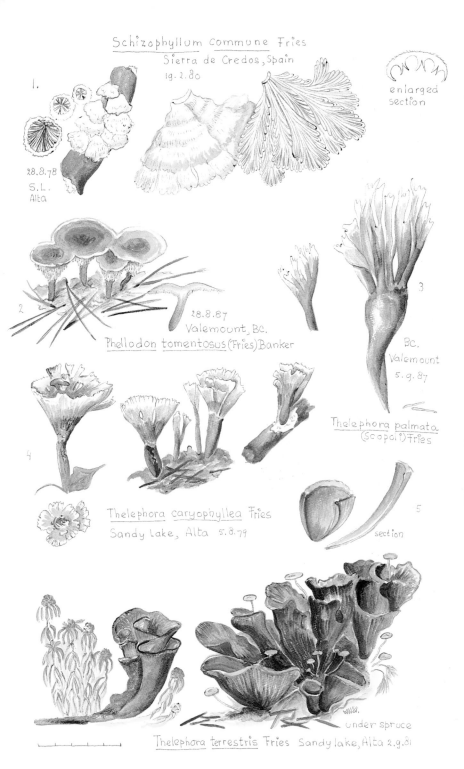

Schizophyllum commune Fries
Sierra de Credos, Spain
19. 2. 80

enlarged section

1.

28.8.78
S.L.
Alta

2
28.8.87
Valemount, BC.
Phellodon tomentosus (Fries) Banker

3
BC.
Valemount
5. 9. 87

Thelephora palmata
(Scopoli) Fries

4

Thelephora caryophyllea Fries
Sandy lake, Alta 5.8.79

5
section

under spruce
Thelephora terrestris Fries Sandy lake, Alta 2.9.81

5. **earth fan**   *Thelephora terrestris*   p.365
Can be found in smaller and bigger groups than shown in the illustrations; grows in spruce bogs and coniferous forests. They form in irregular groups of dark purplish-brown outsides and lighter insides of fan, lobe or vase shapes. Inedible.
(The miniature white mushroom in this plate, *Inocybe petiginosa*, growing on and around the earth fan, is discussed with the species on p. 119.)

Page 171

THELEPHORACEAE

All species of *Hydnellum* are tough, becoming woody when dry; all have colourful zoned flesh and brown spores forming on teeth (or spines). *Phellodon* (p. 169) has white spores on teeth; *Sarcodon* (p. 172) has brown spores, unzoned flesh.

1. **pine Hydnellum**   *Hydnellum pineticola*   p.366
Pink velvety cap in the young stage, later turns brown on top. Flesh zoned in pale wine colour and rust. Taste unpleasant but not bitter; occurs under pine.

2. **blueish Hydnellum**   *Hydnellum caeruleum*   p.366
Pale, velvety purplish-blue or grey-blue cap, browning in the centre, with irregular bumps; very short or no stalk; flesh zoned in yellow ochre and brown. Mild taste, odour of drying hay; a very heavy mushroom; grows under spruce.

3. **orange Hydnellum**   *Hydnellum aurantiacum*   p.367
Velvety to tomentose, orange and rust cap; smaller than the others; zoned orange and brown flesh; bitter taste; unpleasant odour; grows under spruce in mixed forest.

4. **sweet-smelling Hydnellum**   *Hydnellum suavolens*   p.367
Light-grey, velvety cap, browning in the centre, uneven, bumps; can have a striking deep blue, indigo stalk with a black base; flesh in cap is zoned in blue and brown; flesh in the stalk is black; particularly interesting odour of fenugreek; very bitter taste; occurs in alpine forest.

Page 172

THELEPHORACEAE

This plate shows three species of the genus *Sarcodon* (or fleshy tooth). They are more fleshy than species of the other genera of Thelephoraceae. Only the scaly hedgehog is edible. Brown spores form on teeth; unzoned flesh.

1. **bitter hedgehog**   *Sarcodon scabrosus*   p.367
Medium to large mushroom, distinguished by its small scales, short teeth and very bitter taste. Inedible.

2. **burnt hedgehog**   *Sarcodon ustalis*   p.368
Medium to large mushroom; dark smoky brown cap with appressed hair; pointed teeth of at least 1 cm in length. Rare North American species; mild taste; edibility is unknown.

3. **scaly hedgehog**   *Sarcodon imbricatus*   p.368
A very large mushroom, especially the dark reddish-brown form which occurs in the west. A light, smaller form also occurs in the west. The scales are prominently raised and the teeth are longer than in no. 1 and shorter than in no. 2. This one is edible, but some forms are bitter tasting.

Hydnellum pineticola
(Harrison) Harrison
Valemount, B.C.
28.8.87

1.

2

Hydnellum caeruleum (Hornemann:
Persoon) Karsten
Athabasca falls, Alta
25.8.78

3

Hydnellum aurantiacum
(Batsch:Fries) Karsten
Edmonton River valley,
Alta 14.9.82

4

Hydnellum suavolens (Scopoli:Fries) Karsten
Kootenay National Park, 30.8.77 BC.

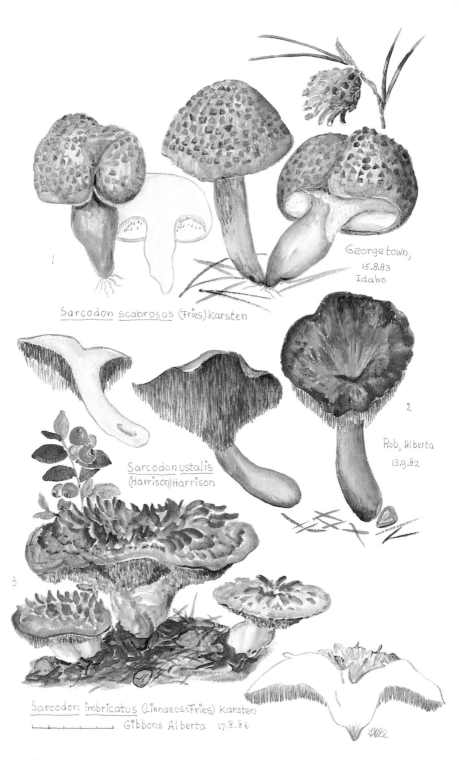

Georgetown,
15.8.83
Idaho

Sarcodon scabrosus (Fries) Karsten

Sarcodon ustalis
(Harrison) Harrison

2

Rob, Alberta
13.9.82

3

Sarcodon imbricatus (Linnaeus:Fries) Karsten
Gibbons Alberta 17.8.86

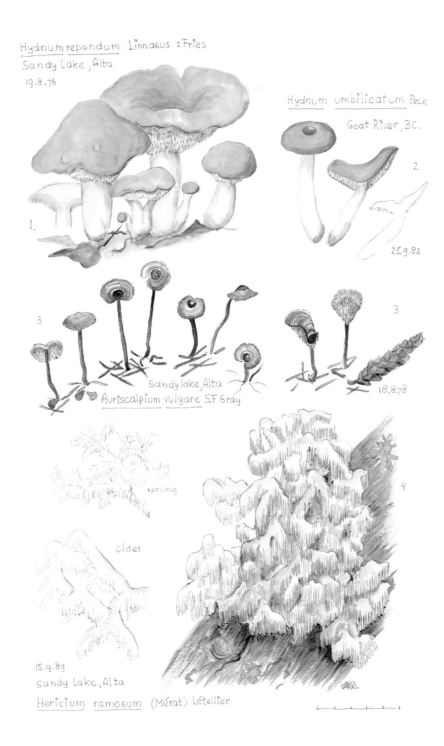

Hydnum repandum Linnaeus : Fries
Sandy Lake, Alta
19.8.76

1.

Hydnum umbilicatum Peck
Goat River, BC.

2

25.9.82

3

3

Sandy lake, Alta
Auriscalpium vulgare S.F. Gray

18.8.78

young

older

4

15.9.89
Sandy Lake, Alta
Hericium ramosum (Mérat) Létellier

Page 173

The families of Hydnaceae, Auriscalpiaceae and Hericiaceae are represented on this plate. Both *Hydnum* and *Hericium* are edible and taste excellent. All form their spores on teeth.

1. **yellow tooth fungus**   *Hydnum repandum*   p.368
Grows in the woods under all kinds of trees; this mushroom is very easy to recognize; looks as appetizing as a freshly baked bun; the small white spore-bearing teeth on the underside, white spores and tender flesh cannot be mistaken. Edible and choice.

2. **navel tooth fungus**   *Hydnum umbilicatum*   p.369
Looking somewhat like no. 1, these mushrooms are daintier; the smaller cap is usually darker; it has a definite navel; and the stalk is white and slender; even if it is mistaken for no. 1, it does not matter, for it is edible and tastes excellent itself.

3. **earspoon fungus**   *Auriscalpium vulgare*   p.369
Small spoon-shaped fruiting body with pinkish teeth, which turn brown; grows on spruce and pine debris. The difficulty is not recognition but spotting the mushroom.

4. **branched Hericium**   *Hericium ramosum*   p.370
Only when moisture conditions have been right for a while do beautiful — often large — clusters of white-branched *Hericium* appear on the plentiful deadwood of deciduous trees in our northern forests. Easily recognized because the pendant teeth grow along the whole branch. When young it is edible and good-tasting.

Page 175

The two large polypores on this plate have stalks and could, at first sight, be mistaken for a bolete, especially no. 1. They have dense, heavy flesh, and the tube layer is very shallow (not a sponge as in boletes) and is not detachable.

BONDARZEWIACEAE

1. **giant mountain polypore**   *Bondarzewia montana*   p.370
Compound, giant polypore; grows near old conifers and is connected to them by a rhizomorph or rootlike structure; sometimes grows on old conifer wood. Hairy caps; white structure covered with pores; heavy, dense white flesh. Aromatic odour but inedible.

POLYPORACEAE

2. **rooting polypore**   *Polyporus radicatus*   p.371
Resembles a bolete somewhat, but has very dense flesh, a black rootlike base and a shallow tube layer, which shows that it is one of the fleshy polypores. The thick stalks have a crust-like appearance. Edible when young, but tough.

Melanopus radicatus (Schweinitz) Pomerleau ≡ Polyporus radicatus Schweinitz

2

near stump
2 o'clock creek, 1.8.82
kootenay Plains, Alta
Rocky Mountains

1.

under Thoja plicata

Bondarzewia montana
(Quélet) Singer

28.9.82 Lakelse Lake, BC

Page 177

POLYPORACEAE

Four more stalked polypores are shown on this plate. In reality most polypores are bracket shaped, woody and tough, but I can only show a minimum number of those. The Canadian tuckahoe is very interesting.

1. **penny size blackfoot** *Polyporus varius* forma *nummularius* p.371
The name "nummularius" means small coin. Penny-size specimens grow on very small branches and somewhat larger ones on larger branches. A round yellow-ochre cap, small round pores and a partly or totally black stalk define the species. Dry old fruiting bodies are very persistent.

2. **winter polypore** *Polyporus brumalis* p.372
It is called winter polypore because in temperate climates it often fruits in winter. Grows on dead branches. These small mushrooms are distinguished by a brown stalk and oval, radially arranged pores, which are bigger than those of the penny polypore.

3. **spring polypore** *Polyporus arcularius* p.372
Also called fringed polypore because young specimens have hair around their cap edge. This stalked, annual polypore is recognized by its very large hexagonal pores. Another small bracket-shaped polypore, *Favolus alveolarius* (former name: *Polyporus mori*) also has large angular pores, but it is soft-fleshed, smells of apricots and has no stalk, or a very short one, and a golden cap.

4. **fungus stone or Canadian tuckahoe** *Polyporus tuberaster* p.372
A fleshy mushroom with a scaly cap; large angular pores underneath the cap, with the pattern of the pores continuing on the stalk. Most important, it emerges from a stone-like sclerotium (or pseudosclerotium as a sclerotium with some sand and soil included is sometimes called). The fruiting body is annual, but the stone can produce fruiting bodies for several years. Edible when young, but requires lengthy cooking.

Page 179

POLYPORACEAE

One species each from seven genera in the Polyporaceae: some edible annual fruiting bodies with soft flesh; some have woody brackets, annual or perennial (every year a new tube layer is added); some woody brackets with gills instead of pores (nos. 5 & 6). This is just a sample of variations possible in Polyporaceae. When annual or perennial is mentioned, it refers to the fruiting bodies; the mycelium lives in the wood until its food source is exhausted.

1. **sulphur shelf or chicken of the woods** *Laetiporus sulphureus* p.373
Easily identified; bright sulphur yellow, large, shelved clusters with very small yellow pores on the underside of the cap; annual. Edible with caution because there are some people who have trouble digesting them.

2. **birch polypore** *Piptoporus betulinus* p.374
Growing only on birch, the distinctive lantern-shaped conks can be found in the tops of old birches or on branches on the ground; annual. Inedible.

3. **tinder conk or horse's hoof fungus** *Fomes fomentarius* p.374
Easily recognized by its shape, comes in grey and brown colours. The specimen in the illustration is growing on birch but it also grows on other deciduous trees. Perennial; the lines on the conk show that it has been growing for quite a few years. Woody.

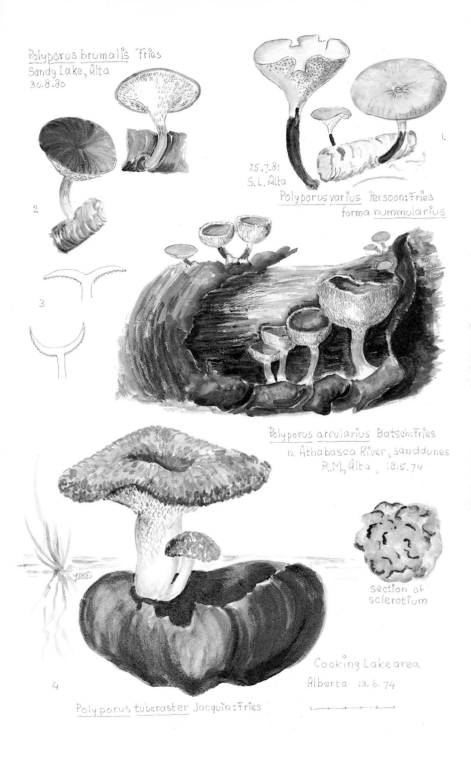

Polyporus brumalis Fries
Sandy Lake, Alta
30.8.80

2

3

25.7.81
S.L. Alta
Polyporus varius Persoon: Fries
forma nummularius

1.

Polyporus arcularius Batsch: Fries
n. Athabasca River, sanddunes
R.M., Alta, 18.5.74

section of
sclerotium

Cooking Lake area
Alberta 13.6.74

4

Polyporus tuberaster Jacquin: Fries

4. **vermilion polypore**   *Pycnoporus cinnabarinus*   p.375
The colour of this bracket mushroom makes it stand out; the red pigment, cinnabar, is present in great quantities and is even visible in the wood and bark of the birch log it grows on; occurs on the wood of various deciduous trees, sometimes on conifers. Woody, annual but persistent fruiting bodies.

5. **white-gilled polypore**   *Lenzites betulina*   p.375
Colourful, tough brackets with hairy concentric zones and with whitish gills on the underside. Despite these characteristics, they belong to the Polyporaceae. The combination results in easy identification. Annual but persistent; woody.

6. **rusty-gilled polypore**   *Gloeophyllum sepiarium*   p.375
A fan-like, tough bracket; hairy; when young it has brightly coloured zones around a dark centre; white or yellow margin; underside gilled, with a smooth infertile border; grows on coniferous wood; often on fences, telephone poles, etc. Annual but persistent.

7. **orange sponge polypore**   *Pycnoporellus alboluteus*   p.376
Soft, spongy polypore, growing along the bark grooves of dead conifers. Its orange colour, ragged pore openings that give the impression of teeth and the size make this species easy to recognize. Annual fruiting bodies, decaying relatively quickly.

Page 180

GANODERMATACEAE
The lacquered bracket family includes the famed reishi fungus, honoured in Japan.

1. **cedar lacquer fungus**   *Ganoderma tsugae*   p.377
The beautiful, red lacquered fruiting bodies can be found on various conifer logs: cedar, hemlock, larch, spruce, pine or fir. Glistening in a ray of sunlight, these fruiting bodies stand out. Annual fruiting bodies. Only no. 2 is perennial

2. **artist's bracket**   *Ganoderma applanatum*   p.377
The name has been used for a long time, but I do not approve of it as an artist. The pore surface has a white, waxy layer on top of the brown tubes, which can be damaged with a fingernail. The lovely big conks can survive for at least 50 years, so it is better to make a sketch on paper or a painting on canvas and keep track of how many years the fruiting bodies survive.

3. **reishi or ling chih**   *Ganoderma lucidum*   p.378
Famous mushroom of immortality and youth and a suppressor of cancer. The intense colour of the lacquered crust can be found in the bark of the stump it grows on. See the sugar maple bark in the illustration. The whimsical shapes the fruiting bodies take on are delightful. Annual fruiting bodies.

Page 181

MORCHELLACEAE
Everybody who loves to eat mushrooms, wants to find morels. The secret is to know when they fruit! When you find them, check to see which tree is budding out and which spring flower is in bloom at the same time. Then you know every year when the true morels are fruiting.

1. **wrinkled thimble or early morel**   *Ptychoverpa bohemica*   p.380
Easily recognized by its brown wrinkled cap, sitting like a thimble on the top of the stalk and attached only there. Off-white to yellowish to almost orange stalk. The whole mushroom is very fragile. Edible with caution. They have to be cooked well. Never eat too many. Some people are sensitive to these.

Laetiporus sulphureus
(Bulliard : Fries) Bondartsev & Singer
Soeren) Holland
7.7.73

Piptoporus betulinus
(Bulliard : Fries) Karsten
Wolf lake Alta
12.8.78

2

Sandy L, Alta   Fomesfomentarius
15.7.72   (Linnaeus : Fries) Fries

3

Pycnoporus cinnabarinus
(Jacquin : Fries) karsten

4

Sandy Lake, Alta
26.8.74

bottom

5

L, 1.10.78

↓ bottom

26.8.73
Sandy L., Alta

Gloeophyllum sepiarium
(von Wulfen : Fries) Karsten

bottom

Lenzites betulina
(Linnaeus : Fries) Fries

7

Pycnoporellus alboluteus (Ellis & Everhart) kotlaba & Pouzar
Assiniboine Pass, Mount Turner, Alta 25.7.76

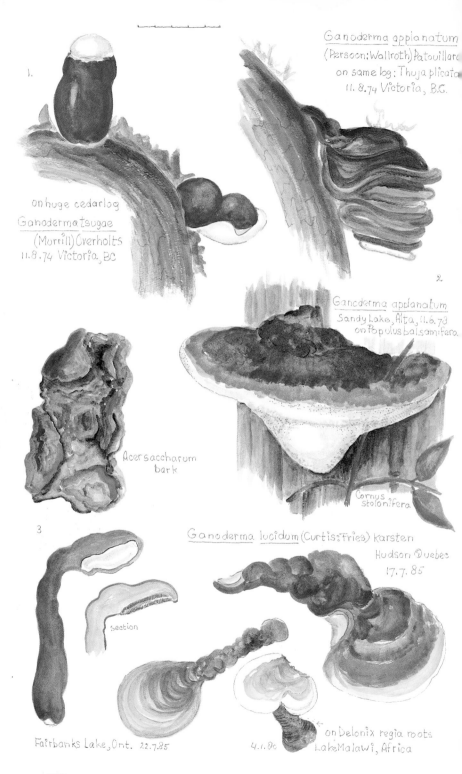

1.

Ganoderma applanatum
(Persoon: Wallroth) Patouillard
on same log: Thuja plicata
11. 8. 74 Victoria, B.C.

on huge cedar log
Ganoderma tsugae
(Murrill) Overholts
11. 8. 74 Victoria, BC

2.

Ganoderma applanatum
Sandy Lake, Alta., 11. 6. 78
on Populus balsamifera.

Acer saccharum
bark

Cornus
stolonifera

3

Ganoderma lucidum (Curtis: Fries) Karsten
Hudson Quebec
17. 7. 85

section

Fairbanks Lake, Ont. 22.7.85

4. 1. 80

on Delonix regia roots
Lake Malawi, Africa

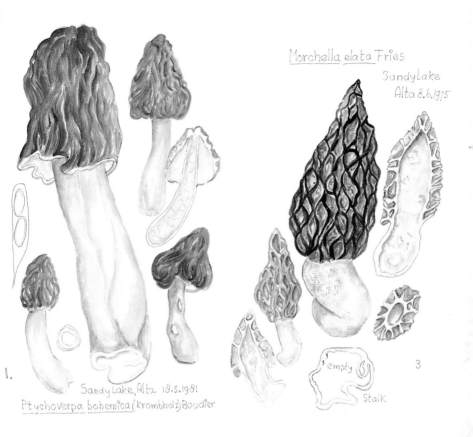

Morchella elata Fries
Sandy Lake
Alta 8.6.1975

3

empty

Stalk

1.

Sandy Lake, Alta. 18.5.1981
Ptychoverpa bohemica (krombholz) Boudier

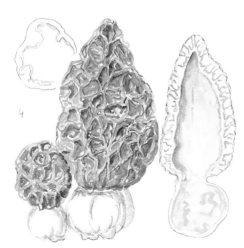

4

Morchella esculenta Fries
Canal Flats, BC. 11.9.86

Verpa conica Fries
Sl. 3.6.82

2,

2. **smooth thimble mushroom**   *Verpa conica*   p.380
While the wrinkled thimble appears nearly every spring, the smooth one can only
be found at the end of the morel season in damp spots when the spring weather
remains cool. Dark brown, smooth cap attached to the stalk only at the apex, like a
thimble on a finger; pale stalk. Easy to recognize. Edible when cooked, but caution
is advised for the same reasons as no. 1.

3. **black morel**   *Morchella elata*   p.381
Very easily recognized mushroom with its honeycombed head with dark ridges
and light-coloured stalk. Head and stalk are one piece, which can be seen when a
lengthwise cut is made. The mushroom is difficult to spot because at that time of
spring it blends in well with the primarily brown and dark colours of the leafless
forest. Edible and good, but do not eat them raw.

4. **yellow or sponge morel**   *Morchella esculenta*   p.381
Recognized by its yellowish sponge-like head and short, pale stalk. This is for many
people the choice mushroom for the table. They have been eaten in many countries
for hundreds of years. People tend to keep their collection sites secret, but these
morels can be found in burnt-over areas, old orchards and in the woods, usually in
spring. Edible only when cooked, and the taste is excellent. **Do not eat them raw.**

Page 183

HELVELLACEAE
False morels have convoluted heads looking like exposed brains. True morels look
more like honeycombs. False morels can be deadly.

1. **hooded false morel**   *Gyromitra infula*   p.382
Mitre or saddle-shaped mushroom; head at first relatively smooth, getting more
and more convoluted and wrinkled as it matures. It stays smoother when it has a
parasite living on it, which happens frequently (see illustration 102). Stalk is whitish
to brownish or vinaceous in colour. Grows in mixed or coniferous woods on
ground rich in lignin or on rotten wood. **Poisonous**: causes vomiting, diarrhea and
temporary paralysis.

2. **brain mushroom**   *Gyromitra esculenta*   p.382
More or less round, brain-like convoluted head, in shades of brown. The buff to
pinkish stalk is swollen in the centre or has a basal bulb; medium to large size.
Although very different from morels, this mushroom, fruiting in the morel season,
has often been mistaken for a true morel — with dire results; it has often caused
death. **Poisonous.**

Page 185

HELVELLACEAE
Four *Helvella* species with distinct head and stalk; the stalk is often pitted and the
head saddle-shaped or irregular but rarely cup shaped. All *Helvella* species should
be treated with extreme caution, although they are not as dangerous as Gyromitras.
Edibility is often unknown.

1. **fluted white Helvella**   *Helvella crispa*   p.383
Once you have seen this white mushroom, you can easily recognize it from thereon
by its fluted stalk and saddle-shaped, irregular head with margins that are loose
from the stalk.

parasitized by *Sphaeronaemella helvellae*
(Karsten) Karsten

IB

A

I

healthy

log

3.9.75

Annie's L. Yukon
4.7.81

Gyromitra infula
(Schaeffer: Fries) Quélet
16.8.80 Sandy L., Alta

solid

2

4.7.81
Annie's Lake, Yukon

2

soft loose
stuffing

near Elk Island P.
24.5.86

Gyromitra esculenta (Persoon) Fries

2a. **fluted black Helvella**   *Helvella lacunosa*   p.383
Another recognizable mushroom, with its grey fluted stalk and saddle-shaped,
black head; edges of the lobes are attached to the stalk in several places. Grows on
disturbed areas in grass, where trees were cut, or on burnt areas in campgrounds.

2b. *Helvella lacunosa* with parasite   p.383
The same species but parasitized by another fungus, as happens frequently. The
explanation is in the detailed descriptions of the species on p. 191.

3. **long-stalked grey cup**   *Helvella macropus*   p.384
A cup on a long stalk. There are other stalked cups, but those stalks are short. The
cup of *H. macropus* is grey and felty on the outside; the spores are formed inside the
dark grey-brown cup. The stalk is also grey and felty.

4. **slender stalked Helvella**   *Helvella elastica*   p.384
Small elegant fruiting bodies; a saddle-shaped brown head with loose hanging
margins on a very slender, white stalk; the stalk is tougher than you think; the head
can be very irregular.

Page 186

PEZIZACEAE
On this plate four genera of Pezizaceae are represented; the fruiting bodies are cup-
or ear-shaped with a smooth or scalloped rim (no hairs on it). They are "sitting"
(sessile) on the ground or on wood or have a short stalk.

1. **home or cellar cup**   *Peziza domiciliana*   p.384
Dirty-white cup mushroom; grows in damp basements on earth or rugs, etc.

2. **charcoal cup**   *Peziza anthracophila*   p.385
Buff-coloured cups with notched edges; brownish inside; grows on scorched
ground.

3. **brown cup**   *Peziza repanda*   p.385
Grows on decaying wood; brown on the inside and whitish on the outside, when
young. Said to be edible.

4. **blackish-brown cup**   *Peziza brunneoatra*   p.385
Not common and hard to see, because of the dark, blackish-brown colour; grows on
the ground along paths in the woods.

5. **violet cup**   *Peziza violacea*   p.385
Pale violet outside and darker inside; grows on old burns on the ground.

6. **red-brown cup**   *Peziza badia*   p.386
Several cup mushrooms resembling this one exist. Grows on the ground under
spruce. Dark brown interior; red brown exterior.

7. **small dung cup**   *Peziza vesiculosa*   p.386
Very small yellowish cup mushroom growing on dung heaps and animal
droppings.

8. **grey goblet**   *Tarzetta cupularis*   p.386
Greyish, stalked, small cup; grows under spruce.

9. **brown bowl fungus**   *Tarzetta catina*   p.386
Bigger, stalked cup with brown bowl and bone-coloured stalk. Easily identified but
rare; grows in mixed forests.

10. **donkey's ears**   *Otidea onotica*   p.387
Tall, yellow, lopsided cups; easily recognized. Look just like donkey's ears; grow on
the ground in coniferous forests; said to be edible.

Helvella macropus (Fries) Karsten
Sandy Lake, Alta
13.8.72

3

Carson L., Alta
13.8.77

Helvella lacunosa
parasitized by
Mycogone cervina Ditmar

2 B

2 A

25.9.82
B.C.
Prince George

Devon, Alta 27.8.80
Helvella lacunosa Afzelius: Fries

15.11.78
Vancouver Island
Francis Park, BC

1.

16.8.80
Sandy Lake, Alta

11.8.79
Sandy
Lake

4

2.9.77

Sandy Lake, Alta
Helvella crispa Scopoli: Fries

15.8.77
Moberley Lake, BC.

Helvella elastica Bulliard: Fries

Tarzetta catina (Fries) Korf & J. K. Rogers

9

Edmonton 1.8.84
Peziza domiciliana
Cooke

1.

Edmonton, Alta
2.6.81

Tarzetta cupularis
(Fries) Lambotte

8

Sandy Lake,
Alta 2.8.81

2

9.7.77
Cypress Hills,
Alberta
Peziza anthracophila
R.W.G. Dennis

7

18.9.82
Ministik Hills,   Alta
Peziza vesiculosa Bulliard: St. Amar

6

Carsonlake, Alta   13.8.77
Peziza badia Persoon: Mérat

3

Peziza repanda Persoon
S.L. Alta 16.8.80

5

Sandy L. 30.8.75
Peziza violacea Persoon

4

25.9.82
gravel
Peziza brunneoatra
Desmazières
Goat River, BC.

11

10

Sandy L., Alta
30.8.75

18.7.83, Alta
above Kootenay Plains
Sarcosphaera crassa (Santi: Steudel)
Pouzar

Otidia onotica (Persoon) Fuckel

Melastiza chateri (W.G.Smith) Boudier
Edmonton, Alta
garden 22.9.80

2

forest
Carsonlake
13.8.77 Alta
ground

Humaria hemisphaerica (Wiggers ?
Fries) Fuckel

1.

18.7.71
Sandy L. Alta
stump

Scutellinia scutellata (Linnaeus: St Amans)
Lambotté

4

log

2.10.75
Sandy L., Alta

3

ground
15.11.78
Prior L, BC
Aleuria aurantia (Fries) Fuckel.

Trichophaea woolhopeia (Cooke & Phillips)
Boudier

6   20.8.73
S.L. Alta

ground

5
26.8.79
Sandy Lake, Alta
Scutellinia pennsylvanica (Seaver)
Denison

8

2.8.84
Sandy L, Alta
Sepultaria pellita (Cooke & Peck) Seaver

7

burnsite
E.of Jasper N.P.
18.5.74

Geopyxis carbonaria
(Albertini & Schweinitz: Fries) Saccardo

11. **violet star cup**   *Sacrcophaera crassa*   p.387
Quite large, dirty-white to pale grey cup mushroom; starts underground as a ball,
then opens up like a pointed crown; pink to purple inside; grows on the ground in
coniferous forests.

Page 187

HUMARIACEAE
The Humariaceae have cup- to saucer-shaped fruiting bodies; no stalk (sessile) and
with hairy underside and margin.

1. **hairy fairy cup**   *Humaria hemisphaerica*   p.387
Cup shaped; keeps that shape; brown hairy exterior, white interior and dark hairy
edge; this is an easily recognized species; grows on rotten logs or rich humus.

2. **red saucer**   *Melastiza chateri*   p.388
Somewhat like nos. 4 and 5 but bigger, smooth margin and flat when mature; a little brown hair on the bottom.

3. **orange peel fungus**   *Aleuria aurantia*   p.388
Easily recognized species because it is a bright orange, large cup mushroom,
which grows on newly made paths and dirt roads; the contrast of orange and off-
white makes one think of orange peel.

4. **red eyelash cup**   *Scutellinia scutellata*   p.388
Red to orange-red, small discs with prominent dark hairy fringes make these easy
to identify.

5. **Pennsylvannia eyelash cup**   *Scutellinia pennsylvanica*   p.388
This one is like no. 4 but has shorter brown hair and is smaller; grows on decaying
coniferous and deciduous wood.

6. **white eyelash cup**   *Trichophaea woolhopeia*   p.389
Another small disc fringed by brown hair; grows on the ground; coloured white.

7. **earth box**   *Geopyxis carbonaria*   p.389
Small cups in colours from pale yellow to tan to orange or brown; auburn
hymenium; grows on burnt ground. (I left the ground a light brown colour in the
illustration.)

8. **orange crown cup**   *Sepultaria pellita*   p.389
Brown, buried, hollow ball which opens up into a cup with an orange interior and
crown.

Page 189

The nine species belong to five families. The scarlet elf cup and the black urn may
be found in very early spring, even before the morels, and the blue-green cup may
be the last one in the fall.

SARCOSCYPHACEAE

1. **scarlet elf cup**   *Microstoma protracta*   p.390
Goblet-shaped cup mushroom; cup scarlet inside, orange outside; paler orange-
buff rim; slim white stalk; grows in very early spring.

SARCOSOMATACEA

2. **black urn fungus**   *Urnula hiemalis*   p.390
Large, dark brown to black, urn-shaped cup; grows on old wood or near it; short
stalk; becomes completely black with age.

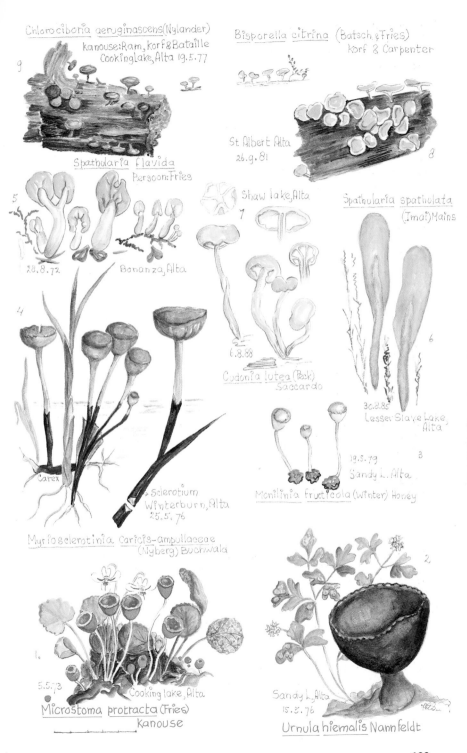

Chlorociboria aeruginascens (Nylander)
kanouse: Ram, korf & Bataille
Cooking lake, Alta 19.5.77

9

Bisporella citrina (Batsch & Fries)
korf & Carpenter

St Albert Alta
26.9.81

8

Spatholaria flavida
Persoon: Fries

5

28.8.72   Bonanza, Alta

Shaw lake, Alta

7

6.8.88

Cudonia lutea (Peck)
Saccardo

Spatholaria spatholata
(Imai) Mains

6

30.8.85
Lesser Slave Lake,
Alta

4

Carex

s Sclerotium
Winterburn, Alta
25.5.76

19.5.79   3
Sandy L. Alta

Monilinia fructicola (Winter) Honey

Myriosclerotinia Caricis-ampullaceae
(Nyberg) Buchwala

1

5.5.73

Cooking lake, Alta

Microstoma protracta (Fries)
kanouse

2

Sandy L. Alta
15.5.76

Urnula hiemalis Nannfeldt

SCELEROTINIACEAE

3. **cherry cup**   *Monilinia fructicola*   p.391
Small, pale, tan cup mushrooms growing on overwintered, mummified wild cherries. Are found away from the cherry trees; birds eat the cherries and deposit them elsewhere.

4. **sedge cup**   *Myriosclerotinia caricis-ampullaceae*   p.391
Good-sized goblets in shades of brown; grow in bogs, on their host plant sedge, in which they form black sclerotia (see description in family).

GEOGLOSSACEAE

5. **yellow earth tongue**   *Spathularia flavida*   p.392
Yellow, fan-like fruiting body with a whitish or pale yellow stalk; grows under spruce.

6. **spatula fungus**   *Spathularia spatulata*   p.392
Tall, spatula- or leaf-shaped mushroom; brown stalk and buff, flattened head; leathery upper part; rare.

7. **yellow Cudonia**   *Cudonia lutea*   p.392
Fruiting body with cap and stalk. Spores form on the outside of the cap. Saved in the refrigerator overnight, it released a cloud of spores as soon as it was taken out. Yellow in colour.

HELOTIACEAE

8. **minute lemon cups**   *Bisporella citrina*   p.393
Tiny cups; grow on old wood. Visible because they appear *en masse*. Yellow stalked cups.

9. **green cups**   *Chlorociboria aeruginascens*   p.393
Small green stalked cups, which can be found by examining a log that shows the typical blue green discolouring of the wood caused by this mushroom; fruits in cool seasons. Pink balls on the wood are from a Myxomycete, *Lycogala epidendron*. The pink balls turn brown when they mature.

Page 191

Pyrenomycetes or flask fungi are only lightly touched upon, but some of these are often encountered as colourful parasites of gilled mushrooms and boletes, e.g., the lobster mushroom. The hosts give them shape. The parasite forms a thin colourful layer on the surface of the host mushroom. Nos. 1 and 2 are flask fungi with their own "independent" fruiting bodies.

1. **soft leather pillow**   *Podostroma alutaceum*   p.394
Looking like an old puffball with a longer or shorter stalk, this mushroom can only be properly identified by using a microscope. The ascospores emerge on the outside from perithecia (see Ascomycotina), while a puffball develops powdery basidiospores on the inside.

2. **carbon balls**   *Daldinia concentrica*   p.394
Black, round, hard fruiting bodies, growing on deciduous stumps. The flesh shows concentric circles when cut.

3. **Gyromitra parasite**   *Sphaeronaemellae helvellae*   p.395
A parasite of the mitred false morel (see also p. 183). The head of this mushroom looks dark brown and fuzzy when it carries the parasite; on a poisonous host.

Podostroma alutaceum (Persoon:Fries) Atkinson
13.8.77 Moonshine Lake
Alta

on stump of
horsechestnut
Edmonton garden

haeronaemella helvellae (Karsten) Karsten
Gyromitra infula (Fries) Quélet

1

2

21.8.80
n. Elk I.P.
Alta

15.7.87

Daldinia
concentrica
Bolton: Fries
Cesati & de Notaris

20.7.83
Chambers Creek, Alta
Hypomyces chrysospermus
on Leccinum

Tulasne

5

Mycogone cervina
Ditmar

4

6

Carson L., Alta
13.8.77

28.9.32

on Lactarius volemus (Fr.) Fr.

on Helvella lacunosa

Lakelse Lake, BC

Hypomyces lactifluorum
(Schweinitz) Tulasne

and

7

Sandy Lake, Alta
23.8.80

on Lactarius torminosus (Fries)
S.F. Gray

8

Sandy Lake, Alta
26.7.81

13.7.75

7.8.92

Hypomyces luteovirens (Fries) Plowright on Russula spp.

4. **Helvella parasite**   *Mycogone cervina*   p.395
   A parasitic ascomycete on a saprophytic ascomycete. The host, *Helvella lacunosa*, is
   black, but it is covered by the white layer of the parasite (see also p. 185).

5. **golden Hypomyces**   *Hypomyces chrysospermus*   p.395
   A parasite on boletes. This is an ascomycete on a basidiomycete. It plugs the tubes
   and prevents the bolete from forming its own spores. Not edible.

6. **lobster mushroom**   *Hypomyces lactifluorum*   p.396
   Vermilion parasite on a bright orange *Lactarius* (apricot milkcap). Not difficult to
   recognize the lobsters, but you have to know the host too. Edible with caution (see
   p. 47 for the host).

7. **lobster mushroom**   *Hypomyces lactifluorum*   p.396
   The same parasite, orange in colour, grows on a poisonous host (woolly milkcap).
   Poisonous (see p. 44 for healthy host of this specimen).

8. **yellow green Hypomyces**   *Hypomyces luteo-virens*   p.396
   This species is very easy to recognize, but the hosts (a species of *Russula*) are not,
   because the gills and stalk are often completely covered and spore production is
   prevented.

Species Descriptions

Class HYMENOMYCETES

The name *Hymenomycetes* means fungi with a fertile layer or hymenium. The hymenium contains the spore-bearing cells which produce the basidiospores. Four orders are discussed here: Boletales, Russulales, Agaricales and Aphyllophorales.

The reason I placed plates and text of the Gasteromycetes (puffballs, etc.) between Agaricales and Aphyllophorales, is to show the closeness of some of these groups to certain families of Agaricales. This will become apparent when pages 143 and 152 are compared for example.

In Hymenomycetes spores are formed on exposed surfaces: both sides of the gills; inside the tubes; the surface of teeth, etc., and spores are forcibly discharged at maturity. In Gasteromycetes spores are formed internally and are not forcibly discharged.

Order BOLETALES   boletes and relations

The Greek name *Boletus* means mushroom, in general, and was used more than 2000 years ago. The family of Boletaceae was grouped with the order of gilled, fleshy mushrooms for a long time and was considered to belong to the Agaricales. Lately the Boletaceae, together with Gomphidiaceae and Paxillaceae have been grouped in their own order, Boletales.

Boletaceae have fleshy fruiting bodies, forming their basidiospores in tubes. The layer of tubes, or sponge, is easily detached from the flesh.

Gomphidiaceae are closely related; their fleshy fruiting bodies have similar solid forms and their thick, fleshy gills are also easily detached in one layer from the flesh.

Paxillaceae are closely related as well; solid, fleshy fruiting bodies; the decurrent gills have connecting veins between the gills and often anastomosing occurs near the stalk. (In the genus *Hygrophoropsis*, the gills are forked.) The fertile layer is easily detached.

Almost all Boletales have similar spores of a long cylindrical shape and most have a mycorrhizal relationship with trees.

Family BOLETACEAE   bolete family

The family of Boletaceae consists of medium to large mushrooms with caps and stalks, with tubes perpendicular to the ground on the underside of the cap. Basidiospores are formed on hymenium inside the tubes. The spores, usually a shade of brown, are forcefully discharged at maturity.

There are many edible species in this group, but species with red tube mouths should be avoided. Genera discussed are: *Boletus, Leccinum, Suillus* and *Fuscoboletinus*.

Genus BOLETUS

The genus *Boletus* has some famous edible mushrooms in it, but also some rather poisonous species. They are easy to tell apart, because the edible ones come in muted colours and the poisonous ones have strong colours. In the latter the sponge has a red surface and the flesh quickly changes from yellow to a strong blue or green when cut, broken or bruised. Generally the mushrooms of *Boletus* species are medium to large in size; the pores have no radial orientation; the stalk is thick and sturdy, often with a fine netlike ornamentation, especially at the top; and there is no ring. All have mycorrhizal relationships with various trees.

yellow cracked bolete

p.27-1

Boletus subtomentosus Fries

subtomentosus: slightly hairy (Latin)

Cosmopolitan, associated with coniferous trees. It occurs along the Pacific coast and in the Rocky Mountains, mostly under pine; fruiting in summer and fall. Frequently it does not occur. Edible but not exciting.

cap	velvety ochre-brown, rounded to flat, often the cuticle cracks exposing the flesh beneath; up to 12 cm across.
pore surface	(or sponge) bright yellow when young, later turning ochre. Pores angular, medium large.
spore print	olive brown
stalk	lemon-yellow top with a bit of a network and decurrent lines lower down (reticulate); further down brownish, streaked; up to 9 cm tall and 3 cm thick at the top. Mycelium at stalk base yellow.
flesh	pale creamy yellow, turning a bit greenish-blue.
taste & odour	mild.

Zeller's bolete

p.27-2

Boletus zelleri Murrill

zelleri: named after Professor S.M. Zeller, mycologist of Oregon State University 1885-1948

Pacific Northwest; associated with alder, poplar or other hardwoods; fruiting in the fall, but further south in the winter; occurs generally in damp places in river valleys, etc.; edible.

cap	dark-brown with some green in it; can be a quite irregular shape; a bit velvety; short skin flap; up to 12 cm across.
pore surface	yellow; large, angular pores; can bruise blue.
spore print	dull olive brown, with a lot of yellow juice on the paper.
stalk	off-white, somewhat lined; top becomes pink and can be quite red from overlay of hair; sturdy; tapering down; up to 10 cm tall and 4 cm thick.
flesh	off-white to very pale yellow, stringy; red-brown in the stalk.
taste	mild.
odour	none.

king bolete

p.27-3

Boletus edulis Bulliard: Fries

edulis: edible (Latin)

Cosmopolitan; associated with coniferous and deciduous trees; fruiting in summer across Canada, and later in the year further south. It has been found in the Yukon and in Alaska; prefers more or less sandy soils; one of the best-loved edible mushrooms in the world, it has a multitude of ethnic names: English - king bolete; French - cèpe; German - Steinpilz (stone fungus); Italian -porcini (pig food); Spanish - rodellon (small round boulder); Ukrainian - borovek; Czech - hrib (mushroom); Estonian - puravikud; Dutch - eekhoorntjes brood (squirrel's bread).

cap	variable shades of reddish yellow-brown, often with a lighter margin; smooth, like a bun; often grows very large, up to 25 cm across.
pore surface	whitish at first, then greenish yellow, finally ochre to coffee-brown; pores round, quite small.
spore print	olive-brown.
stalk	massive; whitish to yellowish, often with some pinkish-brown, especially when handled; top with raised network pattern (reticulate) sometimes over a large area of the stalk; up to 12 cm tall and 4 cm wide.
flesh	solid, white, turning a bit pink under the cuticle; does not stain blue and does not change colour in cooking either.
taste	nutty, excellent.
odour	pleasant.

red-pored bolete

p.28-1

Boletus pulcherrimus Thiers & Watling

former name: *B. eastwoodiae*
pulcherrimus: very beautiful (Latin)

Pacific Northwest; associated with both deciduous and coniferous trees; a poisonous but very beautiful mushroom. I found it under western red cedar and Douglas fir in the Rocky Mountain Trench near Fort McBride. Any bolete, the flesh of which quickly changes colour to blue or blue-green, is inedible or **poisonous**. This is one.

cap	smooth, dry; beautiful, unpolished, deep red-brown, like soft leather; up to 15 cm across.
pore surface	blood-red; tubes are yellow, quickly turning blue-green when cut; pores medium small, red, angular, somewhat radially arranged.
spore print	olive-brown, lots of yellow juice on white paper.
stalk	heavy; enlarging toward the base (club-shape); top orange-yellow with red reticulations, dark red lower down; up to 10 cm tall.
flesh	thick, solid, lemon-yellowquickly turning a strong blue to green, while base discolours to rhubarb-red.
odour	mild; do not taste.

peppery bolete

p.28-2

Boletus piperatus Fries

piperatus: peppery (Latin)

Cosmopolitan; this species occurs all over the North American continent, particularly in the North, including the Prairie provinces, the Yukon, Alaska and the Rocky Mountains; associated with aspen, alder, pine and spruce. Inedible.

cap	mostly dry, chestnut or red brown; semi-spherical at first, sometimes the margin is somewhat hairy; up to 8 cm across.
pore surface	red; in longitudinal section tubes ochre at first , then red; pores large, angular.
spore print	red-brown; the juice staining white paper red.
stalk	orange-yellow with red streaks, equal, solid, slender; up to 10 cm tall and 1.5 cm thick; older specimens sometimes have orange mycelium at their base.
flesh	yellow, with rhubarb red above the tubes; solid.
taste	peppery.
odour	pleasant.

Genus SUILLUS   sticky bolete

of a pig (Latin)

This genus is important for mycophagists (those who eat mushrooms) because it is safe. Easily recognized by their yellow-orange to brown colours, stickiness in wet weather and yellow solid flesh. It is still important to recognize each species. Page 29 shows species with rings and page 31 shows species without rings on the stalks. All have mycorrhizal relationships with a specific conifer, either pine, tamarack, hemlock or Douglas fir. The needles on the caps in the illustrations indicate stickiness as well as the associated tree species. Spore prints are a shade of yellow brown. All are edible, though some are tastier than others. The slimy skin is harmless, but it can easily be peeled off if earth or needles stick to it. The flesh does not discolour in cooking.

peaked Suillus

p.28-3

Suillus umbonatus Dick & Snell

umbonatus: with an umbo or knob (Latin)

Pacific Northwest and the Rocky Mountains; associated with pine; the peaked Suillus fruits in late summer and fall in moist, mossy, mixed pine and spruce forest. Unpalatable.

cap	greenish brown to grey-brown, streaked, slimy, with knob (umbonate); up to 9 cm across (usually small).

pore surface	yellow, turning ochre, then brown; pores are large, angular, irregular; radially arranged, compound, anastomosing.
spore print	medium cinnamon brown; the juice will spot white paper yellow.
stalk	white, often bent, slender, equal, up to 8 cm tall and 1 cm thick, solid.
ring	gelatinous, soon staining cinnamon from the spores; may disappear.
flesh	dirty, white to yellowish, sometimes a bit of viridian green in stem base.
taste	somewhat sour.
odour	pleasant.

slippery Jill   p.29-1

Suillus subolivaceus Smith & Thiers

subolivaceus: about the colour of a fresh olive (Latin)

Pacific Northwest; associated with western white pine and lodgepole pine in the Rocky Mountains; in Alberta and the Western U.S., fruiting in summer and fall. Edible but not recommended.

cap	yellow to olivaceous brown, rounded, sticky when moist, somewhat streaked; skinflap, up to 8 cm across.
pore surface	first greyish buff, becoming olive brown in maturity; pores medium large.
spore print	medium brown.
stalk	pale yellow with glandular dots; white mycelium at the base; up to 7 cm tall and 1.5 cm thick.
ring	broad, white on top, brown underneath, sticky, flaring.
flesh	dirty-yellowish.

western painted bolete   p.29-2

Suillus lakei (Murrill) Smith & Thiers

Lakei: after American mycologist E. R. Lake

Pacific Northwest; associated with Douglas fir in the Rocky Mountains and along the coast; fruits in summer to late fall; on duff, sometimes on wood; edible.

cap	red fibrils on orange-brown background, sticky; bits of sticky veil on the cap edge; up to 8 cm across.
pore surface	yellow at first, then ochrish; pores near stalk sometimes red; pores angular, large.
spore print	dingy cinnamon.
stalk	yellow top with brown glandular dots; below the ring is yellow, but soon turns reddish brown from handling; up to 7 cm tall and 1.5 cm thick; white mycelium at base.
ring	broad, woolly, white to yellowish.
flesh	yellow, a bit of olive-green at base.

heavy bolete   p.29-3

Suillus ponderosus Smith & Thiers

ponderosus: heavy (Latin)

Pacific Northwest; associated with Douglas fir and pine; fruiting in the Rocky Mountains from August into October; the epithet *ponderosus* means that this is a potentially very heavy and large mushroom (and not that it has a special relationship with *Pinus ponderosa*); edible.

cap	salmon pink to reddish brown, smooth, sticky, small skin flap or overhanging sterile edge, up to 25 cm across.
pore surface	yellow at first, turning yellow-brown; large, angular pores; pore pattern continuing on top of the stalk (anastomosing).
spore print	cinnamon-brown.
stalk	light yellow, sturdy; up to 8 cm tall and 2 cm thick, (slugs caused the holes in the stalk of the specimen portrayed).
ring	sticky, whitish band; bits of veil still attached to the cap-edge.
flesh	yellow, unchanging.
taste	like lemon.
odour	very fresh.

hollow-stalked larch bolete

p.29-4

Suillus cavipes (Opatowski) Smith & Thiers

cavipes: hollow foot (Latin)

Cosmopolitan in temperate climates of the Northern hemisphere, including the Arctic; fruiting in late summer and fall. Easy to recognize; edible and good.

cap	dark brown hair tufts on orange background; dry cap margin has skin flap and bits of veil on it; up to 10 cm across.
pore surface	yellow; large, angular pores, radially arranged.
spore print	dark olive-brown; yellow juice stains on white paper.
stalk	yellow above the ring, red-brown below; wider in the middle, hollow; up to 5 cm tall and 2 cm thick.
ring	near the top; narrow and slight, white and wispy.
flesh	pale yellow; solid in cap, hollow in stalk.

tamarack Jack

p.29-5

Suillus grevillei (Klotzch) Singer

grevillei: named after English mycologist R.K. Greville

Cosmopolitan; associated with larch; occurs in the Northern and Southern hemisphere in temperate climates, wherever larch species grow naturally or are introduced; fruiting in late summer and fall. Edible mushroom, remove the slime layer.

cap	striking orange to auburn; shiny with thick slime in wet weather; up to 10 cm across; skin flap.
pore surface	yellow at first, later a bit brownish; pores somewhat radially arranged.
spore print	medium olive-brown.
stalk	yellow, short; often a red-brown band above the ring and red-brown on the base; up to 5 cm tall and 2 cm thick.
ring	white or yellow with some red brown; large, fibrous, flaring.
flesh	bright yellow.
taste	excellent.

slippery Jack

p.29-6

Suillus luteus (Fries) S. F. Gray

luteus: golden yellow (Latin). This name seems to be a misnomer, because slippery Jack is less yellow than other species in this group.

Cosmopolitan on the Northern Hemisphere; associated with conifers particularly pine; fruits in cool weather in summer and fall; closely related to *S. subolivaceus*, which occurs only in our Pacific Northwest. The difference between the two species is mostly in the colour. Edible.

cap	light to dark brown with purplish tinge, very sticky when wet, smooth but streaky; ample skin flap; up to 8 cm across.
pore surface	white, soon turning yellow, then curry; surface uneven, pores angular, medium large.
spore print	olive-brown.
stalk	yellow top with glandular dots; below ring whitish with purple streaks; up to 5 cm tall and 2.5 cm thick.
ring	sticky, white on top, purplish below.
flesh	bright lemon-yellow or whitish becoming yellow with some reddish spots.
taste	good.
odour	spicy.

variable Suillus

p.31-1

Suillus subvariegatus Snell & Dick

subvariegatus: somewhat variable (Latin)

North American; associated with conifers like hemlock, pine and western red cedar; along Pacific and Atlantic coasts in damp locations; fruiting in the fall. Quite rare; edibility unknown.

cap	viscid in wet weather, smooth, may have some tufts of hair, pale orange-brown, up to 9 cm across.
pore surface	warm yellow, almost orange; pores medium large, angular.
spore print	dull cinnamon.
stalk	pale yellow, smooth, relatively tall, equal, a bit wider at the top; somewhat reddish at times, up to 9 cm tall and 1 cm thick.
flesh	lemon yellow, staining blue when cut or injured.
taste	mild.
odour	none.

woolly pine bolete   p.31-2

Suillus tomentosus (Kauffman) Singer, Snell & Dick

tomentosus: covered with hair (Latin)

North American; associated with pine; occurs anywhere pine grows on our continent, particularly in the west; fruiting in August and September, somewhat longer along the coast and in the south; often found in camping areas in the mountains; edible.

cap	sticky when damp; red hair visible when dry, this may disappear; colour varies from orange-yellow to reddish brown; up to 10 cm across.
pore surface	coffee brown, in cross section the tubes are lighter in colour; pores small and angular.
spore print	dark olive brown.
stalk	warm yellow with brown glandular dots at the top, some reddish colouration; white mycelium at base; up to 6 cm tall and 2 cm thick.
flesh	yellow to flesh colour with some blue-green discoloration.
taste	mild.
odour	light aromatic.

milk bolete   p.31-3

Suillus granulatus (Fries) Kuntze

granulatus: dotted (Latin)

Cosmopolitan; associated with pine species; it occurs wherever pine grows naturally or is introduced; fruiting in summer and fall; edible and good.

cap	sticky, smooth, streaky or mottled, cinnamon brown to yellow-brown; up to 8 cm across.
pore surface	warm yellow becoming ochre with age; small, cloudy droplets often cling to the pores, giving rise to the name "milk bolete"; pores medium small.
spore print	light cinnamon brown.
stalk	white, sometimes bright yellow top, glandular dots at the top, almost equal, short, up to 4 cm tall and 2 cm thick.
flesh	yellow; red around wormholes.
taste & odour	mild.

northern pine bolete   p.31-4

Suillus albivelatus Smith, Thiers & Miller

albivelatus: with a white veil (Latin)

Pacific Northwest; associated with pine species; fruiting in late August and September and later in the fall further south, until frost starts. Edible and good.

cap	sticky, with appressed white hair on the yellow-brown cap; sometimes a bit of a fringe shows; up to 8 cm across.
pore surface	yellow, pores medium small.
spore print	cinnamon brown.
stalk	top half bright yellow, bottom half white; sticky; hairy cap-edge often imbedded in stalk in immature specimens. It shows up like an annular zone, often tinted red; short, up to 4 cm tall and 2.5 cm thick.
flesh	yellow, red around wormholes.
taste	mild.
odour	light, aromatic.

short-stemmed bolete   p.31-5

Suillus brevipes (Peck) Kuntze

brevipes: short stalked (Latin)

North American; associated with pine species; occuring in Canada and the U.S.; fruiting in summer and fall. Edible and good.

cap	sticky and smooth, reddish brown fading to streaky purplish brown; up to 8 cm across.
pore surface	pale yellow, small pores, short tubes.
spore print	dull cinnamon.
stalk	white to very pale yellow, short, up to 3 cm tall and 2 cm thick.
flesh	pale lemon yellow, unchanging.
taste & odour	pleasant.

small short-stemmed bolete   p.31-6

Suillus brevipes Peck var. *subgracilis* Smith & Thiers

subgracilis: quite small (Latin); gracilis: small, slim

Pacific Northwest; associated with Jackpine and lodgepole pine; growing on sandy soils; fruiting in summer and fall in boreal mixed forest. Edible and good.

cap	sticky and smooth, tan to ochre, up to 10 cm across.
pore surface	yellow, with age a bit greenish ochre; pores medium large, angular.
spore print	dull cinnamon.
stalk	bright warm yellow with a white base; up to 5 cm tall and 2 cm thick.
flesh	yellow, unchanging.
taste & odour	pleasant.

Genus LECCINUM   rough stemmed bolete

Leccinum species have a white stalk, roughened with ornaments or scabers, which sooner or later turn black. The cap is rounded at first and the edge of the cap rests against the stalk. When the fruiting body grows, a sterile edge extends beyond the cap margin (skin flap). The pores are small and whitish at first and not radially arranged. The flesh, white when cut, turns pink then grey or blackish to some degree. Most of the rough-stemmed boletes have mycorrhizal relationships with aspen. Since more than half of the trees in the northern forest are aspen, it is evident that this genus is important. Six species are described which occur in the northern part of this continent. There is quite a lot of variation in each species in the size and colour of the cap and in the heaviness of the stalk. Older specimens all turn brownish and spongy and can become massive. These should be left to the squirrels. Otherwise this is a very safe genus for mycophagists. The flesh is softer than that of *Boletus edulis* and turns greyish in the pot, so it is considered less palatable than the king bolete. *Leccinum* is the bolete you will find most of the time and is, therefore, very popular.

The species name *L. aurantiacum* is considered by some authors to be a group name for orange to orange-brown species and *L. scabrum* the group name for the brown-capped species.

northern rough stem   p.32-1

Leccinum boreale Smith, Thiers & Watling

Leccinum: Italian word for mushroom
borealis: of the north (Latin)

Northwest North American species; mycorrhizal with poplar species. Earliest fruiting bolete in aspen parkland and boreal mixed forest of the prairie provinces, the Yukon, Alaska and northern B.C. Edible and good.

cap	orange to red-brown; smooth, dry, large skin flaps; up to 16 cm across.
pore surface	off-white at first, sagging with age; dirty pores, small and round.
spore print	medium brown.
stalk	white, grooved at the top, coarse black ornamentation, massive; narrower at the top and the base; up to 10 cm tall and 3 cm wide at the top.
flesh	thick, solid, white; slowly turning pink when cut, then somewhat grey.
taste & odour	mild.

brown rough stem   p.32-2

Leccinum snellii Smith, Thiers & Watling

Snellii: named after W.H. Snell, mycologist

North American species; mycorrhizal relationship with aspen and black poplar. It grows in small numbers in boreal mixed forest in July, August and September. Edible and excellent.

cap	dark brown with an overlay of black fibrils at first; with age becoming mottled with pale yellow spots and nearly smooth; narrow skin flap; up to 7 cm across, sometimes larger.
pore surface	first ivory, later dirty white; small pores.
spore print	medium warm brown.
stalk	white with fine dark ornaments, arranged in vertical lines at top; thickening toward base; up to 8 cm tall and 1.5 cm wide.
flesh	white, hardly discolouring, a bit pink under the skin.
taste & odour	mild.

ochre rough stem   p.32-3

Leccinum ochraceum Smith, Thiers & Watling

ochraceum: ochre-yellow (Latin)

Northwest North American species; reported from Michigan and Alberta under aspen and birch in damp spots; fruiting in July.

cap	ochre-yellow to tan with the texture of fine felt; the skin is sometimes cracked (areolate) at the crown; small skin flap; up to 10 cm across.
pore surface	light tan, medium small pores, a deep well near the stalk; with age the tubes discolour to orange-ochre.
spore print	warm brown.
stalk	relatively slender, the top lined; fine black ornamentation; thickening toward the base; up to 8 cm tall and 1.5 cm wide.
flesh	white; when cut it turns lilaceous pink, then slowly greyish.
taste & odour	mild.

pale rough stem   p.32-4

Leccinum holopus var. *americanum* Smith, Thiers & Watling

holopus: with perfect stalk (Greek)

North American; occurs in boreal mixed forest under spruce and aspen; in the Rocky Mountains under fir. This bolete is associated with conifers, the other five with deciduous trees.

cap	whitish to beige, a tinge of brown on the crown, half spherical; very narrow skin flap; up to 6 cm across.
pore surface	off-white, very small pores.
spore print	a medium yellow-brown.
stalk	white, lined at the top, very fine dark ornamentation, coarser toward the base; up to 6 cm tall and 1 cm wide.
flesh	white, hardly any discolouration, sometimes a little pink under the skin.
taste & odour	mild.

aspen rough stem

p.32-5

Leccinum insigne Smith, Thiers & Watling

insigne: remarkable (Latin)

North American; occurs where natural aspen forests occur: aspen parkland, boreal mixed forest, Rocky Mountains, central U.S.; fruiting in July, August and September.

cap	orange, turning brown and somewhat sticky with age. Large skin flap, often split; up to15 cm across.
pore surface	off-white at first, discolouring to ochre with age and when handled; indented at the stalk.
spore print	yellow-brown.
stalk	white, densely covered wih reddish-brown ornamentation which turns black with age; there are often blue-green spots; heavy, especially at the base, narrowing at the top; up to 10 cm tall and 3 cm wide.
flesh	white, often with blue-green spots, discolours quickly to mauve when cut and then to slate-grey.
taste & odour	mild.

white rough stem

p.32-6

Leccinum niveum (Blume) Smith, Thiers & Watling

niveum: snow-white (Latin)

North American species, not described in field guides so far; I find it regularly although not often; under aspen, saskatoon, buffalo-berry, etc. Fruits in July.

cap	ivory coloured or ivory with a pink blush; smooth, sometimes cracked in patches; skin flap; up to 12 cm across.
pore surface	off-white, becoming dirty looking with age; small pores; indented at the stalk.
spore print	medium-brown.
stalk	white with dark, coarse ornamentation; up to 10 cm tall and 3 cm wide.
flesh	white, the flesh and the tubes turning pink or lilac when cut, then slowly somewhat grey.
taste & odour	mild.

Genus FUSCOBOLETINUS   **darker-spored bolete**

fuscus: dark (Latin)
boletinus: small bolete (Latin)

Fuscoboletinus is close to *Suillus*. It has a darker spore print than *Suillus*; large, angular pores that are radially arranged. Sometimes radial ridges protrude from the sponge, reminding one of gills. Quite a few species have mycorrhizal relationships with *Larix* or larch. These are medium to large-sized boletes with a ring on the stalk. The first *Fuscoboletinus* named was a small bolete; therefore, it was given the Latin diminutive form of *bolete* — *boletinus* — as part of its name. The species described here are not small. All three species discussed are northern species. All three are edible but far from choice.

admirable bolete

p.33-1

Fuscoboletinus spectabilis (Peck) Pomerleau & Smith

spectabilis: admirable (Latin)

North American; associated with tamarack; has been found in eastern Canada and the U.S.; also in boreal forest and cold northern larch-bogs of the Northwest Territories. A very striking mushroom. Edible but not good.

cap	greyish red patches on a yellowish background, viscid, domed; covered at first by a glutinous veil, part of which clings to the cap margin; up to 8 cm across.
pore surface	yellow; pores large, angular, radially arranged; pores continue as lines down the top of the stalk (decurrent).
spore print	purplish-brown.

stalk	top yellow; below the ring there are red fibrils on a yellow background; wider in the middle, tapering down; up to 7 cm tall and 2 cm thick at the top.
ring	double, gelatinous, wine-red, collapses on the stalk.
flesh	yellow, solid in the cap, hollow stalk.

hairy bolete
p.33-2

Fuscoboletinus sinuspaulianus Pomerleau & Smith

sinus: bay (Latin); named after the Baie Saint Paul in Quebec, where this mushroom occurs

Northern bolete, only found in Canada so far. Named by Pomerleau, who found it at the Baie St. Paul in Quebec. Mr. Pomerleau expected this species to grow throughout the boreal forest. I was pleased to find it near Princeton, B.C., in the Cascade Mountains and prove him to be right. Associated with conifers (*Picea, Pinus & Pseudotsuga* species). Said to be edible.

cap	viscous, dark chestnut-brown, tufts of hair on yellowish background; skin flap (sterile edge); up to 18 cm across.
pore surface	brownish-ochre, uneven, more or less decurrent; pores large, radially arranged.
spore print	vinaceous cinnamon; juice turns white paper yellow.
stalk	sturdy; ochre top, reticulate, part of the network is red; base of stalk red-brown, lined and/or reticulate; up to 8 cm tall and 4 cm thick.
ring	fibrous, disappearing.
flesh	yellow, thick and solid, not discolouring. Lots of white mycelium in the needles underneath the mushrooms.

rosy larch bolete
p.33-3

Fuscoboletinus ochraceoroseus (Snell) Pomerleau & Smith

ochraceoroseus: coloured yellow-ochre and red (Latin)

Occurs in the Pacific Northwest and Rocky Mountains; associated with larch; fruiting in summer and fall. A striking mushroom, but not recommended for eating, since it tastes very bitter.

cap	dry, thickly covered by bunches of red hair, sometimes yellow at the margin; it can be brilliant in colour as in the illustration, when its habitat is damp, dense woods; the colour varies all the way to straw-yellow with just a tinge of pink in open sunny places; up to 14 cm across.
pore surface	yellow changing to ochre with age; large, angular pores, radially arranged; surface uneven.
spore print	dark reddish brown.
stalk	sturdy, thick; top yellow and reticulate, quite short; broad annular zone; base whitish, ochrish and pink, often swollen; up to 4 cm tall and 3 cm thick.
ring	white, disappearing with pieces clinging to the edge of the cap and to the stalk.
flesh	solid, yellow; base sometimes discolours green.

Family GOMPHIDIACEAE   sticky pegtops

Members of the small Gomphidiaceae family have a mycorrhizal relationship with conifers. All species are edible though not choice, and they are easily recognized. The name of the family comes from the Greek word for peg (gomphos). The mushrooms are more or less peg-shaped, sturdy, medium-sized and have thick, well-spaced, decurrent gills. Gomphidiaceae are closely related to Boletaceae. The spores are similar in shape to those of a bolete, and the layer of gills peels off as easily as the sponge of a bolete. Four species from two genera are described.

Genus CHROOGOMPHUS   small pegs

skin-coloured peg (Greek)

Members of the genus *Chroogomphus* are smaller and slimmer than *Gomphidius* species; the colour varies from reddish and white to chestnut-brown or burgundy; caps are sticky; stalks are dry; spore colour greyish-black.

Genus GOMPHIDIUS   slimy pegs

like a peg (Greek)

Gomphidius species are generally more robust than *Chroogomphus* species, and the mushrooms are completely covered with a glutinous layer. The flesh is mainly white, but in the stalk base the colour is bright yellow. The two species discussed here are associated with pine, but others, like *Gomphidius maculatus* which is very similar to the two discussed below, are associated with larch. The cap of *G. maculatus* is reddish brown and spotted, as the name implies, and the spore colour is dark purple-brown to black.

pegtop   p.35-1

Chroogomphus rutilus (Schaeffer: Fries) O. K. Miller

rutilus: red-gold (Latin)

Cosmopolitan; associated with conifers — pine, spruce and hemlock — and is widely distributed. It occurs in boreal forest, in the mountains and foothills. It is said to be edible but not choice; turns violet when boiled and black when pickled in vinegar (see next species).

cap	colour variable, copper to crimson or ochre to yellow-brown. The specimens I found were from pink to crimson to red-brown; rounded, often with a small sharp umbo; at first sticky, then dry and slimy; up to 5 cm across.
gills	buff to mud-brown, sometimes with crimson edges, later grey from the developing spores; decurrent, thick and distant; covered at first with a slimy, wispy veil.
stalk	relatively slim, equal, colourful. The base is often white, the middle orange to red; not viscous at the top; often there are left-over pieces of the sticky partial veil; up to 9 cm tall and 8 cm thick.
partial veil	glutinous, leaving a superior (high on the stalk) wispy ring, blackish from spores
spore print	very dark, smoky grey to blackish.
flesh	pale ochre, a bit pinkish under the cuticle of the cap.
taste	mild.
odour	slight.

wine cap   p.35-2

Chroogomphus vinicolor (Peck) O. K. Miller

vinicolor: wine coloured (Latin)

North American; occurs all across Canada and the U.S.; fruiting late in the fall; the further south, the later the fruiting; associated with coniferous trees. Edible. Chroogomphus species are best combined with other food, e.g., stuffing or casseroles. They can be preserved by cutting them into small pieces and drying them.

cap	dark burgundy to purple-brown to dark chestnut; rounded; often with small umbo; sticky when wet. shiny when dry; up to 5 cm across.
gills	ochrish when young; greyish coffee-brown with lighter edges with age; thick, distant, decurrent and broad.
partial veil	covers the gills at first, disappears, once in a while leaving a few whispy bits at the top of the stalk; blackish from spores.
spore print	smoky grey to blackish.
stalk	top widest, slimming down to base; shiny lovely rufous colour; often twisted; base sometimes yellow; up to 9 cm tall and 1 cm thick.
flesh	solid; pale rufous, a bit yellow at the base.
taste & odour	mild.

rosy Gomphidius

Gomphidius subroseus Kauffman

subroseus: almost rosy coloured (Latin)

Cosmopolitan; on our continent primarily a western species although it does occur in Quebec. It grows in coniferous forest; associated with Douglas fir and pine species. Found from the Yukon all through the Rocky Mountains and foothills into California, from sea level up to 2000 m. Fruiting in summer and fall. Said to be edible and good, but be sure to remove the slimy layer if bits of grass, needles or dirt are stuck to it.

cap	pink, glutinous, rounded, edge rolled in at first; specimen on the right in the illustration has an interesting cracked pattern of the cuticle, called areolate. This is often seen in many species in the north as a result of cool, dry growing conditions; up to 8 cm across.
gills	white at first, covered with a thick slimy veil, later grey from ripening spores; decurrent, thick, distant, broad.
spore print	black.
stalk	thick, short, white with bright yellow base; up to 6 cm tall and 2.5 cm thick.
ring	a tattered, sticky zone just below the gills; black from spores.
flesh	solid, substantial, white with bright yellow stalk base and pink under the skin.
taste	mild.
odour	light.

slimy Gomphidius

Gomphidius glutinosus (Schaeffer: Fries) Fries

glutinosus: covered with glue (Latin)

Cosmopolitan, it is native to the whole temperate zone of the northern hemisphere; further south it can be found in mountainous areas in coniferous woods (pine and spruce). Said to be edible and good, fine in soups and stews.

cap	glutinous, lilac to purplish to almost blackish-brown, later dusty brown with a dark margin; rounded, then flattening, sometimes domed; up to 10 cm across.
gills	at first whitish, turning grey-black with age; long-decurrent, thick, distant; covered at first with a thick, slimy veil.
spore print	dark purple-brown to black.
stalk	white with yellow base, sturdy; up to 6 cm tall and 3 cm thick.
ring	the remnants of the white, sticky veil show up prominently because blackish spores get caught in the sticky zone.
flesh	white, thick, solid, with yellow stem base and salmon colour under the cap cuticle.
taste	a bit sour.
odour	slight.

Family PAXILLACEAE   dry pegs or nails

The family of Paxillaceae is closely related to the Boletaceae although spores are formed on gills and not in tubes. In the genus *Paxillus*, connecting veins are often found between the gills and anastomosing takes place near the top of the stalk. In the genus *Hygrophoropsis*, the gills are forked (in *Paxillus* the gills are also forked but not consistently). Paxillaceae grow on the ground, on plant debris or on dead wood. They are mycorrhizal and saprophytic. The spore-producing parts (gills or tubes) are easily separated from the cap, as with all members of the order Boletales. The spores are rusty-brown except in *Hygrophoropsis*, where the spores are cream coloured. Mycologists may not keep this genus in the Paxillaceae very long. It has been placed in Tricholomataceae (because of its spore print colour), in Cantharellaceae (colour of gills) and will probably be in its own family of Hygrophoropsidaceae. *Paxillus* species are not recommended for eating. Although several species had been enjoyed by people in the past, it was discovered, after several deaths, that toxic effects are cumulative. A gradually acquired hypersensitivity can result in the dissolution of red blood cells and kidney failure. *Paxillus involutus* was the culprit, but the others may be suspect also.

spring Paxillus
p.37-1

Paxillus vernalis Watling

Paxillus: small pole or peg (Latin)
vernalis: of the spring (Latin)

North American; reported from the Great Lakes area and Alberta; it is quite common in the city of Edmonton in grass under poplar species, but I found it in aspen parkland and boreal mixed forest as well; fruiting in spring and early fall in cool weather. Not recommended for eating.

cap	sandy to yellow ochre, marbled, smooth, shiny; appressed hair on the margin, edge inrolled at first, later flattening with a dip in the centre; up to 20 cm across.
gills	pale yellow-ochre at first, staining red-brown when handled; decurrent; close, narrow, connecting veins between the gills; often forked (sometimes as much as in *Hygrophoropsis*); anastomosing near the stalk.
spore print	cinnamon brown to chocolate brown.
stalk	pale to bright yellow, staining red to red-brown when handled; confluent with the cap; surface fibrillose; very sturdy, up to 8 cm tall and 4 cm thick; no ring.
flesh	soft to bright yellow, solid, thick, sometimes has white latex.
odour	very aromatic, like roasted corn or papaya.

poison Paxillus

p.37-2

Paxillus involutus (Batsch: Fries) Fries

involutus: inrolled (Latin)

Cosmopolitan; widely distributed, frequently found in spruce-birch bogs all over the north in Europe and North America; fruiting in cool weather in summer and fall; usually grows on the ground, sometimes on old wood. **Poisonous.**

cap	marbled brown, sticky when wet, shiny when dry, appressed hair; margin strongly inrolled; up to 20 cm across, but usually much smaller than *Paxillus vernalis*.
gills	first pale, then ochre; staining brown when handled; close, narrow; sometimes anastomosing near the stalk; decurrent, separable from the cap.
spore print	yellow-brown.
stalk	sandy brown to reddish brown; confluent with the cap, tapering down; up to 5 cm tall and 3 cm thick.
flesh	thick, solid, sandy coloured, changing to red-brown.

blackfoot Paxillus

p.37-3

Paxillus atrotomentosus (Batsch: Fries) Fries

atrotomentosus: with black hair (Latin)

Cosmopolitan; widely distributed but not common; occurs in coniferous forests in the Pacific Northwest and in the Rocky Mountains; on wood debris or on the ground. Not edible.

cap	tan to fox brown; appressed hair; dry, irregular, often in lobes; margin inrolled; up to 18 cm across.
gills	tan or buff, close, decurrent, narrow, often forked.
spore print	yellow-brown.
stalk	dark velvety brown; blackish hairs; thick, short, solid; often several in a bundle and off-centre; confluent with the cap; up to 6 cm tall & 4 cm wide.
flesh	off-white with some yellow under the skin and over the gills; thick, solid.
odour	aromatic.
taste	bitter.

false chanterelle

Hygrophoropsis aurantiaca (Fries) Schroeter
Hygrophoropsis: resembling Hygrophorus (Latin)
aurantiacus: with the colour orange (Latin)

Cosmopolitan; widespread; this mushroom grows in several climate zones from the far north to the warm south, under conifers; fruiting in cool weather; in the north fruits under spruce in summer, in the south fruits under Sequoia in winter, often on squirrel dens or bits of dead wood; not recommended for eating. It has been confused with the real chanterelle, but the gills of the latter are shallow thick folds rather than gills.

cap	orange or brownish; rounded, then flat to shallowly depressed, margin inrolled at first; up to 8 cm across.
gills	brilliant orange, often brighter than the cap; decurrent, regularly forked, close, narrow, thin.
spore print	whitish to pale cream.
stalk	orange, solid, confluent with the cap; equal, often bent or twisted; up to 5 cm tall and 1 cm thick.
flesh	buff or pale orange, soft.
odour	mild.

Order RUSSULALES

Family RUSSULACEAE   brittle mushrooms

The Russulaceae were placed in their own order, the Russulales, because they are anatomically different from the order of gilled mushrooms, the Agaricales. They have a brittle consistency caused by roundish inflated cells which are interspersed with the usual filamentous cells (or hyphae) that make up the flesh of gilled mushrooms. When breaking a stalk of a *Russula* or a *Lactarius*, it comes easily and cleanly apart and that is one of the characteristics to watch for. The spores are variously ornamented with ridges, spines and warts (which fact is used in making a microscopic identification). This and the difference in the consistency of the flesh are the reasons for placing the family in a separate order.

The family is an artist's delight with its colourful palette, especially *Russula*. *Lactarius* tends to be in pastel colours, although an indigo *Lactarius* with dark blue latex exists which I have not found yet.

There are two large genera in the family: *Russula* and *Lactarius*. Both have a confluent cap and stalk, fragile or brittle flesh and no ring or volva. All are mycorrhizal fungi, living in a symbiotic relationship with a tree or woody shrub. The spore prints in both genera range from white to cream to buff, from pale to bright yellow and from orange to yellow ochre. The main difference between the two genera is that *Lactarius* species contain latex, a milklike fluid (see genus description) which is not present in *Russula* species. The edibility of *Russula* and *Lactarius* species is debatable. Ramsbottom writes that in Poland and Russia all species of *Lactarius* and *Russula* are eaten with avidity. People here whose folks originated from Eastern Europe tell me the same thing: they boil them in water and drain them before preparing their favorite dish with them. I have enjoyed the yellow and green Russulas but generally prefer their beauty over the taste. As far as *Lactarius* is concerned, *L. deliciosus* does not quite live up to its billing, but there are strains in that species which are better tasting than others. I advise people to try only the mild-tasting Russulas and not the sharp-tasting species. I would only try those *Lactarius* species whose edibility is well known.

Genus RUSSULA

Russula species usually have an incurved cap-edge when young. That means that the caps look almost spherical, with the margin touching the stalk when young. For identification purposes it is important to take a small cut from the top of the stalk, including some of the gills, on the tongue to determine if it tastes mild, sharp or bitter. Sometimes the sharpness comes slowly. **Spit out the piece after tasting.** This is not dangerous because on this continent none of the Russulas are very poisonous, but some can cause discomfort. It is essential to be able to recognize a *Russula*. In Japan, however, there apparently is one coarse brown species very much like the brown one on p. 43, which is deadly. This is *R. subnigricans* (Imazeki and Hongo 1974). We should always, therefore, take great care, because a very poisonous species may yet be found here. The name "Russula" comes from the Latin word for red (russus). Looking at the first two plates, it can be seen that red is an important colour in Russulas. Identification is difficult, not to genus but to species, because not only do the colours fade in sunshine and rain, there is also variation with the soil they grow on and the trees they associate with. All within certain limits of course. For *Russula* identification I have followed mostly Pomerleau's wonderful book *Flore des champignons au Québec*.

rainbow Russula   p.38-1

Russula olivacea (Secretan) Fries

olivacea: colour of olives (Latin)

Cosmopolitan; associates with old-growth Douglas fir and hemlock. Occurs in the Pacific Northwest; a large colourful mushroom with a variegated cap, often mottled. It is supposed to be edible.

cap	olive green, pink and/or brownish; convex, up to 20 cm across or more.
gills	yellowish, entire, close, adnexed, often with a red edge.
spore print	yellow.
stalk	all white with pink blush or pink all over; up to 8 cm tall and 3 cm thick.
flesh	white, some yellow under cap cuticle.
taste	mild.
odour	nutty.

leathery-looking Russula   p.38-2

Russula alutacea (Fries) Fries

alutacea: resembling thin leather (Latin)

Cosmopolitan; associated with spruce. This is one of the "fading" Russulas. The centre becomes wrinkled; it looks like an aged *R. xerampelina*; edible.

cap	dull vinaceous pink and tan, a bit wrinkled and like tan-coloured leather when old; striate margin; up to 12 cm across.
gills	bone coloured at first, later warm yellow; distant, broad, free, some forks.
spore print	warm yellow, tinged with orange.
stalk	white, with a pink blush and discolouring to brown somewhat; up to 7 cm tall and 2 cm thick.
flesh	white, spongy.
taste	mild.
odour	fruity when young, dirty when older.

Peck's red Russula   p.38-3

Russula peckii Singer

peckii: named after Dr. Charles Horton Peck, State botanist of New York, 1833-1917

North American species; associated with spruce in mixed forest or bogs; this is one of the variable red species, with a pale yellow spore print.

cap	blood red or crimson, smooth, striate margin, up to 6 cm across.
gills	white at first, then cream; some red edges and forks.
spore print	creamy to pale yellowish.
stalk	pink or reddish all over; up to 8 cm tall and 1.5 cm thick at the top.
flesh	white, flushed pink especially under the cuticle, very loose, almost hollow in the stalk, very fragile.
taste	mild.
odour	faint.

fishy-smelling Russula   p.38-4

Russula xerampelina (Schaeffer: Secretan) Fries

xerampelina: resembling dried vine leaves (Latin)

Cosmopolitan; associated with spruce. Despite its fishy smell, it is said to be edible and good tasting.

cap	dusty-looking, purple fading to sandy and smoky brown, leathery, often radially split; up to 10 cm across.
gills	white at first, then tan; distant, intermediates and forks; like in most Russulas, the gill is broadest near the cap margin.
spore print	bright yolk yellow.
stalk	white, blushing pink or purplish pink all over; up to 7 cm tall and 1.5 cm thick, widening toward the base.
flesh	whitish changing to light tan, very loose in the stalk.
taste	mild.
odour	fishy.

bog Russula   p.38-5

Russula paludosa Britzelmayr

paludosa: of the bog (Latin)

Cosmopolitan; occurring in mixed forest, often in damp spots; can have different cap colours, fading spots or fading all together; difficult to identify; fruits earlier than other Russulas; colour of rosehips.

cap	deep red or orange with blotches, fading with age, striate margin up to 12 cm across.
gills	white at first, then buff; intermediates.
spore print	pale ochre.
stalk	white, up to 6 cm tall and 2 cm thick.
flesh	white, soft, spongy.
taste	mild to a bit sharp.
odour	faintly unpleasant.

northern Russula   p.38-6

Russula borealis Kauffman

borealis of the north (Latin)

North American species; large, proud *Russula* of the north; mycorrhizal relationship with spruce and larch; the sight of these beautiful, bright red mushrooms in a dark spruce forest is unforgettable. Fruiting in July and August. Edible

cap	deep blood red and globular at first, then expanding and fading somewhat, almost to white in spots (and not to orange, like *R. paludosa*); up to 20 cm across.
gills	white and close at first, then as the spores ripen, bright yellow and distant with red edges.
spore print	yolk yellow to orange.
stalk	white with pink blush; up to 7 cm tall and 3 cm thick, sturdy.
flesh	white, firm, red under the cap cuticle only.
taste	mild, only once I very slowly noticed a slight sharpness.
odour	faint.

small yellow Russula

p.38-7

Russula chamaeoleontina (Fries) Fries
chamaeoleontina: like a chameleon (Greek)

Cosmopolitan; this small mushroom, in its bright yellow version, used to be called *Russula lutea* (Hudson: Fries) S. F. Gray. *R. chamaeoleontina* is a composite species, appearing in various colours (see Pomerleau): yellow with cherry red spots, pink and orange. I only found one specimen with red striations; all the others were golden yellow, growing in mixed forest in Alberta; small but edible and good.

cap	lemon yellow with deeper yellow in the centre; spherical when young, expanding to plane; up to 6 cm across.
gills	off-white at first, soon yellow from the spores.
spore print	butter yellow.
stalk	white, equal, up to 6 cm tall and 1 cm thick.
flesh	white.
taste	mild.
odour	faint.

brown velvet Russula

p.38-8

Russula velenovskyi Melzer & Zuara
Named after a Czechoslovakian mycologist, Josef Velenovsky, 1858-1949

Cosmopolitan; associated with spruce; not immediately recognized as a *Russula* with its velvety cap surface; it does have the consistency of *Russula* and it has no latex. There are some *Lactarius* species with this kind of cap.

cap	velvety or granular coffee brown, it can also be brick brown or vinaceous brown; up to 8 cm across.
gills	off-white with a yellowish tinge at first, later ochrish; well spaced, entire.
spore print	warm yellow.
stalk	top off-white, lower down salmon pink; enlarging toward the base; up to 8 cm tall and 1.5 cm thick.
flesh	white, spongy in stalk.
taste	mild.
odour	slightly dirty.

green Russula

p.39-1

Russula aeruginea Lindblad
aeruginea: verdigris or coppergreen rust (Latin)

Cosmopolitan and widespread. Growing from Alaska and the Yukon south all across Canada and parts of the U.S. The green colour of the cap can vary quite a lot. I found apple-green specimens with a light yellow spore print under spruce most of the time, while the darker, more verdigris-coloured specimens with a much paler, creamy white to buff spore print occurred under aspen and birch; fruiting in summer; edible.

cap	apple green to dark blue-green; rounded at first, then flattening out with a dip in the centre; smooth; up to 10 cm across.
gills	whitish to yellowish, free.
spore print	pale cream to soft tan.
stalk	whitish, sometimes a bit greenish; up to 7 cm tall and 2 cm thick.
flesh	white, fragile, later becomes spongy.
taste	mild.
odour	faint.

American Russula

p.39-2

Russula americana Singer
americana: of America (Latin)

North American species; described by R. T. Orr from the Olympic Peninsula. I have found it in eastern Canada as well. It is closely related to *R. sanguinea* (former name: *R. rosacea*); associated with conifers, especially larch or spruce; fruiting in the fall; this is one of the red species with white gills and an intensely sharp taste. It is extremely fragile. Inedible.

cap	very bright red; the cuticle peels off easily, margin grooved, up to 7 cm across.
gills	white, relatively distant, almost free, intermediates.
spore print	white.
stalk	white, very fragile; up to 10 cm tall and 1.5 cm thick at the top.
flesh	white, spongy.
taste	sharp.
odour	faint.

fragile Russula
p.39-3

Russula fragilis (Fries) Fries

fragilis: fragile (Latin)

Cosmopolitan; small *Russula* growing in mixed woods on the ground or quite often on pieces of very decayed wood, which is very unusual for a *Russula*.

The next species does this also. Very sharp taste. It comes in a variety of shades, but most of the time I found it in the colour shown. Inedible.

cap	most often vinaceous pink, with a dark cap centre; striate margin, up to 6 cm across.
gills	white, close, entire, a few forks near the stalk.
spore print	white.
stalk	white or very pale pink; up to 3 cm tall and 1 cm thick at the top.
flesh	white.
taste	very sharp.
odour	variable.

the sickener
p.39-4

Russula emetica (Schaeffer: Fries) S. F. Gray

emetica: causes vomiting (Latin)

Cosmopolitan; associated with spruce in coniferous forest, sometimes in mixed woods; deep crimson, but fading as it develops and becoming blotchy. This is another red-capped *Russula* with white gills, white stalk and white spores, but the stalk is not as soft and fragile as that of *R. americana*. Extremely sharp and burning taste. **Poisonous**.

cap	deep crimson; radish red and spherical at first, then expanding and fading to light red with whitish blotches (not fading to orange like *R. paludosa*, see plate 9), up to 10 cm across.
gills	white, quite close, entire, forked near the stalk.
spore print	white.
stalk	white, fragile, up to 6 cm tall and 1.5 cm thick at the top.
flesh	white, but red under the cap cuticle.
taste	very sharp and burning.

blue Russula
p.39-5

Russula parazurea Schaeffer

parazurea: almost sky blue (Persian)

Cosmopolitan; associated with poplar or other deciduous trees. I have not seen this lovely, medium-sized slate-blue species very often, but to find an almost blue mushroom is exciting. The green, blue and grey species are closely related. Fruiting in summer.

cap	slate blue or with a bit of green; with some tan in the centre dip; matt surface, a bit like hoar frost; up to 8 cm across.
gills	white becoming creamy, entire.
spore print	cream colour.
stalk	white, widening somewhat in the middle, up to 5 cm tall and 1.2 cm thick at the top.
flesh	white.

taste	a bit sharp in young specimens, later becoming mild.
odour	faint.

grey Russula

p.39-6

Russula grisea (Secretan) Fries

grisea: old, grey (Greek)

Cosmopolitan; associated with deciduous trees — in Alberta with black poplar. I also found this mushroom in lilac, lighter than the elephant grey of this one and with a much brighter spore print. The taste is mild; edible.

cap	iron grey or elephant grey with a purplish tinge; rounded at first, then flattening with a dip, which often is tan coloured; up to 12 cm across.
gills	light tan, narrowly attached, entire, relatively distant.
spore print	pale buff to soft yellow.
stalk	white or with a lilac tinge; up to 7 cm tall and 2 cm thick at the top.
flesh	white.
taste	mild.
odour	none.

soft white Russula

p.39-7

Russula albida Peck

albida: whitish (Latin)

North American; associated with deciduous trees. Pomerleau writes that a few are found in Southern Québec, but more in Ontario and New York State. He gives the size as 2-5 cm. In Alberta they are bigger, generally 10-12 cm across. Taste mild, edible.

cap	white; rounded at first, then expanding with a dip in the centre; striate margin, up to 12 cm across.
gills	white at first, then pale buff.
spore print	pale yellow.
stalk	white, robust, up to 6 cm tall and 2 cm thick.
flesh	white and brittle.
taste	mild.
odour	none.

greying Russula

p.41-1

Russula decolorans (Fries) Fries

decolorans: changing colours (Latin)

Cosmopolitan and widespread; associated with various conifers. The name has to do with the colour change the flesh undergoes when exposed to air; mild tasting; fruiting in summer; edible.

cap	deep orange, fading to yellowish; convex and staying round for a long time; a bit sticky, but soon dry; up to 10 cm across.
gills	bone coloured at first, then yellowish; free, close.
spore print	varies between creamy and warm yellow.
stalk	white, discolouring to dirty white or grey; up to 10 cm tall and 2 cm thick.
flesh	white, slowly discolouring to grey.
taste	mild.
odour	faint.

chrome-yellow Russula

p.41-2

Russula claroflava Grove

claroflava: bright yellow (Latin)

Cosmopolitan; this bright yellow *Russula* occurs in coniferous and mixed forests. I found the one shown on this plate in a creekbed in the foothills of the Rocky Mountains. Only the top half of the stalk was visible, but it proved to be surprisingly tall. Taste mild; edible.

cap	yellow, fading; where the cap was covered with leaves, some ochre and olive green coloured the edges; convex, up to 12 cm across.
gills	white, lots of intermediates, adnate, discolouring with age.
spore print	whitish (in most descriptions ochraceous).
stalk	white with a bit of salmon pink, discolouring greyish near the base; can be very tall, up to 23 cm, but usually shorter; 2 cm thick at the apex.
flesh	white, discolouring to grey when cut; solid cap, very spongy stalk.
taste	mild.
odour	clean, of northern bedstraw (*Galium boreale*).

almond Russula   p.41-3

Russula laurocerasi Melzer

laurocerasi: with the odour of bitter almonds (Latin)

Cosmopolitan and widespread; the species is associated with deciduous trees, in this case with aspen and birch. I found this specimen in Banff National Park near the ochre beds. Another species, *Russula fragrantissima* Romagnesi, looks a lot like this one, but has a light brown margin and dark brown centre of the cap, a warm yellow spore print and a dirty odour of unwashed clothes or persons. The name *fragrantissima* means strong smelling.

The almond Russula and the fetid Russula intergrade. Soil chemistry has something to do with the colour differences. Discolours with age. Inedible.

cap	yellowish with red-brown centre; ball shaped when young, later flattening out with a dip; margin conspicuously striate. Up to 16 cm across.
gills	white, distant, staining brownish, often beaded with transparent drops, veined, almost free.
spore print	cream coloured.
stalk	white, equal or thickening toward the base, up to 10 cm tall and 2.5 cm thick at the top.
flesh	white, coarse, spongy in the stalk, sometimes hollow, discolouring to tan with age.
taste	very slowly sharp.
odour	pleasant, of dried fruit or almonds, unpleasant when aging.

stinking Russula   p.41-4

Russula subfoetens W. G. Smith

subfoetens: almost like foetens (Latin)
foetens: fetid (Latin)

Cosmopolitan; growing in damp spots under black poplar; a very large species. Obviously related to the group of *R. foetens*, *R. fragrantissima* and *R. laurocerasi*, it has in common with them the strong cap striations, watery droplets on the gills and the slowly sharp taste, but it is very large and has strong discolouration. According to Pomerleau, it should have a pale orange yellow spore print, but my specimens had white spore prints and a disagreeable chemical odour. Inedible.

cap	dirty ochre yellow, slimy, strongly striate margin, discolouring to dark brown, up to 18 cm across.
gills	dirty white, beaded with watery droplets, distant, forks, broad.
spore print	white.
stalk	dirty white, tall and thick, bumpy, spongy, hollow when mature, up to 14 cm tall and 4.5 cm thick.
flesh	not thick in cap; white, spongy in stalk.
taste	slowly sharp.
odour	a disagreeable chemical odour of chlorine or iodine.

Cascade Russula   p.43-1

Russula cascadensis Shaffer

cascadensis: of the Cascades, a western mountain range (Latin)

North American, of the Pacific Northwest; this species has a mycorrhizal relationship with coniferous trees; often has a dirty cap because it develops underground; fruiting in summer. I found it in boreal mixed forest in the prairie provinces and in alpine forest in the Rocky mountains. It also occurs along the coast. Not edible.

cap	off-white, convex first, then developing into a large funnel; earth-encrusted, yellowish discolouration, smooth, up to 22 cm across.
gills	white at first, coarse, distant, discolouring to ochre, decurrent, intermediates, veins between the gills, often forked.
spore print	white.
stalk	white, thick, coarse, equal, up to 5 cm tall and 5 cm thick.
flesh	white, coarse, not discolouring.
taste	slowly acrid.
odour	faint, but when drying unpleasant.

short-stalked Russula   p.43-2

Russula brevipes Peck

brevipes: with short foot or stalk (Latin)

North American species; associated with spruce or pine; widespread. It is not easy to differentiate between the large white Russulas, but *R. brevipes* has a tightly inrolled cap margin; narrow, close, white gills which are sometimes tinged with blue; fruiting in summer and fall; not recommended for eating because this species can be confused with no. 1 and some people get stomach upsets from it.

cap	white, inrolled edge when young, funnel with a rounded margin when mature; dirt encrusted, up to 15 cm across or larger.
gills	bone white, decurrent, narrow, intermediates, interveined, a few forked.
spore print	white.
stalk	white, short, stout, hard; equal or rounded at top and bottom; often with water droplets at the apex; up to 5 cm tall and 5 cm thick.
flesh	white, solid, coarse, hard.
taste	mild to very sharp in a western variety.
odour	none, but smelly when drying.

blackening Russula   p.43-3

Russula nigricans (Bulliard: Mérat) Fries

nigricans: blackening (Latin)

Cosmopolitan and widespread, especially in Europe. On the North American continent it is recorded only in the Northwest. I find it regularly in Alberta in boreal mixed forest. To identify this species properly, it has to be studied in all its colour phases because there is a group of related species (*R. densifolia* has crowded gills and sharp taste and *R. albonigra* has flesh that does not turn red, but goes from whitish to blackish). It is essential to watch the colour in the flesh change from white to red. Spore size and spore decoration are important in making an exact identification by microscope. Fruiting in summer and fall. Inedible.

cap	almost white at first; convex, then flattening with a depression in the centre; turning buff, then brown and finally black, in which state it is often found the next spring; up to 20 cm across.
gills	off-white, staining ochrish, coarse, distant, veins, intermediates, relatively broad.
spore print	white.
stalk	whitish at first, soon staining brown and blackish; thick, solid, sometimes reddish stains; up to 7 cm tall and 4 cm thick.
flesh	white at first, often discolouring red when cut; soon greying and blackening.
taste	mild.
odour	rank, especially when aging.

Genus LACTARIUS   milkcaps

The name *Lactarius* was derived from the latin word for milk, *lac*, and the species of this genus are called milkcaps. When one of these mushrooms is injured or when cutting the gills close to the stalk, a milk-like fluid is exuded. Drops of the milk, called latex, will be seen when the supply is adequate, but sometimes it is not. In that case, cut off the stalk and put pieces with the cut side down on a piece of white paper. In many cases the latex is not the colour of milk. It can be colourless, white, yellow, orange or blue; it can also be white yet stain the flesh and gills yellow or purple. Always do the paper test and note any discolouration of the white paper. Sometimes this happens quickly and sometimes slowly (five minutes). Other differences from *Russula* (other than having latex) include usually having an inrolled cap edge when young and having quite a few species with a hairy or bearded margin. The taste should be noted, too, when identifying *Lactarius* species. As with *Russula*, chew a very small piece and then spit it out again. Species with purple-staining flesh are poisonous and should be avoided.

Lactarius species often have mycorrhizal associations with specific trees. Pages 44 and 45 contain hairy species and pages 47 and 49 contain smooth-capped species.

woolly milkcap   p.44-1

Lactarius torminosus (Schaeffer: Fries) S. F. Gray

torminosus: full of sharpness, causing pain (Latin)

Cosmopolitan and widely distributed; mycorrhizal association with birch species; this very beautiful mushroom is considered to be **poisonous**. It has a very sharp peppery taste and causes gastrointestinal discomfort. Raw, it is a powerful purgative (see introduction to Russulaceae). Fruits in summer and fall across North America, including the Yukon and Alaska.

cap	pinkish, with darker and lighter concentric circles with orange and/or red touches; very hairy, especially the margin which is inrolled when young; up to 12 cm across.
gills	whitish to light salmon pink, close, narrow, decurrent, serrate, forked near stalk.
spore print	creamy white.
latex	milky white, unchanging, scant in quantity, does not stain white paper.
stalk	pink, reddish or yellow; stout, up to 8 cm tall and 2.5 cm thick.
flesh	off-white to pale pink, unchanging.
taste	very sharp.
odour	faint or fruity and pleasant.

downy milkcap   p.44-2

Lactarius pubescens Fries sensu lato

pubescens: becoming downy (Latin)

Cosmopolitan; associated with birch. Smaller, less hairy and less colourful than no. 1; its taste gets slowly very sharp and peppery. Not recommended for eating.

cap	pale peach, smooth with dip, but bearded margin; up to 6 cm across.
gills	pale peach, crowded, short, decurrent.
spore print	white.
latex	creamy, scant, unchanging.
stalk	colour same as the cap, smooth, up to 5 cm tall and 1.5 cm thick.
flesh	off-white to pale peach.
taste	peppery.
odour	faint.

poplar milkcap   p.44-3

Lactarius controversus (Fries) Fries

controversus: controversial (Latin)

Cosmopolitan; associated with willow and poplar; this is a northern and mountain species quite common in the Pacific Northwest. Fruiting in summer and fall. Inedible like a lot of *Lactarius* species.

cap	white, slightly zoned with appressed hair; sticky at first and inrolled, then flattening and extending up, sometimes very much so as in the illustration. Can be up to 20 cm across.

gills	pale, vinaceous pink, narrow, crowded.
spore print	creamy, with pink tinge.
latex	white, not staining white paper.
stalk	white; sticky, but soon dry; thick, squat, relatively short, up to 10 cm tall and 5 cm thick.
flesh	white, hard, stays white.
taste	mild at first, very slowly acrid.
odour	slight.

tan woolly milkcap   p.44-4

Lactarius subtorminosus Coker

subtorminosus: resembling torminosus (Latin)

North American species; associated with birch. It is paler than the woolly Lactarius and is not well known. It has a mild taste. Not recommended for eating.

cap	pale tan, woolly with a bearded margin; inrolled at first, then forming a shallow bowl; up to 9 cm across.
gills	pale pinkish buff, crowded, short decurrent.
spore print	creamy white.
latex	milk white, does not stain white paper, scant.
stalk	white or same colour as cap, up to 4 cm tall and 2 cm thick.
flesh	whitish to cream, a bit pinkish under the cap cuticle.
taste	mild.
odour	faint.

deceptive milkcap   p.44-5

Lactarius deceptivus Peck

deceptivus: deceptive (Latin)

North American species; associated with both deciduous and coniferous trees; a northern species, widespread in the Pacific Northwest. Depending on the growing conditions, this species can be small or large.

cap	white at first, inrolled bearded margin, sticky, woolly, later almost funnel shaped or depressed, earth and leaves adhering to it, up to 25 cm across.
gills	white when young, turning yellowish and brownish when drying; narrow, often forked.
spore print	creamy white.
latex	milky white, not staining white paper.
stalk	very sturdy, thick; white at first, discolouring brownish; hollow, velvety; up to 5 cm tall and 3.5 cm thick.
flesh	white, coarse.
taste	slowly somewhat sharp.
odour	mild, becoming pungent with age, like turnip.

hairy milkcap   p.44-6

Lactarius villosus Clements

villosus: hairy, rough (Latin)

North American; a small to medium-sized, hairy species; mycorrhizal relationship with aspen or birch, occurring in mixed forest. Identified by A. H. Smith. Not recommended for eating.

cap	bright orange, especially in the centre; hairy or felty, edge inrolled at first, bearded, flattening with dip in the centre and fading somewhat; up to 9 cm across.
gills	pale orange, eroded, narrow, close, short decurrent.
spore print	creamy.
latex	creamy, not staining white paper.
stalk	same colour as cap, felty, wider at the top, up to 4 cm tall and 2 cm thick.
flesh	orangy tan, pinkish tan or pink; brighter under the cap cuticle.
taste	very sharp.
odour	faintly of straw.

northern milkcap

Lactarius repraesentaneus Britzelmayr

repraesentaneus: well represented (Latin)

Cosmopolitan; this large northern milkcap is a good example of a *Lactarius*, with a generous supply of white latex, which colours the flesh purple on exposure to air. It is abundant in the Pacific Northwest; it has a mycorrhizal relationship with northern conifers; it grows in damp spots on calcium-poor soils in boreal mixed forest. All *Lactarius* species which stain purple when cut or damaged are considered to be **poisonous** on the North American continent.

cap	a pale golden yellow at first, with darker zones later and a sandy-coloured depression; the surface has appressed hair under slime; the margin is inrolled and bearded when young, flattening out later with a shallow depression in the centre; up to 20 cm across.
gills	pale buff to ochrish later, close, decurrent, eventually broad, discolouring purple when touched.
spore print	pale yellow.
latex	creamy white, changing to purple when exposed to air, staining white paper purple, copious.
stalk	pale yellow with watery depressions under a layer of slime; leaves and debris often stick to stalk and cap; heavy, hollow stalk up to 13 cm tall and 4 cm thick at the top.
flesh	white to pale buff, coarse, discolouring purple when cut.
taste	mild at first, then quite sharp.
odour	pleasant, fruity or of carnations.

purple-staining milkcap

Lactarius uvidus (Fries) Fries

uvidus: moist (Latin)

Cosmopolitan; a well-distributed species, occurring in damp places in mycorrhizal relationships with deciduous trees like poplar, birch and willow; in boreal mixed forest, in the mountains and along the coast, including Alaska. Variations of the species include var. *uvidus* (cap without zones, equally purplish grey) and var. *montanus* (cap with concentric zones of deeper purple, slightly hairy). Other lilac species are *Lepista nuda* (pinkish spore print, no latex) and *Cortinarius alboviolaceous* (medium brown spore print, cortina). As in the northern milkcap, the flesh of this species stains lilac when injured and causes gastro-intestinal disturbances when eaten.

cap	purplish to purplish brown, smooth equal colour or slightly zoned; somewhat viscous; up to 10 cm across.
gills	creamy, edges staining buff or lilac, short, decurrent.
spore print	white to off-white.
latex	white, slowly stains white paper lilac.
stalk	off-white to yellowish or pale cap colour; equal, sometimes with purple-coloured erosions; up to 8 cm tall and 1.5 cm thick.
flesh	off-white, staining purplish when cut.
taste	mild to slowly sharp; in most of my specimens the taste was mild.
odour	faint.

pitted milkcap

Lactarius scrobiculatus (Fries) Fries

scrobiculatus: spotted, with small erosions (Latin)

Cosmopolitan; this species occurs on calcium-rich soil and has a mycorrhizal relationship with conifers. I found this one in the Rocky Mountains. Well distributed in the Pacific Northwest. It resembles *L. repraesentaneus*; the most visible difference is the white latex changing to sulphur yellow and staining the flesh yellow. **Poisonous**.

cap	pale lemon yellow, slimy, hairy, margin inrolled and bearded, getting a bit brownish in age, up to 15 cm across.
gills	yellowish, decurrent, narrow; intermediates and forks.

spore print	white; European specimens have an ochre spore print according to A. H. Smith.
latex	white, changing to sulphur yellow on exposure to air, staining white paper yellow.
stalk	pale lemon yellow with erosions coloured ochre (transparent), up to 6 cm tall and 2 cm thick.
flesh	white, staining yellow when cut.
taste	sharp, with burning aftertaste.
odour	pleasant.

yellow-staining bearded milkcap   p.45-4

Lactarius resimus Fries

resimus: with elevated margin (Latin)

Cosmopolitan; this is mainly a mountain and northern species. Like *L. scrobiculatus*, its latex turns yellow. I found this species in northern B. C. and Alberta. The very similar *L. deceptivus* has white unchanging latex. Growing in mixed forest. Inedible.

cap	creamy white, sticky, hairy mostly toward the bearded margin, deep depression in the centre, elevated wide margin, up to 15 cm across.
gills	white, changing to bright yellow when cut; decurrent, forked and anastomosing near the stalk.
spore print	white.
latex	staining gills yellow, scant, more obvious in young ones.
stalk	creamy white, heavy, up to 6 cm tall and 2.5 cm thick.
flesh	white, coarse.
taste	mild, slowly bitter.
odour	faint.

delicious milkcap   p.47-1

Lactarius deliciosus (Fries) S. F. Gray

deliciosus: full of delight, delicious (Latin)

Worldwide distribution; in countries where the mushroom did not occur originally, it has been introduced along with its mycorrhizal partner, e.g., with pine species in Australia and South Africa. Associated with pine or spruce; it is a variable species. In the West I have not found it as delicious as the name indicates. Easy to recognize by its overall orange colour, latex and green discolouration; it is a safe, edible mushroom.

cap	pale to bright orange and with brick-coloured concentric zones; often with green discolouration, fragile, a bit sticky; inrolled margin when young, later depressed; up to 10 cm across.
gills	bright orange, decurrent, close, a bit forked, staining green where wounded.
spore print	creamy to yellowish buff.
latex	orange, scant, staining white paper orange.
stalk	salmon orange, short, up to 5 cm tall and 2 cm thick at the top.
flesh	bright orange under the cuticle in stalk and cap; inside white or buff; often a hollow stalk.
taste	mild to slightly bitter.
odour	faint.

sweetish milkcap   p.47-2

Lactarius subdulcis (Fries) S. F. Gray

subdulcis: sweetish (Latin)

Cosmopolitan and widespread; occurs in large groups in damp areas under deciduous trees, poplar, willow or alder, often in grass. It looks like a small version of *L. rufus*, but *L. rufus* is associated with spruce. *L. subdulcis* usually has a mild taste and is edible (according to O. K. Miller, the sharpness of the taste varies greatly).

cap	reddish brown, fading to pinkish; broadly umbonate when young, flattening in age but keeping a small knob in the centre; up to 6 cm across.
gills	whitish at first, then tinged like the cap and stalk; narrow, decurrent.
spore print	creamy.

latex	cream coloured, unchanging.
stalk	red-brown with lighter top, equal, up to 8 cm tall and 0.8 cm thick at the top.
flesh	whitish, flesh colour under the cuticle.
taste	mild to slightly peppery (variable).
odour	faint.

gold-drop milkcap

p.47-3

Lactarius chrysorrheus Fries

chrysorrheus: streaming gold (Greek)

Cosmopolitan; grows in mixed woods in association with deciduous trees, in this case alder. The startling fact that the latex of this dull, ordinary-looking species turns quickly from white to bright yellow, makes it easy to recognize. Two more species with yellow latex are described below. None of these are recommended for eating.

cap	yellowish pink or flesh colour, with zones of darker reddish-brown spots; a bit depressed in the centre, slightly sticky, up to 9 cm across.
gills	off-white to yellowish, intermediates, decurrent, narrow, close.
spore print	creamy to light buff.
latex	white, changing to bright yellow on exposure.
stalk	white discolouring to brown, thicker in the middle, hollow, up to 6 cm tall and 2 cm thick.
flesh	off-white, staining yellow when injured.
taste	slowly a bit sharp and bitter.
odour	slight.

spicy milkcap

p.47-4

Lactarius camphoratus (Bulliard: Fries) Fries

camphoratus: spicy (Latin)

Cosmopolitan; associated with conifers; this species grows on the ground or on very decayed wood, as in the illustration. It has an aromatic odour.

cap	foxy red-brown, fading to soft salmon; small umbo, which stays when the cap expands; smooth, dry surface like chamois, wrinkled, up to 5 cm across.
gills	same colour as the cap, decurrent, close, narrow, many intermediates.
spore print	creamy.
latex	white, unchanging.
stalk	same as cap colour, tall, slim, white mycelium on the base; up to 6 cm tall and 0.5 cm thick at the top.
flesh	pale salmon.
taste	smoky, not sharp.
odour	aromatic (like fenugreek), especially when dry.

apricot milkcap

p.47 -5

Lactarius volemus (Fries) Fries

volemus: the size of a pear (Latin)

Cosmopolitan; it has a mycorrhizal relationship with deciduous trees. A striking mushroom; found scattered in mixed or deciduous woods; this is an edible mushroom when well cooked; the odour is slight but becomes fishy when it gets old. I found these in boreal mixed forest in Alberta and northern B.C.; not common

cap	bright apricot colour, smooth, edges inrolled and slightly hairy, depressed in the centre, not zoned; up to 10 cm across.
gills	off-white at first, becoming pinkish buff; short, decurrent, intermediates.
spore print	creamy.
latex	whitish, profuse, not staining white paper.
stalk	light apricot colour, bulging in the middle, up to 4 cm tall and 2.4 cm thick.
flesh	slightly pinkish, hollow stalk.
taste	mild.
odour	slight, becoming fishy when the mushroom gets old.

bright yellow milkcap

p.47-6

Lactarius aspideoides Burlingham

aspideoides: resembling a shield (Greek)

North American species; mycorrhizal relationship with willow and aspen. An interesting species because this bright yellow mushroom has white juice which stains the flesh purple on exposure. It is rare in the Pacific Northwest. I found specimens of it (in mixed boreal forest) only twice over many years. **Poisonous.**

cap	bright yellow, slimy, small umbo when young, smooth, unzoned or very slightly zoned, up to 8 cm across.
gills	white to pale yellow, decurrent, relatively close, anastomosing close to the stalk.
spore print	white.
latex	white, copious, slowly colours gills and flesh purple when injured.
stalk	bright yellow, smooth, sticky, hollow, up to 6 cm tall and 1.4 cm thick at the top.
flesh	whitish, staining purplish.
taste	mild.
odour	none.

red-hot Lactarius

p.49-1

Lactarius rufus (Schaeffer: Fries) S. F. Gray

rufus: red brown (Latin)

Cosmopolitan; a well-known species occurring all over northwest North America in spruce bogs. It can have a mycorrhizal relationship with other conifers as well; fruiting in summer and fall. **Poisonous.**

cap	rufus or chestnut red brown, smooth, dry or moist; inrolled edge, often keeping a small umbo in the depression in maturity; up to 10 cm across.
gills	pale pinkish tan, short, decurrent, close, serrate.
spore print	white.
latex	white, not staining white paper.
stalk	light first, then colour of the cap; often with mycelium at the base, equal, up to 7 cm tall and 1.5 cm thick.
flesh	white to pale pinkish.
taste	slowly exceedingly acrid, with burning aftertaste.
odour	faint.

sticky milkcap

p.49-2

Lactarius affinis Peck

affinis: related (Latin)

North American species; mycorrhizal relationship with conifers; related to *L. trivialis*, which is similar but has a purplish grey cap (not illustrated). Fruiting in summer and fall. Not edible.

cap	pale pinkish buff to pale ochre, slimy, not zoned, small dip, up to 10 cm across.
gills	buff to salmon, decurrent, some forked.
spore print	creamy, a bit pinkish.
latex	copious, creamy, not staining white paper.
stalk	buff, with orangy blush, viscid, equal, up to 8 cm tall.
flesh	whitish, sometimes a bit pinkish or lilac under the cap cuticle.
taste	mild, slowly a bit acrid.
odour	faintly aromatic.

smoky milkcap

p.49-3

Lactarius fumosus Peck var. *fumosoides* (Hesler & Smith) Smith & Hesler

fumosus: smoky (Latin)
fumosoides: almost like fumosus (Latin)

North American species. I find these regularly in boreal mixed forest and aspen parkland under deciduous trees, aspen and hazelnut. They also occur in the area of the Great

Plains. The taste of the *fumosoides* variety is consistently mild. Not recommended for eating.

cap	beautiful velvety, smoky brown; dry; margin inrolled at first, then expanding, finally funnel shaped; up to 7 cm across.
gills	orange buff, narrow, short, decurrent.
spore print	white.
latex	creamy white, staining white paper pink.
stalk	same colour as cap, smooth, more or less equal, up to 9 cm tall and 1.5 cm thick at the top.
flesh	creamy, firm, stains pinkish when cut.
taste	mild.
odour	like turnip.

pale milkcap   p.49-4

Lactarius pallidus (Persoon: Fries) Fries

pallidus: pale (Latin)

Cosmopolitan; mycorrhizal relationship with spruce. More often described in European books than in North American books, this species is quite variable in colour, pale flesh-coloured pink to pink as in the illustration. I have also found pink, lightly zoned and slightly more lilac specimens. This one may be **poisonous**.

cap	pale pink; slimy in damp weather, shiny when dry; not zoned; inrolled margin at first, later with depressed centre; up to 7 cm across.
gills	pale salmon pink, some forked, intermediates, decurrent.
spore print	whitish.
latex	milky, copious, does not stain white paper.
stalk	colour same as cap, up to 5 cm tall and 1.2 cm thick.
flesh	off-white.
taste	mild to very sharp.
odour	light to spicy or fruity.

waterdrop milkcap   p.49-5

Lactarius aquifluus Peck

aquifluus: with a watery flow (Latin)

North American species; occurring in spruce and birch bogs. Can be easily recognized because it has clear latex; fruiting in late summer and fall. Inedible.

cap	reddish brown, like fine leather, smooth, often becoming areolate or developing fine cracks (see illustration); inrolled margin at first, then flattening with more or less of a dip; up to 9 cm across.
gills	pinkish orange or pale salmon, narrow, decurrent.
spore print	whitish.
latex	watery, clear.
stalk	colour like cap, but lighter and with orange tinge, equal; up to 6 cm tall and 1.5 cm thick.
flesh	sandy coloured.
taste	pleasant, of brown sugar.
odour	mild.

Order AGARICALES   gilled mushrooms

Agaricus: mushroom (Greek)

The order is named after Agaricus, a well-known mushroom for twenty centuries, and is represented in this book by 15 families. They are arranged traditionally — according to spore print colour, from light to dark. Making a spore print is just the first step in identifying mushrooms with gills. The keys should also be consulted.

Basidiospores are formed on both sides of the gills and are forcefully expelled from mature mushrooms. To make a spore print, place the cap on a white piece of paper, and after several hours, or overnight, the spore print should be visible (including white spores). The mushroom has to be the right age: not too old or too young.

Family LEPIOTACEAE   parasol mushrooms

The families of Agaricaceae and Lepiotaceae are closely related. Some authors combine them in one family. I agree with the close relationship, but for practical reasons (see under Agaricales) I start with the white-spored Lepiotaceae and describe Agaricaceae with their dark brown spores later on.

The family contains very small, medium-sized and very large species. All Lepiotaceae have free, white gills, a ring on the stalk, which can often be moved up and down, and, most of the time, they have small to large scales on the cap. The scales are part of the cap tissue, the result of the breaking up of the cap cuticle as the cap grows. The family is named for these scales (lepis: Greek for scale).

Genera discussed are *Lepiota*, *Macrolepiota*, *Leucoagaricus* and *Leucocoprinus*. They are saprophytic and terrestrial.

Genus LEPIOTA
scaly ear (Greek)

The genus contains many small to medium-sized, beautiful mushrooms. It is good to be able to recognize them, as several of them are deadly poisonous and occur in the Pacific Northwest. *Lepiota josserandii* caused the death of a man in New York State in 1984; it occurs here as well. *L. helveola* and *L. subincarnata* , both from the Pacific Northwest, are equally poisonous. The latter killed a man on the West Coast (New Westminster, Fall 1988). These three happen to contain amatoxins, like *Amanita virosa*, the angel of death. French mycologist Henri Romagnesi warns that one ought to be aware of the small Lepiotas with some pink discolouration, like these three. To be safe, it is best to leave all small *Lepiotas* alone.

Genus MACROLEPIOTA
big Lepiota (Greek)

Several very large species of parasol mushrooms have been placed in the genus *Macrolepiota*. The famous *M. procera* (*procera*: Latin for tall), which in Europe is considered an excellent edible when young, occurs in North America; it grows in eastern Canada and the eastern U.S. and has been seen in California, but not in the Pacific Northwest. The large parasol mushroom from our area is *M. rhacodes* (the shaggy parasol). In Alberta, B.C. and south of the border, it occurs around compost heaps, grassy areas and open forest, but also often in atria; fruiting in winter.

Genus LEUCOCOPRINUS
white Coprinus (Greek)

Leucocoprinus contains small species of exotic origin, appearing frequently in greenhouses, on pots of houseplants and in atria. They have striate caps, like *Coprinus*, but white gills and white spores like Lepiotas.

Genus LEUCOAGARICUS
white Agaricus (Greek)

Medium-sized species with a smooth cap and stalk. They look very much like the button mushroom, with free, white gills, which even sometimes turn a bit pink. The spores are white.

sharp-scaled Lepiota

p.51-1

Lepiota acutesquamosa (Weinmann) Kummer

acutesquamosa: with sharp scales (Latin)

Cosmopolitan; the sharp-scaled Lepiota occurs in mixed or coniferous forests across Canada and the U.S. Widely distributed but not common. Fruiting in summer. **Poisonous**.

cap	sharp, brown, relatively large warts on a white background; umbo; up to 11 cm across.
gills	white, crowded, broad, free.
spore print	white.
stalk	smooth, light brown above ring and darker below; equal with a small bulb at the base; up to 6 cm tall and 1 cm thick.
ring	fibrous; white, with brown, sharp scales on the edge.
flesh	white.
odour	faint.

shaggy stalked parasol

p.51-2

Lepiota clypeolaria (Bulliard: Fries) Kummer

clypeolaria: looking like a roman shield (Latin)

Cosmopolitan; occurs in Europe, Japan and throughout North America; grows in mixed forest in the prairie provinces, fruiting in August; fruiting in September along the coast and in fall and winter further south. **Poisonous**.

cap	small, medium brown scales on a white background; pronounced dark brown umbo; bits of veil attached to the margin; sometimes the cap edge is bright yellow; quite a bit of variation in colour between individual mushrooms; up to 8 cm across.
gills	white, close, free, with intermediates.
spore print	white.
stalk	white to pale brownish with fluffy, woolly fibres, especially beneath the ring; equal; up to 9 cm tall and 0.5 cm thick.
ring	woolly, fibrous, soft, often in tatters. This and the woolly bits on the stalk give it its name, "shaggy-stalked parasol".
flesh	white, stalk hollow.
odour	sometimes a bit unpleasant.

small white Lepiota

p.51-3

Lepiota alba (Bresadola) Saccardo

alba: white (Latin)

Cosmopolitan; closely related to *L. clypeolaria*; this species occurs in the mountains but also in aspen parkland and boreal mixed forest. In Kamloops I found it growing under sagebrush, and have also found it in grassy places. Not recommended for eating.

cap	white, smooth, sometimes a few scales on the margin; umbo sometimes a bit brown; up to 7 cm across.
gills	white; close in young specimens, distant in mature; sometimes forked, broad.
spore print	white.
stalk	white, equal, sometimes a bit woolly beneath the ring; up to 6 cm tall and 0.6 cm thick.
ring	small; woolly at first, later just a remnant; more delicate than in *L. clypeolaria*.
flesh	white, solid in cap, hollow stalk.

small brown Lepiota

p.51-4

Lepiota castanea Quélet

castanea: chestnut (Latin)

Cosmopolitan; occurs in Europe and Japan but only in western North America. Found in coniferous forests in moss, this small, dark Lepiota is easily overlooked; fruits in summer and fall; a **very poisonous** mushroom, contains **deadly** Amanita toxins.

cap	fox brown, dry, covered with small scales; umbo; later spreading and with uplifted margin; up to 4 cm across.
gills	pinkish, later with rusty edges; distant with many intermediates close to the edge.
spore print	whitish.
stalk	same colour as the cap; above the ring smooth, or a bit hairy, and lighter than below the ring where the stalk is brown and woolly; equal; up to 6 cm tall and 0.3 cm thick.
ring	small, fibrous or scaly.
flesh	a bit rusty brown, thin, hollow stalk.
odour	mouldy.

brown-eyed parasol   p.51-5

Lepiota helveola Bresadola

helveola: yellowish (Latin)

Cosmopolitan; this **deadly** *Lepiota* and several others with pinkish discolourations
(*L. subincarnata* and *L. josserandii*) occur in the Pacific Northwest. At the end of the
previous century it was already known that these mushrooms caused the same symptoms as *Amanita virosa*. After an incubation period of 6 - 15 hours, people died from the
poisoning, as did someone recently in New Westminster, B.C. The specimen illustrated
was found in a park in Edmonton. **Deadly poisonous.**

cap	not umbonate or slightly; the red-brown crown looks like an eye in the centre of the creamy cap, surrounded by scales in concentric circles; the edge of the cap is turned down and striate; up to 6 cm across.
gills	whitish with pinkish cast, eroded edges, free.
spore print	creamy.
stalk	white, shiny, smooth, equal, hollow; up to 7 cm tall and 0.5 cm thick.
ring	flaring, discolouring brown, thin, fragile, disappearing.
flesh	white, sometimes with a bit pinkish discolouration.
odour	slight.

shaggy parasol   p.51-6

Macrolepiota rhacodes (Vittadini) Singer

rhacodes: ragged, shaggy (Greek)

Cosmopolitan; this large stately mushroom occurs in Europe, America and Australia;
grows under conifers but also in grass, on compost, along roads and in greenhouses and
atria; a real people mushroom. Care has to be taken **not** to confuse it with the semitropi-
cal, poisonous, green-gilled parasol (*Chlorophyllum molybdites*). The green colour in the
gills is very slow to appear, and in other respects it is very similar to the shaggy parasol.
The tropical species has been found in masses in a mall in Montreal; also recently in an
atrium in Holland. It could show up at any time in a mall or atrium in the west. *M. rhacodes*
is edible with extreme **caution.**

cap	brown, egg shaped when young, the cuticle cracks while expanding into rounded or domed shape. Large, dark brown scales almost float on cottony white surface, some fall off; up to 22 cm across.
gills	white with pink edges when maturing, free, broad and bruising pink, intermediates.
spore print	white.
stalk	massive; at first whitish, soon reddish brown; enlarging toward the base into an enormous bulb; up to 24 cm tall; 1.5 cm thick at the top and 7 cm at the base.
ring	flaring, double edge up to 6 cm wide, persistent, movable.
flesh	white changing to saffron, then red after cutting, especially under the cuticle of the stalk and stalk base; solid in cap; stalk is hollow and tough.
odour	aromatic.
taste	excellent.

deadly parasol
p.52-1

Lepiota josserandii Bon & Boiffard

Named after French mycologist Marcel Josserand

Cosmopolitan; in Canada it is found in Aspen parkland and boreal mixed forest. Fruiting in the fall. Another **deadly** species.

cap	at first egg shaped, then domed with relatively large scales on a white and pink background; edge radially lined, bits of veil attached to the margin; up to 7 cm across.
gills	white, close, free, relatively narrow.
spore print	white.
stalk	top flushed pink, base white; gradually enlarging from top to bottom. The whole stalk is covered with white woolly fluff; up to 4 cm tall; top 1 cm wide, bottom 2 cm.
ring	woolly, white, cobweb like, disappearing.
flesh	thick, hollow stalk, base turning a lovely salmon pink.

cobweb parasol
p.52-2

Lepiota cortinarius J. Lange

cortina: cobweb (Latin)

Cosmopolitan; growing under spruce in mixed boreal forest; at the base of the stalk a lot of white mycelium is visible with spruce needles imbedded in it. Relatively rare; has been found in Québec, Great Lakes area, Alberta and Michigan. This species has been found repeatedly in a greenhouse of Montreal's Botanical Gardens. A northern species; not recommended for eating.

cap	at first egg shaped; cobwebby veil (cortina) is clearly visible, persistent; surface covered with light brown scales, darker on the umbo; up to 7 cm across.
gills	white, free, crowded.
spore print	white.
stalk	smooth, whitish and a bit lined; equal with a sudden thickening at the base when white mycelium with imbedded spruce needles is attached to it; up to 8 cm tall and 0.5 cm thick.
ring	in the form of fine cobwebby threads, called cortina.
flesh	white.
odour	like radishes.

flowerpot parasol
p.52-3

Leucocoprinus longistriatus (Peck) H. V. Smith & Weber

longistriatus: with long grooves or striations (on the cap) (Latin)

Cosmopolitan; native to warm climates, this species is often found in heated greenhouses and atria in cooler climates; fruiting in winter. Not recommended for eating.

cap	white, soft, striations reach from the margin to the brown disc; egg shaped when young, spreading out later; very small scales all over, fragile; up to 5 cm across.
gills	very white, free, relatively distant, very soft, intermediates.
spore print	white.
stalk	white, bulbous base, smooth, base somewhat smoky brown; up to 3.5 cm tall and 0.5 cm thick.
ring	small, white, fixed.
flesh	thin, very white, soft, hollow stalk.
odour	faint.

yellow Lepiota
p.52-4

Leucocoprinus luteus (Bolton) Godfrin

luteus: golden yellow (Latin)

Cosmopolitan in the sense that this species is found in greenhouses all over the world, but it occurs naturally in warm climates on compost piles, decaying hay, leaf piles, etc. An interesting fact is that it forms white sclerotia. A sclerotium is a small amount of dense mycelium that is able to withstand adverse conditions. **Poisonous**. This species looks a lot like *Coprinus*.

cap	bell shaped, yellow, radially grooved and split, medium brown scales on the umbo; lighter, soft warts all over; powdery looking; colour varies from pale yellow to intense golden or sulphur; 2 - 4 cm across.
gills	white with yellow edge, free, remote.
spore print	white.
stalk	yellow, bulbous base, up to 8 cm tall and 1 cm thick at the top.
ring	yellow, fibrous.
flesh	whitish or pale yellow.
odour	earthy.

smooth Lepiota   p.52-5

Leucoagaricus naucinus (Fries) Singer

naucinus: of little importance (Latin)

Cosmopolitan; occurs all over the world in various climates. Found in grassy areas in summer and fall. A good edible but **extreme caution** is advised, because it resembles a white *Amanita*. However, unlike the *Amanita* it does not have a volva. There is also a grey form that could be poisonous.

cap	smooth, white, perfect half-round before it expands, bits of veil may be on the cap edge; up to 10 cm across.
gills	white, free, broad, close (distant in old specimens).
spore print	white.
stalk	white, sturdy, often but not always enlarging toward the base; up to 8 cm tall and 2 cm thick.
ring	flaring, white, thick, edge often standing up like a collar.
flesh	white, thick, hollow stalk.
odour	mild, sometimes unpleasant.

Family AMANITACEAE

The family of Amanitaceae is characterized by a volva or universal veil enveloping the young mushroom. This stage is called the "egg". There are two genera in this family.

The genus *Amanita* has a membranous veil and the genus *Limacella* , a gelatinous one. *Amanita* species are mycorrhizal fungi; they have a mutually beneficial relationship with a variety of trees and play a very important role in our forests. *Limacellas* are saprophytic, not mycorrhizal. All species have white, free gills and a white spore print.

Some of the most beautiful mushrooms belong to this family and some of the most poisonous. Throughout history, starting with recorded instances in Greek and Roman literature, people have died after eating Amanitas. In 1988 five people ate Amanitas at a dinner party in the U. S. A. Four people needed a liver transplant! The taste is good, and the symptoms of poisoning often don't come until 12 - 24 hours after the meal. **Do not try to eat or taste any Amanitas.**

Genus AMANITA

named after a mountain in Turkey

Fleshy mushrooms; the button in the volva (or universal veil) looks like an egg-shaped puffball, but when cut lengthwise, the shape of a mushroom is visible.The emerging mushroom has a bulbous base often with a cup at the base and small bits of veil on the cap, leftovers of the volva which is different for each species.The cup is often deeply buried, so for identification the mushroom has to be dug up.A ring can either be present or absent.

Genus LIMACELLA
small slug (Latin)

Fleshy mushrooms; the volva consists of slime, and the growing mushroom often glistens and drips slime. No cup is left because the slime disappears, but the free, white gills, white spore print and viscosity characterize the genus. Formerly *Limacella* was placed in the genus *Lepiota*. Now they are a separate genus in the *Amanitaceae* family with which they have more in common. They are medium-sized, mostly terrestrial fungi.

the panther   p.53-1
Amanita pantherina (de Candolle: Fries) Secretan
pantherina: resembling a panther (Latin)

Cosmopolitan; almost worldwide; distribution includes the temperate zone of the northern hemisphere as well as Africa. Rare in the eastern half of our continent, it is widespread along the Pacific coast and the Rocky Mountains, including the Yukon. It has a mycorrhizal relationship with Douglas fir and other conifers. It is **deadly poisonous** and hallucinogenic.

cap	the colour ranges from smoky yellowish brown to dark brown; sometimes with yellow ochre spots on the striate margin; irregular white cottony patches; up to 14 cm across.
gills	white, close, free, some intermediates.
spore print	white.
stalk	white; smooth above the ring, woolly below; bulbous base, hollow; up to 10 cm tall and 2.5 cm thick (at the top).
partial veil	resulting in a white, thick, persistent, drooping ring.
universal veil	the egg is white; volva leaves irregular, white, woolly patches on the cap and a narrow white collar along the top of the bulb.
flesh	white, thick, solid, a greenish semi-transparent layer under the skin of the cap.

fly Amanita   p.53-2
Amanita muscaria (Fries) S. F. Gray
muscaria: having to do with flies (Latin)

Worldwide distribution. Many interesting stories and facts can be told about this mushroom. It is not as poisonous as the two other species, but a grown-up can become very ill and a child may die after eating one mushroom. Fatality rate after ingestion is one percent. It gets its name from the common housefly, *Musca domestica*. East Europeans stun houseflies by putting pieces of fly amanita in a saucer of milk, which draws them. In Japan a pesticide is made from a derivative of one of the chemicals, muscimol, contained in the mushroom. Its hallucinogenic qualities have often been used in stories as in Lewis Carol's *Alice in wonderland*. Alice eats a bit of the fly amanita and shrinks in size! Fruiting in summer and fall, it develops fast in hot weather and slowly in cool. It occurs into far northern latitudes, including the Yukon and Alaska. Mycorrhizal partners include deciduous and coniferous trees.

cap	red, fading to orange and yellow in strong sunlight and to white just before it collapses; loose, white patches, remnants from the universal veil, wash off in rainshowers; convex at first, then plane; striate margin; up to 24 cm across.
gills	white, close, free.
spore print	white.
stalk	white, often heavy, smooth above the ring, gradually enlarging toward the heavy bulbous base; up to 20 cm tall and 2.5 cm thick.
partial veil	white, membranous; leaving large, soft, drooping ring high on the stalk.
universal veil	the egg is white; breaking up, it leaves cottony patches on the cap and cottony rows below the ring but no cup.
flesh	white, solid, a bit of red sometimes under the cuticle of the cap.

destroying angel

p.53-3

Amanita virosa (Fries) Quélet

virosa: stinking or poisonous (Latin)

Cosmopolitan, this mushroom occurs throughout North America. The very elegant, somewhat ghostly looking destroying angel does not fruit every year, but when it does, there may suddenly be a lot of mushrooms, particularly in hot weather. This **deadly** mushroom apparently tastes good! Poisoning symptoms show up 6 - 24 hours after eating and are irreversible. Dreadful suffering is followed by death. No antidote exists so far. The earliest known victim was Emperor Claudius of the Roman Empire.

According to René Pomerleau, most mushroom fatalities in Canada are caused by this species. It grows in mixed or deciduous forests, fruiting in summer and fall.

cap	white, conic or convex to plane, sometimes a bit of an umbo, smooth; up to 12 cm across.
gills	white, free, crowded.
spore print	white.
stalk	white, slender, somewhat enlarging toward the base, a bit shaggy, hollow; up to 17 cm tall and 1.5 cm thick at the top.
partial veil	white, flaring, often torn and irregular.
universal veil	leaving a large cup at the base but no bits on the cap.
flesh	white, odourless.

grisette

p.55-1

Amanita vaginata (Fries) Vittadini

vaginata: sheathed (Latin)

Worldwide distribution; grows under both deciduous and coniferous trees; fruiting in summer. Several of the ringless Amanitas are said to be edible but eating any is **not recommended**.

cap	shiny, dark grey brown; conical at first, then flattening out with a small umbo; margin strongly grooved; the margin splits, showing the white flesh; up to 10 cm across.
gills	white, free, broad.
spore print	white.
stalk	white with a lovely grey flame pattern gradually enlarging toward the base, hollow; up to 15 cm tall and 1 - 1.5 cm thick.
partial veil	absent.
universal veil	egg is white, tall and slim; volva very soft; a bit of veil is sometimes left on the cap, when the mushroom breaks the egg open; the cup is tall but very soft and fragile and it is very easily left behind when digging the mushroom up; loose, lobed, free margin.
flesh	white, relatively thin.
odour	none.

Battarra's Amanita

p.55-2

Amanita battarrae Boudier

former name: *A. umbrinolutea* Secretan
battarrae: named after A. J. A. Battarra, Italian mycologist, 1714 -1789.

Cosmopolitan; this specimen was found at approx. 2000 m in the Rocky Mountains. In Europe it is also found in the mountains. The spores of this species have a second thickened, ornamented wall unlike any other Amanita, according to S. A. Redhead. Occurs in alpine forest.

cap	dirty dull brown with a bit of orange in it; convex; striate margin; a large piece of velum clings to the crown; up to 7 cm across.
gills	off-white, close, free.
spore print	white.
stalk	whitish with a fine, scaled pattern on it; up to 10 cm tall and 1 cm thick at the top.
partial veil	none.

| universal veil | egg is somewhat elongated and the volva opens up so that there often is one large patch on the cap; the cup is tall and relatively slim. |
| flesh | white and quite thin. |

tawny grisette   p.55-3
Amanita fulva Persoon

fulvus: reddish (Latin)

Cosmopolitan; this lovely fox-coloured *Amanita* is widespread; forms a mycorrhizal relationship with deciduous trees; grows all over our continent and well up into the Northwest Territories; fruiting in the summer; said to be edible but **not recommended**.

cap	tawny orange to fox brown, egg shaped to convex, smooth with a strongly grooved margin; up to 9 cm across.
gills	creamy, edges a bit floccose, distant, broad, free, intermediates.
spore print	white.
stalk	peach coloured at top, grooved; tawny lower down with a beautiful pattern of raised fibres; enlarging toward the base; hollow with fluffy stuffing; up to 15 cm tall and 0.8 - 1.5 cm wide.
partial veil	absent.
universal veil	white elongated egg; soft volva, breaking open and forming a large sac at the base of the stalk with a loose floppy edge.
flesh	off-white, thin.
odour	none.

smelly Amanita   p.55-4
Amanita roanokensis Coker

roanokensis: named after the town of Roanoke in eastern Alabama

North American. This white, ringless, very tall *Amanita* with a strong nauseous odour is only described in a book by A. H. Smith. He writes that it grows in the eastern and southern U.S. in the summer and fall. I found it in the summer in aspen parkland which is an additional location for it.

cap	white, smooth; with a large, somewhat smoky, umbo; grooved margin; 11 cm across.
gills	white, distant, free, narrow.
spore print	white.
stalk	white, very tall, flame pattern in white, enlarging toward the base; 22 cm tall; 1 cm wide at the top and 3 cm at the base; buried in the ground for almost half its length.
partial veil	absent.
universal veil	egg elongated, encrusted with earth, leaving a large floppy cup with flaring white edge at the base of the stalk.
flesh	white, sturdy, hollow stalk.
odour	nauseous, peculiar.

purplish or booted Amanita   p.57-1
Amanita porphyria (Fries) Secretan

porphyria: purple (Greek)

Cosmopolitan; widespread in Canada and northern U.S., although it is not very common; it grows in the Rocky Mountains and along the Pacific coast, including Alaska. Fruiting in spring, summer or fall when the temperature is right; occurs in coniferous or mixed forest. **Poisonous.**

cap	grey brown with purplish tinge, smooth; conical at first, then plane with small umbo; cap edge splitting; up to 8 cm across.
gills	white, free, intermediates.
spore print	white.
stalk	whitish above the ring, grey flame pattern below; abruptibulbous base; up to 11 cm tall and 1 cm thick.
partial veil	leaving a grey, flaring ring.

universal veil grey egg, volva leaving some grey patches on the cap edge and a free collar on top of the bulb.

flesh white, hollow in stalk.

odour unpleasant.

the blusher

p.57-2

Amanita rubescens (Persoon: Fries) S. F. Gray

rubescens: reddening (Latin)

Worldwide distribution; it may have been introduced along with its mycorrhizal partner, *Pinus patula*. I found it in several places in Africa; it occurs along the Pacific coast and has been reported from Yellowstone National Park and the Yukon. Not common, but this very beautiful mushroom attracts attention wherever it appears. It is edible but is easily confused with *A. pantherina*, so it is best left alone. It has a mycorrhizal relationship with deciduous as well as coniferous trees; fruiting in summer and fall.

cap a lovely shade of smoky red brown, covered with raised white and pink volval patches; convex at first, then plane; no grooves on the margin; up to 11 cm across.

gills white, free, broad, close.

spore print white.

stalk flushed pink, especially the base; abruptibulbous base, but there is no free collar; the apex, or top of the stalk, is striate; up to 15 cm tall and 2 cm wide at the top and 4.5 cm at the base.

partial veil pendulous, pink striations on the ring.

universal veil the egg is white; volval patches on the cap are numerous; no cup left on the base, not even a collar as in *A.porphyria* or *A.pantherina*.

flesh white; pink under the top cuticle and where insects have burrowed.

white to yellow, slime-veiled Limacella

p.57-3

Limacella illinita (Fries) Earle

illinita: greasy, slimy (Latin)

Cosmopolitan; growing on the ground in coniferous or mixed forest, rare; thick slime drips off the cap. I found a group with white caps and one with yellow caps shimmering through the volval slime; fruiting in the fall; edible but unpleasant because of the slime.

cap white or yellow, glutinous and glistening; rounded, then spreading a bit; very soft; up to 6 cm across.

gills white, free, very soft, relatively broad.

spore print white.

stalk white, glutinous, equal; up to 8 cm tall and 1 cm thick.

partial veil glutinous; when the mushroom matures, the veil hangs in big dribbles on the cap edge.

universal veil the slimy, colourless volva envelops the button but it vanishes as it dries, and no cup remains.

flesh white, weak and very soft.

fox-coloured, slime-veiled Limacella

p.57-4

Limacella glioderma (Fries) Earle

former name: *Lepiota glioderma*

glioderma: with glutinous skin (Greek)

Cosmopolitan; widespread but rare; growing on humus under spruce in mixed woods; fruiting in summer and fall. Edibility unknown.

cap rufus colour fading to buff along the margin; bell shaped at first, then flattening with a broad umbo; slimy at first but drying to granular surface; up to 8 cm across.

gills white, close, free, many intermediates.

spore print white.

stalk pale rufus or tan above the ring and rufus scales below; up to 10 cm tall and 0.5 - 1 cm wide.

partial veil fibrous or disappearing; sometimes there is a little roll right at the top of the stalk (see illustration).

universal veil	slimy but less thick than no. 3, leaving a glutinous layer on the cap and on the scales of the stalk.
flesh	whitish, soft.
odour	mealy.

Family HYGROPHORACEAE   waxgills

The family of waxgills contains many colourful species in the three genera discussed. They often have moist, sticky or slimy caps. The name *Hygrophorus* means carrying moisture. The main characteristic they have in common is the thick soft gills, which feel waxy when they are rubbed between the fingers. The spore print is always white.

Members of the genus *Hygrophorus* are mycorrhizal. All eleven species of pages 58 and 59 grow under spruce: some in spruce forest, others in mixed forest and one in either coniferous or deciduous forest. Members of the genus *Hygrocybe* are saprophytic; they grow in grassy areas or mixed forest. This is the most colourful group. The last genus, *Camarophyllus*, has a lot in common with the other two genera. It is saprophytic; grows on the ground in duff, grass or decayed wood and is small to medium in size. There are microscopic differences in the arrangement of the hyphae in the gills and in the shape of the basidia, which help to identify the genera in this family. Microscopic observation shows that in *Hygrophorus* the interior tissue of the gills is bilateral, in *Hygrocybe* and *Camarophyllus* the gill-hyphae are parallel. In some books all species are placed in *Hygrophorus* and grouped in sections named *Hygrophorus*, *Hygrocybe* and *Camarophyllus*. When comparing books, look under the second name or epithet.

I have not eaten any Hygrophoraceae. They are either small and slimy or bigger and rare. I will mention edibility if it applies. None are really poisonous, but the white species could be confused with poisonous *Clitocybe* species.

Genus HYGROPHORUS
carrying moisture (Greek)

Fruiting bodies are small to large; the caps are sticky to slimy, mostly pastel coloured; stalks often fleshy, rarely hollow; often a slimy or fibrillose veil is present, sometimes both; most of them have a mycorrhizal relationship with spruce. All eleven species described are originally covered with a gelatinous veil, which may leave some evidence in maturity. The colour is variable in each species and may be determined by location and natural soil dyes.

spruce waxgill   p.58-1

Hygrophorus piceae Kühner & Romagnesi

piceae: of spruce (Latin)

Cosmopolitan; frequent on the Pacific coast, in the Rocky Mountains and on the prairies. This species has a mycorrhizal relationship with spruce. One other white species is *H.eburneus* which is more ivory in colour, bigger and more slimy, including the stalk. Fruiting in the fall.

cap	very white, sticky, becoming shiny when dry; convex, then flattening; up to 5 cm across.
gills	white, waxy, distant, decurrent, sometimes forked.
spore print	white.
stalk	white, silky, smooth, equal, up to 8 cm tall and 0.6 cm thick.
flesh	white.
odour	none.

sheated waxgill
p.58-2

Hygrophorus olivaceoalbus (Fries) Fries

olivaceoalbus: olive brown and white (Latin)

Cosmopolitan; occurring on acid soils under spruce or in mixed forest. It has a mycorrhizal relationship with spruce; often found singly, but also in clusters, as in the illustration. This mushroom is covered by a layer of slime, and its partial veil includes a sheath. Lincoff mentions that this one is edible with caution since not everyone can eat them.

cap	medium to dark smoky brown; slimy at first and broadly conical, then expanding; dark radial fibres make it look streaky; up to 6 cm across.
gills	white, can be tinged grey, decurrent, arched at first, distant, beautifully spaced, waxy.
spore print	white.
stalk	white at the top; below the superior ring is a very interesting zigzag pattern of brown fibres on white; equal but narrowing at the apex; up to 8 cm tall and 0.5 cm thick at the apex, 1 cm thick further down.
partial veil	a fibrous sheath, resulting in a small collar-like ring and the interesting, long "sock".
flesh	white, solid.
taste & odour	mild

small grey waxgill
p.58-3

Hygrophorus morrisii Peck

morissii: named after G.E. Morris, an American mycologist

Cosmopolitan; relatively rare, mycorrhizal with spruce. This small grey mushroom has a ridge below the gills, just like the large pink species in the illustration. Fruiting in the fall.

cap	grey to grey brown, slimy; conical at first, then flattening with umbo; up to 3.5 cm across.
gills	white, decurrent.
spore print	white.
stalk	white with small, grey, pointed scales, a small ridge just below the gills.
partial veil	fibrillose, evanescent.
flesh	white, hollow stalk.

veiled waxgill
p.58-4

Hygrophorus velatus Hesler & Smith

velatus: covered (Latin)

North American species; rare. I have found it in Alberta six times in twenty years. Previously only recorded from Idaho. It is an extraordinarily beautiful species when found in moist conditions because it is completely covered by a glistening pink gel and looks glazed. Mycorrhizal with spruce; occurs in small groups or singly.

cap	delicate pink, slimy when damp, looking very ordinary when dry; conical at first, then flattening or with raised edges; up to 10 cm across.
gills	white with pink tinges, decurrent, beautifully spaced, veins between the gills, thick, waxy.
spore print	white.
stalk	white with pink tinges; covered by small white, woolly scales; small ridge just below the gills, slimming toward the base; up to 9 cm tall and 1.5 cm thick.
partial veil	cortina which disappears.
flesh	whitish, pale pink below the the cap cuticle, solid.
odour	fresh.

smoky waxgill
p.58-5

Hygrophorus camarophyllus (Fries) Dumée, Grandjean et Maire

camarophyllus: with arched gills (Greek)

Cosmopolitan; a species widespread in the northwest; mycorrhizal with spruce. Fruiting in late summer and fall. Edible. Another species, *H. agathosmus*, is quite similar, but more grey than grey brown, and it has a white stalk and almond odour.

cap	smoky grey brown, smooth, slightly sticky when damp; convex at first, then expanding up to 7.5 cm across.
gills	white or tinged grey, distant, thick, adnate to decurrent, intermediates.
spore print	very white.
stalk	grey, granular at the apex; often a small ridge often just below the gills, but less than in nos. 3 and 4; up to 3 cm tall and 1.5 cm thick.
partial veil	not noticable, although there is a small ridge sometimes as in no. 3.
flesh	white, soft.
taste & odour	mild.

golden fringed waxgill

p.58-6

Hygrophorus chrysodon (Batsch: Fries) Fries

chrysodon: with golden tooth (Greek)

Cosmopolitan; in the Northwest it is mycorrhizal with spruce. At first covered with a golden yellow veil of slime, which leaves yellow flocs on the cap and edge and top of the stalk. The specimens in the illustration were found in the foothills of the Rocky Mountains under mixed spruce and pine. Fruits in the fall.

cap	off-white to yellowish with yellow flocs on the cap edge, slimy when damp; convex, then flattening; up to 7 cm across.
gills	white, distant, waxy, decurrent, loosening from stalk, pinkish when drying.
spore print	white.
stalk	white to yellow, with yellow granules at the top, equal, hollow; up to 9 cm tall and 1 cm thick.
flesh	white.
odour	slightly unpleasant.

golden waxgill

p.58-7

Hygrophorus aureus (Arrhenius) Fries

aureus: golden (Latin)

Cosmopolitan and rare. This is a beautiful golden and orange species; mycorrhizal with spruce. Because of interbreeding, there are transitional forms between *H. aureus* and *H. hypotheius* (Fries) Fries. The latter is initially covered by a thick olive-brown layer of slime with a pale yellow cap under the slime. The stalk is almost smooth and whitish under the slime; the gills are whitish at first, turning yellow and even orange, in the end. The golden-coloured specimens of *H. aureus* I found in the Rocky Mountains had a translucent slimy veil; a yellow to orange cap with deeper orange-brown-coloured centre, a very floccose stalk (golden flocs) and white gills, which stayed white (see Dähncke). These specimens were found on ochre-coloured soil, which formerly was used by native people to extract yellow ochre and brown ochre dyes. Colour varieties are to be expected in this group. It is said to be edible.

cap	shiny yellow to orange with thick slime layer on young, yellow-brown specimens; bell shaped at first, then flattening with small umbo; up to 6 cm across.
gills	white, decurrent (arched at first), waxy, distant.
spore print	white.
stalk	apex and base white, the main part wider and thickly covered by golden orange flocs, up to 6 cm tall and 1 cm thick at the apex and 2 cm in the middle.
veil	translucent, thick, golden gel; leaving a small ridge in the annular zone and a floccose sheath on the stalk.
flesh	white and bright yellow under the cuticle.

blushing waxgills

p.59-1

Hygrophorus pudorinus (Fries) Fries

pudorinus: blushing (Latin)

Cosmopolitan; growing in boggy places in moss under conifers, mixed spruce and pine. A northern or mountain species; fruiting in the fall. Inedible.

cap	pinkish flesh colour or orange, darker in the centre. In damp weather a bit sticky; broadly conical at first, then expanding with umbo; margin inrolled at first; up to 6 cm across.
gills	off-white to pinkish, distant, waxy, decurrent, intervenose (meaning veins between gills).
spore print	white.
stalk	whitish with orange or pinkish streaks, slightly floccose, sometimes twisted, up to 9 cm tall and 1 cm thick.
flesh	white; orange or pinkish under the cap cuticle; solid.
odour	light, fragrant.

purplish waxgill p.59-2

Hygrophorus purpurascens (Fries) Fries

purpurascens: turning purple (Latin)

Cosmopolitan; this species is widely distributed in the Northwest. I have found it regularly, but not often, in boreal forest as well as the Rocky Mountains. A heavy, purplish pink mushroom with a cortina, which does not immediately appear to be a *Hygrophorus*. It has a mycorrhizal relationship with spruce and emerges from needle duff in small groups. Fruiting from late July until the middle of September. Edible according to Miller.

cap	pale and sticky at first, later coloured fibres — crimson, purplish pink and pinkish brown — radiate from the crown; convex with edge curved in, later showing a zone on the margin where the cortina was attached; up to 15 cm across.
gills	white at first but soon with purplish red margins and spots; subdecurrent with veins between the distant gills, which are sometimes forked.
spore print	white.
stalk	white above the ring, below streaked the same as the cap; solid, relatively short and robust; up to 6 cm tall and 4 cm thick.
partial veil	white cortina visible in immature specimens, resulting in a pink line on the cap margin and a small woolly ring which soon turns purplish.
flesh	white at first, but in maturity streaked pink; insect holes are also pink or purplish.
taste	pleasant.
odour	faint, sometimes of anis, radish or none at all.

reddening waxgill p.59-3

Hygrophorus erubescens (Fries) Fries

erubescens: reddening (Latin)

Cosmopolitan; this is another blushing waxgill, which is a lot like the previous one in colour, but which is smaller, has no ring and has a bitter taste. Grows in mixed woods. It occurs in wet grassy areas under spruce in spring. Fruits in the fall. Inedible.

cap	streaked, vinaceous and reddish on light background; sticky; broadly conic at first with turned in margin, then flattening out; up to 6 cm across.
gills	off-white, a bit pinkish, later spotted, adnate; close at first, distant later.
spore print	white.
stalk	same colour as the cap, streaked, sturdy, equal or slightly club shaped, solid or hollow, up to 7 cm tall and 1 cm thick at the top.
flesh	in the cap off-white, yellowish in the stalk.
taste	bitter.
odour	faint.

waxgill of the Rockies p.59-4

Hygrophorus saxatilis Smith & Hesler

saxatilis: near or between rocks (Latin)

North American species; this is a rare montane species of the Pacific Northwest. This caespitose bunch (or cluster) was growing on a decaying conifer stump on a mountain slope. It is surprising to find out that it is a *Hygrophorus* with its rosy red gills and its awkward, irregular, tall stalks in a bundle.

cap	shiny white and yellow with pink appressed hair, convex, a bit irregular, inrolled margin; pinkish watery spots near the margin, indicating that the cap was attached to the stalk there when inrolled in an earlier stage; up to 9 cm across.
gills	pale at first, then rosy red; decurrent and arched, separating from the stalk.
spore print	white.
stalk	shiny white, staining yellow, a bit pruinose at the top, tall, irregular, in caespitose bundles; up to 17 cm tall, widening at apex and/or base up to 2 cm thick.
flesh	white, hollow stalk.
odour	none or faintly of dried apricots.

Genus HYGROCYBE

with a moist head (Greek)

The genus contains many small to medium-sized, brightly coloured species; the caps are viscid and often the stalks as well; the gills are waxy and free, adnexed, adnate and rarely decurrent. There is no veil. The shape of the cap is frequently conical. Waxiness can be noticed when some gill tissue is rubbed between the fingers. The species are saprophytes and are often growing in grassy areas and open woods.

chanterelle waxgill   p.61-1

Hygrocybe cantharellus (Schweinitz) Murrill

cantharellus: like a small cup (Latin)

Cosmopolitan; this one is reported more often from eastern North America than from the west, but it has been found in Manitoba; growing on acid soil in mixed or coniferous forests or in peat bogs; fruiting in summer or fall. Resembles the chanterelle with its decurrent gills. Is said to be edible, but it is very small.

cap	a beautiful red with yellow shining through near the edge, smooth and dry; convex at first, getting a dip in the slightly felty centre; up to 2 cm across.
gills	bright warm yellow, decurrent and arched, distant, thick.
spore print	white.
stalk	brilliant red, with some yellow at the base, smooth, not shiny, up to 4 cm tall and 0.5 cm thick.
flesh	orange-yellow, more red in cap and under cuticle.
odour	none.

pointed waxgill   p.61-2

Hygrocybe cuspidata (Peck) Murrill

cuspidata: pointed (Latin)

North American species; resembling *H. conica* but not blackening, also resembling *H. acuticonica*, but smaller and more red at first; fruiting in spring.

cap	blood-red and slimy, fading to orange, conic, splitting radially, with lobed margin, up to 3 cm across.
gills	yellow, almost free.
spore print	white.
stalk	yellow, often twisted, striate, up to 4 cm tall and 0.3 cm thick.
flesh	yellow.

orange-brown waxgill   p.61-3

Hygrocybe laeta (Persoon: Fries) Kummer

laeta: glad, shiny (Latin)

Cosmopolitan; growing in forests on wet, poor soil; a variable mushroom, mostly orange brown to flesh colour, but it can have wine or pinkish tinges.

cap	orange brown, very slimy; convex at first, then expanding; up to 2.5 cm across.
gills	pinkish, distant, adnate to subdecurrent.
spore print	white.

stalk	same colour as cap, slimy; up to 4 cm tall and 0.4 cm thick.
flesh	yellow-tan, thin.
odour	fishy.

minute waxgill

p.61-4

Hygrocybe minutula (Peck) Murrill

minutula: very small (Latin)

North American species; occurs in grassy areas and in moss in field, open forest or mountain slope; fruiting spring, summer and fall.

cap	orange red with crinkly yellow margin; slimy, convex or broadly conic, flattening with a slight dip; up to 1.5 cm across.
gills	yellow, thick, distant, intermediates.
spore print	white.
stalk	orange with a yellow base; the specimens from the mountains had a slimmer, taller, twisted, yellow, hollow stalk; up to 5 cm tall and 0.2 cm thick.
flesh	red in cap and on the outside of the stipe, yellow inside.
taste & odour	none.

small waxgill

p.61-5

Hygrocybe parvula (Peck) Murrill

parvulus: very small (Latin)

North American species; occurs in mixed forest; a very elegant, small waxgill, growing in small clusters; quite common in Canada and the U.S.

cap	bright orange to apricot, smooth, hygrophanous, a bit viscid, fading to yellow, becoming radially streaky after picking; hemispherical, then flattening; becoming irregular; up to 3.5 cm across.
gills	orange, decurrent, many intermediates, waxy, distant.
spore print	white.
stalk	yellow with a bit of orange and a white base; crooked, hollow, not viscid, up to 5 cm tall and 0.3 cm thick.
flesh	pale yellow, semi-transparent in stalk.
taste & odour	none.

vermilion waxgill

p.61-6

Hygrocybe miniata (Fries) Kummer

miniata: painted red (Latin)

Cosmopolitan; this species occurs all across Canada from coast to coast, although never in large groups; growing on the ground or wood debris, in mixed forest. The illustrated specimens were found in northern B.C. under cedar.

cap	scarlet or vermilion fading to orange, smooth, a bit rough in the centre when dry, up to 3.5 cm across.
gills	same colour as cap, distant, sinuate to slightly decurrent, many intermediates.
spore print	white.
stalk	same colour as cap, hollow, up to 4 cm tall and 0.5 cm thick, equal.
flesh	vermilion.
taste & odour	none.

golden yellow waxgill

p.61-7

Hygrocybe ceracea (Fries) Kummer

ceracea: waxy (Latin)

Worldwide distribution; known from across Canada, also in the U.S.; often growing in clusters in damp places in mixed forest, sometimes in grassy areas.

cap	golden yellow, viscid; convex at first, edge inrolled, then extending; up to 4 cm across.
gills	yellow, thick, distant, veins irregular, adnate, sinuate with decurrent tooth, waxy.

spore print	white.
stalk	yellow, dry, equal, hollow, bent, some white mycelium on the base; up to 4 cm tall and 0.5 cm thick.
flesh	yellow, fragile.
flavour	none.
odour	none.

parrot waxgill

p.61-8

Hygrocybe psittacina (Schaeffer: Fries) Wünsche

psittacina: parrot green (Greek)

Worldwide distribution, but not common anywhere; occurs in small groups in grassy areas or in open woods. Like all the *Hygrocybe* species, these are saprophytes. It is edible, but there is no taste.

cap	an olive green layer of slime covers the whole mushroom at first, then as it dries, the colour changes to yellowish and pinkish buff, even pinkish brown; convex or bell shaped, then flattening with umbo; up to 5 cm across.
gills	greenish at first, then pinkish buff with green tints; adnate, distant, thick and waxy.
spore print	white.
stalk	green top, yellow base, hollow, up to 5 cm tall and 0.5 cm thick.
flesh	white in stalk, pinkish in cap, thin fragile.
taste	none.
odour	fragrant.

sharply conic waxgill

p.61-9

Hygrocybe acutoconica (Clements) Singer

acutoconica: sharply conical (Latin)

Cosmopolitan; this very beautiful species does occur in Europe, but it is rare; widely distributed on the North American continent, but more in the west than in the east; growing in mixed forest, saprophytic. It does not blacken. It does remind one of *H. conica*, but it is generally yellow and orange. If there is a red touch, it is on the crown or a bit on the cap edge; variation in size and colour are shown in the illustration. Fruiting in summer.

cap	orange and yellow, sometimes with a touch of red; slimy when moist; most often sharply conical, lobed and splitting, sometimes expanding; looks like a chinese hat; up to 6 cm across.
gills	lemon yellow, free to almost free, broader near the cap edge, distant, thick, waxy, eroded edges.
spore print	white.
stalk	apricot orange or streaked orange, red and yellow top, yellow in the middle, white base; sometimes just yellow (see the smaller specimen). The stalk is equal, twisted, up to 10 cm tall and 0.6 cm thick.
flesh	white, stringy, only yellow in the thin part of the cap.
taste & odour	none.

blackening waxgill

p.61-10

Hygrocybe conica (Fries) Kummer

conica: conic (Latin)

Worldwide distribution; occurring in grassy areas or mixed woods; very striking mushrooms containing a latex which stains the flesh black when exposed to air. There is a lot of variation in colour (scarlet, orange, lemon yellow) and in size (taller in the woods). Some authors (e.g., Phillips) separate *H. conica* into two species: *H. nigrescens* and *H. conica*; others (e.g., Arnolds) consider it to be one. It would be hard to tell the two species apart. Fruiting in summer and fall, they turn black as soon as they are touched or when they age.

cap	scarlet, scarlet and orange, completely orange or pale yellow; bell shaped to sharply or bluntly conic, splitting when expanding; up to 5 cm across, but can be much smaller. In the illustration the small red mushroom growing next to the tall red one is a young specimen; the orange, the pale yellow and the red and orange specimens are all mature and were found in different spots; slightly viscid when moist, blackening.
gills	white or yellow (see illustration) depending on the overall colour of the specimen; narrow, almost free, relatively close, blackening.
spore print	white.
stalk	either yellow and orange with white base or orange, white or yellow with red lines and similar variations; often twisted, up to 13 cm tall and 0.7 cm thick at the apex; equal or thicker in the middle, blackening.
flesh	white or yellow depending on the overall intensity of colour, with red caps often red flesh in the cap, blackening as well.
taste & odour	none.

Genus CAMAROPHYLLUS

with arched gills (Greek)

The fruiting bodies are less sticky than either *Hygrophorus* or *Hygrocybe*. There is no veil; they are never bright red or yellow; the gills are decurrent and arched at first. The genus is saprophytic and occurs in field or forest on dead organic material.

snow-white waxgill   p.63-1

Camarophyllus niveus (Fries) Wünsche

niveus: snow white (Latin)

Cosmopolitan; this is one of the more common white *Camarophyllus* species which can be found in grassy clearings or open mixed forest. Saprophytic; it fruits in late summer and fall. Edible but small and easily confused with poisonous small white *Clitocybes*. **Caution.**

cap	off-white and slightly sticky when damp, hygrophanous and fading to snow white; convex, then flattening with a dip, sometimes stretching to funnel shape; up to 3 cm across.
gills	whitish, arched at first and decurrent, thick with a thin edge, waxy; distant with many veins interconnecting the gills.
spore print	white.
stalk	white, more or less equal and narrowing at the base; up to 5 cm tall and 0.5 cm thick.
flesh	white.
taste & odour	none.

meadow waxgill   p.63-2

Camarophyllus pratensis (Fries) Kummer

pratensis: growing in a meadow (Latin)

Worldwide distribution; growing in damp places in field and forest; fruiting in fall in the prairies, later along the coast and further south. Aspen Parkland along the fringes of the prairies is an ideal open forest habitat in which to find this species. Sometimes grows on decaying logs; a good, edible mushroom, easily recognized.

cap	apricot, orange or salmon coloured, with paler margin; fading to buff, dry, unpolished; convex or with broad umbo, later flattening or with edge upturned, retaining the umbo; up to 6 cm across.
gills	pale but showing orange when looking into them; two tiers of lamellulae (intermediate gills); distant, interveined, waxy, thick but with thin edges.
spore print	white.
stalk	pale orange or whitish with orange tinges, equal; up to 9 cm tall and 1 cm thick.
flesh	orange under the cap cuticle, paler in the stalk or off-white; solid in cap, stringy in stalk.
taste	good.
odour	mild.

virginal waxgill

Camarophyllus virgineus (von Wulfen: Fries) Karsten

virgineus: virginal (Latin)

Cosmopolitan; this white waxgill is fleshier and bigger than *C. niveus*; in form it is much like *C. pratensis*. This is said to be a good, edible mushroom, but it can be confused with *Tricholoma inamoenum*, which has sinuate gills and an unpleasant odour, or with certain poisonous *Clitocybes*; **caution** is advised.

cap	unpolished white, convex, dries up yellowish, up to 7 cm across.
gills	whitish, decurrent, distant, interveined, intermediates, waxy, thick, arched.
spore print	white.
stalk	white, drying up yellowish, equal, gills extend with ridges at the top, sometimes twisted, up to 10 cm tall and 1.3 cm thick.
flesh	white.
taste & odour	faint.

violet waxgill

Camarophyllus subviolaceus (Peck) Singer

subviolaceus: nearly purple (Latin)

Cosmopolitan according to Pomerleau, but it is so rare there is little information on its distribution. This very interesting species, with its purple arched gills, produces a white spore print and at first sight is hard to place. It occurs in small groups in open woods throughout northern North America. Grows on the ground or on decayed wood; saprophytic, like the other members of this genus.

cap	dark brownish purple, slightly sticky when damp, broadly conical, up to 6 cm across.
gills	purple with a powdered look, arched, decurrent, broad, thick, waxy, interveined.
spore print	white.
stalk	pale at first, soon tinged like the cap and spotty; tall, enlarging toward the base; surface a bit rough; hollow with a funny loose lining; up to 13 cm tall; 0.5 cm thick at the apex and 1 cm at the base.
flesh	whitish with a thick purple cuticle.
taste	bitter and slightly nauseous.
odour	slight.

northern white waxgill

Camarophyllus borealis (Peck) Murrill

borealis: of the north (Latin)

North American species; this small white mushroom is not restricted to boreal areas; grows in open forests.

cap	white, drying up chalk white; conic at first, then expanding, keeping a small umbo; sometimes there is a small depression; slightly sticky when damp, up to 3 cm across.
gills	white, arched and decurrent, distant, intervenose, thick, narrow.
spore print	white.
stalk	white, slim, equal; up to 7 cm tall and 0.5 cm thick.
flesh	white.
taste & odour	none.

Family TRICHOLOMATACEAE

This family consists of a large and diverse group of mostly white-spored, gilled mushrooms, which do not fit in Amanitaceae, Hygrophoraceae, Lepiotaceae, Russulaceae, Laccariaceae, Pleurotaceae or Xerulaceae. The species forming the last two families have recently been taken out of the Tricholomataceae for various reasons — chemical and physiological, e.g., whether they cause white rot or brown rot (see research by Redhead and Ginns 1985, mycologists at the Biosystematics Research Centre in Ottawa).

In this book 91 species of 26 genera of Tricholomataceae are discussed, but that is still only a modest portion of the huge number of species in the family. I have described and sketched all these from specimens found in the area covered by this book; 99% were spotted by my husband and myself and the rest by friends and interested people in my courses.

The family is named for the genus *Tricholoma* (Greek for with hair on the edge). Not many have hair on the edge, but the genus is easily recognizable nevertheless. That is not the case with some of the other genera. Many people have worked on classifying this huge family, and many more will work on it, clarifying groups and separating out those which deserve to stand on their own.

Species in the genus *Tricholoma* are mycorrhizal; most of the others are saprophytic on duff in the forest or on old wood. *Armillaria mellea* is strongly parasitic, sometimes saprophytic.

Genus TRICHOLOMA

This genus contains mostly robust species with confluent cap and stalk, sinuate gills and white spores. Woodland species, they are divided into two groups, those which have a mycorrhizal relationship with coniferous trees and those which have a mycorrhizal relationship with deciduous trees. There are two plates of each group. Some species are easily recognizable; others have quite a variation in size, colour or shape, so that it really is necessary to find them again and again before one can detect the characteristics which are constant in each species. There are a few choice edible mushrooms, several less than choice and some mildly poisonous, but none are fatal.

Page 64 shows two large ringed species, edible, one very famous.

Page 65 contains some yellow, good edible, medium-sized species and some look-alike poisonous ones.

Page 67 shows species growing in large groups under deciduous trees, mostly poplar.

Page 69 shows species all growing under coniferous trees, several pink staining, which is an important identification feature in *Tricholoma*.

Zeller's mushroom

p.64-1

Tricholoma zelleri Stuntz & Smith (Ovebro & Tylutki)

former name: *Armillaria zelleri* Stuntz & Smith

zelleri: named after S. M. Zeller, American mycologist 1885-1948

Mainly a Pacific Northwest species; it has a mycorrhizal relationship with coniferous trees. A very beautiful, sturdy mushroom; I found it once under Douglas fir and once under spruce in the Jasper area; both times it had a very pleasant odour, while usually an unpleasant odour is mentioned by various authors. Edibility unknown.

cap	sandy to light brown with brown patches or scales mostly on the disc; rounded at first, then flattening with broad umbo, up to 20 cm across.
gills	bone coloured with rusty spots, wavy edge, relatively close, broad, adnate. Looking at the gills from below, one gets the impression that they are tan colored.
spore print	white.
stalk	off-white with brownish, woolly squamules; massive; tapering down, smooth above the ring; up to 10 cm tall and 4 cm thick.
partial veil	a sheath-like cover of the stalk, resulting in a flaring ring with woolly edge; off-white on top.
flesh	solid, white, nonstaining.
odour	fruity, aromatic but variable, can be unpleasant.

pine mushroom p.64-2

Tricholoma magnivelare (Peck) Redhead

former name:*Amerillaria ponderosa* Peck
magnivelare: with big veil (Latin)
Pacific Northwest species; occurs under mixed conifers along the coast and mostly under pine in the mountains. Called the Canadian white matsutake, it is closely related to the Japanese species *Tricholoma matsutake* (S. Ito et Imai) Singer but *T. matsutake* contains more pigment. *T. magnivelare* has a mycorrhizal relationship with conifers. Edible and good.

cap	light buff, smooth, rounded in young specimens, inrolled edge, flattening later with veil remnants on cap edge (evanescent), up to 20 cm across.
gills	bone colour, a bit peachy when you look into them from below, close, broad, wavy edge, adnate.
spore print	white.
stalk	white at first and relatively smooth; appressed fibres, bottom part sheathed; above the ring a bit woolly; large and sturdy, tapering down; up to 10 cm tall and 4 cm thick.
partial veil	a sheathlike cover of the stalk forming one piece with the ring after it breaks away from the cap edge; pieces of it adhere to the cap margin and the rest forms a large flaring white annulus.
flesh	white, hard, firm.
odour	spicy, fragrant.
taste	excellent.

earthy Tricholoma p.65-1

Tricholoma terreum (Schaeffer: Fries) Kummer

terreum: of the earth (Latin)
Cosmopolitan; it occurs across Canada and the U.S. as far north as Alaska. Fruits in the cool seasons, spring and fall, in mixed forest. Not recommended for eating.

cap	grey, from mouse colour to quite dark, greyish brown; fibrous to felty, convex, then more or less plane; edges radially splitting; up to 8 cm across.
gills	off-white to light grey, distant, many intermediates, sometimes forked; adnexed, sinuate.
spore print	white.
stalk	white to light grey, hollow, easily splitting into long fibres; up to 6 cm tall and 1.5 cm thick.
flesh	slightly pinkish, staining brown in cap, fragile.
odour	slightly unpleasant.

western chevalier p.65-2

Tricholoma leucophyllum Ovebro & Tylutki

leucophyllum: with white gills (Greek)
Pacific Northwest species; occurs under aspen in boreal mixed forest, aspen parkland and the mountain ranges; fruiting in summer and fall. Good edible.

cap	chestnut brown centre gradually changing to yellow or off-white toward the margin; bell shaped or convex at first, then umbonate like a chinese hat; smooth, up to 10 cm across.
gills	white, broad, close, eroded, adnexed-sinuate.
spore print	white.
stalk	white with yellow and light brown tinges, slim, sometimes twisted, equal, up to 12 cm tall and 1 cm thick.
flesh	white.
odour	none or lightly of radish.

man on horseback

p.65-3

Tricholoma flavovirens (Fries) Lundell

former name: *T. equestre* (Linnaeus: Fries) Kummer

flavovirens: golden yellow of the spring (Latin)

Cosmopolitan; widely distributed in Canada, occuring across the Prairies, B.C., the Yukon and in Alaska; associating with deciduous trees, mostly aspen and birch, in Alberta, but in other areas pine is frequently mentioned. Excellent edible species.

cap	yellow with fine reddish-brown appressed scales on the crown. I found a paler version as well with a yellowish cap and only a bit of pale brown on the disc; convex and expanding to almost plane with a small umbo; up to 9 cm across.
gills	bright yellow like rapeseed blossoms or lemon; narrow at first, broad in maturity; close, adnexed, sinuate to almost free, serrate.
spore print	white.
stalk	pale yellow varying to white or white with yellow spots, up to 9 cm tall and 1.5 cm thick, equal or a bit wider in the middle.
flesh	white.
odour	varies, none or slight like radish.
taste	good flavor.

narcis Tricholoma

p.65-4

Tricholoma sulphureum (Bulliard: Fries) Kummer

sulphureum: containing sulphur (Latin)

Cosmopolitan; this is a poisonous species with wide distribution; occuring in mixed woods, it is mostly reported as having a dirty odour and a nasty taste. It is best not to go by the odour, because that is a very personal and variable matter. This mushroom probably is called "narcis Tricholoma" because concentrated narcissus odour has some sulphur in it. The specimen portrayed had a pleasant, interesting odour. The sulphur yellow flesh is the best characteristic. Grows under spruce in the Pacific Northwest. **Poisonous.** The poison in this species attacks the red blood cells.

cap	sulphur yellow, often reddish brown with a bit of an olive tinge; convex at first then expanding up to 8 cm across; often irregular, splitting at the margin.
gills	sulphur yellow; narrow at first, then broader; adnexed-sinuate.
spore print	white.
stalk	sulphur yellow streaked with reddish-brown fibres, tapering down or equal, up to 8 cm tall and 2 cm across at the top.
flesh	strong lemon yellow in stalk, lighter in cap.
odour	light aroma of the narcissus plant to nasty, strong coal tar gas.

soapy Tricholoma

p.65-5

Tricholoma saponaceum (Fries) Kummer

saponaceum: soapy (Latin)

Cosmopolitan; the species is common across the North American continent. Locally it is associated with aspen, but in other areas it may be growing under both deciduous and coniferous trees. Colour and odour vary considerably. I found the grey version only once. Most often I find the yellowish kind shown in the illustration, looking a lot like a freshly baked bun, but it is **poisonous**.

cap	the colour of white bread with a golden crust, a bit cracked on the crown; rounded at first with inrolled margin, expanding to almost plane; up to 10 cm across. Can grow to quite large size.
gills	white to off-white, distant, many intermediates, serrate, adnexed-sinuate, relatively narrow.
spore print	white.
stalk	white, a bit rough, a bit brownish in older specimens, often irregular, bent, bumpy or slightly bulbous; short or up to 10 cm tall and 2 cm thick.
flesh	white.
odour	aromatic, like lily of the valley or slightly like raw meal.

the sandy

Tricholoma populinum Lange

populinum: of poplars (Latin)

Cosmopolitan; particularly prevalent in northwest North America; mycorrhizal relationship exclusively with poplar underneath which it grows in dense masses. This fact needs to be established when they are picked for the pot. Fruiting in the fall. It is edible but has a mediocre flavor and needs to be cooked. Be careful not to confuse it with *T. pessundatum* (pp. 69, 244).

cap	pale, dingy reddish brown with white border; rounded at first with inrolled edge, then expanding shapes becoming irregular through crowding; sticky at first with lots of earth, humus and leaves adhering to it; up to 20 cm across.
gills	whitish, distant, coarse, eroded; staining pink, especially along the edges; relatively narrow.
spore print	white.
stalk	white, massive, solid, very heavy.
flesh	white, solid; stringy strands in stalk when mature.
odour	of sweet-scented bedstraw (*Galium triflorum*) but also described as mealy.

burnt Tricholoma

Tricholoma ustale (Fries) Kummer

ustale: burnt cinnabar, a pigment (Latin)

Cosmopolitan; growing under various deciduous trees; this particularly large clump was found in the sand dune area near Gibbons, Alberta, north of Edmonton. I have only found this species described in Pomerleau's book, and he describes it as frequently occurring in southern Québec. Fruiting in the fall, this vivid, maroon-coloured, large mushroom stands out. Mediocre quality for eating purposes. Not recommended.

cap	maroon; rounded at first with strongly inrolled edge, flattening out and becoming depressed in the centre; irregular because of crowding in a large group; smooth, viscid at first, earth and leaves adhering to it; up to 20 cm across.
gills	off-white, changing to pink and then brown, especially when touched; relatively narrow.
spore print	white.
stalk	dirty white with pinkish brown discolouration; heavy, ventricose, with rooting base; up to 15 cm tall and 2.5 cm thick at the top.
flesh	white, discolouring pink, especially around insect holes; solid; in long strands in the stalk.
odour	of wild licorice (*Glycyrrhiza lepidota*).

slimy orange Tricholoma

Tricholoma aurantium (Fries) Ricken

aurantium: orange (Latin)

Cosmopolitan; widely distributed across Canada and the northern U.S. Reported from Quebec, Manitoba and Alberta; growing singly or scattered in mixed forest. An interesting species, the orange Tricholoma is completely covered with a slime layer at first; most easily recognized when the fluffy belts on the stalk stand out. Unpalatable.

cap	orange to rusty brown; convex or broadly umbonate, then flattening; slimy when wet; up to 8 cm across.
gills	off-white, adnexed to free, eroded edges, relatively close at first, many intermediates.
spore print	very white.
stalk	pinkish orange, smooth top, the rest of the stalk covered by sticky, fluffy belts or ridges; the base is smooth and white, also sticky when wet; up to 12 cm tall and 1 cm thick. The tallest specimen on the plate was growing from the base of a rotten stump.
partial veil	a fluffy, slimy sheath on the stalk; covering the stalk and originally attached to the cap edge; when it loosens from the cap edge, the top of it becomes a ring (see illustration).
flesh	white in the stalk, a bit pinkish in the cap.
odour	of bullrush hearts.

girdled Tricholoma p.69-2

Tricholoma cingulatum (Fries) Jacobasch

cingulatum: girdled (Latin)

Cosmopolitan; this small grey mushroom grows in mixed forest under conifers (in Europe it is reported as growing under willow). Not common.

cap	lovely pale blue-grey or velvety brown-grey, radially streaked, light edge, up to 4 cm across.
gills	very white, adnexed, relatively broad; eroded edges and gills often broken up in sections.
spore print	white.
stalk	white, equal, smooth, bent, up to 4 cm tall and 0.6 cm thick, hollow.
partial veil	leaving a small fibrillose ring, which often disappears.
flesh	very white, fibrous bundles in stalk.
odour	slight.

ill-scented Tricholoma p.69-3

Tricholoma inamoenum (Fries) Quélet

inamoenum: unpleasant (Latin)

Cosmopolitan; in Europe this is described as a mountain species. In the Pacific Northwest I found it in the mountains, but also in boreal mixed forest and aspen parkland growing in moss under spruce in boggy areas. Unpalatable, unpleasant odour.

cap	off-white to pale tan; convex or conic to start with, then flattening; smooth, dull, up to 7 cm across.
gills	white, distant, with veins connecting the gills or sometimes forked, adnexed, broad, many intermediates (see illustration of underside of the cap).
spore print	very white.
stalk	white, equal or enlarging toward base, sometimes twisted, up to 7 cm tall and 1 cm thick at the top.
flesh	white, stringy in stalk.
taste	of raw meal.
odour	unpleasant chemical odour.

scaly Tricholoma p.69-4

Tricholoma vaccinum (Persoon: Fries) Kummer

vaccinum: of the cow (pertaining to its colour) (Latin)

Cosmopolitan; the species occurs across Canada and in the northern part of the U.S., under conifers. In the Pacific Northwest it is found in the mountains, in boreal mixed forest and aspen parkland and is associated with spruce or pine. There is quite a variation in the degree of scaliness and shades of colour. Fruiting in late summer and fall and growing in small or large groups or rings. Not edible.

cap	red-brown; fibrillose or scaly with light background showing; conical at first, then expanding; fringed edge, frequently splitting radially, up to 10 cm across.
gills	white, coarse, distant, staining pinkish or brown, adnate to sinuate.
spore print	white.
stalk	colour same as the cap or paler, sometimes with a white top; most often tapering down, hollow, in deep moss can be up to 11 cm tall; 2 cm thick.
flesh	pinkish.
odour	pleasant or mealy.

red-brown Tricholoma p.69-5

Tricholoma pessundatum (Fries) Quélet

pessundatum: low on the ground (Latin)

Cosmopolitan; associated with spruce. In the Pacific Northwest it grows in boreal mixed forest. Occurs occasionally in Québec. This is another red-staining species, and it is **poisonous**.

cap	dark brown, sticky; convex at first with inrolled edge, then flattening; smooth, up to 8 cm across, but can grow larger.
gills	white, distant, serrate, staining pink, adnate.
spore print	off-white when fresh, drying pale yellow.
stalk	striped pinkish, a bit woolly at the base with white mycelium, club shaped, up to 8 cm tall and 1.5 cm thick.
flesh	white, staining pink.
odour	pleasant or mealy.

false Tricholoma   p.69-6

Pseudotricholoma umbrosum (Smith & Walters) Singer

Pseudotricholoma: false Tricholoma (Greek)
umbrosum: in the shadow (Latin)

North American species; growing under conifers, rare. Pomerleau writes that it was first found in Nova Scotia. I found it in the foothills of the Rockies and near Watson Lake in the Yukon. It looks like a *Tricholoma*, but it has microscopic differences in spores and hyphae and it has a hard consistency. Edibility unknown.

cap	golden brown, rounded, inrolled at first, smooth with some cracks, then flattening out, up to 8 cm across.
gills	off-white to light salmon, relatively narrow, adnexed or free; edges brown.
spore print	creamy white.
stalk	red-brown, squat, shaped like an onion, smooth, up to 4 cm tall and 3 cm thick.
flesh	pale, hard, a bit pinkish in the cap, lovely peach colour in the stalk, a big hollow space in the centre.
taste	long lasting, of turnip or cucumber.
odour	clean but slightly unpleasant.

Genus CLITOCYBE

The name of the genus means sloping head. This refers to the cap, which often has a funnel shape and decurrent gills. Cap and stalk are confluent, not easily separable; there is no ring; the spore print is white or creamy. There are small, medium and large species.

Clitocybes are humus saprophytes. Their copious mycelium penetrates the top layers of forest duff and decomposes leaves and needles with their enzymes, freeing nutrients for the green plants. A few grow on rotten logs. There are four pages of illustrations of *Clitocybe* species: small to medium-sized, fragrant species (p. 70); very poisonous species (p. 71); fox-coloured funnels (p. 73); giant Clitocybes (p. 75).

mountain avens Clitocybe   p.70-1

Clitocybe candicans var *dryadicola* (Favre) Lamoure

candicans: becoming white (Latin)
dryadicola: living with *Dryas* or avens (Latin)

Cosmopolitan. These mushrooms were found in a dense bank of the creeping woody plant *Dryas drummondii* along Two O'clock Creek on the Kootenay Plains in the Rocky Mountains. It was the first reported sighting in North America, according to S. A. Redhead. Fruiting in summer. Edibility unknown.

cap	white or buff with darker spots, smooth, dry, margin curved in, striate in older specimens, up to 5 cm across.
gills	white to pinkish, moderately close, many intermediates, adnate to decurrent.
spore print	white.
stalk	white to pinkish, crooked, sometimes flattened, hollow, up to 6 cm tall and 0.5 cm thick.
flesh	off-white, thin, sometimes brownish in the stalk.
odour	none or faintly unpleasant.

slim anise mushroom

p.70-2

Clitocybe fragrans (Sowerby: Fries) Kummer

fragrans: fragrant (Latin)

Cosmopolitan; abundant in the Pacific Northwest. Both this small, purely white *Clitocybe* and the next species grow in city lawns and grassy areas in parks and are often brought to me by fellow Edmontonians. These two, smelling strongly of aniseed, are innocent, but because there are similar deadly poisonous species, my advice is always to leave them strictly alone.

cap	white, smooth, becoming either a shallow or deep funnel shape when mature; up to 5 cm across.
gills	white, decurrent, narrow, close.
spore print	white.
stalk	white with mycelium at the base; up to 2 cm tall and 0.5 cm thick.
flesh	white, thin.
odour	strongly of anise.

sweet-smelling Clitocybe

p.70-3

Clitocybe suavolens (Fries) Kummer

suavolens: sweet smelling (Latin)

Cosmopolitan; for habitat see *C. fragrans*; fruiting in the fall; this species often shares a fairy ring of *Marasmius oreades*. This one is innocent, but deadly poisonous *C. dealbata* is often present also. Take care!

cap	dark brown when damp, hygrophanous, immediately fading after it is picked to pale smoky brown; shallow cup shape with wavy edge, up to 4 cm across.
gills	pale grey, adnate to decurrent, close, forked here and there.
spore print	white.
stalk	velvety brown, base slightly swollen, often bent, up to 2.5 cm tall and 0.3 cm thick at the top.
flesh	brown, thin.
odour	fragrant of anise or sweet-scented bedstraw (*Galium triflorum*).

slim Clitocybe

p.70-4

Clitocybe tenuissima Romagnesi

tenuissima: very slim (Latin)

Cosmopolitan; found growing on pine needles in sphagnum in the foothills of the Rocky Mountains. Do not try to eat small grey or white Clitocybes.

cap	dull greyish ivory, smooth, hygrophanous, small umbo, up to 4.5 cm across.
gills	white, narrow, close, decurrent.
spore print	white.
stalk	white, slim, tall, equal, woolly with mycelium at the base.
flesh	white, thin.

bruised Clitocybe

p.70-5

Clitocybe vibecina (Fries) Quelet

vibecina: bruised (Latin)

Cosmopolitan; woodland species growing under spruce; fruiting in the fall.

cap	greyish brown when damp, hygrophanous, fading to cream colour with a brown, often striate, margin; rounded with big navel; up to 5 cm across.
gills	dirty white to pale brown with eroded edges, relatively distant, decurrent.
spore print	white.
stalk	whitish, streaked with brown; white mycelium mixed with spruce needles at the base; up to 4 cm tall and 0.7 cm thick; white erect hairs at the stalk base called cystidia.
flesh	off-white.
odour	aromatic, of sweet-scented bedstraw.

white anise-scented Clitocybe   p.70-6

Clitocybe odora (Fries) Kummer var. *odora*, pale form

odora: perfumed (Latin)

Cosmopolitan; the white form may be the more common type in the north and according
to Pomerleau, it is the only one found in Québec. Here in the West in boreal mixed forest
and aspen parkland, it is a very common mushroom, too, even during dry summers
when not much else is fruiting. The green form is smaller and is only found in coniferous
woods. Good edible mushroom, but because of its strong flavour best used to spice
dishes. **Caution**, because of possible confusion with white poisonous species.

cap	white, domed at first, with edge rolled in, then flattening with umbo, finally funnel shaped; up to 9 cm across.
gills	white, narrow, close, decurrent, slightly yellowing in age.
spore print	white.
stalk	white, equal or tapering to base, up to 5 cm tall and 1 cm thick.
flesh	white, solid.
taste & odour	of anise.

green anise-scented funnel mushroom   p.70-7

Clitocybe odora (Fries) Kummer

odora: perfumed (Latin)

Cosmopolitan; generally the green anise mushroom is far more common than the white
one. The green form varies considerably with more or less green in the gills and stalk. It
is found occasionally in coniferous forest in the prairie provinces. In B.C., it is more
common than the white form. Edible. Safer than the white form.

cap	bluish to greenish green, smooth, edge rolled in; convex at first, then flattening and somewhat depressed; up to 9 cm across.
gills	white, close, decurrent.
spore print	white.
stalk	white, sturdy.
flesh	white, solid.
taste & odour	of anise.

deadly Clitocybe   p.71-1

Clitocybe rivulosa (Persoon: Fries) Kummer

rivulosa: full of rivulets (Latin)

Cosmopolitan; this small **very poisonous** mushroom has wide distribution. A strong
warning for such a small mushroom is warranted, because they are really beautiful, with
an odour like flowers. I found them included in fairy rings in city parks with *Marasmius
oreades*; also under spruce in the woods. They contain muscarine which makes them
deadly.

cap	zoned rosy and white in concentric circles (the name "rivulosa" pertains to that), darkest in the depressed centre; up to 5 cm across.
gills	off-white, decurrent, narrow.
spore print	white.
stalk	whitish with some pinkish brown at the base, buff mycelium; up to 4.5 cm tall and 0.5 cm thick.
flesh	pinkish, flesh colour.
odour	of flowers, sweet.

lead-white Clitocybe   p.71-2

Clitocybe cerussata (Fries) Kummer

cerussata: painted with white lead (Latin)

Cosmopolitan; growing in coniferous or mixed forest in deep moss; could be mistaken for
the white *Clitocybe odora*, but it does not smell of anise. This is another **poisonous** species

containing muscarine. It grows in the Yukon, and I found it in several places in Alberta.

cap	dull white or off-white; rounded at first with rolled-in edge, then plane or somewhat depressed; up to 8 cm across.
gills	white at first and more or less decurrent, narrow, intermediates, later creamy or yellowish.
spore print	whitish to pinkish cream.
stalk	white at first, later a bit pinkish; brown base, thick mycelium at the base, up to 5 cm tall and 1 cm thick.
flesh	dull white, solid, sometimes a small hollow in the stalk.
odour	faint or a bit sweet.

sweating mushroom   p.71-3

Clitocybe dealbata (Sowerby: Fries) Kummer

dealbata: bleached (Latin)

Cosmopolitan, widespread, growing in groups in grassy areas or open places in the woods; occurring in the prairie provinces, the mountains and B. C.; in cities as well as in the wild. High muscarine content causing acute perspiration. Watch that small children playing near fairy rings don't eat any if this species is growing in the lawn. **Very poisonous**.

cap	frosted grey with some brown in the dip, becoming white, inrolled edge, up to 6 cm across.
gills	greyish white, close, decurrent.
spore print	white.
stalk	frosted grey, short; up to 3 cm tall and 0.8 cm across.
flesh	white, brown in stalk base.
odour	none or mild.

clubfooted Clitocybe   p.71-4

Clitocybe clavipes (Persoon: Fries) Kummer

clavipes: clubfooted (Latin)

Cosmopolitan and widespread; occurring in coniferous and mixed woods, this species grows across the prairie provinces and in the Pacific Northwest. Often called edible, it is known to cause **Coprine poisoning**. When eaten with, before or after using alcohol, it causes hot flushes and miserable internal disturbances (see the smooth inky cap, p.145).

cap	dull brown, smooth, wrinkles like soft leather with age, rounded with slight umbo, up to 8 cm across.
gills	off-white to yellowish, close, forked or interveined, narrow to very narrow, decurrent.
spore print	white.
stalk	greyish deer-brown, fibrous with very enlarged base; up to 7 cm tall, 0.5 cm thick at the top and 2 cm at the base.
flesh	white, solid.
odour	pleasant, a bit spicy.

log Clitocybe   p.71-5

Clitocybe truncicola (Peck) Saccardo

truncicola: living on wood (Latin)

North American; growing in groups on old mossy logs of deciduous trees, unusual for the genus. These mushrooms are recyclers of wood, but they are not good for eating, as they contain muscarine. The ones illustrated were found on the same old poplar log for seven consecutive seasons, fruiting whenever the log was damp enough. **Poisonous**.

cap	off-white; pinkish buff or pinkish brown markings on the disc; sometimes staying white; up to 6.5 cm across.
gills	off-white to faintly pink, close, narrow, decurrent.
spore print	white.

stalk	whitish to brownish, hollow, slender, tough, often bent, up to 4 cm tall and 0.5 cm across.
flesh	off-white.
odour	faintly or strongly aromatic, like Japanese oranges.

cloudy Clitocybe p.71-6

Clitocybe nebularis (Fries) Kummer

nebularis: clouded (Latin)

Cosmopolitan; widely distributed and particularly common in the Pacific Northwest. It grows in large fairy rings under conifers. A very beautiful mushroom which can reach a very large size. I found them up to 25 cm across. The fruiting bodies survive a long time, like many other Clitocybes. This species used to be considered edible, but it is now known that it accumulates heavy metals like mercury and cadmium from the environment and so must be considered **poisonous**.

cap	streaked smoky grey with hints of purple and raw sienna; rounded at first, then expanding to almost plane with a slight dip; the edges stay curved in and split in maturity; usually reach 15 cm across but may be much bigger.
gills	soft yellow, decurrent, close, narrow, especially when young.
spore print	pale yellow.
stalk	white, fibrous, a bit granular at apex, relatively equal, copious white mycelium at the base, up to 7 cm tall and 2 cm across.
flesh	off-white, solid.
odour	faintly of skunk.

small scaly Clitocybe p.73-1

Clitocybe squamulosa (Fries) Kummer

squamulosa: scaly (Latin)

Cosmopolitan; this small brown mushroom is not at all common; it occurs in the Rocky Mountains, usually near conifers, fruiting in summer.

cap	brownish with small scales or felty in the centre; inrolled margin at first, then an interesting funnel shape, grooved and incurved margin; up to 5 cm across.
gills	bone coloured to pale brown, many intermediates, some forked, decurrent, relatively distant.
spore print	white.
stalk	same colour as cap, sturdy, solid or hollow, up to 4 cm tall and 0.5 cm thick.
flesh	white, brown cuticle.
odour	weak.

sturdy or strong Clitocybe p.73-2

Clitocybe robusta Peck

robusta: strong (Latin)

Cosmopolitan; this species has been described from different places, but it has no remarkable features; it looks like a white version of *C. nebularis*. It grows in deciduous and coniferous forests or in grassy open areas; fruiting in summer and fall. **Not recommended** for eating since if *C. nebularis* collects mercury, *C. robusta* might also.

cap	off-white with rolled-in margin at first, then expanding and getting somewhat pinkish buff; up to 10 cm across.
gills	bone colour, crowded, decurrent, narrow, eroded.
spore print	off-white to creamy.
stalk	white to buff, fibrillose base covered with mycelium; up to 5 cm tall and 1 cm thick.
flesh	off-white, solid, thick in cap, sometimes a bit pithy in the stalk.
odour	none or faintly unpleasant.

slim funnel mushroom

p.73-3

Clitocybe gibba (Persoon: Fries) Kummer

former name: *C. infundibuliformis*
gibba: hump (Latin)

Cosmopolitan; widely distributed all over this continent. Like *Marasmius oreades* it contains a small amount of cyanic acid, which disappears in cooking. Grows on dead leaves in mixed forest. Not recommended for eating.

cap	lovely light buckskin to peach colour, deep funnel; long inrolled and then incurved, striate edge; up to 8 cm across.
gills	off-white to pale pink, narrow, close, decurrent, forked.
spore print	white.
stalk	white or slightly blushing; enlarging toward base, which is covered with cottony mycelium; up to 5 cm tall and 0.8 cm thick at the top.
flesh	white, thin.
odour	faintly aromatic.

brick-red Clitocybe

p.73-4

Clitocybe sinopica (Fries) Kummer

sinopica: quartz, coloured red-brown by iron-oxide impurities (Latin)

Cosmopolitan; this colourful species grows on burnt ground (after forest fires or in campgrounds) or along roads. The specimens in the illustration were found in a campground in the mountains.

cap	deep red-brown to orange-brown, rounded with inrolled margin at first, then expanding to plane with a shallow depression in the centre; up to 9 cm across.
gills	light pink, close, decurrent.
spore print	off-white to cream.
stalk	same colour as cap or a bit lighter; up to 6 cm tall and 1 cm thick at apex.
flesh	whitish to pale buff.
odour	mealy or of cucumber.

streaked Clitocybe

p.73-5

Clitocybe ectypoides (Peck) Saccardo

ectypoides: pictured in relief (Greek)

North American species, particularly of the Pacific Northwest. The illustrated specimens were found on decayed wood in a spruce, larch and birch bog in Alberta. The name pertains to the scaly cap centre. The stalk base had an interesting structure buried in the wood. Not recommended for eating; fruiting in summer and fall.

cap	brownish honey colour with darker red-brown scales in the centre; convex at first, funnel shaped when mature with wavy margin with splits, up to 12 cm across.
gills	pinkish buff, close, long-decurrent.
spore print	creamy.
stalk	auburn, lighter near apex, equal, bent, mycelium at the base, an interesting basal structure in the wood debris; up to 8 cm tall and 1.5 cm thick.
flesh	whitish in cap, buff in stalk, solid.
odour	very pleasant, of peach.

large white Clitocybe

p.75-1

Clitocybe maxima (Fries) Kummer

maxima: the biggest (Latin)

North American species; occurring in mixed open forest; in rings, tufts or rows. In Europe the name *C. maxima* is sometimes used as a synonym for *C. geotropa*, but the two are actually very different. This mushroom can reach a very large size. It is edible when young but lives a long time and becomes tough with age.

cap	off-white; edge inrolled at first, irregular with shallow depression in maturity; smooth like soft leather, up to 20 cm across.
gills	white, decurrent, close at first, distant with age; very narrow.
spore print	white to off-white.
stalk	white, tall, slim, equal, stringy, mycelium and leaves clinging to base, up to 12 cm tall and 2 cm thick; sometimes short depending on the thickness of the duff.
flesh	off-white, both colour and consistency like a marshmallow, solid.
odour	faintly aromatic.
taste	mild.

trumpet mushroom   p.75-2

Clitocybe geotropa (Bulliard & St. Amans) Quélet

geotropa: directed to the earth's centre, erect (Greek)

Cosmopolitan; very popular in Europe. Grows in open wooded areas in fairy rings or groups, but not bunched together like *C. maxima*. Each fruiting body stands very erect. A very beautiful mushroom, edible when young, long living.

cap	sandy to peach pink, strongly inrolled margin at first, flat or with small knob, finally forming a huge funnel often with a band of grooves on the margin. Splits and holes may form along those grooves resulting in interesting shapes, up to 30 cm across.
gills	creamy to straw colour, finally tan, narrow, close, long decurrent.
spore print	white.
stalk	peach colour with fluffy white bits scattered on it, enlarging toward the base; covered with white mycelium almost halfway up; develops a very heavy cuticle; up to 12 cm tall; 3 cm thick at the top and 6 cm at the base.
flesh	off-white, soft, buff in the cap when mature, stalk solid or hollow.
odour	aromatic, peaches or amygdalin.
taste	mild.

Genus COLLYBIA

small coin (Greek)

The genus *Collybia* contains mostly small to medium-sized species. The mushrooms are inedible and tough, but it is one of the very valuable saprophytic groups recycling organic materials such as leaves and rotten wood in the forest. Small mushrooms are just as important as big ones in this regard, they grow from similar amounts of mycelium.

Thin fleshed, with hollow cartilaginous stalks, which are often hairy or velvety; narrow, crowded gills, which are never decurrent; mostly white spores, rarely buff; they grow in tight tufts or groups. Collybias often fruit in spring, especially the forest-loving Collybias. The small, white violet blooms very early as well, that is why it is in the illustration.

insignificant Collybia   p.76-1

Collybia ingrata (Schumacher: Fries) Quélet

ingrata: undeserving, thankless (Latin)

North American; very small saprophytic mushrooms growing in large groups on duff in deciduous forest. The mycelium is visible in the duff. I found these after a very heavy rainfall; very aromatic odour.

cap	buff, rounded, very thin, up to 1.2 cm across.
gills	yellowish white, narrow, crowded, free.
spore print	white.
stalk	whitish, felty, equal, twisted, sometimes Siamese twinned, up to 5 cm tall and 0.2 cm thick.
flesh	white, thin, tough.
odour	very aromatic.

tufted Collybia

p.76-2

Collybia confluens (Persoon: Fries) Kummer

former name: *Marasmius confluens*
confluens: flowing together (Latin)

Cosmopolitan; wide distribution, growing in tufts on forest debris, both in deciduous and coniferous forests. I found it on wood, spruce needles and leaves. It is a tough little mushroom which can dry up and then revive after rain, like several other *Collybia* and also *Marasmius* species. A lot of mycelium is visible in the duff.

cap	tan with light brown crown, margin inrolled at first, rounded, smooth like a chamois, later flattening; up to 3 cm across or more.
gills	off-white.
spore print	white.
stalk	flesh colour fading to buff, felty, equal, up to 7 cm tall and 0.4 cm thick.
flesh	buff colour, hollow in stalk, thin.
odour	mild or none.

dark Collybia

p.76-3

Collybia obscura Favre

obscura: dark (Latin)

Cosmopolitan; growing on duff in small groups in deciduous or mixed woods. A small dark, obscure mushroom not easily noted. I found the one illustrated in the mountains on yellow avens debris.

cap	purplish brown, fading to rust brown, smooth, up to 4 cm across.
gills	medium brown, many intermediates, relatively close and broad.
spore print	white.
stalk	very dark brown, velvety, squeezed or with grooves; up to 2.5 cm tall and 0.3 cm thick.
flesh	medium brown in cap, dark brown in hollow stalk.
odour	none.

clustered Collybia

p.76-4

Collybia acervata (Fries) Kummer

acervata: in a bundle or sheaf (Latin)

Cosmopolitan and widespread; growing in tight caespitose bunches on old stumps or buried conifer wood. Bitter taste; inedible. Common in the Rocky Mountains and the Pacific Northwest.

cap	reddish brown, fading to yellow-ochre and buff; convex at first, margin inrolled, flattening later; up to 6 cm across.
gills	off-white, crowded, narrow, free.
spore print	white.
stalk	dark red-brown, may fade with age; smooth, up to 8 cm tall and 0.5 cm thick; white mycelium at the base.
flesh	white at first, then sometimes brownish; thin.
odour	none.

June mushroom

p.76-5

Collybia dryophila (Bulliard: Fries) Kummer

dryophila: tree loving (Greek)

Cosmopolitan and widespread; this species fruits mostly in spring. It is so variable in colour and size, that it takes a long time to know. I have sketched and described it more than two dozen times, thinking I might have finally found *C. butyracea*, but the spore print was always white and that of *butyracea* is buff. I recently was told that *C. dryophila* is a complex of several species. This species grows on forest debris, leaves and rotten wood, mostly of deciduous trees. Revives in moist weather. Some authors call it edible, but severe gastro-intestinal disturbances have been recorded.

cap	can be very dark when young and moist, then chestnut or orange brown, finally buff; hygrophanous, convex when young with inrolled cap edge, flattening in maturity; up to 8 cm across.
gills	off-white to pale yellow.
spore print	white.
stalk	off-white, pale brown or orange; equal or thickening toward the base; mycelium on the base and in the duff; up to 6 cm tall and 0.5 cm thick at the top.
flesh	white to yellowish, sometimes a coloured layer under the cuticle, hollow stalk.
odour	none to very pleasant, of peaches.

hard-to-know Collybia   p.76-6

Collybia confusa Orton

confusa: hard to know, mixed up (Latin)

Cosmopolitan; rare, probably because this very dark small species blends in with the undergrowth in the forest and so is not often found.

cap	dark brown, fading to ash brown; smooth, thin, persistent rolled-in cap edge, up to 3 cm across.
gills	brown, crowded, narrow, free, drying up with space around the stalk (distant).
spore print	white.
stalk	dark brown, velvety, drying up lighter, equal, often twisted, up to 7 cm tall and 0.3 cm thick.
flesh	thin, whitish.
odour	mushroomy.

spotted Collybia   p.76-7

Collybia maculata (Albertini & Schweinitz: Fries) Kummer

maculata: spotted (Latin)

Cosmopolitan; widespread and quite common in the Pacific Northwest. Grows in tufts on decaying wood or lignin-rich soil under conifers. Inedible; the taste is usually bitter.

cap	white and convex at first, flattening and with pinkish to rusty spots with age, up to 10 cm across.
gills	off-white to pinkish, often developing rust spots in age, close, sinuate to almost free, narrow.
spore print	pinkish buff.
stalk	white, grooved, equal or with widening base, sometimes with flattened and narrowing base and "rooting", up to 9 cm tall and 1.5 cm thick.
flesh	white, hollow in stalk.
odour	fresh and pleasant.

Genus MARASMIUS

withered (Greek)

The name of the genus refers to its remarkable ability to revive after withering and drying up if not dry for too many weeks. The majority of species in *Marasmius* are small to very small. Related genera *Marasmiellus* and *Micromphale* contain even smaller species.

In the rain, these very small mushrooms can be seen in the forest in the millions, on leaves, conifer needles, bits of wood and bark, but when the sun comes out, they become invisible in a very short time. All *Marasmius* species are saprophytic, including the fairy ring mushroom, which grows on dead grass.

conifer pinwheel   p.77-1

Marasmius pallidocephalus Gilliam

pallidocephalus: pale-headed (Latin and Greek)

North American species; these small mushrooms grow on fallen needles and cones of pine and spruce when moisture conditions are right. When the sun comes out, they fade and shrink immediately.

cap	reddish brown, soon fading to buff or almost white; convex, thin, up to 0.1 cm across.
gills	buff, narrow, relatively distant.
spore print	white.
stalk	brown, thin, like horse-hair, tough, 2 - 3 cm tall and 0.1 cm thick.
flesh	very thin, pliant.
odour	none.

white pinwheel   p.77-2

Marasmius epiphyllus (Persoon: Fries) Fries

epiphyllus: on leaves (Greek)

Cosmopolitan; this small white mushroom is widespread but not often seen, because it disappears even faster than no. 1. It grows in the forest on dead leaves of deciduous trees after rain.

cap	white, thin, uneven, drying in wrinkles, up to 0.8 cm across.
gills	white, narrow, distant, foldlike.
spore print	white.
stalk	brown, like horse-hair, very thin, lighter apex.
flesh	very thin.
odour	none.

Dryas pinwheel   p.77-3

Marasmius epidryas Kühner

epidryas: on the small woody plant named *Dryas* (mountain avens) (Greek)

Circumpolar distribution as well as in the Rocky Mountains and the European Alps. Growing on the dead part of bark tissue of certain avens species, making it a very specialized small fungus (Redhead et al 1982).

cap	brown and convex, soon fading on top; with navel; striate margin, which stays curved in, up to 1.5 cm across.
gills	ivory to buff, adnate distant, intermediates.
spore print	white.
stalk	dark brown, apex lighter, up to 4 cm tall and 2 cm thick.
flesh	off-white, thin, tough.
odour	none.

navel mushroom   p.77-4

Micromphale sp.

micromphale: small, with navel (Greek)

This specimen is an example of species of the genus *Micromphale*. Growing on wood, it resembles *Micromphale foetidum* in many respects, but it does not have the strong dirty odour described by Hermann Jahn (1979) and Lincoff (1981).

cap	brown, hygrophanous, fading between "ribs", rounded with deep navel, up to 2 cm across.
gills	buff, adnate and arched, many intermediates, strongly eroded.
spore print	white.
stalk	top dark brown, grooved, base broader, tan and fuzzy all-over; up to 3 cm tall and 0.4 cm thick.
flesh	white, solid.
odour	clean, aromatic.

fairy ring mushroom p.77-5

Marasmius oreades (Bolton & Fries) Fries

oreades: growing in the mountains (Greek)

Cosmopolitan and widespread. This species grows in grassy areas and is not always appreciated. People often complain that their grass is killed by *M. oreades*, but there is an easy way to keep the grass green. In the ring of mushrooms the mycelium is quite dense, restricting grass roots somewhat. Since the mycelium is greasy as well, the grass cannot get enough water. Take a garden fork, make holes in the ring and pour water with mild soap or detergent in it on the ring area (to cut the grease). Water and fertilize, and your grass will stay green. Eventually your fairy ring will disappear. Looking at the ring closely, you will notice greener grass inside the circle. This is where the ring was before, and the green is from the extra nutrients the fungus freed for the grass. When no chemicals are used on the grass, the caps can be eaten in soups, omelettes or sauces. They should be cooked in any case. They contain tiny amounts of hydrocyanic acid, which gives the faint almond odour to the mushrooms. They should not be eaten in large quantities. Fruiting in spring, summer and fall; adapted to dry climates.

cap	tawny or pale tan; bell shaped at first, then flattening out, often with an umbo; fading when drying out, reviving in moist conditions; up to 4 cm across.
gills	creamy, distant, broad, almost free, veins between the gills in older specimens.
spore print	white.
stalk	light tan, base sometimes darker, felty, tough; up to 7 cm tall and 0.5 cm thick.
flesh	off-white.
odour	lightly of almonds.
taste	good.

tightly bunched Marasmius p.77-6

Marasmius strictipes (Peck) Singer

strictipes: stalks fitting well together (Latin)

North American species; quite similar to the fairy ring mushroom but a forest species; not growing in rings but in tight bunches as the name "strictipes" indicates. Fruiting in summer. This species has a lot of tan or ochre-coloured mycelium in the leaves at the base of the stalk. Edibility unknown.

cap	lovely reddish and yellowish brown colour; bell shaped at first, flattening with umbo; elevated margin sometimes, up to 6 cm across.
gills	buff to light tan, narrow, crowded, adnexed to almost free, many intermediates.
spore print	white.
stalk	light pinkish buff, equal, often twisted, velvety, hollow and stringy inside, up to 13 cm tall and 0.8 cm thick.
flesh	off-white to light buff.
odour	pleasant, of flowers.

Genus ARMILLARIA

wearing a belt (Latin)

At one time the genus *Armillaria* included a number of species with white spores, adnate gills and a stalk with a ring but which were not really related. For a while the honey mushroom was called *Armillariella mellea* because it was so different from the others, and the name *Armillaria* was used for some large, ringed species like *Armillaria ponderosa* and *Armillaria zelleri*. These have since been shown to have a much closer connection with *Tricholoma* and have been placed in that genus. The name "Armillaria" is now restricted to the type species *Armillaria mellea* and its close relations. "Type species" means the species which is most typical of the genus, to which its name is given. Mycologists follow the rules of the International Code of Botanical Nomenclature in the case of restoration or changes of names and new names.

I will only describe *Armillaria mellea* and only in a broad sense. Generally it is thought to be a complex of several species. In Europe a number of species have been named, and phytopathologist Y. Hiratsuka is conducting research in Edmonton on this tree killer. In the near future we will have a better idea of how many species the complex includes on our continent.

honey mushroom   p.79-1

Armillaria mellea (Vahl: Fries) Kummer s.l.

Armillaria: furnished with an armband (Latin)
mellea: with the colour of honey (Latin)

Worldwide distribution. This mushroom, which people have been collecting under the name honey mushroom (English), tête de Méduse (French meaning head of Medusa), Hallimasch (German), pidpanki (Ukranian meaning at the bottom of the stump) and honingzwam (Dutch meaning honey fungus, because of the colour of the mushroom), is generally so variable and interesting, that it has been studied many times in the past and still is at present. It can be very virulent and spreads in two ways. Its spores can only infect dead wood and stumps, but its mycelium forms black shoelace-like strands or rhizomorphs, which can grow long distances from one tree to another, infecting the roots of living trees. They are parasites and kill all tree species, but they are especially damaging in tree plantations where trees of one kind are planted. Once infected, the wood becomes luminous, which can be easily seen by taking a piece of infected wood into a dark place! Physiologically it is a very intriguing species since this is the only known gilled mushroom with a diploid mycelium, which greatly accelerates the sexual reproductive process.

It fruits in the fall in cold climates and all through the winter in rainy, mild climates. They are not the finest quality for eating, but mycophagists are still happy to find them. Stalks are tough so only the caps should be used. They should always be cooked. Not only that, but they should only be eaten when young because poisonous substances form in older specimens! They are real survivors, tolerating droughts and a certain amount of frost. In the illustration you see some very dark brown specimens which were still sporulating, although they were very old.

cap	honey colour, lighter or darker up to chestnut brown; rounded at first, then flattening; smooth and streaked or somewhat scaly; size varies, up to 12 cm across.
gills	whitish to buff or slightly pinkish, adnate to decurrent.
spore print	whitish.
stalk	same colour as cap or lighter, streaked; the lemon colour just below the ring and the club-shaped base (sometimes equal when growing in bunches) are important characteristics to note.
partial veil	white, fibrous or woolly; sometimes some yellow on the outside; resulting in a cottony roll just below the gills or a ring which stands out a bit more (fibrous); persistent and staying white even when the mushroom turns almost black with age.
flesh	white and solid.
odour	weak.
taste	mild or slightly bitter.

woolly-stalk mushroom   p.79-6

Floccularia albolanaripes (Atkinson) Redhead

Floccularia: woolly mushroom (Latin)
albolanaripes: with white woolly stalk (Latin)

Growing on the Pacific coast, fruiting in fall and winter; this bunch was found in November in Vancouver, B.C. The woolly stalk mushroom is closely related to the honey mushroom. Edible.

cap	dark chestnut brown and viscid when young; later yellowish, covered with fine scales; rounded at first; when mature extending up to 8 cm across.
gills	bone colour, adnexed, intermediates.
spore print	white.

stalk	white, completely woolly including partial veil, when mature smooth white apex can be seen; up to 7 cm tall and 1 cm thick.
flesh	white, solid.
taste	bland.

Genus LEPISTA

The species of *Lepista* which were transferred from the genus *Tricholoma*, have cream or pinkish to flesh-coloured spores. Three of the five specimens in the illustrations are very similar in shape — the purple, the wine-coloured and the pale one; they have adnate to sinuate gills and pinkish spores. The other two — the golden and the orange — have decurrent gills like most Clitocybes, but have buff to pinkish gills as well, and a white to cream-coloured spore print. Taxonomists do not agree yet where these five species really belong. They are sometimes placed in *Tricholoma*, other times in *Clitocybe*. I have followed Pomerleau and put them in *Lepista*. The name "Lepista" means peeled in Greek. The smooth dull surface looks like split leather (chamois).

The purple species is the famous blewit, a well-known edible mushroom, cultivated in various parts of the world. It can be grown on old leaf compost in gardens. The woolly Lepista and blueleg have been reported as edible, but some people report gastrointestinal difficulties with them. Not as easily recognized as the blewit, they are better left alone.

Blewits should be eaten cooked because *Lepista nuda* contains a substance which destroys red blood cells; this substance is broken down by cooking. The Lepistas are terrestial saprophytic mushrooms.

orange funnel cap   p.81-1

Lepista inversa (Fries) Patouillard

former name: *Clitocybe inversa* (Fries) Gillet
inversa: up-turned (Latin)

Cosmopolitan; widespread in northern climates; on our continent occurs particularly in the west; growing in coniferous or mixed forest, often in fairy rings. Not recommended for eating.

cap	variable colour from buff to rust to orange, flat at first with a depression and inrolled margin, finally upturned with wavy edge, funnel shape; up to 10 cm across.
gills	whitish at first, then buff to pinkish or salmon coloured; narrow, long decurrent.
spore print	whitish to cream colour.
stalk	short, red-brown, often partly covered with white mycelium, also visible in the duff, up to 3 cm tall and 1 cm thick.
flesh	whitish to buff, hollow stalk.
odour	faint or aromatic (of peaches).

woolly Lepista   p.81-2

Lepista irina (Fries) Bigelow

irina: woolen (Latin)

Cosmopolitan; growing in deciduous woods, this pale *Lepista*, with its sinuate gills, can easily be taken for a species of *Tricholoma* until a spore print is made, which is pale pink. There are pink-spored, poisonous Entolomas with which this mushroom can be confused.

cap	off-white with buff crown, can be a bit pinkish; smooth, feels like chamois; broadly domed or rounded and later flattening; up to 14 cm across.
gills	buff to pale pink, relatively close, eroded, intermediates, adnate sinuate.
spore print	light pink.
stalk	whitish, top rough with flocks, stringy; equal to slightly enlarged base, which has woolly mycelium cover; up to 8 cm tall and 2 cm thick.
flesh	off-white to pale buff in cap, stringy in stalk, hollow with pith.
odour	faint.

blue leg

p.81-3

Lepista saeva (Fries) Orton

saeva: strong (Latin)

Cosmopolitan; this strong, robust species grows in deciduous forests in boggy open areas or at the edge of the forest in fairy rings. While it may at first appear to be a faded blewit, the vinaceous stalk (rather than violet) and buff flesh (rather than violet) prove otherwise. Not recommended for eating.

cap	off-white to buff with vinaceous tinge; rounded at first with inrolled margin, then flattening; smooth, dull; soft, feeling like chamois; up to 15 cm across.
gills	off-white with vinaceous tinges, adnate, sinuate, crowded, eroded.
spore print	rosy peach colour.
stalk	vinaceous, stringy, sturdy, equal, up to 10 cm tall and 2.5 cm thick.
flesh	white, stringy in stalk, with hollow or with pith-filled centre.
odour	pleasant, aromatic.

golden Lepista

p.81-4

Lepista gilva (Fries) Patouillard

gilva: pale yellow (Latin)

Cosmopolitan; growing in coniferous forests. In Europe it is considered a species of the mountains; I found it in boreal mixed forest in Alberta.

cap	soft yellow with some orange; inrolled margin at first, then flattening with slight depression; up to 8 cm across.
gills	pale pinkish yellow, narrow, crowded, long decurrent.
spore print	whitish to creamy.
stalk	pale yellow, thickening a bit below the gills, up to 4 cm tall and 1 cm thick.
flesh	soft pinkish yellow.
odour	delicately aromatic.

blewit

p.81-5

Lepista nuda (Fries) Patouillard

nuda: naked (Latin)

Cosmopolitan; this very popular edible mushroom has a very wide distribution in Europe, Japan and on our continent. In the prairie provinces it fruits in July, August and September. Along the coast it fruits more in the fall and early winter. In Holland I found them in October growing in profusion on an old pile of leaves in chilly, rainy weather. If a compost pile like that is kept in the same place year after year, that would be **the** place for backyard growing of mushrooms, and it would include the recycling of leaves. *L. nuda* is easily cultivated but has not achieved the same popularity as the button mushroom because it grows more slowly. To get to know them, look especially for young specimens, which are a beautiful violet all over and should have no cobwebby veil. A spore print from an older one in the same ring should be peach-coloured, and the flesh should be pale violet. Edible and excellent but **eat only after cooking.**

cap	lilac and convex at first, then expanding, centre changes to buff or pale tan, finally margin turns up and becomes wavy, losing most of its colour; soft, smooth, up to 20 cm or more across.
gills	violet, close, adnate sinuate, turning pinkish when spores ripen.
spore print	peach coloured to pinkish buff.
stalk	streaked lilac and white; slowly enlarging toward base, which is often covered with mycelium with a lilac tinge; violet mycelial rhizoid extends into the duff, up to 12 cm tall and 3 cm thick at the top.
flesh	violet when young, fading with age but always some lilac present; remarkably free of insects. solid when young, stalk hollow in maturity.
odour	very pleasant, aromatic.
taste	excellent, but has to be cooked for eating.
mycelium	somewhat violet coloured.

Genus LEUCOPAXILLUS

white Paxillus (Greek)

Leucopaxillus is a small genus of medium to large species, which are saprophytic. The field characteristics they have in common are as follows: confluent cap and stalk; dry cap like soft leather; fleshy stalk, not stiff and straight like in *Melanoleuca*; gills usually narrow and adnate to decurrent and somewhat forked; abundant white mycelium present in the duff under and around the mushroom. They are long-living and get tough. Plants near these mushrooms often have a dusting of white spores on them. Most *Leucopaxillus* species are tough, unpalatable and hard to digest, but I ate some young *L. giganteus* which were excellent. One of the chemical characteristics is amyloid spores, meaning the cell wall of the spore turns blue upon contact with an iodine reagent.

spruce leucopax   p.83-1

Leucopaxillus piceinus (Peck) Pomerleau

piceinus: of spruce (*Picea*) (Latin)

North American; this species occurs regularly in Alberta. It is persistent; its copious, matted mycelium is visible in the duff, and surrounding plants are dusted with white spores. The rounded base of the stalk is the only part of the mushroom infested with insects. Grows in mixed forest, fruiting in July. Indigestible.

cap	white at first, rounded with inrolled margin, then buff to light tan with pale margin, surface soft like chamois; tightly rolled-in edge; persistent; up to 11 cm across.
gills	off-white, crowded, adnate to decurrent, forked here and there, narrow.
spore print	white.
stalk	white, relatively short, bulbous base, always with insects in the bulb, which is underground and covered with mycelium; up to 6 cm tall and 2 cm thick at the apex.
flesh	white, solid, very thick in the centre of the cap.
odour	fresh, of drying hay.
taste	bitter.

northern leucopax   p.83-2

Leucopaxillus septentrionalis Singer and A. H. Smith

septentrionalis: northern (after the seven bright stars of "Septentriones" or the big dipper, the northern constellation) (Latin)

North American; this interesting mushroom with the romantic name occurs under conifers. Reported from the Yukon and the east slopes of the Cascade Mountains. I found it east of Edmonton under spruce in August.

cap	tan colour; convex at first, then broadly domed; smooth, like soft leather, small in relation to its massive stalk, margin rolled-in; up to 8 cm across.
gills	extremely narrow, decurrent, anastomosing. Resembling those of a real *Paxillus*, *P. vernalis*, which strongly anastomoses as well but which has a cinnamon-coloured spore print.
spore print	whitish.
stalk	very thick, white with salmon streaks, up to 7 cm tall and 4 cm thick; equal or slightly thickening at the base; showing copious white mycelium in the duff.
odour	peppery.

bitter leucopax   p.83-3

Leucopaxillus amarus (Albertini & Schweinitz) Kühner

amarus: bitter (Latin)

Cosmopolitan; it has a western distribution in Canada and the U.S.; the illustrated specimens were found under fir in the Lac la Biche area of Alberta. Fruiting in late summer. This beautiful mushroom is inedible because of its bitterness.

cap	deep red-brown on the disc, lighter towards the inrolled margin, dry surface, up to 12 cm across.

gills	white, crowded, narrow, adnate to decurrent.
spore print	white.
stalk	white, short, up to 5 cm tall and 1.5 cm thick at the apex, mycelial mat.
flesh	very white, firm.
odour	strong mushroom smell.
taste	bitter.

giant leucopax   p.83-4

Leucopaxillus giganteus (Fries) Singer

former name: *Clitocybe gigantea*
gigantea: very large (Latin)

Cosmopolitan; widely distributed; most common in mixed forest in the Pacific Northwest, the Rocky Mountains and across the prairie provinces. Choice edible mushroom when young. Since they persist a long time and are still around in dry summers when no other mushroom is, they tend to be too old when people try them and, therefore, have a bad reputation.

cap	ivory coloured at first and convex, margin inrolled; then flattening out and becoming a shallow funnel shape; smooth, sometimes with circular cracks and colour changing to pale tan; can become very large, up to 30 cm across.
gills	pinkish ivory, crowded, narrow, decurrent, sometimes forked.
spore print	white.
stalk	off-white with reddish brown fibres, when mature up to 8 cm tall and 3 cm thick; abundant matted white mycelium at the base.
flesh	off-white.
odour	varies — fragrant, slightly of amygdalin, to a bit unpleasant like turnip.
taste	good when young.

Genus MELANOLEUCA
black and white (Greek)

North American species of this genus have not been thoroughly studied. *Melanoleuca cognata* for instance, with its many variations in colour, shape, size, and spore colour, may be a complex of similar species. Generally they are saprophytic, fleshy mushrooms with tall slender stalks, confluent caps and stalks, no ring or cup; the gills range from almost free to adnexed, adnate or decurrent, and the spore deposits are white or creamy to tan. It is not an easy genus to get to know. When found, immediately note the cap colour and the colour of the stalk, gills and flesh because they fade quickly after picking. Some species are said to be edible.

mountain Melanoleuca   p.84-1

Melanoleuca evenosa (Saccardo) Konrad

evenosa: wihout veins (Latin)

Cosmopolitan; this mushroom occurs in mountain meadows in the Rockies, but also in boreal forest and aspen parkland; edible and good.

cap	light sandy and white, smooth, rounded, inrolled edge, then flattening somewhat, up to 8 cm across.
gills	off-white, intermediates, close, almost free.
spore print	white.
stalk	off-white, lined, often twisted, fibrous, thickening a bit toward the base; up to 8 cm tall and up to 1.5 cm wide.
flesh	off-white, loose and stringy in stalk.
odour	of fresh hay, slightly anise.

yellowish-white Melanoleuca p.84-2

Melanoleuca alboflavida (Peck) Murrill

alboflavida: white and yellow (Latin)

North American species; growing in meadows or along roadsides. The ones illustrated were found in a grassy area in Alberta. This is a group of tall mushrooms.

cap	creamy to pale brown; convex with inrolled edge at first, then flattening with umbo; smooth, up to 14 cm across.
gills	white, broadly attached, almost decurrent, close, serrate edges.
spore print	creamy.
stalk	whitish with some tan streaks, equal, very tall, base a bit bulbous with some red discolouration, up to 18 cm tall and 1.5 cm wide.
flesh	white, stringy in stalk.
odour	aromatic.

dark Melanoleuca p.84-3

Melanoleuca melaleuca (Fries) Murrill

former name: *M. vulgaris* (Patouillard)
melaleuca: black and white (Greek)
vulgaris: common (Latin)

Cosmopolitan and widely distributed; this is the darkest of the Melanoleucas, especially when moist; occurs in woods and fields, fruiting in the fall. Not recommended for eating because it is not easily recognized.

cap	mouse grey to brown, very dark when damp, smooth; domed at first, then flattening and arching up; up to 8 cm across.
gills	white, close, relatively narrow, intermediates.
spore print	whitish, drying up yellow.
stalk	grey to grey brown, streaky, enlarging toward the base somewhat, up to 7 cm tall and 1 cm thick.
flesh	pale buff in cap, brown in stalk with white pith in the centre.
odour	light.

small Melanoleuca p.84-4

Melanoleuca humilis (Fries) Patouillard

humilis: low (Latin)

Pacific Northwest; a small drab species found in moss in spruce-birch bogs; fruiting in the fall.

cap	mouse grey, smooth, rounded, then plane, up to 4 cm across.
gills	white, close, adnexed and sinuate.
spore print	white.
stalk	grey, short, lined, up to 4 cm tall and up to 0.5 cm thick.
flesh	brownish.
odour	unpleasant.

striped stalk Melanoleuca p.84-5

Melanoleuca grammopodia (Bulliard) Patouillard

grammopodia: with a lined stalk (Greek)

Cosmopolitan; occurring in forest and grassy areas; once familiar with the genus, you can see that this species is an obvious *Melanoleuca*; fruiting in summer and fall.

cap	brown, darker in the centre, smooth; rounded at first, finally expanding into a shallow bowl; up to 12 cm across.
gills	off-white at first, then buff and darkening with age, close, intermediates, adnexed to free.
spore print	creamy.

stalk	brown like the cap, slender, streaked or lined, sometimes twisted, enlarging toward the base, which is covered with woolly, white mycelium.
flesh	off-white to light buff.
odour	pleasant.

peach-gilled Melanoleuca p.84-6

Melanoleuca cognata (Fries) Konrad & Maublanc

cognata: related (Latin)

Cosmopolitan; this ochre-coloured mushroom grows in the Pacific Northwest in aspen parkland and boreal mixed forest. It is probably a complex of similar species and comes in many shapes and sizes, as can be seen in the illustrations. The specimen with the decurrent gills may look a lot like *Lactarius fumosis*, but does not contain latex nor white flesh turning reddish. Not recommended for eating.

cap	from yellow ochre to chestnut brown, fading to buff; see illustration for variety in shape; up to 10 cm across.
gills	pale ochrish to orange, broad, adnexed and sinuate to decurrent, serrate.
spore print	creamy to buff to yellow ochre.
stalk	a shade of brown, orangy to smoky, tall and slim, enlarging toward the base which has some white mycelium on it, up to 10 cm tall and 1 cm thick at the top, at other times the stalk is thick and heavy, up to 3 cm thick and equal.
flesh	buff to light orange, soft, solid in cap, stringy in stalk.
odour	slightly fruity.

Genus LYOPHYLLUM

with loose gills (pertains to easy separation of gills from the cap) (Greek)

The genus *Lyophyllum* contains several species, which always grow in large groups or tufts. The stalk bases are strongly joined together. There are also smaller ones which grow singly, but they are harder to recognize than the tufted, larger species. Terrestrial and saprophytic, they grow in disturbed places. The mushrooms have a confluent cap and stalk; the gills are adnate or decurrent; there is no partial veil; the spore print is white. Like *Calocybe*, the basidia contain granules which will darken with a carmine stain. This chemical test is used by experts as an added means of identification. Even the large tufted species are not easily identified because of variable cap colour and gill attachment.

One of the illustrated species, *L. loricatum* (3 a, b, c), is dark brown with a hoary bloom on it to start with; as it matures it fades to a lighter brown and eventually it just looks like no. 2, pale tan. These are good edible mushrooms although the white one is not recommended. It is easily confused with poisonous white Clitocybes. As always when trying out a new species, eat just a little bit, because allergic reactions are possible and have occurred with these mushrooms.

white tuft p.85-1

Lyophyllum connatum (Schumacher: Fries) Singer

connatum: born together (Latin)

Cosmopolitan; it grows in tufts in grassy areas along roads and in open areas in forests on the ground, sometimes on decayed wood. Edible, but not recommended because of possible confusion with similar-looking poisonous species.

cap	white or off-white, convex at first then expanding, wavy edge, smooth, up to 6 cm across.
gills	white, close, a bit decurrent, adnate or almost free.
spore print	white.
stalk	white, equal or narrowing toward the base, relatively tall, hollow, up to 7 cm tall and 0.7 cm thick, bases of stalks fused.
flesh	very white.

fried chicken mushroom p.85-2

Lyophyllum decastes (Fries: Fries) Singer

decastes: in numbers of ten (Greek)

Cosmopolitan; this species has a wide distribution in the Pacific Northwest and the prairies; a very popular edible species. It occurs in grassy areas like schoolyards or roadsides; usually there is some buried wood or roots in the ground, or it may grow on decaying wood. Growing in dense clusters with fused stalks. Edible, but make a spore print.

cap	hygrophanous, yellowish brown to greyish brown and fading, shape is irregular because of crowding in the cluster; up to 12 cm across.
gills	creamy white, close.
spore print	white.
stalk	whitish with a bit of tan, fused at the base into large bundles, irregularly formed because of this, central or off-centre, shorter or longer, up to 10 cm tall and 4 cm thick.
flesh	white, solid, sometimes in strands in older ones, semi-transparent layer under cuticle.
odour	aromatic.
taste	good.

frosty Lyophyllum p.85-3

Lyophyllum loricatum (Fries) Kühner

loricatum: armoured (Latin)

Cosmopolitan; found in the west from the Yukon south to California; this species is very closely related to *L. decastes*. When the mushrooms are over-mature, they look exactly alike. In the illustration I have shown them in three phases as we found them in northern B.C. during a cold spring. There were such masses of them, and with a variety of colours, that I thought at first that there were several species present. Blackish brown with a hoary sheen when young, then chestnut brown fading to pale tan. The name refers to a tough skin. Edible with caution, because of the colour variations.

cap	changing from very dark, blackish brown with a hoary sheen to chestnut; finally to pale tan when overmature and full of insects. Growing in large caespitose tufts, their caps become irregularly shaped from crowding, up to 13 cm across.
gills	whitish, close, later relatively distant, edges yellowing, some interconnecting veins, edges eroded, adnate.
spore print	white.
stalk	white, a bit brownish, strongly caespitose, often fused and not only at the base, irregularly shaped, up to 8 cm tall and 4 cm thick.
flesh	white, solid.
odour	slight.
taste	not the best.

Genus CALOCYBE

beautiful head (Greek)

Calocybe is a small rare genus with some colourful species. They have been separated from other genera like *Tricholoma*, *Lyophyllum*, *Clitocybe* and *Collybia* because of certain characteristics which they have in common. One characteristic of the *Calocybe* genus is the presence of iron-loving (siderophilus) granules in the basidia which can be detected by a chemical test. However, in this guide we will depend on the field characteristics. If you are in doubt, then consult an expert. The species I found are orange, pink, lilac and cream coloured; growing in fairy rings in grass, sometimes in moss in coniferous forests. Often years go by in the prairie provinces without fruiting. They are saprophytes.

orange Calocybe

p.87-1

Calocybe fallax (Saccardo) Singer: Redhead & Singer

fallax: deceptive (Latin)

Cosmopolitan; rare in Canada; it has been reported from Québec and Ontario. I found it in Alberta a few times in the summer, growing in moss in a mixed spruce-birch bog; the irregular gills are an interesting feature.

cap	orange and yellow ochre with somewhat darker crown, dry, smooth, convex or slightly umbonate, up to 2 cm across.
gills	warm or ochre yellow, irregular, forked, not always radiating, sometimes feathered.
spore print	white.
stalk	yellow, woolly white base, stipe up to 1.5 cm and 0.2 - 0.4 cm thick.
flesh	yellow, solid.

pink Calocybe

p.87-2

Calocybe carnea (Bulliard: Fries) Kühner in Donk

carnea: flesh coloured (Latin)

Cosmopolitan; widespread in northern North America but rare; may be found in grassy areas in fairy rings, but in Alberta I found it in moss in a spruce bog.

cap	pinkish to flesh coloured to red brown, fading to pale tan; note the colour immediately when found because it fades fast; dry, convex to slightly umbonate, up to 4 cm across.
gills	white, close, crowded, intermediates, adnexed.
spore print	white.
stalk	sturdy, colour of the cap in the top half, streaked, white base, buried in moss and enlarging toward base to club shape; up to 4 cm tall and 0.5 cm thick at the top.
flesh	white with a pink area under the cuticle of the cap and stalk.

violet Calocybe

p.87-3

Calocybe ionides (Bulliard: Fries) Donk

former name: *Lyophyllum ionides*
ionides: violet (Greek)

Cosmopolitan; rarely found in eastern Canada; in Alberta it is found in lawns and other grassy areas during wet summers. It grows in fairy rings.

cap	deep violet, fading with age to pale violet and pale tan; the colour has to be noted immediately when found because of fading; rounded then flattening, smooth, dry, up to 5 cm across.
gills	bone colour; seen from below the cap they look somewhat yellow; adnexed sinuate, crowded, intermediates.
spore print	white.
stalk	white with violet fibres on the top, white base, more or less equal, up to 6 cm tall and 0.8 cm thick.
flesh	white, solid, in older specimens stringy in the stalk.
odour	fresh, of sweet-scented bedstraw.

cream Calocybe

p.87-4

Calocybe gambosa (Fries) Donk

gambosa: with many curves (Greek)

Cosmopolitan; growing in open woods, grassy areas and roadsides in fairy rings. This large, fleshy, edible mushroom is popular in Europe because it occurs early in spring when not much else fruits, but the quality of its taste is not the best. I found it only in the fall in Alberta.

cap	cream coloured, rounded, very thick fleshed; inrolled edge, when expanding, the centre stays rounded and turns brownish, the edge splits and becomes irregular and wavy, partly turning up and partly down; can become very large, up to 26 cm across.
gills	cream coloured, crowded, narrow at first, sinuate with a yellowish impression when looking from below.

spore print	white.
stalk	cream coloured, heavy, up to 7 cm tall and 4 cm thick, swelling towards the base, splitting when expanding.
flesh	cream coloured, solid.
odour	pleasant, of fresh meal or old bread.

Genera PLEUROCYBELLA, TRICHOLOMOPSIS, FLAMMULINA & HYPSIZYGUS

Page 89 shows five species in four genera; all grow on wood and are saprophytic, although both *Flammulina* and *Hypsizygus* are also found on dead parts of living trees. All have white spore prints.

Pleurocybella: thin, white, fan-shaped brackets growing on conifer logs; a very small genus with only one species so far.

Tricholomopsis: another small genus also growing on conifer logs; two species described. They are wood saprophytes. The fruiting bodies have hairy caps, central stalks and yellow or yellowish gills.

Flammulina: a small genus but a very famous one. *Flammulina velutipes*, the velvet foot (called enoki in Japan), is cultivated all over the world but mostly in Japan. It grows naturally in tight caespitose bundles on stumps, logs and dead parts of dying deciduous trees. It is an adaptable saprophyte: in other parts of the world it grows on different tree species. In cultivation, bundles are grown on a sawdust mixture in bottles and sold like small bouquets of flowers. The mushrooms stay pale, like the small ones in the illustration, with very long stalks and small pale caps. It is hard to imagine that this is the same species which is so colourful when growing in its natural habitat.

Hypsizygus: members of this genus grow on the wood of deciduous trees. There has been a lot of confusion about whether European species of similar names were the same species on our continent. This has been definitely sorted out by S.A. Redhead by studying hundreds of specimens from both continents. The one portrayed and described here grows on stumps and in crotches of dead trees. It can develop very long stalks which emerge from between the bark and the wood of a stump. *Hypsizygus* is closely linked to, but distinctly different from, *Lyophyllum*.

angel wings   p.89-1

Pleurocybella porrigens (Persoon: Fries) Singer

former name: *Pleurotellus porrigens*
Pleurocybella: a small head attached on one side (Greek)
porrigens: stretched out and up (Latin)

Cosmopolitan. The popular name "angel wings" seems very apt when finding these delicate white brackets on an old conifer log, seemingly ready to fly in all directions, especially when a ray of sunshine falls on, and through, them. This is a species of the Pacific Northwest, growing in old coniferous forests, particularly on hemlock logs. Fruits in the fall. The brackets are small and thin, but enough can usually be collected for a meal. They are said to be edible and good.

cap	white, thin, fan-shaped, fleshy brackets which grow from the top and the sides of the log in all directions; inrolled margin, up to 6 cm wide and 8 cm high.
gills	white, close, very narrow, many intermediates, some forks, growing fanlike toward the place of attachment to the log.
spore print	white.
stalk	none or maybe a sliver.
flesh	white, very thin.
odour	none.
taste	good.

king's coat

p.89-2

Tricholomopsis rutilans (Fries) Singer

Tricholomopsis: resembling Tricholoma (Greek)
rutilans: reddening (Latin)

Cosmopolitan; this widespread species occurs in Europe, Japan and in North America. Grows on dead conifer wood or roots or on lignin-rich humus in mixed or conifer forests; fruiting in summer and fall in Western Canada. It is said to be a mediocre edible.

cap	red hair on a yellow background; young are often solid red, breaking up in small scales or tufts with age, but still matted in the centre; up to 10 cm across.
gills	yellow or white with yellow edges, broad, more or less adnate, serrate, many intermediates.
spore print	white.
stalk	the same as the cap with less fibrils, base yellow and a bit swollen, up to 8 cm tall and 1.5 cm thick.
taste & odour	faint.

queen's coat

p.89-3

Tricholomopsis decora (Fries) Singer

decora: beautiful (Latin)

Cosmopolitan; widespread distribution, but not found as often as the reddening species. It is quite similar but smaller, and the yellow cap has less hair, which is brown or blackish instead of red; grows on old conifer logs, fruiting in the fall. Edible but not very good.

cap	yellow with brownish black hairs, denser in the centre, convex at first then flattening with a small depression, up to 6 cm across.
gills	yellow, adnate or short decurrent, serrate, intermediates.
spore print	white.
stalk	yellow, equal, smooth or with darker fibrils near the base, up to 6 cm tall and 1 cm thick.
flesh	yellow, thin.
taste & odour	very slight.

velvet foot

p.89-4

Flammulina fennae Bas

Flammulina: like a small flame (Latin)
fennae: named by Dutch mycologist C. Bas after his wife Fenna

A very interesting species, the genus *Flammulina* is easily recognized by its brown velvety stalk, brownish cap and its large tight tufts growing on wood. From correspondence with mycologists S. A. Redhead in Ottawa and C. Bas in Leiden (Holland), I have learned that *F. fennae* is one of our two velvet foot species. Dr. Bas writes that "this species is very similar to the velvet foot or very famous Japanese enoki mushroom, the cosmopolitan *F. velutipes*, but differs by shorter and broader spores (average length-width ratio <2). The North American material with such spores is, however, brighter and deeper coloured than the European *F. fennae* and may represent a still undescribed species."

F. fennae fruits very late in the fall, the fruiting bodies even withstand some frost, reviving when thawing out and sporulating again. Where winters are mostly rainy, it fruits all winter. Growing on both alder and spruce wood, it needs a cold shock to start fruiting.

cap	chestnut to orange-brown with a yellow margin; glistening with a glutinous layer when damp; very young specimens are buff to yellowish and rounded, flattening later and darkening; up to 7 cm across.
gills	off-white; close in small specimens, distant in mature; serrate, adnexed, broad, intermediates and veins.
spore print	white.
stalk	pale brown in very small young specimens; velvety, deep chestnut on the lower part in mature ones, pale at the apex and orange in between (see illustration), up to 7 cm tall and 1 cm thick.

flesh	white, stalks are tough (when it is grown inside, the complete cultivated mushroom is tender and pale in colour).
odour	faint.
taste	good (cap only).

western Hypsizygus   p.89-5

Hypsizygus marmoreus (Peck) Bigelow

Hypsizygus: carrying high (Greek)
marmoreus: marbled (Latin)

North American species; occurring in Canada from coast to coast and north to the Yukon. Preferring poplar wood in the west and birch and maple in other parts of the country. These mushrooms sometimes occur in very large groups in a crotch of a dead tree or in smaller groups on a stump. They can have very long stalks. The gills range from adnexed to decurrent. This species of *Hypsizygus* is found in the west, while another species, *H. ulmarius*, occurs more in the east. Sometimes it takes a long time to develop, and the slower the development the tougher it gets, even becoming woody. Edible but not very good . Fruiting in summer and fall.

cap	light buff with brownish watery spots in the centre of the cap; convex at first with edge curved in, flattening out in maturity; becoming irregular with wavy edges because of crowded space in the bunch, up to 12 cm across.
gills	off-white; relatively close when young, then moderately distant; serrate; can be adnexed, adnate or decurrent; intermediates.
spore print	white.
stalk	white, smooth, tall, often irregular, bent and joined at the base with others in the group.
flesh	white, smooth, solid, tough.
odour	aromatic, anise, apricot or faint.

OMPHALINOID AND CANTHARELLOID SPECIES   funnel and navel mushrooms

Illustrated on page 90 are a group of ten small species belonging to eight genera which do not fit in with the main genera of this family.

All have confluent stalks and cap, a more or less funnel-shaped cap, with a navel in the cap centre and decurrent gills. Three species are from the genus *Omphalina* (Greek for having a navel), and some others are called Omphalinoid because they look like *Omphalina*.

Ripartites has brown spores, which is surprising for such a pale mushroom.

Cantharellula and *Cantharellopsis*, which are called cantharelloid (resembling the chanterelle), both have interesting, conspicuously forked gills. *Chrysomphalina* is actually related to the Cantharellaceae. The most interesting small mushroom on this plate is *Phytoconis*. This is the fungal partner of an alga; together they form a lichen.

Myxomphalia and *Rickenella* species complete the collection.

orange pin mushroom   p.90-1

Rickenella fibula (Fries) Raithelhuber

Rickenella: named after A. Ricken, French mycologist, 1851-1921
fibula: hairpin

Cosmopolitan; growing in moss in the Pacific Northwest and across Canada in mossy places.

cap	orange, hygrophanous, smooth with serrated edge, incurved when young, navel in the centre, up to 2 cm across.
gills	white to buff, decurrent, thin, wavy, with cross veins, many intermediates.
spore print	white.
stalk	orange, tall, slim, 4 cm tall and 0.1 cm thick.
flesh	orange, thin.
odour	none.

small white umbrella mushroom

Phytoconis ericetorum (Persoon: Fries) Redhead & Kuyper

Phytoconis: plantdust (Greek)
ericetorum: of the heath or open places (Latin)

Cosmopolitan. This very interesting species is always found as part of the lichen *Botrydina vulgaris*. The small white mushrooms are the fruiting bodies of the fungus partner in the alga-fungus symbiotic relationship that makes up a lichen. It is one of the most common gilled mushrooms in the Arctic and extends southward across Canada to the cooler places in the U.S. Because it is part of a lichen, it can survive on rocks. The spore print is white, but in the Pacific Northwest there is one variant with a yellow spore print. Unlike most other basidiomycetes, it can have 1, 2, 3, or 4 spores on each basidium. Not only does it grow in the far north, it also occurs high up in the Rocky Mountains, where I found it in many places. Usually it is all white, but once in a while it has a brown stalk and brown markings on the cap.

cap	off-white, smooth, with navel and grooves, rounded, looking like a small umbrella; up to 2.5 cm across.
gills	off-white, distant, decurrent, cross veins.
spore print	white.
stalk	most often white, sometimes brown, pliant, thin, 2 - 4 cm tall and 0.1 cm thick.
flesh	white, thin.

very dark Omphalina

Omphalina obscurata Reid

Omphalina: possessing a navel (Greek)
obscurata: very dark (Latin)

North American; rare, small dark mushrooms which are almost invisible; about the same shape as *Phytoconis*. This specimen was found in short grass along the road in the Rockies.

cap	dark brown; incurved margin at first, then umbrella shaped with navel; striate margin, up to 2 cm across.
gills	dark brown, distant, decurrent.
spore print	white.
stalk	dark brown, bent, up to 2.5 cm tall and 0.1 cm thick.
flesh	brown.

brown goblet

Omphalina epichysium (Persoon: Fries) Quélet

epichysium: a toasting glass (Greek)

Cosmopolitan; grows in mixed or coniferous woods on rotten, moss-covered logs. The name indicates the goblet shape of the mushroom.

cap	dull dark brown, drying up lighter, hygrophanous, deep navel, striate margin, deeper funnel shape than the others, 2 cm across.
gills	brown, close, narrow, many intermediates.
spore print	white.
stalk	brown, hollow, smooth, fuzzy white mycelium at the base, 2 cm tall and 0.2 cm thick.
flesh	brown, thin.

burn site mushroom

Myxomphalia maura (Fries) Hora

Myxomphalia: with slimy navel (Greek)
maura: dark (Greek)

Cosmopolitan; this species occurs on burnt wood and on burn sites in northern mixed or coniferous woods.

cap	grey brown, convex, cuticle glutinous when damp, margin stays incurved, streaked, up to 3 cm across.

gills	whitish to pale grey, close, decurrent and arched because the cap stays curved down, relatively broad.
spore print	white.
stalk	grey brown, equal, up to 4 cm tall and 0.2 cm thick.
flesh	grey.

brown-spored navel mushroom

p.90-6

Ripartites tricholoma (Albertini & Schweinitz: Fries) Karsten

Ripartites: living along a stream (Latin)
tricholoma: with hairy fringe (Greek)

Cosmopolitan; this is a genus with few species. It looks very much like a small *Tricholoma,* but it has light brown spores. Various authors have placed it in Cortinariaceae or Paxillaceae or Tricholomataceae, but it still is an orphan.

cap	pale pink, domed, hair standing out in all directions, up to 2.5 cm across.
gills	pale pink, short-decurrent and arched, narrow.
spore print	light brown.
stalk	pale pink, bent, enlarging toward the base, large lump of white mycelium at the base, up to 4 cm tall and 0.3 cm thick at the top.
flesh	white in cap, pink and semitransparent in stalk and over the gills.
odour	delicate.

leather-brown Clitocybe

p.90-7

Clitocybe diatreta (Fries) Kummer

diabreta: widespread (Greek)

Cosmopolitan but not common. This one was found under spruce. Misidentified as *Omphalina* by the author and corrected by S. Redhead: under a microscope clamp connections in the mycelium prove that this is a Clitocybe more at home on p. 70.

cap	yellowish buff, streaked with some olive colour, hygrophanous, rounded with navel, edge curved in, up to 2.5 cm across.
gills	off-white to yellowish, decurrent, many intermediates, relatively narrow.
spore print	white.
stalk	off-white to brownish, 2 cm tall and 0.2 cm thick.
flesh	whitish with brownish layer under stalk cuticle and over the gills.

fork-gilled funnel

p.90-8

Cantharellopsis prescotii (Weinmann) Kuyper

Cantharellopsis: resembling Cantharellus (Greek)
prescotii: named after Prescot, probably a collector

Cosmopolitan; grows under spruce in sphagnum moss in coniferous and mixed forest. Considered rare in North America. I found it in four places in Alberta.

cap	ivory colour, smooth, with a depression in the centre, incurved margin, 1 - 2.5 cm across.
gills	white, decurrent, close, often (not always) strongly forked, narrow.
spore print	white.
stalk	white, equal, slim, up to 4 cm long and 0.3 cm thick, sometimes slight thickening toward the base.
flesh	white, solid.

grayling

p.90-9

Cantharellula umbonata (Gmelin: Fries) Singer

Cantharellula: somewhat like Cantharellus (Greek)
umbonata: with a knob (Latin)

Cosmopolitan; this medium-sized grey mushroom occurs in conifer bogs. I found it under spruce in Lycopodium and in a larch bog in sphagnum. Fruiting in fall and summer. It is said to be edible, but only after cooking.

cap	light to dark grey; a bit depressed at first but then developing a small knob in the centre; edge inrolled when young with unrolled wavy edge when mature, up to 4 cm across.
gills	white with grey tints, thickish, narrow, strongly forked, decurrent.
spore print	white to greyish.
stalk	grey, felty, equal or gradually thickening toward the base, up to 6 cm tall and 0.5 cm thick.
flesh	white, soft, staining slightly reddish when cut.
odour	faint.

golden-gilled mushroom   p.90-10

Chrysomphalina chrysophylla (Fries) Clemençon

Chrysomphalina: golden navel cap (Greek)
chrysophylla: golden gilled (Greek)

Cosmopolitan; growing on rotting conifer logs. With its bright orange gills, this species is easily recognized. *Hygrophoropsis aurantiaca* is another mushroom with very bright gills, but they are conspicuously forked (see illustration on p. 37). Occurs in the Pacific Northwest. The specimens illustrated were collected in the Rocky Mountains. Also reported from Eastern Canada and the U.S., mostly in the north.

cap	brown appressed hair on buff to orange background giving a streaked look; rounded at first with pronounced navel, flattening later; up to 4.5 cm across.
gills	bright orange to apricot, broad, distant with many intermediates, decurrent.
spore print	varies from white to yellow.
stalk	orange with a white base, hollow (not always), slightly enlarging toward the base, up to 3 cm tall and 0.3 cm thick at the apex.
flesh	pale orange.

Genera PHAEOLEPIOTA and CYSTODERMA

Phaeolepiota and *Cystoderma* species occur on the ground among conifer needles or on wood debris; they are saprophytic. The fruiting bodies are covered with a granular veil which separates at the cap edge, leaving the stalk gaitered or booted; cap and stalk are continuous, gills adnate to adnexed.

Cystoderma: Greek for blistery skin, which refers to the granular cuticle. The species have a creamy white spore print. They look somewhat like colourful Lepiotas, and they are placed in that family by some authors; however, Lepiotas have free gills and Cystodermas do not.

Phaeolepiota: which means sunny *Lepiota* in Greek, indicates by its name that it resembles Lepiotas as well. The cap has a strong orange-yellow colouring, and as the spores ripen, the gills turn ochre yellow. The spore print is orange to ochre yellow. This seems to be a "foundling" species, having been classified in various genera, but in this guide it is placed with *Cystoderma* species because of its physical resemblance to them.

gold cap   p.91-1

Phaeolepiota aurea (Mattirolo: Fries) Maire: Konrad & Maublanc

aurea: golden (Latin)

Cosmopolitan, but uncommon. It does not occur in eastern North America but is fairly common in the Pacific Northwest. Growing on rich soil and wood debris in coniferous and deciduous forests, on sawdust piles and along roads. Fruiting in the fall. These were found along the highway in the Rocky Mountains. This species is so easily recognized that it is a pity that it cannot be eaten, but it gives some people indigestion.

cap	golden ochre to orange, fine granular surface which rubs off; convex at first, becoming irregular in older specimens, up to 25 cm across.
gills	pale honey colour at first, yellow ochre in maturity, adnexed, many intermediates.
spore print	yellow ochre, almost orange.

stalk	same colour as the cap below the ring and white above, massive, club shaped, up to 15 cm tall, 4 cm thick at the apex and 6 cm lower down.
partial veil	covering both gills and stalk base resulting in a collar-like persistent ring; white on top and granular on the outside, continuing downward as a sheath on the stalk.
flesh	pale yellowish, solid; in the mature specimens there is a thick yellowish layer under the cuticle.
odour	peppery.
taste	pleasant.

conifer Cystoderma   p.91-2

Cystoderma fallax A. H. Smith & Singer

fallax: fallacious, misleading (Latin)

North American species; it does occur in Québec but is more frequent west of the Great Lakes; primarily a Pacific Northwest species. It looks like a small brown version of the golden Phaeolepiota, but the spore print is white; fruiting in summer. Edibility unknown.

cap	beautiful warm chestnut brown or rusty brown, surface granular, convex, fringed with bits of veil, up to 5 cm across.
gills	off-white, adnexed, close.
spore print	white.
stalk	same colour as the cap and granular below the ring, top buff, club- shaped base; sometimes equal; up to 6 cm tall and 1 cm thick at the top.
partial veil	collar-like membranous ring plus sheath, the ring can stand up collar-like or can be more crumbly.
flesh	buff to pale brownish or off-white.
odour	weak.

vermilion Cystoderma   p.91-3

Cystoderma cinnabarinum (Albertini & Schweinitz: Secretan) Fayod

cinnabarinum: colour of cinnabar or vermilion (Greek)

Cosmopolitan; not common but I find it every few years in moss under spruce. Fruiting in August, often in the company of some *Hydnum repandum*. Edible but mediocre and hardly worthwhile.

cap	beautiful vermilion colour, granular surface; spherical at first, then flattening; up to 8 cm across.
gills	white or creamy, adnate to adnexed, close, intermediates.
spore print	white.
stalk	same colour as the cap under the ring but broken up in scales showing white underneath; also white mycelium at the base, above the ring either white or pink or both; up to 6 cm tall and 1 cm thick at the top.
partial veil	consisting of scaly sheath and ring which is crumbly and evanescent, often bits of it on the cap edge.
flesh	creamy white.
odour	weak.

unspotted Cystoderma   p.91-4

Cystoderma amiantinum (Scopoli: Fries) Fayod

amiantinum: pure, spotless (Greek)

Cosmopolitan; not common but widespread small mushroom, growing in moss in mixed woods under conifers or birch; fruiting in the fall; found it on Vancouver Island in November.

cap	pale orange to orange brown, fine granular surface, small umbo, up to 3 cm across.
gills	white, close, adnate.
spore print	white.
stalk	base same as cap, paler or the same colour above ring; up to 5 cm tall and 0.5 cm thick.

| partial veil | resulting in a stand-up collar and sheath, sometimes the ring is more wispy (see illustration, in the middle at the top). |
| flesh | pale buff. |

mountain Cystoderma p.91-5

Cystoderma amiantinum forma *montanum* (Scopoli: Fries) Fayod

Cosmopolitan; the mountain form has a more intense colour and more scaly stalk (Dähncke 1980), otherwise it fits the description of no. 4. It is very small and can be found under spruce in moss.

Family XERULACEAE

Fleshy fungi with cap, stalk, gills and white spore print; all have rhizoid bundles of mycelium at the stalk base and some genera have large pseudorhizas. The members of this family were formerly included in the Tricholomataceae, a very large group, which is gradually being sorted out into groups with closer relations to each other. S. A. Redhead mentions that some genera in the Xerulaceae produce important antibiotics in the fight against cancer.

The following genera are discussed:

Xerula (Greek for that which relates to dry materials): The family is named after *Xerula*. The only member of this genus I found was in Holland and was *X. radicata*, which means rooted. It looked like a *Collybia*, but I was surprised by the very long rootlike structure hidden in the ground; this is called a pseudorhiza and is a continuation of the stalk.The cap of the specimen was 7.5 cm across, but its overall length, stalk and pseudorhiza, was 36 cm. I would love to include it, but I have not found it in Canada. *Xerula* does not grow directly on wood.

Hemimycena: The Greek name translates literally as half a *Mycena*, but it probably has to do with the hemispherical shape of the small caps. It is related to *Mycena*, but *Hemimycena* species are white and lack pigments, while Mycenas come in many colours. Notice the small rhizoids.

Mycenella (Greek for small *Mycena*): Very small mushrooms with interesting spore ornamentation and cystidia. I have found a lot of small fruiting bodies while painting in the woods. Luckily my friend Scott Redhead was interested in them as well, and, more importantly, he knows what they are. Notice the small rhizoids here, too.

Strobilurus (Greek for living on cones): This is a small genus.The species grow on fallen or buried cones of conifers and even of Magnolias. The mushrooms are small with a thin cap and stalk and crowded, narrow gills.

Xeromphalina (Greek for a dry mushroom with a navel): Small mushrooms, often with orange, ochre and red-brown colours, decurrent gills, tan-coloured mycelium and rhizoids. It has the capacity to revive when moistened after drying up, like the fairy ring mushroom.

Baeospora (Greek for with small spores): It grows on mossy, well-decayed wood; the conspicuous pseudorhiza can grow through the wood into the ground. Thin consistency and extremely crowded, narrow gills are other characteristics.

Megacollybia (Greek for large *Collybia*): These mushrooms can grow to a very large size. Characteristics include white, broad gills, strongly rooting stalk and no veil.

Mycena (Greek for a fungus): The genus contains many small, fleshy, white-spored, gilled mushrooms, with either a conic or convex cap. When young, the edge of the cap touches the stalk; the gills are beautifully spaced, and mostly adnexed. *Mycena* species are saprophytic, growing on the ground and decaying wood or plants. These mushrooms are easy to identify to the genus level, but are difficult to identify to species without knowing their odour, taste and colour. The stalk of the mushroom has to be crushed to get the odour and broken to see if there is latex. A microscope is important as well to examine the spores. Several of my mycological friends were extremely interested in this genus, and I sent them specimens that they identified. That is why so many species are included in this guide.

slender white bog mushroom   p.93-1
Hemimycena gracilis (Quélet) Singer

gracilis: slender (Latin)

Cosmopolitan; a very small, saprophytic, all-white mushroom growing in groups in boggy areas on leaf and needle duff.

cap	white, hemispherical, thin, striate, sometimes with minute umbo; up to 1.2 cm across.
gills	white, decurrent and arched, relatively distant with connecting veins, intermediates.
spore print	white.
stalk	white, slender, thickening somewhat near the cap; up to 4 cm tall and 0.1 cm thick; rhizoids at the base.
flesh	white, thin.
taste & odour	none.

miniature Mycena   p.93-2
Mycenella margaritispora (Lange) Singer

margaritispora: spores like pearls (Greek)

Cosmopolitan; grows on or near stumps of deciduous trees in moss; very small, relatively long stalk; differs from *Mycena* in spore ornamentation and other mycroscopic features.

cap	grey , felty, small umbo and upturned margin, up to 1 cm across.
gills	light grey, free, crowded.
spore print	white.
stalk	grey, darker than cap, thin, bent, rhizoids; up to 3 cm tall and 0.1 cm thick.
flesh	grey, very thin.
taste & odour	none.

western cone mushroom   p.93-3
Strobiluris occidentalis Wells & Kempton

occidentalis: of the west (Latin)

Northwest North American species; common in Alaska, along the Pacific coast, in the Rocky Mountains and in boreal mixed forest. Growing on old cones (sometimes buried), cone bracts and needles of pine, spruce and Douglas fir, also on leaf stems of poplar.

cap	buff to yellow-brown to dark brown, smooth, flat, thin; up to 1 cm across.
gills	white, crowded, narrow.
spore print	white.
stalk	white apex, mostly brown, thin, rhizoids; up to 4 cm tall and 0.1 cm thick.
flesh	white, thin.
taste & odour	not noticeable or not distinctive.

Douglas fir cone mushroom   p.93-4
Strobiluris trullisatus (Murrill) Lennox

trullisatus: resembling a small planting scoop (Latin)

North American species; usually growing on cones of Douglas fir. This one grew on an old spruce cone. Profuse orange mycelium grew around the stalk base, which is typical for this species.

cap	warm brown fading to buff; hygrophanous, striate, smooth margin; up to 2 cm across.
gills	light brown, close.
spore print	white.

stalk	white apex, the rest is orange; velvety, cartilaginous, dry; floccose orange mycelium at the base and on the cone around it.
flesh	thin, tough, orange.
taste & odour	not distinctive.

orange fuzzyfoot   p.93-5

Xeromphalina campanella (Batsch: Fries) Kühner & Maire

campanella: small bell (Latin)

Cosmopolitan and widespread species; one of the most common in coniferous forests of the northern hemisphere; growing on well-rotted, moss-covered logs or stumps; secondary invaders of wood, which means that it is not the first saprophytic fungus to grow on a log. Fruiting in a cool time of the year: spring or fall. Dry specimens revive when soaked in water.

cap	bright orange, fading to ochre and brown, with a navel in the centre, striate, edge inrolled at first; up to 2.5 cm across.
gills	yellowish to orange ochre, decurrent, distant, intermediates and veins.
spore print	white.
stalk	orange top, rufus base, velvety, stiff, up to 3 cm tall and 0.2 cm thick.
flesh	ochrish, pliant, thin.
taste & odour	none.

rufus fuzzyfoot   p.93-6

Xeromphalina fraxinophila A. H. Smith

fraxinophila: loving the ash tree (*Fraxinus*) (Latin)

Cosmopolitan; this species was first found by A. H. Smith in Michigan on the leaf and branch debris of ash trees, but it grows on the litter of birch and poplar as well and also on spruce and balsam fir needles. Fruiting in the fall.

cap	orange to yellow brown to chestnut colour, darker in the centre, deep navel in rounded cap, margin uneven when expanded; up to 4 cm across.
gills	white, yellow or ochrish, decurrent and arched; distant with intermediates or interveined, sometimes close; relatively broad.
spore print	white.
stalk	chestnut to dark brown with tan mycelium at the base; up to 5 cm tall and 0.3 cm thick, sometimes black rhizoids.
flesh	same colour as the outside.
taste & odour	none.

lavender Baeospora   p.93-7

Baeospora myriadophylla (Peck) Singer

myriadophylla: with 10,000 gills (Greek)

Cosmopolitan; saprophytic, growing on well decayed wood of both deciduous and coniferous trees.

cap	lavender, when maturing the centre turns the colour of leather, hygrophanous; thin, flat, sometimes small, low umbo; up to 4 cm across.
gills	lavender, crowded, narrow, nearly free, intermediates.
spore print	white.
stalk	lavender, tall, bent, bottom half thickening and very woolly, hollow; up to 7 cm tall and 0.5 cm thick at the top.
flesh	pale lavender, thin.
taste & odour	not distinct.

rooting broadgill

p.93-8

Megacollybia platyphylla (Persoon: Fries) Kotlaba & Pouzar

platyphylla: with broad gills (Greek)

Cosmopolitan; this mushroom is common in eastern North America. In Hudson, P.Q., I measured one 27 cm across and with a stalk 7 cm thick at the apex. Also common in the Pacific Northwest, in the mountains and along the coast. It grows in groups on, or near, stumps of both deciduous and coniferous trees; edible when young with caution, since some people cannot digest them and the flavour is poor as well. This mushroom has gone under quite a few different names in the past, but it is placed in Xerulaceae for biochemical and anatomical reasons.

cap	dull velvety brown to grey brown with radiating fibres; convex at first, then flattening; up to 15 cm across, but sometimes much bigger.
gills	white to bone coloured, distant, broad, serrate, intermediates.
spore print	white.
stalk	white, long fibres, sometimes twisted; a large bundle of pseudorhizas at the base, hollow, up to 12 cm tall and 3 cm thick at the apex.
flesh	white.
taste	not much flavour.
odour	faint or fragrant.

bleeding Mycena

p.95-1

Mycena haematopus (Fries) Quélet

haematopus: with bleeding foot (Greek)

Cosmopolitan; saprophytic, growing in clusters on very decayed wood; fruiting in spring and fall; the dark red juice from a broken stalk is very obvious. Common in northwest North America.

cap	purplish red to red-brown crown, pinkish buff margin; striate; egg shaped when young, expanding to lovely chinese hat shape; scalloped margin extending beyond the gills; up to 4 cm across.
gills	white at first, then buff, sometimes with red margins; adnexed to almost free, beautifully spaced, intermediates.
spore print	white.
stalk	dark crimson, white hairy base, hollow, showing dark red latex when broken; up to 8 cm tall and 0.3 cm thick.
flesh	pink to crimson in the stalk and above the gills.
taste	mild to bitter.
odour	none.

orange Mycena or Lea's Mycena

p.95-2

Mycena leaiana (Berkeley) Saccardo

leaiana: named after Thomas Gibson Lea, 1785-1844, an Ohio mushroom collector

North American species; growing on deciduous logs and stumps in caespitose groups. Alexander Smith wrote in 1980 that he found it curious that this species had not been found on alder or other deciduous woods in the Pacific Northwest. A. J. P. Oort, a Dutch mycologist, and I found it in Québec on a beech log, and later I also found it along the Alaska Highway, growing near the ground on low woody plant debris (dwarf dogwood, *Cornus canadensis*). Both collections are shown in the illustration. Said to be edible.

cap	orange, sticky when wet, fading, hygrophanous, slightly striate margin, irregular shapes, up to 4 cm across.
gills	light orange, adnexed, broad, distant, intermediates, brilliant orange edges.
spore print	white.
stalk	orange, bent, hollow, caespitose, orange mycelium at the base, up to 10 cm tall and 0.4 cm thick.
flesh	white, quite tough, orange cuticle.
taste	faint.
odour	slightly mealy.

toque Mycena
p.95-3

Mycena galericulata (Fries) S. F. Gray

galericulata: with a small hat (Latin)

Cosmopolitan; widespread in the entire temperate zone of the northern hemisphere; growing on well-decayed deciduous wood in caespitose clusters, sometimes in great quantities; also on leaves; inedible.

cap	smoky brown to buff with darker centre, bell shaped at first, then flattening with small umbo; smooth or finely striate; up to 4 cm across.
gills	first white, later pink, adnexed with a small tooth, relatively broad.
spore print	off-white.
stalk	same colour as cap, caespitose; up to 10 cm tall and 0.3 cm thick.
flesh	white.
taste & odour	mealy.

Algerian Mycena
p.95-4

Mycena algeriensis R. Maire in Kühner, sensu A. H.Smith

algeriensis: of Algeria; named by R. Maire, a French Algerian (Latin)

Cosmopolitan; growing in caespitose clusters on decaying wood (willow in this case); fruiting in cool weather, spring or fall; this one may have long rhizomorphs.

cap	very dark brown to charcoal black, hygrophanous, bell shaped, silky, up to 2 cm across.
gills	light grey, distant, narrow, adnexed.
spore print	white.
stalk	purplish brown, equal, white at the base, up to 6 cm tall and 0.2 cm thick (found once with a rhizomorph 9 cm long).
flesh	grey, sometimes white in the stalk.
odour	somewhat of raw potato.

yellow-edged Mycena
p.95-5

Mycena citrinomarginata Gillet

citrinomarginata: with yellow edges (Latin)

Cosmopolitan; very small mushroom, growing under conifers on needle and wood debris; fruiting in summer and fall.

cap	yellow with brown crown, pointed, striate margin, up to 1.2 cm across.
gills	white with yellow edge or all yellow, narrow, intermediates.
spore print	white.
stalk	yellow, some brown in the middle; up to 6 cm tall and 0.1 cm thick.
flesh	thin, yellowish.
odour	faint.

parabola Mycena
p.95-6

Mycena parabolica (Fries) Quélet

parabolica: like a parabola (Greek)

Cosmopolitan; this dark grey mushroom grows in small clusters on decaying wood. The striations follow the contour of the conic cap all the way; growing on both coniferous and deciduous wood.

cap	dark grey, strongly striate, hygrophanous, velvety, conic; up to 3 cm across.
gills	pale grey with white edges, distant, intermediates, adnexed.
spore print	white.
stalk	same colour as cap with hairy white base; up to 5 cm tall and 0.2 cm thick.
flesh	grey, thin, fragile.
odour	none.

pink or lilac Mycena

Mycena pura (Fries) Quélet

pura: clean (Latin)

Worldwide distribution, even above the arctic circle; grows on both hardwood and softwood duff; singly or in groups, but not in caespitose clusters. One of the biggest species of the genus, *M. pura* varies a great deal in colour and has been reported as **poisonous**.

cap	pinkish or purplish or in between, convex, striate border, hygrophanous, up to 4 cm across.
gills	same colour as the cap, adnate sinuate, distant with connecting veins and intermediates.
spore print	white.
stalk	same colour as the cap with white hairy base; up to 8 cm tall and 0.5 cm thick.
flesh	pink or purple depending on the exterior, sometimes white in the cap.
taste	mild.
odour	when crushed, it smells of radish.

white-stemmed Mycena

p.97-2

Mycena niveipes Murrill

niveipes: with snow-white foot (Latin)

North American; this species is widespread, but not common; grows all over North America on duff or woody debris of deciduous trees; fruiting from summer to fall.

cap	pale grey to greyish buff; egg shaped when young, like a chinese hat with umbo when mature; striate margin, up to 3.5 cm across.
gills	pale grey, sinuate-adnexed, broad, beautifully spaced.
spore print	white.
stalk	apex a bit grey, the rest white; white mycelium on the base, up to 7 cm tall and 0.3 cm thick.
flesh	pale grey, thin, fragile.
taste	sharp.
odour	chemical.

dark brown Mycena

p.97-3

Mycena macrocystidia Singer

macrocystidia: with large cystidia (Greek)

North American species; growing on spruce needles; like many of the small Mycenas, this one can only be identified with the help of a microscope.

cap	dark brown, unchanging, convex, smooth, up to 2.5 cm across.
gills	white, practically free, close, intermediates.
spore print	white.
stalk	smoky brown, hollow.
flesh	white.

sand Mycena

p.97-4

Mycena (prob.) *psammicola* (Berkeley & Broome) Saccardo

psammicola: living in sand (Greek)

North American species; growing on cone bracts and *Picea* needles. This small mushroom is distinct, with its narrowly conical cap and brown gills, because it looks like a *Galerina*, but it has white spores.

cap	reddish brown crown; ochre, striate margin, bell shaped, hygrophanous, up to 1 cm across.
gills	mocha brown, close, adnate-ascendant, narrow.
spore print	white.

stalk	buff to brown, whitish hairy base, up to 4 cm tall and 0.15 cm thick.
taste	of radish.
odour	of iodine.

pewter Mycena   p.97-5

Mycena stannea (Fries) Quélet

stannea: pewter colour (Latin)

Cosmopolitan; growing on duff of leaves as well as of needles in mixed forest; fruiting in the fall.

cap	grey brown, conical or convex, silky, striate margin, up to 2 cm across.
gills	pale grey, distant, intermediates, narrow.
spore print	white.
stalk	same colour as cap; stiff white hair on base; up to 7 cm tall and 0.3 cm thick.
flesh	thin, greyish, fragile.
taste & odour	none.

conical Mycena   p.97-6

Mycena pectinata Murrill

pectinata: combed (Latin)

North American; growing in mixed forest on duff of coniferous and deciduous trees.

cap	grey-brown with paler edge, narrowly conical; up to 1.5 cm across.
gills	white, close, adnate-sinuate, narrow, intermediates.
spore print	white.
stalk	brown with white woolly base; up to 5 cm tall and 0.2 cm thick.
flesh	greyish.

common Mycena   p.97-7

Mycena vulgaris (Fries) Quélet

vulgaris: common (Latin)

Cosmopolitan; growing in moss on the needle duff of Douglas fir in the Rocky Mountains.

cap	fox-coloured crown with lighter margin, convex or with small umbo, very sticky, needles cling to it, grooved; up to 1.5 cm across.
gills	greyish white, short, decurrent and arched, relatively distant, intermediates.
spore print	white.
stalk	buff top, brown base, thin, up to 3.5 cm tall and 0.1 cm thick.
flesh	greyish, thin, tough.
taste & odour	dirty, unpleasant.

Family LACCARIACEAE

A small family with only one genus so far. Colourful mushrooms, they have rounded caps with fine scales; thick, distant, coloured gills, becoming powdery from spores; a white spore print; a tough, fibrous, often twisted, tall, hollow stalk and coloured thin flesh. They may either be saprophytic or live in a mycorrhizal relationship with various trees; usually occurring in damp areas, in contrast to species like *Suillus grevillei*, which can only survive when it has a mycorrhizal relationship with a larch. The genus and family are named for their colourful appearance (*lac* is the Persian word for paint or varnish). When I find *Laccaria laccata*, the most common species of this group, the fresh mushroom cap reminds me of the lovely lacquered trays and boxes from the far east.

The genus is often said to be edible, but not very good. I would advise against trying any, because *Laccaria amethystea* has been found to accumulate an astonishing amount of arsenicum. This very poisonous element is present in all living creatures in very low concentrations, but the amethyst Laccaria gets "constipated with it," as one scientist told me, a very apt description. It is not known whether the other species in the genus are also collectors of arsenicum. (See *Coolia*, magazine of the Dutch mycological Society, 1980, no. 4; the whole issue is devoted to research on "Accumulation of potentially poisonous elements in mushrooms.")

These are very durable mushrooms, existing longer than usual for gilled mushrooms. They can fade or turn dark and grow into interesting shapes; they can stay small, grow big, stay single or grow in clusters, all without rotting. That is why I painted more specimens than usual in each species to show all stages.

auburn Laccaria   p.98-1

Laccaria purpureo-badia D. Reid

purpureo-badia: purplish red brown (Latin)

Cosmopolitan, but rare in Europe as well as here. In its long mushroom life it grows into elegant shapes. A hole may develop in the thin flesh of the cap above the stalk, and inside the stalk, the colour is as deep auburn as the cap. I found this mushroom growing among ferns in a spruce-birch bog.

cap	purplish auburn; convex at first, then flattening, finally with irregular wavy edges; small scales on surface, up to 5 cm across.
gills	pink at first, then dark purplish red-brown with a powdery look from the spores and eroded edges; thick, adnate-sinuate, distant, intermediates.
spore print	white.
stalk	same colour as cap, fibrous, often twisted, slim, hollow, tough; up to 8 cm tall and 0.5 cm thick.
flesh	purplish pink when young, dark red when mature, thin, tough in stalk.
taste & odour	none.

amethyst Laccaria   p.98-2

Laccaria amethystea (Bulliard: Mérat) Murrill

amethystea: like amethyst, a purplish semi-precious stone (Greek)

Cosmopolitan; widespread; growing in deciduous as well as coniferous forest in open areas or the edge of the forest; in European research these mushrooms were found to be accumulating arsenicum, containing a much higher percentage in the flesh than surrounding plants and soil; to be avoided as **poisonous**.

cap	violet, more vivid when damp, discolouring to brownish, rounded or somewhat domed, flattening, margin sometimes uplifted, often with a dip in the centre, which can become a hole later on; surface has fine scales, this shows when drying; up to 5 cm across.
gills	violet, thick, broad, distant, intermediates; the gills have a powdery look from spores in maturity; finely eroded edges.
spore print	white, sometimes with a lilac tinge.
stalk	same colour as cap, stringy, often twisted, covered with tough short fibres all over; with white or violet-tinged mycelium at the base; hollow, up to 7 cm tall and 0.7 cm thick.
flesh	pale violet or purplish, thin, tough in stalk.
odour	mild.

orange Laccaria   p.98-3

Laccaria laccata (Scopoli: Fries) Cooke

laccata: painted or lacquered (Persian)

Worldwide distribution in the northern as well as the southern hemisphere. *Laccaria* is often called "the deceiver" in different languages because of the many variations in colour, shape and size; very common in Alaska, the Yukon and the prairies, but also in California. Fruiting in cool weather preferably (I found a sturdy, healthy-looking cluster, frozen in mid November on Vancouver Island). A striking characteristic is the colour clash between the pink gills and the orange cap. Occurs in boggy areas, woods, meadows and in silt close to a river — a very adaptable species.

cap	orange brown with buff margin or brownish yellow, fading to tan when dry, with fine fibres; rounded, often with dip, finally flattening with wavy margins; up to 6.5 cm across.
gills	pink or flesh coloured, thick, distant, veins; can have many intermediates, finely powdered look from spores.
spore print	white.
stalk	rusty, twisted, streaky, fibrous, tough, hollow; up to 12 cm tall and 0.7 cm thick.
flesh	thin, buff to tan.
odour	faint.

two-coloured Laccaria
p.98-4

Laccaria bicolor (Maire) Orton

bicolor: in two colours (Latin)

Cosmopolitan; growing in boggy areas in mixed forest on sandy soils; not often spotted, either because it is less spectacular than the other three or because it is really rare; thick gills; called "bicolor" because there are two colours present: tan in the cap and lilac in the stalk.

cap	brownish at first, soon fading to tan; rounded, fine scaliness when dry, dull, up to 3 cm across.
gills	at first pale lilac, then sandy; thick, relatively distant, adnate- sinuate with descending tooth, intermediates.
spore print	white.
stalk	sandy colour like cap but with amethyst blush and white to lavender -tinged mycelium at the base; up to 6 cm tall and 0.4 cm thick.
flesh	off-white to pale yellowish.
odour	none.

Family RHODOTACEAE

There is only one known species in the genus *Rhodotus* and only one genus in the Rhodotaceae family. This is called a monotype. The fungus has had many names and different temporary locations in the taxonomic system, but it is really one of a kind. The Greek name means rosy ear; when "ear" is used in the name, the mushroom is often stemless and attached to the wood like an ear to the side of a head with the gills looking like a fan. In my collections the stalks were either short or long and either central or eccentric but not stemless. The spores are heavily warted.

netted Rhodotus
p.99-1

Rhodotus palmatus (Bulliard: Fries) Maire

palmatus: with the pattern of the lines on the palm of a hand (Latin)

Cosmopolitan, but rarely fruiting wherever it occurs. Pegler writes that it sometimes is found on old posts and beams in England. I found mine on old poplar wood in mixed boreal forest and included all that I collected in the illustration. The fruiting bodies survive quite a long time, and the gelatinous pink layer on the cap dries up and the colour changes to yellow orange with a raised white network of veins. This is a real survivor and one of my favorites; not poisonous, but tough.

cap	gelatinous, apricot-pink surface at first and hemispherical, inrolled margin; changing when drying to yellow and orange with an off-white raised network of veins. Mostly of small size, but in damp weather can be much larger. When wet, it is smooth brick-red and orange, semitransparent, showing red veins in the flesh (see illustration), up to 9 cm across.
gills	salmon coloured; close in young specimens, distant in mature ones; intermediates, serrate.
spore print	cream to pinkish buff to salmon colour.

stalk	white, sometimes pink droplets at the apex, mostly up to 4 cm tall and 0.3 cm thick, but it can grow to a larger size with a 9 cm long stalk and 1.2 cm thick.
flesh	white or pink in cap, sometimes with red veins, thick and rubbery; white and tough in stalk.
odour	aromatic.

Family PLEUROTACEAE

The family is named for the genus *Pleurotus*, a Greek word meaning an ear on the side of the head, and the stalkless specimens do resemble ears somewhat. The family contains decay fungi, which recycle dead wood, and includes both white and brown rot genera. Brown rot is caused by fungi, growing on wood, that remove the cellulose from the wood and leave the lignin, which is brown. White rot fungi have a different enzyme system and leave a white pattern in the wood. A genus has either white-rot- or brown-rot-causing fungi. The Pleurotaceae are actually closer to the Polyporaceae (the polypores or shelf fungi) than to the other gilled mushrooms (Agaricales). All species grow on wood; the fruiting bodies are long living — they dry up rather than rot. All are useful in the conversion of dead wood resulting from windfall or logging operations.

This is one of my favorite groups; they are survivors in dry areas — not fruiting when it is too dry but surviving in very dry wood! This is probably the reason why the trainwrecker is so widespread It has been exported in lumber and railroad ties all over the world. Another well-known member of this family is the oyster mushroom, which is now a cultivated species. Japanese mycologists found that it produces a polysaccharide (a polymer of sugar), which may be a cancer cure. Eight genera are described:

smelly oyster   p.99-2

Phyllotopsis nidulans (Persoon: Fries) Singer

Phyllotopsis: looking like a gilled mushroom
nidulans: nesting, referring to the downy caps, like small nests (Latin)

Cosmopolitan; not common in Europe, but widespread in North America. In the Pacific Northwest, I found it most often on decaying birch. All parts are orange — cap, flesh and gills, and the latter are a deep saffron orange. The bark of the birch log may even take on some orange colouring, although the mycelium near the the place of attachment is white. The illustration shows how the gills are placed when it is growing on the side of a log or stump. When growing on the uneven top of a stump, the cap is elongated into what almost looks like a stalk, while on the smooth top surface of a horizontal log, the place of attachment is central and the fruiting body is flat like a saucer. Edible but the smell of old cabbage makes it unattractive; growing in small or large groups.

cap	orange; paler and felty in the centre, fringed margin, up to 9 cm across; sessile.
gills	deep orange or saffron; see illustration for fan shape or other pattern which depends on the position of the mushroom on the log.
spore print	salmon colour.
stalk	none.
flesh	two layers colour — one, orange and one, buff; deepest colour under the cuticle; gelatinous but tough.
odour	strongly of rotting cabbage, especially when warmed by the sun.

the oyster mushroom   p.101-1

Pleurotus ostreatus (Fries) Kummer

Pleurotus: side ear (Greek)
ostreatus: covered with oysters (literally: like a group of oysters) (Latin)

Cosmopolitan; a collective species! Mushrooms with this name occur in many places, but may look, smell and behave differently. They have been given the same name because they can be hybridized, meaning they will interbreed to produce a hybrid. In higher plants, orchids for instance, species from different genera are hybridized all the time. Personally I do not think that crossbreeding, by itself, can be the deciding factor for a species. The European winter oyster mushroom has a blue-grey to grey-brown cap, has stalks and grows on living but wounded trees; it fruits in winter and does not smell like anise. The variant found in boreal mixed forest and aspen parkland, which is described below, has white caps, no stalks and grows on stumps, logs and standing, dead, deciduous trees (mostly poplar). It fruits in the spring and smells strongly of aniseed. This is one of the early edible mushrooms, fruiting at the same time or soon after the morels. Longlasting, only pick young clusters to eat.

cap	off-white to creamy, yellowing with age, having the shape of an oyster, smooth, dull; margin inrolled at first, then expanding; laterally attached, in shelves, up to 30 cm across. As with *Phyllotopsis* (p. 99), the shape of the cap depends on its position — whether it is on the top or the side of a log.
gills	white, relatively close, becoming broad and distant with age, extending down to a point of attachment, sometimes forked or anastomosing; staining, with age, like the cap.
spore print	white, extremely prolific in the production of spores.
stalk	absent or, rarely, a very short stalk when growing on a horizontal surface (see illustration).
flesh	white, solid, very dense in dry weather, waterlogged and soggy in rainy periods.
taste	of anise.
odour	strongly of anise.

veiled oyster   p.101-2

Pleurotus dryinus (Fries) Kummer

dryinus: of wood (Greek)

Cosmopolitan, widely distributed but not common; growing most often on deciduous trees (alder or Manitoba maple), sometimes on coniferous trees; growing on dead sections or wounds of living trees; long-living fruiting bodies; good edible mushroom when young.

cap	white, felty, convex, later depressed, cap edge with a fringe from the partial veil; later with flat scales; yellowing with age; up to 15 cm across.
gills	white, close, long decurrent, with lines below the gills on the apex of the stalk, narrow, intermediates, serrate edges; sometimes anastomosing near the stalk.
spore print	white.
stalk	white, thick, firm; tomentose at first; later smooth and yellowing; central or eccentric; up to 8 cm tall and 3 cm thick.
partial veil	part of it stays on the cap edge, thin, some remnants on the stalk.
flesh	white, thick, firm, gets tough, dries rather than rots with age.
taste	pleasant when young.
odour	faint or fragrant.

black jelly oyster   p.102-1

Resupinatus applicatus (Batsch: Fries) S. F. Gray

Resupinatus: bent backwards (Latin)
applicatus: fixed against something (Latin)

Cosmopolitan; this small black bracket is very rubbery. When I found it on an old, damp, decaying log, I thought that I had a black jelly fungus, but with a striate top and gills on the bottom, it had to be the black jelly oyster fungus. The greyish-black jelly-like tissue layer under the thick cuticle gives it the rubbery look. The placement on the log affects the shape of the bracket. On the underside of the log, the brackets look like upside down cups.

cap	black, somewhat fuzzy near the place of attachment, lateral attachment on the side of a log, lateral to central when growing on the underside of the log, up to 2 cm across.
gills	brownish black with a powdery look from the spores; shaped like a fan, distant, many intermediates.

spore print white.
stalk none.
flesh greyish black, tougher than in jelly fungi.
odour none.

late fall oyster

p.102-2

Panellus serotinus (Persoon: Fries) Kühner

Panellus: small torch (Greek)
serotinus: late (Latin)

Cosmopolitan and widespread; found in the Pacific Northwest, especially in the coastal areas from Alaska south; also in the mountains. I found the specimens in the illustration in Vancouver late in November! Lovely colours in these fleshy brackets. It is said to be edible and quite good. The name refers to the late fruiting in fall and early winter.

cap orange with an olive green overlay, highly variable in appearance, spotty, sticky when wet, fine short hair, inrolled margin at first, up to 8 cm across.
gills orange when young, later pale yellow; crowded, adnate, narrow to relatively broad.
spore print white.
stalk rust to orange; short, swollen, finely tomentose; up to 2 cm long and 1 cm thick.
flesh white, with brownish gelatinous layer over the gills and under the cuticle; soft like a marshmallow.
taste & odour faint.

sunray mushroom

p.102-3

Heliocybe sulcata (Berkeley) Redhead & Ginns

former name: *Lentinus sulcatus*
Heliocybe: sunhead (refers to the radial pattern on the cap) (Greek)
sulcata: plowed or grooved (Latin)

Cosmopolitan and widespread, but not common; this tough little fungus is an oddity, anatomically; while most hyphae of the Agaricales species have clamp connections, *H. sulcata* has clampless hyphae. It is an elegant small mushroom with raised ribs over the gills like a small umbrella; growing on dry bare logs and even on piers and fences. This species, one of a kind, was originally described from Ohio; a recycler of decayed wood of the brown-rot group. Reported from Ontario, Manitoba, Saskatchewan, Alberta, B.C. and the Yukon.

cap brown ribs over the gills, lighter in between, brown scales in cap centre, small umbo, up to 4 cm across.
gills bone coloured, sinuate, serrate, intermediates, distant, sometimes forked near the stalk.
spore print white.
stalk whitish, lined apex, base with small scales, up to 3 cm tall and 0.3 cm thick.
flesh white, solid, confluent in cap and stalk.

train wrecker

p.102-4

Neolentinus lepideus (Fries: Fries) Redhead & Ginns

Neolentinus: new Lentinus (Latin)
Lentinus: pliable (Latin)
lepideus: scaly (Greek)

Worldwide distribution; a decay fungus, creating brown rot in old logs. I found it fruiting every spring on the same old poplar log for eight years. When fruiting occurs, the mushrooms last for a long time, drying rather than rotting. I watched one from May 22, when the veil was still in place, until July 13, when it was eaten by a squirrel. It took two weeks to become full grown. After three weeks it started to get wrinkled, and the gills turned yellowish; seven weeks after first observation it was still there, but browner. I kept on observing the log for several years, when it started to fall apart no more mushrooms appeared. The fungus got the name "train wrecker" because it grows in dead wood, whether it is windfall, telephone poles or railroad ties; it even tolerates creosote. It grows on coniferous and deciduous wood. A chewy, edible mushroom when young. Research by Redhead & Ginns (1985) on the genus *Lentinus* showed that species causing brown rot and species causing white rot were included in the same genus. Since no homobasdiomycete is known to cause both white and brown rot, the genus *Neolentinus* was created for those species causing brown rot.

cap	cream coloured with brown scales; a fringe around the cap edge, remnants of the partial veil; up to 12 cm across.
gills	white at first, discolouring to yellowish brownish with age; serrate, intermediates, relatively distant, decurrent.
spore print	white.
stalk	white, solid, lines on apex extending from gills to flaring ring; white scales below ring, base often flattened where it comes out of the wood, up to 7 cm tall and 2.5 cm thick.
partial veil	fringe on cap edge and flaring ring.
flesh	white, tough and woody in old specimens.
taste	young caps are good.
odour	fragrant, of anise.

shoehorn oyster p.102-5

Hohenbuehelia petaloides (Bulliard: Fries) Schulzer

Hohenbuehelia: named after Freiherr von Hohenbühel, Austrian cryptogamist 1817-1885
petaloides: like a leaf (Greek)

Cosmopolitan; saprophytic fungi, growing on decaying stumps, buried or burnt wood. *Hohenbuehelia* species have either a gelatinous layer on the cap or under the cuticle. This fungus (and also the oyster mushroom) can catch nematodes for additional needed nitrogen, when that element is insufficient in the old wood. The gelatinous layer holds and stuns the insect so that the hyphae can penetrate it (Greg Thorn). Long-lived mushrooms, not readily decaying. Edible but of poor quality.

cap	buff, tan and somewhat orange; one sided; leaf or scoop shape, fuzzy or with bloom away from the margin; rolled-in edge at first, up to 10 cm across.
gills	whitish; flesh coloured or tan with age; close, narrow, serrate with age, long decurrent.
spore print	white.
stalk	could be considered stalkless, but cap and stalk are one and the gills run down the stalk (see p. 102); sometimes a small fuzzy stalk is visible.
flesh	white, rather tough.
taste & odour	mild.

hairy oyster p.102-6

Lentinus strigosus (Schweinitz) Fries

Lentinus: tough, pliable and slow (Latin)
strigosus: hairy (Latin)

North American species; widespread, but not common at all; this lovely, hairy mushroom has undergone many name changes; saprophytic, causing white rot in wood; tough, thin-fleshed mushroom, too beautiful to pick.

cap	light smoky with reddish brown, deep centre; irregular, covered with dense short hair and bearded, turned-in edge, lightly zoned, up to 7 cm across.
gills	whitish at first, yellowish with age, narrow, sometimes forked.
spore print	off-white.
stalk	off-white, velvety, sturdy, up to 2 cm tall and 1.5 cm thick.
flesh	white, tough, continuous in cap and stalk, very tight.
taste	slightly bitter.
odour	faint.

Family PLUTEACEAE

The Pluteaceae are pink-spored mushrooms with free ventricose gills; the cap separates easily from the stalk and there is no ring. Species from two genera are described.
Pluteus, growing on decaying wood; no volva.
Volvariella, growing on rich soil, manure, straw or wood; with a volva.

Genus PLUTEUS
shield (Latin)

Pluteus is a very distinct genus; free gills; often white at first, then pink as the spores ripen; stalks lacking both an annulus and a volva; always on decaying wood, which is sometimes buried; fruiting in spring, summer or fall; some edible species, none poisonous; a spore print **must** be made to ensure that it is pink. Small to medium mushrooms.

patrician deer mushroom   p.103-1
Pluteus patricius (Schulzer) Boudier
former name: *P. petasatus* Fries: Gillet
Pluteus: shield (Latin)
patricius: noble (Latin)

Cosmopolitan; widely distributed in North America; occurs on old hardwood; fruiting in summer; a beautiful mushroom; edible.

cap	light background with short, or long, dark-brown fibers in a very nice pattern; split margins; up to 8 cm across.
gills	white at first, then pale pink; free, broad, serrate.
spore print	pink, pinkish brown after it dries.
stalk	similar to cap but lighter, enlarged white base; up to 7 cm tall and 1 cm wide.
flesh	white, solid; long fibres in stalk; a bit yellow sometimes.

golden deer mushroom   p.103-2
Pluteus leoninus (Fries) Kummer
leoninus: of the lion (Latin)

Cosmopolitan; widely distributed but not common; reported from the prairie provinces; singly or in small clusters on deciduous or sometimes coniferous wood or woodchips; fruiting in summer and fall.

cap	yellow with a bit of velvety reddish brown crown; hygrophanous, which causes colour change when moisture is lost; striped margin; up to 3.5 cm across.
gills	yellow changing to pink, free, broad.
spore print	pinkish brown.
stalk	yellowish with some brown; base a bit enlarged; 3.5 cm tall and 0.5 cm wide.
flesh	yellow, thin, stalk hollow.

small white deer mushroom   p.103-3
Pluteus tomentosulus Peck
tomentosulus: a little hairy (Latin)

North American, widely distributed; reported from Manitoba, Saskatchewan and Alberta; singly or in small numbers on hardwoods; fruiting in summer.

cap	white, floccose; wavy edge; broadly umbonate; 6 cm across.
gills	white, then pink, broad, crowded, free.
spore print	pink.
stalk	white, bent, often twisted, some thickening at the base; up to 4 cm tall and 1 cm thick.
flesh	white, solid, fibrous strands in the stalk.

the deer mushroom
p.103-4

Pluteus cervinus (Fries) Kummer

cervinus: of the deer (Latin)

Cosmopolitan; common, widely distributed in North America; on hardwoods, old stumps, buried wood and sawdust piles; single or in groups; edible and good; the radish odour disappears in cooking; fruiting in spring, summer and fall.

cap	light smoky to very dark brown; radially streaked, uneven surface; bell shaped at first, then umbonate; up to 8 cm across.
gills	white, then light pink.
spore print	pink.
stalk	white or tan with appressed fibrils, sometimes twisted; up to 10 cm tall and 0.6 cm thick.
flesh	white.
odour	radish
taste	mild

white deer mushroom
p.103-5

Pluteus pellitus (Persoon: Fries) Kummer

pellitus: covered with a skin (Latin)

Cosmopolitan; not common but widely distributed; on wood of deciduous trees; in Alberta on willow and birch; fruiting in summer and fall; edible.

cap	brilliant silky white; shiny, slightly pinkish; rounded at first, then plane with umbo; up to 9 cm across.
gills	white at first, then salmon pink; free, broad, serrate, close; remote from stalk (see illustration).
spore print	pink.
stalk	white, long, solid, narrowing toward the top and widening toward the base; up to 12 cm tall and 1 cm thick.
flesh	white, stringy in the stalk.
odour	radish.
taste	mild.

yellow-stalked deer mushroom
p.103-6

Pluteus lutescens (Fries) Bresadola

lutescens: becoming yellow (Latin)

Cosmopolitan; widely distributed but infrequent. In Alberta, found on the wood of poplar and birch and on chips; fruiting in summer and fall.

cap	dark cinnamon to olive brown; bell shaped at first, then umbonate; folds; up to 5 cm across.
gills	at first yellow then pinkish yellow; free, broad, serrate, subdistant.
spore print	deep pink.
stalk	yellow with white base;, sometimes enlarging toward base; bent, stringy; up to 5 cm tall and 0.8 cm thick.
flesh	yellow, pale in cap, bright in stalk.
taste & odour	mild.

bulbous-stalked Pluteus
p.105-1

Pluteus semibulbosus (Lasch: Fries) Gillet sensu Lange

semibulbosus: slightly bulbous (Latin)

Cosmopolitan; small inconspicuous mushroom; infrequent; on decaying hardwood logs or sawdust.

cap	white; bell shaped, then expanding with umbo; floccose; up to 3 cm across.
gills	at first white, then delicate pink; free, broad.
spore print	pink.
stalk	white, slim, with small bulbous base; up to 3.5 cm tall and 0.5 cm wide.
flesh	white, thin, stringy in stalk.

pink and grey Pluteus

p.105-2

Pluteus atriavellaneus Murrill

atriavellaneus: grey and pink (Latin)

Rare; on decaying wood; found in boreal mixed woods; in Alberta on birch wood.

cap	greyish buff with pinkish margin, bell shape, umbonate; up to 4 cm across.
gills	whitish at first, then delicate pink; crowded, free.
spore print	pink.
stalk	whitish with some brown, enlarging toward the base; woolly white mycelium where it is attached to the wood; up to 5 cm tall and 0.3 cm thick.
flesh	solid, off-white.

small deer mushroom

p.105-3

Pluteus exiguus Patouillard

exiguus: small, not important (Latin)

Found in Alberta on buried wood; however, it is rarely found, perhaps because it is grey and small. It is a lovely little mushroom, and it is nice to be able to include it in the guide; fruiting in the summer.

cap	pale, smoky grey brown with a light brown umbo; radially lined; split margin; up to 4 cm across.
gills	white at first, then pink, free, beautifully spaced, intermediates.
spore print	deep pink.
stalk	white, base brownish, twisted; up to 6 cm tall and 0.3 cm thick.
flesh	white.

Genus VOLVARIELLA

with a volva (Latin)

Volvariella is a very distinct genus characterized by a volva which completely envelopes the immature fruiting body (egg stage), then stays as a cup at the base of the stalk; free gills, usually white at first, turning pink as the spores ripen; pink spores and no ring. Care has to be taken not to confuse Volvariellas with ringless *Amanita* species, which are quite similar except that their white gills stay white and their spores are white.

The genus is mainly a tropical one. *Volvariella volvacea*, the famous, widely cultivated paddy straw mushroom (from the Malayan word for the rice plant: *padi*), which is often found in oriental food, belongs in this group. *Volvariella* species in the temperate zone grow on rich soil or decaying wood. One species, which is not in this book, is parasitic on other mushrooms; the others are decomposers.

grey Volvariella

p.105-4

Volvariella speciosa var. *gloiocephala* (de Candolle: Fries) Singer

Volvariella: with volva (Latin)
speciosa: beautiful (Latin)
gloiocephala: with viscid head (Greek)

Worldwide distribution in a wide climate range; fruiting in cool weather; occurs from the Yukon south to California and from east to west on the North American continent (also in Europe, Australia and Japan); grows on decaying hardwood, woodchips, soil rich in lignin; not recommended for eating, often reported as **poisonous**.

cap	rounded to broadly domed, shiny grey, viscid in damp weather; up to 8 cm across.
gills	white at first, then pink; free, ventricose, serrate, remote from stalk.
spore print	deep pink.
stalk	white, can be massive, solid, stringy inside, sometimes hollow; up to 5 cm tall and 1cm thick at the top.
volva	white, modest to substantial and flaring; completely enwraps the youthful mushroom (egg stage).
flesh	white.

Volvariella speciosa var. *speciosa* (Fries) Singer

speciosa: beautiful (Latin)

Worldwide distribution; solitary or in groups; grows in forests and in parks, on duff, manure or rich soils. Like other saprophytes (*Coprinus* and *Agaricus*), it tolerates and even thrives in disturbed areas. According to some authors, the grey and white varieties are one species. In Arizona I found them side by side, although the grey ones were on woodchips. Not recommended for eating, often reported as **poisonous**.

cap	white to white streaked with some brown or grey; viscid when damp; egg shaped at first, then umbonate when expanding; up to 12 cm across.
gills	white at first, then slowly turning pink; free, remote from stalk, ventricose, serrate.
spore print	deep pink to reddish brown.
stalk	white, tall, slim at top, enlarging toward base, shiny, sometimes twisted; up to 20 cm tall and 1.5 cm thick.
volva	white, thick, fibrous, large.
egg	when found, can be 4 cm wide and 6 cm tall; often underground.

Family ENTOLOMATACEAE

former name: Rhodophyllaceae

The family is named for the genus *Entoloma* (Greek for with inrolled margin). It usually gets short shrift in mushroom guides because for exact identification a microscopic examination is necessary to determine critical characteristics (e.g., shape of spores, structure of cap cuticle, pigmentation and presence or absence of clamp connections). Also this difficult family needs more research. All pink-spored mushrooms used to be in the family Rhodosporae (Greek for with pink spores) but now they are, for the most part, divided between Pluteaceae, with free gills and smooth pink spores, and Entolomataceae, with attached gills and angular pink spores. It is not difficult to tell the families apart, but within the Entolomataceae family identification is difficult. There are quite a few species which can be recognized by macroscopic characteristics, however, and I will give some examples.

Some mycologists have a large *Entoloma* genus and subdivide it into the subgenera *Entoloma*, *Nolanea*, *Leptonia*, etc.; others prefer to have separate genera. There are quite a few **poisonous** species in Entolomataceae; therefore, none should be eaten.

Entoloma (Greek for with inrolled margin): Quite a few are large and similar in shape to *Tricholoma* or *Russula* species, with adnate-sinuate gills; flesh of the cap and stalk continuous; pink angular spores. There are small species too (see p. 107).

Nolanea (Latin for bell shaped): Slender, conical or bell-shaped mushrooms; thin fleshed; margin not inrolled, but pressed straight to the stalk at first; gills adnexed. Many are brown, but the genus also includes some lovely coloured species; pink angular spores.

Rhodocybe (Greek for redhead): Reddish-brown caps; decurrent gills; pink, bumpy to warted spores.

The following genera are not included because I am not sure enough of the identification of *Pouzarella* and *Leptonia* and have not found *Clitopilus*.

Pouzarella (named after mycologist Pouzar): Small, dark and scaly mushrooms with coarse stiff hair at the stalk base; pink angular spores.

Leptonia (Greek for slender): Small, slim, often bluish, mushrooms with thin flesh; gills adnate or somewhat decurrent; pink angular spores; *Pouzarella* and *Leptonia* have no clamp connections.

Clitopilus (Greek for depressed cap): Small genus with a very well known species, the miller, *C. prunulus*. Mostly decurrent narrow gills, whitish to greyish mushrooms; pink spores which are longitudinally ribbed and angular in end view.

earthy Entoloma

p.107-1

Entoloma rusticoides (Gillet) Noordeloos

rusticoides: resembling earth (Latin)

Cosmopolitan; terrestial, growing on dry poor soils. The specimens illustrated grew between patio stones on sand with very fine moss. I was able to include this very small *Entoloma* in the book because S. A. Redhead identified this collection for me. It is not included in any of the literature available to me.

cap	dark brown; small scales in concentric circles; old specimens are very dark with a depression; striate margin; up to 1.5 cm across.
gills	brown, adnate to short decurrent; distant; short intermediates.
spore print	pink.
stalk	dark brown, slim, stiff, up to 2.5 cm tall.
flesh	brown.

strongly scented Entoloma

p.107-2

Entoloma nidorosum (Fries) Quélet

nidorosum: with the odour of frying (Latin)

Cosmopolitan; growing in damp spots in forests or near rivers, singly or in small clusters. **Poisonous.**

cap	tan, fading to almost white; convex becoming slightly depressed, rolled in margin at first; up to 6 cm across.
gills	pale at first, then pink from the spores; adnate-sinuate, uneven, intermediates, relatively distant.
spore print	deep pink.
stalk	same colour as cap, slim, fragile, hollow, somewhat swollen near the base; up to 6 cm tall and 0.5 cm thick.
flesh	white, thin.
odour	pleasant.

shield Entoloma

p.107-3

Entoloma clypeatum (Linnaeus: Fries) Kummer

clypeatum: like a Roman shield (Latin)

Cosmopolitan; often growing in great numbers in grassy areas or in woods; caps are conical, and when maturing, they flatten, keeping a rounded border and a bump in the middle which looks like a Roman shield. It seems like an easily recognized species, but shapes as well as colour vary in different species; therefore, consider all Entolomas as **poisonous.** Even though *E. clypeatum* is sometimes considered to be edible, other Entolomas are extremely poisonous.

cap	dark, medium or light brown; hygrophanous; campanulate (bell shaped), then flattening with umbo; inrolled margin at first; innate radial fibres in cuticle; silky look; up to 7 cm across.
gills	off-white, then pink from ripening spores, adnate-sinuate, distant, intermediates.
spore print	deep pink.
stalk	white, silky, fibrous, up to 6 cm tall and 2 cm thick, widening near the base.
flesh	white, solid, but in wet places sometimes brownish; stalk somewhat spongy, sometimes hollow.
odour	weak, a bit mealy.

rosy Entoloma

p.107-4

Entoloma rhodopolium (Fries) Kummer

rhodopolium: shining pink (Greek)

Cosmopolitan; reported from all prairie provinces; this mushroom grows in the forest and on the edge of it. **Poisonous.**

cap	pale yellowish or grey, silky; convex at first or with small umbo, flattening later; up to 8 cm across.

gills	pale at first, then pink to flesh colour, broad, adnate-sinuate, distant, serrate.
spore print	rosy pink.
stalk	white, shiny, bumpy, up to 12 cm tall and 0.8 cm thick at the top.
flesh	white, thin; stringy and hollow in stalk; fragile.
odour	faint.

slate-grey Entoloma   p.107-5

Entoloma madidum (Fries) Gillet

madidum: moist (Latin)

Cosmopolitan; in North America it is more a western than an eastern species; terrestrial, growing in mixed forest under spruce. This *Entoloma* has the shape of a *Russula*, but does not have the brittle flesh of a *Russula* nor the same kind of spores. **Poisonous.**

cap	slate colour, may get dark brown borders or stains when mature; convex, streaked, looking damp; up to 12 cm across.
gills	pale at first, turning pink as spores ripen; broad, coarse, adnate-sinuate, intermediates.
spore print	pink.
stalk	white, fibrous, staining with age; up to 8 cm tall and 2.5 cm thick, widening toward the base.
flesh	white, thick, firm, staining a bit when mature.
odour	a bit mealy.

redhead   p.107-6

Rhodocybe sp.

The mushrooms in the illustration were found in atria in Edmonton. I like to include these fungi, because they may have been introduced on the roots of tropical plants or have come in with local soil. In the moist warm atmosphere they fruit at odd times. The name *Rhodocybe*, or redhead, was given to them because the caps are often reddish brown.

cap	smoky brown, dull, looks like fine leather; often irregular, inrolled margin; convex at first, then flattening and then depressed; up to 8 cm across.
gills	whitish to buff at first, then pinkish; long decurrent; narrow; intermediates, which continue in lines on the apex of the stalk.
spore print	salmon pink.
stalk	white, covered with fibres in a pattern; sturdy, club shaped; up to 7 cm tall and 1.2 cm at apex.
flesh	white, solid.
odour	earthy.

slim Nolanea   p.107-7

Nolanea juncina (Kühner & Romagnesi) Orton

juncina: slim, like a reed (Latin)

Cosmopolitan; this small mushroom can be found growing on spruce needles.

cap	dark brown, bell shaped at first, then flattening with umbo; up to 4 cm across.
gills	buff to light brown; beautifully spaced, adnate, distant with intermediates; turning pink as spores ripen.
spore print	pink.
stalk	brown with white woolly base; straight, slender; up to 6 cm tall and 0.3 cm thick.
flesh	brown, thin.

silky Nolanea   p.107-8

Nolanea sericea (Mérat) Orton

sericea: silky (from Chinese)

Cosmopolitan; this medium-sized, tall mushroom occurs in Europe and Japan as well as here. It grows in rings in grass and fruits during rainy spells. **Poisonous.**

cap	dark brown, shiny, silky streaky, hygrophanous, fading to buff.

gills	light greyish buff at first, then brownish pink when the spores ripen; broad, relatively distant, adnate-sinuate; wide near the stalk, narrow near the cap edge.
spore print	deep salmon colour.
stalk	streaked grey brown, tall, slim, straight, up to 9 cm tall and 0.5 cm thick.
flesh	grey, fragile, stalk may be hollow.
odour	of clean linen.

breast- or bell-shaped Nolanea   p.107-9

Nolanea mammosa (Fries) Quélet

mammosa: with a nipple (Latin)

Cosmopolitan; growing under spruce in feather moss.

cap	dark brown, campanulate with small umbo, hygrophanous, fading to buff; striate edge, not inrolled when young; up to 4.5 cm across.
gills	light brown at first, later reddish brown; distant, intermediates, narrow, adnexed, almost free.
spore print	reddish.
stalk	greyish top, brown further down, twisted, white base.
flesh	brown, thin.

yellow Nolanea   p.107-10

Nolanea sp.

A pale yellow *Nolanea* found in feather moss in Alberta; it was added just to show a brighter species. It is not identified beyond genus.

cap	pale yellow and buff, small, convex; 1.5 cm across.
gills	pale yellow at first, then pink; broad, adnexed.
spore print	reddish.
stalk	colour of cap in top half, bottom half pinkish tan, base white; 9 cm tall and 0.2 cm thick.
flesh	white, thin.

salmon unicorn Nolanea   p.107-11

Nolanea salmonea (Peck) Pomerleau

salmonea: salmon colour (Latin)

North American, but so far only found east of the Great Lakes. I found this one in Dorset, Ont., in a bog. It is added for the same reason as no. 10. It might be mistaken for a *Hygrocybe*, but the spore print (salmon pink) and adnexed gills indicate that it is a *Nolanea*.

cap	apricot orange or salmon coloured; conical to bell shaped, with or without sharp umbo; radial fibres; fading with age, up to 3 cm across.
gills	salmon coloured, relatively close and broad, adnexed.
spore print	salmon pink.
stalk	same colour as cap, slender; up to 7 cm tall and 0.3 cm thick.
flesh	orange, thin.
odour	faint.

Family CORTINARIACEAE

Cortinariaceae is the largest family of brown-spored, gilled mushrooms. The genus *Cortinarius* alone has nearly 800 taxa (species, varieties and forms) in North America! Many are encountered in the Pacific Northwest. In the genera *Cortinarius*, *Hebeloma*, *Galerina* and *Inocybe* are many poisonous and deadly species, so it is good to be able to recognize them. Most are woodland species with a mycorrhizal relationship with trees. They have a very important role to play in the forest. Many have a cortina or cobwebby veil covering the gills. Most of the time only a few fibres are left on the stalk or only a sticky zone, which shows up when coloured spores stick to it. It is very important to find young and mature specimens in order to check cortinas and the colour of young gills.

Some species have no veil and a few have a membranous partial veil. The spore print may be bright rust, orange-brown or gray-brown; none are purple-brown. The genera of Cortinariaceae that are discussed are:

Cortinarius (Latin for with a cobwebby veil): All species have a cortina and a rusty brown spore print.

Galerina (Latin for with a small fur cap): small species with slender stalks; hygrophanous, often conical caps; many dangerous and deadly; brown spore print.

Hebeloma (Greek for with a rounded margin): a large genus; some species quite poisonous; none are edible; dull brown spore print.

Inocybe (Greek for fibre head): small, medium and large species; most are poisonous, some deadly; radially splitting caps; greyish, earth-brown spore print.

Crepidotus (Greek for attached like an ear): the only genus in this family with stalkless caps; growing on wood; yellow-brown or cinnamon-brown spore print.

Simocybe (Greek for with a flat head): small mushrooms growing on wood; yellow ochre spore print.

Alnicola (Latin for living with alder): These species live with alder; spore print light brown. Identification is mainly by microscope (of special cells in the cap cuticle).

Tubaria (Latin for small trumpet): small genus of small brown species living on wood, chips or small wood debris; yellow to reddish brown spore print.

Gymnopilus (Greek for with naked cap): large and small species living on wood or lignin-rich humus; bright orange or rusty brown spore print.

Rozites (named after mycologist E. Roze): species with a true membranous veil, rare in Cortinariaceae; rusty brown spore print.

Genus CORTINARIUS
with cobwebby veil (Latin)

Cortinarius is the largest genus of the gilled mushrooms. All have a cortina or weblike veil between stalk and cap edge. It is important to notice this on young specimens, because in mature specimens it may have disappeared completely. The same is true for the universal veil: a gelatinous or slimy veil covering the entire fruiting body and which also disappears, particularly in dry weather when you find a very shiny mushroom with only a few needles or a leaf stem stuck to it, in memory of a lost veil. Young gills **must** be seen for proper identification; they may be cream, olive, violet, grey, pale yellow, buff, etc.; mature gills are a shade of red-brown or rust brown.

Because it is easier to identify the many species, seven subgenera are used. The grouping is somewhat different with various authors. I have followed Roger Phillips' book *Mushrooms and Other Fungi of Great Britain and Europe* and, for North American species, Alexander Smith's book *How to Know the Gilled Mushrooms*. European authors place the name of the subgenus in brackets between the genus and species name. I find that it makes a lot of difference in sorting things out properly; therefore, I do that too.

The following subgenera are recognized:

Myxacium (Greek for slimy all over): A gelatinous universal veil covers the whole mushroom, so look for slimy cap and stalk. When dry, the mushroom is shiny as if varnished.

Phlegmacium (Greek for slimy [but only of the cap]): A sticky cap and a dry stalk at first. The stalk can be equal or have a slightly bulbous or heavily bulbous base. A. H. Smith has used a subgenus *Bulbopodium* (meaning with bulbous base), but bulbous bases seem to be more general, occurring in other subgenera as well, and, therefore, I don't use *Bulbopodium*.

Seriocybe (Greek for silky head): The cap has a silky look and is often covered by veil remnants; the stalk can be swollen or have a bulbous base; young gills are often violet coloured.

Cortinarius (Greek for possessing a curtain or cobwebby veil): The cap is dry and often fibrous to scaly. There are not many species in this group.

Leprocybe (Greek for with a scaly head): Olive-yellow and orange-red mushrooms. Some of these are deadly. Not represented in this guide, because I have not found any in this group.

Telamonia (Greek for with a belt): The mushrooms in this group have a cap which is moist and hygrophanous, then smooth (not fibrillose). Watch the colour of veil and gills for identification.

Dermocybe (Greek for fur head): The subgenus of Dermocybe is often promoted to a separate genus, but I have left it as it was. The caps and stalks of the mushrooms are covered with small fibres. They are dry; the stalks are usually slender; the caps are brightly coloured: greenish, yellow or red.

slimy violet Cortinarius   p.109-1

Cortinarius (Myxacium) iodeoides Kauffman

iodeoides: resembling *C. iodes*, a violet-coloured *Cortinarius* (Greek)

North American species with a slimy universal veil, which looks a lot like the European *C. croceocaeruleus*, except that the North American species grows under coniferous trees and has a broader, conical cap instead of a convex one.

cap	violet and buff or yellow, streaked; conical at first and slimy, then broadly conical; sometimes radially splitting, not fading; up to 7 cm across.
gills	pale buff, later medium brown, narrow, adnate.
spore print	yellow brown, mocca.
stalk	whitish with some violet streaking; slimy at first; spindle shaped or slightly thickening at the base; cortina; remnants on the stalk; up to 8 cm tall and 1 cm thick.
flesh	off-white.

very slimy Cortinarius   p.109-2

Cortinarius (Myxacium) subbalteatus Kühner

subbalteatus: with not much of a belt (Latin)

North American species; growing under conifers. I first found this very interesting mushroom in Kootenay National Park in the mountains, still completely covered with slime. I could see the white cortina and the ivory gills and thought of a sturdy *Hygrophorus* species. When the slime dried up, its cortina turned light cinnamon brown from the spores. Later I found an earlier phase at Shaw Lake showing the thickest, red-brown slime layer I have seen (top of p. 109).

cap	red brown with a thick slime layer, conical or convex, expanding and lighter coloured when the slime dries up; the cuticle cracks in the centre and forms scabs; up to 6.5 cm across.
gills	ivory at first, then colouring light brown as the spores ripen; adnate-sinuate, intermediates, broad.
spore print	medium cinnamon brown.
stalk	pinkish, spindle shaped, solid, sturdy, up to 6 cm tall and 1.5 cm thick at the apex, 2.5 cm at the thickest part.
cortina	white, leaving a cortinal zone, brown from spores, on the stalk.
flesh	ivory to pale lemon yellow.

early Cortinarius   p.109-3

Cortinarius (Myxacium) trivialis Lange

trivialis: unimportant (Latin)

Cosmopolitan; a widely distributed species; on the prairies, it is a very early spring mushroom, but it sometimes fruits in the summer. In Québec it fruits in the fall. The name refers to its appearance, but I find this species interesting, not trivial, because it is so well-dressed: first its slimy transparent universal veil on the outside and then the sheath on the stalk, which is white and fibrous. In the illustration it is seen with holes in it showing the yellow stalk. This happens when the stalk lengthens; it leaves a narrow ring where the cap edge was attached. The cortina is present as well. In the mature specimen the spores colour the stalk brownish. Great variation in size. It is said to be a good edible.

cap	slimy orange ochre, conical to convex; drying up shiny, up to 8.5 cm across.
gills	buff at first, later spore coloured; adnexed, intermediates.
spore print	cinnamon brown
stalk	slimy at first, with white partial veil or sheath covering the yellow stalk; stretching stalk breaks up the sheath, which stays in zigzagging patches on the stalk; up to 10 cm tall and 2 cm thick, equal.
flesh	pale buff.

slimy Cortinarius   p.109-4
Cortinarius (Myxacium) mucosus (Bulliard: Fries) Kick

mucosus: full of mucus or slime (Latin)

Cosmopolitan; grows in mixed and coniferous forests. This slimy species is widespread on this continent but most numerous in the Pacific Northwest. Fruits in summer.

cap	slimy dark chestnut to lighter yellow brown, often with a yellow border; convex at first, then expanding to almost plane; up to 7 cm across.
gills	pale yellowish, then gradually spore colour; adnate, broad, intermediates.
spore print	cinnamon brown.
stalk	shiny, silky white; after the universal veil dries up: streaked, no patches like in *C. trivialis*. May split a bit or get a brown base in age; equal, up to 9 cm tall and 1 cm thick.
flesh	off white or yellowish.
odour	mild or fragrant.

pale Cortinarius   p.109-5
Cortinarius (Myxacium) pallidifolius Smith

pallidifolius: with pale gills (Latin)

North American; according to A. H. Smith, the very pale Cortinarius occurs in the mountains of western North America and is abundant at times. These specimens were found in boreal mixed forest and aspen parkland in Alberta. They probably grow in those habitats across the prairie provinces. The slimy, yellow universal veil leaves some colour behind on the cap and stalk. The originally off-white gills in the very pale mushroom reminded me of the white-spored Cortinarius, but the spores are light cinnamon brown!

cap	off-white with some yellowish and brownish streaks; slimy at first, then shiny; dome shaped to flattened dome; up to 9 cm across.
gills	off-white, then pale pinkish greyish, finally light brown, adnate broad, intermediates, serrate.
spore print	light cinnamon brown.
stalk	off-white, sturdy, cortinal zone superior, streaked with yellowish spots of the universal veil and also with spores; equal or a bit spindle shaped; bent; up to 14 cm tall and 2 cm thick.
flesh	white, solid.

beautiful Cortinarius   p.111-1
Cortinarius (Phlegmacium) calochrous Fries

calochrous: with beautiful skin (Greek)

Cosmopolitan; this lovely mushroom grows under both conifers and hardwood. I found this one in mountain forest on Mt. Robson.

cap	golden yellow on top and a lemon yellow margin; sticky; convex at first, then flattening with rounded edge; up to 8 cm across.
gills	pale lilac, narrow, close, adnexed.
spore print	cinnamon brown.
stalk	yellow and violet streaked; sturdy with bulbous base; the yellow colour is from the remnants of the universal veil; up to 6 cm tall and 2.5 cm thick at the top.

	cortina	remnants on the cap edge and stalk.
	flesh	off-white.
	odour	mild.

mountain Cortinarius s

p.111-2

Cortinarius (Phlegmacium) montanus Kauffman

montanus: of the mountains (Latin)

North American species, especially the western mountains according to A. H. Smith, but Pomerleau writes that Smith also found some specimens near Québec City in 1959. Those portrayed on p. 111 were found repeatedly near Sandy Lake in boreal mixed forest.

cap	brown crown, streaked olive green and brown towards margin; convex at first and sticky with edge turned in, then broadly convex; up to 7 cm across.
gills	greenish yellow at first, then cinnamon from spores; narrow, adnexed.
spore print	cinnamon brown.
stalk	whitish with cortinal zone, sometimes streaked brown and greenish; other times just some spore colour; widening toward the base; up to 5 cm tall and 1.5 cm thick at the base.
flesh	off-white.

variable Cortinarius

p.111-3

Cortinarius (Phlegmacium) multiformis (Fries: Secretan) Fries

multiformis: in many shapes (Latin)

Cosmopolitan; widespread, occurring under both coniferous and deciduous trees. Found in large groups, this mushroom has several shapes which can all be seen in the group at any one time. When young, it has a short, very round stalk base; then it becomes tall and slender-stalked with a small bulb or tall with a heavy stalk and round basal bulb. I found an enormous one in the foothills of the Rockies in deep sphagnum, 20 cm tall with a heavy stalk (3 cm at the top) and a cap 20 cm across!

cap	sandy colour, slimy; when fresh and moist, cuticle peels off; convex with inrolled edge, later plane and shiny with bits stuck to it (leaves, etc.)
gills	whitish at first, then pale yellow, finally light brown; narrow to broad; many intermediates; strongly serrate edges.
spore print	light cinnamon.
stalk	white with buff spots, bulbous base big or small when mature; slender or sturdy, short or tall.
cortina	very scanty remnants on stalk.
flesh	white, solid, stringy in the stalk.
odour	fresh, pleasant.

yellow spinning-top Cortinarius

p.111-4

Cortinarius (Phlegmacium) autoturbinatus (Secrétan) Lange

autoturbinatus: with built-in spinning top (Latin)

Cosmopolitan; this strong, bright mushroom has a slimy top, dry stalk and voluminous cortina. It looks like a spinning top because of the rim on the bulb, where the cap edge was connected to the stalk by the cortina. The strongly serrate, pale gills look like those of *C. multiformis*, but all other parts are much brighter; growing under spruce.

cap	sulphur and lemon yellow or orange and very slimy, changing to rust brown except for the margin; convex with a dip or just convex; up to 12 cm across.
gills	pale, then light sandy to pale rust; strongly serrate, adnexed, many intermediates; broad.
spore print	rich cinnamon.
stalk	white apex, yellow to orange lower down; soon covered by a prolific amount of spores; strong rim, usually on shoulder of the bulb; up to 6 cm tall and 2.5 cm at the apex, 4.5 cm in the bulb.
flesh	white and yellow as in the illustration or all yellow.

purple-staining Cortinarius

Cortinarius (Phlegmacium) purpurascens (Fries) Fries

purpurascens: colouring purple (Latin)

Cosmopolitan; purple-staining species with a variegated cap and stalk; often growing in wet spots with poplar or willow.

cap	streaky purple and reddish brown, sticky when young; convex at first, then expanding to domed or flat. In warm, dry areas with cool nights, the cuticle often cracks into patches as in several of the *Cortinarius* species shown; up to 8 cm across.
gills	purple at first, then brown as the spores ripen; adnexed, broad, serrate, intermediates.
spore print	rust brown.
stalk	streaky purplish brown, thickening gradually into bulbous base which is lighter; sometimes the base is rimmed; remnants of the cortina are not very visible on the dark stalk.
flesh	violet, streaked with purple, darker when squeezed.

cedar Cortinarius

Cortinarius (Phlegmacium) cedretorum Maire

cedretorum: of cedars (Latin)

North American species, especially of the Pacific Northwest; grows in coniferous forest. This one was found in the foothills of the Rockies under lodgepole pine.

cap	slimy; yellow and round in youth, but soon changing to brick red and then to the colour of raw steak; expanding to flat; up to 12 cm across.
gills	honey yellow at first, then light brown; serrate, intermediates, broad.
spore print	red brown.
stalk	buff streaked with reddish-brownish fibres, sturdy, tall with an abrupt basal bulb; up to 10 cm tall and 2.5 cm thick at the top.
flesh	pale lavender in cap, shimmery geranium pink in stalk.
odour	of radishes.

pointed Cortinarius

Cortinarius (Myxacium) vanduzerensis Smith & Trappe

vanduzerensis: named after the place where species was originally found: H. B. van Duzer Forest Wayside (Oregon coast)

North American species; not common; originally found in late fall on the Oregon coast. I found the specimens in the illustration northwest of Edmonton, Alberta, under spruce and in the mountains in B.C., under alpine spruce. When young, the mushrooms are covered by a slimy universal veil; fruiting in late summer, solitary or in a ring or group. Rare everywhere except in Oregon.

cap	dark red-brown, streaked with purple, white edge; slimy and smooth at first; when dry the cap is radially wrinkled; almost egg shaped at first, then sharply peaked or rounded with a sharp umbo. An old specimen had lost part of its umbo and was radially split, looking somewhat like an old *Inocybe*, except for the colour of the spores, the gills and flesh. Up to 11 cm across, sometimes larger.
gills	light tan at first, then rusty cinnamon brown; adnate, broad, intermediates.
spore print	cinnamon brown.
stalk	streaked; dark red-brown and purple; booted (sheathed), somewhat lighter above the boot; the shape varies a lot depending on its surroundings: in deep moss the boot becomes tall with a pointed base; can be all the way from 4 to 20 cm tall and up to 2.5 cm thick.
flesh	from light to medium brown (in the mature one at right) to deep maroon dark brown.
odour	of raw potatoes.

booted Cortinarius

Cortinarius (Telamonia) torvus (Bulliard: Fries) Fries

torvus: strong (Latin)

Cosmopolitan; this interesting beauty occurs in the Pacific Northwest. This is a *Cortinarius* with a membranous ring, visible in the young specimen while it disappeared in the mature one. This is rare in a *Cortinarius*. It grows under aspen or other deciduous trees.

cap	brown, sometimes streaked with violet; convex, then expanding with a broad umbo; pale margin; up to 11 cm across.
gills	lilac, then purple, then brown as the spores mature; broad, adnate-sinuate, intermediates.
spore print	medium brown.
stalk	top half lilaceous pink, bottom half white; boot; up to 9 cm tall and 2.5 cm thick.
partial veil one	the boot on the stalk and bits on the cap edge; top of the boots stand up; first ring.
partial veil two	also white, covering the gills under veil one. This is not a cortina, but is fibrous; a second ring; disappearing when mature.
flesh	dirty white; in young specimens somewhat violet.

bracelet Cortinarius   p.112-3
Cortinarius (Telamonia) armillatus (Fries) Fries
armillatus: with bracelet (Latin)

Cosmopolitan and widespread; this mushroom occurs across Canada, but is better known in the northeastern part of the continent; growing under deciduous trees but mostly associated with birch. The red bracelets make it stand out. It is said to be edible.

cap	chestnut brown, bell shaped or convex, shiny; up to 10 cm across.
gills	cream at first, then as the spores ripen, cinnamon brown; adnexed, broad, intermediates.
spore print	cinnamon brown.
stalk	whitish or light brown from spores at the top; one, two or three vermilion bracelets in the middle on a pale background; a bulbous red-brown base, stout, up to 12 cm tall and 3 cm thick at the top.
cortina	disappearing, traces of it above the bracelets.
flesh	pale, then light, brown; thick, soft.
odour	fresh.

little brown Cortinarius   p.113-1
Cortinarius (Telamonia) castaneus (Bulliard: Fries) Fries
castaneus: colour of a chestnut (Latin)

Cosmopolitan; growing with coniferous trees; this is truly an L.B.M. or "little brown mushroom", easily overlooked by most people in the mushroom season. I found it very early in the year (for our climate), growing under Juniper on a hot dry slope above Pyramid Lake in the Rocky Mountains, with the tiny *Arctostaphylos uva-ursi* or kinnikinnick. I also found it in boreal forest, fruiting in the fall under spruce. It just did not fit on the illustration with the large *Telamonia* species, but I wanted to show that there also are many small *Cortinarius* species everywhere as well as the big ones.

cap	dark chestnut with white rim from the cortina when moist; fading somewhat when dry; bell shaped, up to 3 cm across.
gills	at first tinged with pale violet, then brown from spores; adnexed, relatively broad.
spore print	rusty brown.
stalk	lighter brown than cap, more red brown with white base, remnants of cortina; up to 4 cm tall and 0.3 cm thick.
flesh	light tan.

yellow Cortinarius   p.113-2
Cortinarius (Dermocybe) croceofolius Peck
croceofolius: with saffron-coloured gills (Latin)

Cosmopolitan; growing in moss under conifers, often in spruce-birch bogs in late stage of evolution of the bog into dryland, like many of the subgenus *Dermocybe*. The species with yellow and brown colours are difficult to identify. *C. croceofolius* has yellow to saffron gills when young; there are also microscopic differences. In this group we can only approximate identification with field chatacteristics.

cap	raw sienna or yellow brown with yellow margin; bell shaped at first, expanding to broad dome or rounded; up to 6.5 cm across.
gills	yellow to orange to saffron colour, adnate to adnate-sinuate or almost decurrent, intermediates; dusted with rust-coloured spores when mature.
spore print	rusty brown.
stalk	yellow, slim, tall when in deep moss, equal, sometimes remnants of cortina; up to 10 cm tall and 0.5 cm thick.
flesh	yellow.
odour	faint.

red-gilled Cortinarius   p.113-3

Cortinarius (Dermocybe) semisanguineus (Fries) Gillet

semisanguineus: partly blood-red (Latin)

Cosmopolitan; occurring in Northern U.S., Canada, Alaska and Europe. Grows in coniferous forests. The one portrayed was found in the Rockies under lodgepole pine. **Dangerous.**

cap	ochre, dull, silky; convex or slightly umbonate, dry; up to 5 cm across.
gills	orange-red to wine red, adnate, relatively narrow, intermediates.
spore print	rusty brown.
stalk	fibrillose base; ochre-coloured; top lighter, equal; up to 4 cm tall and 0.6 cm thick.
flesh	yellowish.

blood-red Cortinarius   p.113-4

Cortinarius (Dermocybe) sanguineus (von Wulfen: Fries) Fries

sanguineus: blood-red (Latin)

Cosmopolitan, widespread but uncommon; this species has been reported from Québec, Manitoba, Alberta and B.C. In the U.S., it is also widespread, but nowhere common. It is often reported when found with its conspicuous blood-red colour all through the outside, inside and gills; growing in coniferous forests. **Poisonous.**

cap	maroon or dark blood-red; bell shaped at first, then flattening with umbo; dry, silky or with fine scales; up to 6 cm across.
gills	blood-red, then powdered with spores to red brown; adnate to adnexed, relatively broad, intermediates; serrate.
spore print	cinnamon.
stalk	very dark red to purplish red; slightly widening toward base; up to 7 cm tall and 0.5 cm thick.
flesh	very dark purplish brown.
odour	mild.

bog Cortinarius   p.113-5

Cortinarius (Dermocybe) uliginosus Berkeley

uliginosus: of the bog (Latin)

Cosmopolitan, widespread but uncommon; this species occurs in bogs or damp spots. The group in the illustration was found between mossy old logs under willow. **Dangerous.**

cap	orange to rusty orange (can be orange-red), dry; bell shaped first, then flattening; up to 4 cm across.
gills	yellow or orangy, later rusty; adnexed to adnate-sinuate.
spore print	rust brown.
stalk	orange brown top, dirty white base, slender, crooked, tall, hollow; up to 6 cm tall and 0.5 cm thick.
cortina	evanescent.
flesh	yellowish.

brown-stalked Cortinarius

p.113-6

Cortinarius (Dermocybe) cinnamomeobadius Henry

cinnamomeobadius: with a cinnamon brown foot (Greek)

Cosmopolitan, see the remarks made under no. 2. The colours here are more brown; the gills golden to sulphur yellow at first. This could be a colour variation of no. 2, but I have kept them separate. They both grow in mossy conifer forests. **Dangerous.**

cap	burnt sienna with a yellow-ochre margin, or all brown; bell shaped at first, broadly umbonate later; up to 6 cm across.
gills	golden to sulphur yellow, adnexed, intermediates.
spore print	cinnamon brown.
stalk	mostly brown, yellowish apex, equal, somewhat widening at the base, scaly, slight remnant of the cortina.
flesh	yellow.
odour	faintly of radish.

purple Cortinarius

p.113-7

Cortinarius (Cortinarius) violaceus (Linnaeus: Fries) Fries

violaceus: purple (Latin)

Cosmopolitan and widespread. This intensely purple mushroom prefers old growth coniferous or mixed forests. Found in Québec, Ontario, Manitoba, Saskatchewan, B.C., and Alaska. Although nowhere common, this mushroom does not escape notice when it appears. I have not found it in Alberta, but it can reasonably be expected to occur here. The specimen portrayed, was found in Ontario. Edible but not of good quality. Caution is advised.

cap	dark purple, dry, scaly with some metallic sheen; convex, then expanding to cap with a broad umbo and lifted margin; up to 10 cm across.
gills	dark violet, then dark purplish brown, broad, relatively distant, adnexed.
spore print	cinnamon brown.
stalk	dark purple, fibrous, almost equal or thickening in the base; up to 7 cm tall and 1.2 cm thick.
cortina	purplish, evanescent.
flesh	purple, thick.
odour	faint.
taste	weak.

silvery-violet Cortinarius

p.113-8

Cortinarius (Seriocybe) alboviolaceus (Fries) Kummer

alboviolaceus: whitish violet (Latin)

Cosmopolitan and widespread; this is one of the violet *Cortinarius* species. It is covered with a silky white universal veil at first, which leaves a sheath at the stalk base; the flesh is violet and the cap stays silvery violet. Look at *C. iodeoides* (p. 109) with slimy universal veil, white flesh; *C. purpurascens* (p. 111) violet flesh but brown colours in cap and stalk; *C. torvus* (p. 112) greyish violet flesh, but the partial veil is membranous not a cortina and the cap is a different colour. There are many others. For identification **all** characteristics have to fit. This one is said to be edible but caution is advised.

cap	pale silvery lilac; convex at first, covered with white universal veil; flattening somewhat when maturing.
gills	violet at first, then rusty from developing spores; relatively narrow, close, intermediates.
spore print	cinnamon.
stalk	whitish, fibrous, sheath with violet tints on lower stalk; top a bit more violet, sometimes more or less equal; often with a swollen base.
cortina	white, evanescent.
flesh	lavender or violet, sometimes with some white.
taste & odour	faint.

Genus GALERINA
resembling a fur cap (Latin)

The genus contains small and sometimes medium-sized species; some, including two of the three species described here, are deadly poisonous. They contain the same toxin as the angel of death, *Amanita virosa*. For that reason it is extremely important that a mushroom hunter can recognize these species in order to know what to leave alone. They grow in the forest on wood and humus; in bogs on sphagnum or various debris and also in grass.

caps	hygrophanous; striate margins; sticky when moist; rounded or convex with small umbo.
stalks	usually long and brittle.
partial veil	present or absent (all species shown do have it).
spore print	ochre to rusty brown.

bog Galerina   p.115-1

Galerina paludosa (Fries) Kühner

paludosa: of the bog (Latin)

Cosmopolitan; always growing in sphagnum bog. S. A. Redhead (1981) has described how *Galerina paludosa* parasitizes sphagnum. A small but tall mushroom. It is not known if this species is poisonous, but it is too dangerous to try any *Galerina*. Initially covered by a white universal veil.

cap	sticky and coloured brown ochre when moist, yellow ochre when dry; radially lined, bell shaped with small umbo, bits of veil soon disappear; up to 2.5 cm across.
gills	light brown, close, adnate, intermediates.
spore print	rust colour.
stalk	light brown with remnants of universal veil covering it in a flame pattern; up to 12 cm tall and 0.1 cm thick.
partial veil	results in thin cobwebby ring or annular zone.
flesh	yellowish.

fall Galerina   p.115-2

Galerina autumnalis (Peck) Smith & Singer

autumnalis: of the autumn (Latin)

Cosmopolitan and widespread; growing on bits of conifer wood in the forest. These small mushrooms are **deadly!** They contain phallotoxins as well as amatoxins (poisons prevalent in Amanitaceae).

cap	hygrophanous; brown and convex or conical at first; sticky, smooth; then flattening and fading to yellowish or rusty brown; up to 4 cm across.
gills	sulphur yellow, then rusty brown from ripening spores, broad, adnate, intermediates.
spore print	rusty brown.
stalk	light brown and a bit streaked; up to 5 cm tall and 0.3 cm thick.
partial veil	leaving some pieces streaking the lower part of the stalk and a superior ring.
flesh	thin watery brown.

deadly lawn Galerina   p.115-3

Galerina venenata A. H. Smith

venenata: poisonous (Latin)

North American and only known from the Pacific Northwest; growing in grass. This poisonous mushroom is also **deadly** and hard to identify, because of the variation in colour and size. More visible than the other two Galerinas because it grows in relatively large groups in grass. This is one to watch out for.

cap	sticky; pale bay brown to reddish cinnamon and convex at first, sometimes with small navel; then flattening and fading (hygrophanous); up to 4.5 cm across.
gills	tan at first, then rusty from spores; adnate, relatively narrow to relatively broad, intermediates.
spore print	rust colour.
stalk	same colour as cap but lighter, with pattern of partial veil remnants; equal, slender,

	hollow base, white and a bit swollen; up to 7 cm tall and 0.5 cm thick.
partial veil	resulting in superior, almost membranous, ring and pattern on the stalk.
flesh	reddish, semi-transparent in the hollow stalk; brownish and reddish in cap.

Genus HEBELOMA

with obtuse, or rounded, margin (Greek)

Small to quite large mycorrhizal mushrooms in white, buff, pink or some shade of brown. Can be dry or sticky. According to the experts, it is a poorly studied group, but since it contains very poisonous species and no known edibles, the mushroom hunter should be aware of these. The odour can be like that of radishes or raw potatoes; the spore print is duller than that of *Cortinarius* species; the top of the stalk is often granular or scaly; the partial veil is usually absent, so there is no ring, except in a few species; the gills are attached and are often grey brown at maturity, as in *Inocybe*.

small poison pie mushroom   p.115-4

Hebeloma sordidulum (Peck) Saccardo

sordidulum: small and insignificant (Latin)

This small *Hebeloma* was identified for me by mycologist S.A. Redhead. It is not in any of the literature available to me. I found these growing in a meadow on an abandoned farm. It looks like a miniature poison pie (see no. 8) but darker. Consider it **poisonous** (see remarks under no. 8).

cap	reddish brown; convex at first, then flattening with small umbo; up to 3 cm across.
gills	dingy brown, adnate, close, intermediates.
spore print	a bit reddish brown.
stalk	white, grainy on the apex, up to 3 cm tall and 0.5 cm thick.
flesh	white.
odour	dirty.

dark-centred Hebeloma   p.115-5

Hebeloma mesophaeum (Persoon: Fries) Quélet

mesophaeum: dark in the centre (Greek)

Cosmopolitan and widespread; often found in the grass in parks and gardens. Interesting small species. I found it in an Edmonton lawn, then in the sand dunes in Holland and in the French Alps. They all looked the same with their brown crowns and buff margins. This is another small mushroom to watch out for. Small children should be taught not to touch small mushrooms when playing on the lawn. Consider it **poisonous.**

cap	shiny, orange-brown to chestnut centre; buff margin, turned under at first; up to 2.5 cm across.
gills	light yellowish brown at first, dull brown later; relatively close; adnate-sinuate, intermediates, broad, serrate.
spore print	mud brown.
stalk	white apex, remnants of cortina below that; base soft yellow; often bent, sometimes twisted; up to 5.5 cm tall and 0.3 cm thick.
flesh	light buff or yellowish, semi-transparent, thin, hollow.
odour	radish.

veiled Hebeloma   p.115-6

Hebeloma strophosum (Fries) Saccardo

strophosum: with a ring (Greek)

Cosmopolitan; this is another Hebeloma with a cortina, but much heavier than in the previous species. I found this one near Lytton, B.C., under Ponderosa pine in sandy soil. **Dangerous**.

cap	buff to ochrish, radially fibrillose; at first convex, then expanding to plane with dip or small umbo; up to 4.5 cm across.

gills	yellow brown at first, then clay brown; separate easily from the cap, adnate, intermediates.
spore print	clay brown.
stalk	same colour as the cap; fibrous base; equal; up to 3.5 cm tall and 0.5 cm thick.
cortina	hairy and full of dull brown spores, much heavier than that of no. 5.
flesh	buff, solid in cap, stringy in stalk.
odour	radish.

scaly-stalked Hebeloma p.115-7

Hebeloma sinapizans (Paulet: Fries) Gillet sensu American authors

sinapizans: with the flavour of mustard (Latin)

Cosmopolitan; looks somewhat like the European species, but is not quite the same. According to Redhead, the species needs a North American monograph. It is poisonous and causes nausea, vomiting and diarrhea. A large, beautiful mushroom, it has a relationship with deciduous trees of the aspen parkland and boreal mixed forest — mainly aspen and black poplar. In California the relationship is with oak. The field characteristics of the North American *H. sinapizans* differ from those of the European mushroom of the same name in the colour and surface of the cap. The **cap colour** of the North American species is a soft pink with a light margin; in maturity changing to pinkish brown; the gills are pinkish buff at first; many droplets of moisture on the gills are dark from the spores. The **cap cuticle** is dry and silky with scanty appressed hair; I have not noticed viscidity, but in a dry climate, stickiness disappears fast. In maturity a raised hairy ring can be on the cap where the inrolled margin touched the stalk in youth; the surface of the stalk is covered with white squamules, much woollier than in the European variety.

cap	lovely soft pink with a lighter margin; convex; in mature specimens the cap flattens and there sometimes is a hairy ridge inward from the edge where the cap touched the stalk when still inrolled; cap colour darkens somewhat to pinkish brown (see illustration); up to 12 cm across.
gills	pinkish buff at first, adnate, serrate edges, intermediates, adnexed, almost free; dotted with many dark spots, left as moisture drops with spores in them dry up.
spore print	medium to reddish brown.
stalk	shiny white; covered with woolly squamules all along the sturdy stalk to the sudden thickening at the bottom (abruptibulbous); up to 10 cm tall and 2 cm thick.
flesh	solid, white, soft in cap; shiny and stringy in stalk; sometimes with a narrow opening in the centre of the stalk.
odour	very strongly of radish or raw potatoes.

poison pie p.115-8

Hebeloma crustuliniforme (Bulliard: St Amans) Quélet

crustuliniforme: with the shape of a cookie (Latin)

Cosmopolitan and widespread. This mushroom is very common in Northwest North America; it occurs in the forest as well as in city parks in grass close to trees; often growing in fairy rings. It is important to know that not only the fairy ring mushroom, *Marasmius oreades*, forms fairy rings in city parks and lawns but also the small poisonous white *Clitocybe* species, *Calocybe ionides*, and various *Hebeloma* species, especially **poisonous** *H. crustiliniforme*.

cap	mostly buff with darker crown, sometimes off-white, convex, edge inrolled, expanding but staying convex, rarely with uplifted margin; up to 7 cm across.
gills	buff, uneven edges, broad, adnate-sinuate or adnexed, intermediates; sometimes dark droplets, but not as regularly as no. 7; dull brown in maturity.
spore print	medium dull brown.
stalk	white; granulate apex (look against the light), sometimes more pronounced than at other times; equal or base slightly enlarged; up to 6 cm tall and 1 cm thick.
flesh	white, solid.
odour	radish.

Genus INOCYBE
fibrehead (Greek)

The genus is close to *Hebeloma*. It is a large group with, according to various authorities, between 500 and 600 species in North America. Like *Cortinarius, Inocybe* is mycorrhizal; it is a very important member of forest societies. The genus contains more poisonous species, quite a few deadly, than any other genus in the kingdom of fungi. The typical shape of the cap is pointed with a sharp umbo and a fibrillose, silky or scaly, not viscid, cuticle. The cap often splits between the gills when expanding (see pp. 117 and 119). They have long fibres in the stalk. It is important to notice the presence or absence of a bulbous stalk base. The odour is another interesting characteristic: unpleasant and pungent, smelling of raw potatoes, radishes, unripe corn or seedy. The spore print is greyish earth brown to dull brown. Only approximate identification can be made in the field. I am showing some species which can be recognized, but for most, microscopic work has to be done for identification. One more interesting fact — these elegant mushrooms can grow to an enormous size in areas of extreme rainfall. I have noticed that this can happen in dry climates, too, when there suddenly is a period of exceptional wet weather (see *I. sororia*, no. 1 on p. 117: the ordinary size and the giant above it).

cornsilk Inocybe   p.117-1
Inocybe sororia Kauffman
sororia: of the sisterhood (Latin)

North American species; frequently collected in the Pacific Northwest; it occurs in mixed forest, singly to scattered. It can grow to very large size under very humid conditions. **Poisonous**.

cap	pale straw colour, silky, with yellowish radial fibres, strongly pointed umbo; bell shaped at first, then expanding, often splitting between the gills; up to 8 cm across, but sometimes larger. The big one shown was 15 cm across.
gills	off-white at first; narrow, serrate, close, intermediates, adnexed, almost free; when maturing, gills change to yellowish or greenish ochre, broad in the large form, eventually they are dingy brown.
spore print	yellowish brown.
stalk	whitish, solid, shiny inside and out, bumpy, may get brownish in age; up to 8 cm tall but 20 cm or more in giant form; 0.5 cm thick at apex (up to 2 cm).
flesh	white with long fibres in the stalk.
odour	pungent, of unripe corn.

deadly Inocybe   p.117-2
Inocybe fastigiata (Schaeffer: Fries) Quélet
fastigiata: with a pointed gable (Latin)

Cosmopolitan and widespread; occurring in the Pacific Northwest and across the continent, growing under deciduous trees and in grass close to trees. Large quantities of muscarin are present in the mushrooms, which makes them **deadly**.

cap	with yellowish and brownish radial fibres, bell shaped at first; splitting between the gills when expanding, sharp umbo, sometimes a plumper shape; up to 8 cm across (see remarks under *I.sororia* regarding size).
gills	whitish and close at first, finally dull brown; serrate, narrow.
spore print	medium mud brown.
stalk	whitish or colour of cap, shiny, base somewhat widening, tall and slim or much thicker and shorter; up to 18 cm tall and 2 cm thick.
flesh	white, long fibres.
odour	fetid.

full-breasted fibrehead

p.117-3

Inocybe eutheles Berkeley & Broome sensu Singer

eutheles: blossoming, full-breasted (Greek)

Cosmopolitan; a very light, almost white, *Inocybe* with an extremely pointed cap; may stain pale brown. I found the one shown in aspen parkland. **Dangerous**.

cap	almost white, silky, later can be very pale brown; bell shaped with very pointed umbo, radially fibrous; up to 5 cm across.
gills	off-white at first, narrow, adnexed. close, pale clay colour when mature.
spore print	light grey brown.
stalk	off-white, smooth, slightly bulging in the bottom half, may get to be a pale flesh colour; up to 10 cm tall and 1 cm thick at the top.
flesh	white, stringy in the stalk.
odour	earthy, a bit like radish.

bog Inocybe

p.119-1

Inocybe paludinella Peck sensu Kühner

paludinella: small bog mushroom (Latin)

Cosmopolitan; this very small species grew in moss and lichens under spruce; identified by S. A. Redhead, this is an example — along with no. 3 — of interesting tiny mushrooms which cannot be identified with this dangerous genus without microscopic study.

cap	ochrish or sand colour, dome shaped, faintly umbonate, shiny, fine striations; up to 1.5 cm across.
gills	whitish at first, then light grey brown; adnexed.
spore print	pale yellow brown.
stalk	white, bent, bumpy; up to 2 cm tall and 0.2 cm thick.
flesh	white, thin.

lilac and grey Inocybe

p.119-2

Inocybe griseolilacina J. Lange

griseolilacina: greyish amethyst colour (Latin)

Cosmopolitan, growing in spruce-birch bog in moss; this small group occurred in the same forest as nos. 1 and 3. Old bogs are fine areas for detecting different fungi, but they cannot tolerate much trampling, so it is best to follow a game trail.

cap	lavender changing to grey, bell shaped with umbo, radially fibrous; the flame pattern of very small scales is especially visible when the cap is still lilac; up to 2 cm across.
gills	dirty ochrish to dull brown, adnate-sinuate.
spore print	pale ochrish brown.
stalk	same colour as cap, swollen toward base; up to 4 cm tall and 0.2 cm thick at the apex.
flesh	pale lavender.
odour	unpleasant.

miniature Inocybe

p.119-3

Inocybe petiginosa (Fries) Gillet

petiginosa: flown in, dropped by birds (Greek)

Cosmopolitan; this is a very small *Inocybe* which I found growing on and around *Thelephora terrestris* in a spruce bog (see p. 169). Seemingly parasitic, this mushroom grows on the ground and probably in dust or earth on the long-living Thelephora. It occurs on at least one other continent because it appears on a check list of Dutch macrofungi (see Arnolds 1984).

cap	yellowish, a bit brownish on the crown; rounded, then plane; up to 1 cm across.
gills	buff to light brown.
spore print	dull light brown.
stalk	yellowish, thin, long, crooked, up to 2.5 cm tall and 0.1 cm thick.
flesh	off-white, thin.

little white Inocybe p.119-4

Inocybe geophylla (Sowerby: Fries) Kummer
geophylla: with earth-coloured gills (Greek)

Cosmopolitan; growing under spruce in mixed forest; this species is widespread. **Poisonous**.

cap	white, bell shaped, expanding to the chinese-hat shape with umbo of the Inocybes; up to 2 cm across.
gills	whitish at first, later mud colour; adnexed.
spore print	ochrish.
stalk	white, equal; up to 4 cm tall and 0.2 cm thick.
flesh	white.
odour	somewhat dirty.

little violet Inocybe p.119-5

Inocybe geophylla (Sowerby: Fries) var. *violaceus* Patouillard
Violet-coloured variety of no. 4.

Cosmopolitan; found in the same locations as the white form; the description is the same except for the colour. This variety is slightly bigger than no. 4 and has white flesh.

brown scaly Inocybe p.119-6

Inocybe dulcamara (Albertini & Schweinitz: Persoon) Kummer
dulcamara: bittersweet (Latin)

Cosmopolitan; widespread distribution on the northern hemisphere; they are common in Greenland. Quite common in groups in sandy areas. This is one of the hairy or woolly *Inocybe* species, which could easily be confused with small brown *Cortinarius* species, except for their dull brown gills and spore print. Nos. 6, 7, 9 and 10 are in this category; all of these even have a cortina, although it is scant; all are dangerous. *Inocybe dulcamara* is **poisonous**.

cap	yellowish to orange brown, felty, scaly on rounded crown, convex to bell shaped, mostly just rounded in maturity; up to 5.5 cm across.
gills	dirty yellow ochrish, adnate, serrate, intermediates.
spore print	medium dull brown.
stalk	brownish, ochre lower down; base white and sometimes somewhat bulbous; scaly, an almost woolly top with remnants of a cortina; up to 4 cm tall and 0.8 cm thick.
cortina	visible in young specimens.
flesh	yellowish to ochrish.
odour	none.

blonde hairy Inocybe p.119-7

Inocybe mixtilis Britzelmayr sensu Kühner
mixtilis: with mixed hair (Greek)

Cosmopolitan; not a very well-known Inocybe. The name *mixtilis* refers to the short hair all over the cap and the small scales at the crown; difficult to identify; fruiting from June to August, mostly associated with poplar. **Dangerous**.

cap	brownish, umbonate; strongly felty but scaly on umbo; bell shaped to broadly bell shaped, fading, striate, watery looking in maturity; up to 3.5 cm across.
gills	light sandy first, then greyish brown, broad, adnexed, intermediates, very distant in old specimens.
spore print	medium dull brown.
stalk	white, fibrous, up to 6 cm tall and 0.5 cm thick.
flesh	white, stringy.
odour	of radish.

black nipple Inocybe

p.119-8

Inocybe fuscodisca (Peck) Massee

fuscodisca: with dark disc or umbo (Latin)

North American, not common, occurring in south-eastern and Pacific coast regions. Growing under black poplar in Alberta. This is an easily recognized species. **Poisonous**.

cap	medium brown; radially fibrous and split like a lot of Inocybes but with a spectacular, dark brown umbo sitting in the middle like a big brown bead; up to 3 cm across.
gills	whitish at first, adnate sinuate; finally pale greyish ochre, intermediates.
spore print	dull grey brown.
stalk	white at top and base, brownish in the middle; up to 6 cm tall and 0.4 cm thick at the top.
flesh	white.
odour	unpleasant, chemical.

small woolly fibrehead

p.119-9

Inocybe ovatocystis Boursier & Kühner

ovatocystis (Latin): with egg-shaped cystidia (cystidium: a particular end cell)

Cosmopolitan; this is a small rust-coloured, woolly mushroom, growing under spruce. One of the hairy group mentioned under no. 6. There are other mushrooms, looking just like this one, which have a black spore print and purplish gills (*Psathyrella*). It is, therefore, very important to take a spore print and to check the colour of the gills. **Dangerous**.

cap	rust brown, woolly, low umbo, turned-in margin; up to 1.5 cm across.
gills	off-white at first, then light brown; adnate.
spore print	medium red brown.
stalk	same colour as cap, top lighter; up to 2.5 cm tall and 0.3 cm thick.
partial veil	fibrillose, small remnants on stalk.
flesh	light brown, can be lighter in the cap.

woolly fibrehead

p.119-10

Inocybe lanuginosa (Bulliard: Fries) Kummer

lanuginosa: full of down (Latin)

Cosmopolitan and widespread; it occurs in aspen parkland, in the Rocky Mountains and in the Yukon. This is the fourth "woolly" *Inocybe* described here. This one does have special features: it grows on very decayed logs, unlike other inocybes (it can also grow on humus), and it has an overhanging infertile skinflap (see section on p. 119). It is a spring mushroom. **Poisonous**.

cap	dull smoky brown, dry, felty to scaly; bell shaped at first, then flattening with small umbo (watch for skinflap on the margin); when young, a cortina can be seen; up to 6 cm across.
gills	dirty white to sandy at first, then dull greyish brown; adnate-sinuate, intermediates.
spore print	a bit smoky, dull medium brown.
stalk	same colour as the cap, fibrous; no cortina remnants in mature specimens, bent; up to 3.5 cm tall and 0.7 cm thick.
flesh	dirty light brown, hollow in stalk.
odour	none.

Genus CREPIDOTUS

The only genus in Cortinariaceae in which the species are stalkless. The name "Crepi–dotus" means, in Greek, with a base like an ear. All are saprophytic and grow on wood. The gills are fanlike or eccentric, radiating from the place of attachment. Brown spore print.

red Crepidotus

Crepidotus cinnabarinus Peck

p.121-1

cinnabarinus: with vermilion colour (Latin)

North American species primarily. Interestingly this species is distributed in a diagonal line across the continent, from the Smoky Mountains in Tennessee (Eastern deciduous forests) to Alberta following the southern edge of the boreal forest (S.A. Redhead 1989). Also found in Japan, far eastern U.S.S.R. and Denmark. Growing on deciduous wood; the specimens I found were all on black poplar, fruiting in July and August. On the old poplar log on which the nicest collection was found, many different species were growing. Besides the red Crepidotus, there was a white one, as well as a Polypore following the grooves in the bark and several lichens and mosses. In the barkless top of the log, woodpeckers were making holes. I followed the succession of living things for years until the log fell apart.

cap	cinnabar red or vermilion with some crimson; felty, fan shape or eccentric depending on place of attachment; often a narrow yellow edge; up to 2 cm across, sometimes more, when several caps grow together.
gills	pinkish with red edge or red at first, then red brown as the spores ripen, broad, subdistant, intermediates.
spore print	red brown.
stalk	none or rudimentary.
flesh	pinkish.

small white Crepidotus

Crepidotus ellipsoideus Hesler & Smith

p.121-2

ellipsoideus: indicating the ellipse-shaped spores (Greek)

North American species, but in Europe they seem to have the same mushroom, which they call *Crepidotus variabilis*. The small white fleshy *Crepidotus*, growing on deciduous wood, often grows on the underside of a branchlet, also on big logs like in the illustration; fruiting from July until September in Alberta.

cap	white, small, with an in-rolled margin; eccentric or fan shaped, depending on place of attachment; up to 0.5 cm across.
gills	white at first, then buff to tan; subdistant with many intermediates, narrow.
spore print	light brown.
stalk	none.
flesh	white.
odour	none.

flat Crepidotus

Crepidotus applanatus (Persoon: Persoon) Kummer

p.121-3

applanatus: flattened (Latin)

Cosmopolitan; growing on decayed deciduous wood that is barkless or so old that it is not easy to recognize the tree species; fruiting in summer.

cap	white at first, then turning brown; edge inrolled at first, then flattening out and the edge becomes wavy; of varying shape, depending if it grows on top, the side or the bottom of a log; the name *applanatus* refers to extreme flatness of the mature fruiting body; up to 4 cm across.
gills	white at first, turning brown when the spores ripen; radiating from the point of attachment, narrow subdistant, many intermediates.
spore print	medium brown.
stalk	none or rudimentary.
flesh	white, thin.

soft Crepidotus

p.121-4

Crepidotus mollis (Fries) Staude

mollis: soft (Latin)

Cosmopolitan; mostly on decaying wood, fruiting from spring to fall, widely distributed. Originally I thought that there were two species: a hairy one with a yellow brown cap and a white smooth one, but *Crepidotus mollis* has a gelatinous cuticle so that when it dries up or is rained on, it loses its tomentum as well as fading to a dirty white colour. The spores ripen slowly, as seen in the illustration (colour changes in the gills); the gill edges gelatinize, too, and the whole thing looks waterlogged after a while. An important recycler of old wood.

cap	buff with a tawny tomentum, later loosing its hair and fading to dirty white; gelatinous layer makes it feel soft; rolled-in edge at first; up to 7 cm across.
gills	greyish white at first, then turning cinnamon brown as the spores ripen; underside of the cap looks like a small fan, close with intermediates.
spore print	cinnamon brown.
stalk	absent.
flesh	white, thin; looks waterlogged because of gelatinization.
odour	faint.

Genus SIMOCYBE
with a flat head (greek)

The genus contains small saprophytic mushrooms growing on decaying wood of deciduous trees. The spore print is a yellow-ochre colour.

American Simocybe

p.121-5

Simocybe serrulatus (Murrill) Singer

serrulatus: like a small saw (Latin)

Cosmopolitan and widely distributed; this mushroom grows on deciduous decaying wood of primarily birch and poplar, in mixed boreal forest; I found it several years in a row on a barkless poplar log; fruiting in spring, summer or fall if moisture conditions are right. This mushroom has had various names over the years (See Redhead 1984).

cap	yellow brown to olive brown, velvety, convex, flattening somewhat with age; up to 2 cm across.
gills	greenish yellow at first, later brown; adnate-sinuate, broad, edges more or less toothed.
spore print	ochre to olive brown.
stalk	yellow brown to brown, curved, hollow; up to 3 cm tall and 0.3 cm thick.
flesh	yellow; brown in stalk.
odour	aromatic.

Genus ALNICOLA
living with alder (Latin)

The genus is reserved for species which live with alder and have rounded cap cuticle cells and warty spores.

brown alder mushroom

p.121-6

Alnicola melinoides (Fries) Kühner

melinoides: looking like grain (Greek)

A species of the Pacific Northwest. This one and *Simocybe serrulatus* were formerly called *Naucoria*. I found the specimens in the illustration in sand on the beach in Victoria, B.C., near a group of alder. They are small mushrooms, looking like dirty Lepiotas, except that they have adnate brownish gills and a yellow-brown spore print. They were fruiting in November.

cap	yellowish, covered with yellow-brown scales, thickest on the small umbo; up to 3 cm across.
gills	dirty yellow or yellow ochre, close, many intermediates, adnate, broad.
spore print	brownish.
stalk	pale dirty yellow, top smooth, bottom two-thirds full of light brown scales; up to 5 cm tall and 0.3 cm thick.
flesh	yellow.
odour	more or less acidic.

Genus TUBARIA
small trumpet (Latin)

A small genus of little brown saprophytic mushrooms growing on branchlets or old wood, sometimes buried wood. Fruiting in cool temperatures. Both species have remnants of a partial veil on their cap edge; spore print yellow or reddish brown.

spring Tubaria   p.121-7
Tubaria conspersa (Persoon: Fries) Fayod
conspersa: sprinkled upon (Latin)

Cosmopolitan; according to D. W. Malloch, this is a very rare species. It fruits very early in the year, when the first Verpas (early morels) appear in Alberta. Since my first find, I have recorded the species a dozen times, always between May 11 and June 16. At that time of year, when plants just start to grow in this region, not many people look for mushrooms. At a higher elevation in the Cypress Hills, I found them on the 11th of July. This *Tubaria* grows on branchlets, leaf stems, old seed pods of balsam poplar and sometimes on wood chips and wood.

cap	chestnut brown to orange brown with white bits of a partial veil on the margin; conical with small umbo when young, expanding and sometimes with a raised edge when older; hygrophanous, fading to buff starting in the centre; up to 4.5 cm across.
gills	tan to light brown, adnate, close, intermediates.
spore print	light yellow brown.
stalk	brown or orange brown with a fluffy white, mycelium covered base; up to 7 cm tall and 0.4 cm thick.
partial veil	rarely leaves any bits on the stalk, but the cap margin has white flocci on it.
flesh	pale yellow brown.
odour	faint.

fringed Tubaria   p.121-8
Tubaria furfuracea (Persoon: Fries) Gillet
furfuracea: scaly (Latin)

Cosmopolitan; growing on branchlets, wood chips and other debris; fruiting late in the fall and sometimes early in the spring. It needs cool temperatures to fruit.

cap	vinaceous cinnamon to pinkish brown; a bit scurfy, convex or sometimes with a small umbo; hygrophanous; small white scales around the rim; up to 3.5 cm across.
gills	light brown to cinnamon brown, adnate-sinuate, distant, intermediates.
spore print	reddish brown.
stalk	red brown, streaky, sometimes evanescent ring, white fluff at the base; up to 6 cm tall and 0.5 cm thick.
flesh	pale pinkish brown.
odour	faint.

Genus GYMNOPILUS
with naked cap (Greek)

Species in this genus do not have a gelatinous or sticky layer on the cap. They are brightly coloured in shades of golden yellow, orange and red brown. The colour of the spore print is rusty orange, brighter than the spore prints of *Cortinarius, Inocybe* and *Hebeloma*. They usually grow on wood or buried wood. A partial veil is often present; the taste is said to be bitter, but I have not tasted any myself. None are good edibles.

golden-gilled Gymnopilus   p.123-1

Gymnopilus luteofolius (Peck) Singer

luteofolius: with golden yellow gills (Latin)

North American species (as far as I know); I found these three times on birch logs in boreal forest and aspen parkland, but they are described as occurring on decaying conifer wood. They resemble *Tricholomopsis rutilans*, also yellow mushrooms, covered with red tomentum and with yellow gills. The latter grow on conifer wood and have a white spore print (see p. 89). Edibility unknown.

cap	shiny yellow, covered with reddish hairtufts or appressed fibrils; convex with inrolled edge, then flattening; up to 4.5 cm across.
gills	yellow at first, then rusty orange; adnate to decurrent, serrate, distant, intermediates.
spore print	bright orange-cinnamon.
stalk	yellow, fibrillose, later covered with spores, remnants of a cortina; central or off-centre, bent; up to 3 cm tall and 0.5 cm thick.
partial veil	like a cortina or almost membranous, remnants on the stalk.
flesh	yellow or yellow with red streaks.
odour	none.

laughing mushroom   p.123-2

Gymnopilus spectabilis (Fries) Smith

spectabilis: spectacular (Latin)

Cosmopolitan; growing in cespitose groups at the base of coniferous or deciduous trees, which are dead or not very healthy. They are spectacular because of the golden colours, but there is such a variation in shape and colour of the stalk, the colour of the cap (old gold to orange red) and the consistency of the partial veil, etc., that I will only describe the most common form which I found. The popular name in many countries, "big laughing mushroom," refers to the fact that a hallucinogenic substance is found in these mushrooms, but according to Arora (1986), the substance is inactive in mushrooms in the West. Inedible because of the bitter taste.

cap	old gold to orange rust; soft like chamois leather when mature; convex, then nearly plane; up to 13 cm across.
gills	ochre yellow, rusty brown with age, adnate, broad, lightly serrate, relatively distant, intermediates.
spore print	orange brown.
stalk	off-white to buff, almost equal to lightly swollen base; getting a bit more ochrish and spore dusted as time goes by; up to 14 cm tall and 2 cm thick.
partial veil	fibrillose, prolific spores on cortina-like remnants, collapsing or disappearing.
flesh	buff to pale yellow, solid, firm.
odour	weak.

small yellow Gymnopilus   p.123-3

Gymnopilus penetrans (Fries: Fries) Murrill

penetrans: intruding (Latin)

Cosmopolitan; growing in conifer forests on the ground or at the base of stumps or of living trees. The one illustrated seemed to be "intruding" all right; the fruiting bodies grew out of a crack in the base of a living hemlock in the mountains. Inedible.

cap	golden yellow at first, then reddish brown on crown and margin; finely fibrillose, radially splitting when expanding, broadly umbonate; up to 6 cm across.
gills	orange buff, close, adnate.
spore print	medium cinnamon.

stalk	yellow top, bottom half red-brown to dark brown, fibrous, up to 6 cm tall and 0.6 cm thick.
flesh	yellowish.

bitter Gymnopilus p.123-4

Gymnopilus liquiritiae (Persoon: Fries) Karsten

liquiritiae: with the quality of licorice (Latin)

Cosmopolitan; growing in tight cespitose clusters on old wood, often logs which were partly burned in past forest fires.

cap	pale yellow orange at first, later orange brown; convex, then flattening; fitting into available space because of close proximity, up to 6 cm across.
gills	pale buff orange at first, then orange brown; adnate-serrate; getting spotty; relatively broad, close, many intermediates.
spore print	bright rust brown.
stalk	colour of cap or somewhat lighter; no partial veil, bent; up to 6 cm tall and 0.4 cm thick.
flesh	yellowish.
odour	not unpleasant.

spruce Gymnopilus p.123-5

Gymnopilus sapineus (Fries) Maire

sapineus: of spruce (Latin)

Cosmopolitan; growing always under spruce. This collection was found in a spruce-birch bog in fine moss and lichens. It grows on rotting logs or in lignin-rich humus.

cap	rusty brown with yellow orange margin, felty; convex at first, then flattening; up to 3.5 cm across.
gills	golden yellow, then yellow brown, mottled; serrate, adnexed.
spore print	rusty orange.
stalk	yellow top, the rest is brown; tiny scales; up to 3 cm tall and 0.4 cm thick.
flesh	yellowish.

Genus ROZITES

This genus was named after French mycologist Ernest Roze, 1833-1900. There is only one species in this genus. It has been described as a *Cortinarius* with a veil.

the gypsy p.123-6

Rozites caperata (Fries) Micheli

caperata: wrinkled (Latin)

Cosmopolitan; widespread and circumpolar in the northern hemisphere; reported from Greenland, Lapland, the Yukon, Alaska and all across Canada and the northern U.S. Only one species in this genus occurs in the temperate zone, but *R. australiensis*, which has a universal veil, occurs in Australia. A few more species occur in the tropics, one, for instance, which is cultivated by leaf-cutting ants. The gypsy grows on humus in deciduous and coniferous forests, singly or in small groups. It is said to be a good edible.

cap	yellow to orange with violet tinges and frosted appearance; turning buff and orange brown with age; oval at first, then bell shaped, finally with wrinkled uplifted margin; up to 10 cm across.
gills	buff at first, turning light cinnamon with developing spores; close, broad, serrate.
spore print	cinnamon brown.
stalk	white, streaked with pale yellow and violet; equal, up to 14 cm tall and 2 cm thick.
partial veil	resulting in a persistent ring with lines on the white top and yellowish underneath, getting loose with age.
flesh	white to pale honey yellow, fibrous in stalk, thick.
odour	pleasant.
taste	good, mintlike flavour.

Family BOLBITIACEAE

The family contains three genera. All species are saprophytic. Although the name means cow dung, only a few grow directly on dung. The genera have microscopic characteristics in common like spores with germpores and cellular cap cuticles, etc. Macroscopically they are very different.

Bolbitius: consists of slimy soft mushrooms; rust to reddish brown spore colour.

Agrocybe: has darker brown spores and is sturdier; most of the time there is a fibrous partial veil.

Conocybe: consists of small fragile mushrooms, usually growing in grassy areas. They have rust-brown spores. A few are hallucinogenic, and some are deadly poisonous.

The family is closely related to the Coprinaceae. They are suburbanites, according to A. H. Smith, meaning that they are not as sensitive to disturbance and pollution.

Genus BOLBITIUS
bolbitius: pertaining to cow dung (Greek)

Growing on manure, manured soil, wet wood or chips; soft and fragile mushrooms, usually slimy all over; gills in some species almost begin to liquify at maturity; spore print is rust brown.

grey Bolbitius   p.124-1
Bolbitius aleuriatus (Fries) Singer
former name: *Pluteolus aleuriatus*
aleuriatus: resembling wheat flour (Greek)

Cosmopolitan; infrequent, found in the forest living on bits of old wood, lignin-rich soil and sawdust; fruiting in summer in Alberta, further south in the fall. Not edible: too small and slimy.

cap	beautiful grey with lilac tinges; bell shaped; slimy at first, drying up later; margin striate, sometimes small umbo; up to 4 cm across.
gills	ivory at first, then sandy, finally cinnamon; close; adnate at first, free when cap is expanded.
spore print	rust colour.
stalk	pale lemon yellow on the outside, hollow and bright lemon yellow inside (sometimes the stalk is white), minutely scurfy; up to 3.5 cm tall and 0.5 - 0.6 cm thick.
flesh	thin, fragile, yellow in stalk, grey in cap.

white Bolbitius   p.124-2
Bolbitius sordidus C. G. Lloyd
sordidus: dirty (Latin)

North American; rare, growing in forests on bits of old wood or lignin-rich soils in damp spots; fruiting in summer; the name probably has to do with the extreme sliminess of the species. Not recommended for eating — too slimy.

cap	off-white; narrowly conic or bell shaped, very slimy, fringe on the cap edge, up to 3 cm across.
gills	white at first, close, narrowly adnate to almost free; later grey.
spore print	medium brown.
stalk	white, covered with white fibrils under the slime; up to 10 cm tall and 0.8 cm thick at the top.
flesh	white, soft, quickly collapsing.

yellow dung mushroom   p.124-3
Bolbitius vitellinus (Persoon) Fries
vitellinus: resembling egg-yolk (Latin)

Cosmopolitan; growing on manure, richly manured ground, rotting hay, woodchips, etc;

fruiting in summer and fall; edible but not tasty.

cap yolk-yellow and slimy at first; dome shaped, then expanding; flattening out with a small yellow umbo; the margin turns lilac grey; flesh of striate cap very thin, up to 8.5 cm across, stays sticky; sometimes the cap colour is green (see 3b on p. 124).

gills creamy at first, narrow, adnate; light brown later and free, almost deliquescing in the end.

spore print medium reddish brown.

stalk white with fluffy white tufts, hollow; when the cap is green, the stalk may be yellow; very fragile, up to 9 cm tall and 1 cm thick.

flesh yellow in cap, white in stalk.

Genus AGROCYBE
head of the field (Greek)

Grows in grassy areas in the forest, on the ground or decaying wood. Generally sturdier than *Bolbitius* and *Conocybe*, at one time members of this genus were included in the genus *Pholiota*, but microscopically they have more in common with the Bolbitiaceae. Often a partial veil is present. The gills are adnate, and the spore print is dark brown.

plains Agrocybe   p.125-1
Agrocybe pediades (Fries) Kühner
former name: *Naucoria semiorbicularis*
pediades: of the plains (Greek)

Cosmopolitan; widely distributed; this small mushroom with hemispherical cap appears in summer in grassy areas in cities and along roads; edible but not recommended since it resembles many small poisonous species, some deadly.

cap yellowish buff, sometimes close to orange; hemispherical, smooth, up to 2.5 cm across.

gills first lilac grey, then medium cinnamon-brown; adnexed, broad, often seceding from the stalk; many intermediates, close.

spore print dark chocolate brown.

stalk buff, stiff, crooked, hollow, mycelial tufts at the base; up to 6 cm tall and 0.2 cm thick.

flesh white, thin.

odour clean, like sweet-scented bedstraw.

mountain Agrocybe   p.125-2
Agrocybe praecox (Persoon: Fries) Fayod, forma *cutefracta* Lange
praecox: early, precocious (Latin)
cutefracta: fragmented cuticle (Latin)

Cosmopolitan; found in a bed of *Dryas drummondii* along a creek in the Rocky Mountains; fruiting in summer; edibility unknown.

cap warm cinnamon brown, light flesh showing in the cracks, smooth; up to 8 cm across.

gills off-white at first, then deep cinnamon brown, adnexed.

spore print dark brown.

stalk whitish at first and a bit scurfy below the ring, then changing to cap colour; up to 8 cm tall and 1 cm wide, thickened base.

partial veil makes fringe on cap edge or small annulus (brown from the spores).

flesh solid to stringy; off-white to a bit yellowish.

odour a bit dirty.

spring Agrocybe   p.125-3
Agrocybe praecox (Persoon: Fries) Fayod
praecox: early (Latin)

Cosmopolitan; widely distributed, fruiting in early spring; growing on the ground in open areas of forests; edible with caution, because it can be mixed up with poisonous *Hebeloma* species.

cap buff with darker crown, convex, smooth, up to 9 cm across.

gills	pale at first, then light brown; adnexed.
spore print	chocolate brown.
stalk	white, hollow, sometimes thickening either at the apex or at the base, sturdy, rhizomorphs on the base; up to 9 cm tall and 1 cm thick.
partial veil	white, membranous; resulting either in a scruffy ring, coloured by spores, or a fringe around the cap edge (3b).
flesh	off-white, thick.
odour	mealy, not pleasant.

rough Agrocybe p.125-4

Agrocybe dura (Bolton: Fries) Singer

dura: rough (Latin)

Cosmopolitan; often in grassy areas in cities and along roads; a suburbanite species, fruiting in spring and summer; edible but not very good.

cap	off-white to pale yellowish, staying pale or sometimes turning light brown when mature; areolate; beautifully rounded at first, then flattening out; up to 8.5 cm across.
gills	off-white at first, then darkening to medium brown; adnexed, close.
spore print	chocolate brown.
stalk	white, slimy equal, hollow, base sometimes discolouring to brown; up to 10 cm tall and 0.7 cm thick.
partial veil	white, fibrous, thin; when stretched across the gills it is already split, disappearing or leaving a small ring.
flesh	white.

stump Agrocybe p.125-5

Agrocybe acericola (Peck) Singer

acericola: living on maple wood (*Acer*) (Latin)

North American; a northern species, probably first found on maple wood in eastern Canada and New York State, but grows on decaying poplar wood in the west (Yukon, Alberta, down to Wyoming).

cap	light brown in young specimens, fading later; egg shaped at first, then flattening; smooth, up to 7 cm across.
gills	greyish at first, then brown; adnate to adnexed, intermediates.
spore print	medium brown to chocolate brown.
stalk	white, equal or with thickened base; sometimes bits of wood or bark incorporated in the base; rhizomorphs; up to 7 cm tall and 1 cm thick.
partial veil	results in a flaring, persistant ring.
flesh	white, solid.

Genus CONOCYBE

with conical head (cap) (Greek)

Grows mostly in grassy areas, sometimes on dung or wood mulch. They have hygrophanous caps, usually cone-shaped, mustard-coloured gills and a rusty spore print.

white dunce cap p.127-1

Conocybe lactea (Lange) Métrod

lactea: milk white (Latin)

Cosmopolitan and widespread; on this continent it grows in grassy areas; edible, but it disappears so quickly, that it is not worthwhile; fruits in summer.

cap	off-white; very slim cone, seems almost draped on the stalk, higher than wide, up to 2 cm across and up to 3 cm high.
gills	white at first, then pink; close, almost free, narrow.
spore print	bright cinnamon to red brown.
stalk	white, slim, equal, often bent, very fragile, hollow; up to 10 cm tall and 0.2 cm thick, no ring.
flesh	white, thin, soft.

slim Conocybe

p.127-2

Conocybe siliginea (Fries: Fries) Kühner

siliginea: looking like wheat cornels (Latin)

Cosmopolitan; reported both from Europe and North America; my specimens are from the Edmonton, Alberta, area; grows in grassy areas or gardens; a very small, elegant mushroom, hard to spot. Unlike *C. tenera*, it has cystidia that form on the stalk. Fruits in summer and fall.

cap	raw sienna or light brown fading to buff; conical or bell-shaped and keeps that shape; up to 1 cm across.
gills	light reddish brown, beautifully regular, relatively distant, adnexed.
spore print	warm reddish brown.
stalk	reddish brown to buff, thin, relatively tall and a bit crooked; up to 6 cm tall and 0.2 cm thick.
flesh	off-white to light brown, fragile.
odour	of radish.

short-stemmed Conocybe

p.127-3

Conocybe mesospora Kühner: Singer

mesospora: refers to the spore size, which is in between those of other species of *Conocybe* (Greek)

Cosmopolitan; the mushroom has a bigger cap than the previous one, but the stalk is very short. It is not easily spotted in lawns except by small children; fruits in summer and fall. There are some little brown mushrooms (often called L.B.M.'s) and little white mushrooms which are poisonous and even deadly, so if a child has chewed one up, look for more of the same and take them to a mushroom expert to make sure they're not poisonous (doctors or emergency departments have no knowledge of mushrooms).

cap	mocha brown, hygrophanous, fading to buff; dome shaped, uneven edge; up to 3 cm across.
gills	mocha to mustard coloured, intermediates, relatively distant, beautifully spaced, adnexed to almost free, narrow.
spore print	mustard brown.
stalk	shiny white, hollow, short; up to 3 cm tall and 0.2 cm thick.
flesh	off-white, thin.

brown dunce cap

p.127-4

Conocybe tenera (Schaeffer: Fries) Fayod

tenera: fragile, slender (Latin)

Cosmopolitan and widespread; grows well up in northern Canada; occurs in manured grassy areas; fruits in late summer and fall. Another similar *Conocybe* is deadly **poisonous!** (i.e. *Cononcybe filaris* Fries)

cap	reddish brown to yellow ochre; hygrophanous and, therefore, fading; conic to bell-shaped, striate margin; up to 4 cm across.
gills	mustard colour, adnexed to almost free, narrow, intermediates, beautifully spaced.
spore print	reddish brown.
stalk	same colour as cap, equal or a bit of thickening below, hollow, tall, slim; up to 7 cm tall and 0.3 cm thick.
flesh	buff, thin.

Kühner's Conocybe

p.127-5

Conocybe kuehneriana Singer

kuehneriana: named after R. Kühner, a very well-known French mycologist

A European species so far, but this Alberta specimen was identified by Dr. S. A. Redhead, like many of my lesser-known species; growing in open areas in the woods, this species shows its relationship to the Coprinaceae family by its close resemblance to certain *Psathyrella* species. A spore print is necessary to tell them apart.

cap	dull yellow brown at first, fading to almost white, hemispherical, smooth; up to 3 cm across.
gills	rust colour, adnexed to almost free, relatively close, intermediates.
spore print	medium reddish brown.
stalk	white, slim, tall, hollow, equal with a small basal bulb; up to 9 cm tall and 0.2 cm thick.
flesh	buff in cap; white in stalk, thin.
odour	none.

Family STROPHARIACEAE

The family consists of fleshy species growing on the ground, on wood or dung. All species of this family have a partial veil, which is sometimes evanescent. Species of five genera are described.

Pholiota species have a rusty brown spore print; the fruiting bodies occur on wood or are connected to buried wood; some species are parasitic.

Kuehneromyces species have a cinnamon brown spore print; closely related to *Pholiota*, they grow in tufts on stumps.

Hypholoma species have purplish brown spores; the mushrooms grow in small or big tufts on wood or on the ground; the ring is cortina-like.

Psilocybe species are mostly small, with purplish to purple-brown spore print, growing on dung or on the ground. A number of hallucinogenic species are included.

Stropharia is a genus with colourful species. The name is from the Greek word for belt (the conspicuous ring). The family is named after this genus.

Genus STROPHARIA
having a ring or belt (Greek)

Fleshy mushrooms growing on dung, humus and, sometimes, on wood; small, medium or large, often with bright colours; the cap is slimy or sticky; gills are pale at first, then a beautiful pearly grey before darkening to purplish brown as the spores ripen. The partial veil results in a fringe on the cap edge and a radially grooved ring darkened by spores; in some species the ring is fragile; the spore print is a deep purplish brown; gills adnate to adnexed. All species are saprophytic.

dung roundhead   p.129-1

Stropharia semiglobata (Batsch: Fries) Quélet
semiglobata: hemispherical (Latin)

Worldwide distribution; this mushroom can be found on cow or horse dung in meadows; scattered or in small groups. Especially in rainy weather, they can be easily recognized by the glistening yellow layer of slime.

cap	yellow, or yellow and white, and slimy especially when young; hemispherical or bell shaped, smooth, up to 5 cm across.
gills	at first pale, then pearly grey becoming spotty, finally dark purplish brown; broad, adnate and seceding.
spore print	dark purplish brown, almost black.
stalk	yellow and white, slender, equal with a small bulbous base, often rhizoids.
veil	slimy, covers young mushrooms.
partial veil	sticky from slime, sometimes evanescent leaving an annular zone, other times resulting in a grooved annulus, blackened from the spores.
flesh	whitish, stained brown in the base of the stalk and over the gills, hollow stalk.
odour	clean, spicy, like fenugreek.
taste	said to be edible, but can be mixed up with poisonous species, so eating or tasting it is inadvisable.

ochre-yellow Stropharia

p.129-2

Stropharia coronilla (Bulliard: Fries) Quélet

coronilla: with small crown (Latin)

Cosmopolitan and widespread in Canada and the U.S.; grows on road berms and waste places; this small *Stropharia* is said to be **poisonous**. Resembles a small *Agaricus*, but the gills are **not** first pink and then dark brown as in *Agaricus* and neither are the gills free. The gills do have the pearly grey colour stage of *Stropharia*. The specimen illustrated was found on the Kootenay Plains along the upper North Saskatchewan River and has been added to show that not all Stropharias are easily recognized.

cap	dull creamy buff with a tan crown, not slimy like the dung roundhead; convex, then more or less flattening; up to 2.5 cm across.
gills	first a lilac or pearly grey, then purple brown as the spores ripen; close, adnate to adnexed, broad, intermediates.
spore print	purplish brown.
stalk	white with superior ring, bulbous base covered with white mycelium; up to 3.5 cm tall and 0.4 cm thick.
partial veil	results in fringe on cap edge and fragile, radially grooved ring, evanescent.
flesh	white, hollow stalk.
odour	clean, of hay.

Kauffman's Stropharia

p.129-3

Stropharia kauffmanii A. H. Smith

kauffmanii: named after C. H. Kauffman, professor of botany at the University of Michigan (1869-1931)

North American; growing on the ground in areas rich in decaying wood or on the edge of footpaths. D. W. Malloch, who identified this species in 1973, said that it is a rare one. This was the first time it had been found in Canada. Before this it had only been found in the state of Washington. Most of the time it occurs singly. I found it eight more times since then in the same general area. It can be confused with *Pholiota squarrosa*, which has a rusty brown spore print (although it can vary in darkness), grows in clusters and has a skunky odour. Inedible.

cap	red-brown to ochre squamules on a buff background, convex, then flattening, veil remnants on the cap edge, up to 12 cm across.
gills	lovely pearly grey, finally purple brown, relatively close, many intermediates, adnate.
spore print	purple brown, almost black.
stalk	white above the ring, either smooth or with small white scales; below the ring it is buff or brownish with white or ochre-yellow scales; base slightly swollen; rhizomorphs often on the bottom; in the illustration one is connected to a bit of wood; up to 7 cm tall and 1.5 cm thick. at the top.
partial veil	white, resulting in a generous fringe on the cap edge and a persistent, flaring, radially grooved ring which is soon darkened by spores. The grooves are impressions from gill edges.
flesh	solid, white.
odour	faint.

blue-green Stropharia

p.129-4

Stropharia aeruginosa (Curtis: Fries) Quélet

aeruginosa: verdigris or bluish green (Latin)

Cosmopolitan; widespread in the Pacific Northwest according to Lincoff. The one illustrated was found in the dunes in Holland. Growing on woody debris and lignin-rich soils at the edge of forests, they are easily recognized by their unusual colour. The heavy layer of green slime can be washed away in rain, exposing the ochre-yellow cap. Not recommended for eating.

cap	blue-green, slimy, convex to bell shaped; yellow-ochre crown is visible in older ones; flattening out when maturing, veil remnants on the edge, up to 7 cm across.
gills	grey then purplish brown when spores ripen, adnate, close, broad, intermediates.

spore print	purple brown.
stalk	blue green, scaly, superior ring, up to 7 cm tall and 0.7 cm thick.
partial veil	resulting in fringe around the cap edge and a radially grooved ring; in mature specimens, squamules, ring and veil remnants disappear. See illustration.
flesh	white and blue green, a bit brownish in stalk base.
odour	of fresh tomatoes.

Winecap or giant Stropharia p.129-5

Stropharia rugoso-annulata Farlow in Murrill
rugosa-annulata: with wrinkled ring (Latin)

Cosmopolitan; this species has moved around with migrating people. I have read that in Europe it came west from Russia with Napoleon's army. Another story is that it came from the Andes together with the potato. In any case, it is a people mushroom, only described from man-made environments: on compost, mulch in gardens and greenhouses. I saw it in a show greenhouse in the Devonian Botanic Gardens near Edmonton. The charming name winecap does not apply to the tan forms, which were developed in cultivation. The name giant Stropharia is more appropriate for them. It is easily cultivated and an excellent, edible mushroom.

cap	wine red or red-brown, fading with age; convex then flattening, often with sooty spots from spores of surrounding specimens and fringed by veil fragments; young specimens often a bit sticky and some veil fragments adhering to caps, up to 20 cm across.
gills	whitish at first, then greyish violet turning blackish or dark purple brown as the spores ripen.
spore print	deep purple brown, almost black.
stalk	white with brownish or pinkish tinges; smooth, slowly widening base, rhizomorphs, up to 20 cm tall and 2.5 cm thick at the top.
partial veil	white, leaving remnants at the cap edge and a large flaring, double ring which is grooved at the top, darkened by spores and often radially splitting.
flesh	white, solid, a bit yellowish under the cap cuticle.
taste & odour	mild.

Genus PHOLIOTA
with scaly cap (Greek)

Mostly scaly species with confluent cap and stalk; yellowish flesh and adnate to adnexed gills; a rusty brown spore print; veil leaving a ring or disappearing and leaving bits on the cap edge. All species grow on wood, some at the tree base, some high up in trees; others on woodpiles or stumps. The one which appears to grow on the ground is connected to buried roots. Different species attack different woody parts of a tree, e.g., *P. squarrosa* will enter trees through a wound in the bark or the roots to attack the living part of the wood and will slowly kill the tree; *P. aurivella* is often found high up in a living tree. It enters through a frost crack and grows in the heartwood or dead centre of a tree. The genus contains both parasitic and saprophytic species.

golden-skinned Pholiota p.130-1

Pholiota aurivella (Fries) Kummer
aurivella: with golden skin (Latin)

Cosmopolitan, widely distributed in North America; this species grows high up on the trunks of living deciduous trees. I have always found them in frost cracks of birch trees. Found on alder and maple along the Pacific Coast. A striking mushroom, growing singly or in small groups; causes wood rot. It is said to be edible.

cap	pale, warm yellow or orange, sometimes with a red-brown crown; sticky to gelatinous when damp, with a few appressed scales which disappear with age, rounded and then flattening somewhat, up to 18 cm across.

gills	pale, a bit olive yellow, then light brown, finally medium chocolate brown, broad; intermediates, adnexed; uneven edges.
spore print	medium warm brown.
stalk	white above the ring, fibrillose, a bit grooved, below the ring yellowish and floccose or rough, base turning brown, tapering and flattening where it fits in the crack of the tree; up to 6 cm tall and 1.5 cm at the top.
partial veil	whitish, fibrillose, leaving narrow ring or annular zone, rusty from the spores.
flesh	pale whitish yellow, solid.
odour	slight.
taste	somewhat bitter.

pointed Pholiota   p.130-2

Pholiota acutoconica Smith & Hesler

acutoconica: sharply conic (Latin)

North American; rare; was found in Alberta in September and in Oregon in October. Grows on or around conifer stumps in large tufts or groups.

cap	yellow with tufts of brown hair, sharply conic with inrolled edge, crown brownish, up to 7 cm across.
gills	ochre-yellow, later brown-ochre, close, relatively narrow, intermediates, easily separable from cap.
spore print	chocolate brown.
stalk	lemon yellow above the ring, yellow below and scaly, base red-brown, bent, equal, up to 11 cm tall and 1 cm thick
partial veil	fibrous, leaving bits on the cap edge and narrow superior ring, brown from spores.
flesh	lemon yellow, solid.
odour	light skunk.

slender Pholiota   p.131-1

Pholiota subflavida (Murrill) Smith & Hesler

subflavida: yellowish (Latin)

Pacific Northwestern species, belonging to the *spumosa* complex; it occurs on spruce debris; the cap becomes spotty green when handled and is smooth. Fruiting in summer. Edibility unknown.

cap	yellow with a brown crown, rounded, then flattening, smooth, viscid, up to 7 cm across.
gills	olive yellow, then medium brown, adnate to adnexed, relatively broad.
spore print	rust brown.
stalk	top yellow, bottom brown; equal, fibrillose, not scaly, white mycelium at the base, up to 7 cm tall and 0.6 cm thick.
partial veil	pale yellow and thin, evanescent, hardly leaving any trace on cap edge or stalk.
flesh	bright yellow in stalk, pale yellow in cap.

alder tuft   p.131-2

Pholiota alnicola (Fries) Singer

alnicola: living on alder (Latin)

Cosmopolitan; this species grows on the decaying wood of deciduous trees, e.g., alder, willow and birch. Reminiscent of *Hypholoma*, but the colour of the spores is an important difference, as well as other features. Fruiting in summer. Edibility unknown.

cap	sandy yellow with streaked rusty brown crown, viscid when damp; rounded, then flattening; up to 6 cm across.
gills	pale grey at first, turning rusty brown as the spores ripen; adnate-decurrent, continuing as lines on the stalk apex.
spore print	dark rusty brown.
stalk	bright yellow top half, base a bit brownish; fibrous, hollow, equal, up to 12 cm tall and 0.5 cm thick.
partial veil	fibrillose, leaving a little on the cap edge and a narrow ring which may disappear.
flesh	shiny, yellow.

lemon yellow Pholiota

p.131-3

Pholiota limonella (Peck) Saccardo

former name: *P. squarrosa-adiposa* Lange
limonella: resembles a small lemon (Latin)

North American species, particularly frequent in the Pacific Northwest: the Yukon, Alaska and B.C. Found on the living wood of deciduous trees, next to a living tree or on logs in tufts. The one illustrated grew on willow. Said to be edible but of poor quality and can be confused with poisonous species.

cap	yellow with some large, flat, brown scales; very slimy, losing its scales and cracking when it dries, up to 6 cm across.
gills	pale yellow at first, later brown; close, adnate-sinuate, serrate intermediates.
spore print	rust brown.
stalk	top smooth, scaly lower down; same colour as the cap or lighter, up to 6 cm tall and 1 cm thick.
partial veil	most of it fringes the cap edge, leaving a sticky annular zone on the stalk.
flesh	pale yellow.
odour	slight.

ground Pholiota

p.131-4

Pholiota terrestris Overholts

terrestris: of the land (Latin)

North American; western species common in the Pacific Northwest in the fall and, unlike all other species, growing on the ground on packed earth in lawns, along paths and old roads. According to Smith, however, it just appears to be on the ground and is actually connected to buried wood. Edible but of poor quality.

cap	buff with darker small, flat scales; centre brown; convex or with small umbo; the scales wash off in rain, up to 8 cm across.
gills	buff to ochrish becoming brownish, close, adnate-sinuate, relatively narrow.
spore print	rust brown.
stalk	same colour as cap, smooth above very narrow ring, scaly below; up to 9 cm tall and 0.8 cm thick.
partial veil	flimsy, evanescent, leaving a very narrow band on the stalk, brown from the spores.
flesh	pale yellow, brown in stalk base.
odour	slight.
taste	mild.

flaming Pholiota

p.131-5

Pholiota flammans (Fries) Kummer

flammans: flaming (Latin)

Cosmopolitan; this bright yellow Pholiota does a lot of damage to conifer wood in the west. Edible but of poor quality.

cap	flaming yellow with red-brown scales, convex or broadly conical with incurved margin, up to 7 cm across.
gills	yellow turning ochre, relatively narrow, close, adnexed.
spore print	rust brown.
stalk	top smooth, the rest like the cap with erect or recurved scales; reddish-brown base, equal, up to 8 cm tall and 1 cm thick.
partial veil	scaly, leaving bits on the cap edge and a scaly, evanescent ring.
flesh	yellow.
odour	unpleasant.

poplar Pholiota

p.133-1

Pholiota destruens (Brondeau) Gillet

destruens: destructive (Latin)

Cosmopolitan; in North America it is better known in the west than in the east. Growing on dead wood, it is often found on piled logs, causing rapid decay. Also grows on standing dead trees, particularly poplar, as is the one in the illustration which I found near Sandy Lake, Alberta. Fruiting in the fall. Inedible.

cap	white to cream, domed or convex, feels slippery after rain, sometimes tan on top; smooth in the centre, but the rest has scattered buff scales; large veil fragments on the cap edge, up to 12 cm across.
gills	pale grey at first, then spotted as spores ripen, finally brown; broad, many intermediates, eroded, adnate-adnexed.
spore print	bright to dark cinnamon.
stalk	white with bulbous base; silky above the superior ring, scaly below; can be quite heavy, flattened where it fits in the wood, often with rhizoid at the base; up to 9 cm tall, 2 cm thick at the apex and 4 cm in the base
partial veil	white, fibrillose, substantial, leaving large pieces on the cap edge and a superior ring coloured by plentiful spores.
flesh	white, solid, hard.
odour	weak.
taste	unpleasant.

scaly Pholiota p.133-2

Pholiota squarrosa (Fries) Kummer

squarrosa: scurfy (Latin)

Cosmopolitan and widespread; damages living trees, both coniferous and deciduous, attacking them when they are in distress. There is a similar smaller species, *P. squarrosoides* (looking like squarrosa), which is generally paler and has whitish flesh, less odour, and a slimy layer under the scales, which wash off more easily in rainy weather. The scaly Pholiota was long considered edible although not choice, but is now known to be **poisonous** to some people. It grows in large clusters. Fruiting in summer or fall.

cap	buff to yellowish with light brown crown and brown scales, small in the centre and larger towards the edge, up to 14 cm across.
gills	greyish or greenish yellow, then ochre, spotted, finally brown ochre.
spore print	coffee brown.
stalk	whitish to yellow and smooth above the ring, below the ring squamulose and cap colour, up to 12 cm tall and 2 cm thick.
partial veil	fibrillose, resulting in either a substantial ring, a smaller ring with a fringed cap edge or most of it on the cap edge.
flesh	yellow, solid or with hollow stalk.
odour	varies; lemon, radish, oniony or of skunk.

Genus HYPHOLOMA

with fringed margin (Greek)

Four *Hypholoma* species are described. The three on p. 135 are all decomposers of decaying wood. I have seen a lot of these in October and November in the Netherlands. They seem to light up the wet forest in the rain, occurring in large tufts. If they seem to occur on the ground, then they are connected to dead roots. All three are widespread on this continent, but the bricktop is quite rare in the Pacific Northwest. Besides growing in tufts, they also have a cobweb-like evanescent partial veil, leaving small remnants on the cap margin; attached gills; and dark purplish-brown spore prints. The fourth *Hypholoma*, a small species occurring in sphagnum bogs, is on p. 136. (*Naematoloma* is a synonym for this genus.)

sulphur tuft p.135-1

Hypholoma fasciculare (Hudson: Fries) Kummer

fasciculare: tufted (Latin)

Cosmopolitan and widespread; small to medium-sized mushroom growing in bundles on stumps of coniferous and deciduous trees. Common in the Pacific Northwest. This is a **poisonous** mushroom, but because it is so bitter not many people will try to eat it.

cap	bright yellow with a rust-brown crown; convex with, or without, small umbo; smooth veil remnants on the cap margin; up to 6 cm across.
gills	sulphur yellow, adnate, close, relatively narrow, intermediates, turning purple brown as the spores ripen.
spore print	purple brown, almost black.
stalk	yellowish, smooth above annular zone, a bit fibrous below; up to 10 cm tall and 0.5 cm thick.
partial veil	cortina-like, leaving some remnants on the cap margin and an annular zone or very narrow ring, darkened by spores.
flesh	yellowish, tough in the hollow stalk.
odour	faint.
taste	very bitter.

conifer tuft
p.135-2

Hypholoma capnoides (Fries: Fries) Kummer

capnoides: smoky (Greek)

Cosmopolitan. The conifer tuft is especially common in the Pacific Northwest. It is a small to medium-sized mushroom which grows in large clusters on conifer wood or debris. They can grow quite tall and vary considerably in size and colour, but they never have the strong sulphur-yellow gill colour of the sulphur tuft nor the brick-red colour of the bricktop. The smooth cap of this species is soft yellow to orange. The specimens illustrated were found under alpine fir and spruce near Lake Louise in the Rocky Mountains.

cap	orange with soft yellow margin, can also be brown orange with paler margin; convex, smooth, veil remnants on the margin, up to 7 cm across.
gills	pale yellowish grey at first, then grey, then purple-brown; close, uneven, adnate, intermediates.
spore print	purple brown.
stalk	white above ring or ring zone, darkened by spores later, shiny yellowish below ring, equal, hollow, up to 15 cm tall and 1 cm thick.
partial veil	cortina resulting in bits on the cap (somewhat above the cap edge because the cap was inrolled at first) and an annular zone or small ring darkened by spores.
flesh	pale yellow in cap, brown in stalk.
odour	pleasant, slight.
taste	slightly bitter or mild; edible according to some sources, not edible according to others.

bricktop
p.135-3

Hypholoma sublateritium (Fries) Quélet

sublateritium: almost brick colour (Latin)

Cosmopolitan; this species is common in Manitoba, but less so further west. Growing on stumps of deciduous trees in tufts of large and small fruiting bodies, it is a lovely colourful find. The illustrated group was found in November on a moss-covered oak stump in Holland. There is quite a variation in size, colour and shape, but the pale yellowish-grey gills changing to dark purple-brown; the white remnants of the veil on the cap margin; and the red cap colour with yellow margin make it easily recognized. Fruiting in the fall. Edible according to some authors.

cap	brick red with yellow margin, in-rolled at first, convex to domed, smooth and streaked, the white tufts are veil remnants which do not hang on the edge of the cap because it was in-rolled in the immature mushroom. Can be quite large, up to 15 cm across, although usually smaller.
gills	whitish at first, then yellowish grey and finally purplish brown as the spores ripen; close, intermediates, adnate-sinuate.
spore print	purplish brown.
stalk	whitish yellow at first, later reddish brown at the base and coloured by purplish spores above the annular zone; equal or bulging in the middle, up to 10 cm tall and 2 cm thick at the apex.

partial veil	cottony, leaving hairy white flocs or scales on the cap margin.
flesh	white, sometimes brownish in the base.
odour	typical mushroom.

Genera HYPHOLOMA, PSILOCYBE AND KUEHNEROMYCES

All species on p. 136 have been in other genera or in more than one other genus. New developments in technology, e.g., electron microscopes, have made it possible to find out more about fungi, giving us new information to evaluate their relationships. Collections from many different herbaria in various countries are carefully compared and studied in order to get international understanding and acceptance. In the case of this group of six species, the genera of *Stropharia, Pholiota, Panaeolus, Galerina, Hypholoma, Psilocybe* and *Kuehneromyces*, as well as names which are now invalid, were involved. I will only mention a few of their previous names.

The genus *Hypholoma* was briefly discussed before. The small slim species discussed here is different in that it does not grow in tufts on wood and the spore print is more reddish brown than purplish brown.

Psilocybe (Greek for with bare head): species in this genus are mostly small to medium in size, the gills are pale at first and darken when they mature. The spore print is purple-grey, purple-brown or nearly black. Some of these species are psycho-active or hallucinogenic.

Kuehneromyces (named after R. Kühner, well-known French mycologist): this genus is closely related to *Pholiota*. The mushrooms have a smooth — not scaly — hygrophanous cap and a cinnamon-coloured spore print, grow in tufts on wood and are saprophytic. Both species described here are edible but can be easily confused with very poisonous *Galerina* species, e.g., *G. autumnalis*. It is not advisable to collect these from the wild if you do not know what you are looking for.

long-legged Hypholoma   p.136-1

Hypholoma elongatum (Persoon: Fries) Ricken

former name: *Psilocybe elongatum*
elongatum: stretched (Latin)

Cosmopolitan; can be found in sphagnum bogs; scattered or gregarious rather than in tufts. Found in Canada and the Northern U.S.

cap	chamois yellow; rounded, then flattening, hygrophanous, up to 2 cm across.
gills	pale at first, then brown; not close, intermediates, adnate, broad.
spore print	dark red-brown.
stalk	yellow-ochre, light apex, white felty base, equal; up to 10 cm tall and 0.2 cm thick
flesh	thin, pale buff in cap, brownish in stalk.
odour	weak.

round dung mushroom   p.136-2

Psilocybe coprophila (Bulliard: Fries) Kummer.

former name: *Stropharia coprophila*
coprophila: dung loving (Greek)

Cosmopolitan and widespread; growing on manure; contains low amounts of psilocybin when fresh.

cap	yellow brown, semispherical, sticky surface, striate border, up to 2 cm across.
gills	grey brown with white edges, broad, distant.
spore print	violet brown.
stalk	yellowish brown, paler than cap, bent, relatively smooth, no ring.
flesh	thin, dirty white.

dung mushroom

p.136-3

Psilocybe merdaria (Fries) Ricken

former name: *Stropharia merdaria*
merdaria: pertaining to dung (Latin)

Cosmopolitan; growing on dung or on manure-rich soil. I found the 3a specimen on horse manure, partly dried up. They were much smaller than the specimens (3b) I found in Holland on ground rich in manure. The latter group really resembled *Stropharia* species. This *Psilocybe* also contains low amounts of psilocybin.

cap	buff or sand colour with very pale border, in-rolled when young, small umbo, smooth, remnants of veil in circle on the border, up to 4 cm across.
gills	light grey at first, relatively distant, eroded, broad, intermediates, dark purplish brown when mature.
spore print	purplish brown, almost black.
stalk	yellowish, smooth above the ring, with lines below the gills and scattered fibres, up to 5 cm tall and 0.5 cm thick, white mycelium at stalk base.
partial veil	hairy to fibrous, leaving bits on cap border and a dark annular zone.
flesh	white, solid.

✳ liberty cap

p.136-4

Psilocybe semilanceata (Fries: Secretan) Kummer

former name: *Panaeolus semilanceata*
semilanceata: somewhat spear shaped (Latin)

Cosmopolitan; growing on the world's seacoasts. This is the famous, or infamous, liberty cap (depending on your point of view). Many people look for this small mushroom with hallucinogenic properties. They are like invading ant colonies, intruding on public and private lands. I have collected newspaper articles, sent to me by friends, with headlines like: "Rain mushroom lovers face prosecution trip" (Vancouver); "Mushroom madness erupts into war" (Queen Charlottes). They are beautiful mushrooms, but it can be most inconvenient to have them on your property. *P. similanceata* fruits in the rainy season, late summer and fall. The mushroom does not occur inland, but a small form of *Panaeolus sphinctrinus* which grows inland on manure can look amazingly similar to the liberty cap and may be mistaken for it (p. 147).

cap	a shade of tan; sticky in damp weather; the sticky layer can be pulled off; bell shaped with a sharp umbo (looking like a small snout); striate edge, incurved, not expanding, up to 2 cm wide.
gills	pale greyish at first, finally purplish brown.
spore print	purplish brown.
stalk	whitish to straw colour, slim, equal, curved, up to 10 cm tall and 0.2 cm thick.
partial veil	disappears.
flesh	thin.

changeable tuft mushroom

p.136-5

Kuehneromyces mutabilis (Fries) Singer & Smith

former names: *Pholiota mutabilis*, *Galerina mutabilis*
mutabilis: changeable (Latin)

Cosmopolitan; this mushroom is widely distributed on this continent. It can be easily cultivated (as it is in Europe) in the same way the oyster mushroom, the velvetfoot (or enoki) and shiitake traditionally were: on pieces of inoculated wood. In the case of this species, it is best to buy a kit because it is very easy when collecting it from the wild to confuse it with deadly *Galerina* species (see p. 115). Grows in tight caespitose tufts on deciduous logs. Abundant in the Pacific Northwest. Edible with extreme caution.

cap	rusty to reddish brown with a yellowish buff centre, broadly bell shaped to convex with small umbo, flattening, hygrophanous, drying to buff, up to 6 cm across.
gills	off-white at first, turning cinnamon brown as the spores ripen, adnate, broad; close at first, later relatively distant.

spore print	cinnamon brown.
stalk	off-white and silky above the ring, later brown from falling spores; brown and very scaly below the ring, up to 10 cm tall and 0.7 cm thick at the apex.
partial veil	membranous, resulting in a superior flaring ring.
flesh	pale in cap, can be slightly darker in stalk.
odour	pleasant, like freshly sawn wood.

small changeable tuft p.136-6

Kuehneromyces lignicola (Peck) Redhead

former names: *K. vernalis*, *Pholiota vernalis*
lignicola: living on wood (Latin)

Cosmopolitan; the distribution of this species is circumpolar like no. 5 although it is not as common. It has been collected in North America, Britain, Switzerland, the U.S.S.R. and Japan; growing on both deciduous and coniferous logs in small tufts or singly. Edibility unknown.

cap	cinnamon brown with buff centre, hygrophanous; bell shaped at first, then flattening with small umbo; up to 3.5 cm across.
gills	buff at first, then cinnamon brown, close, adnate, very narrow.
spore print	cinnamon brown.
stalk	same colour as cap, central but strongly bent, equal, slim, silky, up to 4 cm tall and 0.3 cm thick.
partial veil	fragile, resulting in bits on the cap edge and narrow ring or annular zone.
flesh	pale pinkish brown.

Family AGARICACEAE

A small family, Agaricaceae has only three genera, two of which contain only a few rare species (*Melanophyllum* and *Micropsalliota*). The third genus, *Agaricus*, is large.

Genus AGARICUS

of the land (Greek)

Fleshy, terrestrial, saprophytic mushrooms; they have a purplish-brown to chocolate-brown spore print; gills are free, first pink then brown; dark brown spore print; cap and stalk are easily separated; there is a ring around the stalk and no basal cup; the flesh is white, pink-staining white or yellow-staining white.

Agaricus is a very popular and safe genus for mushroom hunters. Species are easily recognized; the only thing to watch out for is yellow discolouration of the flesh. Two species with that discolouration are shown: *A. xanthodermis* and *A. hondensis*. When eaten, gastro-intestinal difficulties may occur. Often found in cities and on farms because they prefer well-manured soils. Meadow mushrooms, horse mushrooms and a yellow-staining species may all be found together in a city park, where they often form fairy rings. Spore prints should be made, of course, and as usual, mushrooms should be identified to species. Ten edible species are discussed, three of which are not recommended, and two poisonous species.

Sitka spruce Agaricus p.137-1

Agaricus perrarus Schulzer

perrarus: very rare (Latin)

Cosmopolitan; on our continent this mushroom appears most often in the Pacific Northwest, preferring a Sitka spruce habitat. The specimen in the illustration was found in Northern B.C. Edible and excellent.

cap	tawny, rounded, some appressed yellow-ochre squamules or scales; half of the surface of the cap was cracked in areolate pattern (like dried mud). This happens in a cool, dry climate close to the Yukon border. Cap flattens out in maturity; up to 20 cm across.
gills	pinkish buff, later dark brown; free and remote from the stalk, crowded.

spore print	dark chocolate brown.
stalk	white and bronze, very heavy; abruptibulbous, split in several places; up to 16 cm tall and up to 3 cm wide (base up to 6 cm).
partial veil	leaving some bits on the cap edge and a large flaring, white to yellowish ring.
flesh	white, solid, staining light pink.
odour	of almonds.
taste	very good.

crocodile Agaricus   p.137-2

Agaricus crocodilinus Murrill

former name: *A. macrosporus*
crocodilinus: resembling a crocodile (Latin)

Cosmopolitan; in the west it grows in grassy areas near the coast or along rivers. The specimens in the illustration were found along the North Saskatchewan River. One of the very best edible mushrooms.

cap	crust-brown squamules, coarser near the edge, rounded, then more or less flattening; up to 25 cm or more across
gills	at first pale, then wine pink, then chocolate brown; free, close.
spore print	dark brown.
stalk	white, very sturdy, ring midway down, smooth, up to 9 cm tall and 3.5 cm wide.
partial veil	double, leaving a few patches on the cap edge and a flaring ring with brownish bottom layer clinging to the stalk.
flesh	white or changing slowly to pale pink, very thick in cap and stalk.
taste & odour	faintly of almond; in maturity may have a dirty smell, but it is never wise to eat overmature specimens.

the Prince   p.137-3

Agaricus augustus Fries

augustus: blessed (Latin)

Cosmopolitan; this woods mushroom occurs more in Western North America than in the East. Frequently found along the Pacific Coast, it grows under coniferous trees, on disturbed soil and in waste places. It is called "the Prince" because many people think that it provides a princely meal. This specimen was from Vancouver Island.

cap	covered with numerous small, brown, fibrillose squamules; can reach a very large size of up to 30 cm across and more.
gills	pale greyish-pink, narrow, crowded, free and remote from the stalk, dark brown in maturity.
spore print	dark brown.
stalk	white, smooth above ring, woolly below; stalk buried deep in the ground, so that the mushroom seems to squat; up to 14 cm tall and 2 - 3 cm wide.
partial veil	double, white, resulting in a large, droopy, persistent ring, hanging from high on the stalk; the cottony patches underneath disappear.
flesh	white, thick, meaty, turning reddish.
taste	sweet.
odour	lightly of almond.

spring Agaricus   p.139-1

Agaricus bitorquis (Quélet) Saccardo

former name: *A. rodmani*
The name *A. bitorquis* was published a few weeks before the name *A. rodmani* and so has priority.
bitorquis: with a double necklace (Latin)

Cosmopolitan; occurs on hard-packed soil in parking lots, garbage dumps and grassy areas in city parks and streets. The common names of this species say a lot. In English it is simply spring Agaricus; French: champignon des trottoirs (sidewalk mushroom); German: Stadtchampignon (city mushroom); Dutch: straat champignon (street mushroom). The mycelium of this fungus can break up sidewalks or pavingstones, when it bundles together. Occurs everywhere there is human habitation. A choice edible mushroom.

cap	white and smooth or with some large tan squamules; rounded with a flat top; up to 15 cm across.
gills	pink, turning dark brown in maturity; free, narrow, never more than one third of the thickness of the cap flesh, crowded
spore print	dark brown.
stalk	white, thick, tapering down or equal, solid; up to 10 cm tall and 3 cm thick.
partial veil	white, producing a collar-like ring; broad with both top and bottom loose and quite low on the stalk (inferior).
flesh	white at first, changing to pale pink; solid, hard, often no insect damage.
taste	nutty, a good keeper.

dark scaly Agaricus   p.139-2
Agaricus pattersonae Peck

pattersonae: named after Ms. Patterson, the collector, who found it in the San Francisco Bay region

Western North American urban species; growing on disturbed and packed soil, developing partly underground so that it often has some earth on the cap; fruiting in cool weather: May-June and September-October. A good edible mushroom, but much infested by insects. I found these in a border on the northside of our house for five consecutive years.

cap	dark reddish-brown, hairy tufts cover the cap, darker on the crown; rounded, then flattening; up to 12 cm across.
gills	pink, then light mocca-brown, finally blackish-brown; relatively narrow at first, free, close.
spore print	very dark brown.
stalk	white, solid, smooth above and below the ring; mycelium, encrusted in earth at bottom; up to 8 cm tall and 2.5 cm wide.
partial veil	white, double, resulting in a fringe around the cap edge and a flaring ring, usually dark brown from spores.
flesh	white, hard, thick, staining pink slowly; no yellow.
taste & odour	pleasant, like button mushrooms.

bleeding Agaricus   p.139-3
Agaricus haemorrhoidarius Fries

haemorrhoidarius: bleeding (Greek)

Cosmopolitan but rare everywhere; occurs along the Pacific coast including Alaska. I found it three times in twenty years in Alberta, once in mixed forest under spruce and the other times in grassy areas. Fruiting in the fall. Edible and good.

cap	covered with red-brown appressed hair; rounded at first, then expanding; the cap is adorned with a white woolly edge, part of the partial veil; up to 12 cm across.
gills	white at first, then beautiful salmon-pink, finally dark brown; moderately broad, close.
spore print	dark brown.
stalk	white, shiny, silky, bruising pink, up to 12 cm tall and 1.5 - 2.5 cm thick.
partial veil	white, fragile, thick, part of it stays on the cap edge, the rest forms a fragile flaring ring.
flesh	quickly discolours from white to bright red, particularly in the top of the stalk.
taste & odour	mild.

wild button mushroom   p.141-1
Agaricus brunnescens Peck

former name: *A. bisporus*
brunnescens: becoming brown (Latin)

Cosmopolitan; this species is easily identified if a microscope is handy, because it carries two spores on each basidium instead of the usual four. According to Dr. D. Malloch (1976) *A. brunnescens*, rather than *A. campestris*, is the original cultivated mushroom. *Agaricus* had been a well-known edible since Roman times. However, it does not make a difference to mycophagists; button mushrooms with 2- or 4-spored basidia both have an excellent taste. In 1650, cultivation started in Paris by accident. Droppings of horses (which were used a lot in the city) were deposited in abandoned quarries. Mushroom spores were naturally mixed in with the manure, and the mushrooms fruited in quantity! This showed the Parisian gardeners how the mushrooms could be cultivated.

I found the mushroom in the illustration in the Rocky Mountains in B.C.

cap	white at first, then brown; some scales; rounded, then flattening out; up to 12 cm across or more.
gills	flesh coloured, then dark brown; crowded, free.
spore print	dark brown.
stalk	whitish, more or less equal, base discolouring to red-brown, up to 8 cm tall and 1.5 cm thick.
partial veil	white, resulting in a ring about halfway down the stalk, membranous.
flesh	white, thick, sturdy, turns pink slowly, sometimes hollow in stalk.
taste	choice.
odour	strong but pleasant.

field mushroom or meadow mushroom   p.141-2

Agaricus campestris Linnaeus: Fries

campestris: of the plains (Latin)

Worldwide distribution; a very popular mushroom, gathered most by mushroom lovers; grows in grassy areas, fruiting after rain in cool seasons, primarily in the fall; grows as far north as the Yukon and Alaska.

cap	white or off-white; smooth and silky or with a few white scales; rounded and remaining so for a long time; a fringe on the cap edge; 3 - 10 cm, sometimes bigger.
gills	pink, even in the button stage, then vivid pink, followed by flesh-red, chocolate-brown and finally very dark brown.
spore print	dark brown.
stalk	white, solid, smooth above and below the ring, relatively short, 4 - 8 cm tall and 2.5 cm thick.
partial veil	white, fragile, leaving a fringe on the cap edge and a narrow, single, evanescent ring.
flesh	white or sometimes lightly pink above the gills and under the skin, firm and solid.
taste	excellent.
odour	pleasant.

wine Agaricus   p.141-3

Agaricus semotus Fries

semotus: remote (Latin)

Cosmopolitan; this species has been reported from Europe and across Canada. Growing in grassy areas, often in the city but also in the forest. A good edible species but rather small. Fruits in the fall. I found it in several places in Alberta.

cap	reddish-brown, appressed hair, darker crown and light border; convex at first, then flattening with raised margin; up to 7 cm across.
gills	at first very light pink, then pale mauve, finally dark brown; free and remote, close.
spore print	purplish-brown.
stalk	white with fine squamules below the ring; up to 4 cm tall and up to 1 cm thick, sometimes hollow
partial veil	results in a narrow ring, evanescent.
flesh	white or white with a bit of pink.
odour	aromatic, slightly of almond or anise.
taste	mild.

small slender Agaricus   p.141-4

Agaricus comptulus Fries

comptulus: small and elegant (Latin)

Cosmopolitan; the distribution of this small *Agaricus* is not fully known on our continent, according to A. H. Smith; occurs in grassy areas or open woods. I found them in mixed woods in Alberta. Not recommended for eating.

cap	creamy to pale yellow, silky; convex at first, then broadly convex; 3 - 6 cm across.
gills	pink then brown, free, crowded.
spore print	dark brown.
stalk	white, slim; smooth above the ring, fine squamules below; abruptibulbous, does not bruise yellow; up to 7 cm tall and 0.5 cm thick.
partial veil	resulting in a flaring ring.
flesh	white, hollow in stalk, very pale yellow-brown discolouration.
odour	lightly of almonds.

atrium Agaricus   p.141-5

Agaricus fusco-fibrillosus (Moeller) Pilat

fusco: very dark, almost black (Latin)
fibrillosus: full of fibres (Latin)

Cosmopolitan. First identified by F. H. Moeller in Denmark in 1943 (under beech); it has been reported by Arora growing wild in California (under Cypress). In Edmonton, Alberta, we find it growing in atria under Ficus. A rare mushroom growing under different trees in different environments as a saprophyte; not recommended for eating.

cap	very dark, almost black, innate fibrils, crown black; spherical at first, then expanding, splitting radially between fibrils and showing white flesh; up to 7 cm across.
gills	rosy flesh colour, narrow, remote from stalk, finally dark brown.
spore print	dark brown.
stalk	white at first, discolouring to a light-brown; somewhat fibrillose below the ring; up to 8 cm tall and up to 1 cm thick, white rhizoids (rootlike bundles of mycelium) at the base.
partial veil	woolly and thick, resulting in a movable ring when it loosens from the stalk and the cap edge.
flesh	white, thin with a pinkish line between cap flesh and gills.
odour	a very strong chemical smell.

horse mushroom   p.142-1

Agaricus arvensis Schaeffer: Fries

arvensis: of the field (Latin)

Worldwide distribution on northern as well as southern hemisphere. Has been reported as far north as Alaska. Grows in grassy areas. *A. arvensis* is a lot like *A. silvicola*, but does not grow in the forest and its spores are larger than those of the latter. Edible and good.

cap	white, smooth, a bit buff on the crown; rounded at first, flattens out; veil fringe around the cap edge; up to 15 cm across.
gills	whitish at first; remain whitish much longer than in other *Agaricus* species, then slowly changing to greyish-pink before turning purplish black.
spore print	purple-brown.
stalk	white, sturdy, equal, no basal bulb, slight thickening of the base; below the ring sometimes fibrillose scaly, bruising yellow when handled; up to 10 cm tall and 2 cm wide.
partial veil	double, bottom layer consists of cottony patches; part stays on the cap edge, the rest forms a large flaring ring.
flesh	white, solid, not discolouring.
odour	of anise, sometimes almond.
taste	good.

yellow-staining Agaricus   p.142-2

Agaricus xanthodermus Genevier

xanthodermus: with yellow skin (Greek)

Pacific Northwest from the Yukon to California; also occurs in Europe; fruiting in summer and fall.This mushroom shares its habitat with other *Agaricus* species: grassy areas, gardens and forest, but this one is poisonous. It can be recognized by its carbolic

odour and yellow discolouration of flesh and cuticle. I found this one in the Yukon.
Poisonous.

cap	white and yellow with brownish streaks, smooth; semi-spherical at first, then flattening; edge splits radially; up to 8 cm across.
gills	white, then pink, then brown; free, narrow, close.
spore print	purplish brown.
stalk	silky white above the ring, white and yellow below, equal; up to 10 cm tall and 2 cm thick.
partial veil	forms a superior, flaring ring, white on top and yellow below.
flesh	white in the cap, yellow in the stalk with pinkish brown streaks, solid.
odour	nasty, of phenol.

felt-ringed Agaricus   p.142-3

Agaricus hondensis Murrill

hondensis: originally described from La Honda, Cal., by W. A. Murrill

Pacific Northwestern species; occurs from B.C. south to California. This specimen was found north of Edmonton in mixed forest. It is one of the yellow-staining group and is poisonous to many people.

cap	covered with small, grey-brown, fibrillose scales; rounded at first, then flattening; up to 10 cm across.
gills	greyish pink, then purple-brown, narrow, free, crowded.
spore print	dark brown.
stalk	white, smooth, base discolouring brown; spindle shape or bulbous base; up to 8 cm tall and 1 - 2 cm thick.
partial veil	white, felty, leaving a thick, flaring ring high on the stalk, underneath coloured like the cap.
flesh	white at first, then discolouring to pinkish grey in the cap and yellowish in the stalk.
odour	unpleasant, creosote.
taste	metallic.

wood Agaricus   p.142-4

Agaricus silvicola (Vittadini) Fries

silvicola: living in the forest (Latin)

Worldwide distribution; occurs all over North America in forested areas; appears as far north as the Yukon and Alaska. This is a collective species and many variations can be found. Often it looks like *Agaricus arvensis*, at other times it is slimmer with a domed cap, or it can be either slim or squat and have a brown squamulose, or scaly, cap. *A. arvensis* does **not** appear in the forest and has larger spores. The woodland species bruises yellow more easily or has yellow tinges when found, but the flesh stays white. It is not recommended for eating because of the variations and, therefore, the chance to mix it up with similar poisonous species. The illustrations show some of the forms I found.

cap	off-white, silky, almost smooth; convex or domed at first, then plane; some yellow discolouration when handled, up to 17 cm across (4a) or yellow to red-brown, squamulose, convex or domed (4b).
gills	light pink and relatively narrow, then dark brown in maturity and broad, free, crowded.
spore print	dark purplish brown.
stalk	white, smooth, equal or sometimes abruptibulbous, thick or quite slender up to 13 cm tall and 2.5 cm wide, bruising yellow when handled.
partial veil	double, underlayer consists of cottony patches, resulting in flaring ring.
flesh	white, solid, unchanging; sometimes has a narrow hollow tube and sometimes some yellow discolouration.
odour	anise.
taste	mild. Exercise caution.

Family COPRINACEAE dung mushrooms

This family contains six genera. All have black to purplish-brown spores, more or less conical caps and they are quite fragile. The six genera are:

Coprinus (Greek for dung mushroom): a large genus with some good edible species, generally with deliquescing caps.

Panaeolus (Greek for dazzling): dung inhabiting and containing several hallucinogenic species.

Anellaria (Latin for with ring): closely related to *Panaeolus*, the only species with a persistent ring.

Lacrymaria (Latin for with tears): a hairy species closely related to *Psathyrella*.

Psathyrella (Greek for strawlike, fragile): a very large genus with many very fragile, small species in it.

Panaeolina (Latin for small Panaeolus): an intermediate species between *Panaeolus* and *Psathyrella*.

The name of the family comes from the Greek word for dung (copros). All members recycle dung, either living on fresh manure or in richly manured meadows, gardens or woods. All species are saprophytic except one, a *Psathyrella* which is parasitic on a *Coprinus* species.

Genus COPRINUS dung mushroom

Coprinus species have smooth black spores. Immature caps are usually egg-shaped, the edge is never inrolled. In most species the cap never expands, but as the spores ripen, autodigestion of the cap takes place. This is triggered by an enzyme which causes the ripening of the spores from the margin inward, gradually dissolving the cap into a black, inky liquid. The majority of the spores is ejected before the dissolution of the cap tissue. In fragile thin-fleshed species, the cap does expand; the gills, beautifully spaced by miniature structures between them, dry up rather than autodigest. In damp weather these too get a little inky. The caps are often grooved and covered with small scales. The gills are crowded and free. The flesh is usually white and the stalk hollow. A ring is not always present. *Coprinus domesticus* and related species may develop a brown woolly mycelium, which perpetuates itself in the dark without fruiting. Saprophytic fungi, they grow on well-manured (rich) soil, dung of herbivores, rotten wood or human refuse. It is a very important species for recycling purposes.

miniature woolly inkcap   p.143-1

Coprinus radiatus (Fries) S. F. Gray

radiatus: radiating (Latin)

Cosmopolitan; the miniature woolly inkcap grows on manure; it grows on herbivore droppings and can occur anywhere in the world.

cap	up to 1 cm high and 1 cm wide; cylindrical to bell shaped, covered with greyish-white woolly fibres; the cap expands and rolls up like *C. plicatilis*.
gills	white, soon turns grey, free, crowded.
spore print	black.
stalk	short at first, then quickly expanding up to 6 cm; white, equal, with a rooting base and white, radiating mycelium at ground surface (hence the name).
flesh	very thin and soft.

domestic inky cap   p.143-2

Coprinus domesticus (Fries) S. F. Gray

domesticus: domestic (Latin)

Cosmopolitan; it is found in all kinds of domestic situations, even in coal mines — wherever it is damp. It is closely related to *C. micaceus* and *C. ellisii*, both found on wood debris in the forest, gardens or parks. Fruits in cool periods in summer and fall. This saprophyte was found on the hulls of sunflower seeds under a birdfeeder.

cap pale ochre in colour; egg shaped at first, then bell shaped; deeply grooved all the way to the crown; covered with small scales at first which soon disappear; up to 4 cm across and up to 5 cm high; splitting easily at the cap edge.

gills white, free, crowded, broad; not deliquescing right away, first turning a delicate orange-brown with spotty grey-brown at the cap margin, then finally turning black and dissolving.

spore print black (purplish).

stalk white, smooth, enlarging a bit toward the base, hollow, up to 7 cm tall, 0.5 cm (or 5mm) thick, no ring visible.

flesh very thin, white, fragile.

woolly inky cap
p.143-3

Coprinus flocculosus de Candolle: Fries

flocculosus: covered with woolly flakes (Latin)

Cosmopolitan; saprophytic, terrestrial; found after wet periods in the garden between the vegetables and among the potted plants in the house, also grows on mineral soil; fruiting in spring.

cap pale yellow-ochre; at first egg-shaped, covered with a lot of white scales (parts of universal veil), then spreading out and deliquescing; up to 6 cm high and 4.5 cm wide when in egg shape.

gills white, relatively narrow, grey near the margin before blackening.

spore print black.

stalk white, smooth, up to 12 cm high and 1 - 1.5 cm wide; broadening a bit toward the base, the base obviously with remnants of a volva; broadened and showing the edge where the cap was attached before the stalk grew out; hollow.

flesh white, thin in cap.

Japanese umbrella
p.143-4

Coprinus plicatilis (Curtis: Fries) Fries

plicatilis: with fine folds (Latin)

Cosmopolitan; growing on old leaves or wood debris; occurs all across Canada, U.S., Japan and Europe. A small form is found in the home among potted houseplants; fruiting in spring, a very fragile species.

cap orange-brown, egg shaped, then opening into a lovely round Japanese umbrella shape; translucent when the gills dry up rather than deliquesce; crown stays brown, rest is greyish covered by white bloom, dark gills showing through the thin flesh; up to 3.5 cm wide.

gills tawny before turning black, narrow, free from the stalk but attached to the collar around the top of the stalk, beautifully spaced.

spore print black

stalk white, slim, equal, up to 7 cm tall; growing with potted plants; earth imbedded in mycelium at base.

flesh thin and brown in cap.

shaggy mane
p.143-5

Coprinus comatus (Müller in Oeder: Fries) S. F. Gray

comatus: covered with hair (Latin)

Worldwide; often grows in grass, on well-manured soils, along roadsides, in lawns, parks, farms and forests; fruits in cool weather from August through October; later along the coast; often in large numbers. During very dry fall weather I have found specimens which did not sporulate and stayed completely white; spore development and autodigestion had stopped. Edible and good.

cap	white with brown scales (parts of the cap cuticle) and brown crown, cylindrical, not expanding, standing erect like a closed umbrella; up to 15 cm tall; up to 8 cm wide; autodigesting from the margin in, leaving the stalk, in the end, with a dripping, small, black-edged "hat".
gills	white at first, then turning pink at the margin before turning black and deliquescing.
spore print	black.
stalk	white, tall, partly inside the cap, very straight, hollow, enlarging toward the base, which often has a bit of a rooting shape; up to 20 cm tall; up to 2 cm thick.
ring	clearly visible on the small ones, loose on the stalk, often disappearing.
flesh	white, fragile, high water content.
odour	mild.
taste	good, particularly in soup.

scaly inky cap
p.143-6

Coprinus quadrifidus Peck

quadrifidus: divided in four (Latin)

North American species; occuring across Canada and in the U.S.; growing on wood debris, buried roots and compost; fruiting in the fall. I found these in a badger hole in the Badlands of Southern Alberta.

cap	egg shaped at first, yellowish with brownish scales; quite solid but splitting in rather large sections (hence the name although there are not always four sections); up to 10 cm across when expanded.
gills	white, soon turning, from the margin inward, first violet-pink, then grey, then black.
spore print	blackish.
stalk	white, smooth top; base full of brown scales in between an area where the attachment of cap edge divides the smooth upper from the scaly lower part; hollow; brown rhizomorphs at base. Scales on the base of the stalk and on the cap are from the universal veil; up to 12 cm tall; up to 1.2 cm thick.
flesh	white, thin, turning brown in cap, hollow in stalk.
taste & odour	mild.

magpie inky cap
p.145-1

Coprinus picaceus (Bulliard) Fries

pica: magpie (Latin)

Cosmopolitan but rare; known on our continent in western North America along the Pacific coast, also in Alberta; growing on wood fibres or on the ground near buried roots; in small groups; fruiting in the fall

cap	at first white when there is a white felty cover (universal veil); this breaks up in pieces and eventually falls away and then the dark background shows; the black and white appearance is the origin of the name "magpie inky cap;" cylinder shaped like a small shaggy mane; matures into a tall, fragile, translucent, striate bell. The grooves go up to the disc (crown) beautifully distanced. This structure dries up and falls apart at the slightest touch. Hardly any ink. Up to 7 cm high and 5 cm across.
gills	grey-brown, crowded, with white bloom on the gill edges; drying up rather than deliquescing.
spore print	black.
stalk	white, woolly, hollow; up to10 cm tall and 1 cm thick, equal; some rooting mycelium at the base.
flesh	whitish, very fragile.
odour	unpleasant.

woodchip Coprinus

p.145-2

Coprinus ellisii Orton

ellisii: named after American mycologist J.B. Ellis

North American; small mushrooms growing on mossy logs or woodchips; closely related to *C. domesticus*; fruits in spring.

cap pale sandy; egg shaped at first, then bell shaped; margin becomes grey and grooved; crown covered wih small brown scales; 1.5 - 2.5 cm tall and 1.5 cm wide; grooved halfway to the centre of the cap.

gills shades of brown before becoming grey-black; relatively narrow; free.

spore print black.

stalk white, hollow, enlarging somewhat to the base or equal with a small thickening at the base; 3 - 4 cm tall.

flesh whitish, thin.

hare's foot Coprinus

p.145-3

Coprinus lagopus (Fries) Fries

lagopus: hare's foot (Greek)

Cosmopolitan; the fastest growing and vanishing mushroom; it grows in different parts of the world, but because it is so fragile and lasts such a short time, it may not be seen so often. Found all across Canada in woods and gardens. Grows in small groups on the ground, on leaves, compost and chips and on burnt areas.

cap young fruiting bodies are woolly and greyish white, looking like very small hare's feet. They grow up fast to become tall mushrooms with a cap like a Chinese hat; grooved right to the centre, with bits of the broken-up universal veil regularly distributed on it. In dry climates the cap finally rolls up and dries up rather than deliquesce. Up to 7 cm across.

gills white at first, then blackening; narrow; free.

spore print black.

stalk originally short, white and woolly, later smooth, straight, hollow, enlarging toward the base and ending in a rooting point; up to 13 cm tall; 0.4 cm (4 mm) thick at the top. (The small specimens on the illustration grew on compost.)

flesh brown, thin.

glistening inky cap or mica cap

p.145-4

Coprinus micaceus (Bulliard: Fries) Fries

mica: crumb (Latin)

Cosmopolitan; it grows on, or near, old rotten stumps in dense clusters in forests, parks and gardens; though small, they grow in such tight bunches that it may be worthwhile to pick them; fruits in spring and summer. Edible and good in omelettes.

cap tawny with orange-brown crown; brown bits on it , which soon get lost; grooves about halfway up the cap; up to 4 cm high, up to 3 cm wide.

gills white, crowded, turning dark brown, then black, dissolving somewhat.

spore print black.

stalk white, smooth, fragile, hollow; up to 6 cm tall and up to 5 mm thick.

flesh thin, fragile, white in stalk, brownish in cap.

tree Coprinus

p.145-5

Coprinus truncorum (Schaeffer) Fries

truncorum: of tree trunks (Latin)

North American; grows close to living trees; fruits in summer; further south it fruits in winter.

cap light brown, bell-shaped, grooved halfway up the bell, disappearing brown bits on the crown; up to 4 cm across.

gills white with grey edges; crowded; later brown and then black, deliquescing.

spore print black.
stalk white, smooth; thin annular zone on lower stalk; rootlike bundles (rhizomes) at base; up to 9 cm tall; up to 7 mm thick.
flesh white, thin, fragile.

smooth inky cap   p.145-6

Coprinus atramentarius (Bulliard: Fries) Fries
atramentum: ink (Latin)

Worldwide distribution; occurs on or around rotten stumps; fruits in summer and fall.

The French mycologist P. Bulliard, who named the species, pointed out in 1784 that an intensely black ink can be made out of the overmature mushroom cap, which can be used for pen-work or wash drawing. Boil the inky liquid with some water and a few cloves to preserve it. This mushroom is edible and good but should not be eaten along with alcoholic drinks; even drinking in the next few days gives the same bad reaction. It causes nausea and hot flushes and has the same effects as the drug Disulfram or Antabuse which is used in therapy for alcoholics.

cap smooth, bell shaped, greyish white with a bit of brown on the crown; up to 8 cm across and up to 6 cm high.
gills crowded, broad; white at first, then brown before turning black and deliquescing.
spore print black.
stalk white, hollow, annular zone near the base; equal, narrowing down beneath the annular zone; up to 10 cm tall and up to 1 cm thick.
flesh white.

The three genera - *Anellaria*, *Panaeolina* and *Panaeolus* are closely related. *Anellaria* looks like *Panaeolus* but has a ring (annulus). *Panaeolina* is an intermediate between *Panaeolus* and *Psathyrella*. They are combined on p. 147. *Panaeolina* has a purple-brown spore print, the others have black spores. Several of these species are hallucinogenic or have other toxic properties. They are not easily recognized because of the variation in colour; the caps are often hygrophanous. In addition there is a great difference in size between members of a species (see illustrations 4 and 5). All have mottled, adnate gills with lighter margins because the spores ripen unevenly.

dung mottle gill   p.147-1

Anellaria semiovata (Sowerby: Fries) Pearson & Dennis
former name: *Panaeolus semi-ovatus*
Anellaria: with ring (Latin)
semiovata: with the shape of half an egg (Latin)

Cosmopolitan; occurs in the Pacific Northwest, the prairie provinces, the Yukon and Alaska. It grows on dung in fields or woods and can be found in various sizes; sometimes it is hallucinogenic; fruits from spring to fall.

cap off-white to yellowish, very sticky when wet, shiny when dry; disc slightly brownish, sometimes cracked when dry; bell shaped to campanulate; 1.5 - 8 cm across.
gills pale at first, changing to mottled brown, then black with light edges; adnate, broad.
spore print black.
stalk white, enlarging toward base, eventually hollow; up to 15 cm tall and up to 6 mm thick at the top.
partial veil fibrous, white, blackened by spores, forming a persistent ring.
flesh off-white.

belted Panaeolus

p.147-2

Panaeolus subbalteatus Berkeley & Broome

Panaeolus: dazzling (Greek)
subbalteatus: belted (darker border on the cap) (Latin)

Cosmopolitan; widely distributed across North America; occurs in well-manured gardens and lawns; hallucinogenic.

cap	dark brown; depending on humidity, the hygrophanous cap soon fades, giving a belted appearance; broadly rounded or conic; the cuticle cracks sometimes with age; up to 4 cm across.
gills	dirty mottled brown; appears dusted with white, later black with light edges; adnate, narrow, close.
spore print	black.
stalk	pinkish-brown, equal, slim, stiff, hollow; up to 8 cm tall and up to 3 mm thick.
flesh	brown in cap, brownish or whitish in stalk.

haymaker's mushroom

p.147-3

Panaeolina foenisecii Fries

former names: *Psathyrella foenisecii, Panaeolus foenisecii*
Panaeolina: small Panaeolus (Latin)
foenisecii: literally dry hay (Latin)

Cosmopolitan; growing in grass, not on dung or wood; it is one of the common lawn mushrooms in North America but widely scattered. Related to both *Panaeolus* and *Psathyrella*. The spore print is not black but dark purplish-brown; hallucinogenic. Fruits through the summer on the prairies, through spring to late fall along the coast.

cap	dark smoky brown when moist, hygrophanous, fading to buff; cuticle sometimes cracking, conic to convex, sometimes slight umbo; up to 3 cm across.
gills	medium brown, then dark purplish-brown with light edges; adnate, intermediates, very nice spacing.
spore print	dark purplish brown.
stalk	light brown, hollow; up to 6 cm tall; up to 3 mm thick.
flesh	off-white to light brown.

pinched Panaeolus

p.147-4

Panaeolus sphinctrinus (Fries) Quélet

sphinctrinus: pulled in, tied up (Greek)

Cosmopolitan; occurring throughout the Pacific Northwest but widely scattered; growing on animal droppings in woods and meadows; very variable in size and colour and not easy to distinguish from *Panaeolus campanulatus*, but *P. sphinctrinus* is generally smaller and the cap edge is more constrained; does not expand; hallucinogenic.

cap	dark grey to brown, campanulate; smooth, not expanding, with remnants of partial veil on the cap edge; up to 4 cm across.
gills	grey, then black with white edges, relatively narrow; adnate.
spore print	black.
stalk	brown to brownish-grey, enlarging a bit toward the base; up to 10 cm tall and up to 3 mm thick at the top.
partial veil	present, remnants showing on the cap margin, but not resulting in a ring.
flesh	grey, hollow stalk.

bell cap Panaeolus

p.147-5

Panaeolus campanulatus (Linnaeus) Fries

campanulatus: bell-shaped (Latin)

Cosmopolitan and widely distributed throughout our continent; dung is necessary for the growth of this species; fruiting in summer and fall, fruiting in winter further south. It contains not only the hallucinogenic substance psilocybin but also, like *Amanita muscaria,* ibonetic acid which causes nausea. **Poisonous.**

cap	bell-shaped, grey with brownish crown or light brown, depending on humidity; toothlike remnants of partial veil on cap edge of young specimens; cap expands when maturing; up to 6 cm across.
gills	mottled brownish changing to mottled black, light margins, broad, distant in mature specimens, many intermediates, adnate.
spore print	black.
stalk	rufus-brown to almost charcoal; stiff, shiny, straight, equal, hollow; white mycelium at the base; up to 16 cm tall and up to 5 mm thick.
partial veil	toothlike remnant on the cap edge, leaving no annulus.
flesh	thin, rufus, shiny in stalk, sometimes whitish.

Genus PSATHYRELLA
straw-like, fragile (Greek)

A very large genus of about 450 species; mostly small, very fragile mushrooms; saprophytic on dead leaves, decaying wood, and lignin-rich humus; caps are usually buff, brown or grey but because they are hygrophanous, the cap colour has to be noted for all three stages: when freshly found, when fading and when fully dry. Any purplish tint should be duly recorded. Gills adnate, mottled with light edges; spore print ranges from dark brown to purple-brown to blackish. All but one of the Psathyrellas are saprophytes, the exception is *P. epimyces,* which is parasitic on *Coprinus comatus* (the shaggy mane). A gilled mushroom growing on another gilled mushroom is quite rare. All species on p. 151 of Psathyrellas have a partial veil covering the gills. Most of the time the partial veil leaves a fringe on the cap edge which disappears; sometimes the partial veil results in a ring on the stalk.

Also on p. 151 is one species of the genus *Lacrymaria* (lacrymaria: Latin for tearful), which is closely related to *Psathyrella.* It is more hairy, and cortina-like remnants of the partial veil are visible on the stalk because dark spores cling to it. In damp weather droplets cling to the gills; hence, the name tearful. It is not known of most of these mushrooms whether they are edible. They are small and fragile, and the one sturdy species has an unattractive odour of raw potatoes.

bell-shaped Psathyrella   p.149-1
Psathyrella conopilea (Fries) Pearson & Dennis
conopilea: with a conical cap (Greek)

Cosmopolitan; widely distributed; grows on well manured soil, on sticks and debris; has rather characteristic setae (bristle-like hairs) on the cap; fruiting in summer and fall.

cap	grey-brown, fading to light buff; bell shaped at first, then broadly conical; fragile, up to 4 cm across.
gills	at first pale, then dark brown with light edge; close, adnate.
spore print	blackish.
stalk	white with some brown in the middle, slim, tall and fragile, hollow, up to 12 cm tall and up to 4 mm thick.
flesh	thin, white.

rooted Psathyrella   p.149-2
Psathyrella microrhiza (Lasch) Konrad & Maublanc
microrhiza: with small root (Greek)

Cosmopolitan; grows in mixed forest, with half of its long stalk underground or in leaves; bunched mycelium at its base (microrhiza); fruiting in summer in Alberta.

cap	warm brown crown, tan margin, hygrophanous, streaked with dark brown; low dome shape; up to 2 cm across.
gills	mottled dark brown, light edge, relatively distant, broad, adnate.

spore print blackish-brown.
stalk streaky white, slim, tall, hollow, bottom half buried in leaves; rhizoid covered with white mycelium bundles; up to 10 cm tall, including buried part; up to 3 mm thick.
flesh thin, white.

big-spored Psathyrella   p.149-3

Psathyrella megaspora A. H. Smith

megaspora: with big spores (Greek)

North American; occurs on paths, on leaves or on rotten wood; fruiting in summer. Reported from Michigan by A. H. Smith. I found the illustrated specimens in several places in Alberta.

cap brown, striate, fading to buff; hygrophanous; thin; bell shaped, expanding a little; up to 2 cm across.
gills greyish-brown with white edges; adnate, relatively broad.
spore print black.
stalk white at first, later the base is brownish; crooked, hollow, up to 4 cm tall and 2 mm thick, equal.
flesh whitish.

path Psathyrella   p.149-4

Psathyrella limicola (Peck) A. H. Smith

limicola: living on paths (Latin); limes: path (Latin)

North American; grows in mixed forest near wet spots and on paths; fruiting in spring and early summer. Also reported from Michigan, Wyoming and New York; the illustrated specimens were found northwest of Edmonton, Alberta.

cap brown at first, hygrophanous, fading to buff; smooth; convex, expanding somewhat, up to 3.5 cm across.
gills off-white at first, then dark brown with light edges; close, narrow, intermediates, adnate.
spore print purplish black.
stalk white, slim, crooked, tall, hollow, up to 11 cm tall and 2 mm thick.
flesh thin, fragile, off-white.

crowned Psathyrella   p.149-5

Psathyrella pseudocoronata A. H. Smith

pseudocoronata: looks crowned (Latin)

North American; occurs on the ground in mixed forest or in grass under poplar; fruiting early in spring, at the same time as morels. Reported from Wyoming. I found the illustrated specimens in various places in aspen parkland in Alberta.

cap dark brown at first, hygrophanous, soon fading to buff; domed at first, then flattening out and turning up somewhat; dull, smooth, margin finely furrowed; up to 7 cm across.
gills ochrish at first, changing to greyish-brown, then dark brown with light edges; adnate.
spore print very dark purplish-brown.
stalk shiny white, equal, hollow, up to 9 cm tall and up to 5 mm thick.
flesh whitish, fragile, fleshy in cap.

smooth-capped Psathyrella   p.149-6

Psathyrella subnuda (Karsten) A. H. Smith

subnuda: almost naked (Latin)

Cosmopolitan; grows in damp places in meadows, on lawns and paths; fruiting in spring. This species reported from California, Oregon and Washington but also from Finland. The specimens illustrated are from the Edmonton area.

cap light brown at first, hygrophanous, soon light buff; convex to domed, flattening out to plane; up to 4 cm across.

gills	light buff in young, bit darker in mature; adnate, many intermediates, gills loosen easily from the stalk.
spore print	dark purplish-brown.
stalk	white, fragile, stuffed with fluffy material, very crooked; up to 10 cm tall; up to 4 mm thick.
flesh	white in stalk, tan in cap.

date-coloured Psathyrella

p.149-7

Psathyrella spadicea (Fries) Singer

spadicea: with the colour of fresh dates (Latin)

Cosmopolitan; growing in tufts on dead poplar stumps or on the base of living old poplars, probably on the dead bark; fruiting in summer and fall.

cap	fresh date colour, hygrophanous, fading to tan; rounded, up to 7 cm across.
gills	pale at first, then reddish-brown; mottled, light edge; adnate.
spore print	dark grey-brown.
stalk	white with brownish streaks, hollow, up to 6 cm tall and up to 6 mm thick.
flesh	white.

bog Psathyrella

p.149-8

Psathyrella uliginicola McKnight & Smith

uliginicola: living in humid conditions (Latin)

Western North American; growing under poplars in the Rocky Mountains and in humid spots in boreal mixed forest and aspen parkland; fruiting in spring, summer and fall, wherever it is damp enough; fruits even when other fungi forego fruiting. A beautiful mushroom but inedible.

cap	domed to globose, not hygrophanous; lovely light-grey, felty, streaked cap, later a bit brownish on the crown, wavy edge, up to 10 cm across; cap separates easily from the stalk.
gills	white at first, then a pearly pinkish grey, many intermediates, eroded edges, finally purple-brown with age, semideliquescing.
spore print	dark purplish-brown.
stalk	shiny, silky white, base sometimes a bit pink, equal, hollow, sturdy, rigid but brittle; up to 9 cm tall and up to 1.5 cm thick.
flesh	white, thick, often with a semi-transparent line over the gills, sometimes pinkish.
odour	of green raw potatoes.

clustered Psathyrella

p.151-1

Psathyrella hydrophila (Fries) A. H. Smith

former names: *Hypholoma hydrophila, Drosophila hydrophila*
hydrophila: water loving (Greek)

Cosmopolitan and widespread; it grows in large clusters on or around hardwood and softwood stumps; fruiting in cool weather in early spring or late fall. Edibility unknown.

cap	dark brown at first, bell shaped expanding to conic, can have some white fuzz on the margin; hygrophanous, fading to yellowish and pale streaky brown; up to 5.5 cm across.
gills	bone coloured at first, then spotty grey-brown, finally dark chocolate brown; adnate, close.
spore print	dark purplish-brown.
stalk	whitish, hollow, up to 9 cm tall and 0.6 cm thick.
partial veil	white, fibrous, resulting sometimes in a ring which is often darkened by spores; most of it forms an evanescent fringe on the cap edge.
flesh	whitish in stalk, brown in cap, fragile.

dubious Psathyrella

p.151-2

Psathyrella incerta (Peck) Smith

incerta: dubious (Latin)

North American species, growing all through the continent on hardwood debris in the forest or in grass; fruiting in summer. Edibility unknown.

cap	whitish, a bit brownish on crown; bare, dull, very fine striation on margin; up to 3 cm across.
gills	bone coloured at first, then muddy; close, adnate, narrow, many intermediates.
spore print	very dark purplish-brown.
stalk	white, equal, hollow, almost smooth, thickened base, up to 6 cm tall and 0.5 cm thick.
partial veil	sometimes leaving a finely striate annulus, mostly a fringe on the cap edge.
flesh	off-white, thin, fragile.

moist-disc Psathyrella

p.151-3

Psathyrella madeodisca (Peck) A. H. Smith

madeodisca: with a moist disc (Latin)

North American; growing on decaying stumps; fruiting in spring; occurs infrequently; edibility unknown.

cap	potato brown, dull, fading to very pale, hygrophanous, rounded, spreading out; the edge connected to the stalk in young specimens by a conspicuous partial veil; up to 4 cm across.
gills	pale at first, later mottled brown with light edges; close.
spore print	purplish-black.
stalk	whitish with a bit of lilac; hollow; up to 7 cm tall and 0.5 cm thick.
partial veil	white, quite visible from the side in young specimens because it sags somewhat (see illustration); evanescent, not resulting in an annulus.
flesh	white, thin.

stiff-legged Psathryella

p.151-4

Psathyrella rigidipes (Peck) Smith

rigidipes: with a rigid stalk (Latin)

North American; growing along roads and in grass; fruiting in summer.

cap	light yellowish-brown with off-white, appressed hair; lighter margin; rounded; up to 3 cm across.
gills	brown with a wavy white margin, adnate, serrate, narrow, finally dark.
spore print	blackish-brown.
stalk	white and sandy coloured, hollow, enlarging toward the base, smooth, sometimes bumpy, often oddly bent; up to 8 cm tall and 0.5 cm thick.
partial veil	white, fibrous, leaving remnants on the cap edge (evanescent).
flesh	thin, whitish.

weeping widow

p.151-5

Lacrymaria velutina (Persoon: Fries) Konrad & Maublanc

former names: *Psathyrella velutina*, *Hypholoma velutina*
Lacrymaria (lacrimaria): with tears (Latin)
velutina: covered with hair (Latin)

Cosmopolitan and widespread; grows in bundles in the grass; white mycelium at the base holding dead grass; fruiting in summer and fall; is said to be edible.

cap	yellowish-brown, hairy, rounded, margin fringed from the partial veil; cap becomes smooth and smoky brown with age, often cracked; up to 6 cm across.
gills	first pallid, then mottled brown, finally very dark purple-brown; relatively distant; many intermediates; adnate, but often loosened from the stalk; in damp weather beaded with droplets.
spore print	blackish-brown.

stalk	top is white or light brown, hairy at first; later has brownish pattern underneath the annular zone (visible due to dark spores), hollow; up to 7 cm tall and up to 5 mm thick.
partial veil	white, hairy, leaving a fringe at the cap edge and a hairy annular zone on the stalk which catches spores.
flesh	light brown, thin.

parasitic Psathyrella p.151-6

Psathyrella epimyces (Peck) A. H. Smith

epimyces: on a fungus (Greek)

Northern North American; infrequent; has been reported from Quebec, Alberta and the Yukon; undoubtedly occurs elsewhere across the prairie provinces and in B.C. The only *Psathyrella* which is parasitic and then only on shaggy manes; fruiting in the fall when shaggy mane fruits.

cap	whitish, silky, later dirty white; first rounded, then extended; fringed margin from partial veil remnants; up to 5 cm across.
gills	pale grey at first, then blackish brown with light edges, adnate.
spore print	blackish.
stalk	white, woolly, up to 6 cm tall and up to 15 mm thick.
partial veil	white, leaving an evanescent ring near the base of the stalk which resembles a volva.
flesh	white, in stalk hollow.

suburban Psathyrella p.151-7

Psathyrella candolleana (Fries) Maire

candolleana: named after A.P. de Candolle 1778-1841, French mycologist

Worldwide distribution; a people species, thriving in an urban environment; occurs on dead grass in lawns and around stumps. This is a complex of species which is variable and, therefore, hard to recognize. Is said to be edible. Caution.

cap	light brown at first, then pale buff, margin lighter and a bit hairy, striate; rounded at first, then expanding, up to 8 cm across.
gills	whitish at first, then purplish brown; close, adnate, narrow, intermediates.
spore print	purplish-brown.
stalk	white, smooth, hollow, fragile; up to 8 cm tall and up to 5 mm thick.
partial veil	white, evanescent remnants on cap edge.
flesh	white, thin.
odour	delicate mushroom odour.

Class GASTEROMYCETES

The Greek word *Gasteromycetes* translates literally as stomach fungi and refers to the fact that the spores are formed inside the more or less round fruiting bodies. Basidiospores are formed inside a skin (**peridium**) which may be multilayered. The spore-producing tissue (**gleba**) consists of sterile hyphae (**capillitium**) on which **basidia** are formed, which produce the spores. Usually the spore mass becomes dry and powdery, but there are exceptions. With the closed spore "containers" the group is well suited to the dry western climate. The group includes false and true puffballs, earthstars, bird's nests, stinkhorns, stalked puffballs and toughskins. Early mycologists had a frank sense of humor when naming their finds in this group.

Orders HYMENOGASTRALES AND PODAXALES

The Greek name *Hymenogastrales* indicates that the hymenium (spore-bearing layer) is contained in a skin. The Greek name *Podaxales* means strong footed, and members of this order have a tough stalk.

Some mycologists place these groups of fascinating fungi in the Agaricales, the order of gilled mushrooms. They are obviously in an evolutionary stage between Hymenomycetes and Gasteromycetes. The first species described looks like a small, somewhat misshapen *Coprinus comatus*, while the second one looks like a very large version of the same mushroom.

Hymenogastraceae (the false truffles) is a family which also belongs to the Hymenogastrales. So far I have not found any of these. The fruiting bodies are potato-like and subterranean. The main difference from true truffles is that the Hymenogastraceae carry basidiospores, while true truffles have ascospores. If you find a truffle-like specimen, you need a microscope to identify it. False truffles are related to more than one group of Agaricales, and so like Secotiaceae and Podaxaceae, they are in an evolutionary stage. The reason they are placed in the class of Gasteromycetes is the thick-walled spores, which ripen slowly and unevenly in a fruiting body which has lost the ability to discharge spores forcibly. Often rudimentary gills are found in immature specimens, and they have a columella, which is a continuation of the stalk, inside the gleba. The families Secotiaceae and Podaxaceae each are represented by one species of one genus.

Family SECOTIACEAE

false puffball   p.152-1

Endoptychum agaricoides Czerniaiev

former name: *Secotium agaricoides* (Czerniaiev) Hollós
Endoptychum: inside the fold (Greek)
agaricoides: looking like a gilled mushroom (Greek)
Secotium: resembles an enclosed space (Greek)

Cosmopolitan; a rare saprophytic fungus, occurring after rain in arid regions; found in the Rocky Mountains up to 3000 m in elevation, but also in cultivated areas. I repeatedly found the ones in the illustration in grassy areas in Edmonton parks. First found in the Ukraine in 1845 by B. Czerniaiev and in the U. S. in 1882 by Peck. Also recorded from Asia, Australia, Algeria and New Zealand. In Canada, found in Ottawa and Winnipeg as well. Is said to be edible when young.

fruiting body smooth and white at first, later scaly with small tufts; up to 11 cm high and up to 7 cm wide with a short stalk. The edge of what looks like the cap stays attached to the stalk.

gleba white at first, often rudimentary gills are visible; turning patchy yellow and white, then yellowish brown, almost orange.

spore print not possible to make, but colour of the gleba varies from pale ochre to brownish; solid mass to a somewhat powdery consistency.

stalk white, up to 3 cm tall but often no visible stalk; inside the cap is a columella, the name for the continuation of the stalk. There is a lot of variation both in length, consistency and flesh colour (see illustration). Rhizoids at the base.

flesh white, turns pinkish; solid consistency, fibrous or with holes in stalk and columella (see illustration).

odour mature specimens smell like cabbage.

Family PODAXACEAE

false shaggy mane   p.152-2
Podaxis pistillaris (Persoon) Morse
Podaxis: strong foot (Greek)
pistillaris: like a pestle (Greek)

Cosmopolitan; occurs in desert regions throughout the world. They have been reported as far north as Idaho, and I think that they may also be found in the dry hot valleys of the Rocky Mountains, for instance in the Fraser Valley near Kamloops. I found the specimens in the illustration on a "working" termite hill in Africa. The fruiting is triggered by rain after a hot dry period.

cap (or head) shaped like a shaggy mane cap, white with brown to blackish ragged scales; up to 20 cm tall and 7 cm across, narrowly elliptic, margin permanently connected with the stalk. The young cap has an interesting fringe like an annulus at the cap base.

gleba white at first, changing to yellow brown with red tones, then to black (see section on p. 152). The colour varies. Rudimentary gills may be present. In the African specimen, black spores fell out of an opening at the head base, but usually remain inside. Miller reports that the gleba can occasionally be slightly deliquescent, proving its connection with *Coprinus comatus*.

spores yellow brown to black, irregularly ripening; thick-walled with an apical pore. The caps usually stay enclosed until disintegration or eaten by an animal; a massive amount of spores is slowly released when disintegration occurs.

stalk white with large scales, tough, equal with small bulb underground; extending in cap as columella; altogether up to 35 cm tall; up to 2 cm thick at the top.

flesh dirty white and tough.

odour slight.

Order LYCOPERDALES

Two families of the Lycoperdales will be dealt with: Lycoperdaceae and Geastraceae. Spores are formed inside and form a powdery mass at maturity. They are not forcibly expelled but emerge through the action of an outside force, e.g., raindrops, wind or an animal. The peridium or skin can consist of two or more layers. In Lycoperdaceae, or true puffballs, either a pore forms in the top or the top crumbles away. In Geastraceae, or earth stars, the **exoperidium,** or outer layer, splits in a star shape and the **endoperidium,** or inner layer, holds the spores, which escape from a hole in the top.

Family LYCOPERDACEAE   true puffballs

True puffballs are not always easily identified to species because mature and overmature specimens, as well as fresh ones, are needed to see colour changes inside and out, the colour of the spores and the way the fruiting body opens up. In some cases a positive identification can only be achieved through a microscopic examination.

Generally a puffball, as such, is easily recognized, and they are completely safe to eat as long as completely white flesh without any visible shape in it is seen when a longitudinal cut is made. None are known to be poisonous and quite a few are edible and good (but see p. 163 because there are some poisonous tough skins).

Puffballs occur in large numbers throughout the west, the prairies, the mountains and the north, including the Yukon and Alaska.

I repeat that a longitudinal cut should always be made in order to avoid a dangerous mixup with devil's eggs (see *Amanita*). The following genera will be described: *Lycoperdon, Morganella, Calvatia, Bovista* and *Vascellum*.

All true puffballs have a one- or two-layered skin or peridium (Greek for little pouch). The outer skin (or exoperidium) usually crumbles away, and the inner skin (endoperidium) contains the spore mass.

Inside the puffball is the spore-producing tissue, which at first looks like a white marshmallow then changes colours as the spores develop and ripen. This tissue, in all stages, is called the gleba (Latin for lump of earth). Then there is the sterile base, which can be either present or absent. The spores can either come out through a hole in the top, called the **apical pore**, or are released when the top crumbles away.

Genus LYCOPERDON
wolf wind (Greek)

Small to medium-sized puffballs with a considerable sterile base and a two-layered peridium. The exoperidium consists of spines, warts, granules or floccose material which sloughs off at maturity; the endoperidium, or sporesac, opens with an apical pore. A small extension of the base into the gleba, or columella, is sometimes present. This can be important for identification.

Genus MORGANELLA
Morganella: after Prof. A. P. Morgan, botanist 1836-1907, Preston, Ohio

Small puffball, quite similar to *Lycoperdon*, but there are microscopic differences in the spore-producing tissue.

These two genera are saprophytic and grow on the ground or on decaying wood.

snow-white puffball   p.153-1

Lycoperdon candidum Persoon
Lycoperdon: flatulence of the wolf (Greek)
candidum: white (Latin)

Cosmopolitan; found in open woods or pastures; growing on the ground or on decayed wood. Occurs across Canada; also widely distributed in the U.S. This species may have hallucinogenic qualities (see Pomerleau 1980).

fruiting body	rounded, white, well-developed sterile base; up to 3 cm high and up to 4 cm across.
peridium	two-layered; exoperidium consisting of a thick layer of pointed white spines which comes off in patches, showing a dark (olive brown) endoperidium underneath; apical pore.
gleba	at first white, then olive brown and finally powdery.
sterile base	white also turning brown.

soft puffball

Lycoperdon molle Persoon: Persoon

molle: soft, fine (Latin)

Cosmopolitan; terrestrial in hardwood and coniferous forests; recorded in Quebec, Alberta and the U.S.

fruiting body	pear shaped; head rounded; stalklike sterile base; up to 4 cm across; up to 5 cm high, rhizomorphs.
peridium	two-layered; exoperidium covered with soft short grey-brown spines in a very attractive pattern; brown granular surface between the spines; cream to yellow-brown endoperidium; smooth after the spines fall away; apical pore.
gleba	at first white, then olive brown becoming powdery.
sterile base	cream coloured, unchanging; showing a definitive rise into the gleba. A lengthwise cut through a mature specimen shows this clearly. Do this outside so that the powdery spores can be blown away. Observe some tissue that is attached to the rise into the gleba. This looks like a brown beard (capillitium: Latin for long hair) and is the tissue on which the spores were formed.

flesh-coloured puffball

Morganella subincarnata (Peck) Kreisel & Dring

former name: *Lycoperdon subincarnatum* Peck
subincarnata: almost flesh coloured (Latin)

North American species; grows on decayed wood or on the ground in coniferous or mixed forests. Reported from Quebec, Alberta and the U.S.

fruiting body	almost round or with a short, pinched, yellowish sterile base; up to 3.5 cm in diameter.
peridium	two-layered; exoperidium brown with pyramidal cones of medium long, brown spines; when this layer disappears, the endoperidium shows a lovely patched design (reticulate); apical pore.
gleba	white at first, then purplish brown, powdery.
sterile base	white; small or rudimentary.

spiny puffball

Lycoperdon echinatum Persoon: Persoon

echinatum: like a hedgehog (Greek)

Cosmopolitan, terrestrial in mixed forests; infrequent. Reported from the prairie provinces: Manitoba, Saskatchewan and Alberta; growing on the ground in moss in woods.

fruiting body	round to pear shaped with short conical base; up to 4 cm diameter; white rhizomorphs (wool-like bundles of mycelium).
peridium	two-layered; brown exoperidium, consisting of long coarse spines, 3 - 5 mm (the longest in this group); white at first, soon turning brown; spines quite persistent but leaving a well-marked pattern on the endoperidium when they do fall off; apical pore.
gleba	white at first, then purplish brown, powdery.
sterile base	slight.

umber puffball

Lycoperdon umbrinum Persoon

umbrinum: dark brown (Latin)

Cosmopolitan; occurs across Canada on the ground in mixed forests; looks like a brown version of *L. perlatum*, the warted puffball, but is a little smaller and usually has a shorter base.

fruiting body	pear shaped; rounded head, squat base up to 4 cm across and 5 cm high.
peridium	two-layered; exoperidium consists of dark brown spines in pyramidal cones, interspersed with granular warts; persistent; endoperidium yellowish and smooth; apical pore.
gleba	white at first, then yellow, then olive brown; powdery.
sterile base	white; start of a columella.

warted or gem-studded puffball
p.153-6

Lycoperdon perlatum Persoon

perlatum: widespread (Latin)

Worldwide; occurs in groups on the ground in open spots in the woods. Grows from Alaska and the Yukon right across Canada and all over the U.S. Edible and good.

fruiting body	pear shaped, head round, a bit flattened; base prominent; up to 6 cm wide and up to 7 cm high.
peridium	two-layered; exoperidium white to pale tan, composed of conical spines interspersed with smaller spines and granular warts; endoperidium smooth; apical pore.
gleba	white at first, then ochrish, finally olive brown; powdery.
sterile base	well developed with small spines on the outside; staying white.

pear-shaped puffball
p.153-7

Lycoperdon pyriforme Schaeffer: Persoon

pyriforme: shaped like a pear (Latin)

Worldwide; on old wood or connected to wood with rhizomorphs; usually in tight groups in mixed forests. I found these on decaying birchwood and on a dead tinder fungus fruiting body, *Fomes tomentarius*, p. 179, no. 3. Fruits in late summer and fall.

fruiting body	pear shaped with a well developed sterile base; up to 3 cm across and 4 cm tall, attached to white mycelial cords.
peridium	2-layered; exoperidium consisting of floccose material and fine warts, sloughing off at maturity; brown papery endoperidium; apical pore.
gleba	white at first, then ochrish; finally powdery olive brown.
sterile base	stays white.

Genus BOVISTA
Bovista: from the German word Bofist (latinized old German)

Small, smooth, round puffballs; rudimentary sterile base or none; two-layered peridium. Outer unpolished layer usually peals off; opens with an apical pore. Only one of the species portrayed is an original *Bovista*, all the others were previously *Lycoperdon*, but there are microscopic differences between the two genera; therefore, they were renamed. The capillitium is loose inside *Bovista*, while in *Lycoperdon* it is attached in the lower part (see illustration on p. 153 of *L. molle*). Attached to the soil with mycelial tufts, *Bovista* often come loose at maturity and are blown around by the wind in meadows.

Genus VASCELLUM
Latin for small pitcher

Small and medium-sized species; intermediate between *Lycoperdon* and *Calvatia*; the difference is that *Vascellum* has a papery membrane separating the sterile base from the gleba.

lead-coloured puffball
p.155-1

Bovista plumbea Persoon: Persoon

plumbea: lead coloured (Latin)

Cosmopolitan; occurs in open grassy areas, common across the West, very persistent, often blown around by the wind.

fruiting body	white, smooth, round, attached to the ground with mycelium tufts; size up to 3.5 cm wide.
peridium	smooth and white surface, showing just a few cracks in the top, then the outer skin peels off like an eggshell, leaving the grey to lead-coloured endoperidium intact; then, becoming detached from the ground, eventually forms a pore for distribution of the spores.

gleba	at first white (when it is edible) then eventually purplish and powdery.
sterile base	none.

small tumbling puffball

p.155-2

Bovista pusilla (Batsch) Persoon

former name: *Lycoperdon pusillum* Batsch
pusilla: small (Latin)

Cosmopolitan; occurs on our continent in cool grassy areas, for instance along roads in the mountains; this small puffball occurs mostly in the west.

fruiting body	white, round, a bit pinched at the base, up to 2.5 cm wide and 3 cm tall, base with mycelium tuft.
peridium	surface at first covered with fluffy bits or fine spines; when the exoperidium disappears, the pale dark brown endoperidium looks dotted. The apical pore has lobed edges like *Bovista plumbea*.
gleba	white at first, then olive brown and powdery.
sterile base	none.

Curtis' puffball

p.155-3

Vascellum curtisii (Berkeley) Kreisel

former name: *Lycoperdon curtisii* Berkeley
curtisii: named after Rev. M. A. Curtis (state botanist of North Carolina, 1808-1872)

North American species; it occurs in grassy areas throughout our continent.

fruiting body	round head with a short base; covered by numerous small spines; up to 2 cm wide and 3 cm high.
peridium	small spines quite persistent on outer skin, a bit greyish brown; endoperidium pale brown, opens up on top like a small glass.
gleba	first white, then yellow brown, powdery when mature.
sterile base	rudimentary and grey.

golden puffball

p.155-4

Bovista colorata (Peck) Kreisel

former name: *Lycoperdon coloratum* Peck
colorata: coloured or painted (Latin)

North American; all over Alberta, but also in Africa in the indigenous forest. Fruits in summer and fall; occurs in meadows, open woods, sometimes on decayed wood.

fruiting body	rounded, pinched at the base, diameter up to 5 cm, with yellow mycelial cords attached to the ground.
peridium	one layer, bright yellow at first with some white at the bottom, young specimens have some discreet, small darker warts; the spores escape through an apical pore; the white becomes yellow and the top deeper orange-yellow to bronze with age.
gleba	white at first, then yellow, then olive brown and powdery.
sterile base	none or small.

western lawn puffball

p.155-5

Vascellum pratense (Persoon em. Quélet) Kreisel

former name: *Lycoperdon hiemale* Bulliard: Vittadini
pratense: of the meadow (Latin)

Cosmopolitan; on well-manured meadows; especially common on the west coast and on the prairies.

fruiting body	base is barrel or drumstick shaped with a round head; after spores disperse through a large apical pore, the top flattens. Eventually last year's long-lasting base can be found the following spring with a shallow bowl on top; up to 5 cm wide and 8 cm tall.
peridium	at first the surface has a layer of fine spines and granules; when the outer skin disappears, the inner skin is white and smooth, turning yellow brown to metallic with age.

gleba	white at first, turning to yellow, then greenish yellow, then olive brown and powdery.
sterile base	well developed, seperated from the gleba by a thin membrane, turning olive-brown like the gleba.

Genus CALVATIA
a bald object (Latin)

Medium to very large puffballs; sterile base may be present or absent; two-layered peridium; the exoperidium often breaks up in patches; the tops disintegrate and bowl-like remnants stay around for a long time. The western giant puffball, *Calvatia booniana*, stays closed long after it has reached maturity and starts to smell like curry. The smooth giant puffball, *C. gigantea* (former name: *Langermannia gigantea*), is not described, but is very easily recognized. It cannot be mistaken for anything else. For edibility see the family *Lycoperdaceae*.

box puffball   p.155-6

Calvatia excipuliformis (Persoon) Perdeck
former names: *Lycoperdon excipuliforme*, *Calvatia saccata*
excipuliformis: with the form of a container (Latin)

Cosmopolitan; this puffball grows in grassy areas, meadows, along the roadside in the same places as *Calvatia utriformis*. It occurs throughout the prairies; is widely distributed but not common. The shape varies from pestle to pear shape.

fruiting body	beautiful round head on elongated sterile base, up to 15 cm tall and 7 cm wide at the head.
peridium	two-layered; the outer layer at first consisting of fine spines and granules, light ochrish brown; the inner skin is yellowish; splits open at the top and eventually looks like an old-fashioned birdbath or bowl on a pedestal.
gleba	at first white, later olive brown and powdery.
sterile base	same colour as top, tall.

checkered puffball   p.157-1

Calvatia utriformis (Bulliard: Persoon) Jaap
utriformis: shaped like a womb or wine skin (Latin)

Cosmopolitan; fruits from summer to fall in open woods and grassy areas; widely distributed on our continent, edible when immature.

fruiting body	can be pear shaped, up to 20 cm high, or more squat (see illustration), up to 20 cm across.
peridium	outer skin white and smooth at first, then cracking into a checkered pattern, leaving a nice design on the inner skin. The top breaks open to expose the spores.
gleba	first white, then yellowish olive brown, finally dark brown and powdery. Often some sticky spores are left in the bowl-like persistent old fruiting body next spring.
sterile base	the shape varies considerably in this species; up to10 cm in height and 0.8 cm wide, dull brown.

tall puffball   p.157-2

Calvatia elata (Massée) Morgan
elata: tall (Latin)

North American species, growing on low ground under brush in moss or in grass, persistent, edible when immature.

fruiting body	more or less pestle shaped, up to 10 cm tall, head up to 7 cm across.
peridium	outer skin whitish and granular at first, later dull brownish; endoperidium thin; long lasting, can still be intact next spring in dry areas.
gleba	white at first, then olive brown and powdery.
sterile base	first white then also olive brown.

giant western puffball

Calvatia booniana A. H. Smith

booniana: named after Dr. Wm. Judson Boone, first president of the College of Idaho

Western North American species, prevalent in semiarid regions after heavy rain in summer and fall, edible when immature.

fruiting body large, up to 60 cm across and up to 30 cm high; a flattened ball.
peridium thick exoperidium, which cracks into large scales, gradually breaking apart as the fruiting body expands; endoperidium stays intact a very long time. The scales can be very thick, up to 2 cm.
gleba solid, firm, white at first, turning bright yellow, then greenish, then starts to smell strongly of curry; finally olive brown and powdery.
sterile base rudimentary or none.

Family GEASTRACEAE earthstars

Geastraceae are saprophytic, terrestrial fungi, closely related to the Lycoperdaceae. There is only one genus, *Geastrum*, in this family. The immature fruiting body is like a puffball, but the peridium is multilayered. When it matures, the outer layers split starlike into **rays** which open up and bend out and down.

In several species the fruiting body ends up standing on the tips of the rays, lifting the endoperidium or spore sac off the ground. The spores escape through an apical pore, and as with *Lycoperdon*, falling raindrops cause the spores to puff out.

Species differ in the shape of the endoperidium: the area around the pore can be raised and be a different colour (called a halo), the pore may or may not be fringed. Further differences in the exoperidium include: the number of rays; the way the layers break up, dry up or disappear.

The small, young fruiting bodies are not easily found because they are often partly underground in moss or duff and often encrusted with earth. The mature specimens show up better. They are all interesting, but *G. floriforme* especially because it has hygroscopic features. It is imbedded in earth to start with, but when it matures, it opens up in damp weather and closes again when it is dry. Obviously this is a defense mechanism for dry climates. In addition it has a very small pore.

four-pointed earthstar

p.158-1

Geastrum quadrifidum Persoon: Persoon

former name: *G.coronatum* Persoon
Ge: earth; astrum: star (Greek)
quadrifidum: divided in four (Latin)

Worldwide distribution; growing in coniferous forests; fruiting in the fall; persistent, dry fruiting body. Occurs in the Pacific Northwest, Rocky Mountains, the prairies and also in Eastern Canada.

fruiting body small depressed puffball at first, partly submerged in duff; opening to up to 5 cm across and 6 cm high, standing on ray tips.
peridium four layered; grey, egg-shaped spore sac; tan, conical, fringed halo; exoperidium splitting starlike into four, sometimes five, rays; top layer breaks up irregularly and falls away in patches; the middle layer forms the arch, brown in colour; bottom layer stays on the ground attached to the ray tips as its mycelial nest, shows up white.
spore powder brown.

sitting earthstar p.158-2

Geastrum sessile (Sowerby) Pouzar

former name: *G. fimbriatum* Fries
sessile: suitable to sit on (Latin)

Cosmopolitan; coniferous and mixed forests in the Pacific Northwest, Rocky mountains, prairies and eastern Canada; fruiting in the fall. Further south in the U.S., it fruits in the fall and winter.

fruiting body small depressed puffball at first, partly submerged in duff; opening up to 4 cm across and 4 cm high.

peridium multilayered; spore sac grey, a bit egg shaped, considerable fringe around the mouth (was at one time named *G. fimbriatum* — Latin for fringed); no halo; exoperidium splits starlike into 6 - 11 rays which bend under; the earthstar sits on its bent tips, hence sessile; the top layer is cream coloured, cracking and turning brown.

spore powder brown.

flower-shaped earthstar p.158-3

Geastrum floriforme (Vittadini) Cunningham

floriformis: in the shape of a flower (Latin)

Cosmopolitan; growing under a variety of trees in different areas of the world. I have found it in Arizona and Hawaii, but it is also reported from Saskatchewan and the western U.S. This is a species with hygroscopic rays, not raising itself on its raytips, but truly sessile.

fruiting body small puffball half in the ground, with mycelial cords at the base, light coloured, earth encrusted, opening up to 5 cm wide and 3 cm high.

peridium four layered; spore sac light buff, round, with small smooth pore, no halo; exoperidium splitting into 5 - 10 rays, light buff, upper layer eventually disappearing; the bottom, dirt-encrusted layer crumbling away, leaving the brown rays, which miraculously close in dry weather and open in dampness. Long after the spores are gone, *G. floriforme* still opens up when put in water!

spore powder brown.

rounded earthstar p.158-4

Geastrum saccatum Fries

saccatum: in a sac (Greek)

North American; grows in conifer forests under spruce; fruiting in summer and fall; persistent dry fruiting bodies. One of the sessile species, starting partly underground and not raising itself up very much.

fruiting body round, partly submerged, light ochre brown; opening up to not more than 5 cm across and 3.5 cm high.

peridium multilayered; round to oval sessile spore sac which is dull brown with buff, raised, conical halo, small fringed mouth; exoperidium splitting into 5 - 8 rays, buff coloured, brown in maturity after the top layer dries up.

spore powder brown.

beret earthstar p.158-5

Geastrum pectinatum Persoon

former name: *G. striatum*
pectinatum: like a comb (Latin)

Cosmopolitan, but rare everywhere; growing in mixed forest or coniferous forest; persistent, reported from the prairies (also Québec and eastern North America).

fruiting body round, covered with earth or debris, opening up to 5 cm across and 6 cm high when standing on its tips.

peridium multilayered; grey spore sac, eventually looking like a plumed beret (barette, biretta) or artist's cap, the fringed mouth is like a small plume; the base of the spore sac is stalklike and striate, set in a small collar-like extension of the exoperidium; this splits into 6 - 8 rays, pale brown with darker brown patches of the broken up upper layer on it. Attached to the raytips are the leftovers of the outer layer of the peridium mixed with duff (mycelial nest). (Look at the illustration to make all of this clear.)

spore powder brown.

collared earthstar   p.158-6

Geastrum triplex Junghuhn

Cosmopolitan; it grows in mixed forests under hardwoods across Canada and the U.S. Persistent, a nice find among the autumn leaves.

fruiting body at first like a tulip bulb, partly submerged; opens up to 10 cm across and 5 cm high, the largest of the earthstars (varies in size). It stands on the raytips.

peridium multilayered, thick; spore sac light brown, round, with lighter, conical halo; fringed mouth sitting in a saucer formed by the buff, upper layer of the exoperidium, which splits into 5 - 8 rays (see illustration). The collar-like part stays. The earthstar stands on the tips of its star and is loose from the ground; eventually the whole thing is brown.

spore powder brown.

Order PHALLALES

Fungi in this order have a mucilaginous spore mass at maturity, which is born on a specialized receptacle, and a cuplike volva at the base. Many more species occur in the tropics than in the North temperate zone. Three species of one family are described.

Family PHALLACEAE   stinkhorns

Immature fruiting bodies of species in this family start out in a round or egg-shaped form often called devil's eggs. The wall is multilayered and the tough outer layer breaks open and forms the cup or **volva** at the base. The whole mushroom is inside the egg, including a stalk which stretches out very quickly and carries the sticky spore mass, right on top in the case of *Mutinus* and on top of a cap-shaped reticulum in the case of *Phallus*. The caplike structure of two of the species is not really a cap, but I will call it that.

Dispersion of spores is done by flies and slugs, which are attracted by the carrion- or foxy-smelling, slimy spore mass. All have thick mycelial cords at their bases which are used for survival in resting periods. People in Europe sometimes eat the eggs. The fruiting bodies have been used in ointments and as powders for gout, epilepsy and rheumatism, as well as in a brew for an aphrodisiac. All are terrestrial saprophytes and not poisonous. More are reported from Eastern Canada and the U.S. than from the west. *P. impudicus* has been reported from B.C.; a similar species with a smooth cap from the prairies; *P. hadriani* from Edmonton; and *Mutinus caninus* from Manitoba westward.

stinkhorn   p.159-1

Phallus impudicus Persoon

Phallus: rod (Greek)
impudicus: shameless (Latin)

Cosmopolitan; growing in forests and gardens and on compost; rare in Canada's coastal provinces; fruiting in the fall. The strong foul odour can be smelled from a considerable distance.

fruiting body develops just underground or under leaves; round or egg shaped with mycelial cords at the base (this is the devil's egg); approximately 6 cm tall, up to 20 cm tall when fully developed.

egg white; outer skin (peridium) consisting of two thin white layers with brownish jelly in between (broken-down hyphae). The complete mushroom is inside. The peridium breaks and the stalk stretches up; a process which takes one and a half hours.

stalk	white, porous, hollow.
volva	at the base, white.
cap	like a thimble on top of the stalk. The crown is pierced and has a ring around the opening (circlet), which is the continuation of the hollow stalk; top surface of the cap is strongly pitted like a honeycomb.
gleba	olive green and slimy, containing basidia with 6-8 spores on each basidium, in contrast to the usual four. The gleba covers the top of the cap. The slimy mass is very quickly eaten by flies and slugs.
odour	very strong, of carrion to attract flies.

dog's stinkhorn p.159-2

Mutinus caninus (Persoon) Fries

Mutinus: small penis, rod (Latin)
caninus: of the dog (Latin)

Cosmopolitan (northern hemisphere); occurs across Canada from west to east, fruiting in summer and fall, not common, in gardens and parks.

fruiting body	long, oval egg 1.5 cm by 2.5 cm with white mycelial cords at the base, up to 12 cm tall when fully developed.
egg	white, some transparent jelly between two thin layers of peridium; complete mushroom inside; egg breaks and stalk stretches out fast.
stalk	white, porous, hollow; white volva-like cup at the base; at the top the stalk ends in a point and is red and orange. There is no caplike structure.
volva	soft white volva-like cup at the base of the stalk.
gleba	is a slimy dark green, almost black, glistening layer sitting directly on the stalk. The tip of the stalk sticks out like a red pimple. After the flies remove this, just the stalk is left and the red top. The stalk quickly falls over.
odour	lightly foxy.

Hadrian's stinkhorn p.159-3

Phallus hadriani (Ventenat) Persoon

hadriani: of Hadrian (see below) (Latin)

Cosmopolitan, but rare everywhere; grows in waste places and sandy areas. Ramsbottom writes that this species was the first phalloid to be described. Hadrianus Junius (Adriaan de Jonghe) found it in the sand dunes in Holland and in 1564, published an account of it both in prose and verse with illustrations on two plates. They had a frank sense of humor in those days in naming fungi. I repeatedly found the species in the centre of the city of Edmonton.

fruiting body	purple, egg shaped, up to 10 cm high and 14 cm across; on top of the ground; strong purple mycelial cords at base, up to 22 cm tall when fully mature.
egg	tough multilayered peridium; a thin gelatinous layer between the purple outer and the white inner skin; complete mushroom inside; the hollow stalk is filled with jelly. This helps the rapid development of the stalk once the peridium breaks open. In most of my specimens a piece of peridium stayed on top of the reticulum, like a bonnet.
stalk	whitish, porous (or chambered), hollow and yellow inside; purple volva stays at base; the stalk of a specimen in a large bottle in my studio only took a few hours to stretch out.
volva	forms large, purple cup at base of stalk.
cap	under the gleba, white and honey combed, attached at the top where the white ringlet is. Through the ringlet one can see the inside of the stalk.
gleba	brown and slimy; 8 spores on each basidium! The spore mass was still on the cap when I painted it (no flies in my studio). This wouldn't be possible with the foul-smelling *P. impudicus*, but the **odour** of Hadrian's stinkhorn is actually quite pleasant with a slightly foxy edge.

Order NIDULARIALES

Family NIDULARIACEAE   bird's nests

The Nidulariaceae are saprophytic fungi, often growing on decaying wood, stumps, logs, small branches, chips, conifer debris (like needles or conebracts), but also on other old wood on the ground (see illustration no.1 on p. 161). *Cyathus olla* was found on a bit of decaying plywood in the corner of a city garden.

The fruiting bodies are small, up to 2 cm high and 1.5 cm wide and, at first, resemble small hairy puffballs. The genera dealt with here all have mature fruiting bodies, which look like miniature bird's nests with a number of eggs in it. Initially there is a thin cover which breaks up. In a puffball a powdery spore mass is exposed, but in a bird's nest the spore mass is packaged in lens-shaped containers, the "eggs" (or **peridioles**). They are lying in a clear gelatinous liquid. In *Cyathus* and *Crucibulum*, each egg is attached to the nest with a mycelial cord (or funiculus). In *Nidula* there are no cords, but a sticky substance holds the eggs in place. In all three genera, raindrops cause the eggs (containing basidiospores) to be splashed out. This wonderful mechanism has been described by Dr. Harold Brodie in his book *The Bird's Nest Fungi*. The end of the cord is sticky and it may attach itself to a passing animal or an object (leaf or branchlet). *Nidula* eggs are splashed out, too, but they have a sticky covering and adhere to grass or other objects. Animals may eat the plants providing further dispersion.

deep splashcup   p.161-1
Cyathus olla Batsch: Persoon
Cyathus: cup (Greek)
olla: pot (Latin)

Worldwide; occurs on decaying wood, plant remains or soil. Fruits in the fall; the empty cups are persistent.

fruiting body	brown, hairy and cylindrical at first; up to 1.8 cm high and 1.5 cm across when mature.
peridium	thick three-layered cup, closed with a light cover. After this cover ruptures, up to 10 lens-shaped peridioles, or eggs, are visible; at first they are embedded in a gelatinous liquid which dries up quickly. The cup is shaped like a trumpet and is smooth and brown outside; with a flaring edge in maturity. Inside it is silver grey.
peridioles	white, containing spores; attached to the cup by a funiculus (cord) and dispersed by raindrops.

ribbed splashcup   p.161-2
Cyathus striatus Hudson: Persoon
striatus: ribbed or fluted (Latin)

Worldwide; occurs in lawns and in woods on the ground and on spruce debris; fruiting in the fall.

fruiting body	brown hairy cylinders at first; when mature up to 1 cm high and 8 mm across.
peridium	thick, three-layered cup; at first closed over with a thin cover; opens wide, showing 3 - 5 lens-shaped eggs attached to the conical cup with mycelial cords; the outside of the cup stays brown and woolly; the inside is silvery white and ribbed.
peridioles	relatively large and white; dispersal by raindrops splashing in the cups. The peridioles can be flung for more than 0.5 m and attach themselves to something by the sticky end of the funiculus, which then may wrap around the object.

yellow bird's nest fungus

p.161-3

Crucibulum laeve (Bulliard: de Candolle) Kambly

former name: *C. vulgare*
Crucibulum: lamp (Latin)
laevis: light or soft (Latin)

Worldwide distribution; occurs on wood debris or soil with a lot of wood particles in it. In all temperate zones of the world, including the Arctic regions. Fruiting in the fall.

fruiting body round when immature; when mature, yellow cups are up to 1 cm wide and high.

peridium yellow to tan; at first with yellow cover; single-layered peridium; after the cover ruptures, numerous white lens-shaped eggs are visible, each with their funicular cord. The outside is velvety at first, later smooth; the inside is pale yellow and smooth.

peridioles numerous; pale ochraceous at first, later white; splash cup dispersal (see *Cyathus*).

white barrel bird's nest

p.161-4

Nidula niveo-tomentosa (Hennings) Lloyd

Nidula: small nest (Latin)
niveo-tomentosa: snow-white, hairy (Latin)

Cosmopolitan, abundant in the Pacific Northwest, west coast of the U.S. and South America; also known from New Zealand and Japan. It can easily be overlooked because it is so small.

fruiting body small white woolly cylinders at first; snow-white furry cups later; up to 6 mm high and 6 mm across.

peridium multilayered, thick; furry outside, smooth inside; white cover; when open, a lot of eggs are visible, embedded in a shiny glutinous substance.

peridioles small, mahogany coloured; not attached by funiculus, but when splashed out, the sticky layer has the same role as the funiculus; the eggs stick to things.

jellied bird's nest fungus

p.161-5

Nidula candida (Peck) White

candida: shining or glistening (Latin)

Pacific Northwest, common from Alaska to Oregon; grows on rotten wood or on the ground; fruits in fall or early winter. New fruiting bodies often grow on top of old ones (see the two right-hand specimens in the illustration).

fruiting body cup shaped, the young fruiting body same shape but closed by a brown furry cover. Mature fruiting body up to 1.5 cm high and 1 cm across.

peridium thick, three layered; outer surface shaggy in shades of grey to brown; when it opens, relatively large, light brown, lens-shaped eggs can be seen embedded in glistening mucilage.

peridioles light brown, relatively large, are splashed out by raindrops. They are covered with a sticky layer but have no funiculus or cord.

Order TULOSTOMATALES   stalked puffballs

Two species of the family Tulostomataceae are described: one *Tulostoma* species and one *Battarraea* species. Both develop well below ground level, and as they mature, a strong stalk pushes the spore sac above ground.

Family TULOSTOMATACEAE

stalked puffball   p.163-1

Tulostoma simulans Lloyd

tulos: tumor; stoma: mouth (Greek)
simulans: imitating (Latin)

Cosmopolitan; on our continent found mostly in the West. Occurs in dry areas, on sandy soil in deserts, in the mountains, along the coast and across the prairies. This one grew in the badlands of Alberta with prickly pear cactus and sagebrush.

fruiting body	develops well underground; a real stalk develops up to 5 cm tall, pushing the spore sac above ground.
peridium	(or skin) is double layered; the exoperidium disappears; the endoperidium is red-brown at first, up to 1.5 cm in diameter; loosening around the stalk, often leaving a bit of a collar; the spore sac turns papery and grey; has an elevated pore on top ("with a mouth like a tumor").
stalk	buried, tough, rough and fibrous, red-brown; equal, with a clump of sand-encrusted mycelium at its base.
gleba	white at first, then brown.
spore powder	varying from pale yellow-brown to rust brown.

desert drumstick   p.163-2

Battarraea stevenii (Liboschitz) Fries

Battarraea: named after Italian mycologist A.S.A. Battarra
stevenii: after Finnish botanist Christian von Steven

Cosmopolitan; the genus occurs worldwide but is rare; on our continent found mostly in the West. It has been reported from the Yukon, Alaska and Idaho, but also from Australia. I have found it in Arizona and Kamloops, B.C. Solitary to scattered in arid and semi-arid regions; fruits in all seasons during wet periods. Mature fruiting bodies persist a long time, slowly releasing their very sticky spores.

fruiting body	young specimens rarely found due to underground development; enclosed in a volva, it develops 15 - 20 cm deep in dry, sandy banks; extensive greenish yellow mycelial cords at the base.
volva	white, two layered, stays at the base of the stalk.
stalk	heavy, shaggy, twisted, a mixture of yellow brown and some blue colours; up to 20 cm high.
spore case	flattened, round; opening at the periphery; the top membrane falls off leaving the very sticky spores on the bottom half, which is concave on the underside. It looks like a hat on a stick (see illustration; only the underside is left).
gleba	a flattened sticky mass in which the very thick-walled spores gradually ripen so that they can be released over a period of time.
spores	mocca-brown, masses of them adhering to the sac and to the ground all around the area where they grow. They adhere to anything that comes close enough.
flesh	tough, stringy; the section was made of a mature fruiting body.

Order SCLERODERMATALES
tough-skinned earthballs

The family of Sclerodermataceae bears a superficial resemblance to the puffballs or Lycoperdaceae; however, the Sclerodermataceae have a tough, thick skin, a gleba with no well-defined hymenium (fertile layer) and basidia that develop throughout the entire fruiting body. The spores are large and ornamented and do not develop all at once, but ripen gradually, giving the gleba a mottled appearance. The Sclerodermataceae are not edible and some are poisonous. These mushrooms have adapted to harsh climates and develop completely underground as protection against them, appearing only when they are mature. They look like potatoes, and some have been called false truffles and used as such to the detriment of the user.

The mycelial cords form a matlike mass with enclosed soil. This is a special structure for the resting stages. Many occur only in the West and the Pacific Northwest. *Pisolithus tinctorius* also has a tough skin and contains lovely natural dyes. It has been called dyemaker's false puffball and is still used for dying wool (yellow) in the Canary Islands.

All Tulostomatales and Sclerodermatales are terrestial, tough and non-edible, and some are poisonous. *Pisolithus* is mycorrhizal; it is in the Pisolithaceae family.

Family SCLERODERMATACEAE

small potato   p.163-3

Scleroderma areolatum Ehrenberg

former name: *S. lycoperdoides* Schweinitz
Scleroderma: tough skin (Greek)
areolatum: dry inside (Latin)

Cosmopolitan; widely distributed but rare; sometimes thought to be mycorrhizal. Has been reported from Quebec. I found this specimen in Victoria, B.C. Occurs on poor soil in gardens and woods, fruiting in late summer or fall.

fruiting body	rounded, often irregular, 3 - 6 cm across; smaller than the other two species discussed; covered with small dark-brown scales on a yellowish background.
peridium	fairly thick, one layer; opens at maturity with a slit.
gleba	white at first, then dark greenish grey, eventually dark olive-brown.
stalk	short, light-coloured, longitudinally lined base with "rooting" mycelial tuft.

pigskin poison puffball   p.163-4

Scleroderma citrinum Persoon

former name: *S. aurantiacum*, but was renamed because the colour is more yellow than orange
citrinum: lemon yellow (Latin)

Cosmopolitan, circumpolar in the temperate zone; also found in North and South Africa and Asia; prefers poor, hard soil in woods or open places. In young form, it has been used as a truffle, because of its underground development and its marbled interior, but it is **poisonous** causing nausea and vomiting. Fruits from July until late fall.

fruiting body	is rounded, shaped like a potato; light brown scales on a dirty yellow background; 5 - 15 cm across.
peridium	one layered. Thick, pink in lengthwise section, opens with a ragged-edged hole, exposing the spore mass.
gleba	white at first but soon purple, marbled, then very dark.
stalk	none but at place of attachment, peridium is sometimes folded and there are strong mycelial bundles.

rooting toughskin p.163-5

Scleroderma verrucosum (Bulliard) Persoon

verrucosum: full of small warts (Latin)

Cosmopolitan, rare; a typical survivor in arid and semiarid places with its underground development, pushing up the soil strongly at maturity, and its very thick skin. It has the strongest and most solid rooting bundle that I have ever seen. It almost looks like a stalk with holes in it. Found in the sandhills in Northern Alberta in the fall.

fruiting body is substantial when the whole structure is considered, because the underground part, the pseudorhiza, is so large although the spore sac is not much bigger than that of *S. citrinum*. The fruiting body completely develops underground, then pushes up the sand when it is mature. The potato-shaped spore sac is rust brown.

peridium thick walled, one-layered skin is white in section and is covered with fine warts in a very nice pattern. These disappear when the mushroom matures.

gleba when the mushroom is quite young, the gleba is already mottled grey and of firm consistency. When it breaks open, the exposed spore mass is very dark, almost black. The spores ripen gradually, and they escape when the mushroom weathers.

stalk-rhizome or rooting stalk is white in longitudinal section, changing to pinkish; it is a larger and more substantial structure than I have ever seen in comparable species.

Family PISOLITHACEAE

dyemaker's puffball p.163-6

Pisolithus tinctorius (Micheli: Persoon) Coker & Couch

piso: pea; lithus: stone (Greek)
tinctorius: used for dying (Latin)

Cosmopolitan; this species is found (rarely) in England, Germany, France and Japan, but more often in California and the Pacific Northwest. I found the illustrated one under Eucalyptus in Africa. It forms a mycorrhiza with a variety of trees; it has been used in many experiments and is sold commercially as mycorrhizal inoculum (for use in research).

fruiting body large, irregular and shaggy with interesting colours showing through the cracks; yellow mycelial cords at the base.

peridium crusty in shades of brown, black and ochre; it soon breaks away in maturity, showing pealike islands of spores (for which it is named). These shapes are yellowish at first then brownish, then purplish brown, ripening unevenly as the outer layer flakes off.

gleba in section the gleba is marbled with ripening islands of spores in different stages. The Nidulariales, or bird's nest fungi, with their eggs or peridioles, seem to have something in common with *Pisolithus*. The spores are dark mustard-ochre.

stalk (or base) heavy, shaggy, covered with earth and showing interesting blues and browns and at the base yellow and orange. There are extensive greenish yellow mycelial cords at the base. The fruiting body persists for months as the spores gradually ripen. The bright yellow pigment of the dyemaker's fungus has been used for a long time to dye wool.

Order APHYLLOPHORALES non-gilled mushrooms

Fungi with fruiting bodies of many different shapes, with a hymenium producing basidiospores but not on traditional gills like the Agaricales, nor in a sponge, like the Boletales have. For a list of the families included, see the Classification table.

Family CANTHARELLACEAE

In this family the fruiting bodies are flared to cap shaped at the top; the margin is lobed, some more than others; and there is a stalk. The famous chanterelle is in this group. Interestingly, these mushrooms have ridges below the cap instead of gills. In *Cantharellus cibarius* the ridges look like blunt gills, but when the mushroom is sectioned, it can be seen that the ridges are covered with a thin, smooth, fertile layer and that there are no gills. In this species the flesh is solid. The second species described belongs to the same genus, but there is a hole in the centre of the cap, connected to the hollow stalk, so that the mushroom has a trumpet shape; the ridges are more irregular. The third species belongs to the genus *Craterellus*. This species has even more of a trumpet shape and its spore-bearing surface is unevenly wrinkled. Cap and stalk form one piece.

golden chanterelle   p.165-1

Cantharellus cibarius Fries

Cantharellus: small cup (Greek)
cibarius: edible (Latin)

Worldwide distribution; occurring in mixed or coniferous forest; saprophytic or mycorrhizal with various kinds of trees. A well-known, famous, edible species, it has disappeared from certain parts of the world because of overpicking, pollution and the use of fertilizers in forests. At an experimental station for mushroom culture in Holland, research has been going on for years on the cultivation of chanterelles, with painfully slow progress. The mycelium grows very slowly, and the challenge is to find a tonic to speed up the process. Also during a visit to Holland, I found some people eagerly collecting orange mushrooms, mistaking *Hygrophoropsis aurantiaca* for chanterelles. When I told them that they were picking the wrong mushroom, they said "Oh, that is why we felt ill yesterday!" (see Paxillaceae). In Holland people are really not allowed to pick mushrooms!

The golden to orange chanterelle is the most common one in the west, in the mountains and along the coast. On Vancouver Island I have seen the white chanterelle, *Cantharellus subalbidus* A. H. Smith & Morse; it is all white, spores included, but bruises orange brown. A red chanterelle, *Cantharellus cinnabarinus* Schweinitz, occurs in eastern North America and so far was not known from the west. However, a friend who used to collect these mushrooms in Estonia told me that she has collected them regularly in the foothills of the Rocky Mountains! She calls them rooster mushrooms. They have a pinkish spore print. The golden, the white and the red chanterelles are all good edible mushrooms.

cap orange, yellow discolouring to ochrish; margin lobed and irregular, up to 10 cm across.
ridges same colour as cap, somewhat paler.

spore print	buff to ochraceous.
stalk	colour of cap, sturdy, more or less equal, up to 7 cm tall; 15 cm thick.
flesh	varies in colour — white flesh in the specimens from Vancouver Island, orange in those from Yellowstone Park in Wyoming.
taste	excellent when cooked well.
odour	fruity.

trumpet chanterelle   p.165-2

Cantharellus tubaeformis Fries

tubaeformis: trumpet shaped (Latin)

Cosmopolitan. In the Pacific Northwest and across Canada, it occurs in moss in bogs, on humus or on decayed wood, often in a fairy ring. This mushroom is well camouflaged with its streaky cap and its bright stalk hidden in the moss; fruiting late in the season, it is called "winter chanterelle" along the coast and further south where winters are not frosty; further inland it fruits in late summer or fall. Said to be edible but not everybody agrees on this.

cap	smoky brown, fibrous and rough with a streaky radial pattern; convex at first, then flattening, soon with a depression with a perforation; looking down, the bright yellow of the stalk is visible through the hole; up to 3 cm across.
ridges	buff to light brown, irregular and forked, distant.
spore print	creamy.
stalk	beautiful orange yellow, a bit smoky brown at the top and white at the base, flattened, hollow, up to 7 cm tall and 1 cm thick.
flesh	thin and fragile.
taste & odour	faint.

horn of plenty   p.165-3

Craterellus cornucopioides (Linnaeus: Fries) Persoon

deceptive horn

Craterellus fallax A. H. Smith

Craterellus: small mixing cup (Latin)
cornucopioides: like the horn of plenty (Latin)
fallax: deceptive (Latin)

Cosmopolitan, terrestrial, growing in clusters in mixed forest; in France it is called *trompette de mort* (trumpet of death) because of its somber colours, but often also "horn of plenty" because of its shape. Both look-alike species occur in the west, but only *C. fallax*, a North American species, occurs in the east. The only differentiating feature when using a field guide is the spore colour: whitish for the horn of plenty; salmon or yellow for the deceptive one, named *fallax* by Alexander Smith because the spore colour is not immediately apparent. Good edible mushroom, dried or fried.

cap	smoky brown, a bit warty, forms a deep funnel continuing down to the very base of the stalk; up to 6 cm across and 12 cm high.
outer surface	including the stalk, purplish brown; unevenly wrinkled at the top (where the fertile layer is).
spore colour	whitish in *C. cornucopioides*, salmon or yellow in *C. fallax*.
stalk	purple brown, not exactly clear where it begins, but no spores are formed on the stalk.
flesh	thin and fragile.
taste & odour	faint and pleasant.

Family SPARASSIDACEAE

A small family with one genus, *Sparassis*, from the Greek word for torn apart. Only one species is described here, but it is an important and interesting one. The fruiting body consists of a heavy "rooting" stalk and flat branches with "leafy" lobes rising from that base. The lobes are covered on both sides with hymenium which produces the basidiospores. The fungus is a root parasite and occurs year after year at the base of the same tree until the tree dies and continues for several more years until the food supply is exhausted.

sponge fungus or cauliflower fungus p.165-4

Sparassis crispa Wulfen: Fries
crispa: curly (Latin)

Cosmopolitan and widespread in cool coniferous forests. It also occurs in the Swiss Alps, the Himalayas (found by Arora), Japan and many other places. It is particularly prevalent along the Pacific coast. In the Pacific Northwest it grows to enormous size; often weighing more than 20 kg. It is a well-known edible mushroom, but when old, it gets too tough. It has to be cooked for a relatively long time even when young. Dried and powdered it has a good flavour.

fruiting body	more or less spherical, up to 75 cm across, consisting of flat branches with curly, leafy lobes; whitish with lots of yellowish colourations, turning brown with age.
base	heavy, tough, rooting.
spores	white, forming on both sides of the lobe.
flesh	quite tough.
taste	good.
odour	fragrant.

Family CLAVARIACEAE AND OTHER CLAVARIOID FUNGI

Of the Clavariaceae family, three species of *Clavariadelphus* and one of *Clavaria* are described. The other multibranched, coral-like specimens were previously grouped in the Clavariaceae but *Clavicorona*, *Clavulina* and *Ramaria* are now placed in Ramariaceae, Clavulinaceae and Clavicoronaceae. As with the Cantharellaceae, *Fungi of Switzerland* is followed for non-gilled fungi.

This is a large and diverse group of club- and coral-shaped basidiomycetes, which carry their hymenium on the surface of the clubs and coral branches. All are saprophytic. The flesh of *Ramaria* species is tough. One species, not described here, is poisonous. All the others are edible, but not all are palatable.

Genus CLAVARIADELPHUS
brother of Clavaria (Greek)

"Brother of Clavaria" is used to indicate that it is related to *Clavaria* (it has also been linked with the Cantharellaceae). The fruiting bodies are mostly simple and pestle shaped; occurring singly or in groups in coniferous woods. The spores are produced on most of the exterior surface. The surface is smooth at first but becomes wrinkled at maturity. The tops are rounded, truncate or pointed. The spore deposit is white to ochraceous. All three species are edible and can be eaten raw.

pestle fungus p.166-1

Clavariadelphus pistillaris (Fries) Donk var. *americanus* Corner
pistillaris: pestle shape (Latin)

North American; found in deciduous and coniferous forests. The specimens in the illustration were found growing in moss under spruce in the Sandhills north of Edmonton, Alberta. The fungus does not fruit often, but when it fruits, there are many. It is said to be edible but of poor quality, particularly when it is bitter.

fruiting body	shaped like a pestle or top, sometimes twinned. It can grow up to 20 cm tall and up to 7 cm across in the top, double that when two-headed; often has bunched mycelium at the base.

top	rounded at first and smooth, in colours of yellow, orange and ochre; wrinkled in maturity; gradually thinning toward the stalk.
stalk	red brown, yellow and white; solid, equal or with a somewhat swollen base.
spore print	white to buff.
flesh	white, unchanging, soft and spongy.
taste	mild to slightly bitter.
odour	none.

strap-shaped pestle p.166-2

Clavariadelphus sachalinensis (Imai) Corner

sachalinensis: named after the Russian island of Sakhalin, where it was first found

Cosmopolitan; named by Japanese mycologists in the thirties when the island was still part of Japan; this species is widespread in the Pacific Northwest and is also reported from Alaska. I have found it repeatedly in B.C., the Rocky Mountains and in Alberta in boreal forests, growing under pine or spruce. The shape is varied, as can be seen in the illustrations; often occurring in one spot in different shapes. A. H. Smith mentioned that it frequently intergrades with *C. ligula* (Schaeffer: Fries) Donk and that this may be the reason for the differences in shape and colour. The Latin word *ligula* means shoestring.

fruiting body	yellow with a white base; slim and pointed, or rounded, top; sometimes comb shaped, as if several have grown together side by side; other times they are somewhat sturdier and club shaped; in maturity they are more ochrish and rufus coloured; up to 7 cm tall and 2 cm across.
spore print	buff.
flesh	white, unchanging.
taste	slightly bitter.
odour	none.

northern pestle p.166-3

Clavariadelphus borealis Wells & Kempton

borealis: of the north (Latin)

North American; well-known species in the Northwest. The illustrated specimens were found under spruce in Northern Alberta. Somewhat smaller than the pestle fungus, the northern pestle is flattened on the top. Spores form more on the sides than on top. The flesh melts in the mouth and can be eaten raw.

fruiting body	club shaped at first, but soon depressed and wrinkled on top; orange in the centre, ochrish around it; red brown on the downslope of the fruiting body; up to 10 cm tall and 6 cm across.
base	covered with white mycelium and a bit swollen.
spore print	white.
taste	sweet and excellent.
odour	slight.

Genus CLAVARIA

small club (Latin)

Many species now in *Clavulina*, *Clavulinopsis*, *Clavicorona* and *Ramaria* were formerly in *Clavaria*. Now the genus is restricted to species which are primarily terrestrial, but when a *Clavaria* does grow on wood, that wood is covered with algae. They range from simple to repeatedly forked. Only one species is described here.

purplish Clavaria p.167-1

Clavaria zollingeri Léveillé

zollingeri: named after Swiss mycologist Heinrich Zollinger, who was especially interested in this group; 1818-1859

Cosmopolitan; occurs in Europe, North America and Australia, but is quite rare. These are very elegant small, irregular fruiting bodies; growing on poor soil in meadows or open spots in mixed forest. The specimens illustrated are from aspen parkland. Edible, but it hardly seems worthwhile.

fruiting body	single or in small, or coral-like, bunches; forked, whitish with smoky purplish tinges or pink-violet and tips like tiny fingers; up to 7 cm tall and 2 cm wide.
spore print	white.
flesh	lilaceous, brittle.
taste & odour	none.

Genus CLAVICORONA
Clavicorona: crowned club (Latin)

Clavicorona looks superficially like other coral mushrooms, but the way it branches is different: branches arise from the margin of the broadened apex of the branch below; on the very top of the branch is a small cup, circled by teeth. This kind of branching is called pyxidate. There are anatomical differences with Clavariaceae as well. This genus belongs to the family Clavicoronaceae.

crowned coral   p.167-2
Clavicorona pyxidata (Fries) Doty
pyxidata: like a small box (Greek)

Cosmopolitan and widespread; it occurs in Europe and Australia, as well as North America; growing on rotten wood, needles or leaves. It looks rather like *Ramaria* with its many upright branches, but the pyxidate branching, the tender flesh and the white spore print, make the differences noticeable. This is a nice edible mushroom. (A similar one that grows on conifer logs tastes bitter).

fruiting body	pale flesh colour or yellowish; turning chestnut at the base; many branches starting from one point, each branch with a crown of smaller branches, ending with a small crown; up to 10 cm high and 10 cm across.
spore print	white.
base	can be white and felty and in one piece growing on old wood, or the brown branches may twist and grow on (or continue like that in) decaying wood (see illustration).
flesh	white to yellowish, quite tender.
odour	spicy, aromatic.
taste	mild.

Genus CLAVULINA
small nail (Latin)

Another genus which was separated from *Clavaria* and placed in its own family of Clavulinaceae. The basidiospores develop in pairs on the basidia, not in groups of four as in the others on this page. The species are mostly terrestrial; spores are white.

white-crested coral fungus   p.167-3
Clavulina cristata (Fries) Schroeter
cristata: with a comb (Latin)

Worldwide distribution; growing on the ground in forests, either singly or in small to large tufts. They are edible, but often are parasitized by other fungi and turn black or grey; fruiting in late summer or fall.

fruiting body	white; grooved branches flattened and subdividing at the top in many small teeth; up to 6 cm tall.
spore print	white.
base	sparingly branched, whitish or cream.
flesh	soft and fragile.
taste	mild.
odour	none.

Genus RAMARIA
branched (Latin)

The genus *Ramaria* contains many species. Formerly all were called *Clavaria* but now they are in their own family, Ramariaceae. They grow on wood or on the ground; they have many branches; the flesh is tough; and the spores are coloured, ranging from pale yellow to ochre to cinnamon. Some species are said to be edible, but the flesh is tough and works as a laxative. One of them, *R. formosa*, works as an extreme laxative and is poisonous. *Ramaria* species are difficult to identify without a microscope.

green-staining coral p.167-4

Ramaria abietina (Persoon: Fries) Quélet
abietina: belonging to *Abies* (fir) (Latin)

Cosmopolitan; growing under conifers on needle duff; occurring in the Pacific Northwest and in boreal forests; fruiting in summer and fall, inedible.

fruiting body	whitish to yellowish with some brown or cinnamon; staining blue green when bruised or with age; up to 12 cm tall and 8 cm wide.
branches	coral-like, many-branched; branches upright but somewhat roomier than in *R. stricta*; branches ending in 2 - 4 pointed tips.
spore print	yellow.
stalk	pale, up to 2 cm tall, 15 cm thick.
flesh	whitish, pliant, discolouring to brownish.
taste	slightly bitter.
odour	strong, of coconut.

straight coral p.167-5

Ramaria stricta (Fries) Quélet
stricta: straight (Latin)

Cosmopolitan; common along the Pacific coast, in the Rockies and in northern forests; growing on the wood of deciduous or coniferous trees, sometimes on buried wood. Many Ramarias have lovely colours, and this is one of them: a lovely greyish orange. Others can be yellow, golden, pink or purple. Edible but a bit tough. In the illustration, the large one is fresh, and the smaller, wine-red specimen was much handled and discoloured but was still orange in the forks.

fruiting body	yellowish orange with lighter tips, bruising wine red, very compact, up to 20 cm tall and 10 cm across.
branches	many, often twinning; parallel, erect, ending in four to five thornlike tips.
spore print	warm yellow.
base	one or more brown branches with white mycelium at the bottom.
flesh	whitish to yellowish, tough.
taste	peppery.
odour	spicy.

Family SCHIZOPHYLLACEAE

In this family there is one genus and one species known in temperate climates. The Greek word *Schizophyllum* means splitleaf or splitgill and describes the structure. In dry weather the grey or pinkish gill halves roll across the hymenium, a hygroscopic action to guard against drying out. When the moisture increases, gill halves straighten up, the fertile tissue is exposed and sporulating starts again. The species described here is an extremely interesting one. The species name *commune* means common, and it occurrs all over the world in any season. It is a real survivor. Experiments by A. H. R. Buller, a Canadian mycologist, who was particularly interested in this fungus, show that specimens enclosed in glass tubes for 35 years and having undergone all kinds of extreme conditions were still able to sporulate (Ramsbottom 1953)!

Hermann Jahn (1979) describes a fascinating theory about the splitgills, namely that they are not gills at all, but the outside of elongated cup-shaped fruiting bodies, growing in a fan-shaped "commune." In each bracket there is a group of these cup-shaped fruiting bodies with felty outsides! Survivors in dry climates have very intriguing lifestyles. One more curious fact is reported by the McKnights in the Peterson *Field Guide to Mushrooms*. People who had eaten these brackets were found to have abnormal growths in their mouths and throats, which, on isolation, were proven to be *Schizophyllum*. This was reported from both Europe and North America.

splitgill   p.169-1

Schizophyllum commune Fries

Schizophyllum: splitgill (Greek)
commune: general, common (Latin)

Worldwide distribution; brackets growing on the wood of all kinds of trees and shrubs; also on reeds. I have found it on birch, poplar, pine, spruce, guava, Eucalyptus and Acacia, to name a few. It occurs on all continents, is very common in the tropics but is just as much at home in the far north. It is a wood saprophyte, which does not do much damage. In dry climates the modest, hairy, little brackets are a dirty, chalky-grey. The most beautiful and biggest specimens I found in Spain in Sierra de Credos on *Pinus radiata*. The intricately lobed brackets can be seen in the illustrations. Inedible.

cap	greyish, chalky white most of the time, but can have greenish and orange zones; hairy; rolled in at first, later lobed; sometimes growing singly but mostly overlapping, fanlike clusters; single brackets up to 9 cm across but smaller most of the time.
gills	fanlike, whitish to pinkish; split lengthwise, hairy in the split; in dry weather the gill halves roll up to protect the hymenium from drying out.
spore print	white.
stalk	absent or very short.
flesh	leathery, tough, whitish.
odour	none.

Family THELEPHORACEAE

Species belonging to genera in this family are mostly leathery or woody and tough; in one genus the flesh is firm and fleshy. I am following the taxonomic system of J. Breitenbach / F. Kränzlin as described in *Fungi of Switzerland*, Vol. 2. Species of four genera are described:

Thelephora (Greek for bearing nipples): in this genus the hymenium is warty or smooth and covers part of the leathery fruiting body, which can be lobed, cup-shaped or like coral.

Phellodon (Greek for corky tooth): tough fruiting bodies with hymenium covering teeth on the underside of the caps; white spore print.

Hydnellum (Greek for small spongy plant): the fruiting bodies can get quite big in some species. Tough, irregular fruiting bodies, mostly with cap and stalk; spores formed on teeth; brown spore print.

Sarcodon (Greek for fleshy tooth): firm fleshy mushrooms, most of which are inedible and bitter; cap and stalk are continuous; spores are formed on teeth; brown spore print.

zoned Phellodon   p.169-2

Phellodon tomentosus (Fries) Banker

tomentosus: velvety (Latin)

Cosmopolitan; growing in mixed and coniferous forests on needle debris and humus; mycelium often forms a lump of needles and humus at the stalk base. Tough little mushrooms resembling *Hydnellum aurantiacum* (p. 171), but less colourful and with a white spore print (*Hydnellum* has brown spores). The caps are often joined when growing in groups. In some years they are very plentiful in the Pacific Northwest. A quite similar species, *Phellodon confluens*, grows in deciduous forests. Inedible.

cap	velvety, zoned in shades of warm brown, darkest in the centre where the hair is a little longer and with a white growing edge (the white rubs off); up to 3 cm across.
teeth	or spines, short, whitish, becoming pale brown with white tips.
spore print	white.
stalk	brown, tough, up to 2 cm tall and 0.3 cm thick.
flesh	light brown in cap, darker in stalk, tough.
odour	fragrant, of fenugreek or lovage (maggi), especially when drying.

fetid false coral   p.169-3

Thelephora palmata Scopoli: Fries

palmata: palmfrond or broom (Latin)

Cosmopolitan; growing on the ground in coniferous forests. This species looks a lot like *Ramaria* or *Clavulina* (p. 167) but is not related. It has a dark red-brown spore print and a terrible odour when drying. Easy to recognize. Inedible.

fruiting body	consists of a rootlike solid base with an erect, much-branched top; up to 13 cm high in total.
top	dark, upright, purplish-brown branches, with whitish tips when growing; the flattened branches carry the spores; palmlike fringed tips; up to 7 cm tall.
spore print	dark red-brown.
stalk or base	carrot shaped, sometimes very short but can be up to 6 cm tall and up to 3 cm thick.
flesh	tough and leathery, brownish.
odour	fetid, of rotting cabbage or garlic; disappears when drying.

funnel-shaped Thelephora   p.169-4

Thelephora caryophyllea Fries

caryophyllea: with walnut-coloured ridges (Greek)

Cosmopolitan but rare in many places. It is also possible that this small brown species, not often being spotted in brown leaves or needles, is, therefore, not reported or described in books and is actually widespread. When it grows on a branchlet, white mycelium can be seen.

fruiting body	upright, up to 6 cm tall; consists of cap and stalk.
cap	upper surface: streaked, brownish radiating fibres, with smooth or lacerated margin, a bit zoned; often a double rosette shape; up to 5 cm across. Lower surface: zoned, light near margin, medium brown in the middle, purplish brown nearstalk, slightly grooved.
spore print	yellowish brown.
stalk	chestnut brown, equal, cylindrical, central, a bit hairy and crusty, up to 3 cm tall, but sometimes stalk is absent.
flesh	deep brown, thin, leathery.
odour	slight or none.

earthfan   p.169-5

Thelephora terrestris Fries

terrestris: of the earth (Latin)

Cosmopolitan and widespread; growing in open spots in woods on the ground on the debris of needles, branchlets and wood; more or less creeping along over everything. Although not a parasite, it can strangle seedlings in plantations! Under certain conditions it can have a mycorrhizal relationship with pine species. The group in the illustration occurred in a spruce bog with very small mushrooms growing all over and around it. *Inocybe petiginosa* (Fries) Gillet is the species growing in between the rosettes, and it is not parasitic on the earthfan.

fruiting body	consists of lobes of irregular shapes in big clusters; on the lefthand side in the illustration is a young specimen, smoother and more purplish than the bigger group, growing on a stick.
cap	rusty to dark brown, fibrous and uneven; the top is infertile; the edges often look fringed and tattered; up to 5 cm across and 7 cm tall.
underside or backside	covered by hymenium, purplish brown; grooved, or wrinkled, and warty; the growing margin is light, later the edge becomes torn and hairy.
spore print	purplish brown.
stalk	short or absent.
flesh	purplish, leathery.
odour	earthy.

Genus HYDNELLUM

The name Hydnellum means small spongy plant, but some of the species can grow to be quite big; terrestrial; an extremely bitter-tasting group; the flesh is tough and fibrous, becoming woody when dry; the colour of the flesh is strong and varied, most often in zones; cap and stalk are continuous; basidiospores are found in a hymenium covering teethlike structures on the bottom of the cap; the spore print is brown.

pine Hydnellum   p.171-1

Hydnellum pineticola (K. Harrison) K. Harrison

pineticola: living in pine forest (Latin)

North American; terrestrial, growing in pine forests; not a very well-known species. The ones illustrated were found in Jasper National Park; fruiting in the fall.

cap	velvety salmon pink at first, brownish on top with age or when handled; rounded edges; imbedded pine needles and moss; up to 12 cm across.
teeth	very small and pimple-like near cap margin; brown and short in the middle; long, brown and thin near the stalk.
spore print	brown.
stalk	whitish, discolouring brown, dried moss and pine needles stuck to it; thick and short, up to 3 cm tall and 3 cm thick.
flesh	zoned pale wine colour and brown.
odour	mild.
taste	a bit disagreeable but not sharp.

blueish Hydnellum   p.171-2

Hydnellum caeruleum (Hornemann: Persoon) Karsten

caeruleum: bluish (Latin)

Cosmopolitan, widespread but quite rare and often not seen for years; occasionally appearing in wet seasons. Reported from the Pacific Northwest, the Rocky Mountains and boreal forests; growing under conifers. Inedible.

cap	velvety, pale purplish blue or grey blue, later brownish in the centre; smooth or with bumps, rounded edges; caps of several individuals may be joined; up to 20 cm across.
teeth	white and small, sometimes tinged blue or violet near the cap margin; a bit longer and darkening to brown as the spores ripen; finally rusty.
spore print	brown.
stalk	brown, very short; present or absent; up to 1 cm tall and up to 5 cm thick.
flesh	zoned yellowish and shades of brown; tough and woody; the mycelium is sand coloured.
taste	mild.
odour	aromatic, of drying hay.

orange Hydnellum

p.171-3

Hydnellum aurantiacum (Batsch: Fries) Karsten

aurantiacum: orange (Latin)

Cosmopolitan; terrestrial, in mixed forest in eastern as well as western Canada, on the Prairies and in the Rockies; bitter tasting. Inedible.

cap	tomentose to velvety, orange edge, rusty and bumpy centre; white at the growing edge; up to 7 cm across.
teeth	first whitish, then pale orange; thin, fine points, approx. 0.5 cm long, decurrent, close to the stalk, brown.
spore print	yellowish brown.
stalk	orange brown; bulbous orange base; the round part is bunched mycelium; up to 2 cm tall and 1.5 cm thick.
flesh	pale orange in cap, zoned orange and brown in the stalk.
taste	not pleasant, bitter.
odour	not pleasant.

sweet-smelling Hydnellum

p.171-4

Hydnellum suavolens (Scopoli: Fries) Karsten

suavolens: sweet smelling (Latin)

Cosmopolitan; terrestrial, under conifers in moss; fruits in summer and fall in alpine forests in the Rocky Mountains and in fall and early winter along the Pacific coast; an interesting fungus with its deep blue colouring in stalk and flesh; very bitter tasting; inedible.

cap	velvety, pale grey when young, then brown in the centre and bumpy; thick edges; up to 15 cm across.
teeth	whitish, small; lower ones getting brown.
spore print	light brown.
stalk	sturdy; bumpy in older ones; a startling, deep blue indigo at the top, black at the base; the mycelium is blue as well.
flesh	zoned brown, blue and white in cap, black in the stalk; tough and leathery.
taste	bitter.
odour	a very nice clean odour of fenugreek or warm hay.

Genus SARCODON

Large fleshy mushrooms with cap and stalk. Basidiospores develop in a hymenium covering teethlike structures on the underside of the cap. The shape is often somewhat irregular. The teeth are light coloured at first, darkening later. The spore print is brown. They occur in coniferous forests. The taste is often sharp or bitter. None are poisonous but few are palatable.

bitter hedgehog

p.172-1

Sarcodon scabrosus (Fries) Karsten

Sarcodon: fleshy tooth (Greek)

scabrosus: scurvy (Latin)

Cosmopolitan; terrestrial under pine; not easy to spot in the brown pine needles. It looks like a stone, pine cone or a bit of old wood. Inedible due to its bitter taste.

cap	cuticle broken up into medium-sized scabs; between these scabs the colour is pinkish; up to 12 cm across.
teeth	short, uneven lengths; first light greyish pink, later brown from the spores; decurrent.
spore print	medium warm brown.
stalk	red brown like the cap, sometimes a bit scaly; base blackish, sturdy, some rhizoids; up to 6 cm tall and 2.5 cm thick.
flesh	off-white to light sandy, solid, not discolouring.
odour	fresh, like sweet-scented bedstraw.
taste	very bitter.

burnt hedgehog
p.172-2

Sarcodon ustalis (Harrison) Harrison

ustalis: burnt (Latin)

North American species; terrestrial, growing under conifers. Found under spruce in the foothills of the Rockies and under pine in Northern Michigan. Fruiting in the fall. Although the taste is mild, it is not known if it is edible.

cap	sepia brown, appressed hair, not scaly, up to 15 cm across.
teeth	at least 1 cm long, running down the stalk; light at first, then turning brown.
spore print	brown.
stalk	darkish red brown, sometimes off-centre, more or less equal; up to 6 cm long and 1.5 cm thick.
flesh	off-white to light brown, solid.
taste	mild.
odour	pleasant mushroom smell.

scaly hedgehog
p.172-3

Sarcodon imbricatus (Linnaeus: Fries) Karsten

imbricatus: covered with scales (Latin)

Cosmopolitan; occurring across North America, including the Yukon and Alaska. Terrestrial, usually in coniferous forests. This is a very interesting species. In the west there are two forms; a medium-sized brown one and a very large, deep red-brown form with very coarse black scales. The latter can reach 25 cm in size across the cap. According to K. A. Harrison (who is an expert in this group), the large dark form only occurs in the west. This species is edible, and when the mature form is bitter tasting, it can be improved by boiling the mushrooms first, discarding the water and then frying. This is the only Sarcodon which is used regularly and is especially popular with people of East European descent.

cap	brown with prominent, more or less erect, scales; margin inrolled at first, later flattening out; up to 25 cm across in the dark form.
teeth	light at first, then brown; not as long as in no. 2 but longer than in no.1.
spore print	medium coffee brown.
stalk	brown, short, thick, with dark pointed base; up to 5 cm tall and 6 cm thick.
flesh	off-white, thick with brownish stalk base.
taste	slightly bitter to very bitter.
odour	light.

Family HYDNACEAE

Hydnum means spongy plant in Greek. Many of the mushroom species which develop basidiospores on teethlike structures used to be placed in this family. This has changed and *Hydnum* now has its own family. *Hydnum* species have fruiting bodies with cap and stalk; hymenium on toothlike spines; a white spore print and brittle flesh.

yellow toothed fungus
p.173-1

Hydnum repandum Linnaeus: Fries

former name: *Dentinum repandum* (Fries) S. F. Gray
repandum: spreading

Cosmopolitan and widespread; growing in mixed forest; fruiting in July and August in the prairie provinces and until late in the fall in the Rockies and along the coast; this is one of the choicest edible mushrooms and hard to confuse with anything else. An almost purely white form sometimes occurs late in the season.

cap	yellow orange to pale rustbrown, looking very much like a freshly baked bun; dry, rounded at first, then becoming irregular; up to 10 cm across.

teeth	white at first, later creamy to pale orange, approx. 0.5 cm long; decurrent.
spore print	white.
stalk	white, dry, solid, discolouring orange when handled and with age; up to 5 cm tall and 3 cm thick.
flesh	white, sometimes yellowish under the cuticle and over the teeth; thick, solid.
taste	choice, nutty.
odour	faint.

navel tooth fungus   p.173-2

Hydnum umbilicatum Peck

umbilicatum: with a navel (Latin)

North American; this species is found along the Pacific coast from California north, all the way up to Alaska. The specimens illustrated were found farther inland, near Prince George, B.C., growing under western red cedar. Edible and good.

cap	reddish to orange buff; it can also be of the same colour as the yellow tooth fungus, but this one is smaller and has a navel in the centre; up to 4 cm across.
teeth	white, not decurrent, somewhat longer than those of *H.repandum*.
spore print	white.
stalk	white, can have some spots of cap colour, slim, up to 5 cm tall and 0.8 cm thick.
flesh	white.
taste	mild.
odour	faint.

Family AURISCALPIACEAE

A small family; one species of one genus is described here. The Latin word *Auriscalpium* means earspoon (an old-fashioned, small instrument to clean ears). It is an interesting small mushroom which gives great delight to the naturalist who spots it.

earspoon fungus   p.173-3

Auriscalpium vulgare S. F. Gray

vulgare: ordinary (Latin)

Cosmopolitan; this species is hard to find because of its small size and brown colour; growing in conifer forests; usually it is described as growing on cones. I have not found them on cones but have on spruce needles on top of squirrel dens; cone bracts were present in the duff.

cap	zones of light and dark and red-brown colours, hairy, up to 2 cm across.
teeth	purplish pink at first, very small near the cap edge, turning brown later.
spore print	white.
stalk	dark brown, eccentric, velvety, slender, stiff, equal, up to 4 cm tall and 0.2 cm thick.
flesh	buff, tough.

Family HERICIACEAE

A relatively small family. Only one species of the genus *Hericium* is illustrated. *Hericium* actually means hedgehog in Latin, but since the *Sarcodon* are already called hedghog mushrooms, I refer to *Hericium ramosum* as branched Hericium. It is the most common northern *Hericium* and the only one I have found in the prairie provinces; growing on deciduous wood. Further west in the mountains and along the Pacific coast, the important species is *H. abietis* (Weir: Hubert) Harrison, growing on conifer wood. It looks a lot like *H. ramosum*, but it does not have spines all along the branches, only at the tips, so it is easy to tell them apart. Another one *H. corralloides* growing on both conifer and deciduous wood occurs in the eastern part of the North American continent. A Pacific coast species, occurring in Douglas fir - tanbark oak forests; forms soft, round, unbranched fruiting bodies with long, white, pendant teeth (spines). The name is *Hericium erinaceum*, named after the European hedgehog *Erinacius europeus*, a small gentle animal which rolls up into a ball when it is threatened.

branched Hericium   p.173-4
Hericium ramosum (Mérat) Létellier
ramosum: branched (Latin)

Cosmopolitan; this is a very valuable decomposer of wood in the forest and an excellent edible mushroom when collected young. In early development, it looks like the young branch in the illustration, with young spines reaching up and sideways. When older, the spines are pendant, and the multibranched structure looks more like the other species. The main branches get tough then and it is not palatable any more.

fruiting body	grows on dead poplar and other deciduous wood, from one strong rooting base, branching repeatedly; up to 25 cm across.
branches	white, forking often, yellowing with age.
teeth	white, hanging from the underside of every branch; up to 1 cm long.
spore print	white.
flesh	white, fibrous.
taste & odour	pleasant.

Family BONDARZEWIACEAE

Named after A. S. Bondartsev, a mycologist who worked on Polypores. A separate family was created for this genus because it is one of the Basidiomycotina, which has spores similar to the Russulales but in other ways is closer to the Polypores (see Jahn, 1979). The genus forms a connection between various groups (taxa).

giant mountain polypore   p.175-1
Bondarzewia montana (Quélet) Singer
montana: of the mountains (Latin)

Cosmopolitan; this fungus lives as a weak parasite at the base, or on roots, of old conifers. Seemingly growing on the ground, but when dug up, it has a long rhizomorph, which is connected to the roots of a conifer, in this case western red cedar (*Thuja plicata*). When it grows on a stump, it can form one of the large fruiting bodies annually for several years. It is rare but is very visible when it does fruit. Another species grows only on or with deciduous trees (*B. berkeleyi*). Hybrids of these species exist.

fruiting body	annual; a large heavy clump with a few or many caps with short stalks. These stalks grow out of one mass of flesh, which is completely covered with a shallow layer of pores. The base of the clump continues into a rhizomorph. The specimen shown was 21 cm across and 29 cm tall, including the rhizomorph, but it can be much bigger.
caps	foxy red brown and velvety in the centre and darkest there; a glowing orange yellow margin which is thick in young specimens; the caps or shelves are irregular, and the surface is quite hairy.
pore surface	on the underside of the caps, but there is no division between cap and stalk, it is all one solid, heavy mass, which has protuberances.
pores	off-white, shallow, medium large, angular; the pores are smallest near the cap edges, more elongated and large lower down, very shallow; this clump was rather young; when older the pores can break and form teethlike structures.
spore print	white.
flesh	white, dense, heavy and tough, not changing in colour; parts which stick out, break off easily.
taste	bitter when fresh; not edible.
odour	aromatic, somewhat like anise.

Family POLYPORACEAE

Most of the species in this genus form basidiospores on the inside of tubes, but some have gills, which may be branching or anastomosing (gills join here and there, forming angular pores). Most of these fungi are bracket shaped, but sometimes they are stalked; often woody or tough and leathery, but some are fleshy, even edible. The majority decompose wood: logs, stumps, small branches; others are mild or virulent parasites. This is a large family with many genera. In order not to make the book too large, I chose a few species of nine genera. Stalked species are on two plates, some of which may look like boletes. Then there is a plate with sessile species, which are of special interest for different reasons. All of them have connections with wood, either directly or with a root-like structure (rhizomorph). One more saprophytic member of this family can be seen on p. 121, on the log with *Crepidotus spp. Cerrena unicolor* is the species growing on that log, following the grooves in the bark. It will be described with the species on p. 179.

The Greek name *Polyporus* means with many pores. Formerly all woody pore fungi were included in the genus, but Overholts restricted the name to species with annual stalked, fruiting bodies, growing on wood: seemingly on the ground, but connected to tree roots with rhizomorphs (p. 175) or on a sclerotium, like the Canadian tuckahoe (p. 177). The context is pale; the spores are white and smooth. It is not easy to get a spore print, because the tough fruiting bodies survive long after their fertile period. They do shed enormous amounts of spores though.

rooting polypore

p.175-2

Polyporus radicatus Schweinitz

radicatus: rooted (Latin)
Melanopus radicatus (Schweinitz) Pomerleau

North American species; rare, growing next to stumps of deciduous trees or on buried wood. I found these in the Rocky Mountains growing between the bark and the wood of a large well-decayed poplar stump. When I removed the bark, the rhizomorph was plainly visible. The author of the finest Canadian mushroom book *Flore des champignons au Québec*, Dr. René Pomerleau, originally named this one *Melanopus*. He likes to continue to use the name *Melanopus* for the black-stalked species, but *Polyporus* is the official name. Pomerleau mentions that this species is edible but tough, so if you are in the mountains, very hungry and happen to find this species, you could chew on it, even if it is not very good.

cap	buff when young, browner when mature, velvety or powdery looking, convex with turned in margin, later flattening and edge turned up; up to 20 cm across; fruiting body is annual.
pore surface	whitish or pale peach with extremely small pores, decurrent, tube layer very shallow; pores larger when old.
spore print	white.
stalk	centrally attached to cap, auburn with a peach-coloured top; cuticle cracked, ending in a long black root; either single or in a caespitose bunch; up to 8 cm tall (12 cm including "root") and up to 3 cm across at the apex.
flesh	white, soft when young but tough in maturity.
odour	fragrant, like a flower.

penny size blackfoot

p.177-1

Polyporus varius Person: Fries forma *nummularius*

varius: not always the same (Latin)
nummularius: small coin (Latin)

Worldwide distribution; annual fruiting bodies which vary quite a lot in colour and size. The small form on p. 177 grows on small dead branches. This species was previously called *Polyporus elegans* Fries or *Melanopus elegans* (Fries) Patouillard. It has an ochre yellow cap and a slim stalk which is partially or wholly very dark brown, almost black.

There is a bigger, more fleshy form, which grows on logs or buried wood, and which has a brown cap and a velvety brown stalk. Both have very small pores, almost invisible to the naked eye when young, a very shallow tube layer and tough, dense, white flesh.

cap brown at first, but soon yellow ochre; round, soon flat with turned in edge and a small dip in the centre or with turned up margin, like a small funnel. Frequently very small, the size of a penny when on thin branchlets; up to 6 cm across.

pore surface pale tan when fresh, later brownish; small round pores, decurrent on the stalk.

spore print white.

stalk top like pore surface, base very dark brown to black, slim, up to 6 cm tall and 0.5 cm thick.

context white, thin, leathery, rigid when dry.

winter polypore   p.177-2

Polyporus brumalis Fries

brumalis: of the winter or shortest day (Latin)

Worldwide distribution; called winter polypore in areas with mild rainy winters, but in places with real winters, where plants and fungi hibernate under the snow, young fruiting bodies can be found early in spring and all through the summer. Often found on dead birch branches, these very neat, small mushrooms are annual but can be found year-round, because they dry up and are persistent.

cap dark brown, velvety when young, inrolled margin, with dip, later depressed; light brown and smooth; up to 7 cm across.

pore surface white, pores radially arranged and round at first, stretching to oval with age, a bit angular; larger than those of no. 1; decurrent.

spore print white.

stalk brown, velvety; sometimes the pore pattern continues on the stalk (anastomosing).

context white, thin.

spring polypore   p.177-3

Polyporus arcularius Batsch: Fries

arcularius: like a paintbox (Latin)

Worldwide distribution but rare; often fruiting very early in spring, but I have also found young specimens in summer. I found these three times. The very large, angular pores inspired the name of paint or jewelbox (divided into partitions). The mycelium is very yellow and causes white soft rot.

cap sandy colour with dark centre; hairy, particularly the edge, later light to dark brown; convex, then flattening or with upturned margin; up to 4.5 cm across.

pore surface white to yellowish; pores large, radially arranged, diamond to hexagonal in shape; decurrent; the shallow tube layer is easily peeled off.

spore print white.

stalk velvety; brown hair on white background, pore pattern at the apex; base widening and white; up to 4 cm tall and 0.8 cm thick.

flesh white, solid, tough.

fungus stone or Canadian tuckahoe   p.177-4

Polyporus tuberaster Jacquin: Fries

tuberaster: like a truffle (Latin)

Cosmopolitan but rare; in Canada this fungus occurs in the aspen parkland belt of the prairies (Vanterpool and Macrae 1951). In disturbed areas where aspen have been cleared away to bring land under cultivation, fruiting bodies can be found growing from sclerotia. A sclerotium (or pseudosclerotium) of this fungus consists of a mass of hardened, resting mycelium encrusted with earth or sand in the form of a dark stone. Farmers have brought these objects repeatedly to the Provincial Museum of Alberta, not knowing what they were. On section they show a black and grey pattern. Friends of mine found the specimen in the illustration on their land near Cooking Lake. After painting it, I gave the whole thing to the Provincial Museum, without making a section, not wanting to damage it. The sclerotium was 18 by 10 by 7 cm in size. The next year we found some more in the same spot. This shows again how important it is to dig out a new species carefully to see what is underneath! The same species is found in Italy, and there the sclerotium, or fungus stone, is called *pietra fungaja*. They cultivate edible mushrooms from a pietra brought home.

In 1920 some sclerotia were found in Holland! In Switzerland (see *Fungi of Switzerland*, Vol. 2) the same species is described growing on deciduous wood and causing white soft rot. Hermann Jahn (1979) tells about *P. tuberaster* growing on dead wood but with a connection in the ground with a sclerotium! This means that this species adapts itself to the climate. In dry areas (hot or cold) it can survive with a sclerotium, and in mild climates it does not need it. A related Australian species *P. melyttae* Cooke & Massée is called blackfellows bread. The sclerotium is clear of sand and earth and is gristly and rubbery. The fruiting body is quite similar, with a smooth cap. They use pieces of the sclerotium to cultivate the mushrooms.

cap	white background with brown scales; sterile margin (sticks out), convex at first, then expanding, dip in the centre; 13 cm across.
pore surface	whitish, tube mouths hexagonal; not radially arranged; decurrent.
spore print	white.
stalk	white with vague, raised network.
flesh	soft and white at first, then tough.
odour	of anise.

sulphur shelf or chicken of the woods   p.179-1

Laetiporus sulphureus (Bulliard: Fries) Bondartsev & Singer

laetiporus: with a wealth of pores (Latin)
sulphureus: sulphur colour (Latin)

Cosmopolitan and widespread; it is found in the Pacific Northwest from Alaska south and from sea level up to 2800 m. So far I have not seen it in Alberta. Growing on living, damaged or dead deciduous trees, they can form huge clusters. In September, 1984, at the N. A. M. A conference in Dorset, Ont., many kilo's of this mushroom were picked to feed all the participants. These fungi fruit in the fall. I saw the clusters in the illustration in Holland, and sketched them on the poplar they grew on. My brother-in-law thought I ought to have this specimen. He put some in a bag in my suitcase, where I forgot them. At the time of my return to Canada some weeks later, it was worth it to see the customs officer's face when he opened the plastic bag! The contents not only smelled of eggs but of very rotten eggs. This mushroom is edible when young, particularly the growing edges of the overlapping caps, but it is not a choice species. According to Robert T. Orr, some people in the Pacific region have had violent reactions from the sulphur shelf. He thinks that there may be a toxic strain along the Pacific coast, so caution is advised. The fruiting bodies are annual, taking about four weeks to develop, after which they die off.

cap	soft yellow knobs when first emerging, then they grow into shelves, often forming large clusters weighing several kilos; with age the caps turn wrinkled and tough and become orange on top, the shade varies.
pore surface	bright sulphur yellow.
pores	small, hardly visible when young.
spore print	white.
stalk	none or very short.
flesh	soft and watery when fresh, tough later.
taste	of chicken.
odour	strong egg smell.

birch polypore

p.179-2

Piptoporus betulinus (Bulliard: Fries) Karsten

Piptoporus: with recessed pores (pore surface) (Greek)
betulinus: of the birch (Latin)

Cosmopolitan; widespread in the temperate zone of the northern hemisphere, the fruiting bodies can be noticed on dead branches in the tops of old birches or that have fallen to the ground. This is a well-known birch parasite. the invading mycelium spreads through a branch but only forms a fruiting body after the branch has died. The fruiting bodies are annual as in the sulphur shelf, no. 1, but they are tougher than the latter and can be found the next spring, turned grey brown. They will not grow another layer of tubes over the previous year's, as the next species, no. 3, does. The fungal infection spreads from the tips of the top branches into the wood of the tree. Old birches often die from the top down. The mycelium causes red-brown rot in the wood; ground into powder, this is used in Switzerland for polishing watch parts.

fruiting body	rounded or hoof shaped; soft at first, can be squeezed, unlike woody polypores; when older, they get tough and corky. The pore surface is sunken, as the name implies, and the margin sticks out considerably. They are sessile or there is a very short stalk, which makes them look like bicycle lamps. Mine were 10 cm across, but they can be much bigger.
cap	white with some light brown on the crown; grey or grey brown with age, blending in with the birch bark; cuticle like paper.
pore surface	white, turning brown with age, tube layer shallow.
pores	very small, round.
spore print	white.
flesh	soft, pure white, later corky.
taste & odour	sour.

tinderconk or horse's hoof fungus

p.179-3

Fomes fomentarius (Linnaeus: Fries) Fries

Fomes: tinder (Latin)
fomentarius: dressing for wounds (Latin)

Cosmopolitan; a weak, wound parasite or a saprophyte on deciduous trees; found most of the time on birch, poplar and willow in the prairie provinces and the Yukon; along the coast and further south on other deciduous trees as well. Rarely occurs on conifers. It is the most common "conk" in the forest in this area. The fruiting body is perennial, forming a new layer of tubes below the one from the previous year. The layers are thin and not clearly defined. Concentric markings are visible on the outside. The tubes are vertical; when a dead, standing tree falls over and tubes become horizontal, the power of gravity clearly takes over. Another conk forms, connected to the old one, and it keeps growing with a 90 degree turn so that spores can fall to the ground. The name *Fomes* indicates that the conks have often been used as tinder and *fomentarius* points at its use in medicine. One of the earliest doctors, the Greek Hippocrates wrote in the fifth century B.C. about its use in cauterizing wounds to stop bleeding (with a smoldering conk). For at least 2000 years it was used for that purpose; Commonly used by the French who called it *amadou* in surgery. The fungus causes white soft rot.

fruiting body	hoof shaped, broadly attached; perennial; new layer of tubes growing every spring underneath the previous year's layer. It can continue to form new layers for many years. I found them up to 15 cm high and up to 20 cm across.
cap	grey with concentric lines and indentations with brownish bottom zone, where the new growth is. Hard, brown crust, smooth; the margin finely tomentose.
pore surface	cream coloured at first; consists of small round pores, then ochrish to brownish. It can immediately be established that the conk is alive and growing by touching this layer and feeling its cool temperature.
spore print	white.
context	hard crust, woody, brown; inside, most of it consists of the tubes; the difference between the yearly additions not clearly visible.

vermilion polypore

Pycnoporus cinnabarinus (Jacquin: Fries) Karsten

Pycnoporus: pores close together (Greek)
cinnabarinus: cinnabar red or vermilion (Greek)

Cosmopolitan; this very brightly coloured bracket is the only one in temperate climates with the red pigment cinnabar in it. An exciting find. It is known from the Pacific Northwest and is not often seen in Alberta. In subsequent years my husband and I found the tropical *Pycnoporus* in South Africa on indigenous wood and an old pine stump. This was *P. sanguineus* (Fries) Murrill. We found a similar, very bright vermilion species in Hawaii, growing on sandalwood and on guava. It had orange flesh with brown lines in it and a very thin tube layer. I do not know if it was the same one as in Africa. In the kingdom of fungi, this pigment is only known from the genus *Pycnoporus*.

fruiting body	sessile when on top of the log as on p. 179; laterally attached when on the side; up to 10 cm across; annual; the bright pigment stains the bark and wood of the birch it grows on. Saprophytic; its preference is to grow on recently dead wood.
top of bracket	vermilion or orange red with some yellow mixed in; appressed hair, fan shape.
pore surface	deep cinnabar red, does not fade with age, not even when dried; pores small, somewhat angular, and irregular to rounded.
spore print	white.
context	corky and tough, rigid when old.

white-gilled polypore

Lenzites betulina (Linnaeus: Fries) Fries

Lenzites: named after H. O. Lenz, German botanist 1799-1870
betulina: of birches (Latin)

Worldwide distribution; saprophytic, growing on dead wood of deciduous trees; rarely on coniferous wood; often on birch as in the illustration on p. 179. The fruiting body is annual but persistent. Dry fruiting bodies are sometimes found completely green from algae. Instead of pores, the brackets have gills. Fresh brackets may have many colours: white, buff, yellow, orange red, but may also contain fine velvety brown and ochre zones, which makes for a lot of variation. The fungus causes white rot in the wood.

fruiting body	on rotting wood; when on top of a log, round or in rozettes, at the side they are semicircular; up to 10 cm across.
top of bracket	concentric zones of white, buff, ochre, orange, red and brown or variations of that; green algae often present; hairy.
bottom of bracket	white or light-coloured gills, branched near the margin, a few pores may be included (anastomosing).
spore print	white.
context	white, tough and leathery.

rusty-gilled polypore

Gloeophyllum sepiarium (von Wulfen: Fries) Karsten

Gloeophyllum: with glutinous or fused gills (Greek)
sepiarium: with a fence (Latin)

Cosmopolitan; growing on dead wood, often in dry areas. Not only growing on conifer logs, but also on timber used in shipbuilding, mines and fences, where it can be very destructive. It is a very beautiful bracket fungus when it is fresh; first dark red brown in the centre or at the place of attachment, then in concentric circles of orange, brown and orange yellow with a white trim. On the underside, this bracket is lamellate, like the Lenzites (no. 5). The second part of the name is descriptive of the yellow infertile border encircling the gills — they are fenced in (*sepiarium*). It is a saprophytic fungus, which is very destructive in man-made structures, because it can live on in dry wood! It produces a brown rot.

fruiting body	a fan-like bracket, annual; often growing on cut surfaces, as is shown in the illustration. The brackets did not grow on the wood like that; I wanted to show the top and bottom of the bracket against the wood. Up to 13 cm across; appearing solitary or in groups which often may be overlapping.
top of bracket	strongly coloured in zones of dark red brown, auburn and orange with a yellow or white border, hairy; darker with age, loosing hair.
underside	ochre to orange gills, anastomosing here and there (the fused gills) forming elongated pores; turning brown with age.
spore print	white.
context	yellow to rust brown, leathery when fresh, rigid with age.

orange sponge polypore   p.179-7

Pycnoporellus alboluteus (Ellis & Everhart) Kotlaba & Pouzar

Pycnoporellus: with countless pores (Greek)
alboluteus: yellow and white (Latin)

North American species. This fungus was found on Mt. Turner in the Rocky Mountains at 2400 m, growing on a huge spruce log. The brackets grew on the downward curve of the log, following the grooves in the bark to a length of one meter. The term for this attachment is resupinate, (Latin for lying on the back); annual, the soft, spongy, orange fruiting body takes about a month to develop, starting under snow in spring; fading to yellowish, then whitish and finally turning black. On the underside are large pores with ragged edges, looking like teeth. Insects soon are all through the brackets.

The fungus causes brown rot. The diminutive "-ellus" in the name stems from the time that the first species in the genus was named. It was small, looked like no. 4, *Pycnoporus*, and was called *Pycnoporellus*. Eventually the huge species described here was found and although awkward it is the correct name. This is a very important decomposer.

fruiting body	a bracket in a long resupinate, soft, spongy form; the fertile layer consists of tubes with ragged pores, looking like teeth.
top	orange, the lower down it grows, the less cap surface there is; fading to almost white with age; up to 1 m wide.
pore surface	ochrish orange, large angular pores with ragged edges, which give the impression of teeth.
flesh	orange.

grey polypore   p.121-9

Cerrena unicolor (Fries) Murrill

Cerrena: like Greek shield (Greek)
unicolor: of one colour (Latin)

Cosmopolitan and widespread, but not common; occurs on living deciduous trees as a wound parasite or on logs and stumps; causes white rot; when on standing trees, the brackets have quite a different formation than when growing on horizontal logs. It follows the grooves of the bark in one long line when on a horizontal log, but on standing trees the hymenia grow together in one big "shield".

caps	red brown first and hairy, later grey with brownish edge, even green from algae, projecting up to 5 cm.
pore surface	a labyrinth of irregular pores, grey brown; the pores break up into teeth eventually.
flesh	creamy, tough, corky.

Family GANODERMATACEAE   lacquered brackets

The spores of members of this family are so different from those of other polypores, that they have been placed in their own group. The spore print is brown, and the spores are truncated at one end and ornamented. The fruiting bodies of the three species discussed have a resinous, often shiny, lacquered crust. They all form an enormous amount of spores in their lifetime, which land all over the place. Luckily only a small percentage germinates. All three species occur in Northwest North America, as well as in many other places. They decompose old wood: *G. applanatus* both deciduous and coniferous wood; *G. tsugae*, coniferous wood; and *G. lucidum*, deciduous wood.

cedar lacquer fungus   p.180-1

Ganoderma tsugae (Murrill) Overholts

Ganoderma: with shiny skin (Greek)
tsugae: of hemlock (Latin)

North American; The specimens in the illustration were found on Vancouver Island; Lincoff mentions that it occurs from Eastern Canada to Maine, North Carolina and the Midwest. The fruiting body is soft when young, tougher later; annual; it has white flesh, in contrast to the third species described — the reishi — which it resembles but which has light to dark brown flesh. The epithet "tsugae" was given to it because it was first found on hemlock, but it grows on other conifers as well, for example the cedar log in the illustration; saprophytic.

fruiting body	in various shapes. The crust is shiny red brown, resembling lacquer; a lighter colour near the margin: bright yellow in this case.
pore surface	white when young, darkening with age, pores minute.
spore print	brown.
flesh	white, soft when young, corky with age.

artist's bracket   p.180-2

Ganoderma applanatum (Persoon: Wallroth) Patouillard

applanatum: flattened (Latin)

Worldwide distribution; a decomposer of old logs and stumps of both deciduous and coniferous wood; occurs from the subarctic to the subtropics. The brackets can grow for many years. I watched a particular group, which I had painted, for about 15 years, until somebody must have sat down on it and broke it off. That was a loss! Brackets are still growing when a new white layer grows on the pore surface and a colourful new edge is added to the margin. The older part of the crust, closest to the wood, is brownish to greyish and uneven.

fruiting body	a woody bracket, more or less flat on top; the oldest part greyish or dark brown, the younger additions lighter. In spring a new layer is added on the circumference in chestnut, orange and yellowish colours, following down the shape of the conk on the underside with a new layer of tubes; up to 50 cm across.
underside	pore surface is white, because a waxy layer covers the very small brown pores. This layer bruises when touched.
spore print	rust brown; a layer of spores often covers the whole top as well as the plants underneath it and at a distance of up to a half a meter from the conk, because the spores are forcefully expelled, and the tubes are not only directed to the ground but also sideways and up around the curved margin of the bracket. Of the trillions of spores ejected in its lifetime, only a small portion lands on top.
context	corky or woody. When a conk is sectioned, the age can easily be determined, because a darker layer of mycelium is visible between the brown, annual tube layers. The top grows around the front and sides and the bottom gets a new layer all over and grows downward in thickness. This works like the annual rings in trees. Another perennial conk on p. 179, *Fomes fomentarius*, shows the rings more on the outside, while the new layers of tubes are not so clearly differentiated.

reishi or ling chih

Ganoderma lucidum (Curtis: Fries) Karsten

lucidum: shining (Latin)

Cosmopolitan and widespread. This is the revered reishi mushroom of Japan and ling chih of China. It is hung at the gate to protect the household from evil, and is taken as medicine against incurable diseases. This has been an important mushroom for more than 2000 years. Recent research has indicated that it may be useful in suppressing cancer. Books are available on the subject. The Reishi is cultivated, and when grown in the dark, its fruiting bodies show whimsical antler-like shapes.

fruiting body	annual, soft at first, firm with age, rigid when dry; stalked most of the time, never in the same shape.
crust	chestnut, alizarin crimson or red lacquer, brown, orange and yellow, lighter, even white towards the growing edge, very varied; with irregular curves and bumps. The sugar maple stumps on which my specimens grew had some of the same deep red colour showing in its bark.
pore surface	whitish and facing down. Tube layer brown. When I (regretfully) sectioned one, there were two layers of brown tubes!
spore print	brown ochre.
flesh	light brown in the one I cut.
odour	aromatic.

Class DISCOMYCETES

All of the mushroom species described so far in this book belong to the subdivision of Basidiomycotina. These mushrooms all develop spores, most often four, on club-shaped cells in a fertile layer. That's the hymenium.

The rest of the book contains a limited number of the subdivision Ascomycotina. In the larger-sized sac fungi, spores are produced in asci (Greek for wineskin or bag) which usually contain 8 spores each. In the class Discomycetes, the ascospores are formed on the upper or outer surfaces of the fruiting bodies in a fertile layer.

Species of six families of the class Discomycetes, belonging to the orders of Pezizales and Helotiales, are described (pp. 181,183,185,186,187,189).

Most of the species discussed belong to the order Pezizales. The fertile surface is on the top of a cup fungus like *Peziza* or on the head of a stalked mushroom like *Morchella* (Morel). The sacs in which the spores are formed are operculate, meaning they have lids (*operculum* is latin for lid). When the spores are ripe, they are forcibly expelled. Often the sun's rays are all it takes to trigger this. You can watch this in the forest by observing one of the cup mushrooms in the shade until it is touched by the sun's rays. If the spores happen to be ripe, a small cloud of the white spores will be seen. The touch of a hand, an insect, an animal or the wind can do this too. Species of six families in the order of Pezizales will be described.

A small number of species belonging to three families of the order Helotiales are pictured on p.189. It cannot be seen with the naked eye if they belong to this order, but one microscopic characteristic is that the miniature spore sacs have no lids (called inoperculate). The ascus has a pore at the tip through which the spores are expelled. There are species with delightful colours and shapes in this order—well worth observing.

Order PEZIZALES

Families:
Morchellaceae: species with head and stalk (head is used rather than cap); the head can be honeycombed, folded or smooth.
Helvellaceae: species with head and stalk; head is often brain or saddle-shaped.
Pezizaceae: cup-shaped species; sessile or with short stalks; in quiet colours of off-white, yellowish brown, a few purplish; no hairy rims.
Humariaceae: cup shaped; many colourful species, with hairy exteriors and hairy rims.
Sarcoscyphaceae: only one species included; a bright red, stalked cup.
Sarcosomataceae: one species included; a large almost black stalked cup.

Family MORCHELLACEAE

The family Morchellaceae is small but contains some of the best loved, edible mushrooms in the world. The name *Morchella* is unusual in that it finds its origin in the old German name for mushroom: *Morchel*. Species of three genera are described; they have heads and stalks and are fragile. I will mention something about spores here, because the presence or absence of oil drops in spores is important in the identification of Morchellaceae and Helvellaceae. Members of the Morchellaceae have *no* oil drops in their spores, while members of Helvellaceae have one or two oil drops in the spores. This can be seen in a microscopic examination.

Like most disc fungi *Morchella* and *Verpa* species have 8 spores in their ascus, but *Ptychoverpa bohemica* has only 2 large spores per ascus.

Morchellaceae are edible but *Morchella*, *Verpa* and *Ptychoverpa* require proper cooking. They contain gastro-intestinal irritants which disappear when cooked in an open frying-pan. Verpas need extra caution: they make some people ill and often people eat too many.

wrinkled thimble or early morel p.181-1

Ptychoverpa bohemica (Krombholz) Boudier
former name: *Verpa bohemica* (Krombholz) Schroeter
Ptycho: with folds (Greek)
verpa: male organ, usually translated as "rod" (Latin)
bohemica: named after Bohemia, the area where this mushroom was first found.

Cosmopolitan; this thimble mushroom is particularly abundant in the Pacific Northwest; along the coast, in the mountains and in the prairie provinces in mixed forest. I have kept track for twenty years of when they first appeared. For Alberta this is always in May, occasionally the end of April; this is the first edible species to occur in quantity in spring. It is easy to spot because small plants on the forest floor have not begun to grow. Although this species is edible and agrees with most people, caution is advised. Some people react to them, exhibiting a loss of coordination after eating them in quantity. It is better to dry your surplus, if you picked more than a modest meal. Friends who like to cook mushrooms tell me that drying enhances the taste. Lincoff and Mitchel (1977) mention that it is possible that this thimble mushroom may contain small quantities of Gyromitrin (see p. 382 *Gyromitra*). Drying may be the solution here! In the meantime neither large quantities nor several meals in a row are advised. I like the name *Ptychoverpa* instead of *Verpa*, because there are more differences from the smooth Verpa than just a folded or smooth cap: (a) more people suffer ill effects, and (b) the interesting 2 large spores in the ascus instead of the usual 8 (see description of the family). **Caution.**

fruiting body fragile, thimble-like head and stalk. Quite a variation in size occurs.
head medium to darker brown (when drying); wrinkled or folded; loose from the stalk and hanging down like a skirt; inside off-white; up to 6.5 cm across and 9 cm tall.
spores form all over the cap surface, often seen in large quantity, dried up on the outside of the cap, yellow to ochre in colour; 2 extremely large spores in each ascus.
stalk off-white, ochrish to almost orange, very fragile; hollow, but when young, stuffed with off-white cottony mycelium.
flesh off-white; when cutting the stalk in young specimens, a semitransparent outer layer is visible, then a solid off-white layer and on the inside cottony stuffing, which disappears later.
odour in older specimens of chlorine.

smooth thimble mushroom p.181-2

Verpa conica Swartz: Persoon
conica: cone shaped (Greek)

Cosmopolitan, but not as frequently occurring in this area as the wrinkled thimble cap. In long, early springs the wrinkled thimble appears first, before the aspen buds open; a few weeks later morels start to fruit, just when aspens bud out; then a few weeks later, if cool, sunny spring weather continues, the smooth thimble mushrooms may fruit in big quantities. By that time they are not easy to spot, because every small plant on the forest floor is growing, taking advantage of the sparse foliage on the trees which lets more light through to the forest floor. Old creek beds are a favourite place. When cool spring weather suddenly changes to warm summer, as so often happens, it is the end of the morel and *Verpa* season. Edible with caution, cooking is a must.

fruiting body	consists of a smooth, thimble-like cap and pale stalk. Quite variable in size.
head	dark olive brown, smooth, becomes semitransparent when it dries. Then it lightens and a fine network of fibres is visible; the inside of the cap is brownish ochre; attached only at the top; up to 5 cm across and 5 cm high.
spores	ochrish, forming all over the outside of the cap; 8 quite large spores in the ascus (microscope).
stalk	off-white to yellowish or pinkish, at first stuffed with pale peach, cottony material, then hollow; up to 11 cm tall and 1.5 cm thick.
flesh	thin, fragile, whitish.

black morel
p.181-3

Morchella elata Fries

elata: proud or lofty (Latin)

Cosmopolitan and widespread; this is the most important northern morel, according to D. Malloch, and the only one I find every year in Alberta. There are fewer when the spring is very dry, but some can always be found. In the Rockies I found them a little later and in the Yukon in early July, because it was still cool spring weather, but with 24 hours of daylight. Spring, summer and fall mushrooms were fruiting there all at the same time. For fruiting time it is better to look at the stage other plants are in, than at specific dates, e.g., whether aspen are leafing out or strawberries and white violets are blooming, etc. In mixed woods they often grow close to spruce, sometimes on very decayed wood. The early morel, or wrinkled thimble mushroom, comes first, then the black morel, after that the smooth thimble; all overlap somewhat. Good edible mushroom but cooking is a must.

fruiting body	sturdy honeycombed head with black ridges forming one piece with a pale stalk; mostly pointed but can be blunt; ridges usually more or less vertical.
head	brown pits and black ridges; when young, the cap is light in colour; the ridges are darkest when the fruiting body is mature; then with age the ridges shrink and the honeycombs flatten; up to 11 cm tall and 5 cm across.
spores	form in the pits but not on the ridges; they are yellow to ochre and escape in clouds when the mushroom is touched by light, the wind or an animal.
stalk	off-white to light ochre; not quite smooth, the surface is a bit grainy. In an old specimen all kinds of pits may develop and the stalk looks more massive than the head, which has shrunk by then. When young, the stalk is about 4 cm tall and 3 cm thick.
flesh	whitish; the stalk is a continuation of the cap, and the hollow space in the cap and stalk is one. The inside surface is yellowish and uneven.
odour	older specimens smell of chlorine.

yellow or sponge morel
p.181-4

Morchella esculenta Fries

esculenta: edible (Latin)

Cosmopolitan and widespread. This is the most famous morel of all. Generally this morel looks more like a sponge than the black morel; the ridges are often thinner and the colour is yellowish. There is great variation in shape; it may be more or less pointed as in the illustration or usually more rounded. Many species' names exist for *Morchella*, but mycologists from different countries: Malloch from Canada, Maas Geesteranus from Holland and Dennis from England, think that all these are merely forms of *M. elata* and *M. esculenta*. Habitat and aging play a role in the appearance. Usually growing in old orchards, woods, disturbed grounds and burnt areas; fruiting in spring. The specimens illustrated came from southern B.C., where a large forest fire had raged in the Canal Flats area. They appeared in large quantities in the fall of 1986 and attracted armies of mushroom hunters. Such an unusual fruiting time happens occasionally, especially after fires.

It is an excellent edible mushroom, but cooking is necessary to destroy a gastro-intestinal irritant. This mushroom contains a considerable amount of vitamin D.

fruiting body	consists of a sponge-like head and a stalk. The head and stalk are one piece, but there is more of a "neck" than in *M. elata* (see illustration).
head	yellowish; pits are irregular in shape; ridges thin; up to 10 cm high and 6 cm across.
spores	are formed only in the pits; the ridges are sterile.
stalk	off-white to yellowish or stained; a bit granular; rounded but narrower than the cap, short, up to 5 cm tall and 4 cm across.
flesh	creamy to yellowish in stalk, brownish in head, hollow, one space; narrowed between head and stalk.
taste	excellent, but only when the mushrooms are fresh.

Family HELVELLACEAE   false morels

The family of Helvellaceae (Helvella: Latin for small vegetable) consists of fleshy mushrooms with heads and stalks. The name head is used, rather than cap, because of all the irregular shapes which occur: saddle, brain or cup shapes. Ascospores are formed on the outside of the head or on the upper surface of the cups. *Helvella* species, and especially *Gyromitra* species, contain various amounts of helvellic acid or gyromitrin. This is a dangerous family. Gyromitrin has a strong dissolving action on red blood corpuscles and damages the liver. It is also carcinogenic. *Gyromitra esculenta* has caused many deaths, despite its name which means edible. It is very toxic when eaten raw. Knowing this, a lot of European people only eat these mushrooms after parboiling them and throwing the water away. This is not always sufficient. The fumes of the boiling water make people ill, too. In Scandinavia, the custom is to pick the brain mushrooms, dry them and keep them at least three months before eating. A Finnish mycologist tells about burying dampened newspapers with Gyromitra spawn mixed in them to promote the cultivation of this mushroom. He said they do that even though they know of the danger. Delayed reaction occurs 1 - 24 hours after eating. An Edmonton boy was in a coma for 18 hours in hospital after nibling on a raw *G. esculenta*. The reaction came 8 hours after the event and left him with liver damage. His mother was also very ill from the cooking fumes. There is less Gyromytrin in *Helvella* species, but still none should be eaten raw. *Gyromitra* spores contain 2 oil drops. *Helvella* spores contain one oil drop.

hooded false morel   p.183-1

Gyromitra infula (Schaeffer: Fries) Quélet

Gyzomitra: round turban (Greek)
infula: tied down with a woolen string (Latin)

Cosmopolitan; widely distributed in the Pacific Northwest, the Rocky mountains and in boreal mixed forest. More often than not, in Alberta I found it parasitized by *Sphaeronaemella helvellae* (Karsten) Karsten (1B) which grows on top of the hymenium of *G. infula* and which makes the surface look felty and more rigid. **Poisonous** (see family).

fruiting body	a mitred head and a stalk with folds.
head	ochrish to chestnut brown, mitred to irregularly lobed; lobes first free, then joined with stalk here and there; whitish inside; coloured when parasitized; up to 9 cm wide and 8 cm high.
stalk	off-white to brownish, often with folds but not with ridges and holes; when parasitized, the stalk often is purplish pink in colour.
flesh	pale brownish grey, semitransparent, brittle in head; creamy and hollow in stalk or with pink lines and more complicated. See cross section 1A.
spores	colourless.

brain mushroom   p.183-2

Gyromitra esculenta (Persoon) Fries

esculenta: edible, a confusing name because it can be deadly! (Latin)

Cosmopolitan and widespread; occurs in Northwest North America in Alaska, Yukon,

B.C., and the forested regions of the prairie provinces. Generally in northern and mountain forests. In drier climates it does not fruit every spring; it may fruit a few springs in a row and then not for ten years. Since they fruit at the same time as morels, people may mistake these **poisonous** brain mushrooms for morels (see family). The ones I found in the Yukon had very heavy solid stalks which were very hard to dig up. They seemed cemented in the ground and had a row of small mosses growing on the base at ground level. I figured that these specimens had grown very slowly at cool temperatures night and day and with 24 hours daylight. The specimens were still heavy when dry. Dr. Jim Ginns, curator of the National Mycological Herbarium of Canada, told me that he found some specimens on Vancouver Island with the same kind of stalk. Usually the stalks have loose stuffing or are hollow.

fruiting body	convoluted head and smooth stalk.
head	medium yellow and reddish brown, becoming dark chestnut with age; strongly convoluted, brainlike; the older it gets the more wrinkled it is; sometimes it is somewhat lobed; attached to the stalk in various spots; up to 10 cm across.
stalk	buff to ochrish or pinkish, equal or thicker at the top, middle or bottom; up to 12 cm tall and 4 cm thick.
flesh	creamy, off-white or pinkish; stalk stuffed with creamy stuffing, hollow or sometimes solid and dense.
spores	colourless.

fluted white Helvella

p.185-1

Helvella crispa Scopoli: Fries

Helvella: small vegetable (Latin)
crispa: curled (Latin)

Cosmopolitan and widely distributed in North America; grows in damp, cool spots in boreal mixed forests; solitary or in twos or threes. Absent in hot, dry summers. Is said to be edible, but is indigestible to some people. Should **never** be eaten raw.

fruiting body	consists of head and stalk; spores are formed on the outer surface of the head. The size varies a lot, I found them from 4 - 18 cm tall.
head	hymenium (outside) whitish; with age ochraceous; underside a bit rough, same colour as the hymenium. Irregular, with two or three lobes, sometimes saddle shaped; up to 7 cm broad and high.
stalk	whitish to ochraceous; beautifully fluted or ribbed, with holes between the ribs; up to 12 cm tall.
flesh	white; the interior of the stalk is chambered.

fluted black Helvella

p.185-2

Helvella lacunosa Afzelius: Fries

lacunosa: full of holes (Latin)

Cosmopolitan; grows in mixed or coniferous forests, often along trails; on the ground or on old wood; often in slightly disturbed areas, places charred by fire or public camp-grounds. In Alberta and B.C., I have found the black Helvella healthy and black as often as with a white powdery head. The parasite that grew on the whitish heads (2b) was identified by Clark T. Rogerson, then senior curator at the New York Botanic Gardens. It is an ascomycete as well, belonging to another group, (see 191-4, *Pyrenomycetes*). This information is added because it occurs quite frequently and is then an interesting puzzle. The black-fluted Helvella is said to be edible but tough. It should **never** be eaten raw.

fruiting body	consists of a head and stalk; the latter resembles the stalk of *H. crispa*, but is darker; the head is black and the edge is attached to the stalk in several places.
head	hymenium (outside) black or blackish brown; lobed and saddle shaped or irregularly wrinkled; underside light grey or the colour of the head; up to 5 cm across and 6 cm high.
stalk	grey with brown tints, fluted like *H. crispa* with holes; often short but can be up to 12 cm tall (see 2b).
flesh	greyish, with chambers in stalk or very irregularly hollow.

long-stalked grey cup

Helvella macropus (Fries) Karsten

macropus: with a long leg (Greek)

Cosmopolitan and widespread; a cup-shaped, stalked mushroom, closer to *Helvellas* than to the cup-shaped *Pezizas*, because of microscopic features of the spores (previous names for this species are *Macropodia*, *Cyathopodia* and *Macroscyphus macropus*). Found in bogs under both coniferous and deciduous trees.

fruiting body	consists of a cup on a stalk.
head	hymenium inside the cap dark grey brown, outside grey and a bit rough; up to 3 cm across.
stalk	pale grey, same colour as the outside of the cup, felty, solid, gradually thickening toward the base; up to 5 cm tall and 0.3 cm thick at the top.
flesh	thin.

slender stalked Helvella

Helvella elastica Bulliard: Fries

elastica: stretched or slimmed (Greek)

Cosmopolitan and widespread; another name for this species is *Leptopodia elastica* (Bulliard: St Amans) Boudier. This is a good name too; *leptopodia* means slender stalked in Greek. I found it in August in boreal forest in open areas, e.g. on a path or under spruce where there is not so much undergrowth as a rule.

fruiting body	consists of a small saddle on a stalk; the edge of the saddle is loose from the stalk.
head	light brown, darker brown or buff to yellowish hymenium; smooth; underside white, smooth or a bit uneven; the head can also be irregular (see p. 185).
stalk	white, smooth and a bit bumpy, slender, bent; can be slimmer at the top or at the bottom; up to 5 cm tall and 0.4 cm thick.

Family PEZIZACEAE   cup mushrooms

Named for the genus *Peziza* (Greek for living on the land, close to the ground, on foot). They grow on the ground, decaying wood, burnt ground (from a forest fire or camp fire), manure or even in damp cellars. Cup-shaped, they are sessile (no stalk) or short stalked. The margin of the cup may be smooth, uneven or serrate but not hairy. Ascospores are formed in a fertile layer (hymenium) inside the cup, disc or bowl. They are forcefully catapulted out of the cup when it is warmed by the sun or touched by wind or an animal. All are saprophytes. The following genera are included:

Peziza (Greek for living on the land): fragile cups, sessile or with short buried stalk; no oildrops in spores.

Tarzetta: cup or bowl shaped with a stalk, which is sometimes rudimentary; 2 oil drops in the spores.

Otidia (Greek for resembling an ear): lopsided bowls, brittle flesh; 2 oil drops in the spores.

Sarcosphaera (Greek for fleshball): fruiting bodies develop underground as closed balls, emerging when maturing, splitting open starlike. There is one widespread species in this genus; 2 oil drops in the spores.

home or cellar cup

Peziza domiciliana Cooke

former name: *P. adae* Sadler

domiciliana: of the house (Latin)

Cosmopolitan and widespread; occurs in damp areas in cellars or dirt basements, on earth or old rugs; this one grew on compost in a basement.

fruiting body	dirty white cups, sessile or with a short stalk; up to 4 cm across and 4 cm tall.
hymenium	in the cup, at first whitish or buff, later tan.
exterior	paler or the same.
flesh	white, fragile.

charcoal cup

p.186-2

Peziza anthracophila R. W. G. Dennis

former name: *P. echinospora* Karsten
anthracophila: loving charcoal (Greek)
echinospora: with warted spores (Greek)

Cosmopolitan; one of the species which grows on the scorched ground of forest fires or campgrounds.

fruiting body	a relatively large cup with notched edge; sessile or with a short buried stalk; up to 8 cm across.
hymenium	inner cup surface, ochrish to hazel brown, smooth.
exterior	lighter, scurfy, with white bloom.
flesh	brownish, fragile.

brown cup

p.186-3

Peziza repanda Persoon

repanda: wavy, folded (Latin)

Cosmopolitan and widespread; one of the most common cup mushrooms, growing on decaying logs or buried wood. The name *repanda* refers to the mature cup, which expands to an irregular, wavy form.

fruiting body	whitish outside and brown inside; smooth edge, sessile or with short stalk, up to 8 cm across.
hymenium	in the cup is pale brown to chestnut or darker, smooth or uneven.
exterior	whitish at first with fine scales, dirty brownish later.
flesh	whitish, fragile.

brown-black cup

p.186-4

Peziza brunneoatra Desmazieres

brunneoatra: brownish black (Latin)

Cosmopolitan, widely distributed but not common according to Pomerleau; occurring on damp soil along paths in the forest. The very dark caps are hard to spot. These specimens grew in gravel on a picnic site.

fruiting body	dark brown inside and out; up to 3 cm across.
hymenium	inside cup, brownish black, smooth.
exterior	same colour or somewhat lighter, smooth.
stalk	none, but a small lump of clay adheres to the point of attachment to the soil.
flesh	brown, thin, fragile.

violet cup

p.186-5

Peziza violacea Persoon

violacea: violet (Latin)

Cosmopolitan; not common but widely distributed. This lovely cup grows in old sites where there have been fires. They should occur frequently in boreal mixed forests, where forest fires are natural events. Growing singly or in small groups.

fruiting body	violet cup inside and out, light edge; up to 6 cm across.
hymenium	inside the cup violet, with age becoming darker than the outside.
exterior	pale violet and some ochre, a bit dusty looking.
stalk	none or rudimentary.
flesh	purplish, thin.

red-brown cup

Peziza badia Persoon: Mérat

badia: reddish brown (Latin)

Cosmopolitan and widespread; grows on the edges of paths in forests, under spruce or on sandy soils.

fruiting body	saucer-shaped cup mushrooms; dark brown inside and red brown outside. (There are more of these brown species growing on the ground than those listed here, and they can be distinguished by their spore surface, using a microscope.) The specimens in the illustration are young and regular; when older, they can become wavy and irregular; up to 8 cm across.
hymenium	inside cup dark brown.
exterior	reddish brown and a bit rough.
stalk	none.
flesh	reddish brown, thin, fragile.

small dung cup

p.186-7

Peziza vesiculosa Bulliard: St. Amans

vesiculosa: with blisters (Latin)

Cosmopolitan; these yellowish, very soft cups grow on manure — in this case on elk droppings. The name *vesiculosa* refers to small bulges in the hymenium.

fruiting body	cup shaped, inrolled at first; sessile with very small stalk. These specimens are about 1.5 cm across, but elk droppings are relatively small; they can be up to 6 cm across.
hymenium	inside or topside yellowish; older ones somewhat browner.
exterior	pale yellowish, scurfy.
flesh	yellowish, soft, fragile.

grey goblet

p.186-8

Tarzetta cupularis (Fries) Lambette

cupularis: like a small mug (Greek)

Cosmopolitan; a pale mushroom with a preference for bare or burnt ground under spruce.

fruiting body	cups with incurved margin, finely toothed and a short stalk; up to 3.5 cm across and 4 cm high.
hymenium	in cup greyish buff, smooth.
exterior	greyish, pruinose (pimply).
flesh	white, fragile.

brown bowl fungus

p.186-9

Tarzetta catina (Fries) Korf & J. K. Rogers

catina: bowl (Latin)

Cosmopolitan and widespread, but rare; the specimen in the illustration was found early in spring on a steep riverbank under aspen and hazelnut.

fruiting body	cup and stalk one piece; up to 15 cm across and 6 cm high.
hymenium	in cup a rich chocolate brown, smooth, dull; some folds in the bowl, splits in the edge of the bowl.
exterior	light bone colour with dark granular dots.
stalk	off-white, sturdy; up to 2.5 cm tall and 1 cm thick.
flesh	white, solid, thicker in the bottom of the bowl than most of the other species on this plate.

donkey's ears

p.186-10

Otidea onotica (Persoon) Fuckel

onotica: of the donkey (Greek)

Cosmopolitan; This is a very interesting species with its tall, erect ear-like cups; terrestrial. The species in the illustration was found in boreal mixed forest under spruce, growing in groups. The mycelium is quite visible and ties the needles together. It is said to be a good edible mushroom with an almond taste.

fruiting body	lopsided cups, like donkey ears, edges inrolled; up to 10 cm tall.
hymenium	reddish ochre inside the ear, smooth.
exterior	yellow, a bit scurfy.
flesh	pale, thin, fragile.

violet star cup

p.186-11

Sarcosphaera crassa (Santi: Steudel) Pouzar

crassa: thick (Latin)

Cosmopolitan; this interesting species develops underground as a fleshy hollow ball; when emerging it splits into a crown. The one illustrated was found in alpine forest.

fruiting body	cup split open like a crown; sometimes there is a short, stubby stalk.
hymenium	inside the cup is amethyst to purple, but it can also be blushing pink.
exterior	dirty white, smooth, waxy feeling.
flesh	white, thick.

Family HUMARIACEAE

Humariaceae contains many colourful species; all have hairy exteriors; the hair can be long or short, thick or scant. All are sessile, as I found them, but *Geopyxis* can have a buried stalk. Fruiting bodies are cup shaped, but may become flat discs with a hairy fringe or stay in the original cup shape; growing on the ground or decayed wood. All are saprophytes. The following genera are included:

Humaria (Greek for growing on humus or decaying organic matter): fruiting bodies are cups with a woolly edge.

Melastiza (Greek for with dark markings): bright red cup-shaped species flattening out on the ground; smooth margin, hairy on the underside.

Aleuria (Greek for powdered with wheat flour): exterior of the bright orange cup gives a powdered appearance because of pale tomentum (short matted hair).

Scutellinia (Latin for like a small dish): small saucer-shaped fruiting body with hair on the exterior and an eyelash fringe on the margin.

Trichophaea (Greek for with dark hair): small white eyelash disc growing on the ground.

Geopyxis (Greek for earth box): small, colourful deep cups, which keep their cup shape; always grow in burnt areas, particularly *G. carbonaria*.

Sepultaria (Latin for buried): the name means buried, and this refers to the young stage, when it is underground as a brown, hollow, hairy globe.

hairy fairy cup

p.187-1

Humaria hemisphaerica (Wiggers: Fries) Fuckel

hemisphaerica: half a globe (Greek)

Cosmopolitan; this most picturesque cup mushroom grows in groups on mossy, very rotten stumps or logs, often in the company of various other species: honey mushrooms, false morels, brackets, small russulas and ramarias. A rotten log is a rich find.

fruiting body	sessile, cup shaped with dark, thick, hairy fringe; up to 3 cm across.
fertile surface	inside cup white, like porcelain, somewhat greyish white.

exterior	brown, covered with dark brown hairs; fringe thick, dark brown, like a miniature fur collar.
flesh	white.

red saucer p.187-2

Melastiza chateri (W. G. Smith) Boudier

chateri: named after J. J. Chater, the finder, in 1872; a gardener in Cambridge

Cosmopolitan; according to mycologist K. N. Egger, widely distributed in Canada, including the Northwest Territories, but not often collected; closely related to *Aleuria* but differs in the presence of brown hairs on the outer surface. I found it twice, once in the woods, flat on the ground, with the rim still turned up, showing brown hairs and later in the garden, between a row of carrots — much brighter, completely flat, bigger and no hairy fringe visible. To see the hair on the red exterior, a magnifying glass was necessary.

Melastiza species are usually bigger than *Scutellinia* species.

fruiting body	small hairy knobs at first, then disc shaped with a small upturned edge, finally flat with smooth margin; up to 3.5 cm across.
hymenium	top, bright scarlet, smooth.
exterior	same colour as top with scanty brown hair (when extended).
flesh	red.

orange peel fungus p.187-3

Aleuria aurantia (Persoon: Fries) Fuckel

aurantia: orange (Latin)

Cosmopolitan and widespread in North America; occurs in summer in the Rocky Mountains; fall and winter along the Pacific coast; in summer in northern Alberta, The Northwest Territories, the Yukon and Alaska. Grows in the woods along paths and on freshly broken ground, in large groups or singly. It is said to be edible. Can be used raw to brighten up salads.

fruiting body	a large cup, up to 10 cm across; sessile, irregular and folded when mature.
hymenium	inside the cup is bright orange, smooth.
exterior	lighter, pale buff yellow and downy.
flesh	orange, thin, fragile.

red eyelash cup p.187-4

Scutellinia scutellata (Linnaeus: St. Amans) Lambotte

scutellata: like a small bowl (Latin)

Cosmopolitan and widespread; this species grows on damp decaying wood of deciduous and coniferous trees; it has been found in the Northwest Territories and Alaska on decaying humus in the tundra; in northwest North America in forested areas.

fruiting body	small hairy knob in youth, then flattening to disc with hairy fringe; sessile disc up to 1.5 cm across; "eyelashes" dark brown to black, up to 0.2 cm long.
hymenium	bright scarlet or orange red, smooth.
exterior	felty with dark brown hair.
flesh	red, thin.

Pennsylvania eyelash cup p.187-5

Scutellinia pennsylvanica (Seaver) Denison

pennsylvanica: first found in Pennsylvania

North American; this is a smaller version of *S. scutellata*; it differs from scutellata by its smaller hairs and more coarsely warted spores. A widespread species, but not often collected, according to K. N. Egger, who identified many Ascomycotina species for me. In boreal mixed forest I find this species more often than no. 4.

fruiting body	small hairy knob at first, then saucer shaped with upturned margin with a short fringe of brown hair; up to 0.8 cm across.
hymenium	bright vermilion.
exterior	covered with brown hair.
flesh	very thin.

white eyelash cup p.187-6

Trichophaea woolhopeia (Cooke & Phillips) Boudier

woolhopeia: found during the excursion of the Woolhope Club, 1877 in Britain

Cosmopolitan and widespread; growing on the ground along paths. Found in the Northwest Territories, according to Graves & Elliot (1971).

fruiting body	hemispherical when young, disc shaped when mature, sessile, margin and exterior covered by brown hair, up to 1 cm across.
hymenium	(or fertile surface) white, fringed by stiff brown hair.
exterior	covered by brown hair.
flesh	white, thin.

earth box p.187-7

Geopyxis carbonaria (Albertini & Schweinitz: Fries) Saccardo

carbonaria: growing on charcoal (Latin)

Cosmopolitan; a fungus which grows on burnt ground. My husband and I were on a May holiday near Jasper National Park, Alberta, when we spotted a very black stand of lodgepole pine and white spruce. A very hot fire had gone through, everything on the ground — even the duff — was burned, but the ground was covered with millions of small cup mushrooms. They came in various colours, from pale yellow, yellow ochre, yellow-brown and orange to grey brown with red-brown interiors. This was the very first thing to grow on the dark brown and black ground after the fire. These cups had no stalks. Groves and Elliot (1971) wrote that this species occurs in the Yukon and the Northwest Territories. Of four collections in the National Herbarium, two are stipitate (or with stalk) and two subsessile (or with dry short stalk)! I find that interesting because in European literature they are described with a stalk and the ones I found were sessile (or no stalk). The Canadian authors also mention colour variations of tan and orange.

fruiting body	deep cup, not changing shape when maturing, sessile, up to 1.5 cm across.
hymenium	auburn.
exterior	buff to yellow ochre; orange to brown with lighter margin.
flesh	tan, thin.

orange crown cup p.187-8

Sepultaria pellita (Cooke & Peck) Seaver

pellita: covered with fur (Latin)

North American; a very interesting species to find on the forest floor growing under spruce in brown needles. Like *Sarcophaera crassa* (see p. 186) it develops underground as a hollow ball, emerging when it matures, by opening with a pointed crown, leaving the bottom half in the ground. This is not shown in the illustration because I wanted the full shape to be seen. Two obvious differences from *Sarcophaera* are the orange inside and the dark brown and hairy outside. It has earth and spruce needles sticking to it.

fruiting body	a brown, hairy, hollow ball developing underground; opening with star-shaped splits, the rays irregular, showing above ground up to 3.5 cm across and 2.5 cm high.
hymenium	bright orange, smooth.
exterior	brown, somewhat hairy and encrusted with earth and needles.
flesh	white, quite thick.

Family SARCOSCYPHACEAE

scarlet elf cup

p.189-1

Microstoma protracta (Fries) Kanouse

Microstoma: with small mouth (Greek)
protracta: brought to light (Latin)

A northern species, one of the earliest in Alberta; often fruiting when there is still snow on the ground but small plants have started to grow already. The rare white violets bloom at the same time (*Viola renifolia*). No leaves on the trees yet, so there is a lot of light on the forest floor. The goblet-shaped cups are very attractive, with a scarlet inside and orange outside, with a short or long stalk. The collection in the illustration was the first one in the National Mycological Herbarium according to D. W. Malloch. Fruiting time is May or whenever the snow is almost gone. At the same time bog wintergreen, *Pyrola asarifolia*, may have a few bright red leaves with dots on them. This is caused by a fungus called rust or *Chrysomyxa pirolata*, a plant disease. The leaf with the yellow dots (not red yet) and the green leaf with the red underside carry this rust. The next species (no. 2) has a plant with another rust next to it. Rusts are basidiomycetes with a complicated life cycle.

fruiting body	deep cup on a slender stalk; cup up to 1 cm high and 1 cm across; stalk up to 5 cm tall and 0.2 cm thick; ascospores are forcefully ejected.
hymenium	in the cup, scarlet.
exterior	orange with an orange buff rim.
stalk	slim, white, can be tall, most of it covered by fallen leaves.

Family SARCOSOMATACEAE

with a fleshy body (Greek)

Black urn fungus

p.189-2

Urnula hiemalis Nannfeldt

Urnula: small vessel (Latin)
hiemalis: of the winter (Latin)

Cosmopolitan; a very dark, big cup mushroom, not often found because it is almost black. Rare in Alberta. Growing on the ground near old wood or on a decaying log; this is an exciting find. The stalk is buried in the ground and not visible when the black urn is spotted. Growing near it was *Adoxa moschatellina*, a small plant which develops early in spring when the trees bear no leaves yet; it disappears in summer. *Adoxa* carried rust, a parasitic fungus, *Puccinia argentata* (yellow spots on the leaves), a completely different group. Ascomycetes are often early fruiters, and the black urn is no exception; it fruits before the morels.

fruiting body	urn shaped; a cup, closed in youth, with a short stalk; 8 cm across and 7 cm high, including stalk. Notched rim; cup inrolled at first, then bell shaped; turns completely black with age.
hymenium	blackish brown.
exterior	blackish brown, velvety.
stalk	short, up to 2 cm tall, enlarging toward the base, grey brown to black.
flesh	dark, relatively thin, leathery, tough; a bit gelatinous inside the cup at first.

Order HELOTIALES

The order is named after Helotium (Greek for pin, dowel, bud). Small stalked cups and earth tongues belong to it. The microscopic features in many of the families are fascinating but macroscopic characteristics are just as interesting. The asci are inoperculate, i.e., the ascus has no lid as in the Pezizales but a pore at the tip through which the spores are expelled. Seven species of three families are discussed.

Family SCLEROTINIACEAE

The name is derived from sclerotium (Greek for something which is dry, hard and strong). The species included here have this survival equipment or sclerotium. This is a compact mass of resistant mycelium. It enables a fungus to survive for years in harsh conditions. This feature is not restricted to this family (see the Canadian tuckahoe in Polypores, p. 177, 372). Other survival equipment is the ability to form different kinds of spores for different stages throughout the year. *Monilinia* is one of these fungi.

cherry cup   p.189-3

Monilinia fructicola (Winter) Honey

Monilinia: refers to neck or chain around the neck (Latin)
fructicola: living on fruit (Latin)

Cosmopolitan; this is a parasitic fungus. The small, stalked cup mushroom, which can be found fruiting very early in spring, grows on overwintered, mummified fruit of *Prunus* spp., in this case chokecherry (*Prunus virginiana*). Ascospores are shot out forcefully and land on the chokecherry bush. This produces an imperfect state (a phase in the lifecycle of a fungus in which asexual spores are produced) in early summer, which attacks the leaves and young twigs of the *Prunus* sp. This is a simplified story of the life cycle, ending with infected fruit which falls to the ground so that the cycle can start again. Species similar to *Monilinia* attack other types of fruit, such as blueberry.

fruiting body	small, deep cup, up to 1 cm across, on a slim stalk, up to 2.5 cm long and 0.2 cm thick; attached to a mummified cherry.
hymenium	inside the cup, buff or pale tan.
exterior	same colour as inside.
stalk	same colour.

sedge cup   p.189-4

Myriosclerotinia caricis-ampullaceae (Nyberg) Buchwald

Myriosclerotinia: with myriads (tens of thousands) of sclerotia (Greek) (see family)
caricis-ampullaceae: of the sedge *Carex ampullaceae* (Latin)

Circumpolar; a rare, subarctic species. Decades go by between finds. It was first collected in Finland in 1931. I found the sedge cup very early in spring (1976) in a bog west of Edmonton, in a small run of water next to marsh marigolds. According to J. Ginns, Curator of the National Mycological Herbarium, this fungus has nothing to do with marsh marigolds, but forms sclerotia in sedge stalks. The next spring I was lucky and found them again in the same spot. I was able to collect some sclerotia (which have the triangular shape of the sedge stalk) and some more fruiting bodies. Since these were the first collections in northwest North America, I sent some to the National Herbarium and gave some to the herbarium of the University of Alberta. Fruiting bodies are formed on the previous year's submerged sclerotia at the time when the sedge plants are pollinating. The fungus infects the sedge via the male flower spikes. Development of sclerotia in the sedge plants occurs during the summer, and they stay in the diseased culms (or stalk) until fruiting takes place again in spring.

fruiting body	more or less leathery cups, up to 3 cm across, and strong stalks, half above and half below water, the lower half as black as the sclerotium it is attached to.
hymenium	inside the cup, auburn.
exterior	brown, very finely tomentose, a bit wrinkled with age.
stalk	brown top half, black bottom half, which is submerged, narrowing down from the top; up to 7 cm tall and 0.5 cm thick at the apex.

Family GEOGLOSSACEAE

earth tongues (Greek)

The earth tongues include species with stalks and fertile portions in the shape of a tongue, a fan, a spatula or an irregular cap shape.

yellow earth tongue   p.189-5

Spathularia flavida Persoon: Fries

Spathularia: resembling a spatula (Greek)
flavida: blonde, golden yellow (Latin)

Cosmopolitan and widespread; growing in temperate climates under spruce in northwest North America, as far north as Alaska. In the genus *Spathularia* the upper fertile part is flattened and fan shaped, decurrent on both sides of the stalk.

fruiting body	the fan can be ivory to bright yellow, the stalk white to yellow or pale brown.
head	(or fertile portion) yellow and up to 3 cm across or ivory and small, up to 1 cm across. Flattened, enclosing the upper part of the stalk like a fan, radially furrowed, the division between fan end stalk clearly outlined.
stalk	whitish yellow or light brown, somewhat irregular; I found it divided in two sometimes with two heads; up to 4 cm tall.

spatula fungus   p.189-6

Spathularia spathulata (Imai) Mains

spathulata: like a spatula (Greek)

North American; according to A. H. Smith, only known from California, but this one was found near Lesser Slave Lake, Alta., growing under spruce. Rare so far. A very beautiful species in buff and brown colours, looking like an elegant wooden spatula. The stalk can be seen through the fertile part, like a vein in a leaf, starting one third down from the top.

fruiting body	spatula shaped, leathery, up to 10 cm tall; flat fertile top up to 2 cm across; up to 9 cm tall.
head	orangy buff, enclosing the upper part of the stalk, but, unlike the yellow earth tongues, the division between head and stalk is not clearly outlined — more like a leaf stem continuing into a vein; sides decurrent.
stalk	brown, round below the head, equal.

yellow Cudonia   p.189-7

Cudonia lutea (Peck) Saccardo

Cudonia: refers to beauty or fame (Greek)
lutea: yellow (Latin)

North American species, widely distributed. Another similar species, smaller, brown and white, instead of yellow is cosmopolitan. Occurs in deciduous or mixed forests.

fruiting body	cap and stalk; cap only fastened in the centre, droops around on all sides.
hymenium	on top of cap; yellow or buff yellow; feels buttery; irregular, margin turned in; up to 3 cm across.
underside	white; can have ribs, for strength, from stalk to cap edge.
stalk	same colour as cap, often grooved and/or twisted; base sometimes slightly purplish; up to 6 cm tall.

Family HELOTIACEAE

Fungi of Switzerland is a wonderful book on the subject of Ascomycetes. It is great to have a good taxonomic system to follow. The authors palce *Bisporella* and *Chlorociboria* in Helotiaceae and that is what I do too, in this book. I know that these two are placed in other families elsewhere, but I will follow the Swiss.

minute lemon cup p.189-8

Bisporella citrina (Batsch & Fries) Korf & Carpenter

Bisporella: with two sets of spores (Latin)

citrina: lemon colour (Latin)

Cosmopolitan; bright yellow cup fungus, growing on rotten, damp logs, and although the cups are very small, they are seen because they fruit in big groups. The name *Bisporella* indicates that each of the 8 ascospores in the ascus is ready to divide in two, so that a double amount of spores is actually produced. There are many very small, interesting ascomycetes recycling wood, herbaceous plants, reeds and rushes. I found a miniature species, *Cyathicula coronata*, close to this one on reeds. It was pin sized, but beautiful when magnified. There was no room to show it on this plate.

fruiting body	cup shape with short stalk; up to 5 mm high and 5 mm across.
hymenium	inside the cup; yellow, more orange as it dries.
exterior	yellow and smooth, sometimes white.
stalk	white and short.

green cups p.189-9

Chlorociboria aeruginascens (Nylander) Kanouse: Ram, Korf & Bataille

Chlorociboria: with green cups (Greek)

aeruginascens: becoming copper green (verdigris) (Latin)

Cosmopolitan and widespread; the fungus produces a pigment which colours the wood it grows on a typical blue-green. The wood is often seen without fruiting bodies. Fruiting takes place in cool weather, early in spring and late in the fall. In 19th century England, the green-coloured wood (oak) was eagerly collected and used to make inlaid jewel and snuff boxes. Named after the town of Tonbridge it was called Tonbridge ware. In Canada, oak is also the preferred wood along the coast, but in the prairie provinces, where there is no oak, it grows on other deciduous wood (birch and poplar). Often minuscule mosses grow on the logs too.

fruiting body	stalked cup. I found them up to 2 cm across, but mostly they are smaller.
hymenium	inside the cup, copper green, smooth.
exterior	whitish at first, becoming green as well.
stalk	verdigris as well; central or, when on the side of a log, attached on the side of the cup; up to 0.5 cm long.

Class PYRENOMYCETES

Order SPHAERIALES

Only eight species of several families belonging to the order of Sphaeriales will be discussed. These are really outside the scope of this book, but the colourful parasitic fungi, covering the surfaces of mushrooms are often encountered by mushroom-hunters and it is interesting to know what they are.

Six of the eight species shown are parasitic on well-known mushrooms. They change the colour and appearance of the host mushrooms by growing as a felty layer on top of the cap, stalk, gills, etc., of their "prey". They are sac fungi, developing their spores in asci (sometimes with 16 spores instead of eight). The asci are not formed on the surface as in Discomycetes, but rather in small flasks (called perithecia) which are imbedded in a feltlike layer of mycelium called stroma. The mouths of the flasks form bumps, or small pimples, on the surface, and the spores are expelled through them. It is said that the lobster mushroom is edible, but it is not easy to decide which species of *Lactarius* or *Russula* is the host. Caution is needed. Included are two flask fungi which have their own "independent" fruiting bodies. All belong to the order of *Sphaeriales*.

soft leather pillow   p.191-1
Podostroma alutaceum (Persoon: Fries) Atkinson

Podostroma: pillow on a base (Greek)
alutaceum: like fine leather (Latin)

Cosmopolitan, but rare. I found the specimens in the illustration on a squirrel den under spruce in northern Alberta. Thinking that these were odd-looking puffballs, I sent them to my experts years ago. To my great surprise they turned out to be ascomycetes. J. Walton Groves and Sheila C. Hoare (1954) write that "this fungus was studied in culture in 1905 by Atkinson, who was able to establish that this was an autonomous fruiting body and not a parasite on a *Clavaria* for instance." Numbers 3 - 8 are all parasitic on other mushrooms, either basidiomycetes or ascomycetes; there is no "freestanding" fruiting body, but only a cottony layer or **stroma**. The stroma of this species however has a stalk, hence the name. This species has 16 spores in each ascus.

fruiting body consisting of a fertile head and a stalk; the colour is whitish at first. As the embedded perithecia develop, the top first turns yellow and then the ostioles, or mouths, show as small brown pimples. The upper one- to two-thirds of the fruiting body may be fertile.
flesh white, tough.

carbon balls   p.191-2
Daldinia concentrica (Bolton: Fries) Cesati & de Notaris

Daldinia: round charcoal (Greek)
concentrica: concentric (Latin)

Cosmopolitan; this fungus grows on stumps of deciduous trees, also on wounds of living trees. The specimen in the illustration grew on a stump of a horse chestnut in the City of Edmonton. This species belongs to a group with tough, hard fruiting bodies. They have perithecia with small openings on the surface.

fruiting body black, hard ball, growing in groups on wood. Reddish brown in youth, later dark and shiny. The ostioles, or mouths, are not as visible as in other flask fungi, probably because of the colour.

flesh blackish fibrous at first, eventually like carbon, but concentric zones are visible; sometimes it has to be held against the light to see them.

Gyromitra parasite   p.191-3

Sphaeronaemella helvellae (Karsten) Karsten

Sphaeronaemella: describing round, pimply perithecia with hairy necks (Greek)
helvellae: of *Helvella* (Latin)

Cosmopolitan; occurring in northern Europe and the northern U.S. and Alaska. In Canada in Ontario and Alberta; these specimens, including host and parasite, were the first from Alberta (1975) in the National Mycological Herbarium in Ottawa (pp. 183 and 191). In this case one ascomycete grows on another. The ascospores of the host, *Gyromitra infula* (former name: *Helvella infula*) are not destroyed, so that the host can survive. As I mentioned earlier, they are more often infected than not.

stroma a fertile layer covering the head of *Gyromitra infula*; the long necks of the round flasks have a row of hairs on the rim, giving the host a fuzzy look. Infection occurs after the host reaches maturity; the head of the host is usually involved. (Greek for stroma: something to sleep on; a blanket, a carpet or straw.)

Helvella parasite   p.191-4

Mycogone cervina Ditmar

Mycogone: birth of a fungus (Greek)
cervina: of a deer (Latin)

Mycogone cervina Ditmar is the anamorph or imperfect form of *Hypomyces cervinigenus* Rogerson & Simms. *Hypomyces* species often go through several stages (forms), each of which produces different spores and, in the case of no. 5 and no. 8 (the golden and the yellow green Hypomyces), the parasitized mushroom wears a different colour in each stage as well! Clark T. Rogerson, then senior curator of the New York Botanic garden, identified my specimens for my friends in Ottawa. Mr. Rogerson was especially interested in this group. It is not easy to identify lobster mushrooms and relations.

stroma a white layer covering the head of the host, *Helvella lacunosa* (see pp. 185 and 191). It sometimes extends on to the stalk. The parasite is very visible, since it covers and misshapes the black head of *H. lacunosa*. In the perfect form this fungus' name is *Hypomyces cervinigenus*; it is still white and produces sexual spores.

golden Hypomyces   p.191-5

Hypomyces chrysospermus Tulasne

Hypomyces: a mushroom underneath (Greek)
chrysospermus: with golden seed (Greek)

Cosmopolitan; occurring throughout North America on different species of boletes. I found it on *Boletus piperatus* and on *Leccinum boreale*. This is a *Hypomyces* with three different stages: a white, a yellow and a red-brown stage, each with a different name. I have only found the white stage; a white to greyish, powdery mass, clogging the tubes; the stalk and sometimes the cap are whitish. The tube shapes can still be seen on a section, but they are not perpendicular to the ground any more. In the next stage a yellow colour shows up; this is also an asexual stage, like the white stage. The third stage finally shows the pimples of the perithecia, which hold the sexual ascospores. By this time the mushroom (host) is decaying. According to Arora it is not edible; often associated with bacterial decay.

lobster mushroom

p.191-6,7

Hypomyces lactifluorum (Schweinitz) Tulasne

lactifluorum: refers to the flow of milk (Latin)

North American; a very brightly coloured parasite, growing on *Russula* and *Lactarius* spp. This is said to be a choice edible mushroom but only if you know the host! That would take knowledge of the place you find it, knowing what grows there and then make doubly sure of what you have. Both nos. 6 and 7 grew on *Lactarius* species. The lobster mushroom is bright orange red or vermilion. *Lactarius volemus* (see p. 47) grew next to no. 6 but, as can be seen in the section, the mushroom had changed in shape and the gills had disappeared. I was certain that *Lactarius torminosus* was the host of no. 7. I recognized the specimen, also knew the place and what grew there. This *Lactarius* happens to be poisonous. The latex of the host stops flowing when it is invaded by the parasite.

stroma orange to vermilion; in no. 7 the lines of the gills can still be seen; both gills and part of the stalks are covered and are somewhat pimply. In the lengthwise section the outline of the gills is still visible, although the gills are grown together.

flesh of the host changes somewhat in consistency due to the parasite.

yellow green Hypomyces

p.191-8

Hypomyces luteo-virens (Fries) Plowright

luteo-virens: yellow, becoming green (Latin)

Cosmopolitan; this fungus is widespread in the Pacific Northwest and is the one most often found in Alberta. Frequently grows on *Russula* species, also on *Lactarius*. Growing in all the places where their hosts occur, fruiting when they fruit.

stroma yellow, then yellow and green, finally dark green, so dark that it becomes almost black. Then the white spores, shot out of the ostioles, can be seen on the dark background; perithecia dark green.

flesh of the host changes somewhat in consistency but is firm and white. Not recommended because it is difficult to recognize the *Russula* when the gills and spore print, etc., cannot be seen.

Illustrated Glossary

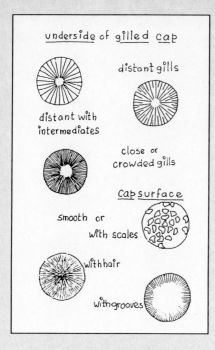

underside of gilled cap

distant gills

distant with intermediates

close or crowded gills

Cap surface

smooth or with scales

with hair

with grooves

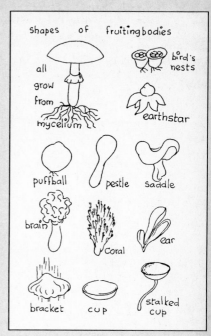

shapes of fruiting bodies

all grow from mycelium

bird's nests

earthstar

puffball

pestle

saddle

brain

Coral

ear

bracket

cup

stalked cup

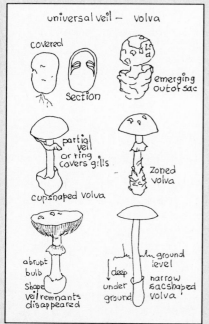

universal veil — volva

covered

Section

emerging out of sac

partial veil or ring covers gills

cup shaped volva

Zoned volva

abrupt bulb

Shape veil remnants disappeared

ground level

deep under ground

narrow sac shaped volva

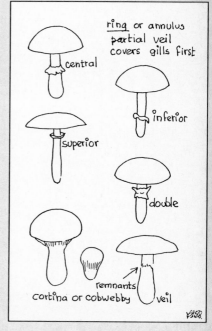

ring or annulus partial veil covers gills first

central

inferior

superior

double

cortina or cobwebby

remnants veil

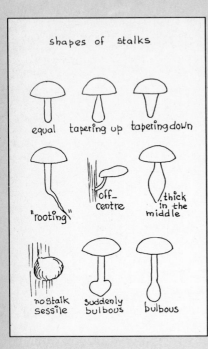

shapes of stalks

equal   tapering up   tapering down

"rooting"   off-centre   thick in the middle

no stalk sessile   suddenly bulbous   bulbous

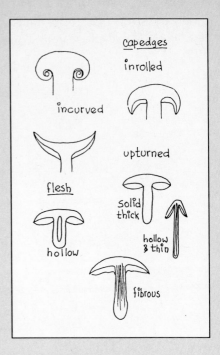

capedges

incurved   inrolled

flesh   upturned

hollow   solid thick   hollow & thin

fibrous

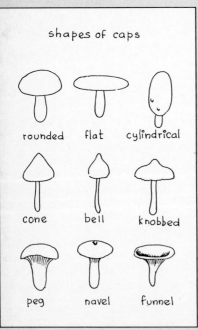

shapes of caps

rounded   flat   cylindrical

cone   bell   knobbed

peg   navel   funnel

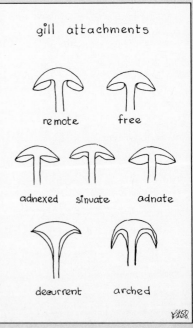

gill attachments

remote   free

adnexed   sinuate   adnate

decurrent   arched

Glossary

A

ABRUPTIBULBUS: sudden thickening of the stalk base.

ADNATE: of gills, broadly attached to the stalk.

ADNEXED: of gills, narrowly attached to the stalk.

ALPINE: vegetational zone producing alpine species;elevation above sea level depends on latitude.

ALVEOLATE: pitted or honeycombed.

AMYLOID: turning purple when treated with iodine.

ANNULUS: membranous ring, resulting from partial veil loosening at cap margin.

APEX: top of the stalk.

APICAL: at the top or tip.

APICAL PORE: hole in top of puffball for spore escape.

APOTHECIUM: exposed hymenium of an ascomycete.

ARCUATE: arched gills, when cap stays convex when gills are decurrent.

AREOLATE: cracked skin (in a regular pattern).

APPRESSED: of hair, closely pressed against surface.

ASCUS: sac in which ascospores develop.

AUTODIGESTION: or deliquescence, dissolving into liquid (Coprinus).

B

BASAL: at the lower end.

BASIDIUM: microscopic club-shaped structure, carrying basidiospores, usually four.

BOOTED: base of stalk closely sheathed by volva.

BROWN ROT: caused by certain fungi in wood, e.g., *Piptoporus* in birch.

BULBOUS: with an enlarged base.

BUTTON: young fruiting body, which looks like a button.

C

CAESPITOSE (or CESPITOSE): groups of mushrooms joined at their stalk bases.

CAMPANULATE: bell shaped.

CAP: pileus (Greek for felt hat).

CAPILLITIUM: (Latin for long hair) sterile hyphae, mixed in with spore mass in puffballs; basidia grow on the capillitium.

CARTILAGINOUS: tough, like cartilage.

CHARACTERISTIC: a feature, helping to identify a mushroom.

COLLAR: part of exoperidium staying around the base of the puffball in the centre (in earth stars).

COLUMELLA: extension of subgleba into the gleba (Gasteromycetes).

CONCOLOR: or concolorous; same colour all over.

CONFLUENT: flowing together; cap and stalk are one piece.

CONIC: of the cap, pointed.

CONNECTING VEINS: connections between gills.

CONTEXT: inside of fruiting body; woody, corky or fleshy.

CONVEX: rounded, of the cap.

CORTINA: hairy partial veil.

CUTICLE: skin.

CYSTIDIA: sterile cells at the end of hyphae; can be on the cap, gills or stalk.

D

DECURRENT: of gills, running down the stalk.

DELIQUESCING: dissolving into fluid or liquid.

DIAPHRAGM: membrane separating gleba and subgleba, e.g., in *Vascellum*.

DIPLOID: binucleate cells.

DISC: centre of cap.

DISCOMYCETE: an ascomycete with a cup or saucerlike fruiting body.

DRY ROT: rot which causes the wood to appear dry, cracked & shrunken.

DUFF: debris on forest floor; leaves, needles, branchlets, dead plants; humus in the making.

E

ENDOPERIDIUM: inner skin.

EPIGEOUS: living on top of the ground.

EPIPHRAGM: membranous cover of cup or "nest" in bird's nest fungi.

ESCULENT: edible.

EVANESCENT: disappearing.

EXCENTRIC: off-centre attachment of stalk to cap.

EXOPERIDIUM: outer skin or tissue layer.

F

FARINACEOUS: smelling of raw meal.

FERTILE LAYER: layer in which spores are formed, gills, tubes, etc.

FIBRILLOSE: with visible fibres or fibrils.

FIMBRIATE: fringed.

FLOCCOSE: fuzzy or with cottony flocs.

FORKED GILLS: gills divide into two like a fork.

FREE: of gills, free from stalk.

FRINGE: hairy little plume around apical pore (in earth stars).

FUNICULUS: cord with which eggs are attached to cup in Nidulariaceae.

FURFURACEOUS: covered with fine scales.

FUSIFORM: spindle shaped.

G

GENUS: taxonomic group including related species.

GEOTROPIC: upright or perpendicular to the earth's surface.

GILLS: lamellae.

GLEBA: (Latin for lump of earth) spore mass in Gasteromycetes.

GLABROUS: bald or smooth.

GLUTINOUS: sticky.

GRANULOSE: covered with fine grains or particles.

H

HAPLOID: having single set of chromosomes or one nucleus.

HIRSUTE: hairy.

HISPID: covered with stiff hairs.

HYGROPHANOUS: (Greek for moist looking) changing colour as moisture is lost.

HYGROSCOPIC: taking up moisture from the air.

HYMENIUM: fertile layer, containing spore-bearing cells.

HYPHAE: hollow threads forming mycelium, without separation into cells.

HYPOGEUS: growing underground.

I

IMBRICATE: overlapping like shingles.

INNATE: part of, not superficial or easily removed.

INOPERCULATE: ascus without lid but with a pore at the tip for expelling spores (Helotiales).

INROLLED: margin of cap edge forms a tight roll.

INTERMEDIATE: of gills, some do not reach the stalk.

INVOLUTE: curled inward (in *Helvella*).

IXOCUTIS: slimy outer layer.

L

LAC: milk.

LACTEUS: of milk.

LACUNOSE: pitted.

LAMELLATE: with gills.

LATERAL: on the side.

LATEX: liquid, moisture.

M

MACROSCOPIC: as seen with the naked eye.

MICROSCOPIC: as seen through a microscope.

MONOTYPIC GENUS: a genus which contains only one species.

MONTANE: vegetational zone lower than alpine.

MOTTLED: of gills, spores ripen unevenly.

MYCELIUM: undifferentiated network of hyphae; vegetative state of fungi.

MYCELIAL MAT: dense mycelium seen in duff.

MYCELIAL NEST: outer or bottom layer of peridium; sometimes stays on the ground when earth star stands on its ray tips.

MYCORRHIZA: symbiosis between fungus and the roots of a higher plant; two types: ectotrophic, hyphae surround the roots and endotrophic, hyphae penetrate the root cells.

N

NOMENCLATURE: the system of naming in biology, including zoology, botany and mycology, following international rules.

O

OMPHALINOID: looking like Omphalina, a small mushroom with decurrent gills and a navel.

OPERCULATE: an ascus with a lid (in Pezizales).

OSTIOLE: mouth of perithecium (in *Ascomycotina*).

P

PARASITIC FUNGUS: takes its nutrition from other living creatures.

PARTIAL VEIL: covers gills in youth, may include sheath on stalk.

PERIDIUM: (Greek for little pouch) skin of puffball, often multilayered.

PERISTOMA OR HALO: the area around the stoma, pore or mouth on the endoperidium, which is delineated, raised or of a different colour (in earth stars).

PERITHECIUM: miniature flask-shaped fruiting body buried in stroma or subiculum (in Pyrenomycetes).

PLANE: flat.

PERIDIOLE: egg-like structure containing spores in bird's nest fungi.

PELLICLE: skin of cap.

PORES: mouths of tubes.

PUCTATE: dotted.

PYRIFORM: pear shaped.

R

RAPHANOID: smelling like a radish.

RAYS: sections into which exoperidium splits (in earth stars).

RECEPTACULUM: stalk-like, spongy structure in stinkhorns.

REMOTE: of gills, distant from the stalk.

RESUPINATE: lying on the back or appressed to the substrate.

RETICULATE: with a raised network pattern.

RHIZOIDS: rootlike bundles of mycelium at the stalk base.

RHIZOMORPHS: form of a root.

RIMOSE: cracked.

ROOTING: having a rhizomorph or rhizoids.

RUDIMENTARY: under developed.

S

SAPROPHYTE: decomposer of dead organic material.

SCABERS: ornamentation on stalk of *Leccinum*.

SCLEROTIUM: resistant compact mycelium with dark covering.

SERRATE: of gills, toothed like a saw.

SESSILE: sitting, no stalk.

SETAE: (Latin for stiff hairs) name for cystidia with thick brown hairs.

SIDEROPHILUS: iron-loving basidia which have granules that darken when heated in acetocarmine.

SINUATE: of gills, wavy; notched near the stalk.

SKIN FLAP: cap cuticle extends beyond gills.

SPAWN: term used in mushroom cultivation for mycelium in resting stage, but ready to fruit when it starts growing.

SPONGE: fertile layer of tubes on underside of bolete caps.

SPORES: reproductive cells of lower plants.

SPORULATING: the forming and dispersing of spores.

SQUAMULOSE: full of scales or hairtufts.

SQUARROSE: covered with recurved scales.

STERIGINATA: small soines-bearing spores on the tip of a basidium, usually four.

STIPE: Greek for stalk.

STRIATE: grooved with parallel lines.

STROMA: cushion-shaped fertile layer in Pyrenomycetes, e.g., in the lobster fungus.

SUBGLEBA: sterile base, can almost be like a stalk, often chambered, e.g., in stinkhorn.

SUBICULUM: felty mat of hyphae in which the flask-like perithecia grow, (Sphaeriales).

SUBSTRATE: substance on which the
   fungus grows.
SYMBIOSIS: interdependence between
   different organisms.
SYNONYM: name which has become
   invalid.

T

TAXON: Greek for group; any group
   large or small in the taxonomic system.
TAXONOMY: classification of
   organisms.
TOMENTOSE: hairy, felty or velvety
   surface of cap or stalk.
TOMENTUM: short, matted hair.
TRUFFLES: underground fruiting bodies
   related to the class of Discomycetes
   (Ascomycotina); not described in this
   book.

U

UMBILICATE: with a navel or dip in the
   cap centre.
UMBO: knob, bump or raised centre on
   cap.
UMBONATE: with an umbo.

V

VENTRICOSE: of gills, wider in the
   centre; of stalk, thicker in the middle.
VERRUCOSE: with warts.
VILLOSE: with long hair.
VINACEOUS: dull pinkish brown to dull
   greyish brown.
VISCID: sticky.
VOLVA: Latin for womb; universal veil
   in youth enveloping fruiting body; also
   used for the sac left at the stalk base.

W

WHITE ROT: wood rot which lightens
   the wood because the lignin is
   decomposed.

Z

ZONED: concentric bands of colour or
   surface consistency.

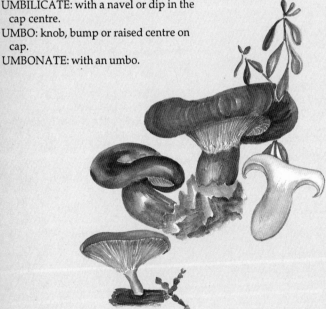

References

F denotes field guides

Abbot, Sean P. and R. S. Currah. 1989. *The larger cupfungi and other Ascomycetes of Alberta*, an annotated checklist. University of Alberta Devonian Botanic Gardens. 96 pp.

Arnolds, E. J. M. 1984. *Standaardlijst van Nederlandse Macrofungi. Coolia*, publication of the Dutch Mycological Society. 362 pp.
A checklist of the macrofungi of the Netherlands.

Arora, David. 1986. *Mushrooms Demystified*. enlarged second edition. Berkeley, Cal.: Tenspeed Press. 958pp. F

Bandoni, R. J. and A. F. Szczawinski. 1964. *Guide to Common Mushrooms of British Columbia*. B.C. Provincial Museum. 239 pp. F
Out of print but at the time it was the only mushroom guide in Western Canada.

Besette, Alan and Walter J. Sundberg. 1987. *Mushrooms: a Quick Reference Guide to Mushrooms of North America*. New York: Collier Books. 175 pp. F
This book has chapters on chemical testing of spores and microscopic spore characteristics.

Bisby, G. R., A. H. Buller, J. Dearness, W. P. Fraser and R. C. Russel. 1938. *Fungi of Manitoba and Saskatchewan*. Preface by H. T. Güssow. Ottawa: National Research Council of Canada.
Important early checklist by six scientists interested in fungi.

Breitenbach, J. and F. Kränzlin, editors. 1984. *Fungi of Switzerland*. Vol. 1, *Ascomycetes*. Lucerne: Mycological Society of Switzerland (Verlag Mykologia). 311 pp.

_____. 1986. *Fungi of Switzerland*. Vol. 2, *Nongilled Fungi: Heterobasidiomycetes, Aphyllophorales, Gastromycetes*. Lucerne: Mycological Society of Switzerland (Verlag Mykologia). 412 pp.
Very important, taxonomically and otherwise.

Brodie, Harold J. 1968. Nidulariaceae of Canada. *Can. Field Nat*. 82: 2-14.

_____. 1975. *The Bird's Nest Fungi*. Toronto: University of Toronto Press. 199 pp.

_____. 1978. *Fungi, Delight of Curiosity*. Toronto: University of Toronto Press. 131 pp.

_____. 1984. *More Bird's Nest Fungi*. Lejeunia, Revue de Botanique Belgique. 70 pp.

Dähncke, Rose Marie and Maria Sabine. 1979. *700 Pilze in Farbfotos*. Aarau, Switzerland: AT Verlag. 686 pp.

Findlay, W. P. K. 1967. *Wayside and Woodland Fungi*. illustrations by Beatrix Potter. London: Frederick Warne and Co. Ltd. 202 pp. F

Groves, J. Walton. 1979. *Edible and Poisonous Mushrooms of Canada*. Rev. ed. Addendum by S. A. Redhead. Research Branch, Agriculture Canada, Publication 1112. Ottawa: Canadian Government Publishing Centre. 320 pp. F

Groves, J. Walton and Sheila C. Hoare. 1954. *Notes on fungi from northern Canada*. I. Hypocreales and Discomycetes. Can. Field-Naturalist 68: 1-8.

Groves, J. Walton and Sheila. C. Thomson. 1955. *Notes on fungi from northern Canada*. II. Boletaceae. Can. Field-Naturalist 69:44-51.

Groves, J.Walton, Sheila C. Thomson and M. Pantidou. 1958. *Notes on fungi from northern Canada*. III. Amanitaceae, Hygrophoraceae, Rhodophyllaceae and Paxillaceae. Can. Field-Naturalist 72:133-138.

Groves, J. Walton and Mary. E. Elliot. 1971. *Notes on fungi from northern Canada*. VI. Additional records of Discomycetes. Rept. Kevo Subarctic Res. Sta. 8:22-30.
Very interesting work.

Guild, Ben. 1977. *The Alaskan Mushroom Hunters Field Guide*. Anchorage: Alaska Northwest Publ. Co. 286 pp.

Hiratsuka, Y. 1987. *Forest Tree Diseases of the Prairie Provinces*. Information Report NOR X 286. Northern Forest Research Centre. 142 pp.

Imazeki, Rokuya and Tsuguo Hongo. 1957. *Mushrooms and Toadstools of Japan*. Osaka, Japan: Hoikusha Publ. Co. Ltd. 181 pp. F

Jahn, Hermann. 1979. *Pilze die am Holz wachsen*. Herford, Germany: Baranek and Frost. 268 pp.
Fungi growing on wood, example of a selected group.

Lange, Morton and F. Bayard Hora. 1963. *Mushrooms and Toadstools*. London: Collins. 257 pp. F
Originally Danish, this is one example of a European mushroom guide which has been translated in many European languages and reprinted many times.

Lincoff, Gary H. 1981. *Field Guide to North American Mushrooms*. New York: Alfred A. Knopf. 926 pp. F

Lincoff, Gary H. and D.H. Mitchel. 1977. *Toxic and Hallucinogenic Mushroom Poisoning*. New York: Van Nostrand Reinhold Co. 267 pp.

Descriptions of poisonous mushrooms, their toxins and treatment of people who have eaten them.

McKenny, Margaret and Daniel Stuntz. 1987. *The New Savory Wild Mushroom*. rev.ed. revisions by Joseph F. Ammirati. Saskatoon: Western Producer Prairie Books. 250 pp. F
An American book, re-issued in Canada by Western Producer.

McKnight, Kent H. and Vera B. McKnight. 1987. *A Field Guide to Mushrooms*. The Peterson Field Guide Series. Boston: Houghton Miflin Co. 427 pp. F

Miller, Jr., Orson K. 1977. *Mushrooms of North America*. New York: E.P. Dutton, Chanticleer Press. 368 pp. F

National Mycological Herbarium of Canada. Biosystematics Research Centre. *Fungi Canadenses*. Ottawa. Ongoing short publications.

Nicholson, Barbara E. and Frank H. Brighton. *The Oxford Book of Flowerless Plants*. Oxford, England: Oxford University Press. 208 pp.
Plants are grouped according to habitat. Lovely Book.

Orr, Robert T. and Dorothy B. Orr. 1979. *Mushrooms of Western North America*. California Nat. History Guide no. 42. Berkeley: University of California Press. 293 pp. F

Pegler, David N. 1981. *The Mitchell Beazley Pocket Guide to Mushrooms and Toadstools*. London, England: Mitchell Beazley. 168 pp. F
Another book grouped according to habitats.

Phillips, Roger. 1981. *Mushrooms and Other Fungi of Great Britain and Europe*. London: Pan Books Ltd. 288 pp. F

Pomerleau, René. 1980. *Flore des champignons de Québec.* Montreal: Les editions La Presse. 652 pp.
Largest Canadian mushroom flora, one of my favourite books.

Ramsbottom, John. 1953. *Mushrooms and Toadstools: A Study of the Activities of Fungi.* London, England: Collins. 306 pp.
A very interesting book.

Redhead, S.A. 1981. *Parasitism of Bryophytes by Agarics.* Can. J. Bot. Vol 59, 1981, 63-67.

_____ 1986. *Xerulaceae, a family with sarcodimitic tissues.* Can. J. Bot. vol. 65, 1987, pp. 1551-1562.
Very important in many ways especially in this case, because of the taxonomy.

_____ 1984. *Mycological observations 13-14 on Hypsizygus and Tricholoma.* Trans. Mycol. Soc. Japan 25:1-9.

_____ 1988. *A biogeographical overview of the Canadian mushroom flora.* Can. J. Bot. Vol. 67, 1989, pp. 3003-3062.
Showing floristic patterns in North America and worldwide patterns in the text.

Redhead, S. A. and J. H. Ginns. 1985. *A reappraisal of agaric genra associated with brown rots of wood.* Trans. Mycol. Soc. Japan 26: 349-381.

Redhead, S. A., O. K. Miller, R. Watling and E. Ohenoja. 1981. *Marasmius epidryas.* Fungi Canadenses no. 213.

Rinaldo, Augusto and Vassili Tyndalo. 1972. *The Complete Book of Mushrooms.* New York: Crown Publishers, Inc. 332 pp. F
Originally an Italian book published by OGAM Verona.

Romagnesi, H. 1963-1970. *Petit Atlas des Champignons.* 3 vols. Paris, France: Bordas. approx. 1000 pp.

Schalkwyk, H. M. E. 1987. *Mushrooms of the Edmonton Area.* rev. ed. Edmonton, Alta.: Schalkwyk. 32 pp. F

Schalkwyk, H. M. E. 1989. *Checklist of Alberta Fungi.* The Stinkhorn, Vol. III, No. 1, pp. 60-65.
A publication of the Edmonton Mycological Club.

Smith, Alexander H. 1975. *A Field Guide to Western Mushrooms.* Ann Arbor: University of Michigan Press. 279 pp. F

Smith, A. H. and Nancy Smith Weber. 1980. *The Mushroom Hunter's Field Guide.* rev. ed. Ann Arbor: University of Michigan Press. 366 pp. F

Smith, A. H., Helen V. Smith and Nancy Smith Weber. 1979. *How to Know the Gilled Mushrooms.* Dubuque, Iowa: Wm. C. Brown Publ. 344 pp. F

Smith, Helen V. and A. H. Smith. 1973. *How to Know the Non-gilled Fleshy Fungi.* Dubuque, Iowa: Wm. C. Brown Publ. 402 pp. F

Stametz, Paul and J. S. Chilton. 1983. *The Mushroom Cultivator.* Olympia, Washington: Agarikon Press. 415 pp.

Vanterpool, T.C. and Ruth Macrae. 1951. *Notes on the Canadian tuckahoe,* its occurence in Canada, etc. Can. J. Bot. Vol. 29, 147-157.

Weber, Nancy Smith and A. H. Smith. 1985. *A Field Guide to Southern Mushrooms.* Ann Arbor: University of Michigan Press. 280 pp. F

Index of Common Names

Page numbers in bold refer to colour illustrations.

Index of Species

Page numbers in bold refer to colour illustrations.

Index of Species

Index of Species

Index of Species

Index of Genera

Page numbers in bold refer to colour illustrations.

Index of Genera

The Author / Illustrator

Helene M.E. Schalkwijk-Barendsen was born in the Netherlands in 1921 and holds the degree of Ingenieur (comparable to M.Sc.) in Horticulture, from Wageningen University. She has been married to J.A. Schalkwijk and has lived in Canada since 1949. They have four children.

A painter and enthusiastic mushroom hunter since 1968, Mrs. Schalkwijk-Barendsen taught courses in field identification at John Janzen Nature Centre in Edmonton for ten years. Some of her exhibitions of paintings have been hung in the Provincial Museum of Alberta in Edmonton, the Glenbow Museum in Calgary, the Edmonton Art Gallery and the Canadian Museum of Nature in Ottawa. She has also been a member of the Edmonton Mycological club since its inception in 1987.